2490

P9-CSC-893

Independent Study & Research

# Methodology in Social Research

# Methodology in Social Research

*Edited by*

**HUBERT M. BLALOCK, JR.**

*Professor of Sociology*
*University of North Carolina*

**ANN B. BLALOCK**

**McGRAW-HILL BOOK COMPANY**

*New York   St. Louis   San Francisco   Toronto   London   Sydney*

**Methodology in Social Research**

# Preface

This text was conceived in order to fill a need for a fairly sophisticated higher-level general work on methodology which would be appropriate for advanced graduate students in sociology, social psychology, political science, and anthropology. The focus of the book is on measurement, design, and analysis. We have assumed that students are familiar with many of the data-collection techniques usually dealt with in courses for advanced undergraduates and first-year graduate students and that they have completed one or two semesters of applied statistics.

Many advanced topics in methodology are sufficiently technical that they should be deferred until the student possesses enough knowledge of statistics to give real meaning to the kinds of questions which they raise. The field of methodology, particularly in its quantitative aspects, has become cumulative in nature. Therefore relatively more time must be devoted to methodological training at the advanced graduate level. The purpose of the present work was to construct a reasonably well-rounded text appropriate to this level of training.

In a highly specialized field it is unfortunately very difficult to find single individuals who have either the technical qualifications or the inclination to attempt to write an entire text at this level. Therefore we solicited individual chapters by specialists in given areas. This immediately created a problem of integrating the various chapters into a meaningful whole. Since we did not wish to restrict any of the contributors by imposing a rigid format—we in fact urged them to raise new issues and pursue important problems as they saw fit—we made the task of integration even more difficult. As a partial resolution of this problem, the senior editor has written two "overview" chapters, one on measurement at the beginning of Part I and the other on the analysis of cross-sectional data at the beginning of Part II. Insofar as possible, we have also attempted to integrate the various chapters by making editorial suggestions where either major overlaps or omissions were evident. The result is a book which is in no sense complete but which we hope will stimulate the advanced student to search out the gaps and fill them with additional readings and original thought.

For the most part, the chapters in this book deal with major methodological questions. Our aim has been to raise questions which we consider highly important, if not crucial, to the advancement of the various social sciences. Several chapters, particularly Chap. 2 by Siegel and Hodge, Chap. 6 by Boudon, and Chap. 11 by Coleman, are quite technical and may be omitted by students who lack a fairly good mathematical background. Some of the statistical chapters might very well be included in second or third courses in statistics or perhaps in courses on mathematical models. Chap. 4 by Jackson and Curtis and Chap. 10 by Wiggins, however, are completely nonmathematical and appropriate for methodology courses given to first-year graduate students.

Curricula in methodology may vary considerably from department to department, and certainly from one discipline to the next, and this is as it should be. However, we hope that this text will stimulate interest in developing higher-level general methodology courses given in the student's third or even fourth year of graduate study. The impression all our contributors wish to convey is that methodological issues are at the core of the social sciences. They cannot simply be raised early in the graduate curriculum and then be ignored once examinations have been passed. As will be clearly evident throughout this book, methodological problems are so closely connected with theoretical questions that the two areas cannot be easily separated.   Our major objective in editing this volume will be achieved if we succeed in convincing the student of the wisdom of this contention.

The editors wish to thank the numerous persons who read drafts of the individual chapters. They are also indebted to Theodore Anderson and Karl Schuessler for reading, criticizing, and evaluating the major portion of the entire manuscript.   The editors are also grateful for secretarial assistance provided by the Institute for Research in Social Science of the University of North Carolina.

*Hubert M. Blalock, Jr.*
*Ann B. Blalock*

# Contents

## Part 3    Experimental Designs and the Analysis of Change Data

# PART 1

# MEASUREMENT AND CONCEPTUALIZATION

Problems of measurement and conceptualization are certainly crucial in the development of any science, and they are especially important during the early exploratory phases. Sociologists, social psychologists, and political scientists are in an excellent position to borrow ideas and techniques from other disciplines, as has been done, for example, in attitude measurement in psychology or in index construction in economics. In some of the more quantitative areas of sociology, such as sociometry and demography, considerable progress has been made in the measurement area. Yet much remains to be done, particularly in the general area of social organization where macrolevel concepts abound, but where operational procedures cannot easily be linked with these concepts.

The early debates over operationalism and measurement that took place in sociology prior to the 1940s helped to state the problem, but in retrospect they seem relatively sterile in terms of positive solutions. Some of these general issues are discussed in Chap. 1, which provides an overview of the basic problem of bridging the gap between theory and research. The central thesis of this chapter is that the measurement process is an indirect one, that there are no purely logical or deductive ways of establishing linkages between theoretically defined variables and actual measures, and that under some circumstances theory and measurement become intertwined in a rather complex manner. A very general way of conceptualizing the measurement problem is discussed, with the hope that such an approach will be useful in specific situations in which one is attempting to link indicators with underlying variables that cannot be directly measured.

In Chap. 2, by Siegel and Hodge, the strategy proposed in Chap. 1 is carried out and elaborated in some detail on a realistic measurement problem of the sort often encountered in empirical research. The approach involves postulating a number of causal models of varying complexity, which make explicit assumptions regarding the linkages between measured and unmeasured variables. The authors make use of path coefficient analysis, which is discussed by Boudon in Chap. 6 of Part 2. Since the Siegel and Hodge chapter is fairly technical, the reader may wish to postpone serious consideration of this material until Chaps. 5 and 6 have been covered.

The question of measuring the unmeasurable has received the most systematic attention within the field of attitude measurement. In Chap. 3, Harry Upshaw discusses some of the major theoretical issues in this complex field. The concern, as is true elsewhere in the book, is not so much with the details of specific techniques (though these are also discussed) as with general approaches and strategies. Sociologists, political scientists, and anthropologists who may not be especially interested in attitude measurement, per se, should note carefully the similarities and differences between issues that arise on the level of individuals and those on the macrolevel, where postulated *group* properties are being inferred from measured indices. Since survey research is a major tool of the social scientist, the field of attitude measurement is also important in its own right. Much of the theoretical literature is highly technical, but the basic techniques can be learned by students with relatively little mathematical background.

Measurement problems can be discussed on a very general level. But there will always be numerous specific and unique questions faced in each substantive field. Therefore we had originally intended to devote an entire section to such specific content areas. However it became apparent that many fields fall into either one of two categories: (1) those in which too little quantitative work has been done (e.g., race and ethnic relations, deviance, medical sociology, sociology of religion) or (2) those using highly specialized techniques (e.g., small groups, demography). The field of social stratification seems to be intermediate in this respect, being reasonably typical of many areas of specialization within sociology and perhaps within political science and anthropology as well. Consequently it is hoped that the kinds of issues discussed by Jackson and Curtis in Chap. 4 are sufficiently general that they are likely to be encountered in numerous other substantive areas. Most certainly, if measurement problems cannot be generalized from one area of specialization to the next, it will turn out to be quite time-consuming and inefficient to rethink them in each and every field of specialization. One of the greatest challenges facing the social sciences seems to be that of stating measurement problems in their full generality, so that we can develop *classes* of measures with properties that have been well studied.

# CHAPTER 1

# The Measurement Problem: A Gap between the Languages of Theory and Research

HUBERT M. BLALOCK, JR.

Few sociologists would disagree with the statement that there is a sizable gap between sociological theory and actual empirical research. The important question, however, involves the extent to which this gap can readily be bridged by a more or less steady improvement of research techniques, on the one hand, and theory, on the other. The purpose of the present chapter is to discuss certain inherent difficulties that produce such a gap, not only in sociology but in all scientific disciplines. I shall take the position—which is certainly not original—that the nature of the scientific method and the ways in which we perceive and analyze the world impose very real limitations that make it difficult if not impossible to close the gap completely. The major concern will be with the limitations that are especially applicable to the social sciences generally and to sociology in particular.

Whenever one points to limitations of the scientific method or stresses the difficulties encountered in closing the gap between theory and research, there is always the danger of encouraging defeatism and pessimism. This is perhaps also true of accounts that compare developments in physics, the most advanced of the physical sciences, with those in the social sciences. Nevertheless, this seems to be a risk worth taking. In the first place, if we pay close attention to parallel problems encountered in other sciences we may profit by borrowing methodological techniques that have proved useful in comparable situations. Many quantitative methods used by sociologists have been borrowed from more advanced fields such as the biological sciences, econometrics, psychology, and statistics.

Secondly, problems cannot be made to disappear simply by ignoring them. It seems much more reasonable to attempt to define them as broadly as possible, so that general strategies or approaches can be worked out, rather than having to resolve difficulties each time they arise with particular variables. Once complexities have been identified, they can often be studied one at a time and their implications noted. In some instances, an investigator may discover that a given difficulty cannot possibly be resolved without collecting additional data or redesigning his study. If so, it would be well to know this in advance.

The operationalism controversies which have taken place within the various social sciences and which reached their height in sociology during the 1930s and 1940s served the useful purpose of raising a number of fundamental questions concerning the measurement process and its relationship to theory. Perhaps the extreme operationalists were naïve and overly optimistic if they believed that measurement processes could be carried out independently of theory construction. Yet they performed the wholesome service of criticizing the practice of developing theories devoid of testable propositions.

In retrospect, the controversy seems rather sterile in two important respects: it did not seem to have much bearing on what most practicing sociologists actually did, and it did not suggest any positive solutions for bridging the gap. The main contribution of the operationalists and extreme empiricists, it seems to me, was that they continually stressed that measurement problems constitute the key to the advancement of any science. Without adequate measurement even the most eloquent theories must go untested. To the degree that there are numerous plausible alternative theories, careful measurement becomes the prerequisite to selecting from among these theories or to modifying those which seem most adequate.

Sociological theorists often use concepts that are formulated at rather high levels of abstraction. These are quite different from the variables that are the stock-in-trade of empirical sociologists. In attempting to bridge the gap between the two levels, we have tended to refer to the latter kinds of variables as *indicators* of the former concepts. We have then been plagued by the problem of *validity* and with deciding on desirable criteria for determining validity. The operationalist criterion of prediction has perhaps been the easiest of these to conceptualize, but, as I shall point out later in the chapter, this criterion leads to theoretical difficulties.

The position taken in Sec. 1.3 of this chapter is that indicator variables can usually be linked to underlying or unmeasured concepts by postulating causal models in which one's assumptions are made explicit. In some simple causal situations, as where correlations among indicators are assumed to be produced by a single underlying variable, operational procedures such as factor analysis can be used to obtain empirical estimates of the unmeasured variable. But in more complex situations, the notion of validity may be far too simple.

In order to develop this thesis more fully, I should like to turn first to a brief discussion of the operational point of view, followed by an account of some criticisms and attempted resolutions. I am in basic agreement with the thesis that there are two very different kinds of concepts, theoretical and operational, which must be linked by common agreement or a priori assumption, rather than by any purely logical process. This point of view has some rather disturbing implications in situations where replication and randomization are not possible. These are discussed in Sec. 1.2, where it is argued that in these instances one's measurement becomes entangled with theory in a rather undesirable way. The suggested resolution is to commit oneself on specific assumptions that can be incorporated into an *auxiliary theory* developed for the purpose of testing the theory in a particular research setting.

## 1.1   THE OPERATIONALISM CONTROVERSY

The notion of an operational definition is commonly associated with the physicist, Percy W. Bridgman, who stated the operational point of view quite forcefully in a work entitled *The Logic of Modern Physics* (4). Arthur S. Eddington, the astrophysicist and philosopher of science, provides an illustrative example that can serve as a useful starting point. Eddington (7, pp. 251–255) asks us to imagine a student confronted with a hypothetical problem in elementary physics. The problem begins: "An elephant slides down a grassy hillside. . . ." Eddington notes that the experienced student need not pay too much attention to this imagery. He reads on and learns that the mass of the elephant is 2 tons. But what *is* this 2 tons to which the problem refers? If we conceive of it as a *property* of the elephant we shall not get very far. The earlier textbooks in physics used to define mass as "a quantity of matter," but it was a mere pious opinion, in the words of Eddington, that such a quantity of matter could be equated with, or represented by, the accepted measurement procedures. Instead, as the student is well aware, mass must be measured or inferred by means of a pointer reading.

Eddington points out that the triumph of science has consisted in establishing the numerical connection among several pointer readings. It might be added that the problem of the elephant on the hypothetical hillside goes on to give the slope of the hill and a coefficient of friction and suggests that one determine the time of descent. All these additional variables, according to Eddington, can also be reduced to pointer readings. The essential point is that, although we seem to have very definite ideas about what objects exist in the external world, these conceptions do not actually come into the problem as handled by science. Before science can deal with the problem, these conceptions—however real they may seem to us—must be replaced by some sort of operations (7, pp. 252–253).

The operationalist position was championed in sociology by George A. Lundberg, whose *Foundations of Sociology* (10) appeared in 1939. Lundberg vigorously denied that certain kinds of variables are inherently unmeasurable or that one should be concerned with hypothetical entities or "common essences." Such a position, claimed Lundberg, is based on the erroneous assumption that "measurement is not a way of defining things, but is a process which can be carried out only after the 'thing' to be measured has been defined" (10, p. 68). If one is asked what is meant by the concept "intelligence," he should be told that intelligence *is* what an IQ test measures.

Lundberg mentions that measurement is a way of defining; Eddington stresses that variables should be defined according to the way they are recognized. Bridgman (4, p. 6) points out that the proper definition of a concept is not in terms of properties possessed but in terms of actual operations. This seems to be the essence of the operational point of view. It means that if variables are defined in terms of properties (e.g., mass as a quantity of matter), there is no possible way of testing directly any hypotheses in which the variables appear. For tests and experiments are performed in terms of operations; it is pointer readings that are related.

Bridgman (4, pp. 9–26) argues that thinking in terms of operations can save one embarrassment about some of the apparent paradoxes in modern physics. For example, if one thinks of the length and mass of a body as inherent properties, he may find it difficult to conceive of such properties as changing according to the velocity of the body relative to the observer. One cannot always assume that different operations or procedures for measuring length will all give the same results or that, stated in nonoperational language, they will measure "the same thing." Bridgman points out that in changing the operation we are in effect changing the concept.

Ideally, then, one should use a different concept for each operation; if the operation is changed, a new word should be used to stand for the new operation. In practice, of course, this is often unworkable. But it might be well to keep the suggestion in mind. A consequence of operational theory, says Bridgman, is that all knowledge obtained by science is inevitably relative (4, pp. 25–26). The statements we are making are about the nature of our descriptive processes. We cannot expect science to give answers to certain types of questions such as, What is length (or intelligence, prejudice, or social class) *really?*

"The essence of an explanation," according to Bridgman, "consists in reducing a situation to elements with which we are so familiar that we accept them as a matter of course, so that our curiosity rests" (4, p. 37). In reply to certain criticisms of operationalism, Bridgman admits that operations are a *necessary* characterization only in the sense that unless one knows the operations he does not know the meaning of concepts; it is not claimed that meaning involves nothing more than operations (5, p. 116). He also admits that there is a certain haziness involved in the idea of operations; some are much simpler than others. There may be other than physical operations, such as the pencil and paper ones of the mathematician. In fact, Bridgman argues, almost any concept can be considered operationally defined if the notion is extended to verbal operations. But, says Bridgman, we want eventually to be able to reduce at least some of our concepts to nonverbal operations. Otherwise we may end up with verbal chains with no exit to something objective that can be directly sensed (5, pp. 126–128).

## Some Criticisms and a Resolution

Operationalism has been criticized on the ground that it does not carry us far enough, that it is insufficient and therefore misleading. Adler (1) points to some of the absurdities in an extreme operationalist position by developing a concept which he chooses to call "$C_N$." An operational definition of $C_N$ consists of questions such as the following:

**1** How many hours did you sleep last night?

**2** Estimate the length of your nose in inches and multiply by 2.

**3** Estimate the number of glasses of ginger ale the inventor of this test drank while inventing it.

There is, of course, no ambiguity as to what $C_N$ is since $C_N$ is what the $C_N$ test measures. The utility of such a concept is an interesting question, however. For where do we go once we have defined the concept? One of Adler's criticisms of operational definitions is that they are inaccessible to constructive criticism even though they may be quite useless. Adler also claims that such operational definitions hamper the advancement of science by their inadequacy in dealing with new situations and with concepts not yet measurable (1, pp. 440–444). A similar criticism that is sometimes made is that operational definitions with an appearance of rigidity and finality may generally tend to discourage further attempts to improve procedures for measurement or classification.

There is the further difficulty—apparent in Adler's $C_N$ concept—of how one arrives at a particular set of procedures involved in the operation. Northrop (11, pp. 126–127) asks us to imagine a Martian visitor, assumed to be quite intelligent but unacquainted with theoretical developments in modern physics, observing a Wilson cloud-chamber experiment. He is quite capable of noting all the operations, all the pointer readings being available to him. But what, asks Northrop, would this experiment prove to him about the existence of electrons? Northrop concludes that without the aid of concepts defined theoretically (nonoperationally) our Martian friend would learn nothing about electrons. The implication is clearly that something in addition to operational definitions is necessary.

Northrop distinguishes between two stages undergone by the maturing science (11, chaps. 3 and 4). The first of these is a natural history stage characterized by the Baconian methods of direct observation, classification, and descriptive analysis. The second, much more advanced, is that of the formulation of deductive theory. Associated with each of these distinct stages are two very different kinds of concepts which Northrop calls *concepts by intuition* and *concepts by postulation.*

Concepts by intuition, associated with the descriptive natural history stage of inquiry, are concepts "the complete meaning of which is given by something which can be immediately apprehended" (11, p. 36). In contrast to concepts by intuition which *denote,* we have concepts by postulation characteristic of deductively formulated theory. "A concept by postulation is one the meaning of which in whole or part is designated by the postulates of the deductive theory in which it occurs" (11, p. 83). The sensed color blue is given as an example of the former type of concept, whereas blue in the sense of the number of a wavelength in electromagnetic theory would be a concept by postulation.

How are these very different sorts of concepts interrelated? We get from one type of concept to the other by means of what Northrop calls *epistemic correlations.* Such an epistemic correlation is "a relation joining an unobserved component of anything designated by a concept by postulation to its directly inspected component denoted by a concept by intuition" (11, p. 119). Epistemic correlations—not to be confused with what we usually think of as correlations, which relate factors known in the same way—join things known in one way to what are in a sense the same things known in another way. Epistemic correlations, then, enable one to go from mass as a quantity of matter to mass as a pointer reading.

If one is to make use of Northrop's distinction between the two types of concepts he will need to know more about epistemic correlations. How are they established? There is no strictly *logical* way of going from one type of concept to the other. Epistemic correlations are not themselves directly observed. One postulates, says Northrop, the existence of unobservable objects. The epistemic correlates are set up *ahead of time* between the postulated entities and factors inspected or observed directly (11, pp. 120–121). Scientists must agree, by common convention, on these associations prior to an actual experiment or test of a hypothesis. In a sense we seem to have two distinct languages, each composed of concepts defined in a very special way. Tests of hypotheses are made in the one language; our thinking is done in the other. At least some of the concepts in what might be termed the theoretical language must be associated (through epistemic correlations) with concepts defined operationally.

But why *two* languages? Why not a single language with two different sorts of concepts? Northrop argues that we will only get into difficulty if we try to short-cut the procedure by mixing the two sorts of concepts. Utter nonsense results, claims Northrop, when the two types of concepts are put into the same proposition. A concern about the color of electrons would be an example of such confusion of concepts belonging to two separate worlds of discourse. It is definitely *not* the case that in a deductively formulated theory there are both concepts by postulation *and* concepts defined operationally. Instead, all concepts of the theory must be concepts by postulation if the theory is not to reach an impasse at some point. Some of the concepts by postulation may, however, be *associated with* concepts by intuition (11, pp. 128–129). A direct consequence of this is that *no deductively formulated theory or any propositions in that theory are ever directly testable*. If one subscribes to this point of view he will see that the process of going from theoretical propositions to testable hypotheses is far from simple.

Ideally it might be preferable to associate concepts in a one-to-one fashion, linking a single operation with each concept by postulation. This is implied in Bridgman's statement that when one changes the operation one should also change the concept. But this ideal is far from being attained in a discipline such as sociology. Let us admit, with the critics of operationalism, that perhaps it is unwise at this point—when research techniques are quite crude—to become overly rigid by tying down a theoretically defined concept to a particular operation. If we associate the term "prejudice" with a specific paper-and-pencil attitude test, then we run the risk either of adding new concepts to our already vastly overcomplicated theoretical language or of losing the flexibility required of a science in its infancy.

If a number of different operations are associated with each underlying concept, however, one runs the risk of obtaining very different empirical results with the various indicators. If so, then either there are true differences in the phenomena being studied or the theoretically defined concept needs clarification. Very commonly it has been found that theoretical variables originally conceived as unidimensional can more satisfactorily be thought of as multidimensional. Items used to tap such underlying variables, when factor-analyzed, turn out to load on a number of distinct dimensions. This is one of the ways, of course, in which the research process contributes to the development of theoretical conceptualization.

Mention has been made of the fact that it is not always necessary for every concept by postulation to be associated with operations. We are likely to find in any theoretical language, then, two sorts of concepts: those which have and those which have not been associated with operations. The important point is that these two kinds of theoretically defined concepts are used in very different ways when it comes to the testing of theoretical propositions. Since tests of hypotheses are actually made in terms of procedures or operations, it is quite evident that *those concepts with which operations have not been associated must be kept out of propositions purporting to be testable hypotheses*. Unless this is done confusion is likely to result.

## Some Related Notions

Before moving on to a specific type of problem that will illustrate some implications of my previous remarks, we must consider briefly some notions that are closely related to the idea of the operational definition.

There are a number of alternative ways of conceptualizing the nature of the gap between theory and research. I have used terminology that implies that there are two distinct ways of *defining* what might be taken as the same concept (e.g., operational and theoretical definitions). Northrop, on the other hand, refers to two types of *concepts* (concepts by intuition and concepts by postulation). Bierstedt (2), among others, refers to nominal versus real definitions. Coombs (6) has adopted the distinction between phenotypic and genotypic levels of analysis. Some writers, such as Francis (8, p. 10), reject the notion of an operational definition on the ground that it is not a definition at all but merely a set of instructions. These authors would prefer another term, such as "operational specifications." Many of the differences in terminology, it would seem, are primarily semantic in nature.

Perhaps the most common practice in sociology is to refer to underlying or unmeasured concepts, on the one hand, and indicators or composite indices, on the other. The problem of bridging the gap between theory and research is then seen as one of *measurement error.* Unfortunately, however, measurement errors can never be known quantities, though they may be estimated if one is willing to make certain untestable simplifying assumptions. The concepts of *reliability* and *validity* are used in this connection in order to clarify the nature of possible measurement errors.

The concept of reliability is built into the notion of an operational definition. If the instructions are not clear enough for two different researchers, working independently, to get the same or nearly the same results, then they are of little use. There is the usual metaphysical assumption that the property being measured is remaining unchanged over a period of time. The physicist weighing a cake of ice and finding that pointer readings are not always the same cannot tell by weighing alone whether his instrument is unreliable or whether the quantity of matter is actually changing. But by performing additional operations—such as collecting the melted ice and weighing it separately—he may infer that it is not his instrument that is at fault. He thus has an indirect check on some of his metaphysical hunches even though the experiment itself deals only with pointer readings. The problem of obtaining such independent checks on the operations performed in social sciences may be considerably more complex, although the underlying logic may be essentially similar.

There is no need, here, to go into a detailed discussion of reliability and validity since these concepts are treated in Chap. 3. It might be worthwhile to make a few comments about the idea of validity, however, since this notion seems to be used in at least two ways, one of which is very similar to Northrop's epistemic correlations. Jahoda, Deutsch, and Cook (9, pp. 100–117) distinguish between a logical and an empirical approach to the problem of validity.[1] From the logical or theoretical standpoint, a measure is said to be valid to the degree that it measures what it is supposed to measure. But how do we decide whether or not it is really measuring what it is intended to measure? Jahoda, Deutsch, and Cook point out that we must make an implicit assumption to the effect that the measuring instrument embodies an appropriate operational definition of a theoretical concept. This kind of assumption is quite a large one. As Eddington would say, it represents merely a pious opinion. Evidently validity in this logical or theoretical sense is being used to link theory and research. It is essentially another term for what Northrop calls epistemic correlation.

Validity is used in a very different sense, however, when one is attempting to interrelate two operational procedures or two concepts by intuition. In the empirical usage, validity may refer to the degree to which a given index can predict to some outside criterion. For example, suppose we accept the judgments of experts in determining the class position of community residents. But we could perhaps find an alternative procedure that might be much cheaper or simpler to apply. Empirically, we might wish to evaluate the validity of this second method.

Here we are interrelating two concepts in the same language, one of which is taken as the criterion. If the criterion is operationally defined, then we say that another operation is valid (with respect to this criterion under specified conditions) to the extent that it yields the same results. In this case there is a very definite procedure for ascertaining the validity of a given index. In the logical approach, however, we seem to have no such procedure (other than reaching common agreement among scientists) since the criterion is not operationally defined. It might serve to lessen the confusion over these two types of validity if they were given completely different names.

## 1.2 THEORY, MEASUREMENT, AND REPLICATION[2]

At this point it is advisable to take up a specific type of problem that illustrates the difficulties involved in passing back and forth from theory to research. We shall see both how theory and measurement can become intertwined in a confusing way and why it is necessary to introduce simplifying as-

---

[1] This discussion is considerably modified in the revised version of the Jahoda text (12), but in the writer's opinion the earlier statement is much more clear and concise. However, both formulations of the concept of validity seem to encounter the same sorts of difficulties, which may very well be inherent in the notion.

[2] This section, quoted by permission of the publisher, represents a slightly modified version of the writer's paper, "Theory, Measurement, and Replication in the Social Sciences," *American Journal of Sociology,* **66** (January, 1961), 342–347.

sumptions in the process. But these assumptions may be more or less realistic depending on the circumstances, and in particular their plausibility will depend on whether or not replication has been possible. We shall encounter a dilemma for the social scientist resulting from the inability, in most studies, to replicate one's results.

In many instances the problem of translating from one language to the other is relatively straightforward. Sex, age, and religion are ordinarily conceived as properties of the individual, and there is little difficulty in actually classifying persons according to one or another of these characteristics. My concern here is with an important special type of property, namely, properties that have been theoretically conceived in terms of their causal implications and that imply measurement in terms of their supposed effects. I shall illustrate in terms of three very different concepts: *mass* as used by the physicist, *power* as defined by both the physicist and social scientist, and *discrimination* as this term is ordinarily used by the sociologist.

Briefly stated, my argument will be that in order to be satisfied with whatever linkage system we may devise in these instances, we must not only find a set of operations with a high degree of reliability, but we must also make a series of *theoretical* assumptions concerning the operation of variables *other than* the one being measured. Thus our measurement problems become entangled in our theory in such a manner that, under some circumstances, it becomes difficult to separate the two. Furthermore, the nature of the relationship between theoretical assumptions and measurement is such as to create special problems for the social scientist, problems which so far at least do not seem to have hampered the development of the physical sciences.

## The Measurement of Mass

We can illustrate the fundamental problem by one of the simplest of physical measurements, the weighing of a block of wood. The operations involved are basically simple; one places the block on one side of the balance, puts bodies with known mass on the other, and observes a pointer reading.[3] As long as one takes the extreme operational point of view that mass *is* what my operations and pointer readings tell me it is, there is no conceptual problem. One is merely measuring mass as operationally defined. But if we wish to establish some sort of link between the pointer reading and the theoretical notion of mass as property, we immediately run into certain difficulties. Suppose, for example, there is some unknown force (in addition to gravity, air currents, dust particles, and so forth) bearing down on the block of wood in such a manner as to increase the value of the pointer reading by 2 grams.

---

[3] Strictly speaking, a body's mass is not known or directly measured but is inferred from its weight at sea level. It would perhaps be more correct to refer to bodies whose weights have been standardized in some way.

Would we then feel comfortable about establishing a one-to-one linkage between the pointer reading and mass as property? Probably not.

In such a situation we would be much happier with the intellectual leap from pointer reading to property if it were somehow possible to *isolate* the effects of the block of wood from those of other possibly unknown variables, such as the mysterious force in the above illustration. The obvious practical solution to our problem involving the unknown force is to replicate the measurement several times, perhaps even interchanging the positions of the block and standard weights according to a table of random numbers. If the pointer readings remained approximately the same over numerous replications, we would perhaps be prepared to accept the notion that the pointer readings gave an accurate indication of the true mass (i.e., mass as a property).

Parenthetically, it should be noted that there seem to be at least two purposes of replication. The first, and the one to which I am referring in the present section, involves rather conscious attempts to vary experimental conditions in order to isolate the effects of disturbing influences. Because of the obvious impossibility of controlling for all such variables, scientists may insist on some form of randomization or at least on the experiment's being replicated by different observers. The second purpose of replication is to obtain more accurate measurement, as when the physicist weighs a block of wood five times and takes the mean figure as his estimate of the true mass. In so doing, of course, he usually assumes both that disturbing influences are operating randomly and that the true mass remains fixed over the several replications.

Now suppose someone raised the question of the possibility of the unknown force always operating in such a manner as to bear down on the same side of the scale as the block of wood. Each time, then, we might be overestimating the true mass by 2 grams. The first reaction of the experimental physicist might well be that the skeptic has raised an operationally meaningless question. After rethinking it, however, he might take either one of two positions. First, he might argue that if in fact such an unknown force were always to bear down on the same side as the block of wood, then one might as well redefine the theoretical notion of mass as property so as to include the effects of such a force. In other words, he might argue that he is measuring the combined effects of two things, mass plus $X$, and then learn to think, always, in terms of mass plus $X$ rather than mass. Before long, however, he would soon go out of his mind, since there is no end to such possible unknown $X$s.

The second possibility is to eliminate $X$ by making a theoretical assumption about the way $X$ operates and then to use probability theory to argue in favor of ruling it out. Thus if it could be assumed that the unknown force always operated on one side of the scale or in some other systematic manner, then by randomly varying the position of the block through a large number of replications, one could calculate the probability of the force and the block always being on the same side. If such a probability were extremely small and if replications yielded (nearly) identical results, then one might assume that there was no such unknown force.

In such a manner, through replication, one attempts to isolate the effects of the block of wood from those of other forces. Where replications fail to yield nearly identical results, one attempts to eliminate disturbing influences until a high degree of reliability is attained. At that point he is usually willing to stop and be reasonably satisfied that his procedure provides an adequate measure of mass as property. But we should note that he is implicitly making the assumption that mass (as a property) has been effectively isolated from other variables that may be operating. And in so doing, he must make certain assumptions about *how* the other variables are operating.

Thus we see that in order to be reasonably satisfied that any given measurement process is yielding the equivalent of certain types of theoretically defined concepts (e.g., mass as property) we must have a theory about how *other* variables may be entering the picture. In some cases the theory may be simple and quite plausible. Indeed, from this point of view the value of replication seems to be in enabling the scientist to get by with as simple a set of assumptions as possible about disturbing factors. Where replication gives nearly identical results, he may decide that the influence of disturbing variables is negligible *under the assumption* that the variables are operating in a given manner. We must now consider what happens when such replication is difficult or impossible. As we shall see, the problem of establishing epistemic correlations then becomes more complex, and the assumptions required about other variables become less plausible.

## *The Measurement of Power*

Power in physics is measured in terms of work accomplished in a given unit of time. Power is also conceived as a property (e.g., a 300-horsepower engine). In labeling the horsepower of an engine, one is, of course, expressing a faith that if actually put to the test the machine would really accomplish a certain amount of work in a particular time interval. To measure its power one would have to isolate its effects from those of other machines or forces, for example, by having it lift a standard weight under carefully controlled conditions.

Again replication is the device whereby certain types of possibilities can be eliminated as extremely improbable. Thus a physicist unaware of the force of gravity, who is attempting to measure the horsepower of an engine by having it push against a machine of known power, could come to several different conclusions if the machines were operating on an inclined plane. But by interchanging the directions in which the machines were pushing and by assuming that the horsepower (as a property) of the two machines remained constant from one replication to the next, he would quickly come to the conclusion that some uncontrolled force was operating.

The social scientist attempting to measure *social* power cannot so easily replicate his experiment and consequently finds himself unable to isolate the effects of disturbing influences. This fact is well known. What I wish to emphasize is that *it is because of problems involved in replication that the social scientist has special difficulties in resolving the differential between his theoretical and operational languages.* Suppose, for example, that one wishes to evaluate the relative power of labor and management in a particular dispute. *If* it can be assumed that there are no independent forces aside from these groups, then relative power can be assessed in terms of whichever side wins the dispute or, perhaps, in terms of how long it takes the one side to move the other a given distance. But how can we decide which of the many additional forces operating in this situation (e.g., police power, public opinion, labor market, demand for the manufacturer's goods, or alliances with other groups) are acting independently of labor and management? Clearly, a theory of social causation is necessary before we can measure the power of either group.

We would probably agree that it would make little sense to attempt to evaluate the power of management stripped of the operation of police powers. In other words, we would probably not consider police powers to be operating independently of the power of management. On the other hand, we might more reasonably conclude that both labor market and demand for sales are in fact operating independently of this particular labor dispute, and we might well imagine an almost identical dispute being carried out under different market conditions. We might even hope to have a crude form of replication. The important point is that in order to isolate and measure the relative power of the two groups, we need a theory about how the other variables are operating. In particular, we need to decide which of the variables are acting independently of labor and management in the sense that neither of these groups can be said to control the other factors.

Perhaps some social scientists would attempt to avoid the problem by arguing that since power is always relative to the situation, it is impossible to measure the actual power of each of the groups except in a particular context. Since the situations may change, their power will likewise vary, and it is therefore meaningless to attempt to measure power in isolation. By implication, whichever group wins the labor dispute is the more powerful under these circumstances. Power is made synonymous with outcome, and the problem of isolating the power of each of these two particular groups is bypassed.

A little thought will convince the reader that there is a profound difference between this perspective on the scientific method and the more analytic approach used by the physicist. If such a perspective were applied to the case of the two machines pushing in opposite directions, it would amount to saying that whichever machine pushed the other was the more powerful, even though one were pushing downhill and the other uphill. To continue the analogy, it should then be claimed that when the directions have been reversed the powers of the two machines have also been changed; this is hardly surprising in view of the fact that the situation has altered! Such a position, if pushed to the extreme, would seem to preclude the possibility of establishing any scientific generalizations whatsoever.

## The Measurement of Discrimination

I have dealt with two concepts, mass and power, which are ordinarily conceived theoretically as properties but which are actually measured in terms of their imputed effects. The concept of racial discrimination is not ordinarily thought of as a property, though it may obviously be regarded as a special type of group property. Discrimination can be defined as a resultant of discriminatory behavior, which, in turn, is often conceived as the differential treatment of a minority because of race or creed.

When we attempt to measure discrimination we may thus become involved with a doubly difficult problem of causation: not only must we decide whether or not the minority is treated differentially *because of* race or creed, but we must also determine the degree to which differences between the majority and minority groups are actually caused by such discriminatory behavior. For example, we may wish to measure discrimination indirectly by taking the difference between the median incomes of Negroes and whites, or perhaps we may develop a measure which compares the percentages of white-collar workers in the two groups. In all such instances, however, we are dealing with a resultant of discriminatory behavior on the part of dominant-group members *plus* a number of other factors, including the behavior of the minority. Differences with respect to income or occupational levels may not be primarily due to discriminatory behavior but to lack of ability, training, or initiative on the part of the minority. Once more we find it necessary to isolate the effects of a particular phenomenon, and again replication under carefully controlled conditions may be impossible.

This specific example will be discussed in somewhat greater detail in the next section, where the focus is on the rationale for controlling or standardizing in such indirect measurement situations. Here it is sufficient to point out that in attempting to pass from a measure of inequality on the operational level to the theoretical notion of discrimination, we need to make certain theoretical assumptions about interrelationships among other variables.

## 1.3  MEASUREMENT AND CAUSAL REPRESENTATIONS

It has been argued that there are two kinds of concepts, or two ways of defining concepts, and that the nature of the linkage between them is often quite indirect. This means not only that one's tests of a theory must also be indirect, but also that difficult problems of conceptualization will arise. It is therefore helpful to attempt to set forth a general mode of attack that will be appropriate for reasonably complex situations, as well as more simple ones. In brief, the procedure recommended is to draw a causal diagram in which both measured and unmeasured variables are assumed interrelated according to some explicit theory. Whenever the linkages are of certain simple types, one may then readily think in terms of validity and may use standard procedures for appraising validity. In more complex situations, however, one may find that the notion of validity is misleading.

Let us first consider those variables which are sufficiently close to the operational level that measurement can be thought of as direct. The variable "age" and the attribute "sex" are ordinarily regarded as directly measured, though of course this is not strictly true. Indicators of sex are so reliable, except in certain deviant quarters, that one usually assumes that there will be relatively minor random errors that occur primarily as a result of the coding process. With respect to age, certain possible systematic errors are expected because some respondents may wish to disguise their true age. In fact, a completely satisfactory operational definition of age would be difficult to construct, unless one could rely on the accuracy of official records. The same is true of formal education or income. But the conceptual problems with such variables are relatively minor compared with those encountered when one deals with more abstract postulated properties. On the empirical level, the difficulties of measurement are considered primarily those of response error.

With regard to the above recommendation that one represent his assumptions in terms of a causal model, these very simple situations can usually be diagramed as follows:

where $X$ represents the true value, and $X'$ the measured value. The side arrows indicate sources of error, such as response error, coding error, and so forth. Thus the measured value of age would be taken as caused by true age plus a number of other factors. If these latter factors can be assumed to have random effects, in the aggregate, then they will be unrelated to the true value $X$. But if one assumes that they are *systematically* related to $X$, then this must be represented in some way, possibly by postulating an additional variable that might be creating a spurious relationship. Or the relationship between $X$ and $X$ may be conditional. Thus suppose women tend to understate their ages more than men. Then sex is said to interact with true age in affecting stated age. If so, this should appear explicitly in the diagram, and the specific nature of one's assumptions should be stated as clearly as possible. This is the basic strategy used by Siegel and Hodge in Chap. 2.

Problems of causal analysis will be considered in more detail in Chaps. 2, 5, and 6. Here it is sufficient to point out that the introduction of unmeasured variables in this manner will lead to complications in the form of additional unknowns. Depending on the simplicity of one's theory in other respects, there may or may not be too many unknowns to yield definite predictions. For this reason, one should keep his assumptions as simple as possible, using only a small number of unmeasured variables in the theoretical system. Usually, therefore, it is convenient to assume that variables such as age, education, and income have been directly measured without error. The number of unknowns may then be reduced to manageable proportions.

There will usually be some variables that can be measured only by very indirect means. These will include postulated internal states of individuals (e.g., needs, attitudes, and values) plus certain types of macrolevel variables taken to characterize entire groups (e.g., cohesiveness, anomie, or political integration). In such cases especially, it is highly important to make one's underlying theory explicit. Where this theory is simple one may use standard procedures, such as factor analysis, for relating indicators to underlying variables.

For example, if it can be assumed that the underlying variable is the single common cause of a number of indicators and that intercorrelations among these indicators are due solely to this common cause, then one may use the factor loadings for each of the indicators as weights in computing an estimate of the factor. The basic model is that of Fig. 1.1, in which it is assumed that there are no additional arrows connecting any of the indicator variables. If, however, it seemed more plausible to assume that some

**Fig. 1.1.   Causal Model Appropriate for Factor Analysis.**

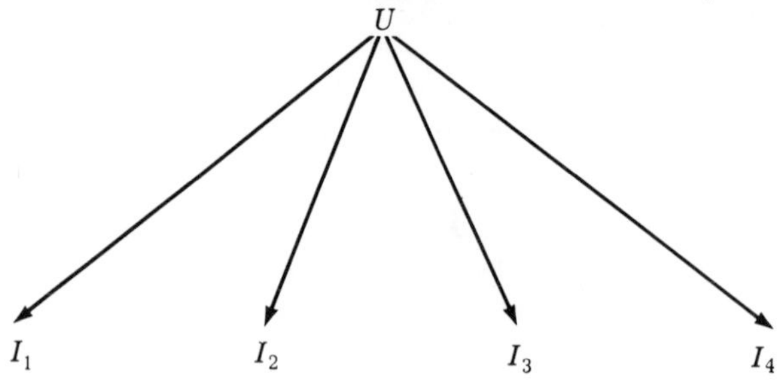

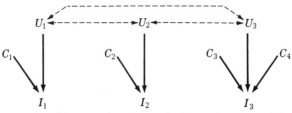

**Fig. 1.2.  Causal Model Appropriate for Standardization by Measured Variables $C_i$.**

of the indicator variables also caused each other, simple factor analysis procedures would no longer be appropriate (3, chap. 5).

Another very common situation is one in which each indicator variable
$I_i$ is linked in a one-to-one fashion with each underlying or unmeasured
variable $U_i$ as in Fig. 1.2. There may, however, be *other* causes $C_i$ of
the indicator variables that may be of no theoretical interest but that need
to be controlled in the measurement process. The rationale behind so-called
standardizing procedures seems to involve this type of assumption. For example, demographers may not wish to deal with crude birthrates, which are
a function of age and marriage distributions. These latter variables may
be treated primarily as nuisance factors that are not theoretically linked with
the major independent variables under investigation. The theory linking
marital status and age distributions to birthrates may be a very simple one,
so simple in fact that it can be ignored for practical purposes.

Let us consider, however, the more complex situation introduced in the
preceding section in connection with the measurement of discrimination. In
particular, suppose one wishes to claim that a given measure of economic
inequality (e.g., the difference between median incomes) is a valid indicator
of economic discrimination against Negroes. One's initial causal diagram
might be similar to that of Fig. 1.3, in which three additional causes of economic inequality have been explicitly identified.

**Fig. 1.3.  Simple Model for Economic Inequality, Standardization Appropriate.**

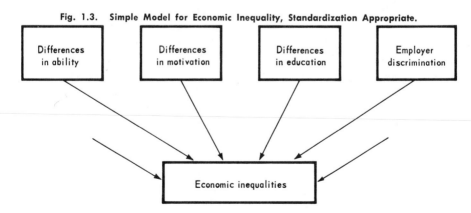

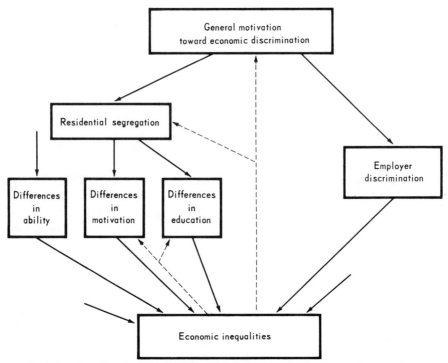

**Fig. 1.4.    More Complex Model for Economic Inequality, Standardization Inappropriate.**

According to the model of Fig. 1.3 it would seem reasonable to standardize for education, ability, and motivation, and then to claim that the standardized measure of economic inequality represents a valid indicator of economic discrimination.    The existence of side arrows not identified with specific variables indicates that one cannot possibly standardize for *all* the causes of racial inequalities.    But at some point one may make the simplifying assumption that remaining variables produce only very minor random disturbances.    As we shall see in Chaps. 5 and 6, some such assumptions about disturbance terms must always be made.

But Fig. 1.3 is far too simple in that the various presumed causes of economic inequality cannot be assumed unrelated.    A more plausible model is given in Fig. 1.4, in which both motivational and educational inequalities are assumed to be consequences of residential segregation, which may be consciously maintained in order to create or perpetuate these same educational and economic inequalities.    Economic inequalities, in turn, may operate to perpetuate segregation and motivational inequalities in a kind of feedback or reciprocal causation relationship, as indicated by the dashed arrows.    It might be reasonable, of course, to introduce further elaborations.    But each time an additional unmeasured variable is used, the problem of linking these with indicators is made more complex.

In this somewhat more complex model, the notion of economic discrimination has been replaced by two unmeasured variables: (1) actual discrimination by employers in the employment office, and (2) a general aggregated motivation to discriminate within the community. This particular reconceptualization, therefore, forces one to ask whether the unmeasured variable of interest is really discrimination by employers in actual hiring or promotion policies, or a more general kind of economic discrimination characteristic of larger social units such as entire communities or subregions.

Suppose one wishes to relate economic discrimination to variables appropriate to these larger units. Suppose, also, that economic inequalities result from some combination of these three paths from aggregated motivation toward economic discrimination. Why should one single out the particular path through employer action? In fact, one could argue that really effective discrimination within the community should make it completely unnecessary for employers to act as gatekeepers. That is, residential segregation could have indirectly made Negroes unqualified for any but the most unskilled positions. It would make sense to control for education, motivation, and ability if one were measuring employer discrimination, but not if one were attempting to get at the more general community level of economic discrimination.

In this particular example, which is certainly no more complex than many other instances of indirect measurement, it is difficult to say exactly what variable should be taken as a single indicator of general economic discrimination. We are not helped by the operationalist's notion that a valid indicator is one that gives accurate predictions. In the first place, one lacks a simple criterion variable. In the second, it may very well be that *all* (measured) variables are highly intercorrelated. If so, then by this criterion alone any one of them might be taken as an indicator of economic discrimination. In fact, if some other variable, such as percentage Negro, were highly related to these variables, one might likewise use it as his indicator of economic discrimination.

The general point, here, is that one may be asking the wrong sort of question when he attempts to locate indicators with a high degree of validity. Instead, it would seem more reasonable to postulate a theoretical model, including both measured and unmeasured variables, and then to see what this implies in terms of verifiable predictions. If the model is simple enough, one may then talk in terms of individual indicators linked with specific underlying variables, and the notion of validity may make sense theoretically as well as practically.

## 1.4 GENERAL VERSUS AUXILIARY THEORIES

In discussing operationalism we noted that we seem to have two distinct languages, one of which is in some sense more complete than the other. The first is a theoretical language in which we do our thinking. The second is an operational language involving explicit instructions for classifying or measuring. The two languages cannot be linked by any strictly logical argument. Instead, a correspondence between two concepts, one in each language, must be established by common agreement or a priori assumption. Not all concepts in the theoretical language need have an operational counterpart, nor is it absolutely necessary to link concepts in a one-to-one fashion. But one must be on guard against creating an extremely flexible theory which cannot possibly be rejected because of too many unknowns and unspecified linkages.

We encounter, here, a basic dilemma for the social scientist. What should he do with theoretical variables that have not been linked with specific operations? One possibility is to do away with such concepts altogether. Another alternative, which seems more reasonable in view of the present state of theory in the social sciences, is to make a clear-cut and explicit distinction between measured and unmeasured variables. This, in turn, implies a distinction between actual research hypotheses and theoretical propositions involving concepts defined in such a manner as to make direct tests impossible. These latter propositions can then be used as theoretical tools for predictive or explanatory purposes, without being labeled as research hypotheses. I would agree with Northrop that, strictly speaking, no theoretically defined concepts are directly measurable. But as noted above, some will be sufficiently close to the operational level that agreement is easily reached. For practical purposes one can conceive of these as directly measured.

It may also be helpful to make a second distinction which partly overlaps the distinction between measured and unmeasured variables. On the one hand, there should be a general theory expressed in abstract terms; on the other, there must also be a specific *auxiliary* theory necessary for testing purposes. Ideally, a theorist should specify the epistemic correlations, linking particular operations with some of his theoretical concepts. He should also state a number of assumptions concerning measurement errors and the behavior of variables he has failed to consider. But this is obviously expecting too much, given the present status of most social sciences. Since there is a wide variety of possible research designs, measurement instruments, and confounding factors, it is much more reasonable to work out a division of labor in the process of theory construction.

The main body of a given theory might consist of a number of definitions, assumptions, and propositions modeled after the ideal of a completely deductive system of thought. General laws of varying complexity might be stated. Again in the ideal, these should not be bound to particular times or places but should be formulated in the hypothetical if-then form. They need not, of course, be stated in a *simple* universal form, such as "the greater the X, the greater the Y." Qualifying conditions can be added, thereby introducing any degree of complexity that may be required to have the law conform to reality. In the process of *constructing* such a theory, the social scientist need not be concerned with the method of testing his propositions or even with specifying populations for which the theory should apply. This is not to say, however, that the theory may not have been *suggested* by empirical data appropriate to particular populations.

Given a main body of theory, anyone wishing to test this theory may then construct an auxiliary theory containing a whole set of additional assumptions, many of which will be inherently untestable. This auxiliary theory will be specific to the research design, population studied, and measuring instruments used. For example, in one population it may be reasonable to ignore a particular set of disturbing influences that would have to be explicitly considered in another population. Certain variables may be taken as measured in one study but not in another. In some situations, measurement error can be assumed minimal or random, whereas in others, such an assumption would be unrealistic. Different operations may be used even within the same study. It is important to note that no main body of deductive theory can ever be tested without the use of some such auxiliary theory, whether explicitly formulated or not.

For illustrative purposes, consider the theory implied by Fig. 1.5. The main or general theory contains variables $X_1, X_2, \ldots, X_6$ interrelated in some specified way, as implied by the arrows in the diagram. All these variables have been placed above the dashed line that separates the main and auxiliary theories. Suppose that $X_1$ through $X_5$ are not considered directly measured, but that $X_6$ is sufficiently close to the operational level that one is willing to

Fig. 1.5. Model Involving Distinctions between (1) Main and Auxiliary Theories and (2) Measured and Unmeasured Variables.

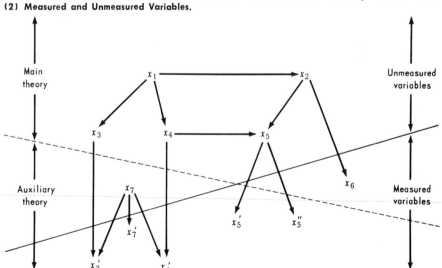

simplify the diagram by referring to its measurement as direct.    In Fig. 1.5 the solid line separates measured from unmeasured variables, with $X_6$ below the line.

The remaining variables have been introduced in the auxiliary theory in order to obtain testable predictions.    No measured variables are directly linked with $X_1$ and $X_2$ in this hypothetical example.    There are two indicators of $X_5$, designated as $X_5'$ and $X_5''$.    The absence of additional arrows implies that these two indicators would be uncorrelated if $X_5$ could be controlled.    Therefore, a procedure such as factor analysis could be used to provide a rationale for weighting the indicators to estimate $X_5$.    In this particular illustration, $X_3'$ and $X_4'$ are taken as single indicators of $X_3$ and $X_4$, respectively, but there are additional arrows leading to these indicators coming from a common source, $X_7$.    In other words, the auxiliary theory allows for biased measures and a partly spurious relationship between the indicators.    According to the auxiliary theory, $X_7$ is measured indirectly by $X_7'$, but it is assumed that the measurement error in $X_7'$ is random.

Thus an auxiliary theory may contain unmeasured variables explicitly brought into the picture to account for disturbing influences.    In this case, $X_7$ operates only to disturb the measurement process, but in other instances it will be necessary to introduce variables, not considered in the original theory, in order to account for possible spurious relationships and other kinds of distortions.    Complications such as these will be considered in Chap. 5.

When main and auxiliary theories are put together in a given research situation, the result should be a series of testable propositions that allow for error terms and unexplained variation.    But although analytically distinct, the two kinds of theory may not be separable empirically.    Referring to the main theory as *A* and the auxiliary theory as *A'*, one will be in the following logical situation.    One may argue that if both *A* and *A'* are true, then certain testable consequences *B* ought to follow.    If *B* is true, then *A* and *A'* *may* be true, though other theories (e.g., *C* and *C'* or *A* and *C'*) may also predict *B*.    However, if *B* is false, then either or both of *A* or *A'* must be modified, but ordinarily we cannot tell which of the two is at fault.

Presumably, the aim of the scientist is to develop main theories which are sufficiently complex that the auxiliary theories can be made relatively simple and plausible.    This may be accomplished, for example, by incorporating many disturbing influences explicitly into the main theory as additional variables.    Clarification of theoretically defined concepts also simplifies the auxiliary theory by facilitating the process of agreeing on operational definitions and by reducing the number of unmeasured variables.    Research design can also be used to simplify the auxiliary theory.    As implied in the discussion of replication, and as will also be seen in Chap. 9, one major function of randomization in experimental designs is to enable the investigator to get by with relatively simple assumptions about certain kinds of disturbing influences.

The implications of the operationalism controversy and of our knowledge about the limitations of the scientific method are quite clear. Some form of auxiliary theory will always be necessary. As a bare minimum, it will be necessary to link theoretically defined variables with operations, and thus untestable assumptions about measurement errors will be required. It will likewise be necessary to make simplifying assumptions about uncontrolled variables. One of the main purposes of a systematic study of methodology is to pinpoint the nature of this auxiliary theory.

Although the division of this text into separate sections on measurement and analysis might seem to indicate otherwise, the major theme of this introductory chapter has been that measurement and analysis problems both require careful theoretical conceptualization before they can be satisfactorily resolved. One of the main arguments in the next chapter by Siegel and Hodge is that the assessment of measurement error is an important aspect of data analysis.

## REFERENCES

1 Adler, Franz: "Operational Definitions in Sociology," *American Journal of Sociology,* 52 (March, 1947), 438–444.

2 Bierstedt, Robert: "Nominal and Real Definitions in Sociological Theory," in Llewellyn Gross (Ed.), *Symposium in Sociological Theory* (New York: Harper & Row, 1959), chap. 4.

3 Blalock, Hubert M.: *Causal Inferences in Nonexperimental Research* (Chapel Hill, N.C.: University of North Carolina Press, 1964).

4 Bridgman, Percy W.: *The Logic of Modern Physics* (New York: Macmillan, 1927).

5 Bridgman, Percy W.: "Operational Analysis," *Philosophy of Science,* 5 (April, 1938), 114–131.

6 Coombs, Clyde H.: "Theory and Methods of Social Measurement," in Leon Festinger and Daniel Katz (Eds.), *Research Methods in the Behavioral Sciences* (New York: Holt, 1953), chap. 11.

7 Eddington, Arthur S.: *The Nature of the Physical World* (New York: Macmillan, 1933).

8 Francis, Roy G.: *The Rhetoric of Science* (Minneapolis: University of Minnesota Press, 1961).

9 Jahoda, Marie, Morton Deutsch, and Stuart W. Cook: *Research Methods in Social Relations* (New York: Holt, 1951).

10 Lundberg, George A.: *Foundations of Sociology* (New York: Macmillan, 1939).

11 Northrop, F. S. C.: *The Logic of the Sciences and the Humanities* (New York: Macmillan, 1947).

12 Selltiz, Claire, Marie Jahoda, Morton Deutsch, and Stuart W. Cook: *Research Methods in Social Relations* (New York: Holt, 1959).

# CHAPTER 2

# A Causal Approach to the
# Study of Measurement Error[1]

PAUL M. SIEGEL

ROBERT W. HODGE

Under the stimulus of Simon's seminal paper on the causal interpretation of spurious correlations (20), the methodology of causal analysis has received substantial attention by research workers in recent years (2,7,19). The effects of measurement error have not, however, been subjected to intensive scrutiny in a causal framework. Even though "actual analyses and interpretations of data usually presuppose that measurement errors can be safely ignored," Blalock notes that "there has been relatively little study of the *kinds* of effects measurement error produces" (3). The need for investigation of the effects of measurement error can easily be seen from a cursory consideration of some logical aspects of causal analysis.

A fundamental postulate of causal analysis is that causal responsibility for *all* the variation in each dependent variable can be allocated among explicit independent variables. As Duncan (9) puts it: "Each 'dependent' variable must be regarded explicitly as *completely* determined by some combination of variables in the system. In problems where complete determination by measured variables does not hold, a residual variable uncorrelated with other determining variables must be introduced." While, as in multiple regression analysis, coefficients of various factors may be distorted by errors of measurement in the data to which a causal model is applied, the use made of this postulate of

[1] Revision of a paper read at the annual meetings of the Population Association of America (April, 1966). The research reported here was undertaken as background to a larger project dealing with occupational stratification in the United States. The study was conducted under a grant to the National Opinion Research Center from the National Science Foundation (NSF #GS725, "Occupations and Social Stratification"). We are grateful to Otis Dudley Duncan both for general guidance and for his discussion of a previous version of this chapter. He bears no responsibility for any errors which may remain.

complete determination serves to disseminate the distortion throughout a system of causal equations. Thus errors of measurement may have extremely pernicious effects upon causal analysis by adding or distorting the coefficients of residual terms in causal equations, as well as by biasing coefficients of measured components of the model. Since comparisons among these coefficients are usually the ultimate step in a causal analysis, it is clear that such analysis should not be undertaken without some knowledge of the kinds of effects that measurement error can produce.

Within the social sciences questions of measurement error have, in large part, been left to psychologists and economists. Psychologists have treated measurement error in the context of assessing the reliability with which an individual can be assigned a score on a test (14,17,21)—an approach similar to that undertaken here. Econometricians have treated the problem in terms of the effects of measurement error upon the estimates of coefficients in linear regression equations (15,18)—a concern also shared by our investigations. Although demographers have developed numerous techniques for adjusting faulty data, often derived from the criterion of internal consistency, most demographic work has been focused on the correction of univariate statistics. Even when demographers have addressed themselves to the question of measurement error in bivariate statistics, they have usually approached the problem as a study in misclassification (6,11,13). Our approach will be to investigate the effects of measurement errors upon statistics derived from bivariate frequency distributions—such as the correlation coefficient—by applying a variety of causal assumptions to models of the relations between measured and true values of variables, using, for the purposes of exposition, data on the reliability of census measures of socioeconomic status.

## 2.1 ANALYSIS OF UNIVARIATE STATISTICS

### *Distribution Parameters of Socioeconomic Variables*

The decennial censuses contain three frequently used measures of socioeconomic status: years of school completed, occupational pursuit, and personal income. The basic data for the present study of the effects of measurement errors in these variables upon associations between them are taken from cross tabulations available in the *1960 Census of Population* and comparisons of census results to those obtained in the *Current Population Survey* (CPS) and the *Post Enumeration Survey* (PES). Estimates of the means and standard deviations of the distribution of years of school completed, personal income, and occupational attainment are presented in Table 2.1 for several different populations from a variety of sources. The means and standard deviations of personal income and years of school completed were derived by scoring the intervals identified in the

TABLE 2.1   Means and Standard Deviations of Selected SES Variables as Observed
in Samples Drawn from Current Population Survey and Post Enumeration
Survey Returns and Matched with Census of Population Returns, c. 1960

| | *Variables\** | | | | | | | |
|---|---|---|---|---|---|---|---|---|
| | *Years of school completed* | | *Personal income* | | | | *Occupational SES†* | |
| *Population* | *Post Enumer-ation Survey* | *Census of Popula-tion* | *Current Popula-tion Survey* | *Census of Popula-tion* | *Post Enumer-ation Survey* | *Census of Popula-tion* | *Current Popula-tion Survey* | *Census of Popula-tion* |
| | | | | *Means* | | | | |
| *Total persons* | 9.84 | 9.97 | $3,697 | $3,811 | $3,793 | $3,761 | 35.6§ | 35.3§ |
| *Whites* | ‡ | ‡ | 3,849 | 3,928 | ‡ | ‡ | 37.2 | 36.8 |
| *Nonwhites* | ‡ | ‡ | 2,160 | 2,236 | ‡ | ‡ | 20.9 | 21.2 |
| *Total males* | ‡ | ‡ | 4,724 | 4,891 | 4,845 | 4,829 | 34.5§ | 24.0§ |
| *Whites* | ‡ | ‡ | 4,909 | 5,022 | ‡ | ‡ | 35.9 | 35.3 |
| *Nonwhites* | ‡ | ‡ | 2,643 | 2,745 | ‡ | ‡ | 21.2 | 21.6 |
| | | | | *Standard deviations* | | | | |
| *Total persons* | 3.61 | 3.58 | $3,556 | $3,762 | $3,109 | $3,130 | 21.2§ | 21.0§ |
| *Whites* | ‡ | ‡ | 3,340 | 3,408 | ‡ | ‡ | 21.0 | 20.9 |
| *Nonwhites* | ‡ | ‡ | 2,011 | 2,038 | ‡ | ‡ | 17.2 | 17.1 |
| *Total males* | ‡ | ‡ | 3,892 | 4,143 | 3,251 | 3,279 | 21.0§ | 20.8§ |
| *Whites* | ‡ | ‡ | 3,549 | 3,608 | ‡ | ‡ | 21.0 | 20.8 |
| *Nonwhites* | ‡ | ‡ | 2,136 | 2,249 | ‡ | ‡ | 17.0 | 16.8 |

\* Those not reporting in either or both surveys are excluded from these figures.
† Scored with Duncan's SES scores (8).
‡ Not available.
§ Figures for "Total persons" and "Total males" refer to those classified as either
employed in CPS and employed or not reported in census, or unemployed in CPS and
unemployed or not reported in census.   All other occupation group figures are for the
former classification only.
Sources: (26, tables 12, 17, and 18); (27, tables 34, 36, 42, and 43).

source tables according to their midpoints.[2]   The mean and standard deviation
of occupational attainment were derived after scoring data tabulated according

[2] The open-ended categories for income distributions were scored as follows: the categories "loss" and "$1 to $99" were combined and scored as $50, the category "$25,000 or
more" was scored as $30,000 in the CPS-census match tabulations; in tabulations from the
PES-census match, the category "$1 to $499 or loss" was scored as $250 and the category
"$10,000 and over" was scored as $12,500; and the category "5 or more years of college" was
scored as 17 years in the PES-census match tabulations.

to major occupation group with Duncan's Socioeconomic Status Index for occupations (8, table vii-4).

The means of the variables shown in the upper panel of Table 2.1 show quite close agreement between the census and the *Current Population Survey* and between the census and the *Post Enumeration Survey*. The differences in means observed in the table *cannot be attributed to differential nonreporting* between the several sources. The figures are based only upon persons reporting in *both* sources for any particular variable. (Under personal income, two census figures are shown: one based only on persons reporting in both the census and *Current Population Survey* and the other based only on persons reporting in both the census and *Post Enumeration Survey*.) The estimated mean occupational socioeconomic status (SES) for persons matched between the 1960 census and the *Current Population Survey* of March, 1960, is about the same in both census and CPS. This is true for each of the subgroups identified in Table 2.1; a similar conclusion holds for the comparison between the estimates of personal income derived from persons reporting in both the census and *Post Enumeration Survey*. However, the *Post Enumeration Survey* does yield a somewhat lower average number of years of school completed, and for every subgroup, the *Current Population Survey* yields an estimate of total personal money income in 1959 which is about $100 less than that observed for the same persons in the *1960 Census of Population*. We have not been able to detect any differences in enumeration procedures which might account for these mean discrepancies.

Given the general tendency to forget income from irregular sources and the higher standards of interviewing demanded by the CPS, one might expect the CPS to yield higher, rather than lower, estimates of personal income. Some other process appears to be counteracting this tendency; study of the sources and patterns of errors enables us to illuminate this anomaly, to which we will return. In any case, the mean differences revealed by the upper panel of Table 2.1 appear to be small and insignificant. The discrepancies never exceed 4 percent of the smallest of any pair of estimates.

Like the means shown in the upper panel of Table 2.1, the estimates of the standard deviations shown in the lower panel of Table 2.1 exhibit close agreement between the census and the CPS and between the census and the PES. Excepting the estimates of the standard deviation of personal income derived from the census and CPS, the estimates from each pair of comparisons are identical to two significant digits. The standard deviation of personal income estimated from CPS reports is, however, always less than the estimate derived from reports of the same respondents in the 1960 census. As we illustrate below, this finding is consistent with the usual assumptions about the relationship between true scores, measurements of them, and errors of measurement. That the estimated standard deviations of years of school completed in the PES and of occupational attainment in the CPS should be larger, even by a small amount, than the corresponding census estimates, is inconsistent with the assumption of uncorrelated errors in usual treatments of reliability theory.

## On the Theory of Measurement Error

In the theory of measurement error, one usually represents the measured value of a variable as the sum of its true value and an error term.   Thus, if $T$ is the *true* value of a variable, $M$ a measure of it, and $e$ an error term, one usually assumes that

$$M = T + e \tag{2.1}$$

Under this condition, the variance of the measured variable, Var $[M]$, may be expressed as

$$\text{Var } [M] = \text{Var } [T] + \text{Var } [e] + 2 \text{ Cov } [T, e] \tag{2.2}$$

where the variances of $T$ and $e$ are given by Var $[T]$ and Var $[e]$, respectively, and their covariance is given by Cov $[T, e]$.   Ordinarily, the errors are assumed to be *uncorrelated with the true scores*, so that Cov $[T, e]$ is equal to zero.   But the variance of the errors is always a nonnegative number, so that under the assumption of random measurement errors, one expects the variance of the measured scores to exceed the variance of the true scores by an amount exactly equal to Var $[e]$ (12, chaps. 1 and 2).

Because of the superior enumeration and data-collection procedures employed in CPS and PES operations, one generally assumes data generated by them to be of superior quality to those obtained in the census.   Letting $I_t$ be the true level of personal income, $I'$ be the CPS observation, $I_c$ be the census observation, and $e_{I'}$ and $e_{I_c}$ be the errors of measurement associated with the CPS and census observations, respectively, we have, on applying Eq. (2.2) and assuming random measurement errors,

$$\text{Var } [I'] = \text{Var } [I_t] + \text{Var } [e_{I'}] \tag{2.3}$$

and

$$\text{Var } [I_c] = \text{Var } [I_t] + \text{Var } [e_{I_c}] \tag{2.4}$$

Subtracting Eq. (2.3) from (2.4) leaves

$$\text{Var } [I_c] - \text{Var } [I'] = \text{Var } [e_{I_c}] - \text{Var } [e_{I'}] \tag{2.5}$$

If the CPS measures of personal income are in fact superior to those obtained in the census, then the variance in the errors of measurement associated with the CPS measures of personal income, Var $[e_{I'}]$, is *strictly less* than the variance in the errors of measurement associated with census readings on personal income, Var $[e_{I_c}]$.   This implies, of course, that Var $[I_c]$ > Var $[I']$.   Inspection of Table 2.1 reveals that, for every subpopulation, the standard deviation of personal income observed in the census exceeds that observed on the same respondents in the CPS.   The measurements on personal income are, then, at least consistent with both the usual assumptions of the theory of measurement error and the belief that the CPS is a superior source of information.

Analysis of the observed standard deviations of years of school completed and occupational attainment in the PES or CPS and census does not, however, prove consistent with *both* the ordinary assumptions of reliability theory *and* the belief that the CPS and PES yield data of higher quality than the census. As one can see in Table 2.1, the census estimates of the standard deviations of these variables are always less—though not much less—than the standard deviations estimated from the PES or the CPS. Unless one is willing to assert that the census provides superior estimates of occupational attainment and years of school completed than the PES and CPS—an anomalous claim in view of the findings on personal income—one's only recourse is to relax the assumption of uncorrelated errors and allow the true scores to be correlated with the errors of measurement. Before providing a numerical illustration, we extend the mathematical analysis.

Using the identity $M = T + e$ to find an expression for Var $[M]$ yields an equation which may be solved for Cov $[T, e]$. Substituting Var $[T] = A^2$, Var $[M] = B^2$, and Var $[e] = 4k^2$ gives

$$\text{Cov } [T, e] = \tfrac{1}{2}(B^2 - A^2 - 4k^2) \tag{2.6}$$

Substituting this expression in the formula for the correlation between $T$ and $e$ gives

$$r_{Te} = f(k) = \frac{B^2 - A^2 - 4k^2}{4Ak} \tag{2.7}$$

Since $(\text{Var } [e])^{\frac{1}{2}} = 2k$ is always a nonnegative number, we consider only nonnegative values of $k$. Thus, if $A^2 > B^2$, $f(k)$ is negative and the correlation between the true scores and the errors of measurement is an inverse one. We may proceed to find the extrema of $f(k)$ by using the derivative test. We have

$$\frac{df}{dk} = f'(k) = \frac{A^2 - B^2 - 4k^2}{4Ak^2} \tag{2.8}$$

which assumes the value zero for

$$k^2 = \tfrac{1}{4}(A^2 - B^2) \tag{2.9}$$

The second derivative of $f(k)$ is given by

$$\frac{d^2f}{dk^2} = f''(k) = \frac{B^2 - A^2}{2Ak^3} \tag{2.10}$$

For $k^2 = \tfrac{1}{4}(A^2 - B^2)$, we have

$$f''(k) = -\frac{4}{A(A^2 - B^2)^{\frac{1}{2}}} \tag{2.11}$$

Thus, at the extremum of $f(k)$ where $k$ is positive, $f''(k)$ is negative and $f(k)$ assumes a maximum. (If $A^2 > B^2$, this maximum is a minimum absolute value of $f$.) Hence, on substituting $k = \tfrac{1}{2}(A^2 - B^2)^{\frac{1}{2}}$ into $f(k)$, we find that

$$r_{Te} = f(k) = \frac{B^2 - A^2}{A(A^2 - B^2)^{\frac{1}{2}}} \tag{2.12}$$

is a maximum value (a minimum absolute value if $A^2 > B^2$) for the correlation between $T$ and $e$ given fixed values of Var $[T] = A^2$ and Var $[M] = B^2$.

Since $f(k)$ assumes a maximum for $k = \frac{1}{2}(A^2 - B^2)$, $f(k)$ assumes smaller values for $k$ less than or greater than this critical number. Since the correlation between $T$ and $e$ is logically restrained between the values $-1$ and $+1$, we are interested only in those values of $k$ where $f(k)$ falls between $-1$ and $+1$. We may find these by setting $f(k) = -1$ which yields the equation:

$$-4k^2 + 4Ak + B^2 - A^2 = 0 \qquad (2.13)$$

This quadratic has zeros for $k = \frac{1}{2}(A + B)$ and $k = \frac{1}{2}(A - B)$. Thus, the correlation between $T$ and $e$ is always negative in case $A^2 > B^2$ and is exactly equal to $-1$ in case the standard deviation of the errors, (Var $[e])^{\frac{1}{2}}$, is equal to $A + B$ or $A - B$. We cannot emphasize too strongly that this analysis applies only in the case where $A^2 > B^2$. The function $f(k)$ has quite different properties in the logically possible situations where $A^2 = B^2$ and $A^2 < B^2$. However, because the variances of occupational attainment and years of school completed estimated from the PES or CPS exceed those estimated from the census, it is the case $A^2 > B^2$ which is of interest in the present context and for which we now provide a numerical illustration.

To utilize the foregoing results in a further evaluation of the relative magnitudes of the variances of either educational or occupational attainment as estimated by PES or CPS and census reports, one must take the additional step of assuming the equivalence of true scores and the PES or CPS reports. Implausible though this assumption may seem to the academic mind, we may note that the Bureau of the Census routinely takes this step in published evaluations of census errors. Indeed, the Bureau apparently regards such an assumption necessary to interpret its own manipulations of the data: "An assumption necessary for meaningful interpretation of the net error is that the CPS is taken as the standard of accuracy" (27, p. 7). Although we are able to relax this assumption below, we accept it for the moment in order to examine the case of years of school completed. Using the figures shown in Table 2.1, we set Var $[T] = A^2 = (3.61)^2$ and Var $[M] = B^2 = (3.58)^2$. Under these conditions,

$$f(k) = \frac{-0.014938 - 0.277008k^2}{k} \qquad (2.14)$$

This function is always negative for positive values of $k$, the only ones considered in this context since the standard deviation of the errors of measurement $(= 2k)$ must be a nonnegative number. The function assumes a maximum for $k = 0.232218$; the value of the function for this value of $k$ is $-0.1287$, which is the smallest correlation *in absolute value* which can be found between the PES estimates of years of school completed and the errors of measurement in the census reports on educational attainment when the PES is taken as the standard of accuracy.

Since $r_{Te}$ can theoretically be equal to $-1$, we can also derive the maximum and minimum values for Var $[e]$. We find that $r_{Te} = f(k) = -1$ holds for $k = 0.015$ and $k = 3.595$. Since Var $[e] = 4k^2$, its actual value must fall between the minimum and maximum values of $0.009$ and $51.6961$; the standard deviation of the errors of measurement must fall between $0.03$ and $7.19$. Thus, the variance in the errors of estimate can, in fact, exceed the variance in the measured and true scores, although this unlikely circumstance will occur only if there is a large negative correlation between the PES estimates of years of school completed and the errors in the census estimates when the PES is taken as the standard of accuracy. In any case, knowing only the variances of PES and census estimates enables one (1) to deduce that the errors of measurement in the census reports on years of school completed are inversely correlated with the PES estimates of years of school completed, and (2) to establish the minimum absolute value this correlation can assume. However, one can place only extremely wide limits on the variance in the errors of estimate. While these results have been illustrated only for years of school completed, the conclusions are similar in the case of occupational attainment. For personal income, the analysis would have to be developed somewhat differently, though even in that case the errors of estimate in census reports on personal income would prove inversely correlated with CPS estimates unless the variance of the errors is small relative to the difference of the variances of measured and true values.

## Some Floor and Ceiling Effects on the Measurements of SES Variables

In the preceding section, we demonstrated that in order to explain the variances in years of school completed and occupational attainment as estimated by PES or CPS and census reports, one needs to posit not only nonrandom errors but also a negative correlation between the PES or CPS reports and the errors in census responses when the PES or CPS replies are taken as the true scores. Such a conclusion is, of course, not surprising, for both years of school completed and occupational attainment have an effective ceiling and floor. Persons who have true levels of education which are high can only report levels of educational attainment which are equal to or less than their actual years of school completed, while those with low true levels of education can only misreport their years of school completed by overstating them. But this implies an inverse correlation between true educational attainment and the errors of measurement. Similar reasoning applies to other measures of socioeconomic status, occupational attainment, and personal income. Thus, in the sections below, there is no necessity for introducing models which assume random errors of measurement. They are considered, however, in order to secure a more complete catalog of causal models which may be applicable in other situations.

The presence of floor and ceiling effects in SES variables may also help explain why the CPS reports on personal income yield a lower mean value than the census replies.  Let us assume that both the CPS and the census yield imperfect measures of personal income, but that the CPS is more accurate than the census.  Under these conditions, persons with high true levels of income will, on the average, underreport their real personal incomes to both the CPS interviewer and the census enumerator, but they will underreport them less in the CPS than in the census.  Likewise, persons with low true levels of income will, on the average, overreport their personal incomes in both the census and the CPS, but they will overreport them more in the census than in the CPS. If personal income were symmetrically distributed, then these differences in accuracy would make no difference in the means estimated from the two sources since the under- and overstatements of personal income would tend to cancel each other out in both the CPS and the census.  However, personal income is not symmetrically distributed and is, instead, skewed to the right, the numbers of respondents having lower levels of income being large relative to the numbers having higher incomes.  This heaping of respondents at the lower-income levels means that the CPS reports, which are the more accurate, should yield a slightly lower estimate of average personal income than the census, though both will still overstate the true mean slightly.   This reasoning yields an expectation which is perfectly consistent with the data shown in Table 2.1, although a more extensive examination would be required to draw a firm conclusion. This is especially so in view of the relative magnitudes of the standard deviations of personal income in the CPS and the census.

## 2.2   ANALYSIS OF BIVARIATE STATISTICS WHEN TRUE SCORES ARE KNOWN

### Reliability Coefficients for Socioeconomic Variables

An assessment of the reliability of census measures of socioeconomic status may be derived by correlating census reports with replies given by the same persons in the PES or in the CPS.  For a variety of subgroups, reliability coefficients derived in this manner are shown in Table 2.2 for years of school completed, personal income, and occupational attainment.  Whether one takes the CPS or PES reports as true scores or regards both the census and survey results as independent measures of the same underlying variable, two important points emerge from Table 2.2.   First, reports on educational attainment appear to be more reliable than reports on either occupation or personal income, which are subject to approximately equal amounts of error.   Second, the reliability of reports on both personal income and occupational attainment is less for nonwhites than for whites.   On the whole, however, the total reliability coefficients are moderately large, indicating that correlations between socioeconomic variables are not likely to be severely attenuated.

TABLE 2.2   Reliability Coefficients for Selected SES Variables as Observed in Samples Drawn from Current Population Survey and Post Enumeration Survey Returns and Matched with Census of Population Returns, c. 1960*

| Population | Years of school completed† | Personal income ‡ | Occupational SES‡ |
|---|---|---|---|
| Total persons | .9332 | .8468 | .8726¶ |
| Whites | § | .8795 | .8711 |
| Nonwhites | § | .7991 | .8175 |
| Total males | § | .8227 | .8607¶ |
| Whites | § | .8522 | .8610 |
| Nonwhites | § | .7618 | .8061 |

\* Data exclude those not reporting on either or both surveys.
† Census-Post Enumeration Survey match.
‡ Census-CPS match.
§ Not available.
¶ Figures for "Total persons" and "Total males" refer to those classified as either employed in CPS and employe d or not reported in census, or unemployed in CPS and unemployed or not reported in census. All other occupational SES figures are for the former classification only.
Sources: (26, tables 12, 17, and 18); (27, tables 34, 36, 42, and 43).

## Correlations between Socioeconomic Variables

The end result of any assessment of reliability and the effects of measurement errors should be the approximation of the correlation between true scores by correction of the observed correlation between measured variables. Before proceeding to the evaluation of several causal models yielding different correction formulas, we introduce in Table 2.3 the intercorrelations between years of school completed, occupational attainment, and personal income observed in the *1960 Census of Population*. These correlations are based either on the total experienced civilian labor force or on those in the experienced civilian labor force over twenty-five. Males and females were combined since one of the reliability coefficients, that for years of school completed, can be derived only for all persons.

The correlations observed between SES variables in Table 2.3 are not large: as many students of stratification in the United States have observed, these variables form a loosely interwoven complex (1,10). Income is by no means completely determined by education and occupational attainment. In turn, occupation and years of school completed are themselves correlated but modestly. These statements are based, however, upon uncorrected correlations;

TABLE 2.3　Correlations between Various SES Measures, Showing Reliability Coefficients in the Main Diagonal, c. 1960*

| Various SES measures | Total personal income | Occupational SES | Years of school completed |
|---|---|---|---|
| Total personal income | .8468 | .3423 | .3189 |
| Occupational SES | | .8726 | .5564 |
| Years of school completed | | | .9332 |

* Correlations are for persons of both sexes aged fourteen years and older with the following exceptions: (1) all correlations involving occupation are for the experienced civilian labor force (ECLF), (2) the reliability coefficient for education is for persons twenty-five years old and over, (3) the reliability coefficient for occupational SES is computed over a population which differs from the ECLF by apparently including the inexperienced unemployed, and (4) all correlations are computed only for those reporting both characteristics or reporting the characteristic both times, except that the census tabulations appear to have allocated the nonrespondents over response categories.
Sources: (26, table 12); (27, tables 34, 36, and 42); (23, tables 6 and 7); (24, tables 9 and 25).

depending upon the particular pattern of errors to which they are subject, they may substantially understate the common variance of each pair of SES variables.

## The Current Population Survey as a Standard of Accuracy

Bogue and Murphy (4) have undertaken an evaluation of the possible effects of measurement errors upon the association between income and education. They approach the data from the perspective of polytomous cross classification, neither imposing a causal model upon the materials nor adopting the strategy of regression and correlation analysis. Following the procedure utilized by the Bureau of the Census, Bogue and Murphy take the PES as the standard of accuracy against which the quality of the census is judged.[3] In this section, we impose causal structures upon the alternatives studied by Bogue and Murphy, retaining the explicit assumption that the PES or CPS reports may be equated to the true scores.

In developing various causal models, we make use of the theory of path analysis developed by the biometrician, Sewall Wright (9,16,30–33). A review of the relevant theory is not appropriate in the present context. It is thoroughly discussed in Chap. 6. According to one of the fundamental assumptions of path analysis, the correlation between any two variables in a causal system may be expressed as the sum of the products of the paths from other variables

[3] Unfortunately, tables 12–14, upon which much of Bogue's and Murphy's discussion (4) is based, are clearly in error, since they do not have corresponding marginal distributions equal.

in the system to the first variable times their corresponding correlation with the second of the two variables whose correlation is at issue. In symbols,

$$r_{ij} = \sum_{k} p_{ik} r_{kj} \qquad (2.15)$$

where $r_{ij}$ is the correlation between $i$th and $j$th variables, $p_{ik}$ is the estimated value of the path *from* the $k$th *to* the $i$th variable, $r_{kj}$ is the correlation between $k$th and $j$th variables, and the summation runs over all variables which have a direct path or net association with the $i$th variable. The theorem may, of course, be successively applied to the $r_{kj}$'s appearing in the initial sum. This theorem, together with a variety of causal assumptions introduced in the context to which they apply, enables us to solve for the paths appearing in the causal models studied below.

### Random Errors

The first model to be considered is exhibited in Fig. 2.1 as a path diagram. The variables shown in the figure are defined as follows: $E'$, reports on years of school completed derived from the 1960 *Post Enumeration Survey; I'*, reports on personal income derived from the *Current Population Survey* of March, 1960; $E_c$, years of school completed as reported in the *1960 Census of Population;* and $I_c$, personal income as reported in the 1960 census. The notation for these variables is used consistently throughout the remainder of the text. For the random error model shown in Fig. 2.1, $p_{E_cE'}$ and $p_{I_cI'}$ are given, respectively, by the known correlations between $E_c$ and $E'$ and between $I_c$ and $I'$. The side arrows shown in the figure represent the residuals of $E_c$ and $I_c$ when regressed on $E'$ and $I'$, respectively. Their values are given by $(1 - p^2_{E_cE'})^{1/2}$ and $(1 - p^2_{I_cI'})^{1/2}$. Applying Eq. (2.15), one finds that the known correlation between $E_c$ and $I_c$ is given by

$$r_{E_cI_c} = (p_{E_cE'})(r_{E'I'})(p_{I_cI'}) \qquad (2.16)$$

which may be solved for the unknown correlation between $E'$ and $I'$. In this model, the implied correlation between years of school completed and personal

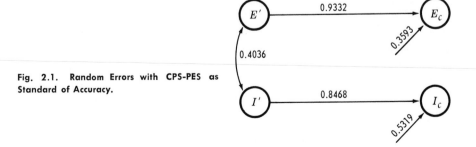

**Fig. 2.1. Random Errors with CPS-PES as Standard of Accuracy.**

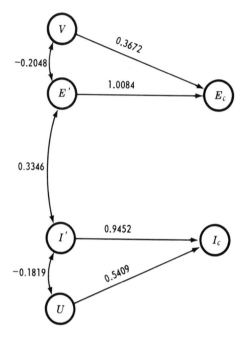

Fig. 2.2. Correlated Errors with Independence of Errors between Variables and CPS-PES as Standard of Accuracy.

income as reported in the *Current Population Survey* is .4036, a value which yields a common variance between education and income about half again as large as that derived from the known correlation of .3189 between the two census measures.

### Correlated Errors with Independence between Variables

In Fig. 2.2 we relax the assumption of random errors, but do not allow the errors of measurement in education to be intercorrelated with the income variables or their errors of measurement and vice versa. To solve for the paths in Fig. 2.2, we first need to work out the relationships between $E_c$, $E'$, and $V$, the errors of measurement in years of school completed, and between $I_c$, $I'$, and $U$, the errors of measurement in personal income. Letting

$$E_c = E' + V \tag{2.17}$$

we may conclude (1) that the regression coefficient of $E'$ in the regression of $E_c$ on $E'$ *and* $V$ is given by $b_{E_cE'\cdot V} = 1$, and (2) that the coefficient associated with $V$ in the same regression is greater than zero. Assuming that $p_{E_cE'} = b^*_{E_cE'\cdot V}$ where $b^*_{E_cE'\cdot V}$ is the regression coefficient of $E'$ in standard form associated with the regression of $E_c$ on $E'$ and $V$, we have

$$p_{E_cE'} = \frac{(\text{Var } [E'])^{\frac{1}{2}}}{(\text{Var } [E_c])^{\frac{1}{2}}} \tag{2.18}$$

With the appropriate standard deviations taken from Table 2.1, we estimate that $p_{E_cE'} = 3.61/3.58 = 1.0084$, a result which may be combined with the equations implied by Fig. 2.2 to solve for the unknown paths. Applying Eq. (2.15), we have from Fig. 2.2,

$$r_{E_cE'} = p_{E_cE'} + (p_{E_cV})(r_{E'V})$$

and $$(2.19)$$

$$r_{E_cV} = p_{E_cV} + (p_{E_cE'})(r_{E'V})$$

Since $E_c = E' + V$, all of the variance in the census reports is explained by $E'$ and $V$. Applying a standard formula for the square of the multiple correlation coefficient *or* using the theory of path coefficients and Fig. 2.2 to derive an expression for the correlation of $E_c$ with itself yields

$$1 = (p_{E_cV})(r_{E_cV}) + (p_{E_cE'})(r_{E_cE'}) \qquad (2.20)$$

With $p_{E_cE'} = 1.0084$ as derived above, with $p_{E_cV}$ greater than zero, and with the known value of $r_{E_cE'}$, this and Eqs. (2.19) may be solved for the values of $r_{E_cV}$, $r_{E'V}$, and $p_{E_cV}$ which are either entered in Fig. 2.2 or may be derived from the values exhibited in Fig. 2.2. The relationships among $I_c$, $I'$, and $U$ may be derived in a manner analogous to the derivation of the relations among $E_c$, $E'$, and $V$.

We may now derive the unknown correlation between $E'$ and $I'$, making use of the correlation between $E_c$ and $I_c$ and the paths from $E'$ to $E_c$ and from $I'$ to $I_c$. Applying Eq. (2.15), we may read from Fig. 2.2 the relationship

$$r_{E_cI_c} = (p_{E_cE'})(r_{E'I'})(p_{I_cI'}) \qquad (2.21)$$

Inserting the known correlation of $E_c$ with $I_c$ and the values of the paths, we may solve this equation for an estimate of the association between $E'$ and $I'$. We find that $r_{E'I'} = .3189/(.9452)(1.0084) = .3346$, a value which is not substantially larger than the correlation of .3189 between the reports on years of school completed and personal income in the *1960 Census of Population*.

## Correlated Errors with Independence between Errors in Different Variables

Figure 2.3 has the same basic format as Fig. 2.2, save that we now allow $V$, the errors in $E_c$, to be correlated with $I'$ and $U$, the errors in $I_c$, to be correlated with $E'$. The relationships among $I_c$, $I'$, and $U$ and the relationships among $E_c$, $E'$, and $V$ which we derived for Fig. 2.2 still pertain in Fig. 2.3. The values of the correlations and paths relating these variables have been carried over from Fig. 2.2 and entered in Fig. 2.3. In order to solve Fig. 2.3 for the unknown correlation between $E'$ and $I'$, we must, however, make some further assumptions. For the moment, we derive a general solution by setting $r_{I'V} = \alpha$ and $r_{E'U} = \beta$.

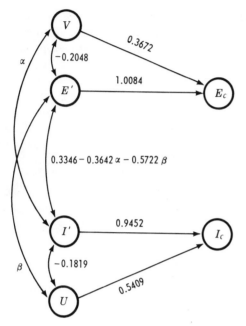

Fig. 2.3. Correlated Errors with Partial Independence of Errors between Variables and CPS-PES as a Standard of Accuracy.

Applying the theory of path coefficients, Eq. (2.15), to Fig. 2.3 yields the following equation for the correlation between $E_c$ and $I_c$:

$$r_{E_c I_c} = (p_{E_c E'})(r_{E'I'})(p_{I_c I'}) + (p_{E_c V})(\alpha)(p_{I_c I'}) + (p_{E_c E'})(\beta)(p_{I_c U}) \quad (2.22)$$

Substituting known correlations and paths in this expression and solving for the correlation between $E'$ and $I'$ yields

$$r_{E'I'} = .3346 - .3642(\alpha) - .5722(\beta) \quad (2.23)$$

In order to solve this equation for $r_{E'I'}$ we need to introduce assumptions which allow us to estimate $\alpha$ and $\beta$. One possibility is that $r_{E_c V} = r_{I_c V}$ and $r_{I_c U} = r_{E_c U}$. In this case, we can, for example, read from Fig. 2.3 that $r_{E_c V} = .3672 - (1.0084)(.2048) = .1607$ and $r_{I_c V} = (.9452)(\alpha)$. Since the identity of these two expressions is assumed, we have $\alpha = .1607/.9452 = .1700$. Similarly, the expressions for $r_{I_c U}$ and $r_{E_c U}$ may be solved for $\beta = .3659$. But these values of $\alpha$ and $\beta$ imply that $r_{E'I'} = .0633$. This seems wholly implausible, so we must conclude that the initial assumptions $r_{E_c V} = r_{I_c V}$ and $r_{I_c U} = r_{E_c U}$ (if not the whole causal model) are untenable.

Failing to solve Fig. 2.3 for a reasonable estimate of the correlation between $E'$ and $I'$ with internal assumptions about the correlations of the errors, we adopt a different strategy. To this point, we have pretended that the correlation between reports of years of school completed and personal income are not directly known from the *Current Population Survey*. Indeed, this is the case for the survey of March, 1960, which was used to check the accuracy of the 1960 census returns.    However, tabulations of years of school completed by personal income are available from the *Current Population Survey* of March, 1964, and March, 1959 (22, 28).    The income measures in these two surveys refer to the total money income of persons in 1963 and 1958, respectively.    Though this concept, identical in census and CPS, produces some differences in population estimates, there is no reason to believe these differences affect the relation of income and education.[4]    We find that, for males and females aged twenty-five and over, the association between years of school completed and total money income in 1963 was .3378, while the association between years of school completed and total money income in 1958 was .3600.    The square root of one-half the sum of the squares of these two correlations is .3491, a value we take as an estimate of the correlation between $E'$ and $I'$.

Inserting the estimate $r_{E'I'} = .3491$ into the expression which gives $r_{E'I'}$ as a linear function of $\alpha$ and $\beta$ yields

$$.0145 + .3642(\alpha) + .5722(\beta) = 0 \qquad (2.24)$$

If $\alpha$ and $\beta$ are of the same sign, this expression will be satisfied only for relatively small, negative values of $\alpha$ and $\beta$.    If either $\alpha$ is less than $-.0398$ or $\beta$ is less than $-.0253$, then $\alpha$ and $\beta$ must be of opposite sign for the expression to be satisfied.    While it seems entirely plausible for $r_{I'V} = \alpha$ and $r_{E'U} = \beta$ to be of opposite sign if both are small in absolute value, it seems hardly plausible for them to be of opposite sign *and* relatively large in absolute value since any argument that $\alpha$ is large can also be applied to argue that $\beta$ is of roughly the same order magnitude and of the same sign.    But with $r_{E'I'} = .3491$, $\alpha$ and $\beta$ cannot be large in absolute value without also being opposite in sign.[5]    We conclude, consequently, that the correlation of $V$, the errors in $E_c$, with $I'$ and the correlation of $U$, the errors in $I_c$, with $E'$ are most likely negligible.    In fact, the estimate of $r_{E'I'}$ derived from Fig. 2.2, where it was assumed that $\alpha = \beta = 0$, was .3346, a value which does not depart in any significant way from the correlation of .3378 observed in the *Current Population Survey* of March, 1964, between years of school completed and money income in 1963.    In case $\alpha = \beta$, the expression $.0145 + .3642(\alpha) + .5722(\beta) = 0$ may be solved for $\alpha = -.0155$.    The weight of the evidence, then, supports the conclusion that $r_{E'U}$ and $r_{I'V}$ are of little consequence.

## Correlated Errors

The final and most general case of correlated errors in the situation where the CPS or PES reports are equated with the true values is shown in Fig. 2.4. Here we not only admit of correlations between $I'$ and $V$ and between $E'$ and $U$,

[4] This disparity appears to have at least partially motivated the census evaluation and research program.    See the discussion of income in 1959 in the introduction and table D of the *1960 Census of Population* (25; also see U.S. Bureau of the Census 27, 28).

[5] Large in this context means orders of absolute magnitude in excess of 0.02 to 0.04.

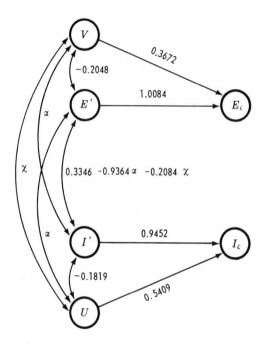

**Fig. 2.4.   Correlated Errors with CPS-PES as a Standard of Accuracy.**

but also allow $U$ and $V$ themselves to be correlated.    As in Fig. 2.3, the relations among $E_c$, $E'$, and $V$ and among $I_c$, $I'$, and $U$ may be carried over from Fig. 2.2.    The numerical values of the relevant paths and correlations have been entered in Fig. 2.4.    The present causal model admits of no solution without additional assumptions.    At the outset we assume that

$$r_{I'V} = r_{E'U} = \alpha \tag{2.25}$$

and for convenience let $r_{UV} = \chi$.

With this assumption and notation, the correlation between the census reports of years of school completed and personal income may be written as

$$r_{E_cI_c} = (p_{E_cE'})(r_{E'I'})(p_{I_cI'}) + (p_{E_cV})(\alpha)(p_{I_cI'}) + (p_{E_cE'})(\alpha)(p_{I_cU})$$
$$+ (p_{E_cV})(\chi)(p_{I_cU}) \tag{2.26}$$

Substituting in the numerical values of the known correlations and paths and solving for the correlation between $E'$ and $I'$ yields

$$r_{E'I'} = .3346 - .9364(\alpha) - .2084(\chi) \tag{2.27}$$

Additional assumptions yielding solutions for $\alpha$ and $\chi$ must now be introduced in order to achieve an explicit numerical estimate of the correlation between $E'$ and $I'$.    First, we study the assumptions $r_{E_cV} = r_{I_cV}$ and $r_{I_cU} = r_{E_cU}$.    On the one hand, we can derive from the theory of path coefficients and the numerical values entered in Fig. 2.2 that

$$r_{E_cV} = .3672 - (1.0084)(.2048) = .1607 \tag{2.28}$$

and

$$r_{I_cU} = .5409 - (.9452)(.1819) = .3690 \tag{2.29}$$

On the other hand, we have $r_{I_cV} = .9452(\alpha) + .5409(\chi)$ and

$$r_{E_cU} = 1.0084(\alpha) + .3672(\chi)$$

With the identities of the correlations assumed above, we have

$$.9452(\alpha) + .5409(\chi) - .1607 = 0 \tag{2.30}$$

and

$$1.0084(\alpha) + .3672(\chi) - .3690 = 0 \tag{2.31}$$

which may be solved for $\alpha = .7088$ and $\chi = -.9414$. However, these values of $\alpha$ and $\chi$ imply that $r_{E'I'} = -.1329$. Thus, as in the case of Fig. 2.3, we are led to a result so wholly implausible that we must reject the assumptions $r_{E_cV} = r_{I_cV}$ and $r_{I_cU} = r_{E_cU}$.

Failing a plausible solution to Fig. 2.4, we again adopt the strategy of attempting to evaluate the likely magnitudes of $\alpha$ and $\chi$ by introducing the value of $r_{E'I'}$, observed in the *Current Population Survey* of March, 1964, and March, 1959. The reader will recall that we selected $r_{E'I'} = .3491$; substituting this value in the expression for $r_{E'I'}$ as a linear function of $\alpha$ and $\chi$ yields

$$.9364(\alpha) + .2084(\chi) + .0145 = 0 \tag{2.32}$$

The equation clearly has no solution if $\alpha$ and $\chi$ are both positive. If $\alpha$ and $\chi$ are both negative, then their absolute values must be small since $.9364(\alpha) + .2084(\chi)$ must equal $-.0145$. In any case, the range of $\alpha$ is severely restricted. For if $\chi = 1$, $\alpha = -.2380$ and if $\chi = -1$, $\alpha = .2071$. In general, by analogy to $r_{E'V}$ and $r_{I'U}$, we might conclude that $\alpha$ is negative, but less in absolute value than either $r_{E'V}$ or $r_{I'U}$. With this plausible assumption, $\alpha$ is no smaller than $-.1819$, in which case $\chi = .7476$. In any event, it seems likely that $r_{UV} = \chi$ will be nonnegative, since the only plausible theory is that persons who over- or understate their years of school completed will reproduce these biases in their statements of personal income. If $\chi$ is nonnegative, then, in order to achieve consistency with the correlations between $E'$ and $I'$ observed in the *Current Population Survey*, we must conclude that $\alpha$ is restricted between $-.0155$ and $-.2380$. For $\alpha = -.0127$, $\alpha = \chi$; for smaller values of $\alpha$, $\chi$ increases rapidly and becomes substantially larger in absolute value than $\alpha$.

Our review of the class of models treated by Bogue and Murphy in the form of polytomous cross classifications is now complete. So long as one holds the reports in the CPS or PES to be the true scores, the errors of measurement can have only a slight net effect upon the correlation between education and income observed in the census. This is so because the values of the association between education and income observed in the *Current Population Survey* do not depart widely from those observed in the census. This does not necessarily mean that the discrepancy between reports in the *Current Population Survey* and in the *Census of Population* is not correlated with both the original and other variables. Though the weight of the evidence is consistent with the assumption that these correlations are not large, our understanding of these matters would be greatly enhanced if the Bureau of the Census routinely published cross tabulations of discrepancies in CPS-census reports on, for example, education by discrepancies in CPS-census reports on other socioeconomic variables.

## 2.3 ANALYSIS OF BIVARIATE STATISTICS WHEN TRUE SCORES ARE UNKNOWN

### *The Current Population Survey as an Imperfect Source of Data*

Much more appealing than the models considered by Bogue and Murphy are causal models which do not equate either reports in the *Current Population Survey* or in the *Post Enumeration Survey* with the true scores. Like most surveys, the *Current Population Survey* and the *Post Enumeration Survey* do not generate error-free data. They are doubtless of higher quality than the census, owing to the use of highly trained and experienced interviewers. In this section, we investigate several causal models in which (1) neither the census nor the CPS or PES data are regarded as error-free and (2) the CPS or PES reports are allowed to be of higher quality than the census reports.

### *The Correction for Attenuation*

Before proceeding to the presentation of alternative models, we introduce the symbols $E_t$ and $I_t$ to represent the true levels of education and income. The previous notation for the census and CPS reports on years of school completed and personal income is carried over to the present section. In Fig. 2.5, the true scores are introduced as explicit causes of the census and CPS reports, which are regarded as independent measures, with random errors, of the corresponding true scores. For ease of subsequent presentation, Fig. 2.5 also introduces further notation: $p_{E'E_t} = a$, $p_{E_cE_t} = b$, $p_{I'I_t} = c$, $p_{I_cI_t} = d$, and $r_{E_tI_t} = \alpha$. The small side arrows placed by the variables $E'$, $E_c$, $I'$, and $I_c$ represent the residuals from the regression of each of these variables on the true scores; the values of the side arrows are indicated as a function of the value of the path from the true scores to the measured variables.

A special case of Fig. 2.5 is the one where $a = b$ and $c = d$. In this situation, $r_{E'E_c} = a^2$ and $r_{I'I_c} = c^2$ which implies, for example, $p_{E'E_t} = a = (r_{E'E_c})^{1/2}$ and $p_{I'I_t} = c = (r_{I'I_c})^{1/2}$. Since on applying Eq. (2.15), we have in this situation $r_{E'I'} = a(\alpha)c$, we conclude:

$$r_{E_tI_t} = \frac{r_{E'I'}}{(r_{I'I_c})^{1/2}(r_{E'E_c})^{1/2}} \tag{2.33}$$

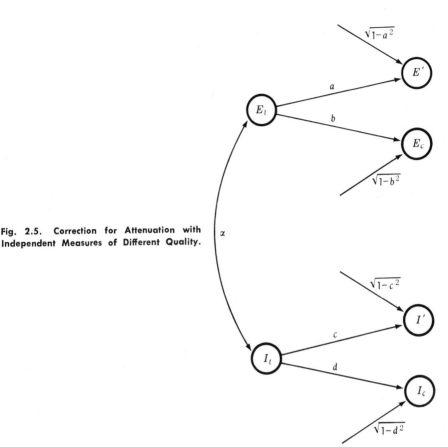

**Fig. 2.5. Correction for Attenuation with Independent Measures of Different Quality.**

This equation will be recognized as the correction for attenuation introduced in many elementary statistics texts (29, p. 300). Sewall Wright demonstrated over two decades ago that Fig. 2.5 is the appropriate causal model underlying the correction for attenuation (33).

The usual correction for attenuation does not concern us in the present situation, where we are unwilling to assume that census and CPS reports are of equal quality. This amounts to asserting that $p_{E'E_t} > p_{E_cE_t}$ and $p_{I'I_t} > p_{I_cI_t}$. However, lacking the critical assumption which allows one to derive the correction for attenuation, we do have an additional piece of information: both $r_{E_cI_c}$ and $r_{E'I'}$ are known. With both these correlations known, application of the theory of path coefficients to Fig. 2.5 yields the following equations:

$$r_{E'E_c} = ab = .9332 \qquad (2.34)$$
$$r_{I'I_c} = cd = .8468 \qquad (2.35)$$
$$r_{E_cI_c} = b(\alpha)d = .3189 \qquad (2.36)$$

and

$$r_{E'I'} = a(\alpha)c = .3491 \qquad (2.37)$$

One further assumption, however, must be introduced to derive an explicit solution for $a$, $b$, $c$, $d$, and $\alpha$. One attractive assumption embodies the notion that the quality of PES relative to census measures of years of school completed is the same as the quality of CPS relative to census measures of personal income. Explicitly, this assumption might take the form, $a^2/(a^2 + b^2) = c^2/(c^2 + d^2)$. By simple algebraic manipulation this expression reduces to $ad = bc$, so the assumption about the relative quality of the CPS or PES reports amounts to assuming the identity of $r_{E_cI'} = b(\alpha)c$ and $r_{E'I_c} = a(\alpha)d$. This assumption, together with the preceding four equations, enables one to solve explicitly for $a$, $b$, $c$, $d$, and $\alpha$. We find, for example, that $p_{E'E_t} = a = .9883$ and $p_{E_cE_t} = b = .9443$, while $p_{I'I_t} = c = .9414$ and $p_{I_cI_t} = d = .8995$. Finally, we find $\alpha = .3754$, a value which implies a common variance between education and income which is about two-fifths again as large as that implied by the correlation of .3189 between $E_c$ and $I_c$.

## Partially Correlated Errors

In Fig. 2.6, we introduce a modest elaboration of the correction for attenuation by considering the differences, $V_1$ and $V_2$, between the PES or census reports on years of school completed, respectively, and the true levels of education. Similarly defined differences, $U_1$ and $U_2$, between the measured and true levels of personal income are also entertained. These differences are allowed to be correlated with the true and measured scores associated with them, but are not allowed to be correlated with either the true and measured scores for different variables or among themselves. These changes render the causal model both recalcitrant to solution and inconsistent with the data at hand.

In Fig. 2.6, the difference $V_1$ is defined by the solution of the equation $E' = E_t + V_1$; the remaining differences are defined by the solution of analogous equations. Thus, the regression coefficient associated with $E_t$ in the regression of $E'$ on $E_t$ and $V_1$ is given by $b_{E'E_t \cdot V_1} = 1$. With $p_{E'E_t} = b^*_{E'E_t \cdot V_1}$, where $b^*_{E'E_t \cdot V_1}$ is the regression coefficient in standard form of $E_t$ in the regression of $E'$ on $E_t$ and $V_1$, we have

$$p_{E'E_t} = \frac{(b_{E'E_t \cdot V_1})(\mathrm{Var}\,[E_t])^{1/2}}{(\mathrm{Var}\,[E'])^{1/2}} = \frac{(\mathrm{Var}\,[E_t])^{1/2}}{(\mathrm{Var}\,[E'])^{1/2}} \qquad (2.38)$$

Similarly, one can find

$$p_{E_cE_t} = \frac{(\mathrm{Var}\,[E_t])^{1/2}}{(\mathrm{Var}\,[E_c])^{1/2}} \qquad (2.39)$$

Taking the ratio $p_{E'E_t}/p_{E_cE_t}$, the unknown standard deviation of $E_t$ vanishes, leaving

$$\frac{p_{E'E_t}}{p_{E_cE_t}} = \frac{(\mathrm{Var}\,[E_c])^{1/2}}{(\mathrm{Var}\,[E'])^{1/2}} \qquad (2.40)$$

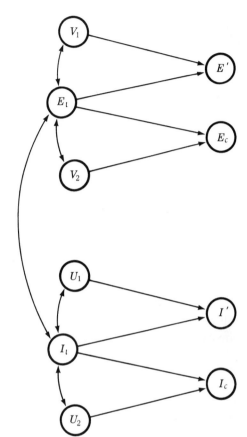

**Fig. 2.6. Partially Correlated Errors with CPS and Census as Independent Measures.**

Selecting the appropriate standard deviation of $E_c$ and $E'$ from Table 2.1, we find $p_{E'E_t}/p_{E_cE_t} = .9917$, or $p_{E'E_t} = .9917(p_{E_cE_t})$. By an exactly parallel derivation, we have $p_{I'I_t} = 1.0579(p_{I_cI_t})$.

At this juncture, we recall our discussion of the previous section, where we indicated that the assumption $r_{E'I_e} = r_{E_cI'}$ was equivalent to assuming that the quality of PES relative to census reports of educational attainment was identical to the quality of CPS relative to census reports of personal income. This assumption is no longer consistent with the numerical results. For if $r_{E'I_e} = r_{E_cI'}$, it is easy to establish that $(p_{E'E_t})(p_{I_cI_t}) = (p_{E_cE_t})(p_{I'I_t})$. But substituting the expressions for $p_{E_cE_t}$ and $p_{I_cI_t}$ in terms of $p_{E'E_t}$ and $p_{I'I_t}$, respectively, leaves us with the clearly false implication that the product of .9917 and a nonzero number is identical to the product of 1.0579 and the *same* nonzero number. Thus, one of the assumptions which enabled us to solve a modified version of the correction for attenuation which allowed the census, PES, and CPS to be of different quality is inconsistent in the present model.

Another source of difficulty stems from one's ability to derive the numerical value of $r_{E'I'}$ once $r_{E_cI_c}$ is known.   From Fig. 2.6, we can obtain, by application of the theory of path coefficients,

$$r_{E_cI_c} = (p_{E_cE_t})(r_{E_tI_t})(p_{I_cI_t}) \qquad (2.41)$$

On the other hand, we have

$$r_{E'I'} = (p_{E'E_t})(r_{E_tI_t})(p_{I'I_t}) = (.9917)(p_{E_cE_t})(r_{E_tI_t})(1.0579)(p_{I_cI_t})$$
$$= 1.0491(r_{E_cI_c}) \qquad (2.42)$$

So with $r_{E_cI_c} = .3189$, we have $r_{E'I'} = .3348$, a value lower than the estimates of .3378 and .3600 derived from the *Current Population Survey* of March, 1964, and March, 1959, respectively.

Despite the inconsistency with the estimates from the *Current Population Survey*, one might choose to disregard the discrepancy as falling well within the standards of precision acceptable in the social sciences.   Similarly, one might surmise that the estimated values of the ratios of $p_{E'E_t}$ to $p_{E_cE_t}$ and of $p_{I'I_t}$ to $p_{I_cI_t}$ are sufficiently close to unity to justify accepting the identities $p_{E'E_t} = p_{E_cE_t}$ and $p_{I'I_t} = p_{I_cI_t}$, despite one's intuition that the reports in the *Current Population Survey* and the *Post Enumeration Survey* are superior to those obtained in the census. This equation of the quality of the census and the PES or CPS also requires the assumption that $r_{V_1E_t} = r_{V_2E_t}$, $r_{U_1I_t} = r_{U_2I_t}$, $p_{E'V_1} = p_{E_cV_2}$, and $p_{I'U_1} = p_{I_cU_2}$. One further set of assumptions allows one to solve for numerical values of the paths in Fig. 2.6.   The critical assumption is that the common variance of $V_1$ and $E_t$ is identical to the common variance of $V_1$ and $E'$.   This assumption and similar ones regarding $V_2$, $U_1$, and $U_2$ yield equations analogous to the following relation:

$$(r_{V_1E_t})^2 = [p_{E'V_1} + (p_{E'E_t})(r_{V_1E_t})]^2 \qquad (2.43)$$

With an effective ceiling and floor imposed on educational attainment, a person with a high true level of education can have only a somewhat lower or equivalent reported level while a person with a low true level can have only a somewhat higher or equivalent reported one.   Either arguing in this way or referring to the underlying mathematical model of Fig. 2.6, i.e., $E' = E_t + V_1$, one can surmise that $r_{V_1E_t}$ is negative, while $p_{E'V_1}$ and the corresponding zero order correlation are positive.   These inequalities and similar ones involving the remaining variables enable one to solve the foregoing equations for numerical values of the paths and unknown correlations in Fig. 2.6.

The numerical solutions imply modest correlations between the errors and both the true scores and measured variables.   We find $r_{V_1E_t} = r_{V_2E_t} = -.1292$, $r_{U_1I_t} = r_{U_2I_t} = -.1957$, $p_{E'V_1} = p_{E_cV_2} = .2585$, and $p_{I'U_1} = p_{I_cU_2} = .3914$.   The most striking result, not evident from the equations themselves, requires $p_{E'E_t} = p_{E_cE_t} = p_{I'I_t} = p_{I_cI_t} = 1$.   Since $r_{E_cI_c} = (p_{E_cE_t})(r_{E_tI_t})(p_{I_cI_t})$, this result gives $r_{E_cI_c} = r_{E_tI_t}$.   Thus, the observed correlation between the census reports turns out under the present assumptions to be identical to the correlation of the true scores. The reader is reminded, however, that this result is not a *general* solution to Fig. 2.6 but a conclusion which can be drawn only under quite stringent assumptions.

Although we have explored a variety of alternative assumptions, we have not been able to devise an entirely plausible solution to Fig. 2.6, much less to the more complicated expansions of it which allow the errors to be correlated with the true scores of other variables and among themselves. Before turning briefly to the three-variable problem, we may note that the causal models employed to this point have not provided any firm reason for holding the correlation between educational attainment and personal income observed in the census to be in substantial error. While our catalog of causal models of measurement errors is far from complete, the models do represent a variety of plausible alternatives which do not require any substantively important revision in the correlation of personal income and years of school completed.

## 2.4 RANDOM ERRORS IN THE THREE-VARIABLE CASE

We conclude our analysis by extending our previous treatment of the association between education and income to include occupational SES as well. We consider only the case of random errors, since more complex models defy explication in the three-variable situation. Students of sociology frequently view income as a function of educational and occupational attainment, noting that education is a kind of investment whereby occupational stock is acquired and upon which income is the dividend. This verbal statement is explicitly introduced as a causal assumption in Fig. 2.7 by regarding the true levels of

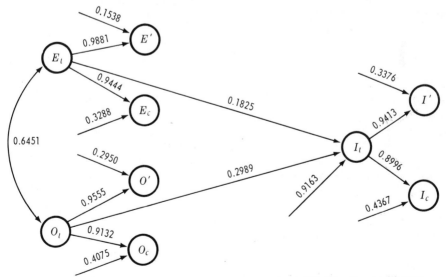

**Fig. 2.7.** Path Diagram for Relationships among Occupational SES, Education, and Income.

education and occupational SES as causes of the true level of income. (The notation in Fig. 2.7 is consistent with that previously introduced; $O'$, $O_c$, and $O_t$ are, respectively, the CPS, census, and true observations on occupational SES.) Although the analysis assumes that the CPS or PES and census reports on each of the variables are independent measurements with random errors, our treatment differs from a generalization of the correction for attenuation (a trivial exercise) by allowing the census to be of inferior quality to the CPS and the PES.

Excepting the side or residual arrows which always have values equal to the square root of the proportion of the variance of a variable unexplained by its direct causal antecedents in the system, there are nine unknown correlations or paths whose values must be estimated to achieve the numerical solution entered in Fig. 2.7. To begin with we allow the quality of the census relative to the CPS and the PES to be constant from one variable to the next. As discussed above in conjunction with Fig. 2.5, this is achieved by setting $r_{I'E_c} = r_{I_cE'}$ and $r_{I'O_c} = r_{I_cO'}$. (The additional assumption $r_{E'O_c} = r_{E_cO'}$ is redundant.) We have already introduced a value for $r_{E'I'}$; six further correlations—$r_{O'O_c}$, $r_{I'I_c}$, $r_{E'E_c}$, $r_{E_cI_c}$, $r_{E_cO_c}$, and $r_{I_cO_c}$—are supplied from Table 2.2, exhausting our information. When the seven correlations are expressed in terms of the paths and correlations explicitly drawn in Fig. 2.7 and set equal to their numerical values, the resulting equations, together with the two initial assumptions, may be solved for the numerical results entered in Fig. 2.7. The only additional assumption required is that all unknown paths and correlations are nonnegative, a condition needed in order to extract the appropriate root of several squared terms which occur in the solution.

The results entered in Fig. 2.7 may be compared with those derived directly from $I_c$, $O_c$, and $E_c$. The correlation between $E_t$ and $O_t$ is entered on the diagram and is substantially higher than the correlation of .5564 between the census measures. We can read from the path diagram that $r_{E_tI_t}$ is given by .1825 + (.2989)(.6451) = .3754. Also, $r_{I_tO_t}$ = .2989 + (.1825)(.6451) = .4166. These values are a little higher than the observed census correlations between education and income of .3189 and between occupational SES and income of .3423. If we consider a very simple, three-variable causal model in which $E_c$ and $O_c$ are entered as causes of $I_c$, then we find that the estimates of $p_{I_cO_c}$ and $p_{I_cE_c}$ by the standardized regression coefficients of $O_c$ and $E_c$ in the multiple regression of $I_c$ on $O_c$ and $E_c$ are given by .2388 and .1860, respectively. These values are about the same as the corresponding values of $p_{I_tO_t}$ and $p_{I_tE_t}$ exhibited in Fig. 2.7. Making use of a familiar equation for the multiple correlation coefficient, we can calculate from Fig. 2.7 that the multiple correlation of $I_t$ with $E_t$ and $O_t$ is given by $[.1825(r_{E_tI_t}) + .2989(r_{O_tI_t})]^{1/2} = [(.1825)(.3754) + (.2989)(.4166)]^{1/2} = .4393$. The multiple correlation of $I_c$ with $E_c$ and $O_c$ is slightly lower (.3757), but on the whole these relationships between SES variables do not appear to be attenuated greatly by unreliability. This conclusion applies, of course, only if the model at hand is deemed appropriate, though several other alternatives have led to a similar conclusion.

## Discussion

We have explored the application of path analysis to the correlation of errors of measurement in SES variables.  Using a causal framework, we studied a variety of models in which, following the example of Bogue and Murphy, the *Current Population Survey* was taken as a standard of accuracy.  Subsequently, some of the difficulties encountered in expanding their conceptualization were explored.

At the conclusion of their own investigation of correlated error in SES variables, Bogue and Murphy assert, "The results obtained here suggest most strongly that the correlation of the errors in direction and degree can powerfully affect the inferences drawn" (4, p. 55).  A casual inspection of the models of correlated error studied herein will convince the reader that this assertion is trivially true in the general case.  However, in the specific case of SES variables, we are cheered by the fact that this assumption is at variance with the known pattern of correlations between CPS and census measurements and the relative magnitudes of their standard deviations.  Bogue and Murphy arrive at their conclusions by consciously making extreme assumptions and trying to set limits on the association between education and income.  In our view, the end result of the study of errors of measurement should be the adjustment of observed correlations to approximate the correlation between true scores.  This goal is not achieved by placing extreme, though logically valid, limits upon correlations, particularly when the limits are established by the use of assumptions which are not wholly explicit or are substantively indefensible.

## 2.5  POINTS OF DEPARTURE FOR FURTHER INVESTIGATIONS OF CAUSAL REPRESENTATIONS OF IMPERFECT DATA

## Correlated Error

In the sections above we have been able to make less than wholly satisfactory progress in many cases because of gaps in the data available to us.  For example, if one chooses to regard CPS-PES as a standard of accuracy, full knowledge of the intercorrelations between the census reports, those obtained in the *Current Population Survey* or in the *Post Enumeration Survey*, and the discrepancies between them would enable one to evaluate the models of correlated error shown in Figs. 2.3 and 2.4 more fully.  On the whole, the Bureau of the Census (and sociologists and psychologists at large) have been more concerned with evaluating the quality or reliability of a single item or test. Ultimately, however, one wants not only to know the quality of particular items, but to evaluate the effects of errors in measurement upon the observed association between *different* items. If nothing else, the exposition in this chapter makes clear that only minimal progress in that direction can be made unless information about the joint distribution of errors in different measures is made available. One strategy is to pursue the numerical solution of the simpler models in which one of several measures is regarded as equivalent to the true scores. Clearly, additional empirical information would enable us to evaluate the models in great empirical detail. The hope, of course, is that further numerical work with these elementary cases will throw light on the more challenging cases in which one assumes not only that all the measures are imperfect, but that the true scores of different variables are causally related.

## Components of Error

By the time data are transcribed to punch cards and transferred to magnetic tape, they have been subject to several sources of error. Consider, for example, reports on occupational pursuit. First, the interviewer may ask for incomplete or incorrect information by soliciting only a broad occupational identification from the respondent or failing to collect such important ancillary details as his industry or class of worker. Second, the respondent himself may misreport his occupational affiliation. Third, the interviewer can, even though soliciting correct information from the respondent, fail to record it properly or in full detail. Fourth, the information returned on the interview schedule may be coded improperly into an erroneous occupational group. Fifth, the coded information may be incorrectly transcribed to coding sheets or erroneously punched onto cards. Sixth, the Wee People may fault an electronic circuit so that (1) the punched cards are not properly transcribed on tape or (2) erroneous information is recalled from memory. Very little, of course, is known about the relative contribution of each of these sources of error to the total unreliability in occupational and similar reports. While one might well presume that coding error and misreporting by respondents are the largest sources of error, even their relative sizes are not known. One useful exercise would be to gauge the relative contributions of these several sources of error and evaluate causal models of their interrelationship. A related problem meriting treatment in the causal framework elaborated in this chapter is the accuracy of respondents' reports about others. Wives, for example, are not infrequently asked in sample surveys to report the occupation of their fathers-in-law. One might assume that their reports would be less reliable than the reports of their husbands on the same person, but precisely how this differential misreporting affects so central a sociological relationship as that between the occupations of fathers and their sons is unknown.

## The Problem of Multiple Indicators

The central focus of this chapter has been the question of reliability.   The situation we have expounded is the one in which two replies to the same inquiry are available and one seeks to understand the relationship of these replies to the correct or true response and the effects of errors in the solicited responses upon the association of the measured variable in question with other indicators. The basic model for this situation is that given in Eq. (2.1), i.e., $M = T + e$, where $M$ is the measured value of the variable, $T$ is its true value, and $e$ represents the error of measurement.   On the whole, however, this formulation focuses only upon the question of reliability and avoids the related problem of validity.

In many sociological investigations one is forced to invoke operational definitions of constructs which do not fully capture the nuances of their theoretical meaning.   Thus, for example, we might decide to operationalize a theoretical construct, say, general social status, with an indicator such as years of school completed.   Doubtless no one thinks the meaning of a person's general social status is exhausted by the number of years of formal schooling he has completed. In this situation and others like it, we can think of our measured variable— reported education—as subject to two distinctive kinds of error: those due to unreliability in reporting and those attributable to the departure of the variable from the meaning of the theoretical construct, i.e., errors arising from the fact that education is not a perfectly valid measure of general social status.

In general, we might write

$$T = C + v \tag{2.44}$$

where $T$ represents the true values of the measured variable, $C$ equals the value assumed by the theoretical construct we are measuring, and $v$ represents departures of the true values of the measured variable from the values of the theoretical variable we are attempting to operationalize.   Substituting Eq. (2.44) into Eq. (2.1) gives the relationship,

$$M = C + v + e \tag{2.45}$$

a form which makes clear that any measure is subject to both errors incurred through definition of a less than completely valid measure of a theoretical construct and errors incurred through definition of an operational measure which is not perfectly reliable.   Questions of validity and reliability are, however, confused in much of the social science literature.   In part this stems from a tendency among some writers to, implicitly or explicitly, amalgamate the errors, $v$ and $e$, in Eq. (2.45).   Other sources of confusion are (1) the adoption of the frequently useful, though often implicit assumption that $T = C$, i.e., that the true values of the measured variable agree perfectly with those attributed to the theoretical construct, and (2) the tendency to ignore questions concerning the consistency (reliability) of repeated measurements of *precisely* the same thing as, e.g., in many factor analytic studies.

In order to make any substantial progress on questions of reliability, one needs, of course, repeated measurements. Similarly, in order to make any progress on questions of validity, one needs multiple indicators, to wit, equally plausible measures of the same theoretical construct with disjoint operational contents. Clearly, a prime problem in further causal analysis of imperfect data is not only to address the question of validity in a manner parallel to the present treatment of reliability, but also to develop models for simultaneously handling both questions of reliability (or about the consistency of identical, repeated measurements of the same thing) and validity (or about the consistency of alternative measures of the same theoretical construct). For example, a useful extension of the results outlined in this chapter might be the introduction of a theoretical variable, such as general social status, and an examination of the effects of regarding the *observed* rather than the *true* values of education, occupation, and income as indicators of such a construct.

## Test Construction and Item Analysis

Any attempt to maintain rigorously the distinction between the validity and the reliability of a measure is blurred in the cases of index formation and test construction. When several items are combined into a single index or test, one generally hopes to achieve a more valid measure of an underlying theoretical construct than would be possible by adopting any single one of the items that make up the instrument. Indicators of the validity of the instrument are, of course, not only the plausibility of all the items and their correlation with an external criterion, but also the magnitudes of the correlations between the items. However, in the testing of many physical or mental abilities, one may expect development or learning to occur between two administrations of the test. One may, then, be frustrated in attempting to evaluate the reliability of the instrument with the strategy of repeated measurements. Consequently, one often turns to the intercorrelations among the various items of a test to establish its reliability—the very correlations which provide evidence concerning its validity. Another useful exercise in the analysis of imperfect data would be the causal representation of alternative strategies of measuring the reliability of tests. Since the intercorrelations among items are used to ascertain an instrument's dimensionality as well as its reliability, this exercise would doubtlessly turn itself into the more challenging task of expounding item analysis and modern factor analysis in a causal framework.

## Conclusions

Neither the solution to the models discussed in previous sections nor further work on the somewhat sketchy overview of related matters discussed in this section can provide a mechanical solution to the problems of estimation engendered by imperfect data.   At best, path analysis can only provide a general framework for the *explicit* representation of *assumed* causal relations.   Every new problem must be evaluated on its own merits; the causal assumptions plausible in some instances may not be viable in others.   Consequently, one cannot hope to devise a general model of error applicable in all specific instances.

The models of error discussed in this chapter make it clear that path analysis provides no answer to the hopeless problem of inferring causality from nonexperimental data.   Instead, the method merely enables one to derive rigorously the implications of alternative causal assumptions; those derivations can, of course, lead one to discard some assumptions, but they by no means establish the veracity of those which cannot be dismissed as erroneous representations of the available data.   Indeed, the applications discussed in this chapter make it clear that the conclusions one draws about the true correlations between SES variables are, in fact, dependent upon the causal assumptions one is willing to defend.   Path analysis can reveal whether alternative assumptions are consistent or inconsistent with the data; the choice between and defense of consistent alternatives are finally governed by the intellectual and theoretical tools available to an individual researcher and the predisposition of current thinking in his discipline.

## REFERENCES

1 Anderson, C. Arnold: "A Skeptical Note on the Relation of Vertical Mobility to Education," *American Journal of Sociology*, 66 (May, 1961), 560–570.

2 Blalock, Hubert M., Jr.: *Causal Inferences in Nonexperimental Research* (Chapel Hill, N.C.: University of North Carolina Press, 1964).

3 Blalock, Hubert M., Jr.: "Some Implications of Random Measurement Error for Causal Inferences," *American Journal of Sociology*, 71 (July, 1965), 37–47.

4 Bogue, Donald J., and Edmund M. Murphy: "The Effect of Classification Errors upon Statistical Inference: A Case Analysis with Census Data," *Demography*, 1 (1964), 42–55.

5 Boudon, Raymond: "A Method of Linear Causal Analysis: Dependence Analysis," *American Sociological Review*, 30 (June, 1965), 365–374.

6 Coale, Ansley J., and Frederick F. Stephan: "The Case of the Indians and the Teenage Widows," *Journal of the American Statistical Association*, 57 (June, 1962), 338–347.

7 Costner, Herbert L., and Robert K. Leik: "Deductions from Axiomatic Theory," *American Sociological Review*, 29 (December, 1964), 819–835.

8 Duncan, Otis Dudley: "Properties and Characteristics of the Socioeconomic Index," in Albert J. Reiss, Jr., and Others, *Occupations and Social Status* (New York: Free Press, 1961).

9 Duncan, Otis Dudley: "Path Analysis: Sociological Examples," *American Journal of Sociology*, **72** (July, 1966), 1–16.

10 Duncan, Otis Dudley, and Robert W. Hodge: "Education and Occupational Mobility: A Regression Analysis," *American Journal of Sociology*, **68** (May, 1963), 629–644.

11 Eckler, A. Ross, and William N. Hurwitz: "Response Variance and Biases in Censuses and Surveys," *Bulletin de l'Institute International de Statistique*, **36** (1953), 12–34.

12 Gulliksen, Harold: *Theory of Mental Tests* (New York: Wiley, 1950).

13 Hansen, Morris H., William N. Hurwitz, and Max A. Bershad: "Measurement Errors in Censuses and Surveys," *Bulletin of the International Statistical Institute*, **38** (1960), 359–374.

14 Hoyt, Cyril: "Test Reliability Estimated by Analysis of Variance," *Psychometrika*, **6** (June, 1941), 153–160.

15 Johnston, J.: *Econometric Methods* (New York: McGraw-Hill, 1963), chap. 6.

16 Kempthorne, Oscar: *An Introduction to Genetic Statistics* (New York: Wiley, 1957), chap. 14.

17 Kuder, G. F., and M. W. Richardson: "The Theory of Estimation of Test Reliability," *Psychometrika*, **2** (September, 1937), 151–160.

18 Madansky, Albert: "The Fitting of Straight Lines when Both Variables Are Subject to Error," *Journal of the American Statistical Association*, **54** (March, 1959), 173–205.

19 Nowak, Stefan: "Some Problems of Causal Interpretation of Statistical Relationships," *Philosophy of Science*, **27** (January, 1960), 23–38.

20 Simon, Herbert A.: "Spurious Correlation: A Causal Interpretation," in *Models of Man* (New York: Wiley, 1957), chap. 2.

21 Spearman, Charles: "Correlation Calculated from Faulty Data," *British Journal of Psychology*, **3** (October, 1910), 271–295.

22 U.S. Bureau of the Census, *Current Population Reports, Consumer Income*, "Income of Families and Persons in the United States: 1958," ser. P-60, no. 33, 1960.

23 U.S. Bureau of the Census, *Census of Population: 1960, Subject Reports, Educational Attainment*, 1963.

24 U.S. Bureau of the Census, *Census of Population: 1960, Subject Reports, Occupational Characteristics*, 1963.

25 U.S. Bureau of the Census, *Census of Population: 1960, Detailed Characteristics, United States Summary*, vol. 1, part 1, 1963.

26 U.S. Bureau of the Census, *Evaluation and Research Program of the U.S. Censuses of Population and Housing: Accuracy of Data on Population Characteristics as Measured by Reinterviews*, ser. ER 60, no. 4, 1964.

27 U.S. Bureau of the Census, *Evaluation and Research Program of the U.S. Censuses of Population and Housing: Accuracy of Data on Population Characteristics as Measured by CPS-Census Match*, ser. ER 60, no. 5, 1964.

28 U.S. Bureau of the Census, *Current Population Reports, Consumer Income,* "Income of Families and Persons in the United States: 1963," ser. P-60, no. 43, 1964.

29 Walker, Helen M., and Joseph Lev: *Statistical Inference* (New York: Holt, 1953).

30 Wright, Sewall: "On the Nature of Size Factors," *Genetics,* **3** (1918), 367–374.

31 Wright, Sewall: "The Relative Importance of Heredity and Environment in Determining the Piebald Pattern of Guinea Pigs," *Proceedings of the National Academy of Science,* **6** (1920), 320–332.

32 Wright, Sewall: "Correlation and Causation," *Journal of Agricultural Research,* **20** (January, 1921), 557–585.

33 Wright, Sewall: "The Method of Path Coefficients," *Annals of Mathematical Statistics,* **5** (September, 1934), 161–215.

# CHAPTER 3

# Attitude Measurement[1]

## HARRY S. UPSHAW

The term *attitude* is used in a variety of ways by social scientists. Most commonly, the term refers imprecisely to the stands people take on controversial issues. Whether implicitly or explicitly, discussions of social attitudes usually focus on three classes of phenomena. One of these is cognitive in nature and refers to an individual's information regarding an issue. Another is behavioral, referring to the acts which an individual performs, advocates, or facilitates with regard to an issue. The third phenomenon is affective, referring to the individual's valuations.

Without presuming to define explicitly the construct of attitude, we shall assume that it includes in some structural relationship cognitive, behavioral, and affective phenomena. Furthermore we set as the task of this chapter to describe current approaches to the measurement of cognitive, behavioral, and affective variables.

A *variable* is an invention, involving the abstraction of certain observable characteristics and the disregard of others. That which varies in a variable is some property which all members of a set of observations have in some kind or in some degree. In defining a variable, an investigator decides the exact property in which he is interested and, as well as he can, provides a set of standard procedures by which the presence or absence or degree of the variable property can be determined reliably in the individual case.

*Measurement* is the systematic assignment of numbers to a set of observations to reflect the status of each member of the set in terms of the variable property. Defining a variable and measuring it are logically equivalent. The

[1] The preparation of this chapter was aided by a grant from the National Science Foundation.

only difference in the two processes is that, in the case of measurement, the rule that serves to classify members of the observational set results in a numerical assignment reflecting their status, whereas, in the absence of measurement, the classification structure is identified by labels other than numbers.

This chapter is devoted to the measurement of some of the basic concepts in the literature on social attitudes. We have already noted that cognitive, behavioral, and affective attitudinal phenomena can be distinguished. We shall return to these three aspects of attitude following a discussion of general principles of measurement. A schema consisting of eight classes of attitude variables will be presented, and the measurement implications of each class will be discussed. The latter part of the chapter will be devoted to the presentation of specific models which have been offered for measurement of particular types of attitude variables. Following the presentation of each, a brief discussion will consider the possible adaptation of the model to other classes of variables in the schema.

## 3.1 THE NATURE OF MEASUREMENT

Let us define a *scale* as a set of elements each consisting of three components: (1) an empirical event (such as a person, an inanimate object, or anything to which the general term *stimulus* might be applied), (2) a number, and (3) a rule or set of rules that links the event and the number. The third component of a scale element, according to this conception, refers to the means by which a concrete event is abstracted into a model of a segment of reality. The rules contained in the third component of a scale element are sometimes called *mapping rules* because they serve to represent concrete events abstractly. The system of numbers which are assigned according to mapping rules constitutes the model. When, therefore, an investigator sets about to construct a scale he focuses attention on a set of observable events. He specifies a variable property in terms of which the events in the set might be described, and he formulates mapping rules by which the events in the set can be distinguished according to their status on the variable property. Finally, he represents by numbers the various statuses which his mapping rules have distinguished. When he has done all these things, he may be said to have measured by means of a scale the variable property as it is manifested by a particular set of observable events.

Although the concept of a scale is defined here in terms of a three-component element containing a particular empirical observation, the generality of the mapping rules and the numerical system, to which the remaining two components refer, imply that a scale transcends any particular group of observations. Thus, adding, deleting, or substituting empirical events does not alter the essential nature of a scale, provided that the observations all derive from what we shall later refer to as the *universe of observations*.

Not only does a scale transcend the particular empirical observations with which an investigator is concerned, it also is more general than any particular mapping rule. Under the rubric of "functional unity," we shall discuss the coherence of the mapping rules incorporated into a particular scale. Insofar as such coherence implies that mapping rules are interchangeable, our later discussion of functional unity may be interpreted as bearing on the generality of scales as regards mapping rules.

A scale is essentially unaltered, furthermore, by changes in the numerical assignments, provided that the changes are within limits that can be specified in each instance. Numbers have many meanings, not all of which are intended for all scales. Following Stevens (38,40), it has become traditional to distinguish *nominal, ordinal, interval,* and *ratio scales* according to the meanings conveyed by the numerical assignments. A nominal scale is a set of observations numbered to indicate their variable classes (and nothing more). As an example of a nominal scale, consider a preelection survey in which respondents are asked to choose among a field of potential candidates. On the basis of his response, each respondent is assigned to a class, all members of which are identical with regard to the basis of classification. The logic of classification is the same whether the classes and their members are identified by the name of their chosen candidate, or by a letter, a word, or a number. The numbers of a nominal scale merely name classes. The meaning of such a scale is, therefore, invariant over any changes of numerical assignment which retain the identity of the classes.

An ordinal scale is a set of observations with numbers indicating which observation has more or less of the underlying property. To extend the example used to illustrate a nominal scale, imagine that the potential candidates among whom respondents are asked to choose differ in degree of liberalism-conservatism. Assuming that the rank order of the candidates in terms of this property is known, we might be able to interpret the classification of respondents based on voting intention as a scale of liberalism-conservatism. To expedite this interpretation, we use numerical assignments for the classes of respondents which indicate their status on the critical property. With a nominal scale, the only restrictions in the assignment of numbers are that all observations receiving the same number must be alike in terms of the scale property and all those receiving different numbers must be discriminably different. The same restrictions apply to the ordinal scale, but in addition, the numerical assignments must reflect the order of the classes on the scale variable. Any change of numerical values which retains that order is a permissible transformation for an ordinal scale.

An interval scale is like an ordinal scale except that its numerical assignments reflect not only the order of the observations, but in addition, the magnitude of the differences in the scale property between pairs of observations. An interval scale of liberalism-conservatism on the set of hypothetical respondents in the earlier example would permit the quantitative comparisons of pairs of respondents. Thus, the difference in liberalism between A and B could be compared with the difference between C and D. In order to preserve such comparisons, we need another restriction in the assignment of numbers in addition to the restrictions imposed for nominal and ordinal scales. This restriction is that the numerical assignments must be such that the difference between a pair of numbers reflects the amount of difference in the underlying property between the corresponding pair of empirical events.

With an interval scale it is meaningful to talk of a unit of measurement and to describe the differences among pairs of observations in terms of this unit. Insofar as the numbers are intended to represent observed differences, the meaning of an interval scale would be unaffected by any linear change in the numerical assignments. Every number, $x$, could therefore be changed to a new number, $y$, according to the rule: $y = a + bx$, where $a$ is any positive number and $b$ is any number, positive or negative. In this rule for a linear transformation of the interval scale values, the term $b$ refers to the constant, albeit arbitrary, unit of measurement, and the term $a$ refers to the arbitrary origin. In saying that an interval scale has an invariant meaning over any linear transformation of the scale values, we are saying that the particular unit of measurement $b$ contributes nothing to the meaning of the scale, nor does the origin $a$ of the scale.

The numerical assignments of a ratio scale reflect identity, order, differences in magnitude, and in addition, the absolute magnitude of the scale property. If the observation has none of the property, then the number zero is assigned to it. All other numbers are assigned to express the difference between the amount of the property possessed by each particular observation and that one, perhaps hypothetical, which has none of the property. The essential difference between an interval scale and a ratio scale is that the point of origin for the numerical assignments of the latter is at zero magnitude, whereas for an interval scale the origin is arbitrarily placed. Because of the rational origin of a ratio scale, its numerical assignments permit an interpretation of the ratios of any pair of elements. Measuring height by a yardstick provides a familiar example of a ratio scale. This instrument provides a choice of arbitrary units: inches, feet, or yards. Measuring height from the bottom of a person's feet to the tip of his head, we speak of a 3-foot child as having half the height of his 6-foot father or as having three times the height of his 1-foot dog. The same ratios apply, of course, whatever the unit, illustrating the fact that the numerical assignments of a ratio scale are invariant in meaning with any change in unit. That a change in origin, however, alters the interpretation of ratios can be seen by imagining the measurement of height from a point arbitrarily drawn 1 foot above the floor. Using the same yardstick as before, the 3-foot child now scores 2 feet; his 6-foot father, 5 feet; and the 1-foot dog now gets a score of zero. By arbitrarily locating the point of origin, we destroy the meaningfulness of the ratios of numerical assignments, and thus convert a ratio scale into an interval scale. The fact that a ratio scale depends on a rational, nonarbitrary origin can be expressed by stating that each numerical assignment $x$ on a ratio scale can be transformed without change in the essential meaning of the scale to another number $y$ according to the rule: $y = bx$, where $b$ is any positive number.

The four types of scales which have been discussed are the four originally proposed by Stevens (38,40). Many more types could be defined by analogy with these, each characterized by a set of permissible transformations of the numerical assignments. [See, for example, Coombs, Raiffa, and Thrall (5).] For present purposes consideration of just the four classical types is adequate to make the point that numerical assignments do not alone constitute measurement. Numbers are assigned by rules that capture only part of the total information available about the observations. If the investigator and his audience are to communicate effectively, both must understand the contingencies governing the numerical assignments. The distinction among scale types aids this understanding.

## Assessment and Prediction

Our discussion of scale construction has indicated that numerical assignments are based on some manifestation of the measured property. It often happens, however, that numbers are assigned to observations to indicate status on some property not immediately observed. Measurement in the first sense is intended as *assessment*, whereas in the second sense, it is intended as *prediction*. The concept of prediction implies two acts of measurement, one leading to the construction of a predictive instrument, and the other, to a criterion measure which is to be predicted. The property of ultimate interest in terms of which the investigator wishes to array the set of observations is represented by the criterion. The criterion measure may constitute an assessment of that property, or it may be another predictive measure. In any event, at the end of any chain of predictive measures is an assessment of the property of interest.

In scoring a predictive instrument, one makes numerical assignments in accord with a manifest property which presumably correlates with the criterion property. Thus, the pull on the spring in the butcher's shop, to use an example provided by Suppes and Zinnes (42), is accepted as a measure of weight because of the anticipated high correlation between it and a more direct assessment of weight. Prediction is an empirical matter; each butcher's scale needs to be independently calibrated. It makes no difference why one is able to estimate a criterion on the basis of a predictive instrument. As long as interest centers exclusively in the criterion property, any feature of an instrument which facilitates the prediction of that property improves the utility of the instrument.

Often, the instrument which serves as a predictor of one property is known in another context as an assessment device for some other property. The status on next year's geometry test might, for example, be predictable for members of a class by means of this year's algebra test. In such cases, the same instrument is amenable to evaluation as both an assessment and a predictive device, albeit with respect to different properties.

## Characteristics of Measurement Instruments

We have already used the term *measurement instrument* in a casual way. Let us now define it more exactly as the means by which stimuli are mapped into a system of numbers. If the length of a table is assessed by averaging 10 scores derived from a yardstick, then, by the present conception, the measurement instrument consists of replicated applications of a yardstick. If the same variable is assessed by averaging the estimates of judges, then the instrument is described as consisting of replicated judgments. A measurement instrument represents the entire set of mapping operations by which a scale is constructed.

An obviously important characteristic of any measurement instrument is the degree of consistency among the various mapping operations in the determination of the scale values assigned to particular stimuli. This variable of coherence we shall call the *functional unity* of the instrument. The concept of functional unity implies some kind of statistical dependency among mapping operations, although the precise nature of the dependency varies according to the theoretical properties of the measured variable and practical considerations involving such matters as whether the instrument is intended as an assessment or a predictive device.

Most attitude-measurement instruments are one of three types: (1) those in which the mapping operations are embodied in judges, (2) those in which they reside in items, and (3) those in which mapping is accomplished by arithmetical operations applied to empirical data. The specific functional unity requirements of these types of instruments refer to relationships among judges, items, or arithmetic operations, respectively. In our subsequent treatment of models for attitude measurement, we shall in each case be concerned with the determination of the functional unity of the resulting instruments.

Besides functional unity there are two other aspects of measurement instruments that require attention, *reliability* and *validity*. Reliability refers to the repeatability of the numerical assignments which are made to a set of observations. The reliability of an instrument is commonly assessed by correlating the instrument with itself. There are three basic approaches to the computation of a reliability coefficient. One involves dividing the mapping operations of the instrument into two equivalent halves. Another involves the actual construction of parallel forms of the instrument, and the third involves a second administration of the single instrument. On purely intuitive grounds, we can see that any departure from perfect reliability is attributable to one of three sources: (1) specific properties of particular mapping procedures, (2) real changes among the observed events in their status on the measured property, (3) momentary changes in status on the measured property due to temporary states (such as fatigue in a human being).

As we have discussed functional unity, that concept refers to the degree of consistency among the various mapping operations as regards their contributions to the numerical assignments. Any inconsistency among operations in this regard is presumably due to the inadvertent introduction of extraneous mapping criteria. Such error factors reduce both internal consistency and the repeatability of the scores assigned to particular observations. Insofar as mapping operations alone determine reliability, functional unity and reliability are equivalent concepts. The latter is, however, a more inclusive notion, for it refers also to influences due to sources other than mapping operations.

As indicated, the correlation of an instrument with itself may be lowered by changes in the values of the variable property which the observations reflect. Real, permanent changes are generally not considered to bear on the reliability problem. It would be undesirable for an instrument *not* to reflect true changes in the measured property. Therefore, in assessing the reliability of an instrument of known functional unity, an investigator faces the task of estimating how much fluctuation in numerical assignments can be attributed to momentary factors associated with the observed statuses of the observations in terms of the variable property. Often it might seem reasonable merely to assume that this source of variance is negligible, as, indeed, it is likely to be in comparison to that attributable to differences in item properties.

To question the validity of a measurement instrument is to ask whether (or to what extent) the numbers assigned to events correspond to the variable quantity that was intended. For example, how do we know that a yardstick measures length or that the Stanford-Binet measures intelligence? Empirically the validity issue is somewhat different for predictive and assessment instruments. The former, as we have noted, are developed for the purpose of estimating the status of a set of observations on some measured trait. Numerical assignments for these instruments are based on rules that are intended to reflect either a degree of confidence that a particular criterion score would be obtained or an estimate of which of a set of criterion scores would most likely be obtained. The numerical assignment rules are based on rational or empirical considerations that the investigator expects to facilitate prediction. In the literature two classes of predictive instruments can be found. There is, first, the purely empirical instrument constructed of items each of which is intended to serve no other purpose but the prediction of the criterion. The second type represents a direct assessment of one trait for the purpose of predicting another.

To illustrate the two types of predictive instruments, let us consider the alternatives available to an investigator who wants to study some behavior, such as making financial contributions to a political party. The particular aims of his research may lead him to establish, first, a criterion measure of the political contributions of a sample of people, to be predicted by an instrument composed of items included because of their demonstrated power to discriminate among people with different criterion scores. Generally items are selected for an instrument of this sort by trial-and-error methods. Understanding the factors which permit the prediction of the criterion comes after the construction of the instrument, if it comes at all.

By contrast, the second approach to the construction of predictive instruments involves a theory, a hunch, or an empirical result linking the criterion property to another property which is assessed by the predictive instrument. Intuitively it seems likely that, other things held constant, a person contributes to a political party in proportion to the outcomes he expects to receive if that party is victorious in an election. In pursuit of this hunch, an investigator might attempt to construct an instrument for the assessment of expected outcomes contingent on the political party's success. Scores on this measure would then be used to predict the criterion of financial contribution. These two classes of predictive instruments differ in their functional unity requirements in that the second type involves direct assessment as an intermediate stage. However, the validity requirements of the two types of instrument are the same. In either case the investigator needs to know the efficiency with which the total score on the instrument predicts the criterion.

The numerical assignments of assessment instruments are intended to discriminate among observations in terms of a specified property. To inquire into the validity of such a measure is to question whether the investigator has correctly identified the property in terms of which the observed discrimination occurs. Empirical evidence of the validity of an assessment instrument most likely consists of a correlation coefficient relating that instrument to another instrument. If the second instrument is regarded as a measure of the same property that is supposedly measured by the first instrument, validity is indicated by a high correlation coefficient. If the second is regarded as a measure of a property which is theoretically distinct from that measured by the first instrument, validity is indicated by a low coefficient of correlation. Validity information, therefore, may be regarded as of two types: *convergent,* referring to the relationship of an instrument to measures of the same or of conceptually similar properties, and *discriminant,* referring to the relationship of an instrument to measures of properties that are conceptually distinct.

Campbell and Fiske (3) have suggested a system for studying the validity of assessment instruments. Their system requires multiple measures of a single trait and the measurement by several methods of related, though distinct, traits. The expected patterns of convergent and discriminant validity indices are evaluated for all the measures in one matrix.

## Generalizing Scale Values

When an investigator makes an observation, his purpose is to represent a concrete event in an abstract model of the domain he is studying. Insofar as his interest is abstract, each particular observation that he makes is intended to be viewed as a sample from a universe, any member of which could have replaced the actual observation. A multitude of factors contribute to any observation, whether in the laboratory or in everyday life. One's view of the setting sun depends on countless space, time, and organismic variables. Similarly, numerical assignments made in the course of measuring a variable are influenced by many features of the observational situation. Consider, for example, the measurement of racial stereotyping on the part of a sample of respondents representing a meaningful social group. Among the contributors to the recorded scores are the following: the particular respondents included in the study, the race and other characteristics of the data collectors, the item format and other characteristics of the data-collection instrument. These variable aspects of a given set of observations are what Guttman (17) calls the facets of the particular hypothetical universe from which the observations are to be regarded as a sample.

When preparing to measure a variable, an investigator must devote some of his attention to the task of delimiting his domain of interest in terms of the facets which will concern him. It is the intended generalization of the numerical assignments which determines this domain. As an example, consider a score assigned to a respondent indicating a degree of hostility toward a target object. Any one of a number of possible interpretations of such a score may be intended. The value of the measured variable may be assumed to be typical of that respondent on any occasion when confronting a particular target object; it may be considered typical of a class of respondents on a particular type of occasion when confronting a class of target objects; etc. The investigator must decide how he wishes to generalize scale values and provide in his design the conditions that permit the desired generalization. The basis of generalization is random sampling. To generalize a scale value to a universe of observations is equivalent to claiming that it is the expected value that would be obtained with repeated random samples from the population. Thus, one might determine the mean score for a sample of Republican voters corresponding to the degree of their expressed approval of the Democratic President. That score can be logically generalized to the population of all Republican voters only if the sample represents a random selection from the population.

Any universe of observations is likely to be multifaceted. Furthermore, it is likely to contain some facets for which there are an infinite number of conditions, such as *persons* when not restricted spatially or temporally. There is no way of knowing whether a sample from a hypothetical universe is random.  It is generally assumed that a sample is random if the following conditions are met: (1) all members of the sample obviously belong to the population, and (2) there is no apparent attribute shared by members of the sample which distinguishes it from the population.  In order to generalize a numerical assignment to any facet of the universe of observations, the investigator must determine the expected value of that assignment on the basis of the observation of a sample which he considers random with respect to the facet.  The members of this sample are considered interchangeable.  They are, in other words, replications of one another.  In discussing particular scale models in a later section, we shall note that some form of random replications is a central requirement of each model.  The reason for this requirement is that the generalization of numerical assignments requires it.

In an empirical discipline a generalization is really a prediction.  The investigator essentially predicts that a particular observation he has made can be reproduced by observing any other sample from the universe of observations, which he delimits as well as he can.  He may be wrong because of the operation of chance or because he inadequately described the universe.  In either case, science thrives on attempts to disprove generality claims.

## 3.2 COGNITIVE, BEHAVIORAL, AND AFFECTIVE ATTITUDE VARIABLES

It was noted earlier that attitude phenomena tend to be cognitive, behavioral, and affective.  Many specific variables have been defined corresponding to these phenomena.  A variable, it will be recalled, is a property in terms of which a set of observations are arrayed.  In discussing cognitive, behavioral, and affective variables we refer to a characteristic of the variable property.  Before proceeding to a discussion of methods for the measurement of attitude variables, we need to be sure that the distinctions among these variable properties are clear.

## Cognitive Scales

As distinguished from behavioral and affective properties, a cognitive variable refers to information or knowledge on the part of a subject about an attitude object.  The fundamental observation for the construction of a scale for the measurement of a cognitive variable is the expression of a belief by a person concerning the characteristics of an attitude object.  As presently conceived, beliefs are by their nature subject to verification according to rules of evidence, however idiosyncratic, which the individual might invoke.  Whether one arrives at the number of teeth in a horse's mouth by direct examination or by theological argument, the result is, in both cases, a belief.  In either event, the number arrived at is subject to appraisal as correct or

TABLE 3.1   Examples of Cognitive-subject, -content, and -object Variables

| *Class of variable* | *Verbal description* |
|---|---|
| Cognitive-subject | Extent to which typical *Americans, Britons, Germans,* etc., perceive Germans to be militaristic<br>Degree to which typical *Republican party officials, independent voters, Southern Democrats,* etc., see John Lindsay as wise-foolish |
| Cognitive-content | Extent to which the typical American perceives that Germans are *militaristic, jovial, practical, industrious,* etc.<br>Degree to which the typical Republican party official sees John Lindsay as *wise-foolish, strong-weak,* etc. |
| Cognitive-object | Degree to which the typical American perceives *Germans, Russians, Israelis,* etc., to be militaristic<br>Extent to which the typical Republican party official sees *John Lindsay, Richard Nixon, George Romney* as wise-foolish |

incorrect by the holder of the belief as well as by any audience who might learn of the belief. The distinguishing characteristic of a cognitive variable is that it is a property of a belief. Examples of cognitive variables are these: the degree to which an attitude object is perceived to display a particular trait, the differential salience of various traits of an object, and the confidence with which people attribute traits to an object.

We can distinguish three types of cognitive scales that can be constructed from a set of observations, each referring to a person's expression of a belief about an object. The basis of this distinction is the designation of the class of observations to which numerical assignments are to be made. There are three components of any belief: the subject who holds it, its content, and the object to which it is directed. In the measurement of a cognitive variable the scale values might be assigned to observations corresponding to any one of these three belief components. We shall designate the resulting scales as *cognitive-subject, cognitive-content,* and *cognitive-object* scales.

Table 3.1 presents two examples of each of the three classes of cognitive scales which we have described. The observations to be scaled are italicized in each example in order to bring attention to the fact that it is this feature of the scales which constitutes the classification principle.

## *Behavioral Scales*

The behavioral aspects of attitudes are those which refer to the acts that a person commits, advocates, or facilitates with respect to an object. As conceived here, behavioral attitude variables have nothing to do with involuntary acts. They refer essentially to decisions people make concerning which of several alternative actions is preferable for coping with a problem involving

TABLE 3.2   Examples of Behavioral-subject, -content, and -object Variables

| Class of variable | Verbal description |
|---|---|
| *Behavioral-subject* | Degree to which *the typical American Legion member, the typical high school graduate, the typical self-employed man,* etc., think it appropriate to punish deliberate draft-card burning by immediate draft into the military<br>Extent to which *the typical white college student, the typical white suburban wife, the typical American Indian,* etc., think it desirable to admit Negroes to close kinship through marriage |
| *Behavioral-content* | Extent to which the typical American Legion member thinks it appropriate to punish those who are guilty of burning their draft cards by *immediate draft into the military, imprisonment, ignoring them,* etc.<br>Extent to which the typical white college student thinks it desirable *to admit* Negroes *to close kinship through marriage, to his club as personal chums, to his street as neighbors,* etc. |
| *Behavioral-object* | Degree to which the typical American Legion member thinks it appropriate to punish by drafting into military service those people guilty of *burning their draft cards, refusing to testify before congressional committees, embezzling money from a bank,* etc.<br>Degree to which the typical white college student thinks it desirable to admit to close kinship through marriage: *Negroes, Canadians, Armenians,* etc. |

the attitude object. Obviously, the decision to do one thing rather than another derives in part from one's beliefs as they relate to the issue. Equally obviously, the decision stems from one's affective involvements as they bear on the issue. From a purely empirical point of view, the prediction of cognitive and affective variables from behavioral variables is probably very efficient. We can, nevertheless, maintain the distinction and define a behavioral variable as one that refers to a person's willingness to perform an act, to allow it to be performed, or to facilitate its performance. The fundamental phenomenon observed in the construction of a behavioral scale is the endorsement or rejection by a subject of an action toward an object.

As in the case of cognitive variables, we can distinguish three classes of behavioral scales by reference to the observations the statuses of which are evaluated: behavioral-subject, behavioral-content, and behavioral-object scales. Table 3.2 presents two examples of each class of behavioral scale. The scaled observations in each example are italicized.

## *Affective Scales*

The concept of affect refers to a person's sentiments, his pleasant or unpleasant feelings associated with attitude objects. Affect is commonly discussed in terms of a degree of favorability-unfavorability. A farmer and a golfer may share the expectation that it will rain on a particular day, but this common belief may be associated with opposite affect in the two individuals. Because the event would bring misery to the golfer, we say that he has an unfavorable attitude, and because it would make the farmer happy, we say that he has a favorable attitude.

The fundamental observation for the construction of an affective scale is the expression by a person of some degree of pro-anti orientation to an object. As with cognitive and behavioral variables, it is meaningful to distinguish between subject and object scales according to the class of empirical events to which numbers are assigned. However, the type of scale which we designated as content does not appear to exist for affective variables. The reason for this is that affect is a logically unitary concept, whereas this is not true of either of the other variables we have discussed. Thus, any single person is thought of as having one, and only one, degree of affect for a particular object. On the other hand, he may attribute any number of traits to a single object or advocate any number of courses of action toward the object without any conceptual inconsistency.

The remarks made in the preceding paragraph concerning the nature of the affective concept may be confusing to one who considers the notion of ambivalence. To define a variable of ambivalence requires either that the single respondent be conceived as having multiple states or that the focal object be conceived as having multiple stimulus values, each of which elicits separate affect. The incorporation of these considerations into the design for scale construction would pose a challenge for an expert in the area. The present work will be concerned with the measurement of univalent affect.

Table 3.3 presents two examples of *affective-subject* scales and two examples of *affective-object* scales. The observations to be scaled are italicized in each example.

TABLE 3.3    Examples of Affective-subject and -object Variables

| *Class of variable* | *Verbal description* |
|---|---|
| *Affective-subject* | Degree to which *teen-agers, retired people, young parents*, etc., like the television show "Peyton Place" |
| | Degree to which *Southern middle-class white people, working-class white people*, etc., would like total racial segregation |
| *Affective-object* | Degree to which the typical television viewer likes *"Peyton Place," "Huntley-Brinkley Report,"* etc. |
| | Degree to which the typical white Southerner would like *total racial segregation, total racial integration, token desegregation*, etc. |

## 3.3 ATTITUDE-SCALE CONSTRUCTION

The remainder of this chapter is devoted to the more common models for the measurement of attitude variables. For each of these models we shall consider the nature of its fundamental data, the numerical assignment rules and functional unity requirements, the assumptions supporting the intended generalization of the numerical assignments, and the applicability of the model to the eight classes of attitude scales which we have discussed.

The empirical basis for attitude-scale construction is likely to consist of a respondent's indicating to the investigator what he believes, feels, or would do about some object. The investigator collects many such data which he organizes in particular ways according to whether he is interested in constructing a subject, content, or object scale. As we have indicated, a subject scale is one in which quantitative comparisons are made among the people who hold specific beliefs, behavioral inclinations, or affective orientations toward an attitude object. A content scale, as defined above, is one in which quantitative comparisons are made among the traits or actions constituting various beliefs or behavioral inclinations of a subject with respect to an object. Finally, an object scale is one in which quantitative comparisons are made among the targets of a particular belief, behavioral inclination, or affective orientation. The data provided by an individual respondent are likely to be the same for subject, content, and object scales. The distinction among these classes of scales refers to the aspect of the basic datum which the investigator chooses to define as the empirical event to be mapped into a numerical system.

In the following discussion of measurement models it will be noted that cognitive-, behavioral-, and affective-subject scales present special methodological problems in addition to those which apply to content and object scales. These special problems derive from the requirement for a subject scale of a basis for interpersonal comparisons that overcomes sources of individual variation, such as unique verbal habits and standards of judgment. Several models for the construction of affective-subject scales have been suggested in the literature. These models, the Thurstone scale, the Guttman scale, the Likert scale, and the semantic differential, will be discussed after the presentation of the more generally applicable models.

The mapping rules of any scaling model accomplish the transformation of information provided by respondents into a set of numbers. In some cases the transformation is subtle, whereas in others it is extremely straightforward. In the latter, respondents are asked to provide direct, quantitative estimates which the investigator essentially averages to determine scale values. We shall begin our discussion with the direct scaling models. Then we shall consider indirect models in which scale values are obtained from raw data by means of assumptions concerning the latent significance of the recorded observations. [The distinction made here between direct and indirect scaling models follows that of Ekman and Sjoberg (8)].

In supplying data for scale construction, a respondent may be called upon to perform a task which resembles nominal, ordinal, interval, or ratio scaling. That is, he may be asked to sort elements into classes, to report perceived order relations among classes, to estimate the amount of difference among classes, or to judge the absolute magnitude or the ratios of stimuli. It is an appealingly simple idea that numerical responses can be interpreted as measures of the variable described in the instructions to the respondents. If such an interpretation could be justified, then virtually the entire labor of scale construction could be assigned to respondents. The only real deterrents to the wholesale adoption of the practice of having respondents do the entire scaling job are fears that they cannot or will not do it.

The uneasiness aroused by the treatment of quantitative data as scale values increases, of course, with the variety of meanings attributed to the numbers. Few people would doubt the ability of the typical respondent to generate a nominal scale, although many might doubt his ability to generate a ratio scale. As regards the nominal scale, everyday conversation presupposes that people can sort traits, actions, and objects into nominal categories. Furthermore, in public opinion polling it is traditional to count the respondents whose nominal scales have one feature or another. A question seldom arises as to whether a respondent is capable of knowing, for example, whether he approves of a particular policy of the government. The more common questions directed toward this kind of attitude measurement concern the stability and predictive value of the respondent's self-examination. Viewed purely as assessment, however, a person's report that he attributes a characteristic to a target, that he endorses a course of action, or that he holds a particular sentiment is prima facie evidence that he has a particular attitude.

A direct scaling model is one in which a respondent is asked to indicate by a number which of a set of alternatives best describes his attitude. The scaling task might require the respondent to replicate his judgment, perhaps in slightly different contexts which are regarded as essentially equivalent. Consistency over such replications would be regarded as evidence of functional unity. This basic model for nominal-scale construction, probably because of its simplicity, has received little formal attention in the attitude-measurement literature. Other direct scaling models, to which we now turn, are more complicated and are more likely to engender controversy about the literal interpretation of the respondents' quantification.

## 3.4  DIRECT ORDINAL-SCALE CONSTRUCTION

Although it is not commonly thought of in this light, the familiar concordance coefficient due to Kendall (27) provides a model for ordinal-scale construction for those situations in which a respondent's task is to rank-order a set of stimuli according to some property. The concordance coefficient is defined by the formula

$$W = \frac{12SS}{n^2(m^3 - m)} \qquad (3.1)$$

where $n$ = the number of respondents

$m$ = the number of stimuli

$SS$ = the sum of squares of the rank sums for each stimulus about the mean of $\frac{1}{2}[n(m + 1)]$

The coefficient $W$ permits the evaluation of the extent of agreement among ranks. It has the value 1.0 if all respondents agree perfectly, and the value of 0.0 if they disagree maximally.

As an example of scale construction under the proposed concordance model, let us imagine that a sample of 10 respondents have ranked eight courses of action according to the judged order of appropriateness for a particular situation. Inasmuch as the respondents are instructed to make ordinal responses which are to be interpreted as ordinal-scale values, this example is an illustration of a direct model for the construction of a behavioral-content scale. The implied scale hypothesis is that the ordinal judgments of the 10 respondents are consistent. If this hypothesis proves to be tenable, a single rank order of the courses of action may be described and generalized to all members of the population of which the 10 respondents represent a random sample. The concordance coefficient provides a means of assessing the degree of consistency among the ranks. If, in accord with the scale hypothesis, the respondents have truly supplied replications of the theoretical class of observations, the expected value of this coefficient will be 1.0. Since every respondent would have given identical data, the common rank order is generalized to the universe of observations.

When the concordance of ranked data which are assumed to represent random replications is not perfect, the investigator must make a decision concerning the implications of this finding. He may choose to consider that some respondents committed errors (misunderstood instructions, purposely falsified the data, etc.). To minimize the influence of such errors, he might remove from consideration all the data supplied by erring respondents (if they can be identified), or he might average the ranks given to each stimulus, generalizing the average rank order to the universe. If the degree of concordance is low, he may decide that his design failed to control some important facets, thus precluding generalization from his data. Alternatively, he may decide that a single ordinal scale does not exist in the universe of observations—that his theoretical conception, not his data, is responsible for the failure to achieve perfect concordance in the ranks of the respondents. In terms of our hypothetical example, a low degree of concordance among the ranks of the 10 respondents may be due to the fact that the population from which the respondents were sampled consists of subgroups who differ systematically in their perceptions of the appropriateness of the eight courses of action. It may be due to different meanings accorded to the instructions or to the descriptions of the stimuli on the part of the respondents. It may be due to the fact that the courses of action thought of by the investigator as alternatives do not appear so to the respondents.

The basis for choosing among alternative interpretations of imperfect concordance cannot be firmly established. Obviously the size of the concordance coefficient is one consideration. An exceedingly low coefficient is more likely to suggest that the scale hypothesis is incorrect than that some respondents made mistakes. Moderate concordance, on the other hand, might suggest inadequate charting of the facets of the universe of observations. In the final analysis, however, the decision is likely to be based on *ad hoc* evidence which the audience may or may not credit in the same way as the investigator.

The rank concordance procedure suggested here applies to any data which consist of the rank order of a single set of stimuli by respondents who are assumed to replicate one another. This requirement rules out the application of the model to subject scales. The model appears to be appropriate, however, for all classes of content and object scales.

## 3.5  DIRECT INTERVAL-SCALE CONSTRUCTION: THE CATEGORY SCALE

Perhaps the most frequently used technique for attitude-scale construction is that leading to a *category scale*.[2] The fundamental data appropriate to this model are a respondent's ratings of a set of stimuli according to the variable property. The ratings are expressed in terms of a group of consecutive numbers referring to categories the boundaries of which are assumed to be equally spaced with regard to amount of the variable property. The decision to assign a particular number to a stimulus is presumably based on the judgment of the respondent that the stimulus possesses more of the variable property than is represented by the lower boundary of the category and less than that represented by the upper boundary.

In our earlier discussion of the nature of measurement we noted that an interval scale is characterized by an arbitrary origin and a constant unit; the origin refers to the level of numerical assignments, and the unit to the dispersion of scale values. When a single respondent has assigned every stimulus in the set to a category, under a direct scaling model he may be said to have constructed a category scale. The origin of the scale has reference

---

[2] The scaling procedure that results in a category scale is frequently called the method of equal-appearing intervals.

to that stimulus, perhaps hypothetical, which he would have assigned to a category labeled 0. The unit refers to that amount of the variable property which defines the width of each response category. If it is further assumed that these scale parameters remain invariant over replications involving additional respondents or involving repeated judgments by the same respondent, the numerical assignments for each stimulus may be averaged. The average ratings constitute a category scale, having the same unit and origin as those employed with the single replications.

The assumption that the scale origin and unit are invariant over replications is unnecessarily restrictive. For a set of numbers to qualify as the interval scale measures of a property they must be invariant in meaning within a linear transformation of the form $y = a + bx$, where $b$ reflects the difference in unit between assumed replications and $a$ reflects differences in origin. If the various replications meet this requirement, then the averaging of numerical assignments for each stimulus results in a new scale, the origin and unit of which are averages of the values of these parameters on the individual replications.[3] If the investigator aspires to nothing more than an interval scale and if he intends no substantive interpretation of the unit and origin of that scale, the more relaxed assumptions that permit variation in origin and unit seem appropriate.

The category-scale model could be used for all eight classes of scales which we have discussed. In each application the intended generalization of scale values would determine what population should be conceived as supplying judgmental replications. The functional unity requirement of the model is, as suggested above, that a linear relationship exists between all pairs of assumed replicates. If this requirement is met, then the unsystematic variance in numerical assignments (i.e., that variance which is not attributable to the linear relationship) might be assumed to constitute perceptual error on the part of the respondent as regards the status of the individual stimuli, the category boundary values, or both. The average numerical response for each stimulus provides the best estimate of the true value, on the assumption that such errors tend to vanish with averaging.

The demonstration of a linear relationship between pairs of assumed replicates, while necessary in support of functional unity, is not sufficient evidence that the scale possesses the degree of invariance characteristic of an interval scale. Such a demonstration merely establishes the similarity of the respondents in their categorical judgments. Measurement at the level of an

---

[3] It will be recalled from statistics that simple averaging procedures have the effect of weighting components directly according to their dispersions. In the present situation this principle implies that simple averaging serves to give more weight to those component replications in which the scale unit is relatively small than to those in which it is relatively large. This conclusion follows from the fact that a smaller unit is associated with narrower response categories and larger dispersions of stimulus-scale values.

interval scale requires this similarity, but, in addition, it requires a constant unit. In the context of our later discussion of the law of categorical judgment we shall discuss some of the evidence that has been collected regarding the constancy of the measurement unit under both the category-scale model and the law of categorical judgment.

If the category-scale model were applied directly to the construction of a cognitive-, behavioral-, or affective-subject scale, the respondent's task would be to rate himself or his group along with any other subjects according to their standing on the scale variable. The use of self-ratings is a very common procedure in the study of attitudes. Typically, however, the investigator asks the respondent to rate himself in terms of the scale property without any explicit reference to other scale stimuli with which the respondent might compare himself. For example, a respondent might be asked to assign a number to himself corresponding to how pro- or anti-Negro his attitude is. In response to these instructions he might implicitly bring to bear a set of other individuals whose attitudes he assumes. Alternatively, he might seek to evaluate his own affect, not by reference to the affective positions of others, but instead, with reference to the affective implications of his beliefs about the Negro or those of the courses of action which he advocates. The point is that when a single respondent judges himself, and only himself, there is no way of assessing functional unity, and it is unlikely that a meaningful substantive interpretation can be based on the routine application of the category-scale model.

Two commonly used models that seek to avoid the pitfalls of a direct application of the category-scale model to subject scales will be discussed later. These are the so-called Thurstone scale and the semantic differential. The discussion of these approaches will be postponed until after the presentation of other general models for scale construction.

## 3.6  DIRECT RATIO-SCALE CONSTRUCTION

Until recently psychologists who study the measurement of sensory experience have tended to assume that the human organism is not capable of rendering judgments about his experiences in the form of numerical assignments which have ratio-scale properties. The persistent work of S. S. Stevens in opposition to this assumption has led to evidence that the human being is, perhaps, more sensitive to his environment than was originally appreciated and that he is a great deal better as a reporter of his experiences than has been imagined. In the course of modern psychophysical research, techniques for ratio-scale construction have been developed which can be applied to social stimuli as appropriately as to physical stimuli. The task set for the respondent is to estimate the magnitude of the variable property for each scale stimulus. The specific response format by which this is accomplished varies considerably (48). We shall illustrate one such format as it might apply to the measurement of a social variable.

Let us consider the construction of a scale to measure the prestige of occupations as perceived by an urban high school population. The respondent might be instructed to consider that a particular occupation, for instance, an insurance adjuster, defines an amount of prestige which will arbitrarily be assigned the number 100. His task is to assign a number to each occupation in the set so that the ratio of perceived prestige of each occupation to that of the standard (insurance adjuster) is reflected in the numerical assignments. If the respondent does, in fact, fulfill his instructions, then averaging over replications the values assigned to each occupation results in an estimate of the ratio values of occupational prestige as perceived by the population to which generalization is appropriate.

The functional unity requirement of an instrument constructed under the magnitude estimation model is an invariance over replications of the sort represented by the equation $y = bx$. This type of consistency is not sufficient to establish that the numerical assignments meet the requirement of a ratio scale. The functional unity requirement could be met if the data represented merely consistent ordinal judgments. In addition to consistency some more direct evidence is required that the scale values actually correspond to the magnitudes of the scale elements in terms of the variable property.

In sensory psychology two types of evidence have been offered in support of ratio-scale construction under the direct magnitude estimation model. One approach has been to vary the context in which a subset of stimuli is included. If, indeed, the method leads to ratio-scale values, the numbers assigned to particular stimuli should be relatively unaffected by which of the alternative subsets of additional stimuli are included with them for the collection of data. The second approach to the demonstration of the required scale invariance has been a type of study known as *cross-modality validation*.

The rationale of cross modality is as follows. For a large class of physical stimuli it has been found that respondents' ratio estimates of their sensory experiences are related to the corresponding physical stimulus values by a power function of the form $R = kS^n$, where $R$ is the respondent's judgment, $k$ is a constant, $S$ is the value of the stimulus measured on a physical scale, and $n$ is a distinctive exponent characteristic of a particular sensory modality. For example, Stevens (41) has reported the exponent in the case of force of hand grip as measured by a hand dynamometer to be 1.7, that of loudness (binaural) to be 0.6, that for the smell of coffee to be 0.5. Respondents might be asked to match a subjective experience in one modality with that in another. Thus to a presentation of a series of sounds differing in loudness, the respondent might be asked to squeeze a hand dynamometer with the force equal in subjective value to the loudness of each sound stimulus. Under the hypothesis that a subjective scale exists which is a power function of the stimulus scale for each of the modalities that are involved, it can be shown algebraically that the matching relation is also a power function. Furthermore, the exponent of the matching function is equal to the ratio of the exponents in the functions relating the subjective scales and the stimulus scales for the individual modalities. Stevens (41) has reported an impressive number of confirmations of this hypothesis involving a variety of different sense modalities. Cross-modal validation is strictly inapplicable to stimuli that are not measurable in terms of physical attributes. Stevens (39) has, however, summarized considerable indirect evidence that the power law formulation applies to judgments of the affective implications of attitude statements, the fairness of prices of wristwatches, the importance of Swedish monarchs, and many other social variables. If the characteristic exponents of variables such as these could be shown to be recoverable from cross-modal matching, the resulting evidence in support of Stevens's position would be impressive. This research has not been reported.

Ratio scaling under a direct model has produced promising results in the area of sensory psychology. It appears to hold the same promise for social stimuli, but very little research has been done to test this promise. The principal advantages of the model, assuming a successful application, are the richness of meaning of the scale values and the relative ease with which scale values are assigned.

## 3.7 THE LAW OF COMPARATIVE JUDGMENT

The law of comparative judgment is an indirect scaling model due to Thurstone (44) for constructing an interval scale to measure the status of a set of stimuli that are imperfectly discriminable in terms of the variable property. The basic assumption of the model is that the degree to which two stimuli can be discriminated is a direct function of the difference in their status in terms of the variable property. The fundamental observation under the model is a decision by a respondent as to which of two stimuli has more of the property. Confusion is assumed to increase to a maximum at that point at which the two stimuli have exactly the same amount of the property. Information concerning the ordinal position of the stimuli on the scale and the degree of confusion among the stimuli is contained in the proportion of times one is judged to be greater than another. The data for any application of the law of comparative judgment are, accordingly, contained in a matrix of probabilities representing the discriminability of all pairs of a set of stimuli.

Thurstone assumed that each presentation of a stimulus arouses in the respondent some undesignated perceptual process which is, in principle, quantifiable. Furthermore, he assumed that the perception of a particular stimulus on any given presentation is distorted somewhat by random and independent factors associated with the experimental procedures and with the respondents. Because the assumed distorting factors are random and independent, the perceptual processes aroused by the repeated presentations of a given stimulus would, if quantified, be distributed normally. If this hypothetical distribution were available as data, its central tendency would be taken as the best estimate of the true position of the stimulus in terms of the scale property. The dispersion of the same distribution, called by Thurstone the *discriminal dispersion* of the stimulus, would provide an index of the magnitude of the error-producing factors that are assumed to be operative.

When a respondent performs the task of deciding which of a pair of stimuli is greater in terms of the scale property, according to Thurstone's conception, he, in effect, selects a sample of one case from the normally distributed perceptual processes associated with each of the stimuli. The resulting model is expressed in the equation

$$S_i - S_j = z_{ij} \sqrt{\sigma_i^2 + \sigma_j^2 - 2r_{ij}\sigma_i\sigma_j} \qquad (3.2)$$

where $S_i$, $S_j$ = the means of the hypothetical distributions of perceptual processes for stimulus $i$ and stimulus $j$

$z_{ij}$ = the normal deviate corresponding to the empirically determined proportion of times that stimulus $i$ was judged greater than $j$

$\sigma_i$, $\sigma_j$ = the discriminal dispersions of stimulus $i$ and stimulus $j$

$r_{ij}$ = the correlation between $S_i$ and $S_j$

The expression under the radical in Eq. (3.2) is recognizable as the variance of the distribution of differences of two random variables. It might also be noted at this point that this distribution of differences in perceptual processes associated with the two stimuli is necessarily normal if the two parent distributions are normal, as assumed by Thurstone.

Of all of the terms in Eq. (3.2) only the $z_{ij}$ term refers to data. If there were $m$ stimuli to be scaled, there would be a total of $m(m-1)/2$ observed proportions from which these normal deviates could be determined. At the same time, there would be exactly this number of unknown correlation coefficients, and, in addition, $m-1$ unknown means (one mean would be arbitrarily designated as the origin of the scale), and $m-1$ unknown variances (one of the standard deviations would, likewise, be arbitrarily selected as the unit of the scale). Because the satisfactory solution of any system of equations requires more observation equations than there are unknowns, some simplification by way of assumption is required in order to make the law of comparative judgment feasible as a scaling model.

Thurstone (44) discussed five cases of the law of comparative judgment. The first case was the complete model expressed by Eq. (3.2) for a single respondent making replicated judgments. The second case was, again, Eq. (3.2), but for a group of judges assumed to replicate one another on the single judgments of all stimulus pairs.  The other cases refer to sets of assumptions that an investigator might impose on the data in order to make the model practical for the measurement of a variable.  The strongest set of assumptions is embodied in case 5, which is probably the most frequently used version of the law of comparative judgment.  The assumptions required in case 5 are:

**1** The arbitrary origin of the anticipated interval scale can be set at any point, thus let $S_j = 0$.

**2** The magnitudes of the correlations between all pairs of stimuli are the same, thus $r_{ij} = r$.

**3** The discriminal dispersions of all items are the same, hence $\sigma_i = \sigma_j = \sigma$.

On the basis of these simplifying assumptions, case 5 can be expressed in this form:

$$S_i = z_{ij} \sqrt{2\sigma^2(1 - r)} \tag{3.3}$$

When the expression under the radical in Eq. (3.3) is defined as the arbitrary unit of the scale, case 5 of the law of comparative judgment becomes a practical model for assigning scale values to a set of stimuli.

The actual scale construction under case 5 of the law of comparative judgment proceeds as follows.  The proportion of times that each stimulus in a set is judged greater than every other stimulus is determined.  These data define a matrix $P$ which is illustrated in Table 3.4.  The general entry in matrix $P$ is $p_{ij}$, corresponding to the proportion of times over replicated judgments that stimulus $i$ was judged greater than stimulus $j$.  Each entry in matrix $P$, according to the model, corresponds to a normal deviate, $z_{ij}$.  Therefore, the matrix $Z$, illustrated in Table 3.5, is constructed from $P$.  In the con-

TABLE 3.4    Matrix $P$ Containing the Proportion of Times That Stimulus $i$ Was Judged Greater than Stimulus $j$

|  | Stimuli | | | | | | |
|---|---|---|---|---|---|---|---|
| Stimuli | 1 | 2 | 3 | $\cdots$ | $j$ | $\cdots$ | $m$ |
| 1 | — | $P_{12}$ | $P_{13}$ | $\cdots$ | $P_{1j}$ | $\cdots$ | $P_{1m}$ |
| 2 | $P_{21}$ | — | $P_{23}$ | $\cdots$ | $P_{2j}$ | $\cdots$ | $P_{2m}$ |
| 3 | $P_{31}$ | $P_{32}$ | — | $\cdots$ | $P_{3j}$ | $\cdots$ | $P_{3m}$ |
| $\cdots$ | $\cdots$ | $\cdots$ | $\cdots$ | $\cdots$ | $\cdots$ | $\cdots$ | $\cdots$ |
| $i$ | $P_{i1}$ | $P_{i2}$ | $P_{i3}$ | $\cdots$ | $P_{ij}$ | $\cdots$ | $P_{im}$ |
| $\cdots$ | $\cdots$ | $\cdots$ | $\cdots$ | $\cdots$ | $\cdots$ | $\cdots$ | |
| $m$ | $P_{m1}$ | $P_{m2}$ | $P_{m3}$ | $\cdots$ | $P_{mj}$ | $\cdots$ | — |

TABLE 3.5 Matrix $Z$ Containing the Normal Deviates Corresponding to Entries in $P$

| Stimuli | Stimuli | | | | | | |
|---|---|---|---|---|---|---|---|
| | 1 | 2 | 3 | $\cdots$ | $j$ | $\cdots$ | $m$ |
| 1 | — | $z_{12}$ | $z_{13}$ | $\cdots$ | $z_{1j}$ | $\cdots$ | $z_{1m}$ |
| 2 | $z_{21}$ | — | $z_{23}$ | $\cdots$ | $z_{2j}$ | $\cdots$ | $z_{3m}$ |
| 3 | $z_{31}$ | $z_{32}$ | — | $\cdots$ | $z_{3j}$ | $\cdots$ | $z_{im}$ |
| $\cdots$ | | | | | | | |
| $i$ | $z_i$ | $z_{i2}$ | $z_{i3}$ | $\cdots$ | $z_{ij}$ | $\cdots$ | $z_{im}$ |
| $\cdots$ | | | | | | | |
| $m$ | $z_{m1}$ | $z_{m2}$ | $z_{m3}$ | $\cdots$ | $z_{mj}$ | $\cdots$ | — |

struction of the new matrix, the element $z_{ij}$ is obtained for the corresponding entry $p_{ij}$ of matrix $P$ by reference to a table of unit normal deviates. In this transformation $z_{ij}$ is given a positive value if the corresponding $p_{ij}$ exceeds 0.50 and a negative value if $p_{ij}$ is less than 0.50. Each entry in matrix $Z$ is an estimate of the difference between the scale values of two elements. The unit in terms of which this estimate of the difference is expressed is, for case 5, the value under the radical in Eq. (3.3). Numerous estimates of the difference in scale values between any pair of stimuli can be derived from matrix $Z$. For example, subtracting the entries in any given row for a particular pair of columns provides an estimate of the difference in scale value of the two stimuli represented by the columns. ($z_{31} - z_{32}$ provides an estimate of $z_{12}$.) Specific computational procedures will not be described here. They are widely available in the literature (6,15,48).

Fortunately, there is available a means of assessing the feasibility of the simplifying assumptions that underlie the numerical values assigned by the law of comparative judgment. This criterion involves a test of internal consistency based on the reconstruction of the values in matrix $P$ from the stimulus-scale values. These proportions are reconstructed by algebraically reversing the process by which the scale values were assigned. For case 5 this amounts to solving Eq. (3.3) for $z_{ij}$. If the reconstructed proportions and the original ones are not in close agreement, then presumably one or more of the simplifying assumptions is at fault. Mosteller (31) has described an application of the chi-square statistic for the evaluation of the discrepancy between observed and expected proportions.

If the test of internal consistency of numerical assignments based on case 5 results in a significant chi-square, the investigator has evidence that at least one assumption underlying the scale construction procedure is not tenable. He may decide that the assumption of equal discriminal dispersions was an error, in which case he may recompute scale values based on procedures that provide an estimate of the individual discriminal dispersions (6). Failure of the internal consistency criterion might also be attributable to the untenability of either the normality postulate or the assumption made concerning the correlation between perceptual processes. Mosteller (31) has indicated that his test is relatively insensitive to violations of the normality postulate. As concerns the correlation coefficients, it should be noted that this term of the equation refers to the relationship between the scale locations of pairs of stimuli over replications. Some degree of correlation might be expected because of fluctuations of implicit judgmental origins and units. Any degree of correlation attributed to these sources, however, would be expected to be constant for all stimuli. It is difficult to imagine the operation of a factor that would lead to inequality of the correlation coefficients, except for the intrusion of extraneous variable properties which the respondents invoke differentially for the various stimuli.

In practice, an investigator is not likely to interpret the failure of the internal consistency (functional unity) criterion as evidence that the respondents judged in terms of more than one variable property unless the inequality of discriminal dispersions has been discarded as an alternative hypothesis. If he is led to the interpretation of multidimensionality, he may decide to abandon scale construction on the ground that a single scale does not fit the data. Alternatively, he may set about to determine the minimum number of dimensions required to account for the respondents' numerical assignments for the particular set of stimuli. Multidimensional scaling procedures are available for this purpose (48).

The law of comparative judgment results in interval-scale values corresponding to the perceptions of a set of stimuli by one respondent or by a group of undifferentiated respondents. The stimuli may be traits, actions, or attitude objects. The model has been used, for example, to measure the perceived severity of crimes, nationality preferences, and the palatability of foods. It is not appropriate for the measurement of subject variables.

Three scaling models incorporating the law of comparative judgment have been suggested for the measurement of affective-object variables at the level of a ratio scale. Each of these models involves pair-comparison judgments of specially contrived, complex stimuli. The model due to Horst (23) requires the pairing of one liked and one disliked object. The respondent's task is to indicate for each pair whether the composite is liked or disliked. The Horst model assumes that a respondent's judgment of the net affect aroused by a pair of objects as favorable indicates that the liked component was farther from a rational zero point in the favorable direction than the disliked component was in the unfavorable direction. This assumption is the key to locating the origin. The logic of the law of comparative judgment is utilized to space the scaled stimuli.

Another variant on the law of comparative judgment for the ratio measurement of affective-object variables is due to Thurstone and Jones (46). Their procedure entails the inclusion in the same data-collection instrument of pairs of objects along with the same objects taken singly. Whereas the Horst procedure requires that the respondent decide for each judgment whether he would take a bad outcome in order to obtain a good outcome, the Thurstone and Jones procedure requires him to decide whether a particular combination of outcomes, whatever their hedonic value, is preferable to another combination of outcomes. This model locates the zero point so that the scale values of the combinations of stimuli are consistent with the numerical assignments to the individual stimuli. This feature of the model is based on the assumption that the affective values of the combinations of objects are a simple additive function of the values of the components. Any form of interaction with regard to the affective values of pairs of objects would invalidate this assumption.

Shuford, Jones, and Bock (37) devised a procedure known as *contingent pair comparisons* which may sometimes prove useful for the construction of affective-object scales. The respondent's task for this model is to choose between pairs of lotteries, each of which is described in terms of the probability with which a valued object may be obtained. The probability of a successful outcome and the probability of lack of success (with lack of success defined as maintaining the *status quo*) in all cases sum to 1. In this procedure the law of comparative judgment is utilized to scale the lotteries. By following a prescribed pattern in constructing the lottery stimuli, an investigator is able to infer the affective values of the objects contained in the lotteries on the basis of the values assigned to the lotteries. Furthermore, if the utility of the *status quo* is defined as a rational zero point, the resulting scale values may be interpreted as ratio values. Comparison of the values of objects scaled by both this procedure and that due to Thurstone and Jones indicated close agreement (37).

## 3.8 THE LAW OF CATEGORICAL JUDGMENT

The logic of the law of comparative judgment has been applied to scale construction based on data derived from the sorting of stimuli into a set of prescribed, ordered categories. A variety of procedures have been described for adapting Thurstone's model to data of this form (1,12,14,36[4],47,48). Names used to refer to these scale construction procedures include, among others, the *method of graded dichotomies,* the *method of successive categories,* and the *method of successive intervals.* Torgerson (47,48) has provided the most general statement of the model, which he designates as the *law of categorical judgment.* We shall use that name here.

[4] The procedure described by Saffir (36) is one due to Thurstone.

In scale construction under the law of categorical judgment the respondent is asked to sort each of a set of elements into its most appropriate category. As in the category scale model, the alternative categories are conceived as representing characteristic amounts of the scale property. In placing a stimulus into a particular category, the respondent effectively assigns a number to the stimulus to represent his perception of its status in terms of the variable property. Unlike the direct scaling model for categorical judgments, the present model does *not* assume that the respondent establishes equal category intervals. It is assumed, however, that the scale constructor knows the rank order of the category boundaries in terms of the scale property. This assumption requires merely that the scale order of response categories be unequivocal as, for example, the following are: "agree very strongly, agree somewhat, neither agree nor disagree . . ."; "a central, dominating trait of the individual, a superficial trait of the individual, a trait not possessed by the individual. . . ." In deriving the law of categorical judgment from the law of comparative judgment, Torgerson treats the boundaries between response categories in the same way that stimuli are treated. Specifically, he assumes that categorical judgment data represent implicit pair comparisons between the particular stimulus, on the one hand, and each category boundary, on the other. As in the law of comparative judgment, the perceptual processes aroused by each presentation of a stimulus are assumed to be distributed normally, and, by analogy, so are the processes aroused by each category boundary. According to this formulation it is meaningful to speak of the scale values of the stimuli and of the category boundaries in terms of the same metric.

The equation that expresses the law of categorical judgment precisely is the following:

$$S_i - C_j = z_{ij} \sqrt{\sigma_i^2 + \sigma_j^2 - 2r_{ij}\sigma_i\sigma_j} \qquad (3.4)$$

where $S_i$ = the mean of the hypothetical distribution of perceptual processes for stimulus $i$

$C_j$ = the mean of the hypothetical distribution of perceptual processes for the $j$th category boundary

$z_{ij}$ = the normal deviate corresponding to the empirically determined proportion of times that stimulus $i$ was judged greater than category boundary $j$

$\sigma_i, \sigma_j$ = the discriminal dispersion of stimulus $i$ and category boundary $j$

$r_{ij}$ = the coefficient of correlation between category boundary $j$ and stimulus $i$

As indicated above, Eq. (3.4), which defines the law of categorical judgment, is identical with Eq. (3.2), which defines the law of comparative judgment, except for the substitution of parameters referring to a category boundary for those referring to a second stimulus. In our discussion of the parent model, we noted that some form of simplifying assumptions is necessary to solve the basic equation for real data. The same requirement exists for the law of categorical judgment.

Torgerson discusses three sets of simplifying assumptions which lead to workable solutions for Eq. (3.4). One of these conditions involves the following three assumptions:

**1** The discriminal dispersions of all stimuli are the same.

**2** The discriminal dispersions of all category boundaries are the same.

**3** All of the coefficients of correlation between stimuli and category boundaries are the same.

With these assumptions Eq. (3.4) reduces to

$$S_i - C_j = z_{ij} \sqrt{k_1 + k_2 - k_3} = z_{ij}k \tag{3.5}$$

A particular set of working assumptions that appear most often in the literature is those associated with a set of procedures that, for historical reasons, is called the *method of successive intervals*. These assumptions are that the discriminal dispersion of all category boundaries are the same and that the correlation between the scale positions of any stimulus and any category boundary is zero. Equation (3.4) with these assumptions becomes

$$S_i - C_j = z_{ij} \sqrt{k + \sigma_j^2} \tag{3.6}$$

The third workable solution suggested by Torgerson is an analog of the last one considered. It involves the assumption that the discriminal dispersions of all stimuli are the same, along with the assumption of zero correlations between stimuli and category boundaries. The law of categorical judgment, taking account of these assumptions, is

$$S_i - C_j = z_{ij} \sqrt{\sigma_i^2 + k} \tag{3.7}$$

In analyzing data according to the law of categorical judgment, the scale constructor constitutes the matrix $P$, the entries of which are the proportion of times that a particular stimulus was judged to have less of the variable property than a particular category boundary. A stimulus sorted into category 1, for example, is considered to have been judged lower on the scale than the boundary between categories 1 and 2, the boundary between categories 2 and 3, the boundary between 3 and 4, etc. Table 3.6 illustrates matrix $P$ showing the general entry $p_{ij}$. Another matrix, $Z$, is then defined from matrix $P$ by representing each entry in $P$ as a unit normal deviate. Table 3.7 illustrates matrix $Z$, each entry of which, $z_{ij}$, corresponds to a term in an observation equation under the law of categorical judgment. The units in which the $z_{ij}$ entries are assumed to be expressed depend on which version of the law of categorical judgment is invoked. Under Eq. (3.5), for example, the various units are assumed to be equal, whereas under Eqs. (3.6) and

TABLE 3.6    Matrix $P$ Containing the Proportion of
Times That Stimulus $i$ Was Judged Less
than Category Boundary $j$

|          | Category boundaries | | | | | | |
|----------|-----|-----|-----|-----|-----|-----|-----|
| Stimuli  | 1   | 2   | 3   | $\cdots$ | $j$ | $\cdots$ | $n$ |
| 1        | $P_{11}$ | $P_{12}$ | $P_{13}$ | $\cdots$ | $P_{1j}$ | $\cdots$ | 1.00 |
| 2        | $P_{21}$ | $P_{22}$ | $P_{23}$ | $\cdots$ | $P_{2j}$ | $\cdots$ | 1.00 |
| 3        | $P_{31}$ | $P_{32}$ | —        | $\cdots$ | $P_{3j}$ | $\cdots$ | 1.00 |
| $\cdots$ | $\cdots$ | $\cdots$ | $\cdots$ | $\cdots$ | $\cdots$ | $\cdots$ | $\cdots$ |
| $i$      | $P_{i1}$ | $P_{i2}$ | $P_{i3}$ | $\cdots$ | $P_{ij}$ | $\cdots$ | 1.00 |
| $\cdots$ | $\cdots$ | $\cdots$ | $\cdots$ | $\cdots$ | $\cdots$ | $\cdots$ | $\cdots$ |
| $m$      | $P_{m1}$ | $P_{m2}$ | $P_{m3}$ | $\cdots$ | $P_{mj}$ | $\cdots$ | 1.00 |

(3.7) the units in each row or in each column, respectively, are assumed to be equal. For those conditions in which equal units are not assumed for the entire matrix $Z$, it is necessary to estimate values of the various units and to use these estimates to weight the entries of matrix $Z$. Computational techniques for accomplishing this and for determining scale values for stimuli and category boundaries are summarized by Edwards (6), Guilford (15), and Torgerson (48).

Edwards and Thurstone (7) have presented the details for an internal consistency check for scales constructed according to the law of categorical judgment. This functional unity criterion involves reversing the scaling procedure in order to obtain a set of expected values for the proportion of times that each stimulus was judged to have a location on the scale lower than that of each category boundary. Edwards and Thurstone suggest as a criterion of internal consistency a small average absolute discrepancy between the observed and predicted proportions. Guilford (15) advocates an adapta-

TABLE 3.7    Matrix $Z$ Containing the Normal Deviates Corresponding to the Entries in $P$

|          | Category boundaries | | | | | | |
|----------|-----|-----|-----|-----|-----|-----|-----|
| Stimuli  | 1   | 2   | 3   | $\cdots$ | $j$ | $\cdots$ | $n$ |
| 1        | $z_{11}$ | $z_{12}$ | $z_{13}$ | $\cdots$ | $z_{1j}$ | $\cdots$ | — |
| 2        | $z_{21}$ | $z_{22}$ | $z_{23}$ | $\cdots$ | $z_{2j}$ | $\cdots$ | — |
| 3        | $z_{31}$ | $z_{32}$ | $z_{33}$ | $\cdots$ | $z_{3j}$ | $\cdots$ | — |
| $\cdots$ | $\cdots$ | $\cdots$ | $\cdots$ | $\cdots$ | $\cdots$ | $\cdots$ | $\cdots$ |
| $i$      | $z_{i1}$ | $z_{i2}$ | $z_{i3}$ | $\cdots$ | $z_{ij}$ | $\cdots$ | — |
| $\cdots$ | $\cdots$ | $\cdots$ | $\cdots$ | $\cdots$ | $\cdots$ | $\cdots$ | $\cdots$ |
| $m$      | $z_{m1}$ | $z_{m2}$ | $z_{m3}$ | $\cdots$ | $z_{mj}$ | $\cdots$ | — |

tion of the Mosteller chi-square statistical test of the magnitude of the discrepancies between the observed proportions and those predicted on the basis of the scaling model. Torgerson (48), however, has noted that for any given stimulus the proportion of times that the stimulus is judged to be greater than any one category boundary is not independent of the proportion of times that it is judged greater than any other category boundary. This fact may introduce a dependency which invalidates the underlying assumptions of the chi-square test.

Another approach to the problem of the goodness of fit of the model is based on the fact that the hypothesis of a single variable property in terms of which both stimuli and category boundaries are ordered implies that the normal deviates in matrix $Z$ for any pair of rows or columns should be linearly related. A graphical test of this hypothesis is appropriate.

As in the case of the law of comparative judgment, failure of the internal consistency criterion suggests that at least one of the working assumptions is not tenable. As a consequence of this finding, a scale constructor might try a new set of scaling assumptions. He might abandon scale construction on the ground that a single variable property is not appropriately measured in the situation in which he has worked. Finally, he may respond to internal inconsistency of the unidimensional model by applying multidimensional scaling procedures of the sort described by Torgerson (48).

Scales constructed under the law of categorical judgment have been shown to approximate closely those constructed for the same stimuli under the law of comparative judgment (7,36). An impressive degree of generality of scale values assigned by the model was demonstrated by Jones (25) who had two samples of one population of respondents judge the same stimuli, one group judging in terms of nine rating categories, and the other, six. He found not only the expected linear relationship between the two affective-object scales, but also that the two scales could be transformed so as to equate their units and origins. Furthermore, the stimulus discriminal dispersions estimated for the two experimental groups were the same. In another study reported in the same paper, Jones found evidence of the invariance of measured category width. These data resulted from eight different surveys made to determine the palatability of various foods for members of the armed forces. The surveys were conducted over a period of two years, with different respondents and different food items. Very stable category widths were observed despite these variations. Taken as a whole these experimental results indicate a desirable degree of invariance of scale properties under the law of categorical judgment. There is, unfortunately, very little research comparing the relative degrees of invariance of different scaling models due to the same experimental conditions. Thus, it is not possible at the present time to compare this model for scale construction with others on the basis of empirical criteria.

Because the respondent's task in scale construction under the law of categorical judgment is identical with that of scale construction by means of the category-scale model, the two models are interchangeable as regards the types of variables to which they may be applied. Scale construction under the category-scale model is easy. The question naturally arises whether there is any reason for an investigator to undertake the considerably greater computational task required of him in scaling under the law of categorical judgment. In answer to this question, the following considerations are relevant. Hevner (20) found a nonlinear relationship between values assigned by the category-scale model and those assigned by the law of comparative judgment, whereas Saffir (36), by reanalyzing Hevner's category-scale data according to the law of categorical judgment, found a linear relationship. Jones and Thurstone (26) found that the relationship between category-scale values and those assigned under the law of categorical judgment is decidedly nonlinear. The demonstrations by Hevner and by Jones and Thurstone both suggest an end effect in the case of the category-scale model, whereby the numerical assignments for extreme stimuli are not spread so far apart as when the same stimuli are scaled under the law of categorical judgment. If the more complex model is accepted as the criterion, this finding indicates that the respondents do not truly make subjectively equal response categories when they are asked to do so. The grounds for accepting the law of categorical judgment as the criterion in this matter are twofold. First, this model provides a means for testing the basic scaling hypothesis. Second, as we have noted, the relationship between values assigned by this model and those assigned under the law of comparative judgment is linear. The accumulated evidence suggests, in summary, that the direct scale model for categorical data leads to an ordinal scale, rather than to the intended interval scale. In those instances in which it is desirable to treat categorical data at the level of an interval scale, the law of categorical judgment is indicated.

Our survey of scale construction procedures has so far included direct and indirect models for the measurement of content and object variables. As indicated earlier, subject variables present special methodological problems. The remainder of this chapter is devoted to consideration of models designed to overcome the difficulties associated with the quantification of comparisons among persons who hold particular beliefs, behavioral inclinations, or affective orientations.

## 3.9  THE THURSTONE SCALE

Thurstone (43,45) proposed a two-step procedure for the construction of affective-subject scales. The logic of the procedure is such that it appears equally appropriate for cognitive- and behavioral-subject scales. The first step in the procedure consists in asking a group of judges to sort a set of statements concerning the attitude object into categories according to the degree of favorableness-unfavorableness toward the object which each statement implies. By means of the previously described category-scale model each statement is assigned a value corresponding to its status on the cognitive variable of pro-anti with respect to the attitude object. The second step of the procedure consists in administering a sample of the scaled statements to the respondent whose degree of affect is to be measured. The task of the respondents is to accept or reject the individual statements. The value on the pro-anti scale of each statement which any given respondent accepts is assigned as a score to that respondent. With multiple endorsements a respondent is given a score equal to the average (mean or median) of all of the statements he accepts. In this way respondents are located on the same pro-anti scale as the statements to which they respond. The procedure is apparently equivalent to having each respondent appear before the judging group and make a set of statements concerning his attitudes about the specified object, on the basis of which the judging group expresses its belief concerning the respondent's affect toward the object. Thus subjects are assigned values as though they were objects in a cognitive-object scale.

The construction of a Thurstone scale for the measurement of an affective variable starts with the compilation of a large set of statements from which judges can infer affect. It is, of course, important that all degrees of implied affect are represented in the initial set of statements. It is also important that the statements are as precise as possible in their affective implications. Thurstone made no distinctions with regard to item content except as this factor bears on the clarity with which a statement expresses a degree of implied affect. Specifically, he warned that items should express a single sentiment and that they should not state a presumed fact, the endorsement of which would be based on considerations other than the respondent's attitude.

Only a subset of the original pool of items is included in the questionnaire that is presented to the respondents whose affect is to be measured. Thurstone (43,45) suggested three criteria for the selection of statements for the final instrument. First, the entire range of implied affect should be covered by a set of statements. As well as possible, the scale values of the statements should be evenly spaced on the pro-anti scale. Second, the particular statements chosen to represent any degree of affect should be those which are least ambiguous, ambiguity in this context to be assessed by an index of the dispersion of the judges' ratings of a statement. Finally, Thurstone suggested that statements for the final questionnaire should be selected in terms of what he described as an *objective criterion of irrelevance*. We shall presently examine that criterion in detail, but at this point, some discussion of the ambiguity criterion is in order.

Because Thurstone defined ambiguity as the lack of consensus among judges, invoking his suggested ambiguity criterion serves to eliminate from the final instrument statements that contain features that judges react to differently. Weaknesses of grammar or syntax which lead some judges to perceive one degree of implied affect and other judges to perceive another degree of affect tend to cause items to be eliminated. Similarly, the inclusion in some of the statements of fringe issues regarding the attitude object, issues which only some of the judges consider to have implications for the object, tends to lead to the elimination of items. The functional unity criterion for the cognitive-object component of the Thurstone scale is a linear relationship between the pro-anti values assigned to statements by all possible pairs of judges. The ambiguity criterion obviously serves to improve functional unity by eliminating those statements most likely to contribute to nonlinearity.

When a respondent accepts or rejects a statement, he may do so, especially if not instructed otherwise, on the basis of whatever idiosyncratic consideration appeals to him. He may, but need not, choose to accept a particular statement because of its degree of implied affect concerning the attitude object. Consider, for example, the following statement reported by Ostrom (33): "If I were president I would order an invasion of Cuba." This item appeared in a set of statements regarding Castro's Cuba. There is little doubt about the affective implications of the statement as regards Cuba. One can speculate, however, about a variety of considerations which a respondent might take into account in deciding whether to endorse the item. Thurstone felt that it was desirable to restrict the items in the final instrument to those which respondents tend to choose or to reject on the basis of their affective implications alone. As a matter of fact, he argued strongly for this feature of the scale: "Now it is, of course, necessary to select for the final attitude scale those statements which are endorsed or rejected primarily on account of the degree of pacifism-militarism which is implied in them and to *eliminate those statements which are frequently accepted or rejected on account of other more or less subtle and irrelevant meanings*" (43, p. 230, italics supplied).

Thurstone's criterion for the elimination of so-called irrelevant items involves determining an index of similarity between statements based on the observed probability of joint endorsement. The statements to be eliminated by this criterion are those which do not show a high probability of joint endorsement with other items of similar scale value. The eliminated items are, in other words, those for which there is not a high degree of correlation between subject scores, on the one hand, and acceptance-rejection of the item, on the other. The employment of the criterion of irrelevance in the construction of a Thurstone scale requires that a sample of the subject group participate in construction of the scale instrument along with a sample of judges. It is a second sample of subjects whose positions are ultimately measured on the subject scale.

The criterion of irrelevance has not often been used in the construction of Thurstone scales. Whether it should be employed appears to be a basic issue that has received surprisingly little attention. A statement which survives the ambiguity criterion but fails the test of relevance is, despite its failure, scalable on the pro-anti variable at the point corresponding to its numerical assignment. The criterion of irrelevance provides no information concerning the affective implications of a statement. A respondent who endorses an item with a scale value of, let us say, *s*, expresses thereby a sentiment equal to *s*, whether or not that statement is relevant. If the item is declared irrelevant by means of the criterion, this merely means that some people whose sentiment is equal to *s* do not endorse it and some whose net affect is different from *s* do.

It should be noted that the systematic elimination of statements on the basis of the criterion of irrelevance represents a selection bias in sampling from the hypothetical universe of unambiguously pro and anti statements. Because of this bias, it would be very difficult to know how to generalize a subject's score. There are probably some research problems for which this generalization restriction would subvert the entire program.

Certainly the criterion of irrelevance should not be applied routinely in scale construction under the Thurstone model. The basic issue concerning its use at any time can perhaps be stated in these terms: Does the question of whether respondents subscribe to statements because of their affective implications have any bearing on the measurement of attitude variables? Is it, alternatively, a second question to be examined in addition to the construction of an affective-subject scale? Thurstone clearly linked the measurement question and that of the basis for item endorsement. The present author prefers to separate them.

A critical role in the development of the Thurstone scale is played by the group of judges who evaluate the status of each statement in terms of its favorability toward the attitude object. The central tendency of their judgments defines the scale value for each statement. The dispersion of their judgments serves as the objective criterion of ambiguity for each item. The Thurstone scale is intended to provide interval measurement of the affective orientations of a set of respondents. This goal presupposes that the items are measured on an interval scale. It was noted earlier that the category-scale model which Thurstone described for measuring the pro-anti implications of the statements probably does not provide an interval scale. That model was adopted by Thurstone because it was feasible practically, whereas his preferred model, the law of comparative judgment, was not (43). At the time that Thurstone published his work on attitude measurement, the law of categorical judgment had not been formulated. It is apparent that his original intentions would be better served by substituting the newer model for the direct model in Thurstone scaling.

Whatever scaling model is used to assign values to the items, the various

judges are assumed to replicate one another. The functional unity requirement of the scale is that the categorical judgments of any pair of judges
should be linearly related. Thurstone wished to generalize item values to
a population of judges consisting of everyone who can read the language
in which the statements are written and is familiar with the attitudinal issue.
A great deal of research effort has been invested in testing Thurstone's assumption that the judge's own attitude is independent of his item judgments. Systematic differences in origin and unit have been observed (24,30,34,51,52).
As discussed earlier, differences in origin and unit are consistent with a linear
relationship among the values assigned by assumed replicates. The typical
result from studies designed to assess the invariance over linear transformations is a correlation between judges of differing attitudes in the .90s
(2,9,10,21,22,35,49,50). Thus, the accumulated evidence appears to support
the functional unity requirement of the category-scale component of the
Thurstone model.

Our discussion of Thurstone's procedures has been directed to their use
in the construction of affective-subject scales. This was the use for which
the model was developed. As indicated earlier, it can be readily adapted
to the construction of cognitive- and behavioral-subject scales. In such adaptations the original item pool would, of course, reflect the degree of implied
readiness to attribute characteristics to the attitude object or willingness to
engage in actions involving the attitude object. In a study by Ostrom (33),
item pools corresponding to cognitive, behavioral, and affective variables were
constructed. He had judges evaluate the affective implications of the statements in each of the three pools, whereas the present suggestion is that judges
can be instructed to evaluate cognitive and behavioral, as well as affective,
implications.

## 3.10  THE LIKERT SCALE

Likert's *method of summated ratings* (28) for constructing affective-subject scales resembles the Thurstone method in that it involves an initial compilation of a set of statements related to the attitude object. Whereas the
scale constructor under the Thurstone model presents the statements to judges
to be rated according to the degree of affect implied by the acceptance of
the item, following the Likert procedures, he presents the statements to a
group of respondents to be rated according to the degree to which they accept
or reject them. On the basis of data obtained from this group of respondents,
some items are eliminated. The usual form of item analysis at this step
in the procedure involves the correlation of the item response with the total
score. The twenty or so items having the highest correlations with the total
score are retained as the final instrument. Sometimes the item analysis procedure consists of a statistical test (such as a t test) between the respondents

whose scores were highest and those whose scores were lowest, based on the total set of items. In such cases the items that are retained are those which meet some statistical criterion.

The statements that survive the culling procedure are assembled as the instrument by which the affect of a set of subjects is to be measured. The respondent's task at this point is to select for each statement one of five or so response categories, such as: strongly agree, agree, undecided, disagree, strongly disagree. These categories are weighted to reflect intensity of agreement with statements that are favorable to the attitude object and intensity of disagreement with statements that are unfavorable. Thus, an arbitrary weight of 5 may be assigned to the category expressing most intense agreement with a pro item, while the weight of 0 is assigned to the category that expresses strongest disagreement with that item. If this is done, then any item in the same set which expresses an unfavorable attitude toward the object will have weights assigned to the response categories which are the reverse of those assigned for a favorable statement. Hence, a weight of 5 is given to strongest endorsement of a favorable item and strongest rejection of an unfavorable item. Finally, each respondent is assigned a score corresponding to the sum of the numerical values associated with his responses to the statements in the set.

Several features of the Likert scale as outlined above warrant special comment. First, it is clear that the numerical assignments made to respondents on the basis of their endorsement and rejection of statements are intended to be generalized to a population of statements implying favorable or unfavorable affect. There is, however, no feature in the model that aids in any way the selection of statements so as to represent this hypothetical population. There are, for instance, no judges employed in this procedure to evaluate the affective implications and ambiguities of items, as in the Thurstone procedure.

A second feature warranting comment concerns the item analysis component of the Likert technique. The items retained on the basis of that analysis are those to which respondents in the initial sample react consistently. Thus, the culling of items serves to ensure a degree of functional unity for the final instrument. The degree of functional unity, however, depends upon the similarity of a particular sample of respondents in their patterns of acceptance and rejection of the statements. Presumably each respondent brings to bear some particular set of considerations when he decides whether to accept or reject any given item. These considerations constitute what we might call the respondent's *decision criterion*. Functional unity, as evidenced by the selection of statements on the basis of the Likert item analysis, suggests that the nature of the decision criteria employed by respondents is homogeneous in quality, although differing in degree from one respondent to the other. The question of whether the functional unity of the final instrument can be generalized to other respondent samples appears to be a question of whether one can assume the generality of the decision criterion. As a minimal precaution it seems prudent to select the item analysis respondents from the same population as those whose affect is subsequently to be measured. In any event, the common practice of ignoring the sampling issue with regard to the initial group of respondents is not defensible.

A third feature of the Likert procedure which warrants comment is the arbitrary manner in which numbers are assigned as weights for the response categories. In an earlier version of the procedure, Likert (28) employed a more elaborate weighting function. It was found empirically that the simple weights correlated very highly with the more elaborate weights, and that is the reason the simple integer weights are almost always used nowadays.

The category values of each item on a Likert scale are intended to reflect the variable of intensity of agreement-disagreement with the item. If each statement could be characterized by a number indicating its degree of implied affect toward the attitude object, then it should be possible to write some function of the item values and the response category values that would pro- vide a meaningful assessment of each respondent's affective orientation toward the object. However, the Likert procedure does not differentiate items accord- ing to their degree of implied affect. It is apparent, therefore, that the inter- pretation of the summated ratings as a measure of an affective variable rests on an assumption that the implied affect of every item in the set is the same, at least within the margin of random, replication error. If this assumption of equal item value were not made, data derived from a Likert scale would tend to be chaotic. Suppose, for example, that one item implied neutrality and another extreme favorability. In order for summation over these two items to be meaningful, the weight assigned to the most intense acceptance of the neutral item would have to be approximately in the middle of the range of values reserved for intense acceptance and rejection of the more extreme, second item. The model has no provision for evaluating any aspect of an item except whether it is generally favorable or unfavorable toward the object.

Ferguson (10) demonstrated that the item analysis procedure employed in Likert scale construction serves to eliminate statements that are *not* expres- sions of extreme sentiments. He submitted statements that survived the item analysis criterion to a group of judges who rated them, as in the Thurstone procedure, according to the degree of implied affect. For four out of five attitude objects, the Likert statements were clustered toward either end of the pro-anti continuum.

We have argued that the functional unity of a Likert scale is specific to a population of respondents, and we have argued that the statements which fare best under the item selection criterion tend to be those expressing extreme affect toward an attitude object. These two considerations suggest that a scale constructor might obtain statements for the initial pool of items by asking a sample from the respondent population to describe positions which they believe define the two extremes of the pro-anti scale. The present writer once compiled an item pool in this fashion and found that 17 out of a total of 18 of these items were found subsequently to discriminate between high and low scorers at the 0.05 level.

There is no apparent reason why the Likert model should not apply as well to cognitive- and behavioral-subject scales as to affective-subject scales. The only modification required for application to these other classes of scales is in the content of the item pool.

### 3.11   THE SEMANTIC DIFFERENTIAL

Much of the recent research on attitude change has utilized a measurement technique known as the *semantic differential*. This technique derives from the work of Osgood, Suci, and Tannenbaum (32) on the measurement of meaning. In the course of their work in semantics, these investigators performed a number of factor analyses on data consisting of ratings of diverse concepts on properties described by polar adjectives. A recurring factor in the various analyses was one which they labeled *evaluative*. Among the polar adjectives found to have high loadings on the evaluative factor, regardless of the concept that was rated, were good-bad, optimistic-pessimistic, positive-negative. To measure the status of a group of subjects on an affective variable, Osgood et al. suggest that each respondent be asked to rate the attitude object on a set of properties which have been shown to have high loadings on the evaluative factor. The respondent's score is taken as the sum (or average) of his ratings of the object on the evaluative properties.

According to the model underlying the semantic differential, every pair of evaluative, polar adjectives approximates in meaning a hypothetical pair of adjectives which defines a pro-anti variable, exactly. The particular adjectives actually utilized in any application of the technique are assumed to be random replicates of each other, and the extent to which each approximates the hypothetical pair of purely evaluative adjectives is assumed to be invariant over respondents. These assumptions provide the functional unity requirements of a semantic differential scale. Evidence in support of the assumptions and, therefore, of functional unity derives from the factor analyses reported by Osgood et al. (32).

The semantic differential seeks to base interpersonal comparisons on the demonstrably similar meanings among subjects of the scale property. However, the model does not control for possible differences among respondents in judgmental origin and unit. If, for example, two respondents are observed to evaluate an attitude object differently, it is not possible to distinguish among three possible explanations. First, the person whose rating is more favorable may, in fact, hold more favorable affect toward the object. Alternatively, his standards of judgment may be such that he is more willing than the other person to describe any of his feelings as favorable (an origin effect). Finally, he may be more or less willing than the other person to describe any of his feelings as extreme (a unit effect).

The semantic differential has been shown to correlate highly with a Thurstone scale measuring affect toward agricultural crop rotation and a measure of the same variable based on a model due to Guttman (16), which is the model to be discussed next.

## 3.12   THE GUTTMAN SCALOGRAM MODEL

Scalogram analysis is an approach to the measurement of cognitive-, behavioral-, and affective-subject variables which, when its conditions are met, yields an ordinal scale. Scale construction under this model begins with the specification by the investigator of what Guttman has called the *universe of attributes*. Specifying the universe of attributes amounts to deciding what facets of a cognitive, behavioral, or affective variable shall be deemed critical insofar as the generalization of ultimate scale values is desired. Statements embodying these critical facets are constructed for administration to a sample of respondents drawn presumably at random from a population in whom the investigator has particular interest. If it can be assumed that the items represent a random sample from a population of items embodying the critical facets of the universe of attributes and if it can be assumed that the respondents are a random sample from a known population, then the behavior of the respondents with regard to the sample of items can be generalized to both populations. What is of particular interest is whether that behavior can be adequately represented by a specific pattern known as a *scalogram*. If so, certain implications are accepted regarding the universe of attributes and the population of people.

The aim of scalogram analysis in any particular application is to determine whether a set of respondents and a set of items can be logically ordered together on a scale in terms of a property described in variable degree in the items and invoked in variable degree by the respondents when they decide to accept or reject each item. What it means for a set of respondents and a set of items to be ordered together on a single scale can, perhaps, be illuminated by the following consideration. As in our discussion of the Likert scale, we may imagine that each individual has certain criteria which he invokes in deciding whether to accept or reject a statement that expresses some belief, an advocated action, or a degree of affect. Furthermore, both qualitative and quantitative differences in decision criteria are likely to be observed in the comparison of respondents. Consider, for example, the issue of the involvement of the United States military forces on the Asian continent. In

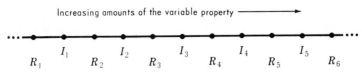

Fig. 3.1.  **Representation of a Hypothetical Guttman Scale on Which Five Items and Six Respondents Are Located.**

deciding whether to say yes or no to a statement relating to this issue, one respondent may evaluate it in terms of its implications regarding the power position of the United States in world politics. Another respondent might evaluate the same statement according to its implications regarding the taking of human life for whatever purpose. Even if two respondents were alike in the item properties that they evaluate in the course of accepting or rejecting items, they might still differ in how much of the property each requires to be present in an item before he will accept it. Thus two individuals might agree on their view that the critical aspect of American military involvement in Asia is, let us say, America's status in the world power struggle. Even so, the two respondents might disagree in what they think America's status in this hierarchy should be. A set of respondents and a set of items are said to be scalable in the Guttman sense when all respondents in the set invoke the same criterion property, albeit in different amounts, in deciding whether to accept or reject each item in the set. If the item is perceived by the respondent to embody less of the scale property than that which defines his decision criterion, he will, under the model, accept the statement. Otherwise, he will reject it.[5]

Figure 3.1, which constitutes a scale as that concept is defined within the scalogram model, pictures the situation with regard to a set of items, on the one hand, and a set of respondents, on the other. Five dichotomous items (i.e., items with two possible response categories) are represented in Fig. 3.1 by the points labeled $I_1, I_2, \ldots, I_5$. Six respondents are represented in that figure by points labeled $R_1, R_2, \ldots, R_6$. The location of each point on the line is assumed to correspond to an amount of the variable property. The amount of the property by which each item is characterized

[5] This assumption of the scalogram model presupposes that the statements are expressed in a form that logically permits the probability of acceptance to be a monotonic increasing or decreasing function of the respondent's scale position. The appropriate type of item is one that conveys the idea that "my decision criterion requires no more of the variable property than $X$," where $X$ varies quantitatively over items in the set. In contrast, the type of item which is *not* appropriate for the scalogram model is one that conveys the idea that "my decision criterion requires at least as much of the property as $X$, but no more than $Y$," where $X$ and $Y$ vary quantitatively over items in the set. The type of items required by the scalogram model has been distinguished from the inappropriate type by the names *increasing probability* versus *maximum probability* (45), *cumulative* versus *differential* (29), and *monotone* versus *nonmonotone* (4).

corresponds to the boundary between the two response categories. Thus, agreement with the premise stated by an item signifies an imprecise amount of the property corresponding to the region to one side of that item's scale location, and disagreement signifies an amount corresponding to the other side of that point. The locations of the respondents in the figure correspond to the magnitude of the variable property which each respondent requires by his decision criterion in order to accept or reject a statement. If the situation described by Fig. 3.1 exists, a respondent will accept any item that implies less of the scale property than that required by his decision criterion. Consequently, the number of items endorsed by each respondent is a function of his position on the scale. According to the assumption of the model, respondent $R_1$ endorses no items, respondent $R_2$ endorses one item, and so forth, with respondent $R_6$ endorsing all five items.

Figure 3.2 is equivalent to Fig. 3.1 as an illustration of the Guttman scale. In Fig 3.2 the items define the columns of the response matrix, called the *scalogram matrix*, and the respondents define the rows. The columns have been arranged in rank order to reflect the position of the items with respect to the variable property in Fig. 3.1. By convention, items are arranged in a scalogram matrix from most to least degree of the property. The respondents are arranged in the rows from top to bottom according to the decreasing rank order of their decision criteria. The entries in the matrix are $+$'s, signifying the acceptance of an item by a respondent, and $-$'s, signifying rejection.

According to the response rule underlying the model, it follows that the

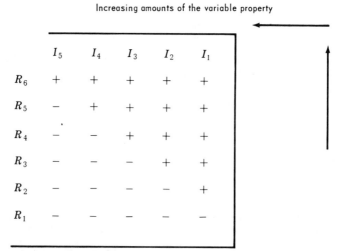

**Fig. 3.2.  Scalogram Matrix Illustrating the Response Pattern Characteristic of the Hypothetical Guttman Scale Depicted in Fig. 3.1.**

relative frequency with which respondents in a group accept an item is an inverse function of its scale position. Similarly, if items in a set have different scale positions, the frequency of item endorsements signifies the respondent's scale position, the more extreme respondents endorsing the greater number of items. Thus, in the practical situation, an approximation to Fig. 3.2 may be made by ordering items according to the frequencies with which they are endorsed and ordering respondents according to the number of items they endorse. For dichotomous items, the matrix of real data will show the triangular pattern of endorsements depicted in Fig. 3.2, provided that the response rule assumed by the model is correct and that the respondents do, in fact, invoke differing amounts of the same criterion property in applying this rule. The various computational procedures which have been suggested for the Guttman scale [see Edwards (6)] generally entail the rearrangement of rows and columns of a data matrix in order to approximate as closely as possible the characteristic response pattern expected on the basis of the scale hypothesis.

The existence of a Guttman scale implies a particular dependency among the component items such that the conditional probability that a respondent will endorse item $I_i$, given that he endorses any item higher on the scale than $I_i$, is 1.00. With real data some amount of measurement and model error is expected, and this causes the computed values of these conditional probabilities to be less than 1.00. Furthermore, more than one variable property may have been invoked by the respondents in reacting to the items, a state of affairs which would serve to lower the critical conditional probabilities. In any event, at the opposite extreme, assuming that the items and the respondents do not belong on a common scale, the items would be statistically independent, and the joint endorsement of every pair of items would be attributable to chance. Under the chance hypothesis, the conditional probability of the acceptance of the item $I_i$, given that an item of higher value was accepted, is simply the probability of endorsement for item $I_i$. For illustration, suppose that 30 percent of the group of respondents accept $I_2$ and 20 percent accept $I_1$. Under the scale hypothesis, 100 percent of those who accept $I_1$ are expected to accept $I_2$. Under the chance hypothesis, however, this figure is only 30 percent. As a consequence of the scale hypothesis as it relates to these conditional probabilities, for dichotomous items, the largest number of response patterns that would be observed with a set of respondents is one more than the number of items. (There may be fewer than this number of response patterns if there are no respondents whose decision criteria fall between pairs of adjacent items.) Under the chance hypothesis, the maximum number of response patterns for $m$ dichotomous items is $2^m$.

If the chance hypothesis is correct, a respondent who accepts a single item might choose any one of the $m$ items for his endorsement. If the scale hypothesis is correct, on the other hand, the respondent who selects a single item for endorsement can be confidently expected to choose that item with the least amount of the scale property. As a general rule, under the scale hypothesis the investigator is able to specify on the basis of knowledge of how many items a respondent endorsed exactly which items these were. This important consequence of the scale hypothesis is called *reproducibility*.

With real data, an ideal, errorless Guttman scale is not to be expected. The practical problem is, therefore, to determine whether the data approximate the ideal scale closely enough to justify dismissing as errors the observations that do not fit. As a means of assessing the goodness of fit of the scale model to data, Guttman's procedure requires, first, that each respondent be assigned to the *scale type* which his response pattern most closely resembles. For this purpose a scale type is defined as a group of respondents who give any of the response patterns predicted by the scale hypothesis, e.g., $+++$, $-++$, $--+$, $---$. The criterion for resemblance among response patterns is, for this purpose, the number of errors of reproducibility engendered by treating a nonscale pattern as though it were a scale pattern. Consider the nonscale pattern $+--$. Under the scale hypothesis, a respondent endorsing only one of three dichotomous items should give the pattern $--+$. The response pattern $+--$ when compared with the scale type with one endorsement contains two errors of reproducibility, one due to the fact that an item was endorsed unexpectedly and the other due to the unexpected rejection of an item. The same nonscale pattern, however, when compared with the scale type with three rejections contains only one error of reproducibility, that due to the endorsement of the most extreme item. Therefore, the nonscale pattern $+--$ is said to most closely resemble the scale pattern $---$, since there is no other scale type with a response pattern to which this one could be compared with fewer errors of reproducibility.

Having accomplished an optimal arrangement of the data, the scale constructor then computes the *coefficient of reproducibility*, which is defined as one minus the proportion of the total responses, summing over items and respondents, which are classified as reproducibility errors. By convention, a coefficient of reproducibility greater than .90 is required as evidence of an adequate fit of the scale model to data. This critical value, an arbitrary choice, corresponds to a maximum of 10 percent of the total observed responses classified as errors.

A criterion of 10 percent error, unfortunately, has differing implications according to the number of items and the popularity of the modal response category for each item (11,19). Furthermore, by arranging the response matrix so as to minimize errors of reproducibility, the scale constructor capitalizes on chance effects, serving to make the coefficient of reproducibility spuriously high. Because of these limitations of the reproducibility criterion, Guttman suggests the following additional criteria:

**1** *Range of frequencies of modal response for items.* The coefficient of reproducibility which serves as the major criterion for the existence of the Guttman scale may be viewed as the average of separate coefficients for each item. Regardless of whether the scale hypothesis is tenable, the item reproducibility can never be less than the proportion of respondents giving the modal response. For this reason it is advisable to include some items with modal response frequencies close to 50 percent and to avoid items with extreme modal response frequencies.

**2** *Error pattern.* It is conceivable that a single set of items might be scalable in terms of more than one variable property. Items dealing with race relations in America, for example, might be responded to differently according to the time perspective of the respondent. Thus, one subgroup of respondents might invoke decision criteria referring to the final state of society implied by the items, whereas another subgroup might invoke decision criteria referring to the means toward some social end. The best evidence that such a division exists among the respondents supplying data for scale construction is the pattern of reproducibility errors. The fairly frequent occurrence of particular nonscale response patterns suggests the invalidity of the one-scale hypothesis, whatever the value of the reproducibility coefficient.

**3** *Number of items.* As is generally true in matters of sampling, the greater the number of items, the greater the confidence that a universe of attributes is scalable. (A similar argument could be made for employing the largest possible sample of respondents.) The discussion of the Guttman scale to this point has been in terms of dichotomous items. For present purposes it should be mentioned that multiple response categories for a single item are formally equivalent to multiple dichotomous items, as will be explained shortly. Hence, the argument for large numbers of items can be generalized to call for a large number of response categories, without regard to how these categories are distributed among the items.

An unsettling degree of intuition is required in deciding whether a set of data forms a Guttman scale. Without a great deal of vigilance, an investigator seems fairly likely to decide that a scale exists when it does not. This peril is dramatized by the fact that the coefficient of reproducibility computed for small numbers of items known to be statistically independent is very high. Guttman (19) showed that for independent, dichotomous items endorsed, respectively, by 0.2, 0.4, 0.6, and 0.8 of the respondents, the coefficient is over .90. Even with as many as nine independent, dichotomous items endorsed by 0.1, 0.2, 0.3, 0.4, 0.5, 0.6, 0.7, 0.8, and 0.9 of the respondents, the coefficient of reproducibility is .83 (13), a high value for the principal scale criterion when the chance hypothesis is known to be correct.

This consideration suggests that scale construction under the Guttman model might prudently be restricted to large numbers of items. This recommendation runs counter to prevailing practice; it is not at all uncommon to find three- and four-item scales in the published literature. One can only speculate concerning the extent to which this folkway is due to the spirit of the numbers game which causes the investigator to be personally challenged to attain a coefficient of reproducibility of .90 by any means. More likely, it is due to the fact that the Guttman scale model is often applied to survey data collected from respondents whose tolerance for repetitive tasks motivated by methodological nicety is limited.

Given the danger of wrongly deciding that a set of data forms a Guttman scale, the following procedure which tests the chance hypothesis might be employed as a minimal safeguard:

**1** Arrange the data matrix so as to minimize errors of reproducibility.

**2** Determine from the real data matrix the proportion of respondents who endorsed each item.

**3** Generate a hypothetical data matrix, assuming the chance hypothesis. In order to do this, an investigator may write response patterns for hypothetical respondents by consulting a table of two-digit random numbers. Suppose, for example, that the real data matrix refers to four items, $I_4$ endorsed by 30 percent of the respondents, $I_3$ by 40 percent, $I_2$ by 50 percent, and $I_1$ by 60 percent. If the first two-digit number consulted in the table of random numbers is 30 or lower,[6] hypothetical respondent, $R_1$, will be considered to have endorsed $I_4$. If it exceeds 30, he will be considered to have rejected $I_4$. The second number consulted in the table determines $R_1$'s response to $I_3$. Thus, acceptance will be scored if the number is equal to or less than 40, and rejection if it exceeds the popularity of the item in the real data matrix. In this way the entire response pattern for each hypothetical respondent, in turn, can be generated. In the present illustration, after $R_1$'s response to $I_1$ is determined based on the popularity value of 0.60, the data for $R_2$ may be generated simply by recycling and continuing to use the random number table. The total number of hypothetical respondents should equal the number of respondents contributing to the real data matrix.

**4** According to the same rules employed for the real data matrix, rearrange the hypothetical data matrix to minimize errors of reproducibility.

**5** Compare the best estimates of the Guttman scales for the real and hypothetical data. For this purpose it is suggested that the respondents, both

[6] The suggested use of two-digit random numbers does not, of course, permit a value of 100 percent. To prevent bias on this account, the investigator might simply ignore the equally extreme entry 00, restricting the range of possible values to 01–99. According to the arguments offered earlier with respect to item popularity, even this restricted range of values exceeds that of items to be seriously considered as scalable.

real and hypothetical, be partitioned into those with no errors of reproducibility, those with one error, those with two errors, etc. A chi-square test applied to the resulting contingency table allows the statistical evaluation of the chance hypothesis for the particular set of real data.

The procedure outlined above appears to have the advantage of providing experimental control for number of respondents, number of items, item popularity, and the employment of procedures which may capitalize on chance variations. It leads, however, to an explicit test of the hypothesis that no systematic relationship exists among the items, whereas the Guttman hypothesis is that a relationship exists which is almost perfect. Therefore, as suggested, the safeguard provided by the procedure is minimal.

The present discussion has assumed that each item employed in scale construction under the Guttman model is dichotomous. The model is in no way restricted to items that are simply accepted or rejected. As a matter of fact, it is possible for the various items that are tested for scalability to have differing numbers of response categories. As we indicated in the beginning of our discussion of the Guttman model, it is the boundary between response categories which is considered to be located on the scale. According to this formulation, each dichotomous item defines one point on a continuum, whereas each trichotomous item defines two points, an item with four categories defines three points, etc. One trichotomous item is formally equivalent to two dichotomous items, except for the fact that a respondent typically selects only one response category, no matter how many are offered. In the spirit of the model, the acceptance of any ordered category for a particular item implies the acceptance of any category lower than it on the scale. The usual procedures employed for scale construction under the Guttman model, in effect, credit the respondent for such implied endorsements of response categories below those that are actually endorsed. When data matrices are arranged to reduce errors of reproducibility, category boundaries for multi-category items are treated in the same way as those for dichotomous items. Sometimes, in order to improve reproducibility, adjacent (on the hypothesized scale) response categories for a particular item may be combined. This procedure serves only to reduce the order of the data matrix and to reduce the number of stimuli on the scale.

Our discussion of the Guttman model has been centered on the question of whether a table of data conforms to the scale hypothesis. The criteria used to make this decision are functional unity criteria which refer to a particular type of consistency to be observed within the data. If the scale hypothesis is accepted, it is assumed that a set of people (subjects) *can* be ordered in terms of a cognitive, behavioral, or affective variable by means of a set of items which are perceived by the respondents to be located on a cognitive-object scale. The criteria for deciding the tenability of the scale hypothesis do not imply any particular rules by which numerical values are to be assigned to respondents and item categories. Most often, scale values are assigned to respondents to reflect their assumed ordinal position in terms of the measured variable. This is done by determining the number of item endorsements included in the response pattern for the scale type which the individual most closely resembles, according to the principle of minimum reproducibility errors. In a similar fashion, category boundaries may be given ordinal scores according to the position of each in the data matrix which has been arranged to minimize errors of reproducibility.

Guttman (18) has provided a seldom-used analytic procedure for assigning numerical values to respondents and to item category boundaries. That procedure assigns scale values such that, for any given data matrix, the ratio of the variance between categories to the total variance is maximum, and, at the same time, the ratio of the variance between people to the total variance is maximum. Scores assigned to respondents by this procedure are proportional to the mean values of the categories which they endorse, and the values assigned to the categories are proportional to the scores of the respondents who endorse them. Guttman's analytic solution to the metric problem provides a criterion against which to evaluate scores deriving from the arrangement of a data matrix so as to minimize errors of reproducibility. Unfortunately, there appears to be no research in the literature evaluating the conventional numerical assignment procedures in this fashion.

The Guttman model is equally appropriate for cognitive-, behavioral-, and affective-subject scales. The only difference among these classes of scales would be in the item content.

Guttman, it will be recalled, argues that the existence of the scale can be generalized to the population from which the particular respondents were drawn as a random sample and to the population of items from which the particular set was drawn as a random sample. Whereas this claim is logically valid, its practical implications are probably not often important because it is impossible to define in any rigorous way the item universe. Furthermore, as many critics have commented, it is difficult to imagine that an investigator who had at his disposal a universe of items would sample from it on a random basis, thus sacrificing obviously better items in terms of clarity of expression and other nonscale attributes.

## 3.13  CONCLUSION

Scale construction under all the models that have been discussed in this chapter proceeds with data deriving from verbal behavior of respondents. The study of attitudes is certainly not restricted to a verbal domain; one can imagine many nonverbal manifestations of the cognitive, behavioral, and affective variables that are subsumed under the attitude concept. The traditional reliance of social scientists on verbal indices of attitude is probably due to two interrelated factors. First, verbal behavior permits much more convenient and efficient data collection than do other, usually more subtle, indices. Second, the level of theoretical development in the study of social attitudes is not so well advanced as to require specific types of behavioral manifestations for the definition of variables. In the absence of conceptual rigor, methods tend to be chosen on the basis of convenience.

The eventual need to broaden the scope of attitude research to include nonverbal behavior may be less important, however, than that of elevating the level of theoretical aspirations of investigators on the contemporary scene to establish firmly some necessary distinctions among existing verbal indices. The simple distinctions that were drawn in this chapter among subject, content, and object scales and between cognitive, behavioral, and affective scales are not always made in substantive research. As a consequence, lively controversies exist between antagonists who may not even be studying the same variables.

There has been an unfortunate tendency among students of social attitudes to divorce theory and method or, at least, to try. Books and chapters on attitude measurement have sometimes apparently presented scale construction models so formidably that investigators seek to avoid them and to rely on unrationalized self-ratings and single questions. Other investigators appear to view scaling models as a set of alternatives to be chosen as whimsically as one selects a salad at a cafeteria. It was not many years ago that a subsequently important monograph appeared in which the extended use of Guttman scales was justified exclusively on the ground that it was not feasible to have separate judges rate statements or to include very many statements in the final instruments. What a disservice it would be to the field it is designed to help if the present chapter leaves any reader with the impression either that he can avoid problems of measurement by ignoring them or that he can arbitrarily take up a measurement model without regard to substantive considerations.

Research may be viewed as a process of systematically comparing stimuli in terms of variable properties. Measurement allows the quantification of these comparisons. In attitude measurement, nonmethodological considerations dictate what stimuli are to be compared and the precise property in terms of which the comparisons are to be made. The functions of scale construction models in this area are to provide a logical basis for particular types of comparisons and quantification procedures. These functions are, of course, integral parts of attitude research. As theory develops and the relevant comparisons are ever more precisely delineated, it seems likely that the variety of scaling models will become too great to encompass in a chapter such as this one.   The basic work which has been surveyed in this chapter is the product, by and large, of methodologists.   The next steps must be made by people whose primary interests are in the subject matter of social attitudes.

## REFERENCES

1 Attneave, F.: "A Method of Graded Dichotomies for the Scaling of Judgments," *Psychological Review,* 56 (1949), 334–340.

2 Beyle, H. C.: "A Scale for the Measurement of Attitude toward Candidates for Elective Governmental Office," *American Political Science Review,* 26 (1932), 527–544.

3 Campbell, D. T., and D. W. Fiske: "Convergent and Discriminant Validation by the Multitrait-Multimethod Matrix," *Psychological Bulletin,* 56 (1959), 81–105.

4 Coombs, C. H.: *A Theory of Psychological Scaling* (Ann Arbor, Mich.: Engineering Research Institute, University of Michigan, 1952).

5 Coombs, C. H., H. Raiffa, and R. M. Thrall: "Some Views on Mathematical Models and Measurement Theory," in C. H. Coombs, R. M. Thrall, and R. L. Davis (Eds.), *Decision Processes* (New York: Wiley, 1954), pp. 19–37.

6 Edwards, A. L., *Techniques of Attitude Scale Construction* (New York: Appleton-Century-Crofts, 1957).

7 Edwards, A. L., and L. L. Thurstone: "An Internal Consistency Check for Scale Values by the Method of Successive Intervals," *Psychometrika,* 17 (1952), 169–180.

8 Ekman, G., and L. Sjoberg: "Scaling," *Annual Review of Psychology,* 16 (1965), 451–474.

9 Eysenck, H. J., and S. Crown: "An Experimental Study in Opinion-Attitude Methodology," *International Journal of Opinion and Attitude Research,* 3 (1949), 47–86.

10 Ferguson, L. W.: "A Study of the Likert Technique of Attitude Scale Construction," *Journal of Social Psychology,* 13 (1941), 51–57.

11 Festinger, L.: "The Treatment of Qualitative Data by 'Scale Analysis,'" *Psychological Bulletin,* 44 (1947), 149–161.

12 Garner, W. R., and H. W. Hake: "The Amount of Information in Absolute Judgments," *Psychological Review,* 58 (1951), 446–459.

13 Green, B. F., Jr.: "Attitude Measurement," in G. Lindzey (Ed.), *Handbook of Social Psychology* (Reading, Mass.: Addison-Wesley, 1954), pp. 335–469.

14 Guilford, J. P.: "The Computation of Psychological Values from Judgments in Absolute Categories," *Journal of Experimental Psychology,* 22 (1938), 32–42.

15 Guilford, J. P.: *Psychometric Methods,* 2d ed. (New York: Mc-Graw-Hill, 1954).

16 Guttman, L.: "The Basis for Scalogram Analysis," in S. A. Stouffer et al., *Measurement and Prediction* (Princeton, N.J.: Princeton, 1950), pp. 60–90.

17 Guttman, L.: "An Outline of Some New Methodology for Social Research," *Public Opinion Quarterly,* 18 (1954), 395–404.

18 Guttman, L.: "The Principal Components of Scale Analysis," in S. A. Stouffer et al., *Measurement and Prediction* (Princeton, N.J.: Princeton, 1950), pp. 312–361.

19 Guttman, L.: "Problems of Reliability," in S. A. Stouffer et al., *Measurement and Prediction* (Princeton, N..J: Princeton, 1950), pp. 277–311.

20 Hevner, Kate: An Empirical Study of Three Psychophysical Methods," *Journal of Genetic Psychology,* 4 (1930), 191–212.

21 Hinckley, E. D.: "A Follow-up Study on the Influence of Individual Opinion on the Construction of an Attitude Scale," *Journal of Abnormal and Social Psychology,* 67 (1963), 290–292.

22 Hinckley, E. D.: "The Influence of Individual Opinion on Construction of an Attitude Scale," *Journal of Social Psychology,* 3 (1932), 283–296.

23 Horst, P.: "A Method for Determining the Absolute Affective Value of a Series of Stimulus Situations," *Journal of Educational Psychology,* 23 (1932), 418–440.

24 Hovland, C. I., and M. Sherif: "Judgmental Phenomena and Scales of Attitude Measurement: Item Displacement in Thurstone Scales," *Journal of Abnormal and Social Psychology,* 47 (1952), 822–832.

25 Jones, L. V.: "Some Invariant Findings under the Method of Successive Intervals," *American Journal of Psychology,* 72 (1959), 210–220.

26 Jones L. V., and L. L. Thurstone: "The Psychophysics of Semantics: An Experimental Investigation," *Journal of Applied Psychology,* 39 (1955), 31–36.

27 Kendall, M. G.: *Rank Correlation Methods* (London: Griffin, 1948).

28 Likert, R.: "A Technique for the Measurement of Attitudes," *Archives of Psychology, New York,* no. 140 (1932).

29 Loevinger, Jane: "The Technic of Homogeneous Tests Compared with Some Aspects of 'Scale Analysis' and Factor Analysis," *Psychological Bulletin,* 45 (1948), 507–529.

30 Manis, M.: "The Interpretation of Opinion Statements as a Function of Recipient Attitude," *Journal of Abnormal and Social Psychology,* 60 (1960), 340–344.

31 Mosteller, F.: "Remarks on the Method of Paired Comparisons: III. A Test of Significance for Paired Comparisons when Equal Standard Deviations and Equal Correlations Are Assumed," *Psychometrika,* 16 (1951), 207–218.

32 Osgood, C. E., G. J. Suci, and P. H. Tannenbaum: *The Measurement of Meaning* (Urbana, Ill.: University of Illinois Press, 1957).

33 Ostrom, T. M.: "A Multitrait-Multimethod Matrix Assessment of the Affective, Behavioral, and Cognitive Components of Attitude." Paper to Midwest Psychological Association, Annual Meetings, Chicago, Ill., 1966.

34 Ostrom, T. M.: "Perspective as an Intervening Construct in the Judgment of Attitude Statements," *Journal of Personality and Social Psychology,* **3** (1965), 135–145.

35 Pintner, R., and G. Forlano: "The Influence of Attitude upon Scaling of Attitude Items," *Journal of Social Psychology,* **8** (1937), 39–45.

36 Saffir, M. A.: "A Comparative Study of Scales Constructed by Three Psychophysical Methods," *Psychometrika,* **2** (1937), 179–198.

37 Shuford, E. H., L. V. Jones, and R. D. Bock: "A Rational Origin Obtained by the Method of Contingent Paired Comparisons," *Psychometrika,* **25** (1960), 343–356.

38 Stevens, S. S.: "Mathematics, Measurement, and Psychophysics," in S. S. Stevens (Ed.), *Handbook of Experimental Psychology* (New York: Wiley, 1951), pp. 1–49.

39 Stevens, S. S.: "A Metric for the Social Consensus," *Science,* **151** (1966), 530–541.

40 Stevens, S. S.: "On the Theory of Scales of Measurement," *Science,* **103** (1946), 677–680.

41 Stevens, S. S.: "Ratio Scales, Partition Scales, and Confusion Scales," in H. Gulliksen and S. Messick (Eds.), *Psychological Scaling: Theory and Application* (New York: Wiley, 1960), pp. 49–66.

42 Suppes, P., and J. L. Zinnes: "Basic Measurement Theory," in R. D. Luce, R. R. Bush, and E. Galanter (Eds.), *Handbook of Mathematical Psychology* (New York: Wiley, 1963), pp. 1–76.

43 Thurstone, L. L.: "Attitudes Can Be Measured," *American Journal of Sociology,* **33** (1928), 529–554.

44 Thurstone, L. L.: "A Law of Comparative Judgment," *Psychological Review,* **34** (1927), 273–286.

45 Thurstone, L. L., and E. J. Chave: *The Measurement of Attitude* (Chicago: University of Chicago Press, 1929).

46 Thurstone, L. L., and L. V. Jones: "The Rational Origin for Measuring Subjective Values," in L. L. Thurstone, *The Measurement of Values* (Chicago: University of Chicago Press, 1959), pp. 195–210.

47 Torgerson, W. S.: "A Law of Categorical Judgment," *American Psychologist,* **9** (1954), 483 (abs.).

48 Torgerson, W. S.: *Theory and Methods of Scaling* (New York: Wiley, 1958).

49 Upshaw, H. S.: "The Effect of Variable Perspectives on Judgments

of Opinion Statements for Thurstone Scales: Equal-appearing Intervals," *Journal of Personality and Social Psychology*, 2 (1965), 60–69.

50 Upshaw, H. S.: "A Linear Alternative to Assimilation and Contrast: A Reply to Manis," *Journal of Abnormal and Social Psychology*, 68 (1964), 691–693.

51 Upshaw, H. S.: "Own Attitude as an Anchor in Equal-appearing Intervals," *Journal of Abnormal and Social Psychology*, 64 (1962), 85–96.

52 Zavalloni, Marisa, and S. W. Cook: "Influence of Judges' Attitudes on Ratings of Favorableness of Statements about a Social Group," *Journal of Personality and Social Psychology*, 1 (1965), 43–54.

# CHAPTER 4

# Conceptualization and Measurement in the Study of Social Stratification[1]

ELTON F. JACKSON

RICHARD F. CURTIS

Validity—the ultimate problem of measurement—may be reduced to the task of fitting theoretic elements to a set of possible observations, or vice versa. Depending on the state of the discipline, then, the problem of validity may be attacked either by developing conceptual schemes which promise to yield order among quantities of existing empirical data or by establishing explicit ground rules for the collection of data required by an existing detailed theory. Since the student of social stratification is beset on the one hand by diverse theories as difficult to express operationally as they are grand, and on the other hand by mountains of useful and interesting data, he must concern himself with conceptualization as well as technique if he is to confront the problem of validity.

To complicate matters further, there are two generally distinct research interests in the study of stratification. The methodological problems that concern a specialist in stratification are different from those which concern a specialist in some other aspect of sociology who feels that the pervasive influence of status in human life makes it an important independent, dependent, or (most likely) control variable.

Like all specialists, the student of stratification needs to refine his general concepts into specific, purified components. His concern is to relate the components of status to consequences for the individual and for the development of the several forms of status, and most importantly, to describe accurately

[1] The authors gratefully acknowledge helpful criticism and advice from H. M. Blalock, Jr., Ann Blalock, Gerhard E. Lenski, and Karl F. Schuessler and exempt them from any responsibility for use of their comments.

the *processes* of stratification, i.e., the relationships among the components of stratification over time.

The researcher focusing on problems other than stratification makes contrasting demands on measurement. He needs to summarize as much status information as possible in as simple a scale as possible. Therefore, he is frequently concerned only with large differences in status, for he cannot afford to waste his sample size with numerous status variables or with many detailed categories along one dimension. He may not care what particular aspect of status as a control variable makes the relationship between his independent and dependent variables disappear, but only whether any status measure can do so. Use of a general status index is also very economical; because status is so pervasive, it is often possible to control a large number of status and associated variables simultaneously with a simple gross index.

To expect the specialist and the nonspecialist to employ completely different techniques of measurement and analysis would, of course, be absurd. Yet their strategy in selecting from a common set of alternative methods will differ. Ideally, we should have a precise theoretical view of the stratification process which would give meaning to both sorts of measures (the complex of distinct variables and the compound index) and which would allow translation from each type to the other. This calls for a set of pure, accurate, precise measures of independent status components which can be collapsed into a theoretically meaningful unitary scale for use in general sociological research. Much theoretical and methodological work remains to be done before such a goal can be reached.

In this chapter we shall describe, from the perspectives of both the stratification specialist and the nonspecialist, the current state of measurement within stratification research and discuss some of the issues which remain unresolved. Since issues of validity involve problems of conceptualization and of measurement, we shall begin by outlining the conception of stratification upon which we shall base our search for measurement solutions. Then we shall treat in turn what we regard as the central measurement tasks[2] in stratification research: (1) the establishment of rank systems—orders of superiority-inferiority along which individuals and groups are ranked—and the construction of indices combining such rank measures into measures of general status, and (2) the measurement of the contradictory or unstable aspects of status, such as status inconsistency and vertical mobility.

[2] It should be noted, although we shall not treat such issues in this chapter, that the stratification area also raises distinctive problems of analysis, i.e., demonstration of relationships between independent and dependent variables, particularly in the control of variables other than the presumed cause. Status variables are often closely related to one another (raising the issue of multicollinearity) and the effects of such aspects of status as mobility and inconsistency are easily confounded, in their effects on dependent variables, with the effects of rank variables.

## 4.1   A CONCEPTUAL ORIENTATION TO SOCIAL STRATIFICATION

The difference between the conceptual orientation presented here and *a* theory of stratification lies in our general avoidance of detailed substantive propositions.  Our purpose is to provide a conceptual basis for interpreting the measures we shall discuss later.

We take *stratification* to be *the study of units* (roles, individuals, families, groups, or whatever a given theorist wishes to specify) *distributed along one or more rank systems* (dimensions of value, facilities, or evaluation).  To specify the units and rank systems under consideration (e.g., hens distributed along a pecking order or occupational roles distributed along an income continuum) is to state the substance of an investigation.

We shall use *rank* to mean the *location* of a unit along a rank system, and *status* to mean some (specified) *composite* of a unit's ranks.  A *status system* will refer to *the set of rank arrangements* within a group.  Rank systems rest on some (variable) amount of *consensus* concerning what is desirable.  We regard consensus concerning who holds what rank as an interesting but different matter.  In addition, the placement of units along the rank system, the form of the distribution along a rank system, and the social arrangements based on rank differences may be institutionalized, but the extent and nature of such institutionalization may vary widely.

Theorists differ regarding which values or evaluations ought to be included in the study of stratification, about the causal relationships among them, and about their relative importance.  Without answering any of these questions, we shall illustrate in the next section the measurement of rank systems in general by discussing a few which we regard as important.

Individual status is always taken to be relative to a system of status; it is necessary to establish *what* system is involved and *in what way* an individual status is related to that system.  Once this has been done, the *meaning* of a status has been specified, and therefore it is possible to discuss comparisons between systems and between individuals in different systems.

Students of stratification have not always been entirely clear in specifying the system within which a measured status exists.  It has been convenient to assume that isolated small towns, small groups in laboratories, dominant metropolitan centers, or American society itself acted as status systems because they appeared to be independent and in some sense closed.  Yet at the same time one would assume that if a person held a status in one of these systems, he also held a status in the others.

As mass transportation and communication transform the American scene, the assumption of independence between status systems becomes less and less tenable.  In practice, this fact is usually ignored and extraneous statuses are rarely held constant in any given study.  If this were not problematic enough, there are other potential systems of status with even less clearly defined boundaries, e.g., one's position in his family, clique, or neighborhood. Think also of important statuses, such as those within a profession, church, club, or political party, as complicated by the relative positions of the professions, churches, clubs, and political parties themselves. In sum, measurements of status are misleading and comparability between statuses is impossible unless the relevant systems of status are clearly specified.

Similarly, comparability between systems depends upon establishment of points of status equivalence between systems *or* demonstration that the two systems to be compared can be subsumed under a larger system.

*How* is a rank related to a status system? There are two basic theoretical approaches to the nature of ranking. First, it may be assumed that individuals or other units are ranked solely in relation to one another. This is to assume, for example, that income status is not properly a dollar amount, but rather that in income one stands below a certain proportion of the relevant population and above the rest, no matter how rich or poor either proportion may be. Percentile scores are proper rank measurements in this view. On the other hand, it may be assumed that status is possession of or access to values and that quantitative measurement of a particular value (where possible) is the proper measure of status. The latter approach still does not make rank independent of a defined status system, since rank can represent the share an individual has in the total amount of the value (e.g., income) distributed within the relevant population.

It is evident that the study of system properties is crucial in establishing comparability of rank. Sociologists have turned to the study of individual status largely because measurement of system properties requires so many data. Yet the theoretical desirability of research on system properties is emphasized by the problems posed by earlier theorists, such as the relationships between system properties discussed by Marx and the relationships between system properties and individual characteristics discussed by Sorokin (62).

The basic set of relationships in this conception of stratification is that among the set of individual rank systems constituting a status system. We may hypothesize generally that all these relationships will be positive, that all will be less than perfectly strong, and that the strength of the relationships will vary from one pair of rank systems to another. If causal sequences among these rank systems can be established, these sequences constitute the process of *rank stratification.* Causal or not, the structure of relationships among a set of rank systems is of intrinsic interest to the stratification theorist and suggests at least one approach to construction of a single overall index of status for the sociologist with other interests.

Since the relationships among rank systems are all assumed to be less than perfect, social units may be categorized by the extent to which they deviate from typical combinations of ranks. Since ranks may change over time, singly or in concert, social units may be categorized by the extent of status change experienced. These variables, status inconsistency and social mobility, respectively, may be regarded as the primary aspects of flexibility in status systems.

*Class stratification* is a term which we shall use to denote *social arrangements,* invidious in character if not in intent, *which stem from rank differentiation.*[3] Similarities of rank give rise, to a variable extent, to interacting groups, cliques, or networks of interaction and communication. Furthermore, communication within groups and the lack of communication between groups at different levels of rank give rise (again to a variable extent) to relatively distinct subcultures and life styles. Treating rank systems, associated networks of interaction, and subcultures as separable and causally related clusters of variables is useful because it (1) focuses attention on the processes of stratification and (2) suggests mechanisms through which aspects of social status have effects on assorted dependent variables. The three primary clusters of such mechanisms are motivation through reward and deprivation and access to resources; agents of social control and interpersonal relations; and socialization and similarity of values, social perspectives, and ideology.

The associations among rank position, group membership, and subculture are by no means perfect; there are variations within as well as between status systems. The extent to which rank differentiation produces differences in group membership and culture and the extent to which an individual participates in such groups and subcultures based on his rank are secondary aspects of flexibility in status systems at the level of the system and of the individual, respectively. Such flexibility not only influences behavior directly, but also conditions the effect of rank or class position on individual behavior.

Status systems are also perceived in variable ways by populations. The nature of the perceptions, the extent of consensus in perception within groups, and differences in perception between groups are further factors influencing the effects of rank and class stratification. As in many areas of sociology, it is fruitful to distinguish between an individual's more or less direct perceptions of the status system and his familiarity with ideology concerning status and class. Individuals may behave primarily in terms of one or the other, or in some cases, both.

Objective class interest is a powerful concept which raises many new problems. The most easily defensible but theoretically least powerful approach is to dispense with the idea of objectivity and define class interest as the interests members of a class think they have. But perhaps they are wrong, duped, or simply altruistic. If the investigator is confident enough,

[3] "Class" can be used to denote an aggregate of individuals located at roughly the same level of rank, but the term becomes sociologically significant only if something else is true: if such individuals therefore share a common interest, interact, identify with one another, or share a common culture.

he may define objective class interest, in which case it is possible to talk about mistaken interest and false class consciousness. Logically, of course, the terms "mistaken" or "false" could apply to the sociologist's definition as easily as to the views of the population.

The central problems of measurement suggested by this conception of stratification, then, are (1) measurement of single rank systems and combining ranks into indices of general status, and (2) measurement of aspects of flexibility in status systems such as social mobility and status inconsistency.

## 4.2 THE MEASUREMENT OF RANK AND SOCIAL STATUS

Measurement is most fruitful when the theoretical concept being measured is clearly specified. In our discussion of various possible measuring devices we shall therefore ask from time to time whether the device indeed orders the units of investigation in a theoretically meaningful way. Measures of occupation and socioeconomic status (SES) are very common in the study of social stratification; less common are attempts to design measures of occupation or SES so as validly to measure a specific theoretical concept.[4] For example, the respondents in a survey may be arranged by occupational status in rather different ways depending on whether the ranking is in terms of the prestige contributed by the possession of an occupation or the extent of power conferred on the incumbent.

Our general position, then, is that attempts to attain precise measurement should not precede attempts to specify carefully the concepts measured. We therefore generally favor the strategy of beginning with the measurement of more or less narrow rank systems, the meanings of which are easier to spell out in detail, and then cumulating from these to measures of social status as a general concept. One advantage of this procedure is that the interrelations of specific rank systems can help us to form a more valid idea of what the term social status might mean.

We shall begin this section with a discussion of the process of abstraction which we consider basic to all measurement in this area. Then we shall turn to methods used to measure rank systems, and to various indices of social class, and end with a discussion of methods of characterizing communities or societies according to the status distributions of units within them. The list of methods discussed will not be exhaustive; nor shall we attempt to give detailed instructions on how to use any given method (although references will be provided for potential users). We aim here for a review of certain significant measures and approaches to measurement, selected and organized in terms of the theoretical guidelines outlined above.[5]

[4] The authors do not exempt their own work from this criticism.
[5] For fuller summaries of some of the most widely used past methods, the reader is referred to Gordon (23, pp. 108ff. and chap. 7), Lasswell (44, chap. 4), Miller (51, sec. IIIA), and Svalastoga (64, chap. 2).

## *Abstraction*

Whether we wish to specify ranks on a single rank system or collapse ranks into a general social status index, the basic procedure is formally the same: the process of extracting a unidimensional measure from an abundance of information on more specific variables. As one example of the abstraction process, consider Ivy League football standings. From the infinite multitude of things about football we could measure—game scores, summed team weights, band size, extra points scored per touchdown, etc.—we ignore all but one datum: wins versus losses. Since each team plays each other team, the data are represented in an array cross-tabulating each team by the teams it played. The rank system, team standing in the Ivy League, is an abstraction from this array: which team won the most games? This rank system, team standing, has an interest all its own quite apart from single victories since it represents a social goal in itself: an Ivy value, distributed among the eight teams, which has social consequences, is expressed culturally, and motivates behavior.

Transitivity need not be present in the multidimensional data from which a single rank system is abstracted. Typically, Yale may have lost to Princeton and defeated Harvard while Harvard drubbed Princeton, which is as clear and recurrent an example of intransitivity as may ever be found in nature. But depending on the results during the rest of the season, any one of these teams may, in fact, have won the league championship. If Yale's season standing was higher than Harvard's, and Harvard's was higher than Princeton's, then Yale's season standing must be higher than Princeton's. Thus, the assumption of transitivity is justified with respect to the derived rank system, league standing.

Starting with status-relevant information about a complex social world, we construct rank systems by abstracting a *transitive, unidimensional* scale which summarizes the socially significant standing of units. We shall see below that even such apparently straightforward rank systems as income or education properly represent an abstraction process. The relative standing of units may be socially significant in two senses, however. The status dimension may be part, of people's cultural apparatus, and hence the scientist's abstraction procedure should parallel the general cultural abstraction process in order best to predict social relations of persons with various ranks on these systems. On the other hand, the scientist may be interested in arraying persons on what he considers an influential aspect of inequality, even though that aspect is not enshrined as a cultural definition.

The procedures of abstraction also vary because there are two basic types of status-relevant information: relative positions of units along variables and interactions between units. We shall discuss these in turn. For both sorts of procedures, however, our guides in choosing among the many different possible abstractions are of three kinds: (1) theoretical demands, (2) empirical relationships among component variables, and (3) relationships with criterion variables justified as (*a*) identities of, (*b*) causes or consequences of, or (*c*) merely correlates of the concept to be measured.

**Abstracting from relative positions of social units on component variables.** This approach to measurement involves two problems: choosing the variables upon which the measure is to be based and deciding on the relative weights of the basic variables. For example, we might be interested in conspicuous consumption as a rank system, and have data on type of yacht, Greek language skills, use of vacations, amount of alimony payments, design of family crest, and size of lawn for each family head to be studied. Other data might be ignored on theoretical grounds or for suspected unreliability. Thus, each unit occupies a position in six-dimensional space which we plan to reduce to a single dimension. The raw data need be intrinsically no more unidimensional than Ivy League football. There may well be in our sample a yachtless divorced man with a small lawn who speaks Greek fluently, yet whose standing on the conspicuous consumption rank system may be expressed unambiguously with assumptions of unidimensionality and transitivity.

It is instructive to think of the problem geometrically as a swarm of points (representing social units) in N-dimensional space (representing the N status-relevant variables concerning which we have data). Through this N-dimensional space we construct a single line, representing the abstracted rank system. The rank of a given unit is represented by the distance between an origin point and the perpendicular projection of this point on the line. Now, any number of different lines could be drawn through the space. The relative positions of points projected on one of these lines will differ from the relative positions of the same points projected on a different line.[6] Thus the problem of obtaining a unidimensional transitive scale can be translated into the question: Which of the different possible lines through the N-dimensional space should be selected as the rank system? This selection may involve ignoring some data as well as determining how to combine remaining data.[7]

In making these decisions about which component variables to ignore and how to properly combine the rest, we are guided by the above three criteria. First, purely theoretical concerns dictate many decisions of relative importance. For example, one must decide whether source of income is a theoretically valid component of an economic rank system or should be omitted. Another crucial theoretical decision is whether or not to arrange the abstracting procedures so that the resulting rank system will match a culturally defined rank system. Although such decisions are properly the duty

---

[6] For a discussion of such ambiguities in measurement, see Coleman (8, pp. 77ff.).

[7] For example, if a rank system line is at right angles to one of the N dimensions, differences between points on that dimension will not affect the ranks of the points, i.e., that dimension is ignored.

of theory, sociological theories are seldom detailed or precise enough to make all the necessary decisions. In addition, the question of which of several variables fits the generalities of a theory is often deliberately left open.

Second, empirical relationships among potential components of a rank system may serve as the criterion for selecting a line through the N-dimensional swarm of points. The justification for this criterion is parsimonious representation of as much of the actual variation along the different variables as possible. Think of the swarm of points not as random, but as forming a solid in space with greater density at some places than others. If that solid is social reality, then we might argue that a line through the dense parts of the swarm, minimizing the average perpendicular distance of each point from the line, approximates that reality as well as a line can. For example, suppose we had interval scale data on the degree of cleanliness and the degree of authority of each respondent's job in a sample. One approach to ranking the jobs would be to distribute the respondents in a scattergram and calculate the line that minimizes the perpendicular deviations from the respondent points to the line. The projection of each point onto the line would place the respondents on an occupation rank system abstracted from cleanliness and authority.

Third, we might select an outside variable as a criterion, either because we have reason to believe that it validly represents the rank system we are attempting to measure, because it is specified as a concomitant of that rank system by the theory, or because it is a theoretically specified cause or consequence of the rank system. The line through our swarm which exhibits the closest association with this criterion variable could be selected on the ground that it maximizes the fit between theory and data. To continue our example, instead of deciding on the relative weights of cleanliness and authority by the relationship between these component variables, one might wish to find the line through that two-dimensional swarm which would rank the respondent points in the manner which would best correlate with their ranking on a direct measure of occupational prestige. If the correlation were high enough, this abstraction from cleanliness and authority could be used as a measure of prestige rather than the more expensive or difficult direct criterion measure. Note, however, that criteria thought to be identical to, causes of, caused by, or merely correlated with the rank system represent quite different types of justification, even though the formal techniques of scale construction are the same.

The relative advantages of guiding measurement by theory, relations among components, and criterion variables will be further discussed below in the specific context of indices of social status.

**Abstracting rank systems from a matrix of interactions.** Such a matrix could involve deference, power, visiting patterns, reciprocal exchange, patterns of communication, sociometric choice, or many other types of abstractions from behavior, singly or in combination. The problem is the same: to ignore some data and combine the rest into one or more systems of rank which meet theoretical objectives.

Several elegant formal solutions to the problem of how to abstract from such data exist (29,39). To choose among the available alternatives, one needs to decide on theoretical grounds (or to explore the issue empirically) whether to weight direct deference relationships most heavily or to emphasize the importance of indirect relationships. For example, we might ask whether getting deference directly from a number of subordinates is more or less important than getting deference from one subordinate who gets deference from one of his subordinates who in turn gets deference from subordinates who receive deference.

Graph theory and other formal solutions to sociometric ranking problems represent promising models for abstracting rank systems from interactive types of data. Ideally, reputational studies of community status should gather data on the entire matrix of choices, visits, and communications in the community. However, at the community or societal level of analysis, which forms the central focus of our present interest, this is obviously impossible. Therefore, the elegant solutions employed in research on small groups or (occasionally) complex organizations are essentially useless for our *measurement* problems. They do, however, provide useful detailed models of social structure which should underlie the more elliptical measures of this sort of rank system in communities. We shall return to this topic below in discussing reputational measures of status.

We have tried above to provide a general orientation to the measurement of rank systems. Such an orientation, of course, presents (and leaves unsolved) pressing technical problems which are beyond the scope of this chapter, especially the problem of attaining valid measures which form true ordinal or, hopefully, interval scales.[8] We turn now to discussions of specific types of measurement which have been employed in stratification research. Throughout, our concern will be to show how various types of information may be employed in the production of a measure of rank or status which reasonably meets the assumptions required by our theoretical approach to stratification.

## Measures of Rank Systems

**Income and education.** These are among the most straightforward rank systems. Nevertheless, they too are abstractions from sets of more detailed information, and these abstractions depend fundamentally upon theoretical decisions. For example, income may be used to indicate earning power in

[8] See Coleman (8, chap. 2) for an introduction to these measurement problems.

the system of production or it may indicate consumption resources. The former conception would lead an investigator to measure relative incomes of family heads, whereas the latter would suggest concern for after-tax total family incomes.

Stratification researchers have often argued the importance of such aspects of family finances as source of income (salary versus wages versus dividends), fringe benefits, stability of income, and gross versus net income. Yet these considerations seldom find their way into the final analysis of data, because income must often be analyzed in gross categories, and the number of men falling into certain cells (e.g., receiving dividends or showing unstable income) may be quite small. To cross-classify all the different dimensions of family finances would be to reduce most samples to essentially meaningless comparisons. Unless one is concerned primarily with the study of income, the solution would seem to be to reduce such complexities to a single dimension, for example, a set of dollar equivalents. Over the years, how many dollars of income are added, in effect, by a major medical insurance policy underwritten by an employer? More importantly and less thoroughly explored, what salaried dollar income is the equivalent of a $2,000 annual dividend?

Detailed answers to such questions depend on initial decisions as to what theoretical dimension is being measured—prestige versus simple consumption power, for example—as well as on considerable future research to establish exact weights. One problem especially requires more work—the equating of the dollar scale and, let us say, a prestige scale. Even if we consider two persons whose incomes come from the same source or are equally stable, it may not be accurate to equate prestige with dollars in a simple fashion. For example, Schmitt's research (61) suggests that an increase of $1,000 brings a considerable jump in prestige to a man making $6,000 per year, but has little influence on the prestige of a millionaire. This would suggest that income-as-prestige be measured, not by income per se, but by a transformed income, perhaps by the logarithm of received income. Once again, future research must establish the exact form of the transformation. However, it might be very helpful in any research project to explore the use of cut-and-dry abstractions and transformations of the sort suggested above.

An education rank system presents similar problems. Individuals can be ranked with respect to years in school, type of degree, subject of specialty, reputation of school, and grade-point average. Just as graduate school admissions officers adjust a B average from Harvard before comparing it to an A average from East Texas State Teachers College, all these types of information can profitably be expressed as school-year equivalents in order to use education as a single rank system.

**Occupation.**   Several writers on social stratification have concluded on quite different bases that occupation is the rank system which is the single best representative of social status generally, or even of social class membership and participation. The methodological problem here is to find ways to place occupational positions upon ordinal or cardinal scales which reflect underlying theoretical concepts such as prestige or power. These scales, once again, are abstractions from the ranking of occupations along multiform subdimensions: earning power, prerequisites in training or skill, functional importance, authority, working conditions, and so on. The problem is to identify the subdimensions along which occupations differ and to project those differences onto a single theoretical rank system. Then we can describe individuals through their occupations.

Historically, sociologists have been unwilling to settle on such a rank system. Rather, they have tried to (1) retain detailed information concerning each unique occupation, and (2) collapse this detail in a standardized way into a simple seven-, four-, or two-category scale which could be used for as many different purposes as possible. The prime example of such a procedure is the Edwards occupational classification (18) and the Census Bureau's current revision of it. The census three-column code of occupations preserves great detail in categorizing the tens of thousands of distinct occupations reported by Americans, but it is far too detailed for most analytic purposes and represents no particular dimension at all. However, since it is very convenient to code occupations with this three-column code (50), the ability to assign such detailed codes to the categories of a more theoretical measure is a desirable quality.

The Edwards classification places each of the three-column occupational codes into one of seven more or less socioeconomic groupings, which also separate occupations to some extent by function, skill, training, prestige, and relation to the means of production. A simpler set of categories of greater *general* utility would be hard to conceive, but in being so general it is highly inaccurate with respect to any given dimension.

Many of the best-known uses of occupation in stratification research employ revisions of the Edwards scale (e.g., 7 and 34). In an attempt to make the scale more meaningful, the revisions may move certain managers or proprietors up, for example, and others down, so that there is greater correlation of the scale with income or prestige. Yet such a procedure loses much of the easy comparability of the Edwards scale and introduces the question of what criteria, exactly, are employed in the revision.

The clearest attempt to provide a unidimensional scale of occupations was begun in a 1947 National Opinion Research Center (NORC) study which inquired into the general standing or prestige of 90 selected occupations (54,59). The ranking established by this national sample study has been confirmed with respect to various United States subpopulations and by a recent national replication (31). Despite certain technical inadequacies, the North-Hatt study (59) provides empirical justification for a unidimensional prestige ranking of occupations.

The usefulness of the North-Hatt study has recently been greatly extended by Duncan's attempts to construct a socioeconomic index for all occupations (14). He chose for study 45 occupations for which the North-Hatt titles corresponded to census categories and attempted to predict the prestige scores of these occupations from the average education and income of men working in them. These indicators accounted for 83 percent of the variation in the percentage of respondents rating the given occupations as good or excellent. Duncan then presented the linear equation for predicting from education and income to prestige score and the predicted scores for each title in the Census Bureau's detailed occupations list.

This is as good an example as can be found of the abstraction process discussed above. Taking 45 occupations scaled by education and income, Duncan converts their bivariate position into scores on a single scale, using the NORC prestige scores as his criterion variable.

Duncan's scores afford a very practical, if insufficiently explored, measure of occupational status. Not only are scores available for the entire range of occupations, as defined by the Census Bureau, but also the analysis itself is readily replicable. One may justify his measure as a reasonable approximation of the prestige scores occupations would have received if the North-Hatt study had asked about them and if respondents had had enough knowledge to rate them. That is, we may argue that education and income are adequate predictors of occupational prestige, since they reflect the training required and the rewards supplied by an occupation.

One way of exploring the theoretical meaning of the Duncan and North-Hatt scores is to ask what the respondents did when asked to give their opinions of the general standing of an occupation. Gusfield and Schwartz (26) report semantic-differential research to clarify whether the respondent ranked occupations according to his own personal evaluation of them or whether he reported his perceptions of how other people rank them or simply how many rewards various occupations receive. Their findings, on a student sample, lend support to the last interpretation. Rank of occupation seemed generally to be more highly correlated with rank on descriptive semantic-differential items than with rank on evaluative items. However, the particular ranking standards employed by different respondents may be quite beside the point. Reiss shows that in the original NORC study there was little consensus on what gives a job excellent standing, but the ranking of occupations was not affected. For example, he reports (59, p. 193) a correlation of +.99 between the prestige scores given occupations by those who evaluate an occupation by whether it pays well and by those who evaluate according to service to humanity. One can therefore conclude either that a general prestige continuum exists for occupations or that it does not, but all specific modes of evaluation produce highly similar rankings.

There are other dimensions of occupational rank—power, authority, functional importance, and so on—on which individual occupations might be scaled. The empirical research deriving measures of occupational rank from such approaches has yet to be carried out. But if occupation is to be treated as a rank attribute, rather than as a catchall classification, the particular dimension along which occupations (and therefore individuals) are ranked should be clearly specified.

**Racial-ethnic membership.** The way in which data on race and ethnicity are to be employed depends on a purely theoretical decision: What kinds of social phenomena are these? Most studies have been based on one of two different answers to this question: race and ethnicity are treated as rank systems, or racial-ethnic groups are treated as nonstatus groups with some of the same characteristics and consequences as social classes.

Considering the latter assumption first, racial-ethnic groups have always confused social class analysis because, like social classes, they consist of interacting groups (or at least loose networks of interaction and communication) and associated subcultures, and they often have opposed group interests. Nevertheless, these categories are regarded as conceptually independent of rank systems; that is, society is regarded as vertically differentiated into classes and horizontally differentiated into racial-ethnic groups, so that a class structure exists within each group, and vice versa (23,24,33). The resulting categories, e.g., class 1 Latvians and class 4 Mexicans, represent more or less homogeneous subpopulations, within which values of dependent variables are calculated for comparison with other subpopulations.

The alternative approach is that race and ethnicity act as rank systems, as values distributed in the population. Hence, a Polish name would contribute to a low-status evaluation just as a low-ranking occupation would. This may be historically due to past low status of such groups, and current low status may reinforce such evaluations. Whatever the reasons, however, this approach assumes that racial-ethnic position is an independent basis of evaluation in the society. To proceed confidently from this point of view, we must confirm the assumption that there is consensus concerning the ranking of racial-ethnic groups, just as the North-Hatt study showed that the evaluations of occupations were generally quite similar in all parts of the social structure.[9] Complete consensus would mean that members of groups ranked as low by other groups would agree that they had low rank. Usually, however, we should expect that members of a given group would accord their group somewhat higher status than it would be accorded by members of other groups. Indeed, we would expect this effect to be stronger for racial-ethnic rankings than for occupation, because the former trait is probably a more integral part of the person's self-concept and thus more subject to perceptual defense. However, if there is considerable agreement about the rank of each

[9] Current research on this question is being conducted by Peter Rossi and Robert Hodge at the University of Chicago.

racial-ethnic group between raters not belonging to that group, a racial-ethnic rank system can justifiably be said to exist.

The relative accuracy of the above two assumptions about the nature of racial-ethnic groups varies from society to society and time to time. If the researcher assumes that racial-ethnic status *does* represent an independent value founded on some consensus, how is the rank of an ethnic group to be ascertained? The most fully explored method is exemplified by the social-distance scale developed by Emory S. Bogardus (3,4). A scale of this kind reflects the degree of social intimacy to which a population will admit persons of various ethnic and racial categories. The problem facing the student of stratification who wishes to employ social-distance scales to rank racial-ethnic groups is that he must assume either that prestige rank and social intimacy are identical or that they are extremely closely related.

One school of thought makes social intimacy the central concept in stratification, but the present orientation takes social intimacy as a *consequence* of rank. There is evidence that individuals prefer to associate with a collection of people at an average rank slightly higher than their own, but without stepping entirely out of their own range of status (42,47). This throws doubt on the assumption underlying the use of the social-distance scale to rank racial-ethnic groups, that is, that as the rank of a group increases, so does desire for social contact with the group. Social intimacy, furthermore, is a consequence of other factors besides status—cultural similarity, for example, or common interest. At any rate, the relationship between status and intimacy involves an empirical question to be answered, not assumed in the definition of status. On the other hand, social-distance scales can profitably be used to measure predispositions toward interaction of persons from different socio-economic groups. A scale of such predispositions could be taken as a measure of actual or potential differential association, class or status consciousness, and reciprocal attitudes between such groups, as well as an indication of the relative importance of various rank dimensions in affecting interaction (67).

On the whole, it would seem more reasonable to determine the rank of racial-ethnic groups on the basis of the North-Hatt sort of study mentioned above. If consensus were found, the results would provide a much-needed foundation for the use of race-ethnicity as a rank system.

**Judges' ratings of personal prestige.** One common procedure in the study of social stratification, especially in the small-community context, is to ask a selected group of judges to rank all or a portion of the families in the community (33,40,41). The judgments are thought to reflect the way in which community residents rank other residents using an implicit system of weights for combining a variety of status-relevant individual attributes. The assumption that such a weighting and summarizing procedure actually occurs is not directly examined, although it probably deserves to be, for it may well be that small-town residents are much more likely to make summarizing global status placements, whereas members of large cities react singly to individual and readily observable rank systems such as income (or its symbolic display) and occupation (55).

This measurement process may seem entirely different from those considered above in that the individual is not placed on a narrow rank system (although one could regard the judges' placement as one's prestige rank). However, the procedure is formally similar to the North-Hatt sort of rating study: judges (instead of the total population or a sample thereof) are asked to rank individuals or families (instead of occupations) with regard to their general standing in the community, with the meaning of "standing" left ambiguous.

The ideal data for deriving a class structure by such a procedure would be the matrix in which each family rated each other family in the community. To what extent is this procedure applicable to large (or even medium-sized) communities? In any but the smallest communities, only a few people are known to the whole population, and only a few people, if any, know all the families in the population. Judgments of a few well-known people by all or judgments of all by a few judges yield insufficient data, since the sample of ratees or raters is likely to be extremely nonrepresentative with respect to any class distribution that exists. One partial solution to this problem would be to obtain ratings from a representative sample of the community population in reaction to detailed verbal portraits describing a variety of individuals. Such a study would provide information on how community residents rate others and the degree of consensus in such ratings. A prediction equation might then be developed to estimate the rank each individual would have obtained had the population ranked him (in the same way that the Duncan index estimates the rank that a poorly known occupation would receive if it were widely known). If it is found, for example, that respondents rank a set of descriptions of individuals such that the ranking can be largely accounted for by occupation, residential area, and type of automobile, weighted 0.6, 0.2, and 0.1, respectively, then ratings of personal prestige for each individual in the population could be estimated.

A last problem in this sort of analysis is that of getting judges to respond similarly enough to make analysis possible and responses comparable without forcing them, in effect, to adopt the investigator's a priori view of the class structure of the community. This is an even greater problem in obtaining respondents' self-ratings of status position.

**Self-placement in the stratification system.** The way in which an individual places himself in a status structure is often a basic concern in stratification research, either as an independent measure of status or as a means of contrasting objective with subjective status.  Self-placements are correlated with, and thus validated by, objective status measures.  They are further validated by their utility in the explanation of dependent variables.  It appears that adding subjective identifications to objective measures of class improves the explanation of such matters as political behavior and political-economic attitudes and orientations.  Finally, where differences between objective and subjective measures of class exist, the differences themselves can help in the explanation of status-relevant behavior (7,10).

The basic problem in this sort of measurement is interpreting the respondent's self-placement.  To understand the response fully, one must understand the respondent's view of the class structure.  If the respondent has no clear view or if there is no consensus from one respondent to another about the class structure, the responses may be hard to organize and analyze.

Forced-choice questions concerning perceptions of status describe the investigator's perception of the class structure and allow the respondent only to place himself within that structure, if he is cooperative enough.  Studies (25,28,38,48) in which United States respondents were asked to describe the class structure in their own terms indicate that somewhere between 20 and 50 percent of the population is unable to give a minimally coherent description of a class order.  And among those giving such a description in answer to open-end questions there is little consensus concerning number or names of classes.  Thus forced-choice self-placement questions certainly do not indicate how United States respondents place themselves in the class structure as they see it.

At the same time, most people probably have some general notion of societal superiority and inferiority and also some notion of where they stand on this general scale.  Closed-answer questions, demanding that the respondent place himself in one of several given classes, may help to tap these general notions and provide analyzable and comparable data.  For example, Kahl and Davis conclude, "The closed answers provided more information than the open because they forced the common man group to sub-divide themselves and the doubters to commit themselves.  Yet these forced answers appeared consistent with the earlier free answers if interpreted with occupational data at hand" (38, p. 325).

One promising technical approach to the measurement of status perceptions was employed by Davis in a study of housewives in Cambridge, Massachusetts (12).  Respondents were provided with 24 photographs of living rooms and asked to sort them into four piles according to "the social standing of the people who live in the homes."  This much of the method establishes rankings of living rooms as prestige symbols by an absolute (if rough) standard.  Davis went on to ask each respondent to divide the pictures into three piles: those higher than, those lower than, and those the same as the respondent's own standing.  Guttman scale analysis then yielded a scale of living rooms measured in relation to the respondent's own perceived rank.  Interviewers matched the respondents' living rooms to the pictures, providing a third standard employing interviewers, in effect, as expert judges. Living rooms, of course, constitute a narrow basis for social class judgments. But the method could easily be extended to use verbal portraits of persons and their relevant status characteristics.

## Composite Indices of Status

The problem of constructing an overall measure of social status out of component rank systems is formally similar to that of deriving rank systems in the first place. The same two problems present themselves: choosing the component indicators and the method by which they are to be combined. Selection of indicators is always a crucial issue, even in factor analysis, but we shall take the indicators, a set of rank systems, as given in the following discussion.

Three rational grounds for assignment of weights to indicators have already been discussed. Of these, the purely theoretical may be treated quickly: we know of no theory of stratification which unequivocally specifies weights for combining different rank systems. The other two approaches will be discussed in the light of specific examples of their use in stratification research.

**Use of a criterion.** Whenever the researcher has a measured variable which in some sense represents the overall concept he wishes to measure, he may develop weights using this variable as a criterion. Often the criterion is assumed to be an intrinsically valid measure of the concept, but one which is too difficult to obtain in the usual research situation. For example, a criterion measure of general status might be developed on a limited population by a detailed study of social interaction (66) or by asking respondents to judge the general standing of a number of verbal portraits of persons with different combinations of rank positions.

Several rank systems may then be combined in a prediction equation which minimizes error in predicting values of the criterion. Hollingshead and Redlich (34), for example, based a criterion status score on total judgments made by Hollingshead and Myers on each interview protocol. They then obtained a multiple correlation of .942 between residence, education and occupation (the indicators), and judged class (the criterion) with weights of 0.18 for residence, 0.15 for education, and 0.27 for occupation. As in most indices, these 'rank scales were combined in a simple additive manner. Other modes of combination might be more meaningful in some situations, however. For example, if low rank on one rank system always led to low general status in a given community, then that rank system would be best included in the prediction equation in a *multiplicative,* not additive, fashion (2).

Rather than representing an assumed valid measure of the desired concept, the criterion selected may represent one or, preferably, a battery of dependent variables assumed to be caused by social status (of course, if this assumption is false, the method is of no value). Relating each potential component of an index to each of a number of dependent variables helps to screen out invalid components, may aid in reconceptualization of the nature of the independent concept, and provides information for estimating the relative weights of components (11). Component indicators would be weighted heavily either because they were strongly related to certain dependent variables (predictive strength) or because they were related at least moderately to a wide range of different dependent variables (predictive generality).

This approach is at least partly exemplified by a study by Haer (27). He compared five measures of status according to how well each predicted 22 dependent variables. He concluded that Warner's Index of Status Characteristics (ISC) was the best of the five measures, attributing its superiority to the fact that it provides a continuous scale and combines several component rank systems. These findings would have been more interesting if Haer had expressed each component in the same measurement terms (e.g., all dichotomies or all continuous scales) and highlighted the comparison between single indicators, rather than emphasizing the superiority of an index over single indicators. Nor does he distinguish between predictive strength and predictive generality. Indeed, as far as generality is concerned, the single factor of education surprisingly outperformed the ISC by a slight margin.

The method should probably be extended beyond simply relating each possible indicator of status to each dependent variable. If the sample were large enough, the indicators could be related simultaneously to each dependent variable in order to ascertain how well each one related to the dependent variable independently of the others. Predictive strength and generality then could be gauged in these terms. Another possibility should be noted: such a simultaneous analysis might reveal that there is no simple additive relationship between the status indicators and the dependent variable. For example, the effect of education may not be the same within control categories of the other status indicators, but it may differ, let us say, for persons of high versus low income.

One interpretation of this is that the person's status inconsistency is related to the dependent variable. And since there is no simple relationship between the status indicators and the dependent variable, there may be no simple status structure in the community that can be conveniently indexed. The use of an overall status index in such a situation would mask such inconsistency effects and prevent the researcher from fully understanding the variety of status effects on the dependent variable in question. This suggests that combination indices of social status should normally not be related to dependent variables until after the dependent variables have been run against a simultaneous cross tabulation of the rank systems involved.

A second example of the use of presumed consequences of stratification as criteria occurred in the Hollingshead-Redlich study mentioned above (34, appendix 3). The problem was to show that Hollingshead's five classes did, in fact, divide the population into relatively discrete cultural groupings. The population was divided into 33 status groups, and several items representing patterns of use of the mass media for each group were correlated with those of each other group. As expected, correlations declined with the distance between two status groups in the class hierarchy. The intercorrelations were factor-analyzed, yielding three factors, which varied monotonically along the scale of status groups. Discontinuities in the distribution of scores of the status groups were used to establish class boundaries. In this case the method was employed to validate the existence of cultural discontinuities and the location of class boundaries previously fixed by Hollingshead, but it could equally well have been used to establish class boundaries in the first place.

**Use of relationships among components of an index.** On the assumption that indicators of a concept correlate with one another to the extent that they reflect that concept, indices also can be constructed based on the pattern of relationships among potential components of an index. Scaling, for example, is a technique for establishing unidimensionality in an index on the basis of empirical relationships between classifications. A more sophisticated method, calling for somewhat more rigorous assumptions, is factor analysis. In this application, factor analysis enables the investigator to search for underlying patterns, simple or complex, in an array of data felt to be relevant for theoretical reasons.

An example of this approach is provided by Kahl's and Davis's analysis (38) of the intercorrelations among 19 indicators of rank in a Cambridge sample. They concluded that two common factors accounted for most of the variation in these indicators. The first factor showed high loadings on such indicators as occupation, education, and respondent's self-rating, and the second combined such items as residential status and status of parents. The writers suggest that these factors reflect current and past status, respectively, since residential status tends to resemble parental status for a time and to lag behind current occupational status. Factor loadings from such analyses could be used as weights in index construction; the two indices could be used together or singly, depending on the interests of the investigator. For general use, of course, factor weights based on an analysis of a national sample and on continuous rather than dichotomized rank variables would be desirable.

**Relative advantages of the different approaches.** Of the specific indexing methods described here, the criterion variable method has the greatest theoretical and empirical justification, provided that three assumptions can be met. First, the predictors must account for most of the variation in the criterion:

moderately strong correlations are not good enough, for one must be able to reason that the derived index actually represents values of the criterion, plus or minus a small random error term. Second, the criterion must be justified, for nothing is gained if one achieves great precision with the use of excellent predictors of an irrelevant or specious criterion. Third, prediction equations developed using known values of a criterion variable within one population can be used on a different population only if the two populations are not fundamentally different. One oft-cited limitation of Warner's work on class measurement is that prediction equations based on evaluated participation in Jonesville should not be used for metropolitan samples (66, p. 128; 56, p. 209).

In the use of a dependent variable as a criterion, tautology must be avoided with great care. To construct an index of an independent variable by virtue of its close association with political preference, for example, and then to show that this index is related to political preference would be hardly worth the effort. Use of several dependent variables has the advantage of directing attention to the predictive power and generality of an index of a common factor underlying all the dependent variables. This common factor may indeed be the independent variable under study, but may just as well not be. Which interpretation is correct cannot be determined, save through the face validity of the resulting index.

Basing an index on relations among component indicators has the advantage of avoiding issues of tautology or result guiding, since index construction is technically independent of other variables to be analyzed. But are we justified in assuming that those indicators which are most closely related to one another therefore most adequately represent the underlying concept? In many areas of research, different indicators represent weakly related aspects of an underlying concept, and the weaker the association between the indicators, the more powerful the index is in representing variation along the basic conceptual dimension. For example, there are distinct aspects of status, if we are to believe Weber, which are generally, but by no means perfectly, related. Perhaps economic rank, political power, and social honor should all receive heavy weights in a general status index despite the fact that they are less closely interrelated than are the indicators of any one of them. In this situation, theoretical considerations might well override empirical criteria in the construction of an index.

## Measurement of Rank Systems as Group Properties

Accurate description of the status system per se is necessary if status systems are to be compared and if individual status is to be expressed in relation to the system in which it occurs or compared with the status of an individual in another system. We shall discuss measures of consistency and mobility in stratification systems below; here we confine ourselves to measures describing how social units are distributed along rank systems. Such measures generally describe three aspects of such distributions: central tendency, dispersion, and form. Measures of such group properties are necessary, first, to analyze their effects (so-called structural or compositional effects) and, second, as a base for expressing the relative position of individuals within the system.

*Measures of central tendency* are useful in comparing social systems in terms of the amount of a value commonly available or available per capita in a system. For example, one could compare two communities, finding that one had a higher mean or median income than the other (controlling for cost of living differences). This might well be relevant as a description of the context in which the individual responds to class stimuli. It may be, for example, that the political implications of status are more important in communities with low average incomes than in communities in the same society where even the relatively deprived are fairly well-off in absolute terms. Even where no such interaction effect exists, measures of central tendency might be useful simply to measure the individual's relative deprivation on various rank systems within the context of his community. For such an analysis, the positions of individuals could be expressed as deviations from measures of central tendency for occupation or education for their community. In some studies such relative measures might well have more predictive power for individual behavior than measures of absolute level of values.

Perhaps the hallmark of stratification analysis is the study of *dispersion,* or the amount of inequality in the distribution of the value under consideration. Communities or societies can be compared in terms of standard deviations, average deviations, and other such measures. Another very useful general technique for measuring dispersion is to compare the cumulative distribution of a value in a system against a theoretical norm. The amount and nature of the deviation from a theoretical standard of equality is often the most useful measure of inequality.

The grand theorists of stratification would lead us to believe that degree of inequality is predictable on the basis of certain characteristics of the communities or societies involved and that such inequality, in turn, affects societal characteristics such as political organization, citizen unrest, motivation, and so on. To test such propositions, dispersion must be measured. Also, for many purposes we may want to express an individual's deviation from a community or society mean in terms of standard deviation units, thereby allowing another aspect of the community context to enter into the measure of the individual's relative rank position. Making $1,000 less than the average income might mean a great deal in a community in which the difference between the highest and lowest incomes was $2,000, but very little in one where the difference was $100,000.

The *form* of a distribution, however, severely qualifies the extent to which measures of dispersion represent the extent of inequality. For example, two societies with the same amount of dispersion in income would still represent very different contexts for class processes if income were distributed normally in one and bimodally in the other. Descriptions of form, that is, are relevant in the measurement of such theoretical properties as polarization. For a stimulating summary and comparison of many measures of inequality taking both form and dispersion into account, the reader is referred to Alker and Russett (1).

On the whole, when one considers the actual distributions of income, education, and occupation in large American cities, he is struck not by their difference, but by their general similarity (16). The processes of rank stratification may be sufficiently general that distributions of some typical form are usually produced in most social circumstances. If this can be established, then all rank distributions can be expressed as deviations from a general model of rank distributions, thus facilitating intersystem comparisons. Svalastoga (63) has suggested that most rank variables in most situations take the form of a lognormal distribution; that is, the rank values are distributed as if their logs were distributed normally, thus generating a right-hand skew in the distribution. Whether this particular suggestion receives future empirical validation or not, measurement of rank distributions will continue to have important implications for the measurement of individual rank.

## 4.3 THE MEASUREMENT OF STATUS INCONSISTENCY AND VERTICAL MOBILITY

At both the individual and group levels, continued empirical research makes it increasingly evident that static and unidimensional analyses of stratification are not sufficient in changing urban-industrial societies. Modern status systems and the positions of individuals within them are above all flexible, but the extent of that flexibility varies from person to person and from society to society. To study such forms of flexibility as status inconsistency and vertical mobility is to add new, nonvertical dimensions to the analysis of social stratification and to create a new set of measurement and conceptual problems as well.

### Status Inconsistency

Since rank systems are imperfectly correlated, individuals may hold inconsistent, contradictory positions: one may occupy high rank on one system and low rank on another. To measure the existence, extent, or pattern of status inconsistency, the researcher must face a series of problems: (1) selection of the population or system to be studied, (2) specification of the sense in which two rank systems may be inconsistent, (3) selection of rank systems to be analyzed, (4) measurement of inconsistency, and (5) extension of the measurement to the group level of analysis.

The basic problem in choosing a population for the study of status inconsistency is that some choices of status system can define status inconsistency out of existence. A population of great homogeneity with respect to a given rank system will usually not exhibit sufficient extremes of rank on any rank system to allow for any but negligible inconsistency between different ranks held by individuals. Also, in the study of such a status system, the effects of inconsistency are *necessarily* confounded with those of status per se. For example, Fredrickson (19) presents findings refuting the hypothesis that status inconsistency is related to low rates of social participation, but since the sample consists only of families with annual incomes less than $4,000, the value of the data is limited. Most inconsistency in the sample is slight, and the few sharp inconsistents must by definition be persons with high education or occupation. In addition, the choice of such a sample probably severely restricts the amount of variation in the dependent variable.

Even with status pyramids that have not been truncated by the investigator, sampling is a problem. Sharp status inconsistency, like extreme social mobility, is relatively rare, so random samples must be large if they are to capture enough cases for analysis. Stratifying the sample to increase the number of respondents of high rank in one or more dimensions can help, but is likely to call for a doorstep screening process and hence to be very expensive.

In making decisions about which rank systems are to be analyzed and how inconsistency is to be measured the researcher must be guided by his notions about the conceptual meaning of inconsistency. Critics of status-inconsistency research (13,52) have asked in what sense different rank systems can be said to be incompatible or contradictory. Possible answers are (1) that certain combinations of ranks present the viewer with an ambiguous status stimulus, and hence the viewer cannot tell where to place the inconsistent person; or (2) that each of the ranks generates expectations which contradict those generated by other ranks. Either or both of these phenomena may occur because (3) a particular combination of ranks deviates from a social consensus regarding what ranks should or do go along with what other ranks.

Such considerations suggest that inconsistency research should employ rank systems which are important status stimuli and which generate strong behavioral expectations; normally these would be dimensions upon which there was substantial consensus on which ranks are higher than which other ranks and how much higher. A second suggestion is that status-inconsistency effects are to be found especially when a strong consensus exists that certain combinations of ranks are right and/or normal. Brandon (5) has shown that the strength of status-inconsistency effects diminishes when the rank systems upon which the sample is jointly distributed do not each strongly imply a corresponding rank on the other.   Research on the content of such implications is needed to verify the (usually implicit) assumptions now used in selecting rank systems for analysis.

Status inconsistency has been measured in several ways in the past, although here again the assumptions underlying the choice of a measure or justifying the choice in terms of the above conceptual definitions have often remained implicit.

One approach has been to regard rank systems as purely ordinal variables and to define inconsistency as the difference between one's ordinal positions along rank system 1 and rank system 2.   For example, in his research on inconsistency and political liberalism, Lenski (45) assigned each member of his sample a percentile score along each of four rank systems.  The standard deviation of the four percentile scores for each individual represented the consistency, or crystallization, of the person's status.   Unfortunately, this approach merges different patterns of inconsistency: the high-income, low-education individual might receive the same consistency score as a low-income, high-education person.   Lenski met this problem by simply sorting out persons whose percentile scores on one rank system were a given number of points higher than on another rank system.   Thus, the high-income, low-education inconsistent group was composed of those persons with income percentiles 30 or more points higher than their education percentiles.

A similar measure of status consistency has been devised by Charles Nam (53) for the Bureau of the Census.   He assigns each person three percentile scores representing relative standing on the rank systems of income, education, and occupation.   If the percentile scores on two ranks are more than 20 points apart, the person is considered inconsistent.   These data, available for the 45,000 household heads in the Bureau's 1/1000 sample, separate consistents from inconsistents and also separate the different types of inconsistency.

As another method for the analysis of contrasting patterns of inconsistency, Lenski (46) later suggested dividing each rank system into three (high, medium, low) sections.   The choice of cutting points to divide each rank system can be based on order (i.e., division into tertiles) or on considerations of which sorts of positions should go together.   Persons falling into the same category along each rank system (e.g., high, high, high) are considered consistent, those with ranks differing by one step (e.g., high, high, medium) are moderately inconsistent, and those bridging extremes (e.g., medium, low, high) are taken as sharply inconsistent.   Although this measure is less precise than Lenski's first measure, it permits calculation of rates of some dependent variable for each combination of ranks and allows for at least a rough control of status per se [see also Jackson and Burke (36)].

The above methods can be termed *ordinal* approaches.   They seem to involve the assumption that *similar relative ranks* generate compatible expectations or are expected to go together.   Alternately, one may assume that *fre-*

*quent or usual combinations of ranks* involve little conflict and are therefore consistent (whether they represent similar percentile scores or not), while unusual combinations are inconsistent. Two justifications for this assumption are possible: if certain status combinations are very common, a consensus may tend to develop defining them as normal; on the other hand, combinations not so defined may be so painful to incumbents that they move out of them whenever possible. Gibbs and Martin (21), for example, deal with consistency of expectations regarding combinations of many sorts of social positions, such as age and marital status, as well as ranks. They assume that a given combination of positions is nonintegrated to the extent that it is relatively infrequently occupied. This sort of assumption forms the basis for what we might term a *regression* approach to the measurement of inconsistency.

For example, one might compute a regression line showing the relationship between two rank systems in a sample or population and use the sign and size of deviations from the regression line to measure the pattern and degree of status inconsistency. In this way the empirical relationship between two rank systems provides the measure of consistency. This general type of analysis has been carried out by Hodge (30), using occupational groups as units and education and income as the rank systems, but in principle the technique could just as well be extended to more than two rank variables and to individuals as units.

One at least partially theoretical decision confronting the analyst who would employ this method is selection of an appropriate regression line. Two rank systems yield two regression lines, and higher-order correlations potentially involve many more. If the rank systems involved can be causally ordered, such as education and occupation, the issue may be resolved by using the regression line showing values of the dependent rank system predicted by values of the independent rank system. In Hodge's research, for example, the central question dealt with the extent to which the average income of an occupational group did or did not exceed that justified by its average level of education, so that the regression of education on income was of no interest.

In cases where such an ordering is not clear or where such a rationale does not seem to be appropriate, the regression line which minimizes the *orthogonal* deviations would seem to be a reasonable choice. One possible interpretation of such a line is that it represents a general status dimension and that perpendicular deviations from it represent status inconsistency. In other words, two new axes, general status and status inconsistency, are substituted for the original axes representing rank systems.

The ordinal and regression approaches outlined above might well yield very different measures of a given person's degree of status inconsistency. In an extreme case, if one rank system were negatively related to another, a person high on one rank system and low on another would be scored as consistent by a regression measure and as highly inconsistent by an ordinal measure. This case seems improbable, yet the measurement of the status inconsistency of Jews involves elements of just such a dilemma.

A third general approach to the measurement of status inconsistency would be direct investigation of the assumptions of ambiguity, conflicting expectations, or violation of norms concerning appropriate combinations of rank which underlie the two general methods discussed above. For example, a measure of consistency might be developed from respondents' reports of feelings of uncertainty, ambivalence, conflict, or confusion in situations where status was relevant. Similarly, measures of inconsistency might be constructed on the basis of research on status expectations themselves. Is there consensus in the population that certain positions go together? At the very least, would most Americans feel puzzled if presented with certain status combinations? Regardless of the actual relationship between, e.g., income and education, is there an association between these variables which is regarded as morally right or at least acceptable? Perceptions of associations between rank variables, as well as normative prescriptions for status combinations, could be used to construct a set of inconsistency measures or at least to validate the preceding approaches.

Finally, all these methods can be adapted to measure the extent of status inconsistency within a social unit such as a community or a society, and this is essential if structural effects of inconsistency are to be studied. For example, the rank-order or product-moment correlation coefficient between occupation and education could be regarded as a measure of the extent of that type of inconsistency in the status system. And as a further extension, Landecker (43) has analyzed the pattern and structure of inconsistency in Detroit as a method of locating boundaries between classes.

Although little research on group rates of inconsistency has been done, the problem is analogous in many ways to the analysis of rates of social mobility in a society or community. This latter problem has received considerable research attention, which we shall summarize in the next section.

## Vertical Mobility

The analysis of vertical mobility involves comparisons between ranks along the same rank system at different points in time, while inconsistency analysis involves comparisons between current ranks on different rank systems. Except for the peculiarities of time, then, and the advantage in mobility research of using the same rank system, the issues in measuring the two variables are the same, and many of the techniques analogous. For brevity's sake, we shall discuss only occupational mobility, since it is the most thoroughly studied type, and since the methodology of mobility along other rank systems will involve the same problems.

The most obvious definition of mobility (such a clear-cut definition was not possible in the study of inconsistency) involves simply stating the absolute difference between the ranks occupied by the person at different times. Hence occupational mobility may be studied even if the occupational scale is regarded as purely nominal, without any ordering, by simply stating whether or not an individual currently has the same occupation as his first occupation or his father's occupation. If occupation is measured on an interval scale, by the use of Duncan's index, for example, one can measure mobility by subtracting a father's occupational score from his son's: the sign indicates direction (positive for upward and negative for downward mobility), and the absolute value indicates the amount of mobility.

In addition to these absolute-difference methods, the ordinal and regression approaches used in measuring inconsistency can also be employed. For example, if deprivation relative to society generally or some specific group, such as siblings, looms large among the mechanisms through which mobility is thought to influence dependent variables, then mobility must be measured in relation to some standard other than simply initial or father's occupation. The simplest relative measure would be a difference between percentile scores: father's occupation would be expressed as a percentile in the ranked distribution of fathers' occupations, son's occupation would be represented by a percentile in the ranked distribution of sons' occupations, and the former would be subtracted from the latter. The score would thus represent changes in relative occupational standing in the society or community. If the sons' distribution of occupations had a higher central tendency than the fathers' distribution, a son following in his father's occupational footsteps would be measured as downwardly mobile by this approach. One problem with this method, however, is that the occupational distribution within which fathers actually lived is not the same as the occupational distribution of fathers of respondents in a sample.

Tumin and Feldman (65), in their Generational Occupation Mobility Score (GOMS), carry the measurement of relative mobility a step further. Each person's mobility is expressed as a deviation of his current occupation from the mean occupation of men from the same occupational origin, divided by the standard deviation of that distribution. Empirically, this method measures sons in the top occupations whose fathers held top occupations as upwardly mobile, since the average destination of sons' of top-stratum fathers is usually lower than the top stratum. Similarly, stable lows are measured as downwardly mobile.

This method of measuring mobility is essentially an application of regression analysis. The mean occupational scores of sons from each origin describe a line of regression, and deviations from that line are taken as the measure of mobility. Just as in the regression measures of inconsistency mentioned above, the base for the measurement of stability is the empirical relationship between father's (or initial) occupation and son's occupation. Current occupations differing from those predicted by past rank constitute mobility.

Our next problem is the extension of these methods to the measurement of *group rates of mobility* in order that we may provide a context for the measurement of individual mobility as well as make intersociety or intercommunity comparisons. Measuring rates of mobility in populations involves all the problems of measuring individual mobility, but also the issue of just what aspects of change are relevant. Every measured rate of mobility has some meaning; the problem is, What specific question does this measured rate answer? And the meaning depends upon the detailed method used in obtaining the rate. To say that 30 percent of the sons in a given society are no longer in their fathers' occupations would be impressive if the occupational distribution were dichotomized, but not if it were broken into ten distinct categories.

Consider, first, measurement of the total amount of movement, ignoring for the moment the causes of occupational shifts. Assuming comparability of occupational categories, we might compare the rates of mobility in two societies by comparing the proportions of sons who did not inherit their fathers' occupations (or the proportions of persons now employed in a different category from their first occupation). Proportions in single cells, e.g., craftsmen sons of unskilled fathers, could be compared to locate specific types of movement. To become more analytic, we might then ask in which society boys have better opportunities, which suggests outflow percentages: proportions from a given father's occupation who hold specified present occupations. Inflow percentages—proportions in a present occupation who come from specified origins—describe the recruitment and present composition of occupational strata. A total-movement measure, reflecting the distance as well as the amount of mobility, may be devised if the strata are ranked or assigned places along an interval scale. Each movement would be weighted by the number of ranks crossed or by the difference between scale scores of origin and destination occupations.

But if we are interested in the relative openness of societies or in the conditions relating ability to achievement, we are obliged to consider the causes of mobility rates and to hold constant some characteristics of the societies within whose contexts mobility occurs. Are high rates of mobility associated with urbanization, for example, because viable industrial economies must allocate crucial roles on the basis of achievement criteria or because the relative demand for clerical and managerial work increases with the size and complexity of the labor force?

In particular, it may be desirable when comparing one society with another to consider changes in occupational structure and differential birthrates, since these factors produce differences between the occupational distributions of fathers and sons, and such differences produce mobility beyond that generated by openness or the societal circulation rate (37, pp. 252–262). In this way two societies similar in total amount of movement might differ greatly in amount of circulation. Since regulation of societal rates of change for experimental purposes is ethically questionable, such factors must be controlled statistically. (The following methods could also be used in comparing communities or societies in terms of status inconsistency, screening out inconsistency forced by differences between, for example, education and occupation distributions.)

To achieve the desired comparability, we must express the amount of mobility in each population in relation to some standard. That standard is a model which shows how mobility patterns would look in each population if perfect equality of opportunity prevailed, if a minimum of opportunity prevailed, or if some other condition were present. The perfect-equality model, for example, shows how the pattern of mobility would appear in a given community if all persons had equal opportunities to move, *given the differences in fathers' and sons' occupational distributions.* Two populations can then be compared by showing that the mobility pattern in the first more closely approximates perfect equality than does that in the second. The fact that differences between fathers' and sons' occupational distributions force more actual mobility in one population than in the other does not disturb the comparison. Intersocietal comparisons, then, are comparisons of actual deviations from some model, and the question answered by the comparison is defined by the precise nature of the model.

One possible baseline for comparison is a maximum-stability model, which generates mobility figures on the assumption that only as much movement occurs as is forced by differences between original and current occupational distributions. For example, in Table 4.1*a*, a hypothetical distribution is shown of fathers' occupations cross-classified by sons' occupations, forming a square matrix with occupational inheritance located along the diagonal. If it were assumed that as much inheritance took place as possible, how many persons would have moved? Since the number of white- and blue-collar positions is greater in the current (sons') occupational distribution than in the fathers' distribution, all sons from these positions could have inherited. However, 40 of the 100 sons of farmers *must* move since the number of farm positions was sharply reduced. Hence, as Table 4.1*b* shows, 260, or 87 percent, of the persons would have inherited under maximum-stability conditions, and 13 percent would have been forced to move.

The destinations of the 40 movers in this specific example are determined, but in general this model does *not* fix the placement of those who do not inherit, but only yields the maximum proportion who may inherit, given the marginal distributions, as well as the proportion forced to be mobile. These figures can then be compared with the number who actually did move, deviations from the model representing the extent to which there was more mobility

TABLE 4.1 Actual and Model Mobility Distributions

| | *Respondent's occupation* | | | |
|---|---|---|---|---|
| | *White-collar* | *Blue-collar* | *Farmer* | |
| *a. "Observed" mobility* | | | | |
| *Father's occupation* | | | | |
| *White-collar* | 80 | 20 | 0 | 100 |
| *Blue-collar* | 30 | 70 | 0 | 100 |
| *Farmer* | 10 | 30 | 60 | 100 |
| | 120 | 120 | 60 | 300 |
| *b. Maximum stability model* | | | | |
| *Father's occupation* | | | | |
| *White-collar* | 100 | — | — | 100 |
| *Blue-collar* | — | 100 | — | 100 |
| *Farmer* | 20 | 20 | 60 | 100 |
| | 120 | 120 | 60 | 300 |
| *c. Perfect equality model* | | | | |
| *Father's occupation* | | | | |
| *White-collar* | 40 | 40 | 20 | 100 |
| *Blue-collar* | 40 | 40 | 20 | 100 |
| *Farmer* | 40 | 40 | 20 | 100 |
| | 120 | 120 | 60 | 300 |

in a society than could be accounted for simply by the differences between the fathers' and sons' occupational distributions. In our example, 90 persons actually moved, and 50 of the moves can be regarded as circulation rather than forced movement. Hence 17 percent of the population experienced circulation. This is a measure of openness which can be compared with similar measures for other populations, and such comparisons will not be contaminated by differences in the amount of forced mobility in the two populations.

A second type of model is generated from an assumption of perfect equality of opportunity. It assumes, that is, a random association between occupation of father and occupation of son. Numbers of sons from each origin who are expected in each present occupation are calculated, using the proportions of sons from all origins who have attained each occupational status (thus giving each son an equal chance, regardless of his origin). Table 4.1c shows such expected frequencies for our hypothetical data. [For details of this method, see Carlsson (6, chap. 5); Glass (20, pp. 218–259); and Rogoff (60, chap. 2).] The expected frequencies can then be compared with actual frequencies in whatever way best answers the questions asked by the researcher. The ratio of actual to expected frequencies for each cell or group of cells can be calculated, or a coefficient of association can be computed which summarizes the size of the deviations. In any case, comparison with the model expresses the extent to which the actual movement falls short of perfect openness, given the occupational distributions observed for fathers and sons.

By comparing actual data for a society with both of the above models, one may locate that society between the extremes of perfect equality and total stability (35). This comparison is restricted to the amount of mobility versus stability—the diagonal versus nondiagonal cells of a mobility table— since the stability model only generates expected frequencies for the diagonal.

A method for combining this double comparison into a single ratio has been developed by Durbin (17) and elaborated by Yasuda (68). First, the number of actual movers from each origin less the number forced to move by structural change (i.e., the number moving that can be attributed to circula-tion) is calculated. This is called the amount of pure mobility. For our men of white-collar origin, for example, we would calculate 20 actual moves less zero forced moves equals 20 pure moves. Similarly, there are 30 pure moves in the blue-collar row. In the farm row, all 40 moves are forced; hence there is no pure mobility. Next, the mobility table is computed as it would look under conditions of perfect equality of opportunity (as in Table 4.1c), and the amount of pure mobility for each origin is computed for this hypothetical table. This produces figures of 60, 60, and 40 pure moves for the three rows. Then the actual amount of pure mobility can be compared with the expected amount under conditions of perfect equality, producing a comparison in which forced mobility and perfect equality are both explicitly taken into account. For instance, our hypothetical data show that the ratio of total observed to total expected pure mobility is 50/160.

If population mobility rates are measured using either the ordinal or the regression approach, the above problems are to some extent avoided by definition. Both of these approaches define movement in relative terms, either in comparison with the labor force generally or with other men from the same origin. In either case, differences in central tendency between the occupational distributions of fathers and sons do not affect the measurement. Thus, if the correlation coefficient relating fathers' to sons' occupation is .20 in one society and .80 in the other, this difference in mobility rate cannot be ascribed to the fact that in the first society, but not in the second, there was an increase in the mean occupational score over the span of a generation.

In addition to the methods cited above, two somewhat more analytic approaches to mobility tables may be mentioned:

The first approach attempts to predict from current mobility patterns to future states of the occupational system. *Assuming that given patterns of mobility are constant over time,* Prais (57,58) has predicted occupational distributions of successive future generations by multiplying each successive occupational distribution times an assumed constant mobility matrix which gives the probabilities that a son from each orgin will enter each occupational destination.   Since mobility rates form a regular stochastic matrix, the successive occupational distributions tend toward an equilibrium state.   Using this result, Matras (49) shows that the equilibrium occupational distributions generated by the mobility matrices of various notions are somewhat different, despite considerable similarities in the original mobility tables.

This approach takes the mobility probabilities as given and the occupational distributions as derivative.   In the long run, however, most of the causal flow is surely in the other direction.   This suggests that it would be more fruitful to work out models to predict changes in the mobility rates that would occur in response to changes in occupational demands of the society. The most significant application of the Prais-Matras approach would probably be to show the ultimate implications of a set of mobility probabilities.   One might argue, for example, that these specific mobility rates will have to change within $x$ generations, because if they don't, the occupational structure will begin to look like this.

The second analytic approach is developed by Goodman (22).   He shows that although occupational inheritance—represented by the diagonal cells of a mobility table—is not a random process, and hence may vary from society to society with social conditions, the cells off the diagonal fit a random model reasonably well.   Replacing the diagonal cells in English and Danish mobility tables with zeros and predicting the remaining nondiagonal cells on the basis of marginal frequencies, he concluded that apart from occupational inheritance, father's occupation had essentially no effect on son's occupation.   This finding, taken together with Yasuda's caution (68) that the measures discussed earlier inadequately represent nondiagonal cells for comparative purposes, suggests that international or time comparisons of mobility rates are on safest ground when restricted to the total amount of movement versus stability or to specific forms of occupational inheritance.   Beyond this specific suggestion, however, Goodman's general approach has promise in terms of leading to a model of the mobility process which will predict observed mobility rates closely.   Such a model essentially constitutes an easily testable theory concerning the antecedents of patterns and rates of mobility.   The degree of fit between model predictions and observed mobility, as well as the patterns of deviations, can be of great aid in understanding the nature of the mobility process.

## 4.4   SUMMARY

This chapter has attempted to confront a problem implicitly defined as unmanageable from the very first paragraph, namely, the problem of validity in the measurement of social status.   It would be impossible to determine in isolation whether a given measurement of a given concept is valid according to our conception of validity.

If a set of models of specific instances of social behavior in widely varying contexts may unambiguously be deduced from a single systematic theory, the problem of validity admits of solution. For if the models do not fit parallel sets of observations, then we may reject either the theory (in whole or in part) or the validity of measurement of one or more variables. If, on the other hand, the models do fit the observations, then both the theory and the validity of the measured variables have withstood a set of tests; we have some reason *not* to reject either.

Yet the body of this chapter consists of many alternative approaches to the measurement of different status variables on the specific grounds that each approach bears a distinct theoretical meaning and that the time for theoretical closure in the study of social stratification is not at hand. In the absence of closure, we have argued for a set of decision rules to be used to justify particular measurements of particular variables. It is our contention that if researchers are guided by these forms of justification at the present stage of investigation into social stratification, then validity in measurement will be more likely when theoretical closure becomes appropriate. We have discussed three such rules: theoretical justification; justification on the ground that a set of presumed measures of the same thing are empirically associated with one another; and justification through the use of one or more criterion variables.

Despite our resistance to premature theoretical closure, we have suggested in our general orientation to the study of social stratification that the measurement of status involves three essentials: (1) selection of a particular set of abstract rank systems, (2) description of the stability of given ranks through time and of the relationships among the rank systems at a point in time, and (3) description of the status system(s) within which the selected rank systems operate. Depending upon the theoretical posture of the investigator, a fourth might be involved, namely, determination of the procedure for combining ranks into a single measure of general status.

A host of other considerations, such as perceived status, self-placement, institutional arrangements based on rank, class consciousness, class interest, and so on, *may* be important, depending upon the circumstances and purposes of the investigation. But without the essentials listed above, a measure of social status would be incomplete, regardless of the substantive content or theoretical stance of the investigator, since each point mentioned necessarily and significantly affects the meaning of status in the life of the individual.

## REFERENCES

1 Alker, Hayward, Jr., and Bruce M. Russett: "On Measuring Inequality," *Behavioral Science,* 9 (July, 1964), 207–218.

2 Blalock, Hubert M., Jr.: "Theory Building and the Statistical Concept of Interaction," *American Sociological Review,* 30 (June, 1965), 374–380.

3 Bogardus, Emory S.: "A Social Distance Scale," *Sociology and Social Research,* 17 (January, 1933), 265–271.

4 Bogardus, Emory S.: "Racial Distance Changes in the U.S. during the Past Thirty Years," *Sociology and Social Research,* 43 (November–December, 1958), 127–135.

5 Brandon, Arlene C.: "Status Congruence and Expectation," *Sociometry,* 28 (September, 1965), 272–288.

6 Carlsson, Gosta: *Social Mobility and Class Structure* (Lund, Sweden: CWK Gleerup, 1958).

7 Centers, Richard: *The Psychology of Social Classes* (Princeton, N.J.: Princeton, 1949).

8 Coleman, James S.: *Introduction to Mathematical Sociology* (New York: Free Press, 1964).

9 Curtis, Richard F.: "Conceptual Problems in Social Mobility Research," *Sociology and Social Research,* 45 (July, 1961), 387–395.

10 Curtis, Richard F.: "Differential Association and the Stratification of the Urban Community," *Social Forces,* 42 (October, 1963), 68–78.

11 Curtis, Richard F., and Elton F. Jackson: "Multiple Indicators in Survey Research," *American Journal of Sociology,* 68 (September, 1962), 195–204.

12 Davis, James A.: "Status Symbols and the Measurement of Status Perception," *Sociometry,* 19 (September, 1956), 154–165.

13 Demerath, Jay: "Status Discrepancy and Vertical Status: Criticisms and Suggested Remedies." Paper read at annual meeting of the American Sociological Association, Washington, D.C., 1962.

14 Duncan, Otis Dudley: "A Socio-economic Index for All Occupations," in Albert J. Reiss et al., *Occupations and Social Status* (New York: Free Press, 1961), chap. VI.

15 Duncan, Otis Dudley: "Methodological Issues in the Analysis of Social Mobility," in Neil J. Smelser and Seymour Martin Lipset (Eds.), *Social Structure and Mobility in Economic Development* (Chicago: Aldine, 1966), chap. 2.

16 Duncan, Otis Dudley, and Albert J. Reiss, Jr.: *Social Characteristics of Rural and Urban Communities, 1950* (New York: Wiley, 1956).

17 Durbin, J.: "Appendix Note on a Statistical Question Raised in the Preceding Paper," *Population Studies,* 9 (July, 1955), 101.

18 Edwards, Alba M.: *A Social-economic Grouping of the Gainful Workers of the United States, 1930* (Washington, D.C.: U.S. Government Printing Office, 1938).

19 Fredrickson, Roderic M.: "The Utility of the Status Equilibrium Index as a Methodological Tool in Predicting Social Participation." Unpublished master's thesis, University of California, Berkeley, 1959.

20 Glass, D. V. (Ed.): *Social Mobility in Britain* (New York: Free Press, 1954).

21 Gibbs, Jack P., and Walter T. Martin: *Status Integration and Suicide: A Sociological Study* (Eugene, Ore.: University of Oregon Press, 1964).

22 Goodman, Leo A.: "On the Statistical Analysis of Mobility Tables," *American Journal of Sociology,* **70** (March, 1965), 564–585.

23 Gordon, Milton M.: *Social Class in American Sociology* (Durham, N.C.: Duke, 1958).

24 Gordon, Milton M.: *Assimilation in American Life* (Fair Lawn, N.J.: Oxford, 1964).

25 Gross, Neal: "Social Class Identification in the Urban Community," *American Sociological Review,* **18** (August, 1953), 398–404.

26 Gusfield, Joseph R., and Michael Schwartz: "The Meanings of Occupational Prestige: Reconsideration of the NORC Scale," *American Sociological Review,* **28** (April, 1963), 265–271.

27 Haer, John L.: "Predictive Utility of Five Indices of Social Stratification," *American Sociological Review,* **22** (October, 1957), 541–546.

28 Haer, John L.: "An Empirical Study of Social Class Awareness," *Social Forces,* **36** (December, 1957), 117–121.

29 Harary, Frank: "Status and Contrastatus," *Sociometry,* **22** (March, 1959), 23–43.

30 Hodge, Robert W.: "The Status Consistency of Occupational Groups," *American Sociological Review,* **27** (June, 1962), 336–343.

31 Hodge, Robert W., Paul M. Siegel, and Peter H. Rossi: "Occupational Prestige in the United States, 1925–63," *American Journal of Sociology,* **70** (November, 1964), 286–302.

32 Hodges, Harold M., Jr.: *Social Stratification: Class in America* (Cambridge, Mass.: Schenkman, 1964).

33 Hollingshead, August B.: *Elmtown's Youth* (New York: Wiley, 1949).

34 Hollingshead, August B., and Frederick C. Redlich: *Social Class and Mental Illness: A Community Study* (New York: Wiley, 1958). (Appendix 3 written with Theodore R. Anderson.)

35 Jackson, Elton F., and Harry J. Crockett, Jr.: "Occupational Mobility in the United States: A Point Estimate and Trend Comparison," *American Sociological Review,* **29** (February, 1964), 5–15.

36 Jackson, Elton F., and Peter J. Burke: "Status and Symptoms of Stress: Additive and Interaction Effects," *American Sociological Review,* **30** (August, 1965), 556–564.

37 Kahl, Joseph A.: *The American Class Structure* (New York: Holt, 1953).

38 Kahl, Joseph A., and James A. Davis: "A Comparison of Indexes of Socio-economic Status," *American Sociological Review,* **20** (June, 1955), 317–325.

39 Katz, L.: "A New Status Index Derived from Sociometric Analysis," *Psychometrika,* **18** (March, 1953), 39–43.

40 Kaufman, H.: *Prestige Classes in a New York Rural Community* (Ithaca, N.Y.: Cornell University Agricultural Experiment Station, Memoir no. 260, 1944).

41 Kaufman, H.: "Members of a Rural Community as Judges of Prestige Rank," *Sociometry,* 9 (February, 1946), 71–86.

42 King, Morton B., Jr.: "Socioeconomic Status and Sociometric Choice," *Social Forces,* 39 (March, 1961), 199–206.

43 Landecker, Werner S.: "Class Boundaries," *American Sociological Review,* 25 (December, 1960), 868–877.

44 Lasswell, Thomas E.: *Class and Stratum* (Boston: Houghton Mifflin, 1965).

45 Lenski, Gerhard E.: "Status Crystallization: A Non-vertical Dimension of Status," *American Sociological Review,* 19 (August, 1954), 405–413.

46 Lenski, Gerhard E.: "Comment," *Public Opinion Quarterly,* 28 (Summer, 1964), 326–330.

47 Lundberg, George A., and Mary Steele: "Social Attraction Patterns in a Village," *Sociometry,* 1 (April, 1938), 375–419.

48 Manis, Jerome G., and Bernard N. Meltzer: "Attitudes of Textile Workers to Class Structure," *American Journal of Sociology,* 60 (July, 1954), 30–35.

49 Matras, Judah: "Comparison of Inter-generational Mobility Patterns: An Application of the Formal Theory of Social Mobility," *Population Studies,* 14 (November, 1960), 163–169.

50 McTavish, Donald G.: "A Method for More Reliably Coding Detailed Occupations into Duncan's Socio-economic Categories," *American Sociological Review,* 29 (June, 1964), 402–406.

51 Miller, Delbert. *Handbook of Research Design and Social Measurement* (New York: McKay, 1964).

52 Mitchell, Robert Edward: "Methodological Notes on a Theory of Status Crystallization," *Public Opinion Quarterly,* 28 (Summer, 1964), 315–325.

53 Nam, Charles B.: *Methodology and Scores of Socioeconomic Status.* Working Paper no. 15 (Washington, D.C.: U.S. Bureau of the Census, 1963).

54 National Opinion Research Center, "Jobs and Occupations: A Popular Evaluation," *Public Opinion News,* 9 (September, 1947), 3–13.

55 Parker, Seymour: "Status Consistency and Stress." Letter to the Editor, *American Sociological Review,* 28 (February, 1963), 131–132.

56 Pfautz, Harold W., and Otis Dudley Duncan: "A Critical Evaluation of Warner's Work in Community Stratification," *American Sociological Review,* 15 (April, 1950), 205–215.

57 Prais, S. J.: "The Formal Theory of Social Mobility," *Population Studies,* 9 (July, 1955), 72–81.

58 Prais, S. J.: "Measuring Social Mobility," *Journal of the Royal Statistical Association,* ser. A, 118 (1955), 56–66.

59 Reiss, Albert J., Jr., with Otis Dudley Duncan, Paul K. Hatt, and Cecil C. North: *Occupations and Social Status* (New York: Free Press, 1961).

60 Rogoff, Natalie: *Recent Trends in Occupational Mobility* (New York: Free Press, 1953).

61 Schmitt, David R.: "Magnitude Measures of Economic and Educational Status," *Sociological Quarterly,* 6 (Autumn, 1965), 387–391.

62 Sorokin, Pitirim A.: *Social and Cultural Mobility* (New York: Free Press, 1959).

63 Svalastoga, Kaare: "Social Differentiation," in Robert E. L. Faris (Ed.), *Handbook of Modern Sociology* (Chicago: Rand McNally, 1964), chap. 15.

64 Svalastoga, Kaare: *Social Differentiation* (New York: McKay, 1965).

65 Tumin, Melvin M., and Arnold S. Feldman: "Theory and Measurement of Occupational Mobility," *American Sociological Review,* 22 (June, 1957), 281–288.

66 Warner, W. Lloyd: *Social Class in America* (Chicago: Science Research, 1949).

67 Westie, Frank R.: "Social Distance Scales: A Tool for the Study of Stratification," *Sociology and Social Research,* 43 (March–April, 1959), 251–258.

68 Yasuda, Saburo: "A Methodological Inquiry into Social Mobility," *American Sociological Review,* 29 (February, 1964), 16–23.

# PART 2

# DESIGN AND ANALYSIS IN COMPARATIVE RESEARCH

For numerous practical reasons, social scientists often find it necessary to work with data that are comparative in nature. These data may or may not have been collected at a single point in time, but the essential characteristic is that they are appropriate in static analyses in which time sequences do not play a crucial role. Such static analyses are often stereotyped as inferior or unsatisfactory, as compared with dynamic analyses, which presumably constitute the ideal or best form of scientific endeavor. But dynamic analyses have their own special difficulties or drawbacks, as will be discussed in Part 3. For one thing, they require a good deal more mathematical sophistication, as well as adequate data collected at more than two points in time. Therefore comparative or cross-sectional data are often more adequate to the task.

This being the case, it is necessary for social scientists to understand both the possibilities and limitations of comparative designs and analysis. Comparative analyses presuppose that populations studied tend to approach equilibrium states, although once-and-for-all changes produced by exogenous factors can be handled in the analysis. If one wishes to specify time paths or to study reciprocal causation, however, it is ordinarily necessary to obtain time-series data. Otherwise, a number of a priori assumptions must be made. Some of these considerations are discussed in Chap. 5 of Part 2 and again in James Coleman's treatment of change data in Chap. 11 of Part 3.

Questions of design and analysis cannot easily be separated. Of course, in actual research one's design and data collection precede analysis. But *knowledge* and *anticipation* of analysis problems are absolute prerequisites to a satisfactory design. This explains the ordering of chapters within this section. Chapters 5 and 6 are concerned with analysis and causal inferences. Chapter 6, by Raymond Boudon, is the more specialized and technical of the two and can be omitted on first reading. Both of these chapters deal with rather abstract questions: the use of simultaneous equations, estimating and testing procedures, the rationale for controlling, statistical interaction, and the measurement of relative importance of variables.

Chapter 7, on problems in cross-cultural research, by Raoul Naroll, constitutes a second substantive case in which design, analysis, and measurement problems are discussed in the context of cultural anthropological data. Naroll suggests resolutions to six central methodological problems, many of which parallel those evident in the social sciences generally. For example, he applies influence analysis (a special causal model) to the problem of causal inference, uses a control factor method to deal with data quality control, constructs a definition for the culture-bearing unit to handle the problems of consistency, and indicates possible directions in resolving sampling bias and the problem of the comparability and validity of indices for major variables.

The final chapter in this part, by Bernard Lazerwitz, covers major topics in the field of sample design and analysis. Although entire courses and books have been devoted to this subject and the reader interested in obtaining a technical knowledge of sampling must pursue the topic in far greater detail, anyone wishing to acquire adequate knowledge of survey research procedures must have some understanding of the basic strategies and techniques of sampling presented in this chapter.

In general, comparative studies require multivariate analyses involving large numbers of variables, which require working with simultaneous equations. In the case of static analyses, these can be algebraic in form, whereas dynamic formulations require either differential or difference equations. Dynamic analyses become exceedingly complex unless the number of variables can be kept to a minimum. It is also probably true that it is easier to grasp the central methodological issues in the case of the relatively more simple static formulations.

# CHAPTER 5

# Theory Building and Causal Inferences

HUBERT M. BLALOCK, JR.

In Chap. 1 it was emphasized that there is a major disparity between the languages of theory and research and that this gap is especially difficult to close in the social sciences. One facet of this problem which we shall encounter in the present chapter is the difficult question of making causal inferences in nonexperimental research. Most scientists may find it helpful to think theoretically in causal terms regardless of the terminology they may use to avoid philosophical objections to causal language. But strictly speaking causal arguments cannot be verified empirically, as they are not on the operational level. They involve purely hypothetical if-then statements and require simplifying assumptions that are inherently untestable (2, chap. 1). Before discussing these matters in more detail, however, I would like to consider briefly some general problems introduced by the necessity of dealing with large numbers of variables and unknown disturbing influences.

## 5.1 WHAT KIND OF THEORY?[1]

I take as my starting point a goal which I presume to be shared by most sociologists: that of developing theories that go considerably beyond common sense but also lead to specific predictions which can be put to empirical test. We wish to avoid those theories which are so vague and highly flexible that, whereas they may be used to account for almost any phenomenon ex post facto, they do not imply sufficiently precise predictions that they can be readily rejected. Most sociological theories, at present, seem to be

[1] Portions of this section are taken with permission of the publisher from H. M. Blalock, Jr., "Some Important Methodological Problems for Sociology," *Sociology and Social Research,* **47** (July, 1963), pp. 398–407.

so top-heavy with unmeasured variables and untestable assumptions that they yield only a very small number of imprecise predictions.

It is not necessary that a theory yield numerous empirical predictions. A small number of exact predictions make it extremely easy to reject the theory. Likewise, a theory that makes a large number of relatively less precise predictions may also be rejected rather easily. But if there are only a small number of imprecise predictions, then there will always be quite a few alternative theories—many of which involve simple common sense—which also cannot be rejected on the basis of the evidence. The result may be an extremely large number of equally satisfactory explanations remaining to clutter up the literature.

Perhaps the ideal model of a theory which is capable of yielding either precise or numerous predictions is the completely deductive system. Because of its logical tightness, one can see exactly how the various predictions are interrelated. In contrast, most sociological theories seem to involve sets of propositions that are merely plausibly interrelated. Each seems to make sense in the light of the others, but there is no rigorous derivation of one set from another. As a result, one can usually insert a number of alternative propositions—leading to quite different predictions—and the new theory will seem equally plausible. There may be no strictly defined procedures for deciding which propositions are logically inconsistent with the others.

Nagel (18) points out that one of the reasons for the inexactness of laws in the social sciences is that they are presumably meant to apply to real-life situations rather than to ideal types or models of reality. In contrast, the much more exact laws of the physical sciences are stated as though they held without exception, but the conditions under which they apply are so strictly delimited that they can be only approximated in real life. For example, if one attempted to apply the law of falling bodies to real objects in the earth's atmosphere, one would be able to establish only statistical regularities.

It is presumably easier to arrive at theories that approximate the deductive ideal if we confine ourselves to simplified models of reality involving isolated systems, a small number of variables, and no measurement errors. Such theories stand a much better chance of being logically tight and capable of yielding a number of exact predictions. But when we state laws in statistical terms, allowing for large amounts of unexplained variation, it becomes much more difficult to develop deductive systems. For example, the simple line of reasoning, if $A$ then $B$, if $B$ then $C$, therefore if $A$ then $C$ becomes translated into if $A$ then usually $B$, if $B$ then usually $C$, therefore if $A$ then sometimes $C$. Such a theory no longer has much predictive value, unless precise values can be supplied for the probability of $B$ given $A$, and so forth. Even then, it might have little predictive value for individual cases.

We might follow the strategy of formulating deductive theories that apply only to ideal models. But how would these theories be tested? We run into a fundamental problem. The testing of such theories depends on our being able to approximate the ideal conditions to some relatively high degree. In general, the more precise the predictions the closer the approximation must be. In laboratory settings one may successively arrive at better and better approximations until a limiting value can be inferred. For example, the behavior of falling bodies can be studied under varying degrees of approximation to a perfect vacuum.

The *testing* of exactly formulated deductive theories depends, then, on our being able to approximate the ideal conditions specified. Laboratory experiments are not necessary if one can find natural systems that are for all practical purposes effectively isolated from outside influences. One need not manipulate the bodies in the solar system, for example, in order to test the accuracy of some rather precise predictions. But when one can neither approximate the ideal experimentally nor find these approximations in the real world, the problem is made extremely difficult. Needless to say, the theory must also specify more or less exactly the nature of the ideal conditions so that the investigator can determine whether or not these are being approximated to a reasonable degree.

Let us assume that in the foreseeable future sociologists will seldom find it possible to test theories under any such ideal conditions. It remains possible that the best strategy is to formulate rather precise deductive theories but to be satisfied with very crude tests of such theories. Another alternative—which may turn out in many instances to be almost equivalent to the first—is to construct deductive theories that allow for unexplained variation. Such variation may be due to a combination of measurement errors and variables that have been left out of the theoretical system. But as soon as we begin to allow for such disturbances, we must make certain simplifying assumptions about *how* they are related to the other variables. Otherwise, although a theory may be formulated in completely abstract terms, testable predictions cannot be made.

Many of our major difficulties involve the fact that in most sociological research we encounter substantial unexplained variation. Whenever this occurs there are at least three rather obvious possibilities which, unfortunately, seem to have rather different implications for theory building and research strategy. The first is that we are dealing with the wrong set of independent variables but that if we could find the right ones, a much higher percentage of the variation in the dependent variable could be explained. A second possibility is that there are in fact a very large number of variables operating more or less independently of one another and that in order to arrive at an adequate theoretical explanation we might have to consider simultaneously a much larger number of variables. Third, we may be dealing with the correct variables, but most of the error may be due to inadequate measurement.

Theoretical schemes that allow for unexplained variation or poor measurement may imply a number of very weak predictions if the number of variables is large and if linkages between important variables are very indirect. For example, consider the simple causal chain argument in which a given factor influences another by way of a series of intervening variables. *If* it could be assumed that no other variables operated on the system, then the indirectness of the linkage would be of no serious consequences to the theory. Thus if $V$ causes $W$, which causes $X$, which causes $Y$, which causes $Z$, then a change in $V$ should produce a determinate change in $Z$. But if $W$ has causes other than $V$, $X$ has causes other than $W$, and so forth, the relationship between $V$ and $Z$ may be extremely weak. For example, we shall see that if all outside influences operate completely randomly and if each of the pairs of adjacent variables is correlated moderately highly (say .7), then the correlation between $V$ and $Z$ will be the product of these separate correlations (i.e., $.7^4$ or .24).[2] Since there would usually be a large number of alternative theories also accounting for such a weak relationship, the initial theory cannot easily be shown superior to its rivals.

Similarly, a theory that specifies rather imprecise relationships among a large number of variables may lead to completely indeterminate predictions. Suppose, for example, we have a theory that predicts the following:

**1** Increases in $X$ produce increases in $Y$,

**2** Increases in $X$ produce increases in $W$,

**3** Increases in $Y$ produce increases in $Z$, and

**4** Increases in $W$ produce decreases in $Z$.

What can be said about changes in $Z$ indirectly produced by $X$? Very little, since increases in $X$ could result in either increases or decreases in $Z$ depending on the magnitude of the coefficients in each relationship. Without a more exact theory, and without accurate measurement, no really adequate predictions can be made. Where the number of variables is increased beyond five or six, I suspect that in most instances the number of such indeterminate predictions will sharply increase. This is completely aside from the attenuations produced by outside disturbing influences.

Because of difficulties involved in carrying out close approximations to the experimental ideal, where randomization may be used to rule out many types of disturbing influences, sociologists and most other social scientists will ultimately have to learn to deal with large numbers of variables simultaneously. Since rigid controls on most disturbing influences can seldom be made, substitute procedures will have to be found. Such substitutes will undoubtedly require the use of certain kinds of simplifying assumptions that

[2] Costner and Leik (8) show that the simple deductive sign rule implied in this type of argument is invalid unless one makes restrictive assumptions concerning either the magnitude of the correlations or the behavior of outside variables.

may not be completely satisfactory. But it may very well turn out that this is the sort of price one must pay whenever there are nonisolated systems in which a large number of variables are changing more or less simultaneously and where it would be unrealistic simply to ignore important variables while focusing attention on a smaller number.

The implications of these remarks should become more apparent as we proceed. The process of relating theory and research involves postulating theoretical models representing oversimplified versions of reality. The assumptions required by these theories are seldom if ever directly testable. But if the theories are to be at all useful scientifically, one must be able to derive from them a set of propositions which, when the appropriate concepts have been linked with suitable operations, lead to empirically verifiable predictions. Although no theory can be verified, since there will always be alternative theories that imply the same predictions, one can at least proceed by eliminating or modifying the inadequate ones. In constructing such theories, the scientist is always confronted with the dilemma of how much to oversimplify reality. On the one hand, simple theories are easier to construct and evaluate. On the other hand, the more complex ones may stand a better chance of conforming to reality. This kind of dilemma will be seen quite clearly in the next section in which we deal with some of the important issues that arise in connection with attempts to construct causal models.

## An Example

Since the discussion in the remainder of the chapter will be rather abstract, it might be helpful at this point to introduce a concrete example for illustrative purposes. Suppose one wished to construct and actually test a theory explaining how individuals select or are sorted into various occupational careers. One can imagine a number of possible research designs, as well as specific variables that can be considered. Eventually, however, the investigator would have to commit himself to one or two alternative designs and to a manageable number of variables.

The ideal design might involve a longitudinal analysis carried out over a period of perhaps twenty years, beginning in junior high school and ending when one could be reasonably sure that most of the subjects were finally settled in permanent occupational positions. Data might be collected at regular intervals, at which times motivational and achievement inventories could be systematically collected. These could be supplemented by school grades, ability tests, and intensive interviews. Although randomization procedures would probably not be possible in this kind of situation, one might very well carry out the kind of analysis of change data proposed by Coleman in Chap. 11.

Such a longitudinal study would be extremely expensive and time-consuming, however.  Since a large sample would undoubtedly be necessary, and since geographic mobility and refusals would probably produce large attenuation rates, one would want to be reasonably sure of a substantial payoff before undertaking such an ambitious study.  As is true with many other practical research situations, it would ordinarily be necessary to reduce the time span of such a longitudinal study or to confine the follow-up studies to one or two later periods.  For a more exploratory or small-scale project, a cross-sectional study would usually be much more feasible, provided that reasonably good standardized data were available for an earlier period of time.  With such a cross-sectional study the investigator would have less information about exact time sequences, and he might have to rely on data collected for other purposes and therefore not completely adequate for his own theoretical formulation.  This means that he would be able to obtain only covariations or correlations, plus knowledge of some of the temporal sequences.  Many of his measured variables would have to be taken as indirect indicators of his theoretically defined variables, and his theoretical formulations would thereby be somewhat more complex.

Bruce Eckland (9) faced many of these decisions before deciding to use a questionnaire distributed to about 1,300 males who had matriculated at the University of Illinois ten years prior to the time of the study (1962). Eckland was particularly interested in the degree to which college graduation, per se, contributed to occupational careers.  The study design required locating a very high percentage of the original population, including those who had dropped out of the University of Illinois but completed college elsewhere. Various records were available, including scores on entrance examinations, grade-point averages while at Illinois, and high school rankings for many of the students.

One of the models used by Eckland is given in Fig. 5.1.  In addition to whether or not the student had finished college, two other independent variables were used to explain occupational achievement.  Both of these variables, socioeconomic status of father and academic ability (as measured by test scores), would be expected to affect college graduation.  But they might also have a direct effect on careers, independently of whether or not the student had completed graduation requirements.  In other words, one would predict that these would be closely linked with stable personality traits that continued to operate after the graduation decision had been made.  The theoretical and empirical problem, of course, is that of separating the direct effects of graduation from those of the remaining variables, given the possibility that all three independent variables could be interrelated.  This must be done by using the available data on covariations and time sequences, plus a number of theoretical assumptions, many of which are not directly testable.

Many important questions arise in this type of analysis situation.  Should one control for father's status and ability?  Why?  What would one infer

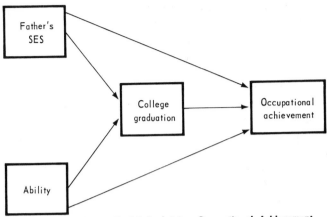

**Fig. 5.1.  Eckland's Model Explaining Occupational Achievement.**

from the behavior of different coefficients? Are the temporal sequences and theoretical rationale sufficiently obvious that one-way causation can be assumed? If not, what complications would be introduced? Are the measured variables actually the ones in which there is theoretical interest? If not, how are they presumed to be linked with these variables? What kinds of measurement errors can be expected, and what do these imply? Are the relationships simple linear additive ones? And finally, assuming that all the above questions have been satisfactorily resolved, what is the best way to measure the relative contributions of these variables to occupational career choice?

Questions of this sort cannot be satisfactorily answered by means of common sense or *ad hoc* rules of thumb. It is therefore necessary to develop a methodologically sound rationale for making analysis decisions designed to answer such questions. The remainder of the chapter is devoted to these and similar problems that commonly arise in nonexperimental comparative research.

## 5.2   THE CONSTRUCTION OF CAUSAL MODELS

There have been a number of philosophical debates over the concept of causality and its appropriateness in scientific discourse. Space considerations do not permit a discussion of these debates (2,7,10,22). In brief, many of the objections to causal thinking reduce to the two points that causality can never be verified empirically and that the notion of cause and effect is far too simple to describe reality, with causal laws being much more a property of the observer than of the real world itself. I will admit to the essential validity of both objections, and in fact have already noted that in a very real sense *no* theoretically defined concepts can be directly translated into operations, nor can theoretical propositions be directly tested empirically.

Yet it remains exceedingly difficult for most persons to think without the aid of some such notions as forces, causes, producing agents, drives, or needs.

One of the ways commonly used in sociology for dodging causal terminology is to speak in terms of structures and their functions. But "function" is characteristically defined in terms of "consequences," which appears to be merely another word for "effects." Presumably, the functionalist objects primarily to the gross types of oversimplifications implied in single-causation theories or those which stress a very small number of factors. Gouldner and Peterson, perhaps somewhat facetiously, point out that the fundamental postulate of functionalism—when stripped of pretentious verbiage—reduces to the assumption that "everything causes everything else" (11, pp. 2–3). Few functionalists would go this far, of course, but functional arguments often stress the notion of reciprocal causation.

The postulate that everything causes everything else is perhaps in a literal sense an accurate description of reality and on the surface seems quite profound. But it is analytically useless, except under ideal circumstances. For if scientific predictions are to be made and evaluated empirically, one must say something about the nature and relative importance of each factor in relation to the others. If one were dealing with variables that could be measured in terms of some metric, this would mean the specification of all coefficients in a system of equations in which each variable appeared once as the dependent variable. Allowing for disturbances created by variables not explicitly considered, this would require in the case of static linear systems a set of equations as follows:

$$X_1 = a_1 + b_{12}X_2 + b_{13}X_3 + \cdots + b_{1k}X_k + e_1$$
$$X_2 = a_2 + b_{21}X_1 + b_{23}X_3 + \cdots + b_{2k}X_k + e_2$$
$$\cdot$$
$$\cdot \qquad\qquad\qquad\qquad\qquad\qquad\qquad\qquad (5.1)$$
$$\cdot$$
$$X_k = a_k + b_{k1}X_1 + b_{k2}X_2 + \cdots + b_{k,k-1}X_{k-1} + e_k$$

where the $e_i$ represent contributions due to omitted variables.

Conceivably, the theorist might be able to specify all values for the $b$ coefficients. This would then give the relative contributions of each variable to the others. For example, if $b_{12} = .4$ and $b_{21} = -.3$ this would mean that if $X_2$ were changed by 1 unit through the actions of some outside agent, then $X_1$ would change by .4 units. But this, in turn, would produce a change in $X_2$ of $(-.3)(.4) = -.12$ units, and so forth. I am, of course, ignoring the changes produced in the remaining variables, which presumably would also affect $X_1$. The major point is that the system of equations implies a series of predicted changes in all variables, given an initial change in one.

Presuming that such an exact theory could be constructed, could it be verified empirically? As is well known, a set of general equations of this sort has an indefinite number of solutions for the $b$ coefficients. Practically, this means that there are an infinite number of combinations of values for the slopes, all of which imply the same empirical predictions. Furthermore, if one were to attempt to reverse the process—as is usually necessary in most sciences—by *developing* the theory from the empirical data, there would be no way of estimating the true values of the coefficients except under very special circumstances.

If each of the hypothetical changes were to occur discretely, with a long enough interval between each change for the observer to note the temporal sequences involved, then the various contributions of each factor could be sorted out. But in reality most such changes occur either almost simultaneously or continuously rather than discretely. To make matters worse, in many nonexperimental situations the observations are taken at a single point in time or at relatively infrequent intervals. In effect, there will be too many unknowns, and unless values for some of these can be supplied a priori, none of them can be determined. This necessity of specifying unknowns a priori rules out any chances of verifying the theory completely.

The existence of too many unknowns can be noted quite easily if the theory has been formulated in mathematical language. But when it has been stated verbally, the situation may not be so obvious. The theorist may dismiss the matter as merely a problem for empirical research. Or he may rest contented with a qualitative listing of the various supposed effects of each variable, with perhaps a rough guess of the weight each should receive. Such theories are obviously not in a form that could lead to testable predictions.

## The Use of Exogenous Variables

Econometricians have found it useful to distinguish between exogenous and endogenous variables. The latter are the variables whose interrelationships are to be explained by the theory under consideration. Some may be causally or mathematically dependent on others, and in the extreme case mutual dependence may exist among all pairs of endogenous variables. Referring to these variables as $X_i$, we might represent the most general linear system of algebraic equations as in Eqs. (5.1), where the disturbance terms $e_i$ could be intercorrelated. Exogenous variables are taken as givens in terms of the theory, though other theories may, of course, be used to explain such variables. But while they appear as independent variables in the system described by the theory, their values cannot simply be ignored. Any particular endogenous variable is thus conceived to be caused by a combination of the exogenous variables and some of the remaining endogenous variables, plus a number of unknown or unmeasured factors whose effects are summed up in the disturbance terms $e_i$. Letting the symbols $Z_i$ represent the set of $j$ exogenous variables, we may then write out a linear system of the following form:

$$X_1 = a_1 + b_{12}X_2 + \cdots + b_{1k}X_k + (c_{11}Z_1 + c_{12}Z_2 + \cdots + c_{1j}Z_j) + e_1$$
$$X_2 = a_2 + b_{21}X_1 + \cdots + b_{2k}X_k + (c_{21}Z_1 + c_{22}Z_2 + \cdots + c_{2j}Z_j) + e_2$$

$$\cdot$$
$$\cdot \qquad\qquad\qquad\qquad\qquad\qquad\qquad\qquad\qquad\qquad (5.2)$$
$$\cdot$$

$$X_k = a_k + b_{k1}X_1 + \cdots + b_{k,k-1}X_{k-1} + (c_{k1}Z_1 + c_{k2}Z_2 + \cdots + c_{kj}Z_j) + e_k$$

There will again be too many unknown coefficients for a unique solution, meaning that an indefinite number of alternative sets of values will be empirically indistinguishable. But it is possible to specify some conditions under which a single set of coefficients can be uniquely identified. Although the literature on this subject is highly technical, it is instructive to note the *necessary* (though not sufficient) conditions for this to occur if no restrictions are placed on the errors $e_i$. These essentially reduce to the following requirement: that in order for the coefficients of any particular equation to be identified, the number of endogenous variables appearing in this equation cannot exceed by more than one the number of exogenous variables that have been left out of the equation (13, pp. 249-252). In effect, this ordinarily means that some of the coefficients must be assumed equal to zero (or some other specific value), and one cannot use too many exogenous variables in any equation that also contains a large number of endogenous variables.

An example will illustrate the point. Suppose we take $X_1$ to be caused by $X_2$ and $X_3$ plus some of the exogenous variables. The equation for $X_1$ would then contain three endogenous variables. In order for the coefficients to be identifiable without further restrictions on the model, it would be necessary that two or more of the exogenous variables *not* appear in this equation. But if we also assumed the coefficient of $X_3$ to be zero, meaning that $X_1$ is dependent on $X_2$ but not $X_3$, then we would need to omit only one of the exogenous variables. If $X_1$ did not depend on any of the other $X_i$, then we could use all the exogenous variables in the equation for $X_1$.

Thus by dealing with specific types of mathematical models, one can show deductively exactly what restrictions are implied by the statement that there may be too many unknowns. Certain restrictive assumptions will be necessary, and perhaps the simplest of these consist in setting some of the coefficients equal to zero. This is equivalent to assuming that certain of the variables do not cause the others. As will be seen below, in one-way causation some rather simple assumptions about error terms may also be used to avoid the identification problem.

## General Recursive Systems

A somewhat less general type of model can be constructed while still allowing for reciprocal causation. In a so-called recursive system, none of the variables considered endogenous at time $t$ can be taken as both a cause and an effect of another endogenous variable. The essential feature of a recursive set of equations is in the triangular form of the slope matrix, in which at least half of the $b$'s have been set equal to zero. By properly arranging the variables, we can write a recursive system in the following way:

$$X_1 = e_1$$
$$X_2 = b_{21}X_1 + e_2$$
$$X_3 = b_{31}X_1 + b_{32}X_2 + e_3$$
$$\cdot$$
$$\cdot \quad (5.3)$$
$$\cdot$$
$$X_k = b_{k1}X_1 + b_{k2}X_2 \cdots + b_{k,k-1}X_{k-1} + e_k$$

where for convenience $a_i$ has been omitted by assuming that all $X_i$ are measured in terms of deviations about their respective means.

As the equations in this system have been written, it would appear that all reciprocal causation has been ruled out. For example $X_1$ depends only on outside variables summed up in $e_1$; $X_2$ also depends on $X_1$; $X_3$ on $X_1$ and $X_2$, and so forth. I shall focus on such one-way causal models in the next section under the heading of special recursive systems. More generally, however, we may take certain of the dependent variables as independent or exogenous at earlier time periods. For example $X_1$ may be the same variable as $X_3$, but at an earlier time. Thus the first three equations in this system might be relabeled with temporal subscripts so as to give

$$X_{t-1} = e_1$$
$$Y_t = b_{21}X_{t-1} + e_2 \quad (5.4)$$
$$X_t = b_{31}X_{t-1} + b_{32}Y_t + e_3$$

Here $X$ at time $t$ is taken as a function of $Y$ at that same time, while $Y$ at $t$ is conceived as caused by $X$ at an earlier period.

Recursive systems of this type are associated with Herman Wold (20,22), who argues that such systems are better suited for causal interpretations than are the more general systems represented by Eqs. (5.1) or (5.2). They can be given a stimulus-response type of interpretation, provided that an autonomous behaving unit can be associated with each of the dependent variables. Such units act and react to the behavior of each other, with finite lags in between. Wold and Jureen give an example of a cobweb model in which consumer demand at time $t$ is caused by prices at that same time, the supply at $t$ is caused by prices at $t - 1$, and prices at time $t$ are caused by past prices plus a function of the difference between demand and supply at time $t - 1$ (22, p. 12). In order to provide such a recursive system with a causal interpretation, one may imagine three autonomous behaving units: consumers who demand goods, producers who supply them, and retail and wholesale merchants who actually set the prices in response to supply and demand.

Strotz and Wold (20) argue that mutual causation is best conceived in terms of dynamic models in which time periods are explicitly considered. To say that $X$ causes instantaneous changes in $Y$, *and vice versa,* is to claim something that could never be verified in laboratory experiments and would be appropriate only under equilibrium conditions. As soon as one allows for finite time lapses, however, he may set up equations that can be given an operational interpretation in terms of stimulus and response.

The practical problem is to specify the proper time interval and to obtain observations at the various times. In the study of consumer-producer behavior, it is often reasonable to assume that production levels are determined perhaps a full year (or season) ahead of time, in response to prices (and other factors) at that time. Consumer responses, on the other hand, can be presumed to be more or less instantaneous. Therefore if annual (or seasonal) data can be collected and the proper lags in the equations introduced, recursive systems may be used to provide reasonably good approximations to reality.

Unfortunately, most sociological phenomena are not so neatly described in terms of fixed time periods. Contrast the behavior of producers, whose production periods often coincide reasonably well, with decisions of individuals to migrate, to commit acts of delinquency, or to discriminate against Negroes. An individual may decide to migrate as a response to present conditions and his migration may in turn affect these conditions at a somewhat later time, but we can seldom fix a realistic time interval appropriate to the process. Intervals for different individuals will not coincide. Although the act of migrating may constitute a discrete act for one individual, when aggregate migration *rates* are formed, the process appears to be a more or less continuous one.

The same applies to other macroscopic or aggregated variables, making the question of temporal sequences a highly complex one. In many situations of interest to social scientists, all variables seem to be changing at once, and recursive models of the type suggested by Wold would not seem to lend themselves to empirical validation. Furthermore, for cost or other practical reasons it may not be possible to obtain time-series data except at very infrequent intervals. Thus if one wishes to retain the notion of reciprocal causation in his model, it may be necessary to resort to nonrecursive systems, with all of the difficulties of interpretation and identification that these involve.

## Special Recursive Systems and One-way Causation

As was pointed out in the previous section, recursive systems can be used to describe situations in which simple one-way causation is assumed. In the equations of (5.3) each successive dependent variable is presumed to be caused by some of the previous variables but not by any which appear as dependent variables in equations listed below it. Thus if $b_{ij} \neq 0$ we must automatically have $b_{ji} = 0$, meaning that if $X_j$ causes $X_i$, then $X_i$ cannot cause $X_j$.

Provided one can make certain assumptions about the error terms, which will be discussed below, these one-way causal models have some very simple properties. In the first place, there is no longer any need for the distinction between exogenous and endogenous variables. In the equations of (5.3), $X_1$ is, of course, exogenous since its value is taken to be independent of any of the other variables explicitly considered in the system. But other exogenous variables can also be formed by merely setting some of the remaining $b$'s equal to zero. For example, if $b_{21} = 0$, then $X_2$ is also exogenous since it no longer depends on $X_1$. As Boudon notes in Chap. 6, the problem of identification also disappears, since each of the coefficients can be uniquely estimated by ordinary least squares. Finally, such a system of recursive equations provides the rationale for interpreting the behavior of partial correlation and regression coefficients. We shall see that this rationale is perfectly consistent with commonsense rules of thumb currently in use. But it also supplies checks on common sense, as well as rules appropriate for the more general $k$-variable case.

All the types of equation systems discussed above require certain assumptions about the behavior of the disturbance terms represented by the $e$'s. Such assumptions need not be too restrictive, but generally speaking, the fewer restrictions we impose the less definite we can be about both the estimating process and the interpretation of coefficients. It is commonly assumed that the $e$'s have mean values of zero. In order to make conventional parametric significance tests (e.g., the t and F tests), we must assume that the $e$'s are normally distributed. It is usually also assumed that the $e_i$ appearing in the equation for $X_i$ is uncorrelated with any of the remaining $X$'s taken to be causes of $X_i$. Otherwise, it is difficult to give a meaningful causal interpretation to the various slopes. Finally, in order for ordinary least squares to give unbiased and efficient estimates, we must also assume that the $e_i$ are uncorrelated with each other. As Boudon shows in the following chapter, this particular assumption permits the unique identification of all coefficients except in the special case where one or more of the $e_i$ are zero.

These last two assumptions have been considered overly restrictive in econometric research. They essentially require that outside variables operate in such a manner as not to produce systematic distortions in the least-squares estimates. Put differently, any outside factor that influences $X_i$ cannot also be a major cause of one of the remaining $X$'s. Practically, we can tolerate minor exceptions, as in the case where the systematic effects of one outside influence are canceled statistically by those of another. But we cannot tolerate the existence of any outside disturbing influence which is an important cause of more than one included variable. If such an influence exists, it should be brought into the model explicitly as an additional variable. Otherwise, faulty causal inferences are likely to be made.

If one is willing to make these and other assumptions (to be discussed later), the system of recursive equations provides a very simple but insightful set of rules for interpreting the results of controlling operations. Put briefly, we postulate a given model as specified by a particular set of equations. This then implies a set of predictions concerning the disappearance of certain partial correlation and regression coefficients. Alternative models may imply the same predictions, making it necessary for us to choose among these on *other* grounds. Where temporal sequences are known, this may provide the kind of supplementary information necessary for choosing among alternative models, all of which yield the same predictions. This particular question will be treated in the next section when we consider problems of interpretation in terms of specific causal models.

The recursive equations of (5.3) do not actually yield testable predictions unless further assumptions can be made. But if additional restrictions are imposed, then we will reduce the number of unknowns to less than the number of equations in the system, and thus the equations will not always fit the data. In effect, this means that the data must satisfy a number of conditions, one for each restrictive assumption we impose. If the conditions are not satisfied, then the model in question must be rejected or modified.

Actually, the restrictive assumptions can be very simple ones, namely, that some of the $b$'s are equal to zero. This means that some of the variables are not directly linked causally to each other. By direct causal links I mean direct relative to the variables explicitly considered. For example, the equation

$$X_3 = b_{31}X_1 + b_{32}X_2 + e_3 \qquad (5.5)$$

implies that changes in either $X_1$ or $X_2$ will produce changes in the mean value of $X_3$. Here we are taking $X_3$ to be directly caused by both variables. But if we set $b_{31}$ equal to zero, then we are assuming that $X_3$ is not *directly* caused by $X_1$, though since $X_2$ is in turn caused by $X_1$, one could say that $X_1$ is an indirect cause of $X_3$ via $X_2$. Given the above assumptions, we can estimate the coefficients $b_{ij}$ by ordinary least squares, using the standard formulas for *partial* slopes. Thus the estimate of $b_{31}$ in Eq. (5.5) would be $b_{31.2}$ in conventional least-squares notation. Thus setting $b_{31}$ equal to zero leads to the restrictive condition that the least-squares estimate $b_{31.2}$ should be approximately zero, subject to sampling errors. This of course means that the corresponding partial correlation $r_{13.2}$ should also be close to zero. But this will be true only if the model conforms reasonably well to reality, and therefore this imposed condition may be used as a prediction of the model in question.

With each pair of variables for which there is no direct causal link, there will be a corresponding prediction that the appropriate partial slope or correlation will be approximately zero. Thus suppose we have the following four-variable model:

There are no direct causal links between $X_1$ and $X_4$ and between $X_2$ and $X_3$. This corresponds to the situation where $b_{41.23}$ and $b_{32.1}$ have been set equal to zero. In this case the recursive equations become

$$
\begin{aligned}
X_1 &= e_1 \\
X_2 &= b_{21}X_1 + e_2 \\
X_3 &= b_{31.2}X_1 + OX_2 + e_3 \\
X_4 &= OX_1 + b_{42.13}X_2 + b_{43.12}X_3 + e_4
\end{aligned}
\tag{5.6}
$$

I am now making use of the familiar dot notation for partial coefficients since ordinary least squares can be used to estimate the slopes. Notice that neither $X_3$ nor $X_4$ appears in the subscripts for the first two equations, and $X_4$ does not appear in the third equation. This is a property of recursive systems involving one-way causation (2, chap. 2).

The above model therefore predicts that both $r_{14.23}$ and $r_{23.1}$ should be approximately zero, since the ordinary least-square formulas for correlations and regression coefficients involve the same numerators. According to this model, $X_1$ is an indirect cause of $X_4$ through both $X_2$ and $X_3$ which act as intervening variables. The first prediction says that when controls are introduced *simultaneously* for the intervening variables, the relationship between $X_1$ and $X_4$ should vanish except for sampling errors. The relationship between $X_2$ and $X_3$, however, is spurious and due to $X_1$. The second prediction states that a control for $X_1$ should wipe out the relationship between $X_2$ and $X_3$. These prediction equations (i.e., $r_{14.23} = r_{23.1} = 0$) are thus perfectly consistent with common sense and with one's research expectations.

In general, we may write a prediction equation for each pair of variables that have *not* been linked directly by a causal arrow, and these predictions will take the form of the disappearance of some higher-order partial correlation. These higher-order partials *may* involve controls for all variables that either are antecedent to or intervene between the two variables under consideration. But they will *not* involve controls for dependent variables that appear only in equations which are found beneath the equations for the two variables being related. For example, one should not control for $X_4$ when relating $X_1$ and $X_2$. Although $r_{23.1}$ should be approximately zero in the above model this will ordinarily not be true for $r_{23.14}$.

If a number of arrows have been erased, certain simplifications may occur. This will take the form of the predicted disappearance of some of the *lower-order* partials. For example, suppose the arrow between $X_1$ and $X_2$ were erased. Under the assumption that outside variables do not systematically disturb the picture, this would imply that the correlation between $X_1$ and $X_2$ should be approximately zero.[3] But if both $r_{12}$ and $r_{23.1}$ are zero, it can easily be seen (from the formula for $r_{23.1}$) that $r_{23}$ should also be zero, again subject to sampling errors. In this case we would have the following causal situation:

$$X_1 \quad X_2$$
$$\downarrow \quad\quad \downarrow$$
$$X_3 \longrightarrow X_4$$

and the relationship between $X_2$ and $X_3$ is no longer spurious due to $X_1$. Likewise, having removed the linkage between $X_1$ and $X_2$, one no longer has to control for $X_2$ in order to show that the relationship between $X_1$ and $X_4$ is indirect. While we would still predict that $r_{14.23}$ should be zero, this would also be true for $r_{14.3}$, as can be verified from the formula for $r_{14.23}$.

In this second causal model we have an example of a simple causal chain $X_1 \to X_3 \to X_4$. This gives the prediction $r_{14.3} = 0$, which can be rewritten as $r_{14} = r_{13}r_{34}$. Thus the correlation between the two end variables is expected to be weaker than that for either of the directly linked variables, and in fact should be (approximately) equal to the product of $r_{13}$ and $r_{34}$. This can be generalized to any number of variables, provided that they form a simple causal chain. For example, if $X_4$ also caused $X_5$, which in turn caused $X_6$, then the model would predict that

$$r_{15} = r_{13}r_{34}r_{45} \quad\quad \text{and} \quad\quad r_{16} = r_{13}r_{34}r_{45}r_{56} \tag{5.7}$$

In such chains we thus see that correlations generally become more and more attenuated as they become increasingly indirect, if outside influences act randomly on the system.

More complex models involving large numbers of variables may also be constructed, though at the present stage of theoretical and methodological sophistication in sociology such models may be of greater use heuristically than practically. For example, suppose we had the following five-variable model:

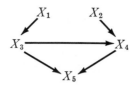

This would give the predictions

$$r_{12} = 0$$
$$r_{14.23} = 0 \quad \text{(reducing to } r_{14.3} = 0)$$
$$r_{23.1} = 0 \quad \text{(reducing to } r_{23} = 0) \quad (5.8)$$
$$r_{15.234} = 0 \quad \text{(reducing to } r_{15.3} = 0)$$
$$r_{25.134} = 0 \quad \text{(reducing to } r_{25.4} = 0)$$

As was pointed out previously, several different models may yield the same predictions, making it impossible to choose among them without introducing further assumptions or additional information. For example, in the simple three-variable case the models $X \leftarrow Z \rightarrow Y$ and $X \rightarrow Z \rightarrow Y$ both give the single prediction that $r_{xy.z} = 0$ or $r_{xy} = r_{xz}r_{zy}$. In the first instance the relationship between $X$ and $Y$ is spurious, whereas in the second $X$ is an indirect cause of $Y$ by way of $Z$. It may make considerable difference both theoretically and practically which of these alternatives is actually correct. Where evidence is based on experimental or time-series data, the actual temporal sequences may be known. If so, one or the other model may be ruled out on the basis of this information. Or we may simply assume, say, that $Z$ cannot cause $X$, thereby eliminating the possibility of spuriousness.

Under certain circumstances it may be possible to add another variable. For example, suppose it can be assumed that $W$ causes $X$ but is not directly linked to either $Z$ or $Y$. Then the two alternatives become (1) $W \rightarrow X \leftarrow Z \rightarrow Y$ and (2) $W \rightarrow X \rightarrow Z \rightarrow Y$. But as can easily be verified, the first model implies that $r_{wz} = 0$, whereas the second implies that $r_{wz} = r_{wx}r_{xz}$. Provided that the latter predicted value is not too close to zero, the introduction of $W$ may then make it possible to choose between these particular alternatives.

It should be emphasized that all these predicted relationships presuppose that a number of assumptions hold true—linearity and additivity, negligible measurement errors, and the proper behavior of outside variables that may possibly be acting as disturbing influences. We shall consider below some of the practical problems that arise whenever certain of these assumptions cannot be realistically met in actual research. In a sense, these difficulties constitute the key to the difficult problem of making causal or explanatory inferences on the basis of the kinds of real data with which the social scientist must learn to deal.

## Some Complications

Whenever the assumptions required by a model cannot be met in realistic situations, one must examine their implications to determine what complications are introduced whenever one or more such assumptions are relaxed. Unfortunately, it is usually not possible to relax too many assumptions at once without introducing indeterminacy into the system in the form of too many unknowns.   Since the problems involved often become quite complex, I shall comment only very briefly on some of the issues that may arise and refer the reader to other sources for further details (2,13,16,22).

Suppose the error terms within a given equation are themselves inter-correlated, regardless of possible relationships with the independent variables. We are then dealing with the problem of autocorrelation in which, in effect, one has fewer independent replications than one would have if errors were uncorrelated.   In time-series data, this problem is well known.   The tendency is for error terms in adjacent time periods to be positively interrelated, particularly when the intervals are relatively short.   From the causal perspective, one would expect that variables not explicitly included in the equation would operate continuously over a given time period, rather than randomly, thereby producing error terms that are systematically related.   Where the cases involve the same units of analysis at several different points in time, this type of confounding influence is quite common.

Essentially the same phenomenon occurs with respect to units that are spatially contiguous.   In Chap. 7, Naroll discusses complications of this sort in connection with cross-cultural data.   Naroll shows that the lack of independence between adjacent units permits alternative explanations that cannot readily be ruled out on the basis of probability theory.   One such explanation commonly used in anthropology is that relationships between $X$ and $Y$ might be spurious in the sense that patterns have merely diffused from one unit to the next.

There may be no direct causal connection between two variables that are correlated across contiguous societies.   Because of the existence of error terms, however, it is quite possible that some cause of $Y$ happens to be correlated with $X$ within a small number of centers of diffusion.   For example, there may be one center that by chance has both a high $X$ and a high $Y$ value and another center with a low $X$ and a low $Y$.   If so, one might find a high correlation between $X$ and $Y$ in a large number of societies (or other units), but one could not thereby claim that these constituted a set of independent replications.   In the extreme, the number of independent replications (centers of diffusion) might be only two.   Hence it would be dangerous to assume that $X$ and $Y$ were causally linked.

Another way in which the assumptions of the model may be violated is that there may be measurement errors in any of the variables.   The problem of measurement has been discussed in Part 1.   Here I wish to make only one major point: that the possibility of measurement errors introduces additional unknowns into the system.   It will *always* be necessary to make certain simplifying assumptions concerning measurement errors as part of one's auxiliary theory (see Chap. 1).   But it is also essential to study the kinds of implications that specific types of measurement errors have for one's inferences.

Systematic or nonrandom measurement errors can, conceivably, have such great effects that almost any inference is possible. If one allows for unknown large systematic errors, it will always be possible to reject or confirm any theory, regardless of one's data. Clearly this is an unsatisfactory state of affairs, and therefore one practically always makes the assumption either that systematic errors are not large or that the magnitude and direction of these errors can be estimated. Where measurement errors are assumed to be completely random, however, it seems possible to make greater headway, at least to the extent of noting how random measurement errors can affect one's inferences and in suggesting techniques for correcting for these errors under special circumstances.

Random measurement errors in a dependent variable will attenuate *correlations* with independent variables, but they will not affect the expected value of estimates of regression coefficients. But if independent variables are also measured with random error, then both types of coefficients will be attenuated. The degree of (downward) bias in the estimate of $b_{yx}$ is a function of the amount of measurement error in $X$, *relative to* the amount of actual variation in $X$ (13,14). This is an important fact: it means that random measurement error is more serious whenever there is relatively little variation in an independent variable.

Certain implications of this fact should be specifically noted. Many types of change studies are especially vulnerable to measurement errors, since for practical reasons it is often difficult to create or find situations in which independent variables change by considerable amounts. This is particularly so where time intervals are purposely kept short in order to minimize distortion from uncontrolled events. Even in decade-by-decade census analyses, real changes may be relatively small as compared with measurement errors.

Whenever two different populations are compared, one must recognize that differences in slopes may be due primarily to measurement error attenuation. The amount of variation in $X$ may be different from one population to the next. This means that populations having the smallest variation in $X$ will have the greatest attenuations. Another possibility is that measurement accuracy may vary, even where all populations have approximately the same variation in $X$. As will be noted below, controls for background variables may have the effect of reducing the variation in $X$. This means that the numerical value of $b_{yx}$ may be reduced with such a control, not because the true value is affected but because the range of variation in $X$ has been restricted, whereas measurement error has not. Statistical tests may show a significant interaction effect (i.e., difference among slopes), whereas this is really a case of spurious interaction due to differential measurement errors.

In effect, the possibility of measurement error means that alternative explanations become rival interpretations for given findings. For example, suppose $Z$ is producing a spurious relationship between $X$ and $Y$ (i.e., $X \leftarrow Z \rightarrow Y$). It can easily be shown (2, chap. 5) that random measurement error in $Z$ will mean that a control for (the measured value of) $Z$ will *not* reduce the correlation between $X$ and $Y$ to zero. This might lead one to prefer some alternative model, such as the possibility that $X$ is a direct cause of $Y$. As another example of how measurement errors may lead one astray, I have noted elsewhere (5) that random measurement errors may make it difficult to use factor analysis correctly.

## 5.3  TESTING FOR SPURIOUS RELATIONSHIPS

It has been pointed out that one must always make assumptions about the behavior of variables left out of a theoretical system if he is to make causal interpretations of his findings. In particular, we have been assuming that omitted variables can have major effects on only one of the included variables. If an omitted variable is a simultaneous cause of two or more included variables, then we are concerned with an important special case in which the assumptions about the error terms will be violated. The error term associated with a particular dependent variable $X_i$ will then be correlated with at least one of the causes of $X_i$, and we will be dealing with a situation in which the association between two variables is at least partially spurious.

Suppose, for example, that we begin with the following model:

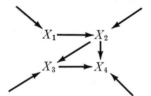

The equation for $X_4$ would be

$$X_4 = b_{42.13}X_2 + b_{43.12}X_3 + e_4 \tag{5.9}$$

where it is assumed that $e_4$ is uncorrelated with $X_2$ and $X_3$. But suppose that $X_2$ and $X_4$ have a common cause $W$. This will ordinarily mean that $e_4$ and $X_2$ will be correlated, and $W$ should be brought explicitly into the model as a variable that is producing a partly spurious relationship between $X_2$ and $X_4$.

The possibility of spuriousness is an important special case because of the need in social research to eliminate at least some of the many potential explanatory factors that might be used in any given analysis. Presumably, one's aim is to focus on a small number of variables that are directly linked to the dependent variable or that are indirectly linked to it by only one or two steps in a causal sequence. Tests for possible spuriousness should therefore be made. In making such tests, however, one should be on guard against two types of errors: (1) inferring spuriousness when in fact another alternative is correct, and (2) believing that one has eliminated the possibility of spuriousness when actually one has not.    Let us examine each of these possibilities.

## Alternatives to Spuriousness

As is well known, a spurious relationship between $X$ and $Y$ in which a third variable causes both $X$ and $Y$ (e.g., $X \leftarrow Z \rightarrow Y$) can easily be confused empirically with the situation in which $Z$ acts as an intervening variable (e.g., $X \rightarrow Z \rightarrow Y$).    In both cases $r_{xy.z}$ should be approximately zero, and one must rely on knowledge of temporal sequences, additional data, or a priori assumptions to choose between these alternatives.    Kendall and Lazarsfeld (15) have used the term "interpretation" to refer to instances where one introduces intervening variables in order to explain indirect linkages between independent and dependent variables.

Whenever such intervening variables are explicitly included in a set of equations, the coefficients of some of the remaining independent variables will change, but the essential nature of one's causal model will not be affected. For example, in the above instance the introduction of $Z$ as an intervening variable between $X$ and $Y$ will change the regression coefficient to zero, indicating that there is no direct link between $X$ and $Y$.    This means that a change in $X$ would produce no change in $Y$ *if* $Z$ were held constant.    But without any such manipulation of $Z$, a change in $X$ would produce a change in $Z$, resulting in the same change in $Y$ that would be predicted by a model that omitted $Z$ entirely.

In most practical instances, the introduction of control variables will not reduce an original relationship completely to zero.    This leaves room for a large number of alternative explanations.    One possibility already noted is that $Z$ alone is producing a spurious relationship, but that there is random error in the measurement of $Z$.    Another is that two or more factors are responsible for a spurious relationship, with only one of these being controlled. A third is that the relationship is only partly spurious, there being a direct (or indirect) causal linkage as well.    Still another explanation is that one has controlled for an antecedent variable in a causal or developmental sequence.

This last possibility can be illustrated in the case of controls for so-called background factors, such as place of residence, education, race, or religion.    A relationship between $X$ and $Y$ may in fact be spurious, owing to such factors.    But another possibility is that the background factor $B$ is a cause of $X$ but not a direct cause of $Y$.    One such simple situation would be where $B$ causes $X$, which in turn causes $Y$.    It can be shown in this case that a control for $B$ will attenuate the correlation between $X$ and $Y$ but will not affect the expected value of the regression coefficient (2, pp. 86–87).    The stronger the correlation between $B$ and $X$, the greater the reduction in $r_{xy}$.

Thus if $r_{bx} = .80$, and if $r_{xy} = .60$, the expected ratio of $r_{xy.b}{}^2/r_{xy}{}^2$ will be .47. But if $r_{bx} = .30$, this same ratio will be .94.[4] This can be interpreted as follows. Controlling for $B$ reduces the variation in $X$. Since uncontrolled factors will continue to produce variation in $Y$, $X$ will explain a relatively smaller proportion when the background factor has been controlled.

The implication is that inferences involving controls for background factors should be based on the behavior of regression coefficients, rather than measures of association such as the correlation coefficient. The mere fact that a correlation goes down is not enough to infer (partial) spuriousness, even where it can be established that $B$ precedes $X$. Where spuriousness is involved, the regression coefficient as well as the correlation coefficient can be expected to approach zero, and thus we have a means for choosing between these two important alternative possibilities (i.e., $B \rightarrow X \rightarrow Y$ and $X \leftarrow B \rightarrow Y$).

## Spuriousness and Independent Replications

The second warning involves the possibility that one may believe that spuriousness has been ruled out when in fact it has not. Sometimes it is thought that randomization removes all possible sources of spuriousness, but this is hardly true, since one can randomize only people, not the manipulations carried out during the process of experimentation. Possible sources of spuriousness in experimental designs are discussed at some length by Ross and Smith in Chap. 9. These authors explicitly deal with effects of premeasurements and uncontrolled events, particularly as they interact with the experimental variable. But as Wiggins notes in Chap. 10, the experimental variable itself is quite likely to be confounded with other factors (e.g., other manipulations, personality of experimenter), and randomization cannot be used to guard against all these possibilities. Its function is to rule out certain types of disturbing influences by relying on the laws of probability. But since others will always remain, the advantages of experimentation over nonexperimental studies are advantages of degree, rather than kind.

It might also be thought that independent replications can be used to rule out the possibility of spurious relationships, but this is generally not the case. There seem to be at least three types of independent replications, two of which involve explicit or implicit controls for certain variables. The first type, which does not involve such controls, is simple replication through the process of drawing repeated random samples from the same population, or in replicating experimental procedures the same way each time. In both instances there is the recognition that there will be chance factors that, it is hoped, will produce only random fluctuation from one replication to the

---

[4] In this model the expected value of $r_{by.x}$ should be zero, i.e., $r_{by} = r_{bx}r_{xy}$. In the first case this gives $r_{by} = .48$, and in the second $r_{by} = .18$.

next. Probability theory can then be used to rule out these disturbances, on the assumption that they are in no way systematically related to the method of sample selection or replication.

The second and third types of replication are basically similar, differing primarily in practical respects. Both involve intentional variations from one replication to the next. In the one case, a single investigator may subdivide his total population into a number of subpopulations (e.g., young male college graduates, old female college graduates), noting whether or not the relationship between $X$ and $Y$ varies from one subpopulation to the next. Where significant variation occurs, this fact may be conceptualized as involving statistical interaction, a concept which will be considered later in the chapter. Where the relationship remains constant, but significantly different from zero, it might be presumed that spuriousness has been ruled out. Alternatively, replication may be carried out on very diverse populations (e.g., in different American cities, rural areas, or other Westernized countries). Obviously, this third kind of replication involves the same principles, except for the fact that in the second case one may obtain exhaustive subpopulations whereas cross-cultural sampling is likely to be much less systematic.

When one breaks up a population into subpopulations he is explicitly controlling for a given set of variables (e.g., age, sex, or education). When larger populations are compared, the controls are less obvious, but nonetheless real. If one finds similar results in different communities, then community is being controlled. In effect, a large number of variables are implicitly controlled in the process, though these may not be easily identified.

Whether or not the sources of spuriousness are controlled by replication depends on their relationships to those factors that are actually being held constant in the replication process. The picture is most clear in the form of replication where an investigator deliberately compares subpopulations. Let us assume that he uses age, sex, and education as bases for subdivision. Let us also suppose that $X$ and $Y$ are spuriously related, owing to $Z$, as in the following models:

1            2

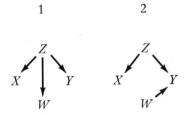

If, as in model 1, $Z$ happens to be highly related to one or more of the control factors, $W$, then $Z$ will also be controlled in the process of subdividing the population. Suppose $Z$ is income level. Then in looking at the old-male-college-graduate subpopulation, we are apt to be looking primarily at high income people as well. In this case, the correlation between $X$ and $Y$ will be reduced. But clearly, if the source of the spurious relationship is unrelated to the control variables, as in model 2, the correlations within each subpopulation may be as large as that within the total population. In fact, if the subpopulation criteria are highly related to either $X$ or $Y$, but not to $Z$, the subpopulation correlations may be *larger* than the total correlation even though the true relationship is completely spurious.

Taking a numerical example, suppose that in both the above models the correlation between $Z$ and $X$ is .80, and that between $Z$ and $Y$ is .60. According to these models, the correlation between $X$ and $Y$ should then be approximately $(.80)(.60) = .48$. Now suppose the factors being controlled in the replication process can be summarized in terms of $W$. In model 1, $W$ is taken as caused by $Z$ or vice versa. If the correlation between $W$ and $Z$ is .80, the expected value of $r_{xy.w}$ is .25; if $r_{wz} = .5$, then $r_{xy.w}$ should be approximately .40, subject of course to sampling errors. In both cases the original correlation is reduced, though not by much in the latter instance. Suppose, however, that $W$ is unrelated to $Z$ but related to $Y$, as in model 2. If $r_{wy} = .8$, then $r_{xy.w}$ should be about .8; if $r_{wy} = .5$, then $r_{xy.w}$ should be about .55.

In this instance, we would be taking out variation in $Y$ that is unrelated to the source of spuriousness, thereby increasing the partial correlation between $Z$ and $Y$ (controlling for $W$). One might then be led to believe that the stronger relationships within the subpopulations are evidence in favor of the theory that $X$ and $Y$ are *not* spuriously related. Needless to say, independent replication will not necessarily rule out the possibility of spuriousness, unless one has independent evidence that the source of spuriousness is in effect being controlled in the replication process.

## 5.4 NONADDITIVE MODELS AND INTERACTION

There are several types of complexities that require modifications in simple linear additive recursive models. One of these is nonlinearity. Since the rather simple forms of nonlinearity occurring most often in sociological research can be handled in terms of algebraic transformations or polynomials, and since nonlinearity presents relatively few conceptual problems, there is no need to discuss specific types of nonlinearity in this very general treatment. The notion of statistical interaction, however, seems conceptually more difficult and also poses some rather interesting challenges with respect to the process of theory building.

In brief, the concept of interaction refers to the nonadditivity of the effects of two or more independent variables on the dependent variable(s). The implication of an additive equation of the form

$$Y = a + b_1 X + b_2 Z + e_y \qquad (5.10)$$

is that if either $X$ or $Z$ is held constant, the slope relating the other independent variable to $Y$ will always be the same, regardless of the numerical value of the control variable. The notion of additivity can obviously be generalized to any number of independent variables. This means that if all such variables have additive effects, one can safely use the phrase "other things being equal" as a simple qualification to any generalization he may wish to make concerning the relationship between the dependent variable and one or more independent variables. In a very real sense he may speak about *the* (single) relationship between $X$ and $Y$.

In the case of three variables where $X$ and $Y$ have been measured as interval scales, additive relationships can be represented as in Fig. 5.2, which allows for the possibility that the relationship between $X$ and $Y$ is nonlinear. The essential point is that additive relationships will give parallel curves, meaning that a change in the numerical value of $Z$, the control variable, will simply shift the level of intercept of the curve but nothing else. The same will hold in the case of curves relating $Y$ to the other independent variable $Z$.

If all variables have been categorized, the additive property can be conceptualized in terms of percentages. Let us illustrate with a simple numerical example. Suppose we have an original relationship between a dependent variable $Y$ and an independent variable $X$ as follows:

|  | $X_1$ | $X_2$ | $X_3$ |
|---|---|---|---|
| $Y_1$ | 370 | 340 | 190 |
| $Y_2$ | 230 | 260 | 410 |
|  | 600 | 600 | 600 |
| Percentage in $Y_2$ | 38.3 | 43.3 | 68.3 |

Suppose we now get the following results when we control for $Z$:

|  | $Z_1$ | | | $Z_2$ | | | $Z_3$ | | |
|---|---|---|---|---|---|---|---|---|---|
|  | $X_1$ | $X_2$ | $X_3$ | $X_1$ | $X_2$ | $X_3$ | $X_1$ | $X_2$ | $X_3$ |
| $Y_1$ | 80 | 140 | 120 | 140 | 120 | 60 | 150 | 80 | 10 |
| $Y_2$ | 20 | 60 | 180 | 60 | 80 | 140 | 150 | 120 | 90 |
|  | 100 | 200 | 300 | 200 | 200 | 200 | 300 | 200 | 100 |
| Percentage in $Y_2$ | 20 | 30 | 60 | 30 | 40 | 70 | 50 | 60 | 90 |

We immediately see that each of the partial relationships is stronger than the total association between $X$ and $Y$ and that the percentage of cases in $Y_2$ is generally the lowest in $Z_1$ and the highest in $Z_3$. From the marginals we also note that $X$ and $Z$ are related, though we are purposely begging the question of causality between $X$ and $Z$. The important fact about the second set of tables is, however, that the relationship between $X$ and $Y$, as indicated by the percentage of cases in $Y_2$, remains the same regardless of the $Z$ category. There are always 10 percent more $Y_2$'s in $X_2$ than $X_1$, and 30 percent more $Y_2$'s in $X_3$ than $X_2$. We could therefore say that,

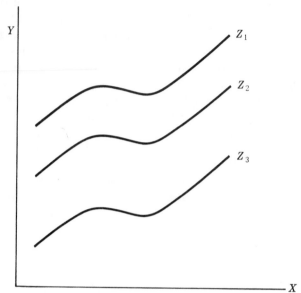

**Fig. 5.2.    Additive, though Nonlinear, Relationships.**

regardless of $Z$, the relationship between $X$ and $Y$ remains the same.    Notice, also, that if a new set of tables were formed by interchanging the role of $X$ and $Z$, one could likewise claim the relationship between $Z$ and $Y$ to be independent of $X$.

Whenever slopes are not parallel, or differences in percentages not the same, we speak of interaction among the independent variables.    Thus the concept of interaction consists essentially of a residual category of all types of effects that are nonadditive.    It should be noted, of course, that interaction always refers to the joint effects of two or more independent variables on some particular dependent variable.    It is quite possible that $X$ and $Z$ will have nonadditive effects on $Y$, while having additive effects on other dependent variables.

Since nonadditive relationships constitute a residual category, it would be rather surprising if interaction effects could always be interpreted in a simple manner.    Let us therefore examine some alternative ways of conceptualizing interaction.

## The Asymmetric Approach: Specification

In many instances the investigator is focusing on a particular set of independent variables using another set as control variables.    His interest in the control variables is presumably secondary.    These control variables may be used to specify the relationship between an independent variable $X$ and the dependent variable $Y$. For example, in the above hypothetical data, the relationship between $X$ and $Y$ might differ from one category of $Z$ to the next. Conceivably, there might be no differences in percentages for $Z_1$, small differences for $Z_2$, and large ones for $Z_3$. Or the differences might even be in opposite directions. If so, one could not speak of a single relationship between $X$ and $Y$ but would have to specify the value of $Z$ as well.

The asymmetry of this approach should be explicitly noted. One might just as well have focused on the relationships between $Z$ and $Y$, using $X$ as a control or conditioning variable. As was mentioned previously, if the relationships between $X$ and $Y$ are found to differ, this will also hold true for those between $Z$ and $Y$. As long as this is clearly recognized, then, there should be no conceptual problem. It would seem preferable, however, to think in terms of the notion of interaction, where by implication one is almost forced to treat both independent variables in a parallel way, referring to their joint effects.

In terms of more ultimate objectives in theory building, the asymmetric specification of conditions ordinarily gives a one-sided picture, a fact that is sometimes not fully appreciated. But in exploratory analyses this is often necessary, particularly in instances where the control variable is a crude indicator of a complex set of factors or when the theoretical role of a control variable is poorly understood. A specific illustration may help to clarify this particular point.

Hyman (12), and Kendall and Lazarsfeld (15), refer to specification by time and place. For example, the relationship between $X$ and $Y$ may differ from one population to another or from one time period to the next. Suppose this were in fact the case. What would one conclude? A pessimistic interpretation would be that generalization is impossible or at least that a generalization must always include a reference to a specific population and time period. But a little thought should convince one that such a practice would be theoretically useless: Chicago on one day is not Chicago on the very next day. Quite clearly, whenever the relationship between $X$ and $Y$ differs one must search for a *general* explanation that involves introducing *variables,* rather than mere references to time and place.

In the search for variables that may interact with $X$ in producing effects on $Y$, one may attempt to order his populations (or time periods) so that relevant factors may be located. For example, suppose that the slopes of the relationships between $X$ and $Y$ become steeper and steeper as city size increases. Then city size and $X$ might be inferred to produce nonadditive effects on $Y$.

The larger and more heterogeneous the populations being compared, or the longer the time periods, the more difficult it may be to locate or infer the existence of specific variables that interact with $X$. Thus if relationships vary from country to country, or region to region, it may be hard to determine why this should be.   If smaller more homogeneous populations differ, however, the reasons for such differences may be easier to specify.   Regardless of whether or not this last assertion proves valid, the essential point is that, whenever interaction is found, an attempt should be made to explain the inter- action in terms of specific variables.   Of course when this cannot be done, it is obviously preferable to specify in terms of time and place than to ignore differences altogether or to obscure the differences by computing single sum- marizing measures.

## The Symmetric Approach

As implied above, it would appear that a symmetric formulation would be superior in terms of its general potential for theory building.   However, it is by no means a simple matter to conceptualize interaction effects theoreti- cally, though they may be *described* empirically in terms of equations that are symmetric with respect to the treatment of the independent variables.

In the statistical literature, interaction is commonly handled by adding terms to ordinary additive models.   Thus one may write

$$Y = a + b_1 X_1 + b_2 X_2 + c I_{x_1 x_2} + e_y \tag{5.11}$$

where the term $I_{x_1 x_2}$ refers to the interaction effect of the two variables.   This may, of course, be extended to any number of independent variables, provided that one also introduces terms representing higher-order interactions involving joint effects of three or more variables.   Thus for three independent variables one could write

$$Y = a + b_1 X_1 + b_2 X_2 + b_3 X_3 + c_1 I_{x_1 x_2} + c_2 I_{x_1 x_3} + c_3 I_{x_2 x_3} + c_4 I_{x_1 x_2 x_3} + e_y \tag{5.12}$$

There are now three first-order interactions among all pairs of independent variables and a single second-order interaction $I_{x_1 x_2 x_3}$ among all three.

A second-order interaction can be interpreted as an interaction of an interaction.   Thus the *interaction* between $X_1$ and $X_2$ varies according to the value of $X_3$, and similarly (by symmetry) for the remaining first-order interactions.   In terms of slopes, this means that a second-order interaction would give a difference of differences in slopes.   With respect to percentages, it would involve a difference of differences of differences in percentages (6).

Allowing for these interaction terms introduces unknown coefficients, in the form of the $c_i$, which must be estimated from one's data.   In many instances there will be too many such unknowns for unique identification, and simplifying assumptions must be made concerning at least some of the coefficients.   The simple additive models of the equations of (5.1) obviously involve the assumptions that all the $c_i$ are zero.

Ross and Smith use this general type of model in their discussion of experimental designs in Chap. 9.   Their essential point is that many earlier treatments of experimental designs did not satisfactorily handle the interaction terms, particularly those involving higher-order interactions. In effect, these terms have been assumed to involve zero coefficients. Ross and Smith show that, depending on the choice of design, one must always make a certain number of a priori assumptions regarding main effects and interaction effects. As the number of independent variables becomes larger, the number of possible interaction terms increases very rapidly, necessitating numerous such a priori assumptions. While one may quite plausibly assume away most higher-order interaction terms, it seems advisable to be explicitly aware of the fact that one is doing so.

In general, one can approximate reality to a high degree by introducing various interaction terms, and furthermore one can often break down total effects empirically into so-called main effects and interaction effects. This is very useful for descriptive purposes and to make statistical tests for interactions. But it does not follow that, if interaction has been found, it is thereby simple to make theoretical sense out of the interaction. This raises the important question of how one goes about *explaining* interaction in terms of causal arguments. Two lines of attack will be discussed; perhaps others can be devised.

One approach involves identifying the interaction term with a specific variable that is simultaneously a function of the remaining variables but also a causal force in its own right. As was noted in Chap. 4, Lenski (17) has argued that status inconsistency may produce strains on individuals which, under certain circumstances, may lead to political liberalism. Liberalism, then, might be explained by means of the main effects of education, occupation, income, and ethnic background plus interaction terms involving various combinations of inconsistencies in status. Since these inconsistency measures are themselves functions of the individual status variables, certain complications are introduced in the form of identification problems (4).

A second approach entails working with specific types of nonadditive models, while attempting to specify a theoretical rationale for making use of such alternatives. For example, multiplicative models of the form $Y = kX_1X_2$ would seem appropriate whenever one wished to argue that *two* conditions were simultaneously necessary in order for $Y$ to occur. Such reasoning extended to continuous variables would suggest a multiplicative model of the above form. As $X_2$ increases, the slope of the relationship between $X_1$ and $Y$ also increases, giving a fan-shaped effect as in Fig. 5.3.

As I have discussed elsewhere (6), the use of indicators as measures of $X_1$ and $X_2$ will ordinarily require one to modify the above simple type of multiplicative model by introducing constant terms into the equation. Using primed values for the measured indicators gives

$$Y = (a + bX_1')(c + dX_2') + e_y \qquad (5.13)$$

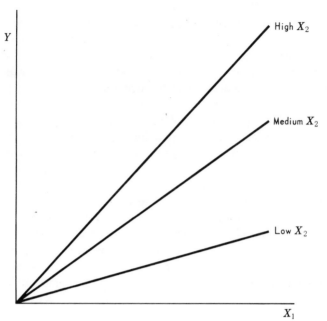

**Fig. 5.3.**    **Nonadditive, Multiplicative Relationships:** $Y = kX_1X_2$.

which, when expanded, reduces to an additive form plus a cross-product interaction term. Thus

$$Y = ac + bcX_1' + adX_2' + bdX_1'X_2' + e_y$$
$$= A + B_1X_1' + B_2X_2' + CX_1'X_2' + e_y \tag{5.14}$$

Where such a theoretical rationale can be developed, one therefore has an explanation for the interaction term, but it might make little sense conceptually to think in terms of main effects and interaction effects. The two independent variables simply fit together multiplicatively rather than additively. Likewise, a general multiplicative model involving three independent variables can be seen to imply one second-order and three first-order interactions.

     This type of multiplicative model may be generally appropriate whenever motivation theory is involved, as a number of social psychologists have made use of theories in which motivated behavior is taken as a multiplicative function of some internal state (e.g., motive, need, utility, drive) and a second factor involving an expectancy term (1,6). A similar approach is also used by Palmore and Hammond (19) who take deviance as a multiplicative function of (1) barriers to legitimate opportunities and (2) access to illegitimate opportunities. This multiplicative model implies that deviance will be low unless there is *both* a denial of access to legitimate opportunities *and* a high degree of exposure to illegitimate ones.

     Such a formulation calls for a definite search for interaction effects among indicators of each of these factors. An examination of pairs of variables supposedly affecting the two opportunity factors should lead to the following results: variables affecting the *same* opportunity factor should not necessarily produce nonadditive effects on deviance, but those which affect *different* opportunity factors should yield interaction terms as in Eq. (5.13). This would lead to a series of predicted interaction effects that would not ordinarily be expected by common sense.

## Implications for Analysis

It is usually difficult to theorize in advance of data collection as to which variables will operate jointly to produce interaction effects. This is particularly so when the number of possible independent variables is large. Furthermore, it is conceivable that standard analysis techniques would show so-called main effects of some variables to be negligible, whereas interaction effects might be substantial. Given the possibility of using high-speed computer programs for the purpose of a preliminary screening or searching for explanatory variables, certain rather general types of strategies are implied by the above discussion.

Where the number of independent variables is not too large (e.g., less than 30) it would seem advisable to form all possible pairs of these variables to look for first-order interactions on each dependent variable. Where first-order interactions are large, one might also combine these particular independent variables into triplets and search for significant second-order interactions. Although there is always the possibility of higher-order interactions in the absence of lower-order interactions, it would generally seem safe to assume such higher-order interactions to be zero unless there were theoretical grounds for suspecting otherwise.

The outcome of this kind of dragnet search for interactions is likely to be that a certain number of statistically significant interactions will be found. Where the number approximates what would be expected by chance, then one is probably justified in simplifying his theoretical argument by neglecting such interactions. Where the number of first-order interactions is relatively large, then one must search for patterns among these interactions. I have suggested (6) that the use of explicit mathematical formulations, such as multiplicative models, may be a useful theoretical device for ordering what might otherwise seem to be a very confusing set of results, in which some combinations of variables produce interaction effects while others do not.

In using these search operations and nonadditive models, one should ordinarily attempt a symmetric approach. Present practice seems too unsystematic. The investigator usually focuses on a relatively small number of major independent variables, trying out selected control variables in order to specify his relationships. Machine techniques seem superior in two respects: they are more efficient in terms of time and money, and they are likely to be more systematic in the sense that all combinations of variables can be investigated without regard to the investigator's individual biases.

## 5.5  EVALUATING RELATIVE IMPORTANCE OF VARIABLES

Social scientists commonly make verbal statements to the effect that one variable is more important than another. It may not be realized, however, that in order to *test* such assertions one must commit himself to a specific causal model. Thus evaluating relative importance constitutes an advanced stage in the scientific process. Furthermore, one must pay careful attention to the types of measures used, their statistical properties, and what is meant by the notion of relative importance.

If it can be assumed that causal factors are operating completely independently of each other, so that they are uncorrelated in a population or independently manipulatable in an experimental design, then the problem is quite straightforward. One of the main advantages of the complex experimental designs studied by statisticians is their symmetry, through which causal variables are made independent of each other. In such designs one can break up the total variation in the dependent variable into components unambiguously associated with each independent variable. But complications are introduced if the causal variables are themselves interrelated. If intercorrelations are very high, one encounters the problem of multicollinearity involving extremely large sampling errors (13,22).

When causal factors are intercorrelated, one must make assumptions about why the correlations exist. This will involve the construction of causal models, as discussed earlier in the chapter. We have thus far been concerned only with the question of *testing* the adequacy of any given model, however. Having decided on some model, one may then wish to say more about the relative contributions, both direct and indirect, of each of the variables in the system. It is here that adequate conceptualization becomes highly important. As Boudon shows in Chap. 6, selection of the proper coefficients is not at all simple.

There seem to be at least two intuitive ways of conceiving of relative importance (3). The first might be labeled a quantitative approach. The underlying idea is that one should compare the relative magnitudes of total or partial correlation coefficients. Whichever variable produces the higher correlations is then called the more important variable. Thus one may compare the relative importance of occupation, race, or religious denomination on voting behavior, using controls on the remaining two variables in each case. This approach seems to involve an extension of analysis techniques used whenever the independent variables are completely unrelated. However, it breaks down whenever the variables are themselves causally connected.

A second theoretical criterion has been more frequently used in historical discussions of causal chains.  In brief, the argument runs as follows.  If *A* causes *B* which in turn causes *C*, then *A* is more important than *B*.  Changes in *A* are more basic in the sense that these changes will themselves produce changes in *B*.  For example, it might be argued that technological or economic factors are more fundamental than ideological ones, the claim being made that changes in the economy produce changes in belief systems that in turn affect other variables.  It can be seen rather simply that this theoretical or causal criterion need not lead to the same conclusions as the quantitative criterion.  As has already been pointed out, in the simple causal chain $W \rightarrow X \rightarrow Y$, the correlation between $X$ and $Y$ will ordinarily be stronger than that between $W$ and $Y$.  Also, of course, the expected value of $r_{wy.x}$ is zero since the effect of $W$ is only indirect.  Thus in this case the quantitative criterion would point to $X$ as more important than $W$, whereas the simple theoretical criterion would favor $W$.

A clarification of issues is therefore needed.  I shall begin by attempting to distinguish between two very different goals, namely, evaluating relative importance and establishing scientific laws.  It will be pointed out that different measures are appropriate to these separate goals.  Specific measures of importance will be discussed by Boudon in the next chapter.

## Causal Laws versus Relative Importance

In order to clarify the basic distinction between evaluating relative importance in some particular instance and establishing a general causal law, let us first consider what we may mean when we say that one variable is more important than another.  We commonly find statements to the effect that *A*, *B*, and *C* were the most important factors contributing to the downfall of Rome or to the differences between race relations in Brazil and the United States.  Or we may ask why a particular building caught on fire or why a bridge collapsed.  Even without the help of general scientific laws, it is easy to see that there may be a multitude of reasons why any change phenomenon *could* occur.  There are any number of reasons why a bridge might collapse or a building catch on fire.  But presumably not all these potential causes would be operative, and we are faced with the problem of determining which of the factors actually did produce a change in the dependent variable in this *particular* instance.

The task is made relatively simple if we already know the appropriate causal laws and if all causal factors operate independently of one another.  To take a very simple example, suppose we have established that a given dependent variable $Y$ is related causally to four independent variables by the formula

$$Y = 5 + 7X_1 - 4X_2 + 11X_3 + 2X_4 \qquad (5.15)$$

Let us assume that there are no errors involved in this equation. Now suppose someone tells us that in some particular instance the $Y$ value has been changed from 23 to 41. How would we evaluate the relative importance of the various $X_i$ in determining this change? Clearly, we could not say that $X_3$ is the most important factor merely because the steepest slope is associated with this variable. We do know that *if* each of the $X_i$ were to change by exactly one unit, then $X_3$ would have more influence in changing $Y$ than any other single variable. But $X_3$ may not have changed at all, whereas $X_4$ may have increased by nine units, thereby accounting for all of the change in $Y$. The point is that we cannot evaluate relative importance from the causal law alone. We must also be given information about the amount of change in each independent variable in the particular case or cases under study.

One must learn to distinguish, then, between *causal laws* that presumably hold true in general or under certain specified conditions and *causes* that are operating in any given case. The former may be much more complex and will generally involve many more variables. But in any given instance, certain of the variables that appear in the causal model may conveniently be ignored. In studying changes in the dependent variable, one may assume that certain independent variables remain essentially constant; thereby it is possible to eliminate such variables from consideration.

One should also be careful to distinguish between situations in which he wishes to account for *variations* or changes in a dependent variable and those in which he is attempting to explain why the average value is at a certain *level*. One may sometimes be primarily interested in accounting for a uniformly high mean value of the dependent variable, whereas in other instances his focus may be on accounting for the size of the standard deviation. The absolute level of the mean $Y$ value will of course be determined by the scores on *all* the independent variables, while variation among $Y$ scores may be due primarily to one or two of the independent variables.

In most instances, scientific interest is concerned with explaining variation. Presumably, if an investigator finds scores that are relatively uniform from one case to the next, he is less likely to ask why such a uniformity should occur than when he is confronted by extreme variation. Of course, there may be a comparison with other cases taken from a *different* population, but in such a situation one is again examining the problem of accounting for variation. Suppose, for example, one finds uniformly high segregation of nonwhites in all large American cities. There may be such a low degree of variation that it is difficult to find explanatory variables that account for more than a very small proportion of this variation. But presumably an investigator must have some basis for comparison in mind when he says that the level of segregation is high, though uniform. Perhaps he is comparing the actual degree of separation of races with what he would expect by chance under a random distribution. Or he may be implicitly comparing the segregation of nonwhites with that of other minorities.

In certain practical instances, the scientist may be called upon to explain mean values of the dependent variable, rather than variation. He may be asked, for example, to find ways of reducing the absolute level of juvenile delinquency, rather than of reducing the variation from one community to the next. If causal laws have already been established, he may then search among the presumed independent variables for those which are most subject to planned manipulation. By changing one or more of these variables he may then reduce the delinquency rates. But there is no implication that the particular variables he has manipulated are in any absolute sense inherently more important than certain others that in this particular case do not happen to vary. Changes produced in one of the latter variables might, under other circumstances, give rise to much greater changes in the dependent variable.

In short, the importance of a variable is always relative to particular problems and purposes. One simply does not ask questions of the sort: Which is more important, volume or temperature, in determining the pressure of a gas? Instead, one states a law interrelating the three variables and then applies the· law in particular instances. This rather obvious point has implications for one's choice of measures and the uses to which the measures are put. Measures are, of course, constructed in order to make various kinds of comparisons. It follows that measures used to compare different sets of data in order to infer general laws may be quite different from those used to evaluate relative importance in specific situations. We turn next to a comparison of standardized and unstandardized measures.

## *Standardized and Unstandardized Measures*

Correlation coefficients are standardized regression coefficients. The standardization procedure has the advantage of yielding a measure that always varies between plus and minus unity, regardless of the units of measurement or the standard deviations in either variable. This has considerable intuitive appeal and affords the scientist a comparative measure that tells him how well he is doing in terms of predictive power: the proportion of the variation in $Y$ associated with $X$. Given this advantage, why shouldn't one always compute standardized measures of this sort?

The answer to this question has already been implied by the previous discussion. Standardization makes sense when one wishes to refer to specific populations and to measure importance in this context. If one is comparing several independent variables with respect to their relative contributions to some dependent variable, given a fixed amount of variation in each of the independent variables, then correlation coefficients make sense. Better still, one should compute standardized dependence coefficients (or path coefficients) as discussed by Boudon in the next chapter. These latter coefficients enable one to sort out the contributions of each independent variable even where one assumes that they are interconnected by rather complex causal paths.

But if one wishes to state general laws in hypothetical form, then standardized measures may be misleading unless one recognizes that the standardized measures may vary from population to population even where the underlying laws are the same. Once the major point is understood, there should be relatively few problems in passing back and forth between the two types of measures. The situation can be seen quite readily in the simple case of two variables $X$ and $Y$. One can think of the correlation coefficient $r_{xy}$ as a dependent variable, being determined by two factors: (1) the (causal) law connecting $X$ and $Y$ as represented by $b_{yx}$ and (2) some features peculiar to each specific population (e.g., means and standard deviations). Thus

$$r_{xy} = b_{yx} \left[ \frac{s_x}{s_y} \right] \qquad (5.16)$$

Similar expressions can be written for partial correlation coefficients. For example,

$$r_{xy.z} = b_{yx.z} \left[ \frac{\sqrt{1 - r_{xz}^2}}{\sqrt{1 - r_{yz}^2}} \frac{s_x}{s_y} \right] \qquad (5.17)$$

In both of the above expressions the terms within the brackets will be peculiar to the population studied.

The coefficient $b_{yx}$ (or $b_{yx.z}$) represents a hypothetical situation. As already noted, it indicates that *if* $X$ were to change by one unit, *then* $Y$ would change by $b_{yx}$ units. There is no assumption that $X$ will actually change or vary, and if $X$ is taken as exogenous the theorist will not be in a position to account for actual variation in $X$. In other words, from the standpoint of the theory, variation in exogenous variables will be taken as accidental or peculiar to each population. Even with endogenous variables, since we have been assuming that unknown disturbance terms (represented by the $e_i$) will be operating on any given population, we cannot account theoretically for the *amount* of variation in any of the variables in the system. We have found it necessary to make simplifying assumptions about *how* the disturbance terms operate, but it is asking too much to require us to specify a priori the *sizes* of the error terms.

The factor $s_x/s_y$ therefore represents a term that cannot be predicted in advance without some very strong a priori assumptions regarding each specific population. One can point out that an unstandardized regression coefficient can likewise seldom be predicted in advance of all data collection. This is certainly true, given the present status of social science theory. But one can at least make meaningful comparisons of regression coefficients across populations. Having found a numerical value for $b_{yx}$ in one population, an investigator can contrast its value in other populations, noting whether or not it remains constant and attempting to explain interaction effects when it does not. Where invariance is found, one infers that the same laws are operative even though the correlation coefficients may be quite different.

It seems advisable to comment briefly on a few apparent difficulties with unstandardized regression coefficients. One problem with these coefficients is, of course, that the numerical value of $b_{yx}$ depends on the choice of measurement units (e.g., dollars versus pennies). This makes comparisons difficult from one *variable* to the next, though not from population to population. In a sense, the numerical value of $b_{yx}$ may be taken as a function of (1) a law itself, and (2) the investigator's choice of units of measurement. But the latter factor is completely under the investigator's control and can be manipulated in terms of perfect mathematical relationships between units (e.g., 100 pennies = 1 dollar). This is quite different from the previous equation linking correlations with regression coefficients; the factor $s_x/s_y$ is an *empirical* quantity which is not known a priori and which depends on variables left out of the theoretical system. When the investigator shifts units of measurement, in other words, he can manipulate the values of $b_{yx}$ very simply. But when he changes populations he has no *theoretical* basis for determining $s_x/s_y$. Therefore if he examines only the correlation coefficients he cannot separate the constant law component from the particular population component.

A more obvious sort of difficulty is encountered in using regression coefficients with ordinal data. There are certain kinds of variables for which absolute variation is meaningless. The only sensible notion may be that of relative position within a given population. For example, prestige or rank involves an ordering of individuals within a particular group. Ruling out ties, this means that two equal-sized populations must, by definition, have the same distribution of scores on such variables (i.e., the ranks 1, 2, . . . , $N$). If this variable is taken as the independent variable $X$, then there can be no variation in $X$ across populations of the same size. Hence $s_x$ (or $\sigma_x$) is a function of $N$ only, and one of the sources of variability in correlation coefficients can be removed. If this is also true for the dependent variable $Y$, then it would make no difference whether standardized or unstandardized coefficients were used, since the latter would automatically be standardized in the measurement process.

How many variables must be measured in terms of rankings is an open question. Certainly this makes sense for most if not all status variables. But what about personality traits, such as authoritarianism? One must be careful not to confuse our *present* measurement capabilities with what is ultimately desirable. Thus one can measure income in dollars, but relative income may be more significant than absolute. On the other hand, measures of personality traits may be so crude that one resorts to ordinal techniques for analysis. But variation in degree might be conceived theoretically in terms of some absolute quantities that are as yet unmeasurable. Thus if we wished to relate authoritarianism to prejudice, it might be better to compare two groups by using absolute scores (as crude as these would be), rather than by converting them to ranks within each group. Authoritarianism might vary much more in one group than in another. If so, we would expect a stronger correlation in the first group, unless other causes of prejudice (unrelated to authoritarianism) also varied more in this same group.

## 5.6   LAWS VERSUS GENERALIZATIONS TO POPULATIONS

As was implied in the preceding section, a number of both philosophical and practical questions seem to be tied to the issue, Should scientific objectives involve generalizations to populations or to relationships among variables? Ideally, one might agree with the proposition that scientific laws should be stated in the if-then form, but that their implications should be tested in terms of predictions appropriate to real populations. Thus in genetics, theories concerning microlevel postulated properties, such as genes, can be tested by studying frequency distributions of measured variables in concrete populations. The problem is not so simple, however, when the populations under study are not closed and are subject not only to outside disturbances but also to unknown differential migration, birth, and death rates.

I have taken the position that if one is to make headway, either in terms of theoretical deductions or empirical tests, he must assume that the theoretical system is closed in some sense. I would also like to argue that it must be assumed that *populations* are closed, if one wishes to use sample or population data for verification purposes. Furthermore, there must be some correspondence between the closure of the theoretical system (consisting of *variables*) and the population (consisting of people or other distinct units of analysis).

It is not difficult to describe what might be called a completely closed system in either the theoretical or empirical sense. We might say that a theoretical system is completely closed if *all* variables assumed to be operative are explicitly included in the system. This would mean that, ruling out the possibility of measurement error, there would be no error terms in any of the equations. The system would be completely deterministic. In a completely closed population, we would have a population which is completely isolated from the impact of outside environmental influences and in which no individuals either enter or leave the population.

In this simple case, one's theory (e.g., the simultaneous equations) would specify exactly what should take place within the population, given a set of initial values. In many instances, such theories might predict that a stable equilibrium would be reached, though it is also possible that there would be continued oscillations or an eventual explosion. The important point is that in such completely closed systems the dynamics for change would be supplied internally and would be specified in terms of equations that might allow for reciprocal causation, delayed feedbacks, and other possible complications. Assuming perfect measurement, the predictions could then be tested on the closed population. As Coleman notes in Chap. 11, if the population were studied at a single point in time, one would have to assume that the system had reached a stable equilibrium in order to make valid inferences. Ideally, one's theory should be formulated in dynamic terms in order to ascertain whether or not stable equilibrium would be implied.

One must now ask whether there is any counterpart, in the case of populations, to error terms introduced by variables left out of the system. I have termed theoretical systems as closed if they meet certain assumptions regarding error terms. Can we define a population as closed in a similar sense, recognizing that such an empirical system will never be completely closed? This is an extremely important question, I believe, because rarely can we find human populations that are anywhere near completely closed. If not, then we must try to determine what assumptions must be made in order that we may make valid inferences from population data.

There seem to be two kinds of reasons why populations are not closed. First, persons within a given population are influenced by outside events and members of other populations. Second, they migrate back and forth between populations, so that persons subjected to causal processes in one population may move to another; such movements give rise to erroneous impressions of what has occurred within the second population. If the theoretical assumptions regarding error terms are to be realistic, then they must not be violated as a result of the outside influence process or through migration. In the remarks that follow I shall confine the discussion to migration, as the influence problem appears to be considerably more complex.

Consider an admittedly ridiculous example. Suppose one is attempting to make probability statements concerning drawings from decks of cards. In the usual deck of 52 cards, suit has been made independent of face value; i.e., there is one card of each suit for each face value. The probability of randomly drawing an ace is $\frac{4}{52}$, whereas that of drawing an ace, given that the card is a spade, is numerically the same, namely $\frac{1}{13}$. Now suppose that there are several decks of cards on a table and that cards can migrate nonrandomly from one deck to the next. What would we have to assume to make probability statements about drawings from some particular deck? This is quite analogous to the situation faced by a sociological investigator whose study is confined to a single population and who is not given information concerning migration to and from the remaining populations.

Suppose that cards move back and forth in order to join other cards of the same suit, but that their face value has no bearing on this movement. Then several spades may move from deck A to deck B, while hearts move to deck A. Knowing nothing more, we would not wish to estimate the proportion of spades or hearts in a given deck. If we could assume perfect knowledge and rationality on the part of the cards, we would expect that ultimately the sifting would result in new decks that were homogeneous with respect to suit. But the distribution with respect to *face values* should be essentially random. Given larger populations, we would expect uniform distributions of face values that differed from each other only by chance.

This particular migration process would result in changes in central tendency and dispersion with respect to suit. But what about the *relationship* between suit and face value? The expected relationship should still be zero. In other words, knowledge of suit should not help one predict face value, or vice versa. An investigator wishing to study this relationship among all cards would not be systematically misled if he examined only one population. If his interest were in central tendency or dispersion of the single variable, however, he would be in difficulty.

Now suppose that cards migrate for *two* reasons, to be with other cards of similar suit *and* face value. Before the sorting process had reached the ultimate stage of double homogeneity, one might expect to find, say, that the diamond face cards were concentrated in one deck, which also contained several spade 2s and 3s. If one were to examine only this single deck he would find a *relationship* between face value and suit owing to this selective migration process.

Returning to the real world, which is considerably more complex, this means that our inferences concerning relationships among variables should not be affected (except for random errors) provided that reasons for migration are directly related to only one of the variables in the theoretical system. Suppose, for example, we are studying the relationship between occupational prestige and political conservatism. Individuals obviously migrate for reasons which are directly relevant to occupational careers. If there are causal mechanisms that work to produce high conservatism among those with prestigeful occupations, then someone with a high occupation will carry his conservatism from one community to the next. If the same causal mechanisms are operative in both populations, we can legitimately infer these by examining the relationship between occupation and conservatism in either community. We could not, however, make valid general inferences concerning occupational levels or dispersions by examining only one population.

Now suppose that persons tend to select communities according to *combinations* of factors. Perhaps high-prestige liberals move into college communities where there is also a disproportionate number of low-income conservatives (e.g., a Southern university town). Conservatism may then be *inversely* related to occupational prestige. It would appear that objections to studying atypical communities refer primarily to just such situations. A study of a large metropolitan area might produce central tendency and dispersion measures that are not at all typical of the nation as a whole or even of other large cities. But we assume, in effect, that selective migration of the above type does not occur. Presumably, there are so many diverse reasons for moving to such communities that we can realistically make the assumption that the effects of migration will not systematically distort relationships among variables.

Whether or not a population can be considered closed in this looser sense therefore depends on the variables under consideration. In the case of conservatism and occupation, one might very well find selective migration (in the double sense) occurring *within* a metropolitan area. That is, high-prestige liberals might congregate in a particular suburb surrounding a local college. If so, one's closed population should be defined so as to include this suburb, but a study focused on this suburb alone would produce misleading results. The practical implication is clear in this instance: the investigator should consider reasons for migration and differential sifting (and perhaps birth and death rates) in selecting the boundaries of his population. Having done so, he should then make his assumptions explicit.

Let me restate the argument quite simply. Reality requires that we deal with populations that are not completely closed. Yet we must make some assumptions regarding distortions produced by lack of complete closure. It seems reasonable to assume, in the case of migration, that movements back and forth may very well affect measures of central tendency and dispersion of single variables. This will likewise be true in the case of outside influences coming from the wider environment. The possibility of selective migration is thus another reason for preferring unstandardized regression coefficients, provided that we are at least willing to make the assumption that the migration process does not disturb relationships among variables.

As long as one is prepared to ignore distortions in means and standard deviations, he can consider populations closed for the purposes of inferring relationships among variables. If the latter relationships are also affected, then either one must redefine his population so that it is reasonable to assume that this is no longer so, *or* he must bring the disturbance factors explicitly into his theoretical system. In the migration example, this would mean locating both the in- and out-migrants, measuring their characteristics separately, and introducing correction factors to compensate for specific distortions.

A discussion of sampling design, such as that of Lazerwitz in Chap. 8, generally presupposes that one is primarily interested in generalizing to specific populations or in comparing various subpopulations. If one's objectives are descriptive he need not go any further than this. Indeed, the field of sampling is sufficiently complex that it would be asking for trouble to compound sampling questions with those of causal or theoretical inferences, which take one's analysis several steps beyond obtaining estimates of population parameters.

Nevertheless, a number of important questions deserving the attention of sampling specialists arise when one attempts to generalize to laws rather than to specific populations. For example, the rationale for stratified sampling seems relatively clear-cut. But suppose, for reasons of convenience, one happens to stratify by a *dependent* variable (e.g., by political party registrations or by membership in voluntary organizations). He may then be manipulating the variation in such a dependent variable in a misleading way. Or perhaps one's clusters in an area sample have been formed as a result of selective migration. What implications, if any, would one's design have for his theoretical inferences? These and other similar questions will have to be answered if we wish to reduce the gap between theory and empirical research practice. As always, one of the first tasks is to pose the right questions.

## 5.7  CONCLUDING REMARKS

To some readers it will undoubtedly seem premature to consider seriously many of the issues raised in the present chapter, to say nothing of the kinds of sophisticated approaches discussed by Boudon in the next chapter. Rarely do sociologists have legitimate interval scales, nor are they in a position to make realistic assumptions to the effect that measurement errors are negligible, confounding influences absent, or linear additive models appropriate. When one is dealing with crude indicators represented as nominal scales, why should he concern himself with such questions?

I believe there are several reasons why these topics should be seriously considered by students of methodology. First, it seems useful to attempt to state the ideal and to clarify issues and objectives even when present practices fall far short of the mark. There is a recognized danger of becoming so perfectionistic that one is immobilized in the process. If one is fully aware of his research limitations and the unrealistic assumptions he is required to make, he may be tempted to give up the venture before he begins. This would appear to be a necessary risk, but one that can be counteracted by the dictum: Don't be afraid to oversimplify reality. It will then always be possible to introduce complexities a few at a time.

Second, it is quite clear that social scientists do in fact attempt to assess relative importance, appraise alternative theories, and interpret their research findings even where adequate guidelines are unavailable. In so doing, they leave many of their assumptions hidden from view. For example, in comparing the supposed effects of two independent variables, an investigator may not recognize that he is implicitly making use of a very simple causal model. Were such a model made explicit, he might be led to the formulation of a more complex one that more adequately reflected his basic argument. The repression of assumptions, like its psychodynamic counterpart, does not make these assumptions disappear. If there is random measurement error, but if this fact is ignored, one does not somehow or other arrive at correct conclusions that would have been missed had measurement error been recognized. Instead, hiding one's assumptions merely makes it more difficult to locate plausible alternatives that might ultimately be more realistic.

Finally, the kinds of considerations discussed here and in subsequent chapters give real insights into the nature of the relationship between theory and research. In the process of theory building one begins with simple causal models, tests to see if they fit the data, modifies them until he is willing to commit himself (temporarily) to a given model, and then finally attempts to estimate standardized or unstandardized regression coefficients. At the same time he is aware that other models may also fit the data and that his measures of relative importance are appropriate for only a given model and a particular set of data. The interplay between theory and research takes on real meaning in the process.

## REFERENCES

1 Atkinson, John W.: "Motivational Determinants of Risk-taking Behavior," *Psychological Review,* 64 (November, 1957), 359–372.

2 Blalock, Hubert M.: *Causal Inferences in Nonexperimental Research* (Chapel Hill, N.C.: University of North Carolina Press, 1964).

3 Blalock, Hubert M.: "Evaluating the Relative Importance of Variables," *American Sociological Review,* 26 (December, 1961), 866–874.

4 Blalock, Hubert M.: "The Identification Problem and Theory Building: The Case of Status Inconsistency," *American Sociological Review,* 31 (February, 1966), 52–61.

5 Blalock, Hubert M.: "Some Implications of Random Measurement Error for Causal Inferences," *American Journal of Sociology,* 71 (July, 1965), 37–47.

6 Blalock, Hubert M.: "Theory Building and the Statistical Concept of Interaction," *American Sociological Review,* 30 (June, 1965), 374–380.

7 Bunge, Mario: *Causality* (Cambridge, Mass.: Harvard, 1959).

8 Costner, Herbert L., and Robert K. Leik: "Deductions from 'Axiomatic Theory,' " *American Sociological Review,* 29 (December, 1964), 819–835.

9 Eckland, Bruce K.: "Academic Ability, Higher Education, and Occupational Mobility," *American Sociological Review,* 30 (October, 1965), 735–746.

10 Francis, Roy G.: *The Rhetoric of Science* (Minneapolis: University of Minnesota Press, 1961).

11 Gouldner, Alvin W., and Richard A. Peterson: *Notes on Technology and the Moral Order* (Indianapolis: Bobbs-Merrill, 1962).

12 Hyman, Herbert H.: *Survey Design and Analysis* (New York: Free Press, 1955).

13 Johnston, J.: *Econometric Methods* (New York: McGraw-Hill, 1963).

14 Kendall, M. G., and Alan Stuart: *The Advanced Theory of Statistics* (London: Griffin, 1961), vol. 2, chap. 29.

15 Kendall, Patricia L., and Paul F. Lazarsfeld: "Problems of Survey Analysis," in Robert K. Merton and Paul F. Lazarsfeld (Eds.), *Continuities in Social Research* (New York: Free Press, 1950).

16 Lawrence R. Klein: *A Textbook of Econometrics* (New York: Harper & Row, 1953).

17 Lenski, Gerhard E.: "Status Crystallization: A Non-vertical Dimension of Social Status," *American Sociological Review*, 19 (August, 1954), 405–413.

18 Nagel, Ernest: *The Structure of Science* (New York: Harcourt, Brace & World, 1961).

19 Palmore, Erdman, and Phillip E. Hammond: "Interacting Factors in Juvenile Delinquency," *American Sociological Review*, 29 (December, 1964), 848–854.

20 Strotz, Robert H., and Herman O. A. Wold: "Recursive versus Nonrecursive Systems: An Attempt at Synthesis," *Econometrica*, 28 (April, 1960), 417–427.

21 Tukey, John W.: "Causation, Regression, and Path Analysis," in Oscar Kempthorne et al., *Statistics and Mathematics in Biology* (Ames, Iowa: Iowa State College Press, 1954), chap. 3.

22 Wold, Herman O. A., and Lars Jureen: *Demand Analysis* (New York: Wiley, 1953).

23 Wright, Sewall: "Path Coefficients and Path Regressions: Alternative or Complementary Concepts?" *Biometrics*, 16 (June, 1960), 189–202.

# CHAPTER 6

# A New Look at Correlation Analysis[1]

RAYMOND BOUDON

One of the major problems in survey research is the following. We have a population and a number of observations on this population which we call variables $x_1$, $x_2$, $x_3$, $x_4$, and $x_5$. The variable we are primarily interested in is $x_1$: we want to explain its variation by means of $x_2$, $x_3$, $x_4$, and $x_5$. We actually find a correlation between $x_1$ and each of these variables. But these independent variables are themselves related. How can we give a clear picture of these relationships? In other words, how can we infer the causal network underlying this set of relationships?

Among the recent discussions of causal inference in empirical sociological research, the most important are Blalock's work (1–3,5) and the discussion of asymmetrical causal models by Polk (20), Blalock (4), and Robinson (21). It appears from these studies that certain problems have not yet been satisfactorily elucidated and that a somewhat different method can be derived.

The core of Blalock's ideas is Simon's analysis (22) of the spurious correlation problem in the linear case. Blalock's recent efforts have been especially oriented toward systematic exploration of the consequences of Simon's logic in the more-than-three-variable cases. This is important, of course, since Simon's treatment was confined to the three-variable case and it was not altogether clear whether the linear specification added much to Lazarsfeld's elaboration formula (12,18). Blalock was able to show that, when one is prepared to admit the linearity of the causal relations, the three-or-more-variable cases may be treated quite easily. Blalock's method, however, takes

---

[1] Sections 6.1 to 6.4, with minor changes and corrections, have been taken from Raymond Boudon (7), with the permission of the publisher.

into account only predictions about the partial correlations that may be derived from a causal scheme.

But, from Simon's causal equations, on which Blalock's models are based, it is possible to derive conclusions concerning not only the partial correlations between variables included in a causal scheme, but also the coefficients of the causal equations. The value of these coefficients is:

**1** That they may be interpreted as a measure of causal influence

**2** That they provide more powerful tests of a causal model than Blalock's method, as will be seen below

Sociological methodologists tend to overlook these coefficients because their meaning is less obvious than that of partial correlation coefficients.

To see the point more clearly, let us recall Simon's example, in a somewhat different notation. (See Fig. 6.1.) The hypotheses were $x_1$ causes $x_2$ and $x_3$; $x_2$ causes $x_3$. A causal structure of this kind might correspond, for instance, to Durkheim's findings (11) on suicide: average age ($x_1$) appears to affect the propensity to suicide ($x_3$) both directly and indirectly (with opposite sign) through the variable "extension of family group" ($x_2$). The corresponding equations would be

$$
\begin{aligned}
x_1 &= e_1 \\
a_{12}x_1 + x_2 &= e_2 \\
a_{13}x_1 + a_{23}x_2 + x_3 &= e_3
\end{aligned}
\tag{6.1}
$$

where the $e_i$ terms are errors in Simon's terminology. I prefer to speak of implicit factors, i.e., factors not explicitly included in the causal scheme. Although it is embarrassing to treat $x_1$ as an error term, and consequently $x_2$ and $x_3$ as a weighted sum of error terms, it seems much more acceptable to conceptualize the $e$'s as factors that act on the explicit variables of the causal scheme without being stated explicitly. Thus, in the previous example, $e_3$ would measure the effects on propensity to suicide of variables other than age

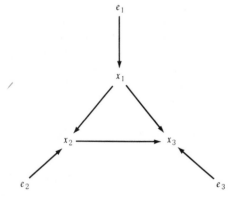

Fig. 6.1. **Abstract Structure Corresponding to the Durkheim-Halbwach Theory of Suicide. Age ($x_1$) Acts on Extension of Family Group ($x_2$); $x_1$ and $x_2$ Both Act Directly on Suicide ($x_3$).**

or extension of family group. Now, if it seems reasonable to assume that these implicit factors are specific, i.e., that each one acts on a single explicit variable, or, in other words, that they are uncorrelated, and if we multiply the equations of (6.1) by pairs and take the mathematical expectations, we get

$$a_{12}E(x_1{}^2) + E(x_1x_2) \qquad\qquad = 0 \quad (6.2a)$$
$$a_{13}E(x_1{}^2) + a_{23}E(x_1x_2) + E(x_1x_3) = 0 \quad (6.2b)$$
$$a_{12}[a_{13}E(x_1{}^2) + a_{23}E(x_1x_2) + E(x_1x_3)] + a_{13}E(x_1x_2)$$
$$+ a_{23}E(x_2{}^2) + E(x_2x_3) = 0 \quad (6.2c)$$

The term in brackets in Eq. (6.2c), being identical to the left member of Eq. (6.2b), is zero, so that if we solve (6.2) for the covariances[2] between age and extension of family group, age and suicide, and extension of family group and suicide, we get, respectively,

$$E(x_1x_2) = -a_{12}E(x_1{}^2) \qquad\qquad (6.3a)$$
$$E(x_1x_3) = (a_{12}a_{23} - a_{13})E(x_1{}^2) \qquad (6.3b)$$
$$E(x_2x_3) = a_{12}a_{13}E(x_1{}^2) - a_{23}E(x_2{}^2) \qquad (6.3c)$$

In his paper, Simon shows that if one assumes that $x_2$ has no effect on $x_3$ and, therefore, that the term $a_{23}$ in Eqs. (6.3b) and (6.3c) is zero, it is possible to deduce from (6.3) that $r_{23} = r_{12}r_{13}$, or in other words, that the partial correlation coefficient $r_{23.1}$ is zero.

But this is not the only kind of deduction one may draw. Of course, Simon's purpose was to formalize the idea of spurious correlation. But from Eqs. (6.3), it is apparent that the linear specification, as well as the hypotheses on the implicit factors, permits deductions regarding not only the correlation coefficients, both partial and total, but the coefficients of the equations as well. Indeed, we get from (6.3), as can easily be seen, three unknown $a_{ij}$ terms and three equations which can be solved. This suggests that for the purpose of causal analysis it may be worthwhile to estimate and use the dependence coefficients[3] of the causal linear equation. If so, however, why has this method been disregarded by most methodologists, at least in sociology?

To answer this question, one must first ask what the dependence coefficients measure, and second, what the connection is between the dependence coefficients and the familiar regression coefficients. As the Polk-Blalock-Robinson discussion shows, the connection between dependence and regression coefficients is far from obvious. The difficulty of assigning clear status to the dependence coefficients is probably one of the reasons why they have been overlooked, and why, among the possible inferences to be drawn from a linear causal structure, those concerning the partial and total correlation coefficients have been considered, while those concerning the dependence coefficients have been ignored.

---

[2] I shall suppose throughout the chapter that variables $x_1, x_2, \ldots, e_1, e_2, \ldots$ are measured from their means.

[3] This usage will be justified below.

## 6.1 DEPENDENCE COEFFICIENTS, REGRESSION COEFFICIENTS, AND THE IDENTIFICATION PROBLEM

To understand the meaning of dependence coefficients and their connection with regression, one must understand the idea of *identification* (1,13,24, for example). Let us suppose that we have a causal structure corresponding to system (6.1), from which we remove the first equation, leaving

$$a_{12}x_1 + x_2 = e_2 \tag{6.4a}$$
$$a_{13}x_1 + a_{23}x_2 + x_3 = e_3 \tag{6.4b}$$

Now, suppose that in a set of observed data the value of each score on each of the variables $x_1$, $x_2$, $x_3$ is known, and structure (6.4) holds. This means that, if appropriate values are used for $a_{12}$, scores plotted in the plane ($x_1$, $x_2$) should cluster in the neighborhood of the line $a_{12}x_1 + x_2 = 0$. The average closeness of observed points to the line depends on the importance of the implicit factors $e_2$. In the same way, we should expect observed points plotted in the space ($x_1$, $x_2$, $x_3$) to cluster in the neighborhood of the plane defined by the equation $a_{13}x_1 + a_{23}x_2 + x_3 = 0$.

This last expectation cannot actually be met however. To simplify, suppose that there are no effects due to implicit factors. In this case, the observed points should lie on the line $a_{12}x_1 + x_2 = 0$, or in the three-dimensional space ($x_1$, $x_2$, $x_3$), in the plane $a_{13}x_1 + a_{23}x_2 + x_3 = 0$. Now, if these equations hold, their sum holds. Thus, we have $(a_{13} + a_{12})x_1 + (a_{23} + 1)x_2 + x_3 = 0$. More generally the equation $(a_{13} + p_{12}a_{12})x_1 + (a_{23} + p_{12})x_2 + x_3 = 0$, where $p_{12}$ may have any value, holds as a consequence of the original equations. This means that the observed points, if the model holds, will lie, not in a specific plane of the space ($x_1$, $x_2$, $x_3$) but in an infinity of planes corresponding to the infinity of possible values of $p_{12}$.

The same reasoning applies to system (6.4). Let us substitute for it the system

$$a_{12}x_1 + x_2 \qquad\qquad\qquad = e_2 \tag{6.5a}$$
$$(a_{13} + p_{12}a_{12})x_1 + (a_{23} + p_{12})x_2 + x_3 = e_3' \tag{6.5b}$$

If (6.4) is true, (6.5) is true.[4] Thus, if the assumed causal structure holds, the observed points will be close to any plane $(a_{13} + p_{12}a_{12})x_1 + (a_{23} + p_{12})x_2 + x_3 = 0$, where $p_{12}$ may have any value; in other words, the observed points do not lie in the neighborhood of any particular plane in the space ($x_1$, $x_2$, $x_3$). As it is impossible to determine a particular set of parameters locating the points in the space ($x_1$, $x_2$, $x_3$), we shall say that the parameters of Eq. (6.4b) are not identifiable.

---

[4] Explicitly, the new error term $e_3'$ in Eq. (6.5b) is equal to $e_3 + p_{12}e_2$. But to write it explicitly is of no use, since it is impossible to separate $e_2$ from $e_3$. For the same reason, we write $Pe = e'$ in Eq. (6.7): the explicit components of the new error vector are in this case $e_2' = e_2$ and $e_3' = e_3 + p_{12}e_2$.

The same argument can be put in matrix form, to facilitate further reasoning. Indeed, system (6.4) may be translated into the single matrix equation

$$Ax = e \qquad (6.6)$$

where

$$A = \begin{pmatrix} a_{12} & 1 & 0 \\ a_{13} & a_{23} & 1 \end{pmatrix} \qquad x = \begin{pmatrix} x_1 \\ x_2 \\ x_3 \end{pmatrix} \qquad e = \begin{pmatrix} e_2 \\ e_3 \end{pmatrix}$$

System (6.5), on the other hand, may be expressed in the following matrix equation:

$$PAx = Pe = e' \qquad (6.7)$$

where

$$P = \begin{pmatrix} 1 & 0 \\ p_{12} & 1 \end{pmatrix}$$

From this, we may define identifiability as follows. If, given a causal system $Ax = e$, it is possible to find a nondiagonal matrix $P$ of appropriate dimensionality, so that the product matrix $PA$ has zeros in the same cells as $A$ (i.e., defines the same causal structure), then the coefficients of the linear structure are not all identifiable.

Conversely, if it is impossible to find a nondiagonal matrix $P$ so that $PA$ has the same structure as $A$, the coefficients of the structure are identifiable: the set of lines, planes, and hyperplanes defined by a matrix $A$ is the same as the set of lines, planes, and hyperplanes defined by a matrix $PA$, if $P$ is diagonal.

The phrase "not all" can be given a more precise meaning. We have just seen that the coefficients of an equation can be linearly combined with another without changing the causal structure. Hence, if we can find a nondiagonal matrix $P$, the rows of the latter which depart from diagonality (i.e., which cannot belong to a diagonal matrix) correspond to the nonidentifiable equations. Thus, as shown in the above example, Eq. (6.4*b*) is not identifiable and the second row of the matrix $P$ is nondiagonal. In this case, $a_{12}$ may be estimated, by least squares, as the regression coefficient of $x_2$ on $x_1$ in the space $(x_1, x_2)$, while $a_{13}$ and $a_{23}$ are not identifiable.

Simon, starting with the same equations, was able to derive definite values of $a_{12}$, $a_{13}$, and $a_{23}$. For the sake of brevity, I have called these coefficients as determined by Simon's method *dependence coefficients*. Thus, two questions arise:

**1** Is $a_{12}$ as calculated by Simon's method a regression coefficient, or more generally, are dependence coefficients equal to regression coefficients in the case of identifiable equations?

**2** What is the meaning of $a_{13}$ and $a_{23}$ as calculated by Simon's method, or more generally, what do the dependence coefficients mean when a structure is not identifiable in the sense defined above?

## 6.2 ARE DEPENDENCE COEFFICIENTS ALWAYS IDENTIFIABLE?

Before answering these questions, we must solve a preliminary problem. In the previous example, dependence coefficients are identifiable, while regression coefficients are not. To what extent can this case be generalized? Are dependence coefficients always identifiable? One useful device for seeing whether this is so is to multiply Eq. (6.6) by $x'$, the row vector that is the transpose of the column vector $x$. We get the matrix equation

$$Axx' = ex' \tag{6.8}$$

and, taking mathematical expectations,

$$E(Axx') = E(ex') \tag{6.9}$$

or

$$AE(xx') = E(ex') \tag{6.10}$$

If there are, as in the example of system (6.4), two equations and three $x$'s, $A$ is a two-rows three-columns matrix and $E(xx')$ is a three-by-three matrix—the matrix of covariances between explicit factors, if the latter are measured from their means. $E(ex')$ is the two-rows three-columns matrix of covariances between the explicit and implicit factors again measured from their means.

Now it is clear that, if $A$ contains a priori zeros (i.e., if some explicit factors are a priori known not to affect certain other explicit factors), $E(ex')$ will contain a priori zeros, assuming that implicit factors are uncorrelated. Going back to our example, to which Fig. 6.1 corresponds, we intuitively see (and can demonstrate by simply applying Simon's method as reported above) that $E(e_2x_1)$, $E(e_3x_1)$, and $E(e_3x_2)$ must be equal to zero if the causal structure holds, i.e., if $a_{21} = a_{31} = a_{32} = 0$. Thus, under the assumption that implicit factors are uncorrelated, any causal structure is associated with structural restrictions both on the matrix $AE(xx')$ and on the matrix $E(ex')$. In other words, whenever we assume a particular causal structure, some definite elements of both $AE(xx')$ and $E(ex')$ must be zero.

Let us now reason in the same way as in the previous section. Premultiplying Eq. (6.10) by a matrix $P$ of appropriate dimensionality, we get

$$PAE(xx') = PE(ex') \tag{6.11}$$

Of course, if Eq. (6.10) is true, Eq. (6.11) is also true. But the important question is the following: Whatever $A$, can $P$ be a nondiagonal matrix such that $PAE(xx')$ has the same structure as $AE(xx')$, and $PE(ex')$ the same structure as $E(ex')$? If the answer is yes, then both $A$ and every $PA$ obtained by assigning arbitrary values to the nonzero elements of $P$ are acceptable sets of dependence coefficients; hence the dependence coefficients will not always be identifiable. If the answer is no, if premultiplication by any nondiagonal matrix $P$, whatever $A$, disturbs the structure either of $AE(xx')$ or of $E(ex')$, then the only acceptable sets of dependence coefficients are the $PA$'s with $P$ diagonal. It follows that the dependence coefficients are always identifiable (up to normalization).

It can be shown (see Appendix, pp. 233–234) that it is impossible to find a nondiagonal matrix $P$ such that $PAE(xx')$ has the same structure as $AE(ex')$, and $PE(ex')$ the same structure as $E(ex')$. Thus we have proved the important result: In the case of one-way causation systems, when the implicit factors are uncorrelated, the dependence coefficients are always identifiable.

In practice, one may determine these coefficients by using either Simon's method as stated in Sec. 6.1 or Eq. (6.10). Simon's method is to introduce equations of the form $x_1 = e_1$ for the explicit factors that do not depend on any other explicit factor, write the equations for the other explicit factors, multiply equations by pairs, take mathematical expectations, standardize to substitute correlation coefficients for covariances, and solve for the dependence coefficients in terms of the correlation coefficients and variances. The other method is to state the elements of the $E(ex')$ matrix that are a priori known to be zero and pick up corresponding elements of the matrix $AE(xx')$. This method, much less cumbersome than the former, is presented in detail in Sec. 6.4.

Before asking what these dependence coefficients measure, I shall add one more remark on Simon's formalization. The matrix notation of Eq. (6.10) shows that it is useless to introduce, as Simon does, equations of the type $x_1 = e_1$, i.e., equations expressing the explicit factors not depending on any other explicit factor in the causal scheme. Moreover, this kind of formalization precludes general reasoning on identification, since if one adds to the matrix $A$ rows corresponding to these factors, it is always possible to find a nondiagonal matrix $P^0$, such that $P^0A^0$ has the same structure as $A^0$. Thus, considering the structure in which $x_1$ causes $x_2$, and $x_1$ causes $x_3$, the corresponding matrix $A$ is

$$A = \begin{pmatrix} a_{12} & 1 & 0 \\ a_{13} & 0 & 1 \end{pmatrix} \tag{6.12}$$

Obviously, no matrix derived from this one, by one or more linear combinations of the rows, will preserve the structure: there is no nondiagonal matrix $P$ such that $PA$ has zeros in the same cells as $A$. On the other hand, Simon's formalization amounts to building a matrix $A^0$ such as the following:

$$A^0 = \begin{pmatrix} 1 & 0 & 0 \\ a_{12} & 1 & 0 \\ a_{13} & 0 & 1 \end{pmatrix} \tag{6.13}$$

which can be premultiplied by a $P^0$ matrix such as

$$P^0 = \begin{pmatrix} 1 & 0 & 0 \\ p_{12} & 1 & 0 \\ p_{13} & 0 & 1 \end{pmatrix} \tag{6.14}$$

without modifying the structure. Here, $P^0A^0$ has the same structure as $A^0$.

## 6.3  INTERPRETATION OF DEPENDENCE COEFFICIENTS

We now know that we can always, if we assume noncorrelation between implicit factors and one-way causation, solve for dependence coefficients in terms of observable quantities (correlation coefficients or covariances between explicit factors, and variances of the latter). We also know that when the matrix $A$ is not identifiable, in the sense defined above, these coefficients are clearly not regression coefficients. But we do not yet know whether they are regression coefficients when the $A$ matrix is identifiable. In any case, we shall have to find a general statistical interpretation of these coefficients.

Such an interpretation was put forward by the biologist Sewall Wright, whose path analysis, although derived from a different approach, is similar to the method of causal analysis advocated here.[5] His argument may be paraphrased as follows. Let us first symbolize any causal equation in the form

$$x_i = a_{1i}x_1 + \cdots + a_{mi}x_m + x_e \tag{6.15}$$

Then, holding constant any variable including the implicit factor $x_e$ except $x_i$ and, say, $x_1$, we have[6]

$$\sigma^2_{i.23...me} = a_{1i}{}^2\sigma^2_{1.23...(i-1)(i+1)...me} \tag{6.16}$$

Now let

$$b_{1i}{}^2 = a_{1i}{}^2\frac{\sigma_1{}^2}{\sigma_i{}^2} = \frac{\sigma^2_{i.23...me}}{\sigma_i{}^2}\frac{\sigma_1{}^2}{\sigma^2_{1.23...(i-1)(i+1)...me}} \tag{6.17}$$

If we now suppose that $x_1$ does not depend on any other factor in the causal scheme, then $\sigma_1{}^2/\sigma^2_{1.23...(i-1)(i+1)...me} = 1$: the variance of $x_1$ is not affected by holding constant factors on which $x_1$ does not depend. Thus, $b_{1i}{}^2$, which is the ratio of the variation of $x_i$ when all factors except $x_1$ are fixed to the total variation of $x_i$, measures the part of the variance of $x_i$ accounted for by $x_1$. On the other hand, if $x_1$ is dependent on some explicit factor(s), it is determined by variables in the system which we wish to hold constant. But holding constant factors on which $x_1$ is dependent will reduce its variance in the proportion $\sigma^2_{.\ 3...(i-1)(i+1)...me}/\sigma_1{}^2$.

Thus, in general, if we want to state the part of the variance of $x_i$ accounted for by $x_1$, holding all other factors constant, we have to correct $\sigma^2_{i.23...me}/\sigma_i{}^2$ to take into account the reduction of variation in $x_1$ by holding these factors

---

[5] See Wright (25, 26). I am grateful to Hanan C. Selvin, who introduced me to Wright's work and stimulated my reflection on causal analysis by his report on "The Logic of Survey Analysis," given in 1964 in Paris (Seminar of the Centre d'Etudes Sociologiques on the epistemology of the social sciences). I use the word "dependence" where Wright uses "path," since the expression "path coefficients" or "path analysis" refers to a mere subsidiary computing device, and in my opinion it obscures the logic of the analysis. Moreover, path analysis is able to deal with linear structures only, while what I call "dependence analysis" may be extended to nonlinear structures as well and take account of interaction effects. This is impossible in path analysis (see Sec. 6.8.)

[6] $N\sigma^2{}_{1.23...(i-1)(i+1)...me}$ is the sum of squares of the distances of the observed points to the regression hyperplane of $x_1$ on $x_2, x_3 \ldots x_{i-1}, x_{i+1}, \ldots x_m, x_e$. See, for instance, Yule and Kendall (27, chap. 12).

constant. If holding these factors constant reduces the variation of $x_1$ to, say, two-thirds of its original value, the correction factor which appears on the extreme right of Eq. (6.17) will be $\frac{3}{2}$, while it will be equal to 1 when $x_1$ does not depend on any other explicit factor. That is what Wright (25) meant when he wrote that $b$ measures "the fraction of the standard deviation of the dependent variable (with appropriate sign) for which the designated factor is directly responsible, in the sense of the fraction which would be found if this factor varies to the same extent as in the observed data while all others (including residual factors) are constant."

Thus, the dependence coefficients, when corrected by the appropriate variances, are really a measure of the direct influence of one variable on another in a causal scheme. Moreover, we know from the previous section that they can always be determined, if the implicit factors in the scheme are assumed to be uncorrelated.

## *Dependence and Regression Coefficients in the Case of Identifiable Structure*

The preceding interpretation of dependence coefficients is, of course, valid whether the regression coefficients are identifiable or not, but it is important to see the connection between both kinds of coefficients whenever the latter may be identified. Going back to Eq. (6.6), we recall that a structure, or a coefficient matrix $A$ associated with this structure, is identifiable if premultiplication of $A$ by any nondiagonal matrix $P$ is such that $PA$ and $A$ have a different structure. Let us suppose then that the matrix $A$ associated with a causal structure is identifiable. Now, from $E(Axx') = E(ex')$, we can derive a set of equations. If, say, $x_i$ depends on $x_j$, we shall have $E(e_i x_j) = 0$, while $a_{ji}$ will be nonzero. Thus, one of the equations allowing for the determination of dependence coefficients will be of the form

$$
\begin{aligned}
E(a_{1i}x_1 + \cdots + x_i + \cdots + a_{ji}x_j + \cdots + a_{mi}x_m)x_j \\
= a_{1i}E(x_1 x_j) + \cdots + E(x_i x_j) + \cdots + a_{ji}E(x_j^2) \\
+ \cdots + a_{mi}E(x_m x_j) = E(e_i x_j) = 0 \quad (6.18)
\end{aligned}
$$

But to estimate the regression coefficients by the method of least squares, one has to minimize the quantity $Q$ where

$$
Q = E(a_{1i}x_1 + \cdots + x_i + \cdots + a_{ji}x_j + \cdots + a_{mi}x_m)^2 \quad (6.19)
$$

Minimizing $Q$ implies that the so-called normal equation, stating that the partial derivative of $Q$ with regard to $a_{ji}$ is zero, will be satisfied. In symbols,

$$
\frac{\partial Q}{\partial a_{ji}} = 2E(a_{1i}x_1 + \cdots + x_i + \cdots + a_{ji}x_j + \cdots + a_{mi}x_m)x_j = 0 \quad (6.20)
$$

This condition is equivalent to

$$E(a_{1i}x_1 + \cdots + x_i + \cdots + a_{ji}x_j + \cdots + a_{mi}x_m)x_j = 0 \quad (6.21)$$

But this is precisely Eq. (6.18).  Hence, the equations allowing for the determination of the dependence coefficients are the normal equations of regression analysis.  Thus, we have the following important result:

If a structure is identifiable, the dependence coefficients are regression coefficients; in other words, when the regression coefficients can be identified, the dependence coefficients are regression coefficients.[7]

## *Why Standardize Dependence Coefficients?*

We have now seen that dependence coefficients are more clearly interpreted if they are standardized, i.e., if one uses $a_{ji}(\sigma_j/\sigma_i)$ instead of $a_{ji}$.  This procedure has one disadvantage: the standardized dependence coefficients are no longer equal to the regression coefficients, when the latter can be determined, except when all the standard deviations are equal.  But this disadvantage is counterbalanced by the ease of interpretation and also by the fact that, if the unknown terms are the standardized dependence coefficients, the known terms in the equations of dependence analysis will be exclusively correlation coefficients, not variances.  To see why this is so, let us go back to Eq. (6.18): if we divide the covariances by the appropriate standard deviations to get correlation coefficients, we get

$$a_{1i}\sigma_1\sigma_j r_{1j} + \cdots + a_{ji}\sigma_j^2 + \cdots + a_{mi}\sigma_m\sigma_j r_{mj} = 0 \quad (6.22)$$

Setting $\quad a_{1i}(\sigma_1/\sigma_i) = b_{1i}, \; a_{ji}(\sigma_j/\sigma_i) = b_{ji}, \; a_{mi}(\sigma_m/\sigma_i) = b_{mi}$, etc., $a_{1i}\sigma_1\sigma_j r_{1j}$ becomes $b_{1i}\sigma_i\sigma_j r_{1j}$; $a_{ji}\sigma_j^2$ becomes $b_{ji}\sigma_i\sigma_j$; $a_{mi}\sigma_m\sigma_j r_{mj}$ becomes $b_{mi}\sigma_i\sigma_j r_{mj}$; so that

$$(b_{1i}r_{1j} + \cdots + b_{ji} + \cdots + b_{mi}r_{mj})\sigma_i\sigma_j = 0 \quad (6.23)$$

But condition (6.23) is equivalent to

$$b_{1i}r_{1j} + \cdots + b_{ji} + \cdots + b_{mi}r_{mj} = 0 \quad (6.24)$$

Thus, the equations of dependence analysis may be constructed in such a way that all the unknown terms are standardized dependence coefficients, and all the known terms, correlation coefficients.

---

[7] Wright has proved a similar theorem.  But his approach through path coefficients prevented him from seeing the validity of the theorem in the general case.  In fact, he proved it only where the postulated causal structure is of the simplest form (a set of independent variables acting on a single dependent variable).  In this case, a causal structure is always identifiable.  But it may be identifiable in much more complex cases as well, and in these, the dependence coefficients, according to the above theorem, will be regression coefficients. Let us, incidentally, note that our distinction between regression and dependence coefficients may be criticized, since the present result can be put in the form: in the case of a nonidentifiable structure, regression coefficients may be determined if noncorrelation between errors is assumed.

## 6.4  ILLUSTRATIONS

### *Blalock's Five-variable Case*

Blalock (2) presents three hypothetical causal models in a five-variable situation. For the present purpose of illustration I shall submit the third model to a dependence analysis. This model is represented in Fig. 6.2. (For the substantive meaning of the causal hypotheses embodied in this model, see Blalock's paper.)[8]

The corresponding equations, i.e., the matrix equation $Ax = e$ in developed form, are

$$a_{12}x_1 + x_2 \qquad\qquad\qquad = e_2 \qquad\qquad (6.25a)$$
$$a_{13}x_1 + a_{23}x_2 + x_3 \qquad\quad = e_3 \qquad\qquad (6.25b)$$
$$a_{24}x_2 + x_4 \qquad\quad = e_4 \qquad\qquad (6.25c)$$
$$a_{15}x_1 + a_{25}x_2 + a_{45}x_4 + x_5 = e_5 \qquad\qquad (6.25d)$$

The a priori conditions imply that in the $E(ex')$ matrix, the elements $E(e_2x_1)$, $E(e_3x_1)$, $E(e_4x_1)$, $E(e_5x_1)$, $E(e_3x_2)$, $E(e_4x_2)$, $E(e_5x_2)$, $E(e_4x_3)$, $E(e_5x_3)$, $E(e_5x_4)$ are zero, yielding 10 equations. The equation corresponding to the first zero term would be obtained by multiplying Eq. (6.25a) by $x_1$ and taking mathematical expectations:

$$a_{12}E(x_1^2) + E(x_1x_2) = E(e_2x_1) = 0 \qquad\qquad (6.26)$$

But, comparing Eqs. (6.18) and (6.24) above, we see that we can write directly

$$b_{12} + r_{12} = 0 \qquad\qquad (6.27)$$

[8] Blalock specifies that "the data were taken from the 1950 Census, the units of analysis being 150 randomly selected southern counties. . . . All . . . relationships were found to be approximately linear. . . . Variable $x_1$, a crude index of urbanization, is the percentage of the county's population classed as either urban or rural nonfarm; $x_2$ represents the percentage of nonwhites in the county. Variables $x_3$ and $x_5$ involve measures of white and nonwhite incomes, respectively (the percentage of families with annual income of $1,500 or more), and $x_4$ is an index of nonwhite educational levels (percentage of males twenty-five and over with more than six years of schooling). (2,6.)

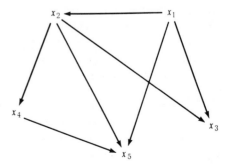

**Fig. 6.2.  Blalock's Third Hypothetical Structure of Causal Connections between Variables** $x_1$ (Urbanization), $x_2$ (Percentage of Nonwhites), $x_3$ (White Income), $x_4$ (Nonwhite Level of Education), $x_5$ (Nonwhite Income).

Skipping intermediate steps for other equations we get the following dependence analysis equations:

$$b_{12} + r_{12} = 0 \tag{6.28a}$$
$$b_{13} + b_{23}r_{12} + r_{13} = 0 \tag{6.28b}$$
$$b_{13}r_{12} + b_{23} + r_{23} = 0 \tag{6.28c}$$
$$b_{24}r_{12} + r_{14} = 0 \tag{6.28d}$$
$$b_{24} + r_{24} = 0 \tag{6.28e}$$
$$b_{24}r_{23} + r_{34} = 0 \tag{6.28f}$$
$$b_{15} + b_{25}r_{12} + b_{45}r_{14} + r_{15} = 0 \tag{6.28g}$$
$$b_{15}r_{12} + b_{25} + b_{45}r_{24} + r_{25} = 0 \tag{6.28h}$$
$$b_{15}r_{13} + b_{25}r_{23} + b_{45}r_{34} + r_{35} = 0 \tag{6.28i}$$
$$b_{15}r_{14} + b_{25}r_{24} + b_{45} + r_{45} = 0 \tag{6.28j}$$

The reader may convince himself that these equations are very easily constructed, and in spite of their number, fairly easily solved. In fact, Eq. (6.28a) gives $b_{12}$, Eqs. (6.28b) and (6.28c) give $b_{13}$ and $b_{23}$, and so forth. Thus, in this case, the number of equations to be simultaneously solved never exceeds three.

Another way of finding the dependence equations is to use Wright's path method (25): if we look at, say, Eq. (6.28b), we see that the correlation between $x_1$ and $x_3$ is the sum of the direct effect of $x_1$ on $x_3$, measured by $-b_{13}$, and of the indirect effect of $x_1$ on $x_3$ through $x_2$; this effect is the product of the effect of $x_1$ on $x_2$, measured by $-b_{12} = r_{12}$, and of the effect of $x_2$ on $x_3$, measured by $-b_{23}$. By applying the same rules to other correlation coefficients, and rearranging terms, we would find system (6.28). Thus, we have the general rule:

The correlation between two variables is the sum of the effects, both direct and indirect, connecting these variables; the *indirect* effects are given by the product of the direct effects which compose them.

In our example, the values of the known correlation coefficients, as given by Blalock, are the following: $r_{12} = -.389$, $r_{13} = .670$, $r_{14} = .264$, $r_{15} = .736$, $r_{23} = .067$, $r_{24} = -.531$, $r_{25} = -.440$, $r_{34} = .042$, $r_{35} = .599$, $r_{45} = .386$. Now, because the original equations were written in the form, e.g., $a_{12}x_1 + x_2 = e_2$, rather than $x_2 = a_{12}x_1 + e_2$, the significant values of the standardized dependence coefficients are the $-b$'s rather than the $b$'s themselves. The solution of the previous system, with reversed signs, is $-b_{12} = -.389$, $-b_{13} = .820$, $-b_{15} = .655$, $-b_{23} = .386$, $-b_{24} = -.531$, $-b_{25} = -.101$, $-b_{45} = .160$.

These values are measures of causal dependence. Thus, if the model is correct, we see that although $r_{25}$ has a rather strong negative value ($-.440$), the dependence of $x_5$ on $x_2$, as measured by $-b_{25}$, is also negative but small ($-.101$). In other words the proportion of nonwhites in the population has, in spite of the correlation, at most a slight direct depressing effect on nonwhite incomes. Such a result is, of course, of great importance to sociologists.

Let us remind ourselves, however, that the validity of a dependence analysis depends on the validity of the hypothetical model. One can sometimes test the model directly by using excess dependence equations; sometimes, too, an interesting result is given, not only by one but by several plausible models. Thus, the value of $-b_{25}$ is much smaller than the correlation $r_{25}$ in Blalock's three hypothetical models. A dependence analysis similar to that of Blalock's third model above shows that $-b_{25}$ is about $-.101$ in the first model and about zero in the second, compared with the $-.071$ obtained above for the third.

Note that in the previous system, the number of equations exceeds by three the number of unknown terms. The solution involved Eq. (6.28$a$) for $b_{12}$; Eqs. (6.28$b$) and (6.28$c$) for $b_{13}$ and $b_{23}$; Eq. (6.28$e$) for $b_{24}$; Eqs. (6.28$g$), (6.28$h$), (6.28$j$) for $b_{15}$, $b_{25}$, $b_{45}$. But this leaves unused the three supplementary equations (6.28$d$), (6.28$f$), and (6.28$i$).[9] This excess of equations will appear in a dependence analysis whenever the number of causal links in a scheme is smaller than the number $n(n-1)/2$ of pairs which can be built from the $n$ variables.

An obvious advantage is that this furnishes a test of the causal model: if a given hypothetical model holds, the corresponding dependence equations should all be consistent, at least if we suppose neither sampling nor measurement error. In the present case, using the values of the $b$'s given above, we get for Eq. (6.28$d$) the value $-.054$ instead of the expected zero value; for Eq. (6.28$b$), we get $-.003$ instead of zero. These two results seem acceptable. Finally, we get for Eq. (6.28$i$) the value $.160$ instead of zero, which seems less satisfactory. Of course, we should judge the goodness of fit by adequate statistical tests, but neither the particular causal model itself nor the estimation problems require attention in this practical illustration of dependence analysis.

## Another Example

Ladinsky (15) tries to explain forms of law practice (solo versus firm) among lawyers by a number of independent variables:

1 Protestant origin versus Catholic, Greek Orthodox, and Jewish

2 Entrepreneurial versus nonentrepreneurial family

3 Father's profession, manual versus nonmanual

4 Quality of law school

One of the inferred best-fit models obtained by using the Simon-Blalock method appears in Fig. 6.3. The Simon-Blalock predictions associated with this model, i.e.,

$$r_{12} = r_{23} = r_{34.1} = 0 \qquad (6.29)$$

[9] In fact, it would have been preferable to use least-squares methods to estimate dependence coefficients. See Sec. 6.5.

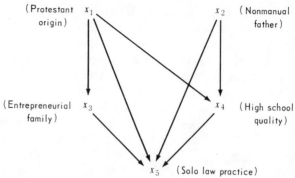

Fig. 6.3.    A Best-fitting Causal Model between Background and Present Law Practice.

seem to be reasonably good, since observed $r$'s are

$$r_{12} = .030$$
$$r_{23} = .153 \qquad\qquad (6.30)$$
$$r_{34.1} = .007$$

Notice that the correlation coefficients used by Ladinsky are the dichoto-mous $\phi$. As will be seen in Sec. 6.6, dependence analysis may be applied to the case where variables are dichotomous.

Dependence analysis was applied to this case by Capecchi (9) from whom we borrow the computations. The causal equations of Ladinsky's model are

$$a_{13}x_1 + x_3 = e_3 \qquad\qquad (6.31a)$$
$$a_{14}x_1 + a_{24}x_2 + x_4 = e_4 \qquad\qquad (6.31b)$$
$$a_{15}x_1 + a_{25}x_2 + a_{35}x_3 + a_{45}x_4 + x_5 = e_5 \qquad\qquad (6.31c)$$

The dependence equations are

$$b_{13} + r_{13} = 0 \qquad\qquad (6.32a)$$
$$b_{14} + b_{24}r_{12} + r_{14} = 0 \qquad\qquad (6.32b)$$
$$b_{14}r_{12} + b_{24} + r_{24} = 0 \qquad\qquad (6.32c)$$
$$b_{15} + b_{25}r_{12} + b_{35}r_{13} + b_{45}r_{14} + r_{15} = 0 \qquad\qquad (6.32d)$$
$$b_{15}r_{12} + b_{25} + b_{35}r_{23} + b_{45}r_{24} + r_{25} = 0 \qquad\qquad (6.32e)$$
$$b_{15}r_{13} + b_{25}r_{23} + b_{35} + b_{45}r_{34} + r_{35} = 0 \qquad\qquad (6.32f)$$
$$b_{15}r_{14} + b_{25}r_{24} + b_{35}r_{34} + b_{45} + r_{45} = 0 \qquad\qquad (6.32g)$$
$$b_{13}r_{14} + r_{34} = 0 \qquad\qquad (6.32h)$$
$$b_{13}r_{12} + r_{23} = 0 \qquad\qquad (6.32i)$$
$$r_{12} = 0 \qquad\qquad (6.32j)$$

Again, in spite of the formidable number of equations, this system is easily solved: Eq. (6.32a) gives $b_{13}$ directly; Eqs. (6.32b) and (6.32c) involve a system with two unknowns: $b_{14}$ and $b_{24}$. Finally, Eqs. (6.32d) to (6.32g) give estimates of $b_{15}$, $b_{25}$, $b_{35}$, and $b_{45}$.

The solution, computed by Capecchi, is the following:

$$
\begin{aligned}
b'_{13} &= -.332 & b'_{14} &= .264 \\
b'_{24} &= .254 & b'_{15} &= -.333 \\
b'_{25} &= -.167 & b'_{35} &= -.168 \\
& b'_{45} = -.313 &
\end{aligned}
\tag{6.33}
$$

where, for convenience, we have let $b'_{ij} = -b_{ij}$. An interesting result of the analysis, as noticed by Capecchi, is that the direct influences of variable $x_1$ and of variable $x_4$ on law practice $(x_5)$ are the same, although the correlation of law school quality and law practice is higher in absolute value $(r_{45} = -.628)$ than the correlation between religious origin and law practice $(r_{15} = -.442)$.

A test of the model may be obtained by comparing with zero the values on the right of Eqs. (6.32$h$), (6.32$i$), and (6.32$j$) when the estimated parameters have been introduced. These values are .006, .143, and .030, respectively. Again there is a question of whether we would consider this a good fit. What we know, if we believe Ladinsky's statement that the causal model of Fig. 6.3 gives the best fit, is that this model fits the data better than any other reasonable one. But, of course, it would be more convenient to have a method which would tell us whether or not the discrepancy between model and observed data is significant. To solve this problem of inference, we must first devise better estimates of the dependence parameters than those used in the previous sections.

## 6.5  PROBLEMS OF ESTIMATION

It is evident that the estimation methods used above are not the best when the number of equations exceeds the number of unknown dependence parameters. Thus, in the previous example, we have used Eq. (6.32$a$) to estimate $b_{13}$. Then, Eqs. (6.32$h$) and (6.32$i$) appear as supplementary equations (an inadequate but expressive phrase). But we could as well have chosen Eq. (6.32$h$) or (6.32$i$) to estimate $b_{13}$. In this case, Eq. (6.32$a$) would have been supplementary. Of course, when we are dealing with fallible data, these different possible choices will lead to different estimates and there is obviously no reason to think that one estimate is better than the other.

A solution to the problem of avoiding arbitrariness in the choice of the estimates is to use the method of least squares. This method is certainly appropriate here, since it provides us with estimates of the dependence parameters by minimizing the sum of squares of differences between observed correlation coefficients and correlation coefficients regenerated by using these estimates. Moreover, the method has the obvious advantage of using all equations instead of introducing an awkward distinction between estimation equations and supplementary equations.

In order to see how this familiar method is applied to our present problem, let us go back to the example of Sec. 6.4.

If we look at system (6.28), we see that only Eq. (6.28$a$) contains $b_{12}$. Similarly, only Eqs. (6.28$b$) and (6.28$c$) contain $b_{13}$ and $b_{23}$. Thus, there are in both cases as many equations as unknowns. On the other hand, it appears that three equations, i.e., Eqs. (6.28$d$), (6.28$e$), and (6.28$f$) contain only one unknown, i.e., $b_{24}$, while the subset of Eqs. (6.28$g$) to (6.28$j$) contains three unknowns, $b_{15}$, $b_{25}$, and $b_{45}$, for four equations. Thus we shall use the method of least squares to estimate $b_{24}$, $b_{15}$, $b_{25}$, and $b_{45}$.

Let us consider for instance the subset of Eqs. (6.28$d$) to (6.28$f$). We want the estimated value of $b_{24}$ to be such that the sum

$$(r_{14}^* - r_{14})^2 + (r_{24}^* - r_{24})^2 + (r_{34}^* - r_{34})^2$$

is minimum, where $r_{14}^*$, $r_{24}^*$, and $r_{34}^*$ are the correlation coefficients regenerated by using the estimated value of $b_{24}$. By Eq. (6.28$d$), we see that $r_{14}^* = -b_{24}r_{12}$, by Eq. (6.28$e$), that $r_{24}^* = -b_{24}$, by Eq. (6.28$f$), that $r_{34}^* = -b_{24}r_{23}$. Thus, calling $Q$ the quantity to be minimized, we have

$$Q = (b_{24}r_{12} + r_{14})^2 + (b_{24} + r_{24})^2 + (b_{24}r_{23} + r_{34})^2 \qquad (6.34)$$

Now $Q$ is a function of $b_{24}$. If this function is to be minimum for a given value of $b_{24}$, its derivative with regard to $b_{24}$ must be zero for this value. Thus, a necessary condition for $Q(b_{24})$ to be minimum is

$$\frac{dQ}{db_{24}} = 2[(b_{24}r_{12} + r_{14})r_{12} + (b_{24} + r_{24}) + (b_{24}r_{23} + r_{34})r_{23}] = 0 \quad (6.35)$$

It remains to solve this equation for $b_{24}$. Dividing by 2 and rearranging terms, we obtain $b_{24}$ by solving

$$b_{24}(r_{12}^2 + r_{23}^2 + 1) + r_{14}r_{12} + r_{23}r_{34} + r_{24} = 0 \qquad (6.36)$$

Substituting the empirical values of the $r$'s into Eq. (6.36), we have

$$1.1568b_{24} + .6366 = 0 \qquad (6.37)$$
whence $\qquad\qquad\qquad -b_{24} = .550 \qquad\qquad\qquad\qquad (6.38)$

In order to estimate $b_{15}$, $b_{25}$, and $b_{45}$, we similarly apply the method of least squares to the subset of Eqs. (6.28$g$) to (6.28$j$). Here we want to minimize the quantity $(r_{15}^* - r_{15})^2 + (r_{25}^* - r_{25})^2 + (r_{35}^* - r_{35})^2 + (r_{45}^* - r_{45})^2$, or, substituting for the starred $r$'s their values taken from Eqs. (6.28$g$) to (6.28$j$),

$$(b_{15} + b_{25}r_{12} + b_{45}r_{14} + r_{15})^2 + (b_{15}r_{12} + b_{25} + b_{45}r_{24} + r_{25})^2$$
$$+ (b_{15}r_{13} + b_{25}r_{23} + b_{45}r_{34} + r_{35})^2 + (b_{15}r_{14} + b_{25}r_{24} + b_{45} + r_{45})^2$$

Let us call this quantity $R$, or $R(b_{15}, b_{25}, b_{45})$ since it is a function of the three parameters $b_{15}$, $b_{25}$, and $b_{45}$.

It is easy to extend the previous reasoning to this new case. A condition for $R(b_{15}, b_{25}, b_{45})$ to be minimum is that the values of the parameters are chosen so that, for these values, the partial derivatives of $R$ with respect to each parameter are zero. Thus, we have to solve the following so-called normal equations:

$$\frac{\partial R}{\partial b_{15}} = 2[(b_{15} + b_{25}r_{12} + b_{45}r_{14} + r_{15}) + (b_{15}r_{12} + b_{25} + b_{45}r_{24} + r_{25})r_{12}$$
$$+ (b_{15}r_{13} + b_{25}r_{23} + b_{45}r_{34} + r_{35})r_{13}$$
$$+ (b_{15}r_{14} + b_{25}r_{24} + b_{45} + r_{45})r_{14}] = 0 \quad (6.39a)$$

$$\frac{\partial R}{\partial b_{25}} = 2[(b_{15} + b_{25}r_{12} + b_{45}r_{14} + r_{15})r_{12} + (b_{15}r_{12} + b_{25} + b_{45}r_{24} + r_{25})$$
$$+ (b_{15}r_{13} + b_{25}r_{23} + b_{45}r_{34} + r_{35})r_{23}$$
$$+ (b_{15}r_{14} + b_{25}r_{24} + b_{45} + r_{45})r_{24}] = 0 \quad (6.39b)$$

$$\frac{\partial R}{\partial b_{45}} = 2[(b_{15} + b_{25}r_{12} + b_{45}r_{14} + r_{15})r_{14} + (b_{15}r_{12} + b_{25} + b_{45}r_{24} + r_{25})r_{24}$$
$$+ (b_{15}r_{13} + b_{25}r_{23} + b_{45}r_{34} + r_{35})r_{34}$$
$$+ (b_{15}r_{14} + b_{25}r_{24} + b_{45} + r_{45})] = 0 \quad (6.39c)$$

or, dividing by 2 and rearranging terms,

$$b_{15}(1 + r_{12}^2 + r_{13}^2 + r_{14}^2) + b_{25}(2r_{12} + r_{23}r_{13} + r_{24}r_{14})$$
$$+ b_{45}(2r_{14} + r_{24}r_{12} + r_{34}r_{13}) = -r_{15} - r_{12}r_{25} - r_{13}r_{35} - r_{14}r_{45} \quad (6.40a)$$

$$b_{15}(2r_{12} + r_{13}r_{23} + r_{14}r_{24}) + b_{25}(r_{12}^2 + 1 + r_{23}^2 + r_{24}^2)$$
$$+ b_{45}(r_{14}r_{12} + 2r_{24} + r_{34}r_{23}) = -r_{25} - r_{12}r_{15} - r_{23}r_{35} - r_{24}r_{45} \quad (6.40b)$$

$$b_{15}(2r_{14} + r_{12}r_{24} + r_{13}r_{34}) + b_{25}(2r_{24} + r_{12}r_{14} + r_{23}r_{34})$$
$$+ b_{45}(r_{14}^2 + r_{24}^2 + r_{34}^2 + 1) = -r_{45} - r_{14}r_{15} - r_{24}r_{25} - r_{34}r_{35} \quad (6.40c)$$

By substituting numerical values for the coefficients of the $b$'s in the above equations, and solving, we find

$$b_{15}' = .781$$
$$b_{25}' = -.020 \quad (6.41)$$
$$b_{45}' = .163$$

If we compare the estimates obtained for the dependence parameters by the arbitrary method of the previous sections and by the method of least squares, we see that they both lead to essentially identical substantive interpretations, although they are somewhat different numerically. Thus, especially in the first trial-and-error phase of a causal analysis, it might be advisable to use the arbitrary method, which gives a rough idea of the best-fit model, and to use the method of least squares only when one is rather sure that a model is better than other reasonable models. Then, it is possible to use the estimates derived from the method of least squares to regenerate theoretical correlation coefficients: this is done by introducing these estimates in the dependence equations. It remains finally to compare these theoretical coefficients with the observed correlation coefficients.

## 6.6 DEPENDENCE ANALYSIS IN THE CASE OF DICHOTOMOUS VARIABLES

In the preceding sections, we have dealt with continuous variables. If dependence analysis were to be limited to this type of variable, its relevance to sociological methodology would be restricted, since continuous variables are the exception rather than the rule in sociology. In the present section, we shall prove that this method is applicable to discontinuous variables, as well, and particularly to the familiar dichotomous variables.

To visualize the proof, we shall use the well-known Durkheim example: marriage $(x_2)$ exerts a (negative) influence on the propensity to commit suicide $(x_3)$; age $(x_1)$ has an effect on the propensity to commit suicide $(x_3)$; being married $(x_2)$ depends on age $(x_1)$.

Let us then introduce some symbols:

$p_{2,1}$: probability of being married for people over thirty years
$p_{2,\bar{1}}$: probability of being married for people under thirty years
$p_{3,12}$: probability of suicide among married people over thirty
$p_{3,\bar{1}2}$: probability of suicide among married people under thirty
$p_{3,1\bar{2}}$: probability of suicide among unmarried people over thirty
$p_{3,\bar{1}\bar{2}}$: probability of suicide among unmarried people under thirty

The problem is to generate these probabilities by a model which would embody the causal hypotheses given above. For this, we may follow Coleman (10). Let us take, for instance, $p_{2,1}$; since being old (over thirty) raises the probability of being married, we may write that this quantity depends on the effect of age on being married, on the one hand, and on implicit factors, on the other hand. Assuming that the relation is linear, this leads to

$$p_{2,1} = a_{12} + e_2 \qquad (6.42a)$$

where $a_{12}$ is a parameter describing the effect of variable number 1 on variable number 2 and $e_2$ describes the effect of implicit factors. Similarly, we shall write

$$p_{2,\bar{1}} = e_2 \qquad (6.42b)$$

This equation says that being married when one is under thirty depends, not on age, but only on implicit factors.

In the same way, if we call $a_{13}$ the effect of age on suicide and $a_{23}$ the effect of marriage on suicide, we may write

$$p_{3,12} = a_{13} + a_{23} + e_3 \qquad (6.42c)$$
$$p_{3,\bar{1}2} = a_{23} + e_3 \qquad (6.42d)$$
$$p_{3,1\bar{2}} = a_{13} + e_3 \qquad (6.42e)$$
$$p_{3,\bar{1}\bar{2}} = e_3 \qquad (6.42f)$$

Thus, Eq. (6.42c) says that among old married people, the propensity to suicide depends on both explicit factors and on implicit factors acting toward committing suicide.   (Notice that in this substantive example we shall expect $a_{13}$ to be positive and $a_{23}$ to be negative.)

We could write still other equations, such as

$$p_{\bar{2},1} = e_{\bar{2}} \tag{6.42g}$$
$$p_{\bar{2},\bar{1}} = a_{12} + e_{\bar{2}} \tag{6.42h}$$
$$p_{\bar{3},12} = \phantom{a_{13} + a_{23} +} e_{\bar{3}} \tag{6.42 i}$$
$$p_{\bar{3},\bar{1}2} = a_{13} \phantom{+ a_{23}} + e_{\bar{3}} \tag{6.42 j}$$
$$p_{\bar{3},1\bar{2}} = \phantom{a_{13} +} a_{23} + e_{\bar{3}} \tag{6.42k}$$
$$p_{\bar{3},\bar{1}\bar{2}} = a_{13} + a_{23} + e_{\bar{3}} \tag{6.42 l}$$

where $e_{\bar{2}}$ and $e_{\bar{3}}$ refer to the effect of implicit factors.   Notice, however, that, since $p_{2,1} + p_{\bar{2},1} = p_{2,\bar{1}} + p_{\bar{2},\bar{1}} = p_{3,12} + p_{\bar{3},12} = \cdots = p_{3,\bar{1}\bar{2}} + p_{\bar{3},\bar{1}\bar{2}} = 1$, this latter set of equations is not independent of the former.

Equations (6.42a) to (6.42f) might be solved directly to give estimates for the effect parameters $a_{12}$, $a_{13}$, and $a_{23}$; on this point, we refer the reader to Coleman (10).   What we are interested in here is using these equations to describe the correlation coefficients $\phi_{12}$, $\phi_{13}$, $\phi_{23}$ as functions of the effect parameters.

Let us first recall that in the case of dichotomous variables, the measure $f_{ij}$ of the effect of a variable $x_i$ on a variable $x_j$ is related to $\phi_{ij}$ in a simple way.

To visualize the meaning of $f_{ij}$ and $\phi_{ij}$, let us use the dichotomous contingency table given below:

| | | |
|---|---|---|
| $p_{ij}$ | $p_{\bar{i}j}$ | $p_j$ |
| $p_{i\bar{j}}$ | $p_{\bar{i}\bar{j}}$ | $p_{\bar{j}}$ |
| $p_i$ | $p_{\bar{i}}$ | 1 |

where $p_{ij}$ is the proportion of people who are positive on both $x_i$ and $x_j$; $p_{\bar{i}j}$, the the proportion of people who are negative on $x_i$ and positive on $x_j$, and so forth. The measure $f_{ij}$ is the difference between two proportions: the proportion of people who are positive on $x_j$ among those who are *positive* on $x_i$ and the proportion of people who are positive on $x_j$ among those who are *negative* on $x_i$:

$$f_{ij} = p_{j,i} - p_{j,\bar{i}} = \frac{p_{ij}}{p_i} - \frac{p_{\bar{i}j}}{p_{\bar{i}}} = \frac{p_{ij} - p_i p_j}{p_i p_{\bar{i}}} \tag{6.43}$$

But

$$\phi_{ij} = \frac{p_{ij} - p_i p_j}{\sqrt{p_i p_{\bar{i}} p_j p_{\bar{j}}}} \tag{6.44}$$

Hence

$$f_{ij} = \phi_{ij} \frac{\sqrt{p_j p_{\bar{j}}}}{\sqrt{p_i p_{\bar{i}}}} \tag{6.45}$$

As $p_i p_{\bar{i}}$ and $p_j p_{\bar{j}}$ are the variances, respectively, of the variables $x_i$ and $x_j$, we may shorten the notation and write

$$f_{ij} = \phi_{ij} \frac{s_j}{s_i} \tag{6.46}$$

where $s_j = \sqrt{p_j p_{\bar{j}}}$ and $s_i = \sqrt{p_i p_{\bar{i}}}$.

Now, if we look at Eqs. (6.42$a$) and (6.42$b$), we see that $f_{12}$ is equal to the coefficient $a_{12}$ which appears in system (6.42), showing that $a_{12}$ is a measure of causal influence:

$$f_{12} = p_{2,1} - p_{2,\bar{1}} = (a_{12} + e_2) - e_2 = a_{12} \tag{6.47}$$

Hence
$$\phi_{12} = a_{12} \frac{s_1}{s_2} \tag{6.48}$$

On the other hand, we know, by the theorems of total and of composed probabilities, that

$$p_{3,1} = p_{2,1} p_{3,21} + p_{\bar{2},1} p_{3,\bar{2}1} \tag{6.49a}$$
$$p_{3,\bar{1}} = p_{2,\bar{1}} p_{3,2\bar{1}} + p_{\bar{2},\bar{1}} p_{3,\bar{2}\bar{1}} \tag{6.49b}$$

Equation (6.49$a$) means the following: if we look at old people (1), the probability that they commit suicide (3) is the sum of the probability that they are married ($p_{2,1}$) and that, being married, they commit suicide ($p_{3,21}$), plus the probability that they are unmarried ($p_{\bar{2},1}$), and that, being unmarried, they commit suicide ($p_{3,\bar{2}1}$). The interpretation of Eq. (6.49$b$) is similar. The only difference is that it applies to young ($\bar{1}$) people.

Thus, by Eqs. (6.42$a$) to (6.42$i$), we have

$$f_{13} = p_{3,1} - p_{3,\bar{1}} = (a_{12} + e_2)(a_{13} + a_{23} + e_3) + e_{\bar{2}}(a_{13} + e_3) - e_2(e_3 + a_{23})$$
$$- (a_{12} + e_2)e_3 = a_{12}a_{13} + a_{12}a_{23} + (e_2 + e_{\bar{2}})a_{13} \tag{6.50}$$

But, by Eqs. (6.42$a$) and (6.42$g$), we have

$$a_{12} + e_2 + e_{\bar{2}} = p_{2,1} + p_{\bar{2},1} = 1 \tag{6.51}$$
and
$$e_2 + e_{\bar{2}} = 1 - a_{12} \tag{6.52}$$
Hence
$$p_{3,1} - p_{3,\bar{1}} = a_{13} + a_{12}a_{23} \tag{6.53}$$
and
$$\phi_{13} = a_{13} \frac{s_1}{s_3} + a_{12}a_{23} \frac{s_1}{s_3} \tag{6.54}$$

But Eq. (6.54) may also be written

$$\phi_{13} = a_{13} \frac{s_1}{s_3} + a_{12} \frac{s_1}{s_2} a_{23} \frac{s_2}{s_3} \tag{6.55}$$

Finally, to get $\phi_{23}$, we would interchange indices 1 and 2 in Eqs. (6.49$a$) and (6.49$b$), and consequently, in the right side of Eq. (6.50). We should get

$$f_{23} = p_{3,2} - p_{3,\bar{2}} = (a_{21} + e_1)(a_{23} + a_{13} + e_3) + e_{\bar{1}}(a_{23} + e_3) - e_1(e_3 + a_{13})$$
$$- (a_{21} + e_{\bar{1}})e_3$$
$$= a_{21}a_{23} + a_{21}a_{13} + (e_1 + e_{\bar{1}})a_{23}$$
$$= a_{23} + a_{21}a_{13} \tag{6.56}$$
Whence
$$\phi_{23} = a_{23} \frac{s_2}{s_3} + a_{21} \frac{s_2}{s_1} a_{13} \frac{s_1}{s_3} \tag{6.57}$$

An explanation is needed for our statement on permutation of indices in order to get $\phi_{23}$. From Eqs. (6.42$a$) to (6.42$i$), it is impossible to describe $p_{3,2}$

and $p_{3,\bar{2}}$ as functions of the effect parameters only: these equations give an expression of $p_{3,2}$ and $p_{3,\bar{2}}$ depending on $p_1$. In order to get for $p_{3,2} - p_{3,\bar{2}}$ an expression independent of $p_1$, we must add to Eqs. (6.42a) through (6.42i) a new subset of equations, i.e.,

$$p_{1,2} = a_{21} + e_1 \qquad (6.58a)$$
$$p_{\bar{1},2} = \qquad e_{\bar{1}} \qquad (6.58b)$$
$$p_{1,\bar{2}} = \qquad e_1 \qquad (6.58c)$$
$$p_{\bar{1},\bar{2}} = a_{21} + e_{\bar{1}} \qquad (6.58d)$$

These equations are obviously compatible with Eqs. (6.42a) to (6.42i). With (6.42a), (6.42b), (6.42g), and (6.42h), they exhaust the three degrees of freedom associated with a $2 \times 2$ contingency table, since $a_{12}$ and $a_{21}$ are not independent. [Indeed, from Eqs. (6.42g), (6.42h), (6.58b), and (6.58c), we have $a_{12} = p_{21} - p_{2,\bar{1}}$ and $a_{21} = p_{1,2} - p_{1,\bar{2}}$. Hence, $a_{12} = f_{12}$ and $a_{21} = f_{21}$. From this and from Eq. (6.46), we conclude $a_{21} = a_{12} s_1^2 / s_2^2$.] Now, Eqs. (6.42a), (6.42b), (6.42g), and (6.42h) differ from Eqs. (6.58a) to (6.58d) only by a permutation of the indices 1 and 2. Hence the rules used to get $p_{3,2} - p_{3,\bar{2}}$.

In summary, the three equations describing the correlation coefficients as functions of the effect parameters are

$$\phi_{12} = a_{12} \frac{s_1}{s_2} \qquad (6.59)$$

$$\phi_{13} = a_{13} \frac{s_1}{s_3} + a_{12} \frac{s_1}{s_2} a_{23} \frac{s_2}{s_3} \qquad (6.60)$$

$$\phi_{23} = a_{23} \frac{s_2}{s_3} + a_{21} \frac{s_2}{s_1} a_{13} \frac{s_1}{s_3} = a_{23} \frac{s_2}{s_3} + a_{12} \frac{s_1}{s_2} a_{13} \frac{s_1}{s_3} \qquad (6.61)$$

But it is easy to see that these equations are identical to the dependence equations one would get in the case of continuous variables: hence, the parameters $a_{12}$, $a_{13}$, $a_{23}$ introduced in Eqs. (6.46a) to (6.46l) may be interpreted as dependence coefficients, while $a_{12}s_1/s_2$, $a_{13}s_1/s_3$, and $a_{23}s_2/s_3$ are the standardized Wright coefficients.

Although we shall not give the proof for the general case, dependence analysis may thus be applied in the case of dichotomous variables as well as in the case of continuous variables.

Let us apply this to an example taken from Stouffer (23) which deals with a three-variable relationship between age, education, and tolerance. By dichotomizing Stouffer's variables so that age $(x_1)$ is less than forty versus forty and more; education $(x_2)$ is grade school or some high school versus high school graduates and more; and tolerance $(x_3)$ is less tolerant and in-between versus more tolerant, one gets, letting $b_{12} = a_{12}s_1/s_2$, $b_{13} = a_{13}s_1/s_3$, and $b_{23} = a_{23}s_2/s_3$,

$$\phi_{12} = -.272 \qquad (6.62)$$
$$\phi_{13} = -.180 \qquad (6.63)$$
$$\phi_{23} = .278 \qquad (6.64)$$

| Whence | $-.272 = b_{12}$ | (6.65) |
| | $-.160 = b_{13} - .272b_{23}$ | (6.66) |
| | $.278 = b_{23} - .272b_{13}$ | (6.67) |

By solving,

| | $b_{12} = -.272$ | (6.68) |
| | $b_{13} = -.910$ | (6.69) |
| | $b_{23} = .253$ | (6.70) |

As an exercise, the reader might solve directly Eqs. (6.42$a$) to (6.42$i$) applied to Stouffer's data, using Coleman (10). He would find that the solutions for the main effects parameters are the same as those obtained by dependence analysis, since $b_{12} = a_{12}s_1/s_2$, $b_{13} = a_{13}s_1/s_3$, and $b_{23} = a_{23}s_2/s_3$ are close to $a_{12}$, $a_{13}$, and $a_{23}$, respectively, in this example.

## 6.7  THE EFFECT OF CORRELATION BETWEEN INDEPENDENT VARIABLES ON A DEPENDENCE ANALYSIS

It sometimes happens that, in a causal model, independent variables are correlated. In other words, there is a causal relationship of some kind between these variables, but we are not willing or able to give it a more precise form. Thus, let us suppose that two variables $x_1$ and $x_2$ are treated in a causal model as independent variables and that they are correlated. Causally, this correlation might correspond to a direct effect of $x_1$ on $x_2$ or of $x_2$ on $x_1$, or to an indirect effect of $x_1$ on $x_2$ through $y$, or to a simultaneous effect of $y$ on both $x_1$ and $x_2$. But the important result is that the estimation of the dependence parameters will be unique, whatever causal interpretation we give to the correlations between independent variables.

Let us consider a hypothetical causal model represented by Fig. 6.4. The dashed curves connecting the independent variables $x_1$ and $x_2$, $x_1$ and $x_3$, $x_2$ and $x_3$ indicate that these variables are correlated although we are not able to interpret the correlations causally.

The results of a dependence analysis applied to such a structure will be identical, whatever causal interpretation we give to these correlations. Thus, the measure $b'_{14}$ of the effect of $x_1$ on $x_4$ will be the same if we suppose $x_1$ causes $x_2$ or, conversely, $x_2$ causes $x_1$ (and similarly for $x_1$ and $x_3$ or $x_2$ and $x_3$). The measures $b'_{24}$, $b'_{25}$, . . . , $b'_{56}$ will likewise be the same, whatever arbitrary causal interpretation is given to the correlations between $x_1$, $x_2$, and $x_3$.

Instead of giving the proof of this important result, we propose to the reader to check, as an exercise, that the dependence equations derived from the causal structure of Fig. 6.4 are the same for any arbitrary causal interpretation of the correlations between the independent variables. For instance, one can write the dependence equations corresponding to the model of Fig. 6.5, with

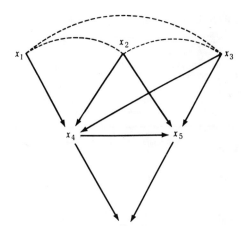

Fig. 6.4. Hypothetical Causal Model Where the Independent Variables Are Correlated.

the arbitrary hypotheses: $x_1$ causes $x_2$, $x_1$ causes $x_3$, $x_2$ causes $x_3$, comparing results with those for any other set of arbitrary hypotheses. The dependence equations giving $b'_{14}$, $b'_{15}$, . . . , $b'_{56}$ are the same, whatever these hypotheses. Thus the rule, when independent variables are correlated, is to connect these variables by arrows arbitrarily oriented and to write the causal and dependence equations as usual.

## 6.8 DEPENDENCE ANALYSIS IN THE CASE OF NONADDITIVITY

At this point, the survey analyst might say: this kind of analysis is fine, but until now I do not see how the important and frequent case where relations are nonadditive may be taken into account.

In fact, we have not yet learned to deal with a case as simple as Lazarsfeld's example (18) of the relationship between age, education, and listening to classical music. Consider the data in Table 6.1. Looking at these familiar data, we see that the relationship between age and listening to classical music is approximately zero. However, when the test variable "level of education" is introduced, an interesting phenomenon appears: among the poorly educated, listening to classical music decreases with age; among the well educated, listening to classical music increases with age. In other words, the effect of age on listening to classical music depends on the level of education. In such a case, we shall speak interchangeably of nonadditivity of effects, of interaction or, following Lazarsfeld, of specification. Since this concept has been discussed in the previous chapter we shall confine our attention to how it can be handled in terms of dependence analysis.

The linear equations used in the previous sections cannot possibly translate a phenomenon of this kind, however simple it may look. Let us examine a

TABLE 6.1    Proportion of Listeners to Classical Music

| Level of education not a test variable | Young | Old |
|---|---|---|
| | 30% | 29% |

| | High education | | Low education | |
|---|---|---|---|---|
| Level of education intro-duced as a test variable | Young | Old | Young | Old |
| | 32% | 52% | 28% | 19% |

Source: Lazarsfeld (18).

typical linear equation such as

$$x_3 = a_{13}x_1 + a_{23}x_2 + e_3 \qquad (6.71)$$

The effect of, say, $x_1$ on $x_3$ is given by taking the partial derivative of $x_3$ with respect to $x_1$. This derivative may be interpreted as the rate of variation in $x_3$ when $x_1$ varies, the third variable $x_2$ having a fixed value. In the case of a linear equation such as Eq. (6.71), this derivative is

$$\frac{\partial x_3}{\partial x_1} = a_{13} \qquad (6.72)$$

Let us note incidentally that Eq. (6.72) points to an interesting interpretation of the dependence coefficient $a_{13}$ as the rate of increase of $x_3$ per unit increase of $x_1$ when other variables are fixed. But the important implication of Eq. (6.72) is that the rate of variation $\partial x_3/\partial x_1$ is constant and, consequently, does not depend on $x_2$. This shows that linearity is here associated with the absence of interaction.

Now, let us look by contrast at an equation such as

$$x_3 + a_{13}x_1 + a_{23}x_2 + a_{123}x_1x_2 = e_3 \qquad (6.73)$$

Or, letting $a'_{13} = -a_{13}$, $a'_{23} = -a_{23}$, $a'_{123} = -a_{123}$,

$$x_3 = a'_{13}x_1 + a'_{23}x_2 + a'_{123}x_1x_2 + e_3 \qquad (6.74)$$

and writing the partial derivative of $x_3$ with respect to $x_1$,

$$\frac{\partial x_3}{\partial x_1} = a'_{13} + a'_{123}x_2 \qquad (6.75)$$

The effect of $x_1$ on $x_3$, as given by the value of the partial derivative, depends on $x_2$. Thus, we have translated algebraically the interaction effect contained in Table 6.1. Depending on the values of $a'_{13}$ and $a'_{123}$, it is possible that the rate $\partial x_3/\partial x_1$ is positive for certain values of $x_2$ but negative for others.

The causal equation (6.74) gives rise to three dependence equations, namely,

$$a_{13}E(x_1{}^2) + a_{23}E(x_1x_2) + a_{123}E(x_1{}^2x_2) + E(x_1x_3) = 0 \qquad (6.76a)$$
$$a_{13}E(x_1x_2) + a_{23}E(x_2{}^2) + a_{123}E(x_1x_2{}^2) + E(x_2x_3) = 0 \qquad (6.76b)$$
$$a_{13}E(x_1{}^2x_2) + a_{23}E(x_1x_2{}^2) + a_{123}E(x_1{}^2x_2{}^2) + E(x_1x_2x_3) = 0 \qquad (6.76c)$$

The equations are obtained by multiplying Eq. (6.73) successively by $x_1$, $x_2$, and the product $x_1x_2$ which is thus considered as a third variable. The introduction of this interaction variable has the effect of giving to the dependence equations, Eqs. (6.76a) to (6.76c), a somewhat unfamiliar appearance. First, we see that covariances of a new type appear: i.e., the covariance between one variable and the square of another. With more complicated causal structures, terms of the form $E(x_ix_jx_k)$ representing, say, the numerator of a coefficient of correlation between three variables would appear. Although quantities of this type are seldom used in practice, they are natural extensions of the ideas of covariance and correlation. The reason that, in practice, only covariances and correlations between two variables are used is that these familiar coefficients have an immediate physical interpretation, while quantities such as $E(x_ix_jx_k)$ have not.[10]

We shall see in a moment how these generalized covariances are to be computed. But let us suppose that they have actually been computed. Then Eqs. (6.76a) to (6.76c) build up a system of three equations with three unknowns, $a_{13}$, $a_{23}$, and $a_{123}$. What is the meaning of these parameters?

To answer this question, let us look at Eq. (6.75). It gives the rate of change in $x_3$ due to $x_1$ when $x_2$ has a fixed value. This rate of change was symbolized by the partial derivative $\partial x_3/\partial x_1$. But suppose we ask: What is the rate of change of $\partial x_3/\partial x_1$ when $x_2$ "moves"? This "second-order" rate of change is given by

$$\frac{\partial}{\partial x_2}\left(\frac{\partial x_3}{\partial x_1}\right) = \frac{\partial^2 x_3}{\partial x_2 \partial x_1} = a'_{123} \qquad (6.77)$$

Thus, Eq. (6.77) may be considered as giving the interpretation of $a'_{123}$. It tells us that $a'_{123}$ is the effect of $x_2$ on the effect of $x_1$ on $x_3$ (or, conversely, the effect of $x_1$ on the effect of $x_2$ on $x_3$). Hence $a'_{123}$ is a measure of interaction. As regards $a'_{13}$ and $a'_{23}$, it is easy to see, by looking at Eq. (6.75), that they measure the effects respectively of $x_1$ and $x_2$ on $x_3$ once the interaction effect has been removed.

Diagrammatically, the interpretation of the causal structure underlying Table 6.1 is given by Fig. 6.5a and 6.5b. In 6.5a, the effect of age is qualified by education; in 6.5b, the effect of education is qualified by age, and both representations are actually indistinguishable. This is exactly what Lazarsfeld means when he introduces a distinction between elaboration types *PI* and *PA*, and says that types *PI* and *PA* have "a simple relationship" (18).

Let us notice, however, that Fig. 6.5 does not adequately represent the structure corresponding to Lazarsfeld's data. If we look, not at the data of Table 6.1, but at the more detailed data it summarizes (see Table 6.2), we see that there is a relationship between age and education. In other words, it would be necessary to complete Fig. 6.5 by an arrow going from age to educa-

---

[10] See, however, how such quantities are introduced in Lazarsfeld (17).

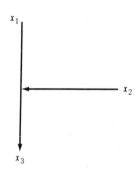

(a)

Fig. 6.5.   Representation of an Interaction Effect.

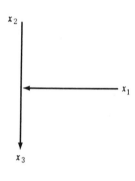

(b)

tion.   (In this case the causal interpretation of the correlation is immediate).
Nevertheless, we know from the previous section that this fact does not affect the
values derived from Eqs. (6.76a) to (6.76c) for $a_{13}$, $a_{23}$, and $a_{123}$.   Incidentally,
we invite the reader to examine carefully these three equations for a confirmation
of the proposition of the previous section, according to which the results of a

TABLE 6.2   Relationships between Age, Education, and Listening to
Classical Music

|  | High education | | | Low education | | |
|---|---|---|---|---|---|---|
|  | *Young* | *Old* | *Total* | *Young* | *Old* | *Total* |
| *Listen* | 192 | 312 | 504 | 110 | 170 | 280 |
| *Do not listen* | 408 | 88 | 496 | 290 | 730 | 1,020 |
| *Total* | 600 | 400 | 1,000 | 400 | 900 | 1,300 |

Source: Lazarsfeld (18).

dependence analysis are unique, whatever the causal structure connecting the independent variables may be. Indeed, the relationship between the two independent variables $x_1$ and $x_2$ appears exclusively in the form of symmetrical covariances. In a world where education would affect age, $a_{13}$, $a_{23}$, and $a_{123}$ would be the same as in our world.

As in the case of causal structures without interaction, one may substitute for the unstandardized dependence coefficients such as $a_{13}$, $a_{23}$, and $a_{123}$, standardized dependence coefficients defined by

$$b_{ij} = a_{ij} \frac{\sigma_i}{\sigma_j} \tag{6.78}$$

$$b_{ijk} = a_{ijk} \frac{\sigma_i \sigma_j}{\sigma_k} \tag{6.79}$$

In the first case, $x_j$ is assumed dependent on $x_i$; in the second case, $x_k$ is assumed dependent on $x_i$ and $x_j$. Indeed, let us call $r_{iij}$ the quantity $E(x_i^2 x_j)\sigma_i^2\sigma_j$; $r_{ijk}$ the quantity $E(x_i x_j x_k)\sigma_i \sigma_j \sigma_k$, and so on. Then, Eqs. (6.76a) to (6.76c) may be written

$$\left( a_{13} \frac{\sigma_1}{\sigma_3} + a_{23} \frac{\sigma_2}{\sigma_3} r_{12} + a_{123} \frac{\sigma_1 \sigma_2}{\sigma_3} r_{112} + r_{13} \right) \sigma_1 \sigma_3 = 0 \tag{6.80a}$$

$$\left( a_{13} \frac{\sigma_1}{\sigma_3} r_{12} + a_{23} \frac{\sigma_2}{\sigma_3} + a_{123} \frac{\sigma_1 \sigma_2}{\sigma_3} r_{122} + r_{23} \right) \sigma_2 \sigma_3 = 0 \tag{6.80b}$$

$$\left( a_{13} \frac{\sigma_1}{\sigma_3} r_{112} + a_{23} \frac{\sigma_2}{\sigma_3} r_{122} + a_{123} \frac{\sigma_1 \sigma_2}{\sigma_3} r_{1122} + r_{123} \right) \sigma_1 \sigma_2 \sigma_3 = 0 \tag{6.80c}$$

But this is equivalent to

$$b_{13} + b_{23} r_{12} + b_{123} r_{112} + r_{13} = 0 \tag{6.81a}$$
$$b_{13} r_{12} + b_{23} + b_{23} r_{122} + r_{23} = 0 \tag{6.81b}$$
$$b_{13} r_{112} + b_{23} r_{122} + b_{123} r_{1122} + r_{123} = 0 \tag{6.81c}$$

Thus, all that we have to do is to compute the $r$ coefficients, both simple and generalized, and to solve Eqs. (6.81a) to (6.81c) to get $b_{13}$, $b_{23}$, and $b_{123}$.

Again, we get a system of equations where the dependence parameters are determined by a correlation analysis. But when interaction effects are present, it is necessary to have more information than the simple two-variable correlation coefficients and to compute generalized correlation coefficients.

Before applying this to Lazarsfeld's example, let us say a word about these generalized correlation coefficients. With continuous variables, there is no special difficulty in this generalization. Thus, the well-known Bravais-Pearson formula

$$r_{ij} = \frac{\Sigma(x_i - \bar{x}_i)(x_j - \bar{x}_j)}{\sqrt{\Sigma(x_i - \bar{x}_i)^2 \Sigma(x_j - \bar{x}_j)^2}} \tag{6.82}$$

will be generalized into

$$r_{ijk} = \frac{\Sigma(x_i - \bar{x}_i)(x_j - \bar{x}_j)(x_k - \bar{x}_k)}{\sqrt[3]{\Sigma(x_i - \bar{x}_i^2)\Sigma(x_j - \bar{x}_j)^2\Sigma(x_k - \bar{x}_k)^2}} \qquad (6.83)$$

$$r_{iij} = \frac{\Sigma(x_i - \bar{x}_i)(x_i - \bar{x}_i)(x_j - \bar{x}_j)}{\sqrt[3]{\Sigma(x_i - \bar{x}_i)^2\Sigma(x_i - \bar{x}_i)^2\Sigma(x_j - \bar{x}_j)^2}} \qquad (6.84)$$

With $\phi$ coefficients the matter is somewhat more complicated but substantively the same.

Let us first recall that $\phi_{ij}$ may be considered a special case of the Bravais-Pearson coefficient: indeed, if we give the arbitrary values 0 and 1 to the two categories of each variable, we have, since $x_i$ has value 1 with probability $p_i$ and value 0 with probability $p_i^- = 1 - p_i$,

$$\text{Var}\ (x_i) = p_i p_{\bar{i}} \qquad (6.85)$$
$$\text{Cov}\ (x_i x_j) = p_{ij} - p_i p_j \qquad (6.86)$$

Hence, the familiar formula

$$\phi_{ij} = \frac{p_{ij} - p_i p_j}{\sqrt{p_i p_{\bar{i}} p_j p_{\bar{j}}}} \qquad (6.87)$$

What is the formula for the generalized $\phi$ coefficients? Let us consider $\phi_{ijk}$. Obviously, its denominator will be the geometric mean of the variances, as in the two-variable case, i.e., $\sqrt[3]{p_i p_{\bar{i}} p_j p_{\bar{j}} p_k p_{\bar{k}}}$. The numerator may be directly computed. If we symbolize the familiar cross products $p_{ij} - p_i p_j$ by $D_{ij}$, we obtain

$$\text{Cov}\ (x_i x_j x_k) = p_{ijk} - p_i D_{jk} - p_j D_{ik} - p_k D_{ij} - p_i p_j p_k \qquad (6.88)$$

and by repeated application of this formula, every covariance of higher order, such as $\text{Cov}\ (x_i x_j x_k x_m)$, can likewise be computed.

Thus the dichotomous case raises no special problems, except one. Consider Eq. (6.88) in the case of a high-order covariance with a repeated variable, such as $\text{Cov}\ (x_i x_i x_j)$. Then, quantities like $p_{iij}$ and $D_{ii} = p_{ii} - p_i p_i$ appear and give rise to these quantities without empirical meaning: $p_{iij}$ and $p_{ii}$. Nonetheless, one might, as a rule, assume that $p_{iij} = p_{ij}$ and $p_{ii} = p_i$, whence $D_{ii} = p_i p_{\bar{i}}$ and $\phi_{ii} = 1$. Then, Cov $(x_i x_i x_j)$ has a definite value.

Let us now apply this to the example of specification given by Lazarsfeld: first, let us refer to the data from Table 6.2.

The two-variable simple correlation coefficients are

$$\phi_{12} = .2926 \qquad (6.89)$$
$$\phi_{13} = .0088 \qquad (6.90)$$
$$\phi_{23} = .2048 \qquad (6.91)$$

where $x_1$ is age, $x_2$ education, and $x_3$ listening.

Next, applying Eq. (6.88),

$$\text{Cov } (x_1 x_1 x_2) = p_{112} - p_1 D_{12} - p_1 D_{12} - p_2 D_{11} - p_1 p_1 p_2$$

$$= \frac{600}{2,300} - 2 \times \frac{1,000}{2,300} D_{12} - \frac{1,000}{2,300} D_{11} - \frac{1,000}{2,300} \frac{1,000}{2,300} \frac{1,000}{2,300} \quad (6.92)$$

Since

$$D_{12} = \frac{600 \times 900 - 400 \times 400}{2,300 \times 2,300} = .0718 \quad (6.93)$$

and

$$D_{11} = \frac{1,000}{2,300} \frac{1,300}{2,300} = .2458 \quad (6.94)$$

we have

$$\text{Cov } (x_1 x_1 x_2) = .0093 \quad (6.95)$$

and

$$\phi_{112} = \frac{.0093}{.2458} = .0383 \quad (6.96)$$

In the same way, applying

$$\text{Cov } (x_1 x_2 x_2) = p_{122} - p_1 D_{22} - p_2 D_{12} - p_2 D_{12} - p_1 p_2 p_2 \quad (6.97)$$

we also find that $\phi_{122}$ has the same value of .0383. As regards $\phi_{1122}$ and $\phi_{123}$, they are respectively equal to .2816 and $-.0653$.

Now we can write Eqs. (6.81a) to (6.81c) with numerical coefficients:

$$b_{13} + .2926 b_{23} + .0383 b_{123} + .0088 = 0 \quad (6.98)$$
$$.2926 b_{13} + b_{23} + .0383 b_{123} + .2048 = 0 \quad (6.99)$$

By solving and reversing signs, we get the solution:

$$.0383 b_{13} + .0383 b_{23} + .2816 b_{123} - .0653 = 0 \quad (6.100)$$
$$b'_{13} = - .0483 \quad b'_{23} = .2287 \quad b'_{123} = .6538 \quad (6.101)$$

Of course, the utility of dependence analysis compared with Lazarsfeld's multivariate analysis would really become obvious only in more complicated situations than the three-variable case dealt with here. Notice that, even with a limited number of explanatory variables, the number of possible causal models increases very quickly as soon as interactions are considered. Thus, although the present method may in theory deal with every situation encountered in survey analysis, however complicated a situation may be, one should not forget that it is not a mechanical tool that can be automatically applied to every situation. On the contrary, its efficiency rests on the degree of precision of our substantive knowledge and on the level of sophistication of our sociological theories. This is the main difficulty. The other one, namely, that computations become rather involved with moderately complicated causal structures, can be easily solved by computers.

## 6.9  APPLICATIONS OF DEPENDENCE ANALYSIS TO PANEL DATA

Dependence analysis provides an interesting tool for the analysis of over-time data collected by the panel method. Let us, for instance, consider a two-attribute turnover table taken from Lazarsfeld's *The People's Choice* (16), and reproduced in Table 6.3. The two attributes were political attitude (Republican versus Democrat) and attitude toward the Republican candidate Willkie (positive versus negative). By looking intuitively at the data, one can see that certain factors are acting to modify attitudes between the first and the second interviews. Thus we see that of the 35 Republicans who were hostile to Willkie, about a third changed their minds on the candidate by the time of the second interview, while 11 Democrats out of 24 became hostile to Willkie. In summary, most people did not change their opinions between the first and second interviews, and most changes consisted of harmonizing attitudes toward Willkie with the basic political attitudes, which appear to be much more stable.

Let us call $x_1^1$ the party identification at time 1, $x_1^2$ the basic political attitude at time 2, $x_2^1$ the attitude toward Willkie at time 1, and $x_2^2$ the attitude toward Willkie at time 2. A model corresponding to the process underlying the data of Table 6.3 may be represented by an arrow scheme as in Fig. 6.6. The arrows from $x_1^{t-1}$ to $x_1^t$ and from $x_1^t$ to $x_1^{t+1}$ symbolize the hypothesis according to which basic political attitudes are likely to persist from one period to the next. The interpretation of the arrows going from $x_2^{t-1}$ to $x_2^t$ and from $x_2^t$ to $x_2^{t+1}$ similarly translates the idea that attitudes toward the candidate tend to persist. Of course, we expect to find, if the model is adequate, that the dependence between two successive observations of $x_1$ is greater than the dependence between two observations of $x_2$. The cross-variable arrows from $x_1^{t-1}$ to $x_2^t$, from $x_2^t$ to $x_1^{t+1}$, and so forth, are supposed to represent the harmonizing process, according to which basic political attitudes and attitudes toward the candidate tend to be consonant. Here again, we expect to observe a greater influence of $x_1$ on $x_2$ than of $x_2$ on $x_1$.

The diagram of Fig. 6.6 is theoretical in the sense that the data of Table 6.3 concern only two interviews. Before the first interview, the harmonization process was going on, and it continues after the second interview. Let us suppose that our interview periods are the periods $t$ and $t + 1$ of Fig. 6.6.

TABLE 6.3    Concurrent Change in Vote Intention and Personal Liking for Willkie

| | | | Second interview | | | | |
|---|---|---|---|---|---|---|---|
| | Party<br>Willkie attitude | | + <br>+ | + <br>− | − <br>+ | − <br>− | Total |
| | Republican for Willkie | (++) | 129 | 3 | 1 | 2 | 135 |
| *First* | Republican against Willkie | (+−) | 11 | 23 | 0 | 1 | 35 |
| *interview* | Democrat for Willkie | (−+) | 1 | 0 | 12 | 11 | 24 |
| | Democrat against Willkie | (−−) | 1 | 1 | 2 | 68 | 72 |
| | Total | | 142 | 27 | 15 | 82 | 266 |

Source: Lipset et al. (19).

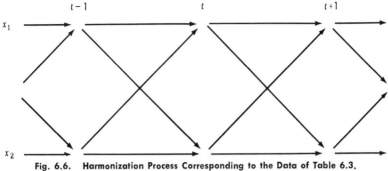

Fig. 6.6. Harmonization Process Corresponding to the Data of Table 6.3.

The fact that the process was already going on in previous periods means that $x_1$ and $x_2$ will appear as correlated at time $t$. Thus the model corresponding to the data of Table 6.3 may be symbolized by the diagram of Fig. 6.7, where the dashed arrow between $x_1^1$ and $x_2^1$ represents this correlation. Notice that we have here a case where the correlation between independent variables $x_1^1$ and $x_2^1$ gives rise to a relatively complex interpretation. Let us, however, recall the result of Sec. 6.9, according to which the causal structure explaining the correlation between independent variables is irrelevant to the subsequent dependence analysis.

At this point, dependence analysis is certainly familiar enough to the reader, and it is unnecessary to write down the causal equations corresponding to the model of Fig. 6.7. Before going directly to the dependence equations, however, let us introduce some modifications in the notations of the previous sections: $a_{11}^{12}$ will be the unstandardized dependence coefficient corresponding to the effect of $x_1^1$ on $x_1^2$; in other words, this coefficient translates the persistence of the basic political attitudes between two successive periods. Similarly $a_{22}^{12}$ will be the unstandardized dependence coefficient corresponding to the effect of $x_2^1$ on $x_2^2$ (degree of persistence of the attitude toward the candidate). On the other hand, $a_{12}^{12}$ and $a_{21}^{12}$ will describe, respectively, the effect of $x_1$ on $x_2$ and of $x_2$ on $x_1$ lagged from the first to the second observation period.

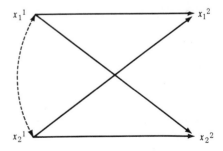

Fig. 6.7. Harmonization Process between Two Successive Periods.

In order to simplify the computations we shall use here, in contrast with the preceding sections, not correlation coefficients but asymmetrical $f$ coefficients. Thus, we will designate by $f(x_1^1, x_1^2)$ the observed effect of $x_1^1$ on $x_1^2$. In other words, $f(x_1^1, x_1^2)$ is the difference between the probability (estimated from the data) $P(x_1^2, x_1^1)$ of being positive on $x_1^2$, when one is positive on $x_1^1$, and the probability $P(x_1^2, \bar{x}_1^1)$ of being positive on $x_1^2$, when one is negative on $x_1^1$. The coefficients such as $f(x_1^1, \bar{x}_1^2)$ and $f(x_2^1, x_1^2)$ have similar meanings.

As it can be easily seen from Sec. 6.6, using $f$'s instead of $\phi$'s has the effect of introducing some computational errors if the variances are not equal. Let us look for instance at Eq. (6.61): it may be written in the form $f_{23} = a_{23} + a_{12}a_{23}$ only in the case where $a_{21} = a_{12}$. This assumes, since $a_{21} = a_{12}s_1^2/s_2^2$, that $s_1^2 = s_2^2$. In the present example, the four variances are respectively (see Table 6.3) $170(96)/(266)^2$, $169(97)/(266)^2$, $159(107)/(266)^2$, and $157(109)/(266)^2$. Since they are approximately equal to one another, $f$'s may be substituted for $\phi$'s. The advantage is that $f$'s are much more easily computed than $\phi$'s; the disadvantage is a slight imprecision of the computations.

The dependence equations corresponding to the model of Fig. 6.7 are, then,

$$f(x_1^1, x_2^1) = a_{12}^{11} \qquad (6.102a)$$
$$f(x_1^1, x_1^2) = a_{11}^{12} + a_{12}^{11}a_{21}^{12} \qquad (6.102b)$$
$$f(x_2^1, x_1^2) = a_{21}^{12} + a_{12}^{11}a_{11}^{12} \qquad (6.102c)$$
$$f(x_1^1, x_2^2) = a_{12}^{12} + a_{12}^{11}a_{22}^{12} \qquad (6.102d)$$
$$f(x_2^1, x_2^2) = a_{22}^{12} + a_{12}^{11}a_{12}^{12} \qquad (6.102e)$$
$$f(x_1^2, x_2^2) = a_{21}^{12}a_{22}^{12} + a_{11}^{12}a_{12}^{12} + a_{11}^{12}a_{12}^{11}a_{22}^{12} \qquad (6.102f)$$

The solutions of these equations are as follows:

$$
\begin{array}{ll}
a_{12}^{11} = .544 & a_{12}^{12} = .329 \\
a_{11}^{12} = .942 & a_{22}^{12} = .593 \\
& a_{21}^{12} = .011
\end{array}
\qquad (6.103)
$$

These results conform to our expectations: the dominant effect is the persistence of party preferences (.942). Attitudes toward the candidate, although less stable, tend to persist (.593). As regards the *cross effects*, basic attitudes have an influence on the attitude toward the candidate in the following period (.329), but the effect of the attitude toward the candidate on the party preferences is close to zero (.011).

It is interesting to regenerate a theoretical turnover table in order to verify the adequacy of the model. Let us first recall a result which may be easily inferred from Sec. 6.6, according to which the dependence equations (6.102) give the same estimates of the dependence parameters as the linear decompositions of conditional probabilities used by Coleman (10), when the variances are equal; thus

$$p(x_2^1, x_1^1) = a_{12}^{11} + e_2^1 \qquad (6.104a)$$
$$p(x_2^1, \bar{x}_1^1) = e_2^1 \qquad (6.104b)$$
$$p(x_1^2, x_1^1 x_2^1) = a_{11}^{12} + a_{21}^{12} + e_1^2 \qquad (6.104c)$$
$$p(x_1^2, \bar{x}_2^1 \bar{x}_2^1) = a_{21}^{12} + e_1^2 \qquad (6.104d)$$
$$p(x_1^2, \bar{x}_2^1) = a_{11}^{12} + e_1^2 \qquad (6.104e)$$
$$p(x_1^2, \bar{x}_1^1 \bar{x}_2^1) = e_1^2 \qquad (6.104f)$$
$$p(x_2^2, x_1^1 x_2^1) = a_{12}^{12} + a_{22}^{12} + e_2^2 \qquad (6.104g)$$
$$p(x_2^2, \bar{x}_1^1 x_2^1) = a_{22}^{12} + e_2^2 \qquad (6.104h)$$
$$p(x_2^2, x_1^1 \bar{x}_2^1) = a_{12}^{12} + e_2^2 \qquad (6.104i)$$
$$p(x_2^2, \bar{x}_1^1 \bar{x}_2^1) = e_2^2 \qquad (6.104j)$$

where $p(x_2^1, x_1^1)$ is, as above, the probability of being positive on $x_2$ at time 1 when one is positive on $x_1$ at time 1; $p(x_2^1, \bar{x}_1^1)$ the probability of being positive on $x_2$ at time 1 when one is negative on $x_1$ at time 1, and so forth.

By substituting the numerical values found by solving (6.102) in the Eqs. (6.104a) to (6.104j), it is easy to see that

$$e_2^1 = .250 \qquad (6.105)$$
$$e_1^2 = .029 \qquad (6.106)$$
$$e_2^2 = .000 \qquad (6.107)$$

One may easily account for the fact that $e_2^1$ has a rather high value compared with $e_2^2$. At the first observation we know only that $x_1$ and $x_2$ are correlated, without being able, as in the second observation, to give a detailed description of the process at work.

From Eqs. (6.104a) to (6.104j) and from the distribution of $x_1$ it is possible, by applying the theorems of total and of composed probabilities, to generate a theoretical turnover table. Thus

$$p(x_2^1, x_1^1) = a_{12}^{11} + e_2^1 = .544 + .250 = .794 \qquad (6.108)$$

Since $n(x_1^1)$ or the number of persons positive on $x_1$ at time 1 is 170 (from Table 6.3), the theoretical number of persons who should be, according to the model, positive on $x_1$ and on $x_2$ at time 1 is

$$n^*(x^1 x_2^1) = .794 \times 170 = 135 \qquad (6.109)$$

where the star means that we are dealing with a *theoretical* value. Of course, the theoretical number of people who are negative on $x_2$ at time 1 and positive on $x_1$ at time 1 is

$$n^*(x_1^1 \bar{x}_2^1) = 170 - 135 = 35 \qquad (6.110)$$

In the same way, we obtain

$$n^*(\bar{x}_1{}^1x_2{}^1) = 24 \qquad (6.111)$$
and
$$n^*(\bar{x}_1{}^1\bar{x}_2{}^1) = 72 \qquad (6.112)$$

In order to determine the theoretical figures corresponding to the cells of the turnover table, notice that we have, for example,

$$p(x_1{}^2x_2{}^2, x_1{}^1x_2{}^1) = p(x_1{}^2, x_1{}^1x_2{}^1)p(x_2{}^2, x_1{}^2x_1{}^1x_2{}^1) \qquad (6.113)$$

But since according to the hypotheses of the model, $p(x_2{}^2, x_1{}^2x_1{}^1x_2{}^1)$ does not depend on $x_1{}^2$, we may substitute for this expression the expression $p(x_2{}^2, x_1{}^1x_2{}^1)$. Empirically, this substitution appears reasonable, since

$$p(x_2{}^2, x_1{}^2x_1{}^1x_2{}^1) = 129/132 = .978 \qquad (6.114)$$
and
$$p(x_2{}^2, x_1{}^1x_2{}^1) = 132/135 = .978 \qquad (6.115)$$

Thus, if we symbolize by $p^*(x_1{}^2x_2{}^2, x_1{}^1x_2{}^1)$ the *theoretical* probability of being positive both on $x_1$ and $x_2$ at time 2, given that one is positive both on $x_1$ and on $x_2$ at time 1, we get

$$
\begin{aligned}
p^*(x_1{}^2x_2{}^2, x_1{}^1x_2{}^1) &= (a_{11}{}^{12} + a_{21}{}^{12} + e_1{}^2)(a_{12}{}^{12} + a_{22}{}^{12} + e_2{}^2) \\
&= (.942 + .011 + .029)(.329 + .593) = .905 \quad (6.116)
\end{aligned}
$$

Whence

$$n^*(x_1{}^1x_2{}^1x_1{}^2x_2{}^2) = p^*(x_1{}^2x_2{}^2, x_1{}^1x_2{}^1)n^*(x_1{}^1x_2{}^1) = .905 \times 135 = 122 \quad (6.117)$$

The same process may be used to find the other figures of the theoretical turnover table. As an exercise, the reader might check the theoretical figures given in Table 6.4. As can be seen, this theoretical turnover table is reasonably close to the observed table.

In this example we have used a very simple case involving two attributes and two interviews. Here again, the utility of dependence analysis would appear more clearly in more complicated cases. With three attributes and three interviews, the panel method gives rise to eight $8 \times 8$ turnover tables.

TABLE 6.4 Theoretical Turnover Table Corresponding to the Observed Data of Table 6.3

|  |  |  | Second interview | | | | |
|---|---|---|---|---|---|---|---|
|  | *Party*<br>*Willkie attitude* |  | +<br>+ | +<br>− | −<br>+ | −<br>− | *Total* |
|  | Republican for Willkie | (++) | 122 | 10 | 1 | 2 | 135 |
| *First* | Republican against Willkie | (+−) | 12 | 23 | 0 | 0 | 35 |
| *interview* | Democrat for Willkie | (−+) | 0 | 0 | 15 | 9 | 24 |
|  | Democrat against Willkie | (−−) | 0 | 0 | 2 | 70 | 72 |
|  | Total |  | 134 | 33 | 18 | 81 | 266 |

This is already too difficult for an intuitive analysis, and it is necessary to have an analytical tool at hand. With more than three attributes or more than three interviews, the amount of information increases tremendously. However, with over-time data as well as with cross-sectional data it is often necessary to consider simultaneously several attributes. For these more complicated situations, dependence analysis provides a powerful tool. One must write down the most reasonable hypotheses concerning the mechanisms underlying a given process and then check to see whether or not the data generated by these hypotheses are sufficiently close to the observed data. Of course, this implies numerous computations, but these can easily be computerized.

### 6.10 CONCLUSION

The basic problem under discussion is the following. Let us suppose we have a deck of punched cards derived from a survey. On these cards the values for a number of variables are recorded. We examine variable $x_1$ and want to explain it. Either intuitively or on theoretical or empirical grounds, we have the feeling that $x_2$, $x_3$, but perhaps $x_4$ and $x_5$, too, have something to do with $x_1$. But, as always in a survey, these independent variables are themselves related to one another. How, then, can we extract from our data a clear picture of these relationships? The answer, given by Blalock, Coleman, Selvin, Simon, and anticipated by Durkheim, is that we should embody our explanatory hypotheses in a model and test it.

In the first sections of this chapter, we have presented the rationale for a general method for dealing with this problem. This method, which owes much to Blalock, Simon, and Wright, is an extension of the familiar one-equation regression analysis. In the remaining sections we have dealt with the special but important problems of the application of dependence analysis to dichotomous attributes, to situations where interaction effects are present, and finally, to over-time data.[11]

**APPENDIX: PROOF OF THE THEOREM** When implicit factors are uncorrelated, the dependence coefficients are always identifiable.

Assume that the $i$, $j$ element of $P$ is nonzero, and that $PA$ has the same structure as $A$. The $i$th equation may be linearly combined with the $j$th. Moreover, $x_{i+1}$ is causally dependent on $x_{j+1}$. Indeed, since the $j$th equation defines $x_{j+1}$, the coefficient of $x_{j+1}$ is not zero in this equation, whence a linear combination of the $i$th and $j$th equations will retain the structure of the former only if $a_{j+1,i+1}$ is not zero, i.e., if $x_{i+1}$ is causally dependent on $x_{j+1}$.

In Eq. (6.11) premultiplication of $E(ex')$ by $P$, where $p_{ij}$ is not zero, will substitute a linear combination of the $i$th and $j$th rows of $E(ex')$ for the original

---

[11] Still other applications may be devised. See Boudon (8).

*i*th row.  But, since $x_{i+1}$ is causally dependent on $x_{j+1}$, the term of the $(j + 1)$th column in the *i*th row of $E(ex')$, i.e., $E(e_{i+1}x_{j+1})$, is zero, while the term of the same $(j + 1)$th column in the *j*th row is not zero.  Hence, premultiplication by $P$ modifies the structure of the *i*th row, and it is impossible to find a non-diagonal matrix $P$ such that Eq. (6.11) satisfies the structural conditions of Eq. (6.10).

To illustrate this, let us go back to system (6.4).  The corresponding causal structure (see Fig. 6.1) implies $E(e_2x_1) = E(e_3x_1) = E(e_3x_2) = 0$.  That is, in our substantive example, implicit factors acting on the extension of family group are not correlated with age, and implicit factors acting on suicide are correlated neither with age nor with extension of family group.  Now, we see from Eqs. (6.5a)–(6.5b) or (6.7) that we may find a nondiagonal matrix $P$ with $p_{12} \neq 0$, such that $PA$ has the same structure as $A$, and, of course, $PAE(xx')$, the same structure as $AE(xx')$ (since the same coefficients are zero).  Now in the equation $PAE(xx') = PE(ex')$, premultiplication by $P$ substitutes for $E(e_3x_2)$ a quantity which we may designate $E(e_3'x_2')$ and which is equal to

$$E(p_{12}e_2x_2 + e_3x_2) = p_{12}E(e_2x_2) + (e_3x_2)$$

But, since $E(e_2x_2)$ is not zero, $E(e_3'x_2')$ is zero if and only if $p_{12} = 0$.  But we have assumed $p_{12} \neq 0$.  Thus, premultiplication by $P$ violates the condition derived from the assumption that implicit factors are uncorrelated, according to which $x_2$ and the implicit factors acting on $x_3$ are independent.

## REFERENCES

1 Blalock, Hubert M.: *Causal Inferences in Nonexperimental Research* (Chapel Hill, N.C.: University of North Carolina Press, 1964).

2 Blalock, Hubert M.: "Correlation and Causality: The Multivariate Case," *Social Forces*, **39** (March, 1961), 246–251.

3 Blalock, Hubert M.: "Four-variable Causal Models and Partial Correlations," *American Journal of Sociology*, **68** (September, 1962), 182–194.

4 Blalock, Hubert M.: "Further Observations on Asymmetric Causal Models," *American Sociological Review*, **27** (August, 1962), 539–548.

5 Blalock, Hubert M.: "Making Causal Inferences for Unmeasured Variables from Correlations among Indicators," *American Journal of Sociology*, **69** (July, 1963), 53–62.

6 Blalock, Hubert M.: "Percent Non-white and Discrimination in the South," *American Sociological Review*, **22** (December, 1957), 677–682.

7 Boudon, Raymond: "A Method of Linear Causal Analysis: Dependence Analysis," *American Sociological Review*, **30** (June, 1965), 365–374.

8 Boudon, Raymond: *L'analyse mathématique des faits sociaux* (Paris: Plan, 1967).

9 Capecchi, Vittorio: "Causalitá e correlazione nella problematica sociologica," *Studi di Sociologia,* anno II, fascicolo III (Luglio-Settembre, 1964), 230–274.

10 Coleman, James S.: *Introduction to Mathematical Sociology* (New York: Free Press, 1964).

11 Durkheim, Emile: *Suicide* (New York, Free Press, 1951).

12 Kendall, Patricia, and Paul F. Lazarsfeld: "Problems of Survey Analysis," in Robert K. Merton and Paul F. Lazarsfeld (Eds.), *Continuities in Social Research* (New York: Free Press, 1950).

13 Koopmans, Tjalling C.: "Identification Problems in Economic Model Construction," *Econometrica,* **17** (April, 1949), 125–144.

14 Koopmans, Tjalling C.: "Statistical Inference in Dynamic Causal Models," Cowles Commission Monograph, 10 (New York: Wiley, 1950).

15 Ladinsky, Jack: "Careers of Lawyers, Law Practice and Legal Institutions," *American Sociological Review,* **28** (February, 1963), 47–54.

16 Lazarsfeld, Paul F., Bernard Berelson, and Hazel Gaudet: *The People's Choice* (New York: Columbia, 1948).

17 Lazarsfeld, Paul F.: "The Algebra of Dichotomous Systems," in Herbert Solomon, *Studies in Item Analysis and Prediction* (Stanford, Calif.: Stanford, 1961), pp. 111–157.

18 Lazarsfeld, Paul F.: "The Interpretation of Statistical Relations as a Research Operation," in Paul F. Lazarsfeld and Morris Rosenberg (Eds.), *The Language of Social Research* (New York: Free Press, 1955), pp. 115–125.

19 Lipset, Seymour M., et al.: "The Analysis of Political Choice Behavior," in Gardner Lindzey (Ed.), *Handbook of Social Psychology* (Reading, Mass.: Addison-Wesley, 1954), vol. 2, pp. 1124–1175.

20 Polk, Kenneth: "A Note on Asymmetric Causal Models," *American Sociological Review,* **27** (August, 1962), 539–548.

21 Robinson, William S.: "Asymmetric Causal Models: Comment on Polk and Blalock," *American Sociological Review,* **27** (August, 1962), 539–548.

22 Simon, Herbert A.: "Spurious Correlation: A Causal Interpretation," *Journal of the American Statistical Association,* **49** (September, 1954), 467–479.

23 Stouffer, Samuel A.: *Communism, Conformity, and Civil Liberties* (Garden City, N.Y.: Doubleday, 1955).

24 Wold, Herman O.: "Causality and Econometrics," *Econometrica,* **22** (April, 1954), 162–177.

25 Wright, Sewall: "The Method of Path Coefficients," *Annals of Mathematical Statistics,* **5** (1934), 161–215.

26 Wright, Sewall: "The Interpretation of Multivariate Systems," in Oscar Kempthorne, Theodore A. Bancroft, John W. Gowen, and Jay L. Lush (Eds.), *Statistics and Mathematics in Biology* (Ames, Iowa: Iowa State University Press, 1954).

27 Yule, Udny, and Maurice G. Kendall: *Introduction to the Theory of Statistics* (London: Griffin, 1958).

CHAPTER 7

# Some Thoughts on Comparative
# Method in Cultural Anthropology

RAOUL NAROLL

For the last ten years, the writer's chief concern has been an attempt
to solve what seemed to him the six or seven leading problems of comparative
method in cultural anthropology.  The present chapter, then, is a progress
report.  The methodological problems I chose to work on were those which
I felt were central, the ones collectively of overriding importance.  But I
doubt that anyone will claim that the problems are easy to solve.  Both the
problems to be discussed and the solutions to be proposed are intricate and
have long scientific histories.  Only a bare outline is given here.

A well-rounded and full discussion of comparative method in cultural
anthropology would need a book at least as large as this one.  The reader
who wishes to know more should look at *A Handbook of Method in Cultural
Anthropology* (54) in which the topics of this chapter are discussed at much
greater length.

Systematic comparative studies have long been carried out in cultural
anthropology for two distinct ends.  First, *idiographic,* historical studies have
been carried out in an effort to reconstruct the specific culture history of
certain regions or certain traits.  Second, *nomothetic,* sociological studies have
been carried out in an effort to discover or verify basic laws of society or
culture, basic principles which presumably would hold good at least as tendencies in any society, anywhere, any time.

Idiographic generalizations hold good only about the specific cultures
compared.  But nomothetic generalizations explicitly or implicitly treat the
cultures studied as samples from a larger universe and hold good for the
entire universe studied, at least as tendencies.  Consequently, if valid, they
permit predictions about cultures not yet studied, indeed about cultures not

yet in existence. For example, the propositions in Murdock (39) imply that if the Hungarians were to develop matrilineal extended family households in the twenty-first century, they could be expected some generations later to develop matrilineal lineages, and still later to develop an Iroquois or Crow type of kinship terminology. While the universe of generalization is rarely explicit in nomothetic studies in anthropology, commonly anthropologists seem to have in mind the entire universe of known human cultures—at least those since the end of the Pleistocene.

This distinction has long been made between the purpose of idiographic and nomothetic studies. By an idiographic study is thus meant one whose purpose is to describe a particular sequence of events. A biography of a person or a history of a city or a country or even of the whole world is an idiographic study if it confines its attention to learning and reporting what happened. By a nomothetic study is meant one whose purpose is to discern a repetitive pattern which reflects a general characteristic of society or culture. If I through interviews collect data on 60 cases of suicide and report what I think happened in each, I have carried out an idiographic study. If I go on to seek in those 60 cases a general pattern of correlation or causation which I believe might well apply to other cases I have not studied, I thereby change the character of my study. The whole effort now becomes a nomothetic study rather than an idiographic one.

## 7.1 IDIOGRAPHIC AND NOMOTHETIC STUDIES

In cultural anthropology, comparative methods have been developed for both purposes. Idiographic comparative studies have had as their goal the reconstruction of the specific culture history of specific tribes or regions. The classic discussion of comparative method for the reconstruction of specific culture history where written records are lacking is still that of Edward Sapir (65). Rather little has been done to carry out Sapir's suggestions in the half century since he wrote. Several important trait-distribution studies have been made, of which the best known is the sun-dance study by Leslie Spier (70). Spier argues that the sun dance must have originated in the area where it is most elaborated. Hoijer (24) has attempted to reconstruct the proto-Athapaskan kinship terminology by comparative linguistic studies. But the most elaborate development of idiographic studies has been the development of the comparative statistical method pioneered by Boas (4) in his study of Northwest Coast folktales.

The progress and problems of this method were well reviewed in two successive papers, by Kluckhohn (29) and Driver (10). This method involves collecting data on a long list of traits from all the tribes of a given region and constructing a correlation matrix in which each trait is correlated in turn with all the others. From a cluster analysis or a factor analysis of this matrix, culture areas and culture climaxes are discerned (31). By a *culture area* in such a study is meant a geographic classification, a geographic area in which a certain complex of traits is to be found. Since most culture traits spread by diffusion, it is to be expected that specific factors elicited by factor analysis will have a clear geographic concentration (13). By *culture climax* is meant the particular tribe or small group of tribes within a culture area in which the characteristic traits are most heavily concentrated. The most impressive recent application of this method has been the studies of North America by Driver and Massey (12).

The idiographic statistical method shares three of the six key problems of comparative statistical study with the cross-cultural survey. The former, too, needs to define its statistical unit, its tribe. It needs to concern itself with trustworthiness of data, for random reporting errors tend to destroy the correlations it seeks, while parallel systematic reporting bias on more than one trait can produce spurious correlations as artifacts of such reporting errors. Finally, as has been repeatedly pointed out by its critics, it too faces Galton's problem—the problem of distinguishing idiographic from nomothetic correlations in comparative statistical studies: in idiographic studies, the idiographic correlations are being sought, and consequently nomothetic correlations produce distorting noise, whereas in cross-cultural surveys, it is the other way around. These three problems will be treated in the discussion of nomothetic studies.

Finally, something needs to be said about *glottochronology*—or lexico-statistics, as it is sometimes called. Glottochronology is a method proposed by Morris Swadesh for finding out how long ago two related languages separated from their common ancestor. French and Spanish are known to be descendants of the Vulgar Latin spoken during the Roman Empire. Linguists, by comparing vocabulary and grammar, have classified nearly all known languages into similarly related groups. Now Swadesh says we can figure out how long ago the Hopi language diverged from the related Serrano language by counting the common elements still in both languages. For this purpose, a standard list of 200 words is used—words believed found in practically all languages—words for such things as hand and foot, fire and water, earth and sky. Much work has been done along these lines, but the validity of the method has been severely challenged (27).

Since Sapir's day, interest in comparative historical studies has waned and interest in comparative nomothetic studies has constantly grown. To most anthropologists of the last two generations, keenly aware of the immense power of culture upon individual behavior and of the wide range of cultural variation, it has seemed almost self-evident that only through comparative studies could scientific laws of human social and cultural behavior be discovered and verified. This attitude has just recently been most spectacularly confirmed by Segall, Campbell, and Herskovits (63,64). These investigators have demonstrated widespread cultural effects on basic visual perceptions. By comparing the responses of Middle Western Americans with those of a variety of African and other tribesmen, they have demonstrated a wide range of perception error from culture to culture in a number of classical optical illusions. When these results are fully studied it will be more difficult than ever to suppose that fundamental laws of social and cultural behavior can be verified without broad cross-cultural comparative studies.

As yet, of course, no fundamental social or cultural laws about the relationships between variables have been established with adequate scientific rigor. Consequently, the development of an adequate comparative method remains the dominant problem of scientific cultural anthropology today. Many hypotheses about such well-studied problems as kinship and cultural evolution seem intuitively to be highly plausible and to enjoy substantial empirical support from systematic studies. But several basic methodological difficulties make all these studies inconclusive, and thus they fall short of scientific adequacy.

## 7.2 LEADING METHODS IN CROSS-CULTURAL STUDIES

### The Case Study

The classic research method of cultural anthropology is the study of a single tribe. Such studies have certainly been a fruitful source of new concepts and analytic insights in cultural anthropology. To be sure, most of the studies are intended to be descriptive rather than comparative, but whether he means to or not, the investigator is always comparing the culture he has studied with his own. And often, as with Holmberg's study of the Siriono (25), a particular tribe is offered as an example of a widespread class and is assumed to be typical. That such an assumption can be misleading indeed was shown by the description of the Punan of Borneo by Needham (57). The Siriono were seen by Holmberg as a typical hunting-and-gathering tribe (even though they did a little crop raising on the side), and Holmberg suggested that the widespread food anxiety found among the Siriono was typical of such tribes. However, Needham pointed out that such a generalization seemed unwarranted since no such anxiety was found by him among the Punan. Needham would have strengthened his case even further if he had cited the statement of the Andamanese pygmy informant Woi of the Oko-juwoi people to E. H. Man (35). Woi told Man: "We . . . go only now and then to get food. We constantly spend our time in dancing and singing." A half dozen other like statements from a half dozen other primitive hunting tribes around the world could be quoted in further support of Needham's position. But such a forensic assemblage of evidence selected to support a particular viewpoint would not decide the issue between Needham and Holmberg. The basic weakness of the case study method is the lack of any assurance that the case selected is really typical. Even if in fact a case is typical, confidence in its typicality can be shaken by producing a single case inconsistent with it.

## The Concomitant Variation Study

Clearly realizing this difficulty, Radcliffe-Brown long ago advocated systematic comparative studies of neighboring, closely related communities of a carefully chosen sort. It is such studies and only such studies that I am here calling *concomitant variation studies.* Two varieties of this approach have been developed in the years since. The first seeks a group of neighboring communities in which the variables of interest to the investigator vary while all other factors remain constant. The classic example of this method is the study of four Yucatan communities by Redfield (62). These four communities differed in size—that is, in population. One was a large city, the second a medium-sized town, the third a large village, and the fourth a small village. Otherwise, the communities seemed alike: their people were of the same racial stock, spoke the same language, lived under the same climatic conditions, and so on. Redfield then examined the four communities to see what else varied concomitantly with community size. Other examples of this first variety include the study of Highland Luzon communities by Eggan (14) and the study of witchcraft among four African communities by Nadel (44). The second variety seeks a group of communities in which the variables of interest remain constant while all other factors vary. The classic example of this method is the Western Pueblo study by Fred Eggan (15); another example is presented by the Yaqui studies of Edward Spicer (68,69). Spicer's studies considered the Yaqui people in three strikingly different situations: first, the normal Yaqui farming villages at home in southern Sonora; second, the community of Yaqui refugees working as casual laborers in Tucson, Arizona; and finally, Yaqui exile communities working in semislavery on the sisal plantations of southern Mexico. All these communities displayed close-knit social organization despite the ecological and sociological variations in their setting. Spicer explained this social coherence in terms of Yaqui ceremonial life, which the Yaqui took with them wherever they went.

These concomitant variation studies have the merit of establishing correlations through direct field study, where the investigator controls his data. They do, however, labor under a number of weaknesses which prevent their results from being conclusive. [Redfield (62, p. 343) himself was careful to emphasize that he considered the results of his Yucatan study highly tentative.] First, the research design really supposes that the investigators consider *all* cultural traits which might conceivably be relevant, but in fact they never consider more than a modest number of fundamental traits, such as ecological setting, economy, language, and social organization.  If the survey of data in these studies is compared with the trait lists of the California trait-distribution studies [e.g., Stewart (71)], one sees at once how much less comprehensive, how informal and unsystematic, are the trait inventories of the concomitant variation studies so far undertaken.

Furthermore, the observer relied upon to detect the relevant lurking variable is usually the investigator himself, who has a strong professional stake in overlooking it.  It is not enough to satisfy us when we recognize in these investigators a strong sense of professional responsibility and scrupulous ethics. Of course we need not fear from men like these any deliberate or purposeful suppression of evidence.  But it is not a matter of scientific fraud, like the Piltdown hoax.  It is simply a matter of the psychology of honest error.  Are not unwitting mistakes more commonly made in favor of the mistaken one than against him?  A critic concerned with this problem often has no ready means of independently checking the investigator's work; only if he deals with such copiously described peoples as the Western Pueblos of Fred Eggan's study can his data be checked by others without going into the field.  After a generation or two has passed, even field restudies can no longer confidently be made of many important elements of fast-changing cultures.

But these problems of quality control are secondary.  The leading weakness of the concomitant variation method is Galton's problem—the problem of distinguishing nomothetic from idiographic correlations.  We must ask ourselves upon reading each of these studies whether the correlations observed might not reflect artifacts of culture-trait borrowing from a common source rather than fundamental tendencies in the nature of society or culture.  Does Redfield in his Yucatan study offer evidence that his urban traits are not European diffusions, his folk traits native survivals?  How do we know that the urban traits are characteristics of all cities rather than peculiarities of European ones?  Does Eggan in his Pueblo study offer evidence that his generalized Western Pueblo traits have not simply diffused together by borrowing as part of a culture complex, like the California Indian culture complexes so intensively studied by Kroeber, and linking such diverse traits with so little apparent functional connection?

Galton's problem can be avoided in comparative studies by choosing widely scattered societies.  For example, Hsu (26) compared Hindu, Chinese, and American societies.  But while such a contrast proves analytically fruitful, it may not provide an effective tool for validating correlations.  By taking three widely separated societies, Hsu greatly increased the total number of culture-trait differences between each; consequently, he was unable to claim that only the variables considered by him were varying and indeed could not attempt to consider in any detail all the ways in which these three societies differed from one another.

Another important difficulty about concomitant variation research design is its unsuitability for causal analysis of the correlations studied. In causal analysis of correlational matrices, as we shall see, differences between the individual correlation coefficients of a group of related traits can be crucially important. But in a concomitant variation research design, such differences cannot be determined. Rather the attempt is merely to classify all conceivable traits into constants or variables, with all the variables varying together. Conceivably, progress with this difficulty might be made by conducting time-depth studies to learn the priority of occurrence of the related traits. However, unless there are adequate written records, time-depth studies are usually difficult, costly, and time-consuming. Furthermore, to establish time priority is not adequate to establish cause-effect relationships, though it is helpful.

Finally, in concomitant variation studies, the correlations observed are observed in a constant, relevant context. That context is the total culture of the society or region studied. Two traits may well be functionally linked in such a situation but not otherwise, so that the correlation between them, even though it is a nomothetic correlation and not an artifact of diffusion, may hold good only in the special local circumstances. For example, in the southeastern portion of the United States today, there is a negative correlation between percentage of Negroes in the population and proportion of people voting in elections. This correlation is a true functional linkage between the traits, but rather than reflecting general characteristics of Negroes or election behavior, it reflects the special Negro-white cultural situation in the region.

## The Regional Study

Another important, though rather little used, method of nomothetic analysis is the regional study. Such a study selects a major region of the world—a continent or a large part of one—and compiles all the data on a number of selected traits. It differs from the trait-distribution study in its aim of analyzing functional relationships rather than merely reconstructing specific historical patterns. The best-known studies of this type are by Schapera (66) and Driver (11,12). These studies are methodologically concomitant variation studies on a larger scale. The importance of diffusion becomes clearly evident in regional studies, especially when the results are mapped. But the evidence for functional linkage remains intuitive in such a study. No method for discriminating idiographic from nomothetic correlations in them has been proposed. They require as much time and effort as a cross-cultural survey (see below) and are subject to most of the methodological difficulties of a cross-cultural survey, but they are far less powerful tests of hypotheses. They are subject in some degree to the problem of the constant regional context. On the other hand, as descriptive, taxonomic studies they can be indispensable handbooks—witness Driver (11).

## *The Cross-cultural Survey*

Because of the profound influence and wide range of variation in human culture, scientifically the most powerful method of hypothesis test is the statistical comparison of a world-wide sample, the cross-cultural survey. This method was first proposed three-quarters of a century ago by Edward Tylor (74). Yet for fifty years it was rarely practiced, and the results of the few studies made before 1940 had almost no impact upon the thinking of anthropologists. Köbben (30) has thoroughly reviewed the reasons for this slow start [compare Whiting and Child (75)]. Fundamental problems must be solved before cross-cultural studies can claim scientific rigor. It is true that many of these difficulties are also often found in regional studies, in concomitant variation studies, and even in case studies. But in these, the difficulties are often less obvious, more subtle, than in cross-cultural surveys.

Furthermore, these other kinds of studies can serve descriptive and historical as well as nomothetic functions. Thus, whether or not we accept the theory in Radcliffe-Brown (60) that among the Andaman Islanders ghost fear produces social cohesion, we can read his book with much pleasure and profit. Good concomitant variation studies, like those of Hsu (26), Spicer (69), or Redfield (62), share the documentary and humanistic appeal of the good case study. On the other hand, if the tables in Hobhouse, Wheeler, and Ginsberg (23) reflect a biased sample, an inconsistent sampling unit, untrustworthy data, and jumbled idiographic-nomothetic correlations, they are of no use to us whatever. Thus a methodologically tentative case study can properly become an anthropological classic while a methodologically tentative cross-cultural survey is of interest only to statistical technicians.

Methodologically, the cross-cultural survey is unquestionably the most difficult and exacting of anthropological research methods. No properly done cross-cultural survey has yet been published. But if done properly, its scientific impact would be greater than that of any other research method in social science. Consequently, the improvement of the cross-cultural survey method is one of the leading tasks facing behavioral science in our time. The best introduction to the method is the collection of readings by Frank Moore (38).

The cross-cultural survey method has not yet proved itself. It has provoked great controversy. Its critics have correctly pointed out the failure of its practitioners to deal adequately with one or another of six fundamental problems. Yet it has been growing increasingly popular in the United States not only with anthropologists but also with sociologists and social psychologists. The writer believes that in decades to come, when its problems have been mastered, it will be generally recognized as an indispensable test of any major theory about human society, human culture, or human history.

A seventh major weakness of the method can never be entirely overcome.

It depends upon the availability of data. Almost all cross-cultural surveys in the past have been library studies—studies of data available in existing field reports. Paul J. Bohannan is now working on a study of divorce in which data are collected instead by having ethnographers answer questionnaires about the people they study. Donald T. Campbell and Robert A. Levine are collaborating on a study of ethnocentrism in which ethnographers not only are given questionnaires but are given funds to enable them to carry out more field work in order to find the answers. However, even such studies must restrict their questions to those which ethnographers can reasonably be expected to answer effectively in a comparatively short time. For a theory to be testable by a cross-cultural survey, it must have clear implications about data which are adequately described in existing literature or which can be adequately dealt with by an ethnographer in response to a questionnaire. The task is to work out particular measures of variables which not only are logically suitable and culturally sensible but are also operational—which can be used in practice. This task usually demands a difficult and time-consuming pilot study.

What specifically are the six fundamental problems of the cross-cultural survey method? I have mentioned nearly all of them in passing already. But let us review them now: (1) causal inferences from correlations, (2) societal unit definition, (3) sampling bias, (4) Galton's problem, the problem of interdependence of cases, (5) data quality control, the problem of trustworthiness of data, (6) categorization, the problem of defining concepts for trait categories which are suitable in any cultural context. The remainder of this chapter will be devoted to a consideration of each of these problems in turn.

## 7.3   CAUSAL ANALYSIS OF CORRELATIONS

This is the most general of the six problems. In one sense, all the others can be thought of as special cases of it. For if we find that two traits (i.e., variables) are correlated, and if we have some reason to believe that one is the cause and the other the effect, our concern about sampling bias, unit definition inconsistency, Galton's problem, data quality, or even concept definition, is simply a concern that the observed correlation is an artifact of one or more of these five elements of our research method. If this fact is always clearly remembered, it will cut in half the difficulties presented by the other five methodological problems. For we will not be concerned with any of the other five methodological problems unless we have reason to think that *both* traits (i.e., variables) being correlated are being similarly distorted or biased.

One of the first warnings received by a beginning student of mathematical statistics is the warning against inferring cause-effect relationships from correlations. For example, if marriage restrictions are correlated with suicide, this correlation is very far from demonstrating that marriage restrictions *cause* suicide. Conceivably, high suicide rates could somehow induce marriage restrictions, for example, as a precaution of parents to guard against their children arranging unhappy marriages which it is feared might later drive them to suicide. Or there may be some lurking variable at work, i.e., some other factor not considered in the research, which produces both marriage restrictions and high suicide rates and thus explains the correlation. The lurking variable is especially to be dreaded when the correlation involved is a so-called ecological correlation. There is no evidence that it is the unhappily betrothed or unhappily married who commit the suicides which are reflected in the correlation between marriage restriction and suicide. The link between marriage restriction and suicide is a mere hypothesis of the observer.

Let me at the outset disclaim any involvement in Aristotelian concepts of necessary or sufficient cause. I prefer not to speak of a strict *cause,* but only of a causal *influence.* For example, I think of divorce rate as a causal influence affecting the suicide rate. In thinking about the relationship between an *influence* and its *effect,* I posit as part of the very definition of the concept that an influence is something which can be thought of as exerted by an actor at the actor's will. (It is enough to merely imagine this relationship between the actor and the influence; there is no need to suppose that in fact such a relationship actually exists. Thus we can imagine Archimedes with a sufficiently long stick and a place to set his lever and in this way imagine him moving the world.)

By an *influence* I mean a variable which when produced by an actor increases the probability of occurrence of another variable, the *effect.* Thus in the study of suicide, I argue that if we change the rules (i.e., the manners and customs of a society with respect to marriage restriction, divorce freedom, and so on), we *thereby* make a corresponding change in the probability of suicide within the society. In other words, we make a corresponding change in the suicide rate. Within the last few decades, several men have sought to develop systems of making causal inferences from correlations (3,5,6,37,59,67,72,73,76). All the systems deal with probabilities, and hence with influences, as just defined, rather than with necessary or sufficient causes. All the systems, furthermore, deal with more than two variables (in one of them time is the third variable). Each system has severe restrictions of one sort or another, making it unsuitable for many cross-cultural surveys. Chapters 5, 6, and 11 of this book discuss these systems at great length. Accordingly, I here submit still another system, which I call *influence analysis.*

Influence analysis deals only with one kind of influence situation. That situation is the one where a number of functionally unrelated but conceptually similar influences independently produce a given effect. Furthermore, taken together, the effects are additive.

Consider the diseases malaria, yellow fever, typhus, and bubonic plague.

They are functionally unrelated: one can fall ill of malaria whether or not yellow fever or typhus or plague is going around the community; the mechanism of any one of these diseases depends in no way on that of the others. Yet one cannot say that the diseases are entirely unrelated; some environments may be especially good both for the *Aedes* mosquito which carries yellow fever and the *Anopheles* mosquito which carries malaria. But while all four of the diseases are functionally unrelated, they are all conceptually similar: they all are produced by microorganisms which travel from person to person by way of insect carriers, and they all frequently cause death. Taken together, they raise the death rate. The mathematical model we have here is that of four independent variables and one dependent variable. According to Boudon (5, p. 371, fn. 12), this mathematical model is the simplest possible form of the general problem of causal analysis of correlation matrices.

Influence analysis has two components, a statistical component and a logical component. The statistical analysis performs a number of tests to see whether in fact the hypothetical influences have little or no correlation with one another while all are highly correlated with the supposed effect. These tests include (1) test of the hypothesis that the mean encorrelation (i.e., correlations between influences and effects) is significantly greater than the mean intercorrelation (i.e., correlations among the various influences); (2) test of hypotheses that true mean intercorrelation is zero; (3) partial correlations in which each encorrelation is controlled in turn by every supposedly irrelevant influence; and (4) factor analysis. In the factor analysis, as many significant factors are expected as there are hypothetical influences; the hypothetical effect is expected to be moderately loaded on all of these, highly loaded on none. Each of the hypothetical influences is expected to be highly loaded on one and only one factor, so that each hypothetical influence can be matched with a corresponding factor and no factor is identified with more than one hypothetical influence.

If all the foregoing tests turn out in this way [and substantially this result was obtained from my study of thwarting disorientation and suicide (49)] and if these relations were predicted in advance of the study (as unfortunately was not true of my suicide study), no rival simple explanation of these statistical data is plausible. Any rival hypothesis which would explain this pattern of correlations otherwise than by supposing a cause-effect relationship between the influences and their common effect *must* posit a number of additional variables at work.

Now since the number of conceivable additional variables which might be at work is infinite, we can never be sure that our probable cause-effect hypothesis is correct. However, this uncertainty differs only by degree from our uncertainty about the validity of even the best established scientific laws, such as Einstein's theory of relativity, since Einstein's revision of Newton's laws reminded us that all scientific generalizations are tentative and subject to revision.

The logical analysis which enables us to distinguish between a validated scientific generalization and a mere speculative hypothesis is the canon of parsimony. Other things being equal, we presume that a hypothesis is correct which most parsimoniously deals with all the available evidence—which presents the simplest explanation that accounts for all the data before us. We do not require that a hypothesis account for imaginary data but only for actually observed data. Consequently, once a study systematically considers a body of data, if it is consistent with a hypothetical explanation, that explanation stands as validated unless we hear some equally parsimonious rival hypothesis which might explain the data as well.

In other words, a well-conducted scientific study shifts the burden of proof from the investigator to the critic. True, the critic need not *disprove* the hypothesis, he need only produce a rival hypothesis which might with equal parsimony explain the data. Indeed, in practice we do not hold our critics to a very strict standard of parsimony; we lean in the direction of scientific caution by requiring of a critic only that he produce a rival hypothesis which might with nearly equal or almost equal parsimony explain the data. If a critic does even this, we usually feel that he has returned the burden of proof to the investigator.

This matter of the canon of parsimony and the burden of proof is the concern of the logical component of influence analysis. In this research design, if the canon of parsimony is to have its greatest weight, all the hypothetical influences need to be particular taxonomic types of one general category. For example, in my suicide study, I argue that seven traits are correlated with suicide report length while all are uncorrelated with one another. The statistical component consists in showing that this correlation pattern indeed is found by applying the four tests mentioned. The logical component consists in showing that each of these seven unrelated traits is a different example of what I call *thwarting disorientation*—a situation in which social ties are broken, weakened, or threatened in such a way that some individual person is seen by the suicide victim as plausibly to blame for his troubles.

Now if evidence is produced suggesting that the encorrelations may be artifacts of some sort of bias in the study, this evidence becomes a plausible rival hypothesis. Since there is no intercorrelation between the supposed influences, no *one* methodological bias could explain all these results. Suppose, for example, that inexperienced field workers tend to overestimate suicide. Take that as an example of a methodological bias. Can we suppose that perhaps such inexperienced field workers also tend to exaggerate divorce freedom, and at the same time exaggerate marriage restrictions, and at the same time exaggerate warfare frequency, and at the same time exaggerate the other three hypothetical influences? Could this single methodological bias explain the results? No. For in such a case, there would be a high intercorrelation among the supposed influences. In the factor analysis, they and the suicide scores would all be highly loaded on a single factor. That factor would be the field-worker-experience factor. Thus no one methodological bias could explain *all* these results. Strictly speaking, six other factors are needed. But if a critic establishes the existence of even four or five such methodological sources of artifact, he will shift the burden of proof back to the investigator, since because of our scientific caution we will always be willing to violate the canon of parsimony a little in favor of the critic by speculating that one or two unknown factors (lurking variables) might well explain one or two of the encorrelations.

It is for this reason that we must give careful attention to the remaining methodological problems of the cross-cultural survey. But in our considerations, we must never lose sight of the point that our concern is with the possibility of parallel bias producing spurious correlations. Other kinds of difficulties, though they might reduce the overall accuracy and scholarly quality of our study, would *not* serve as plausible rival explanations for encorrelations and thus would not help a critic shift the burden of proof back onto our shoulders as investigators.

## 7.4 SOCIETAL UNIT DEFINITION

The problem of defining the culture-bearing unit, the society or tribe, is discussed at length elsewhere (51). Six criteria have been widely considered by anthropologists in defining whole societies or other units of comparison:

1 Distribution of particular traits being studied
2 Territorial contiguity
3 Political organization
4 Language
5 Ecological adjustment
6 Local community structure

I propose a concept, called the *cultunit,* which uses three of these six criteria. A cultunit is defined as *people who are domestic speakers of a common distinct language and who belong either to the same state or the same contact group.*

*Distinct language.* In homogeneous languages the language itself. In language chains, the chain link.

*Homogeneous language.* A set of dialects, the speakers of any one of which can understand all the others, but none of which is intelligible to speakers of dialects of any other set. Notice that only spoken and not written language is considered both in this definition and the next one. Examples: Tikopian, Hopi, Bella Coola.

*Language chain.* A set of dialects which are arrangeable in sequences such that, while each dialect in the sequence is interintelligible with the preceding and following dialects, and all such interintelligible neighbors are included, some dialects in the set are not interintelligible with others in the set. (The term "language chain" is used in this sense by many anthropological linguists today; other linguists often use "linguistic continuum" to mean the same thing.) Examples: English (including Devonshire, Yorkshire, Lancashire, and various Lowland Scottish dialects); German-Dutch; Italian-French-Spanish-Portuguese; Timbira; Basin Shoshonean. One can travel down the Rhine from its headwaters in Switzerland to its mouth in Holland without ever passing two neighboring villages whose local peasant dialects are not intelligible. One can travel from the toe of the Italian boot by land through France and Spain to the coast of Portugal with the same result.

*Chain link.* One of a set of divisions of a language chain made in such a way as to produce the smallest possible number of divisions, each containing only interintelligible dialects. Wherever we can, we draw the boundaries of these links between the least similar neighboring dialects. (Dialect differences along language chains do not ordinarily turn up at a constant rate; some pairs of neighboring villages differ more than others.)

*State.* A territorially ramified territorial team whose leaders assert and wield the exclusive right to declare and conduct warfare.

*Territorially ramified.* Made up of a number of component territorial teams. For example, the United States is made up of fifty territorially defined teams—New York, Massachusetts, California, etc.

*Territorial team.* A group of people whose membership is defined in terms of occupancy of a common territory and who have an official with the special function of announcing group decisions—a function exercised at least once a year.

*Common territory.* A geographically contiguous territory within which are found not only the dwellings of the people of the team but also the lands of their usual subsistence activities ashore.

*Contiguous.* Accessible without crossing the land territory of others. (N.B. Thus water gaps are ignored, however great.)

*Warfare.* Public lethal group combat between territorial teams. (N.B. Thus blood feuds between nonterritorially defined kin groups are not considered warfare.)

*Contact group.* People who belong to no state but who speak a common distinct language and who are all interconnected by successive contact links.

*Contact link.* Two nuclear families make a contact link if someone from each family speaks to someone in the other family at least once a year. (For practical purposes, it is usually necessary to assume that this happens if the two families live within a certain distance of each other.)

*Domestic speakers.* People who predominantly use a given dialect for speech within the nuclear family, that is, among husband and wife and their minor children.

It seems useful to distinguish four types of cultunit:

*Hopi type.* People who belong to no state but who speak a common distinct language and who are all interconnected by successive contact links. Examples: Hopi, Bella Coola, Naron, Hupa, Nuer.

*Flathead type.* People who belong to a state all of whose members speak a common distinct language. Examples: Flathead, Swazi, Tikopia.

*Aztec type.* People who belong to a state in which mutually unintelligible dialects occur and who are domestic speakers of a dialect intelligible to speakers of the lingua franca of the state, that is, the dialect in which the state officials usually transact their business. Examples: Aztecs, Incas, Zulus.

*Aymaran type.* People who belong to a state in which mutually unintelligible dialects occur and who are domestic speakers of a dialect not intelligible to speakers of the lingua franca of the state. Examples: Aymara, Zulu-ruled Thonga.

To apply these rules in practice, remember two things. First, no two people belong to the same cultunit unless they speak the same language at home. Second, no two people belong to the same cultunit unless they are in contact. There are two ways to be in contact. People under the control of any state are in contact with everyone else who belongs to their own state and only with them. People not under the control of any state are in contact not only with all the people they themselves speak to at least once a year but also with the ones their acquaintances speak to, and *their* acquaintances in turn, and so on. Do all people who belong to the same state belong to the same cultunit? Not unless they all speak the same language at home. Do all people who speak the same language at home belong to the same cultunit? Not unless (1) they all belong to the same state, or (2) they all belong to the same contact group. My cousins who live in Toronto speak English at home which is hardly any different from the English spoken by my other cousins who live in Los Angeles. Do they belong to the same cultunit? No, because the Toronto cousins live in Canada while the Los Angeles cousins live in the United States. Some Luiseño Indians living near San Diego speak as good English as many Americans of English descent. Do they belong to the same cultunit? No, because these Indians speak Luiseño in the home. Mr. Robert Burns of Ayreshire in Scotland (like his namesake the poet) reads literary English as well as Mr. Jonathan Bull of London and writes it better. Do these gentlemen belong to the same cultunit? No, because at home with his wife and children, Mr. Burns likes to talk Ayreshire Scottish; but Mr. Bull cannot understand Ayreshire at all.

Our four cultunit types emerge when we consider these two different kinds of boundaries: a linguistic boundary and a communication-link (state or contact-group) boundary. A cultunit boundary is formed by *either* of these boundaries, whichever is least inclusive. If a state has more than one distinct language spoken within it, then the political unit, as established by the political boundaries, is subdivided into cultunits by the linguistic boundaries within the state.   That cultunit formed by the domestic speakers of the lingua franca of the state is classified as an Aztec-type cultunit; the other cultunits within that state are classified as Aymaran type.   Thus by definition we cannot have an Aztec-type cultunit except in association with Aymaran-type cultunits.

Where a state is linguistically homogeneous, the state boundary is followed and we get a Flathead-type unit.   Where there is no state, linguistic boundaries only are followed unless contact gaps occur which break up speech communities into cultunits within which speech communication presumably flows freely but between which speech communication presumably is rare and unimportant; and those in which speech communication flows freely form Hopi-type cultunits.

It is important to remember that some cultunits differ very little in *culture* from one another, whereas others differ greatly.   Frequently, neighboring cultunits may differ not at all with respect to certain traits being studied.   The fallacy of counting neighboring and closely related cultunits repeatedly as independent trials of a functional hypothesis is Galton's problem (Sec. 7.6).

The cultunit concept is far too awkward and cumbersome for most people.   Most people would like something simpler, more elegant.   So would I.   In its defense, I can say this.   I have tried it out on 58 societies, collecting information on language, state membership, and contact-group membership.   There is not room to publish my results here but they are to be published in the *Handbook* (54).   The groupings obtained by using this concept were usually much like the unit concepts of particular tribes in the minds of the natives or in the minds of anthropologists.   I do not believe that any other general concept of a culture-bearing unit has been similarly tried out in practice in a careful and systematic check of each culture studied to see if it conformed to the general concept the investigator had in mind.   (The Human Relations Area Files have no very clear concept of a tribe or society and do not claim to.)   The only merit for the cultunit concept is that it can be used in a rigorous cross-cultural survey.   Crude and awkward as the cultunit is, it offers one way to answer two questions: (1) When you count tribes or societies in a cross-cultural survey, exactly what are you counting?   (2) When you take a probability sample of primitive tribes, what is your sampling universe and what are the units that have a stated chance to be picked for the sample?   As we shall see in the next section, this second question cannot yet be easily or directly answered but only awkwardly and with difficulty—*but it can be answered.*

The urgent need now is for a new concept of a culture-bearing unit—perhaps one fairly similar to the cultunit.   This new concept should be simple and clear.   It must be a concept which can be easily used to sort out tribes and cultures, using the kind of information now usually found in books about primitive tribes.

One can consider a cultunit a society, if one wants to do so.   Much paper has been wasted talking about the difference between a society and a culture. For people, though not for social insects, these two concepts can be easily linked so that, given one, the other is implied. Any culture exists in the minds of a group of people who cooperate to keep the culture going by talking to one another and by teaching their children the culture. One can define such a group of people as a society, even if they have no other social bonds. That is what Murdock does and there is no reason he should not. Consider the Hopi Indians of Arizona. They have a common language, a common set of customs, a common oral literature, and until recently a common religion. There are only a few thousand of them and their villages are all within a square less than 100 miles wide. No one has ever been able to get the Hopi to agree upon a formal permanent tribal organization for any purpose. Hopi not only fail to act in concert as a tribe, they violently refuse to when it seems to an outsider urgently in their interest to do so. Yet Murdock calls the Hopi a single society because they keep up—or used to keep up—their common language, their common set of manners and customs, their common set of moral ideas, their common religion. Contrariwise, any social organization of people must have a common set of rules which defines the membership of the organization and governs the social relationships of its people. To that extent, any social organization has a common culture, consisting of these rules.

I offer the cultunit concept for use in cross-cultural surveys, to answer the two questions just mentioned—what are you sampling and what are you counting? The ethnological report does not always come wrapped in a cultunit package, though it often does. When it comes wrapped in some other package, in a report describing only a fractional part of a cultunit, or describing as a single group more than one cultunit, the comparativist must do his best to infer the cultunit characteristics from the information at hand. If he does so, the cultunit concept is working as a sort of ideal type in his mind. Where the cultunit is made up of a chain link in a linguistic continuum, it has an objective existence *as a society* only in the mind of the comparativist; in this case, the boundaries which the comparativist draws between chain links will not seem particularly important to the people living on either side of them.

For the person making a cross-cultural survey, the best of all possible worlds would be one in which all field reports were monographs on units of the sort he is studying. If he is studying cultunits, then this would require a world in which all field reports were monographs on particular cultunits. (In fact, a good proportion of them turn out to be just that.) Field workers, however, would often find the cultunit an unsuitable unit for their diverse purposes. Let us hope that henceforth field workers, whatever units they choose to describe, will tell us enough about the linguistic, political, and contact situations so that we can see how their units fit into a cultunit scheme.

A student wishing to appreciate the technical problems of ethnic unit definition cannot do better than to study carefully Leach's book on Highland Burma (32). Here language, political organization, religious custom, and economic interrelationships are intertwined in great complexity. Leach describes this tangle beautifully. If you want to use a Shan or Kachin tribe as one case in a cross-cultural survey, you must be able to disentangle it from this knot of complicated interrelationships. Leach thinks that such a task cannot be done at all (32, p. 299)! The cultunit concept, I think, works well in Highland Burma (54).

The problem also arises of defining cultunits in time rather than space. This problem has often been neglected by comparativists in cross-cultural surveys, with results which are sometimes disastrous (58). I think it will always be helpful to confine a cultunit to a single *ethnographic time period*. If data are available on more than one ethnographic time period for a given group of people, those data should be sorted out so that each ethnographic time period can be considered a separate cultunit. I offer as a working definition of an ethnographic time period: that period of time in which the cultunit type remains constant. In practice this definition will usually serve to classify time periods of people who do not keep written records of their own history.

## 7.5 SAMPLING BIAS

To date, all published cross-cultural surveys have depended upon *purposive* sampling to choose the societies being studied. Even Ember (16) studied a small simple random subsample of a large purposive sample—Murdock's World Ethnographic Sample (40). By a purposive sample is of course meant a judgmental sample in which the sampler tries to construct with his sample a model of the universe from which he is sampling. Nor does any purposive sample used so far seem to be based on any formal model, any sampling plan assigning particular quotas to particular characteristics of the universe.

The sampling universe of most cross-cultural surveys has not been defined with much care or precision. All tacitly agree that it includes and chiefly consists of all known primitive tribes of modern times. Murdock's *Outline of World Cultures* (41) tries to include all known cultures, primitive and civilized, ancient and modern. His listing falls short of including all known recent primitive tribes in Australia and New Guinea, but this omission reflects only the difficulty of the task and not any departure from principle. Murdock's World Ethnographic Sample (40) includes some ancient primitive tribes, some ancient civilized societies, and some modern civilized societies. (The distinction between primitive and civilized cultures is not of much concern to Murdock, by the way.)

In the 58-society War, Stress, and Culture probability sample, I took as my universe all human cultures known since the year A.D. 1500, which fulfilled three requirements: (1) They had to be described in publications accessible to an investigator in the cities where I worked. *Accessible* meant not only that these publications had to be listed in standard ethnographic bibliographies but also they had to be on hand in the libraries I was using. (2) These publications had to give certain types of information about either suicide or homicide, two of the problems I was investigating. (3) These publications had to describe the society at a time when it was free to make war if the people wanted to, instead of being under the military control of outsiders. (In other words, Aymaran-type societies were excluded from my sampling universe.)

The Northwestern University *Permanent Ethnographic Probability Sample* takes as its universe all recent primitive societies which we consider well enough known. Primitive societies are taken to be those with no native literature recording their own history. We consider a society well enough known if in standard ethnographic bibliographies we find a body of works by a man or woman who has spent at least a year in the field among the people of that society, makes some claim to know their language, and has published a fairly generalized description of their culture instead of keeping only to one or two narrow specialities. [We have a precise measure of this degree of generality. A writer qualifies if his works devote a chapter or titled paper to each of 10 two-digit categories of the *Outline of Cultural Materials* (43).]

The typical cross-cultural survey sample is one in which the sampler vaguely claims that he has tried to represent the universe faithfully, that he has given thought to representing each of the world's major geographic regions, and that he believes the sample representative. A dominant consideration in such samples has always been the problem of finding societies on which adequate information is available in the library or libraries being used. Sometimes the sampler may claim that he has included all known tribes on which the library has material describing the variables he is studying (16; 39, pp. viii-ix; 40; 75, pp. 48ff.). While the Human Relations Area Files have tried to follow a purposive sampling plan originally drawn up by Murdock, inspection of the list of societies shows that the Soviet Union and its immediate neighbors are disproportionately overrepresented, as is Southeast Asia. Clearly one of the factors influencing the selection of societies for inclusion in the Files has been their interest to officials in Washington, D.C.

It will come as no surprise to those familiar with survey research sampling problems to learn that samples compiled like these have clearly failed to resemble their universe in important respects. Köbben (30, p. 140) pointed out that while in the large sample of Hobhouse, Wheeler, and Ginsberg (23) the ratio of matrilocal to patrilocal tribes was 10 to 13, in Murdock (39) the ratio was 2 to 1. And Murdock (40, pp. 664ff.) himself later expressed the need for "a much more systematic sampling procedure." His World

Ethnographic Sample (40) is an attempt to provide precisely equal representation to all the culture areas of the world, but the areas represented are
themselves intuitively defined, with no objective criteria for classification, and
no claim that each area contains an equal number of societies, and no report
or estimate of the number of societies found in each.

The desired remedy for these sampling difficulties is clear enough. Some
kind of *probability sampling* is needed. By a probability sample is meant
a sample selected in such a way that the probability of choice of any member
of the sampling universe is known. From the point of view of Galton's problem (see next section), simple random sampling would be undesirable, however. The closer two societies are to each other geographically, the more
likely they are to share traits of common historical origin. The more near
neighbors one has in a sample, the greater the influence of diffusion upon
correlations and, therefore, the greater the difficulty of solving Galton's
problem.

Ideally, the sample should be widely scattered. Simple random sampling
(in which every unit in the sample is independently chosen at random and
has an equal chance of selection) often produces clusters of near geographic
neighbors; in Ember (16) a simple random subsample of only 24 societies
from the World Ethnographic Sample produced two pairs of near neighbors,
one pair of South African Bushman tribes, and one pair of North American
Plains tribes. It is better to stratify the sample geographically and to sample
separately from each stratum. To do so brings fewer clusters of near neighbors. Such a stratification method does not require validation of the stratification criteria; the strata may be purely intuitive. This is true because the
purpose of stratification is achieved by *any* geographic grouping whatever,
since any such stratum reduces the probability of two near neighbors being
sampled without affecting the probability that any particular society is chosen.
Each stratum should have a known number of sampling units. If the number
of societies chosen from each stratum does not vary in proportion to the
total number of sampling units in the stratum, this of course affects the probability of choice of its members. Variations in selection probability, if known,
can be allowed for in statistical computations one way or another—either
by weighting the results to compensate or by testing to see whether the selections from *under*represented strata differ in any way relevant to the problem
being studied from the selections from *over*represented strata.

If it be supposed that culture area classification has any value whatever,
if it be supposed that societies grouped together by Murdock in his World
Ethnographic Sample into a single culture area are more likely to resemble
one another than they are to resemble societies in neighboring culture areas,
then stratifying by culture areas gains an additional advantage. For the likelihood of selecting two neighboring, similar tribes is reduced wherever the intuitive culture area classification is sound, without being increased wherever

it is unsound.   In other words, we have much to gain and nothing to lose by using any knowledgeable ethnologist's intuitive culture area classifications as sampling strata.   Another way of putting this point is to say that most though not all culture traits in one tribe or nation are like those of its immediate neighbors.   Because of this fact, any sort of geographical culture area classification is almost certain to reduce the variance within the stratum (culture area) and thus make the within-stratum variance less than the variance between strata.

However, if more than one society is to be drawn from each geographic stratum, it would be well to substratify by some other criterion, such as societal complexity, in order to reduce the cultural resemblances among neighbors in the sample.   Size of the largest settlement in the society provides a simple and useful measure of societal complexity (16,45).

Two basic difficulties remain before such a plan can be carried out.   First, a list of the sampling units in the universe being sampled is needed.   The sampling unit is, of course, the tribe, the society, the cultunit.   No such list exists for the cross-cultural survey.   However, adequate materials for such a list (if only the relevant linguistic and political data were available) is set forth in the *Outline of World Cultures* by Murdock (41).   The *Outline* lists by name nearly all the known world societies outside Australia and New Guinea.   For New Guinea, it can be supplemented by the language lists in Capell (7).   For Australia, we can use the tribal list in Greenway (22).   However, there is no consistency in the social concepts used in compiling these lists.

Second, a large proportion of the sampling units—of the order of half of them, perhaps—are so inadequately known that they cannot usefully be studied.   This proportion varies according to the problem being studied; a study relating settlement pattern to vegetation and rainfall would find adequate data on much more than half the known societies, but a study relating witchcraft techniques to weaning methods would find adequate data on much less than half.

We cannot assume that those societies on which we have adequate information can be taken to represent those societies on which data are lacking.   It seems safer and more conservative—and in my opinion closer to the truth—to suppose that certain sorts of societies tend to be selected by anthropologists, missionaries, and others for study and description, whereas certain other sorts tend to be overlooked.   I would guess that larger societies are more likely to be studied and described than smaller ones, warlike societies more than less warlike ones, societies with highly elaborate ceremonials more than societies without them, societies near main routes of transcontinental or overseas travel more than societies distant from these routes, societies regarded as relevant to current anthropological theory (e.g., segmentary societies in Africa) more than those societies considered less relevant, and finally societies that are relatively hostile to and resistant to European influence and colonial administrators more than societies that are relatively docile and yielding.

By collecting data on *wealth of description* among the societies in a cross-cultural sample studied, we probably can find and allow for any strong effect that the particular bias in the selection of societies for study by field workers might have upon the correlations we find. Only if the selection bias of the field worker is related to a trait with a U-curve relationship to both traits in a correlation would a measure of wealth of description fail to constitute an adequate control for field worker's selection bias. Wealth of description can be measured by the number of entries or the total number of pages shown for a society in an appropriate ethnographic bibliography [e.g., Murdock (42)].

To detect U-curve relationships in selection bias of field workers, an investigation may use either of two methods. If the trait was included on the trait list of any large-scale systematic regional idiographic study, one can rate the societies in that study (which for a regionally defined universe is a 100 percent sample) for wealth of description. Such a procedure will detect a U-shaped curve if one exists. However, if the trait was not so included, then one must conduct a small regional field study in a region where native cultures still survive in numbers in order to make the determination directly. The hypothesis to be tested in the field is the hypothesis that very poorly studied tribes resemble well-studied tribes, but differ from moderately studied tribes, with respect to the trait of interest. Where a research design focuses on a small number of dependent variables, only these variables need necessarily be checked.

For the universe of societies on which adequate documentation exists, probability samples can be selected in one of two ways. The less expensive way permits stratification only by *region* or *culture area*. This way was followed in my War, Stress, and Culture sample. A tentative list of sampling units, such as Murdock's *Outline of World Cultures,* is stratified regionally. The number of tentative sampling units in each region is noted. Within each region, tentative units are examined in turn in some randomly chosen order. The first tentative unit so examined in each stratum which meets the explicit bibliographic criteria of the sample is chosen as the representative of that stratum. The sampler notes whether that tentative sampling unit contained two or more *bibliographically acceptable* cultunits. (Where bibliographic requirements are at all demanding, rarely will it contain more than one.) He also notes whether the selected cultunit forms part of more than one tentative sampling unit. In this way, considering the total number of tentative sampling units in each sampling stratum and discrepancies between the tentative sampling unit chosen and the cultunit concept, the investigator can test to see whether any biases in this sampling method affect his correlations.

A second, more desirable but more expensive, method is to compile a complete list of societies meeting explicit bibliographic standards and to note, for each of them, data on additional stratification criteria. Such a list can become a universe of bibliographically acceptable cultunits suitably stratified, from which a strict stratified random sample can be selected. A list is currently being compiled at Northwestern University as part of the Permanent Ethnographic Probability Sample method.

The bibliographic criteria which determine whether a society is sufficiently well described to be considered part of the universe being sampled must be explicit if measurement of documentation bias is to be confidently performed.

## 7.6  GALTON'S PROBLEM

Galton's problem is widely considered a crucial weakness in the cross-cultural survey method. Galton raised his problem at the meeting of the Royal Anthropological Institute in 1889 when Tylor (74) read his pioneer paper introducing the cross-cultural survey method. Tylor showed correlations ("adhesions" he called them) between certain traits; in the discussion which followed, Galton pointed out that traits often spread by diffusion: by borrowing or by migration. Since this is often so, how many independent trials of his correlations did Tylor have? Boas, for decades the immensely influential dean of American anthropologists, once told his student Lowie (34) that when he first read Tylor's paper, he became greatly enthusiastic. This seemed to him an ideal research technique. On reflecting further, however, Galton's objection seemed to him a devastating one; unless there was a solution to Galton's problem, Boas considered the cross-cultural survey method valueless.

Not all anthropologists have agreed with Boas. Significantly, however, two of the leading recent authors of important cross-cultural surveys—G. P. Murdock (39) and J. W. M. Whiting (75)—were very much worried about Galton's problem. Talk with sociologists leads one to believe that they are more likely than anthropologists to consider the problem trifling. Sociologists are likely to take for granted that any two traits which *seem* functionally related in theory and which in fact are correlated must therefore somehow be functionally related. Accordingly, I have recently published (52) considerable anthropological evidence that traits very often are highly correlated simply because they are found in neighboring tribes and without apparent functional linkage—certainly without any functional linkage strong enough to account for the very high correlations between the traits. For example, in aboriginal California, patrilinear totemic clans are found invariably and exclusively in tribes (namely, the Mohave, the Yuma, and the Kamia of the southeast corner of the state) which also play tunes on flageolets, use carrying frames made of sticks and cords, make oval plate pottery, use a large fish scoop, use a squared muller, and favor twins.

But patrilinear totemic clans are not peculiar to southeastern California. They are found scattered around the world in many other places. Would we expect that in Africa, in Eurasia, or in Oceania, wherever we encountered patrilinear totemic clans, there and there only we would also find people playing tunes on flageolets, using carrying frames made of sticks and cords, making oval plate pottery, using a large fish scoop, using a squared muller, or favoring twins?

Clearly we would not. The perfect correlations found between traits comprising selected elements of the southeastern California complex are explained by joint diffusion and only by joint diffusion. How do we know then that correlations between matrilocal residence and matrilineal descent—traits which *seem* to have a clear functional linkage—might not likewise reflect the influence of joint diffusion, especially since they too are so often found in geographic clusters? That is Galton's problem. It must be solved; it cannot merely be talked away.

I believe that the concept of independence of cases is an unfruitful approach to the difficulty. The difficulty is to distinguish the effect of functional associations (of adhesions, in Tylor's graphic term) from the effect of mere common historical association through diffusion, whether through genetic relationship of common cultural ancestry or through borrowing from a common cultural center. The problem here is to control a correlation between factors considered related functionally to see whether this relationship is an artifact of common historical circumstances. Thus we have, conceptually speaking, a simple problem of partial association analogous to that discussed in detail in Zeisel (77). For instance, Zeisel in one example shows that single people eat more candy than married people, but that if we control for age, this relationship disappears; the apparent correlation between marital status and candy consumption merely reflects the fact that older people eat less candy than younger people and older people are more likely to be married than younger people. Now Galton's problem, as I see it, is to test apparently functional correlations between traits to see if they are mere artifacts of historical relationship—i.e., to control for diffusion. If the correlation merely reflects coincidences of borrowing or migration, I call that relationship a *hyperdiffusional* association, but if, after controlling for the effects of diffusion, we find that the association remains significant, I call that relationship a *semidiffusional* association. (If no diffusion were involved at all, I would call this an *undiffusional* association, but I know of none.)

As Kluckhohn also pointed out (29), the mathematics of probability theory has been given more attention by anthropologists than has the underlying logic—and it is a logical problem we face here. There are three basic approaches to probability logic currently in use among mathematicians; each turns on a different concept of probability—the classical concept, the frequency concept, and the axiomatic concept (28, pp. 2–5). I rest my argument on the classical concept, which has been formally defined by Laplace thus: "If an event can take place in $n$ mutually exclusive ways, all equally likely, and if $r$ of these correspond to what may be called 'success,' then the probability of success in a single trial is $r/n$." This idea is best expressed by a familiar model: consider a jar containing a number $(n)$ of spheres, such as ping-pong balls, all absolutely identical in shape, size, and all other characteristics except color; $r$ of them are black, and the others white. If the balls are thoroughly mixed and then a blindfolded person draws one ball out of the jar, the probability of the ball being black is $r/n$. That is the definition of the classical probability concept. When we say that an event has a probability of 0.05, we mean that it is as likely for that event to occur as for the blindfolded man to get a black ball if there is 1 black ball to every 19 white.

Where events being considered must occur in discrete units or bundles (or as the mathematician says, are discretely distributed), it is a relatively straightforward matter to work out correspondence between these discrete events and the model of a jar full of ping-pong balls. Where, instead, they can occur in magnitudes varying along a continuous scale (e.g., as height, weight, and distance are continuously distributed), the use of integral calculus and the probability density concept lets us work out correspondences between such situations and the model of a jar full of ping-pong balls.

All the various statistical tests which are used to calculate probabilities can be related to the ping-pong ball model; the relationship is worked out mathematically and invariably involves certain stated mathematical assumptions. The logic of statistical inference involves inquiry as to the suitability of the mathematical model of the test being used. The test asks whether observed events can be explained by a given mathematical model. This question is the null hypothesis; if it is answered positively, the observations being tested are considered to lack statistical significance. For example, the chi-square test used by Murdock in *Social Structure* (39) asks: Would a random sample from a universe of two independent and continuously distributed phenomena be likely to produce an association of the kind observed? The t test used by Whiting and Child in *Child Training and Personality* (75) asks: Would a random sample of two independent and normally distributed phenomena be likely to produce an association of the kind observed?

Thus the key point is this: if an event being studied conforms in every way to the mathematical model of the statistical test being used, the result of a statistical test almost always must be to support the null hypothesis—to report the absence of a significant association, or a significant difference, or whatever. The point of the test is to establish the fact that the event being studied *cannot* plausibly be considered to conform to the mathematical model of the test.

It is then a logical and observational rather than a mathematical problem to explain the failure of the data to conform to the mathematical model. If ethnological observations are entirely independent of one another, then by assumption neither historical nor sociological relationships exist among them, and the only plausible explanation for apparent relationships is sampling error. Where a statistically significant result is observed, then *random* sampling error is discredited as an explanation for the apparent relationship. In an ideally controlled experiment, only two possible explanations for any relationship are permitted—the hypothesis being tested and random sampling error. But in ethnological statistical studies, other explanations are also possible. We cannot plausibly explain the correlations in Murdock's *Social Structure* or Whiting's and Child's *Child Training and Personality* or in the University of California trait-distribution studies (31) as the result of random sampling error. That is what their statistical tests tell us and that is all they tell us.

In a recent paper, Naroll and D'Andrade (53) reviewed the logic of Galton's problem and discussed four solutions to it. Geographic propinquity is usually (although not always) a measure of diffusion. If a correlation occurs independently of geographic propinquity, it can hardly be a mere artifact of diffusion, a hyperdiffusional association. It must at least be a semi-diffusional association, in which there is a definite tendency for the two traits to diffuse together, to be borrowed together, to be retained together, or to be dropped together—if indeed it is not an undiffusional association, in which diffusion plays no part at all.

The four solutions discussed in Naroll and D'Andrade all use propinquity as a measure of diffusion, but in different ways and with different degrees of sensitivity and statistical flexibility. The *bimodal sift method* (46, pp. 31–34) and the *interval sift method* (53) are statistically more flexible than the *cluster* and *matched-pair* methods; once the validity of the sift has been verified, the sample can simply be treated statistically as though it were a sample from historically unrelated societies. The cluster method (46, pp. 35–38) alone of the four provides a direct test of the hypothesis that semi-diffusional associations tend to diffuse together, and thus this method is logically the most rigorous; but the matched-pair method (53) alone of the four measures the relative importance of diffusion and functional associations.

A recent publication (50) presents a fifth method, the *linked-pair method*. This method combines the statistical flexibility of the sifting methods with the twofold scope of the matched-pair method. The linked-pair method aligns a society in successive East-West or North-South or diffusion arc oriented lines, as in the interval sift method. Each society is compared in turn with its neighbor in the alignment with respect to the trait being tested. Statistically, the test is whether society A differs from society B with respect to the trait, each society in turn being treated first as society A and next as society B to make up successive linked pairs. In this way, similarity between neighbors can be measured by exactly the same statistical measures as are used to measure relationships among the traits being correlated in the influence analysis.  Where the assumption of linearity of relationship is plausible, coefficients of partial correlation can be directly computed, and thus one can obtain a measure of pure functional or pure historical relationship.

The linked-pair method is simple to use.  You only have to arrange the tribes (societies, cultunits) in your sample in any convenient geographic order which lines up neighbors side by side.  To test a variable for similarity between neighbors, call the tribe's own score on that variable trait A, and call its neighbor's score trait B.  For example, suppose you are studying a selected sample of modern nations, and one variable in your study is the per capita gross national product (GNP).  Going from West to East across Europe, you find your sample includes United Kingdom, West Germany, Czechoslovakia, Soviet Russia, and China (going from West to East between 20 and 40 degrees north latitude).  Call trait A for each country its own GNP; call trait B for each country the GNP of the next country in your sample to the East of it.  This gives you the following data.

| Country | Trait A Own GNP | Trait B Neighbor's GNP |
|---|---|---|
| United Kingdom | 778 | 508 |
| West Germany | 508 | 450 |
| Czechoslovakia | 450 | 250 |
| Soviet Russia | 250 | 100 |
| China | 100 | |

Compute a coefficient of correlation between trait A and trait B.  This gives you a measure of the tendency of nations in your sample to resemble their geographic neighbors.  In this instance, the correlation is obviously high.

## 7.7  DATA QUALITY CONTROL

Conflicts in field reports between ethnographers, such as those between Mead (36) and Fortune (18) or between Redfield (61) and Lewis (33), remind us that even the best of anthropologists make mistakes.  Since cultural anthropologists rarely concern themselves with representative sampling in choosing informants, they may give distorted reports of traits by supposing erroneously that one social class is typical of all or that one community or region is typical of all.  Furthermore, much ethnographic literature is written by scientifically untrained missionaries or government officials who, however familiar they are with the natives they describe, are unaware of the complexities of non-European societies with respect to such things as kinship systems, and who consequently are quite likely to misunderstand or confuse them.

Anthropologists who tend to think of field work in terms of the finest traditions of humanistic scholarship are, however, sometimes given to overestimating the importance to cross-cultural surveys of this kind of error. The descriptive ideal of the humanistic field worker could be termed, paraphrasing Leopold von Ranke's celebrated dictum, *"Das Volksleben wie es eigentlich gewesen"*—the way of life as it really was. To a sensitive field worker, any obvious error or misunderstanding or even oversight in the work of an untrained or careless reporter jars a sensitive nerve and offends aesthetically. Such a field worker often feels like ignoring the writings of such reporters and in private table talk displays shock at cross-cultural surveys which rely upon obviously incompetent reporters as sources of information. (To call such expressions of shock mere gamesmanship ploys seems often to do injustice to the feelings of fine, sensitive scholars who are more concerned with the unquestionably vital problem of accurate field work than they are with the equally vital problem of testing general hypotheses.)

Classical scholars, from whose humanistic tradition all modern European scholarship descends, could, however, remind some of these humanistic anthropologists that patient, discerning study can yield trustworthy information from obviously incompetent or even mendacious sources of information. Were this not so, we would know much less than we do about the histories of ancient Greece and Rome.

In cross-cultural surveys, our task of making trustworthy inferences from untrustworthy sources is made easier by three helpful factors. First, we need be anxious only about systematic bias, not about random error. For detecting systematic bias, the ideal body of data is not a collection of consistently high-quality reports but instead a collection of reports varying widely in quality, given by reporters well trained and ill trained, sensitive and insensitive, careful and careless, discerning and obtuse, conscientious and unscrupulous, veteran and novice, recent and early. Such a range of reporting quality is the range which can best be expected to detect systematic reporting bias, since such bias is less likely to be present in, or is likely to be less influential upon, the better qualified observers than the more poorly qualified ones. Random error need not concern us if we have statistically significant correlations; in such correlations, evidence of random error is evidence that the true correlations must be even higher than we suppose. For random errors tend to lower correlations, not to raise them.

Second, cross-cultural surveys often study theoretical rather than actual systems, plans rather than actual behavior. Where such plans must be generally known and generally agreed upon to work at all, any knowledgeable informant can be presumed to know them and they can safely be presumed to be standard throughout the working group whose cooperation is needed to carry them out. On the other hand, where such working groups are quite small, variations in important elements in the theoretical system can take place unbeknown to informants. Kinship terminology is a good example of this. The system needs to be standard only for the group of relatives involved. One family need not be concerned about the practice of another family unless the two interact *as kin*. Thus it is that in the United States today, two inconsistent systems for particularizing cousins exist unbeknown to almost everyone in the country. (System A terms ego's grandparent's sibling's grandchild his *second* cousin; system B terms that relative his *third* cousin.)

Third, where the trait being studied can function effectively within a single community and does not depend upon intercommunity relationships, the effective unit of *study* (though not of *sampling*) can be the particular local community studied by a field worker rather than the entire cultunit it is taken to represent. Thus relationships between kinship terminology and residence rules, or between weaning practices and witchcraft attitudes, can be accurately studied from a collection of field reports which in fact accurately describe the system only in particular communities, though they purport to describe it for entire cultunits.

Now wherever the theoretical plan rather than the actual behavior is being dealt with, one or the other of the two foregoing benefits will often be enjoyed by the comparativist. If the trait requires a common understanding among a large number of communities, unnoticed regional variation is unlikely. If it does not, and the trait functions independently in each community, unnoticed regional variation is likely but unimportant, since it will not result in spurious correlations. (From a sampler's viewpoint, the unnoticed variant communities are undocumented cultunits, not members of the universe studied.)

While these helpful factors reduce the risk of danger of spurious correlations from data-reporting errors or oversights, they do not eliminate it entirely. I suspect that one or two supposedly functional correlations in well-known cross-cultural surveys actually are mere artifacts of reporting bias. For example, Whiting and Child (75, p. 281) report a correlation between weaning practices and witchcraft. I have elsewhere presented evidence suggesting that less well qualified ethnographers are likely to underestimate the importance of witchcraft (48, p. 153) and to overestimate normal weaning ages (56, p. 25). Such a tendency, if widespread, might conceivably account for the supposed correlation between the two.

The method I have proposed to detect systematic error (bias) is the *control factor method* of data quality control (48). This method involves collecting data on observation conditions thought to affect the likelihood of reporting bias. (Many of these conditions might also affect the likelihood of random error; but it does not matter if they do or not.) For example, field workers studying smaller communities would be less likely to overlook variant local culture patterns than those studying larger ones; those using a larger number of informants would be less likely than those using a smaller number; those studying several, widely scattered communities less likely than those studying only one. The control test consists in testing whether field workers carrying out a study under the presumably more favorable conditions differ in their trait reports from those working under presumably less favorable conditions. If they do differ with respect to both traits involved in the correlation, a plausible rival explanation for this element of the influence analysis has been found. In such a case, it might be well to consider whether the presumably better reports considered alone yield a significant correlation between the supposed influence and the supposed effect. However, even so, unless the presumably better reports are good enough for one to place complete confidence in their accuracy, the influence correlation must be considered suspect until better quality field work is done.

In planning data quality control tests, we need to consider carefully the possible sources of reporting bias. Informant error is only one example of the ethnographer's sampling bias mentioned above. Here the informant, knowledgeable only about his own subculture, mistakenly supposes that his pattern is typical of the culture as a whole and so informs his ethnographer. Informants also may err by describing ideal patterns as actual ones or by following a cultural theory or stereotype. In short, an informant's error can arise from any circumstance which leads an informant to form an erroneous or misleading mental image, or memory, of an event or a culture pattern. An informant may deliberately mislead an ethnographer, misrepresenting his culture for one reason or another. He may, out of a desire to please, simply give the answer he thinks the ethnographer expects or wants. Or he may have, or think he has, some benefit to be gained or injury to be avoided by misrepresenting. Indeed, he may simply wish to avoid embarrassment about a delicate subject, such as sex or (in our society) earnings, or he may wish to represent his culture as more modern, i.e., European, less backward, i.e., native.

Ethnographers thus may be misled by their informants. They may err in other ways. They may notice and record traits which support some preconceived theory they have but overlook traits inconsistent with it.

Finally, the comparativist himself in his coding may systematically bias his results by consistently interpreting doubtful or uncertain cases in a particular way. Such a bias need not be linked with the comparativist's own hypothesis to be dangerous; it might also be dangerous if unlinked. So-called tests of reliability of coding decisions of coders kept ignorant of the hypothesis being tested do not protect against this danger; they protect only against the danger of random errors. Indeed, use of the term "reliability" in its technical sense of a test of consistency of response is unfortunate. The nontechnical, layman's sense of reliability is trustworthiness. Behavioral scientists may be able on demand to quote accurately the technical definition of the term, but I fear that they are nevertheless more likely to feel confidence in a test of reliability than they ought, simply because of the halo effect of the layman's meaning of the term. It would be much better to call such tests *tests of consistency,* which they are, than to call them *tests of reliability,* which in the everyday sense of the word they most certainly are not.

One advantage of using a standard cross-cultural sample like the Human Relations Area Files or the projected Northwestern University Permanent Ethnographic Probability Sample is the ease with which control factor data may be used over and over again by successive comparativists, once the data have been compiled. The number of traits believed useful as control factors is likely to increase. The value of a particular trait as a control factor may be judged in one of two ways. First, common sense may make a trait intuitively appealing. For example, it is common sense to suppose that a field worker who has spent thirty years in a village knows it better than one who has spent only thirty days. Common sense may err here as it has been known to err elsewhere, but use of a length-of-stay control factor nevertheless tends to be reassuring if it fails to turn up any significant correlations with substantive traits.

Second, control factors may turn out to be related to particular trait reports, as witchcraft reports, for example, seem to be related to length of stay (48, p. 89). If this relationship is established, one then has a problem in causal analysis of correlations. A number of control factors, all of which (1) increase the flow of information from informant to comparativist, but which (2) are unrelated statistically to one another, would, if correlated with a particular trait report bias (e.g., witchcraft importance), constitute material for an influence analysis. They would offer evidence difficult to refute that the easier and fuller the flow of information from informant to comparativist, the more accurate the report. Such an influence analysis—which is very far from having been performed at present—would be the most satisfactory way of validating a quality control factor.

Observation conditions which seem promising as quality control factors may include:

**1** *Field time.* How many months did the reporter spend among the people? If there was a research team involved, how many people took part, and how many months did each stay in the field?

**2** *Participation.* Did the reporter live *in* (rather than merely *near*) the native community he studied? Did he seek to share its daily life himself in some ways, such as eating certain meals with the natives, taking part in certain ceremonies, adopting a certain kinship status with some native family (perhaps both reporter and natives used the appropriate kinship terms to one another, for example)? Needless to say, anything like *full* participation in native culture, involving full assumption of marital, economic, kinship, political, and literary obligations, is not often to be expected from reporters.

**3** *Native language familiarity.* What claims to knowledge of the native language does the reporter make? Is there any reason to believe he has carried on conversations in it without the aid of interpreters? Has he compiled any dictionaries or word lists? Has he transcribed and translated any native texts? Has he written any phonetic or grammatical analyses of the language?

**4** *Report length.* How many pages in all did the reporter publish about the people he is describing? The more copiously he describes them, the more he may be likely to tell us about traits which in the past seemed comparatively unimportant to most field workers but which are now of theoretical interest to us.

**5** *Publication date.* When did the reporter do his field work? This date usually is reflected (with a two- to ten-year time lag) in his date of publication, usually the easiest relevant information to find. Field workers and the people they expect to read their field report have changed their general interests considerably from time to time in the course of the last two hundred years.

**6** *Number of native helpers.* Many field workers use natives as assistants to help them collect information. I found a correlation between the number of native helpers used and (*a*) the attention ethnographers paid to suicide and (*b*) the number of craft specialties mentioned by ethnographers.

## 7.8 CATEGORIZATION

The *validity of categories* is a problem which has been of large concern both to those who have done cross-cultural surveys and to those who have criticized their work. Of the six problems I have chosen for special attention and called crucially important, this problem is the one whose importance is least doubted by thoughtful anthropologists of every point of view. Most behavioral scientists from other disciplines also give it great weight. Yet it is a problem which persistently traps the unwary and engages the anxious concern of the sophisticated.

Exactly what is meant by validity of categories? The categories of a cross-cultural survey are its variables. To put it even more sharply, they are the definitions of the variables. Logically, a definition is valid if it is clear and unambiguous, so that we may easily and confidently say that any given object or behavior pattern either is one of the things defined or is not one of the things defined. The definition may be of a measurement; then we must easily be able to report the value of the variable in terms of the stated measurement scale. However, the logical problem of validity of categories is the least of the problem. Take the concept "cannibalism." I can define it for a cross-cultural survey thus: If in a given tribe, the people eat human flesh and say it is right and proper to do so, I call them cannibals. If they never eat human flesh, or if they consider eating human flesh morally wrong and improper, then I say they are not cannibals. Such a definition is clear. It sets up two criteria, both of which must be fulfilled; if either fails, the tribe is called not cannibal; if both are met, the tribe is called cannibal. Logically, there is nothing wrong with this definition.

Yet its validity in any theoretical cross-cultural survey is most doubtful. Here are some objections to it.

Suppose a missionary reports that the Niam-niam are cannibals but says nothing more. How do we know whether he means they are *eaters* of human flesh or that they also *approve* of eating human flesh. (Some people in the Donner party of immigrants to California in the early 1840s ate the flesh of their companions in order to survive the winter when they were trapped in the snows of the High Sierras. Does that make Americans cannibals?)

What kind of cannibalism is meant? The Donner party used human flesh as an emergency survival ration, as did the sailor in the poem by W. S. Gilbert, who reported himself in at last as "The bosun tight/ And the midshipmite/ And the crew of the captain's gig." In some tribes, human flesh is an ordinary article of commerce, sold like any other meat in the marketplace. In others, it is eaten only for magical purposes, because the people think they will gain a person's qualities if they eat his body or certain parts of it. Eat a brave man's heart and you will be braver yourself. Eat a newborn child, old man, and you will grow younger. In still others, the warriors in battle eat their enemies in order to humiliate them. Nothing was thought a greater disgrace in Fiji 125 years ago than for your enemies to eat you; nothing was a greater triumph than to eat your enemies. (The Fijians might later have pointed out that if General Foch had eaten General Hindenburg in 1918, there might have been less doubt later on in Germany about which side lost the First World War.) Among still other tribes, human flesh was eaten only as part of a funeral ceremony. People might eat bits of the flesh of a dead father or mother; they said this helped comfort them, helped console them for their loss.

If like Maurice R. Davie (9) you have a theory that warfare had its origin in cannibalism, clearly you need to think about this second group of questions.

Cannibalism as a category does not describe a behavior pattern which is functionally related to any other behavior pattern or trait. It lumps together a collection of unrelated behavior patterns. Therefore, one cannot learn much if anything about the general nature of human society or culture by a cross-cultural survey which has cannibalism for one of its categories. On the other hand, one might well learn something by studying dietary cannibalism, or trophy cannibalism, or sympathetic magic cannibalism, or emergency ration cannibalism, or funerary cannibalism. By the validity of a category is meant the ability of an investigator to learn something useful about the theoretical problem he is investigating through the use of the category as part of his research design.

The ultimate criterion for validity of categories in cross-cultural surveys then is their theoretical relevance. Cross-cultural surveys, like any other research-seeking generalizations, are part of a larger intellectual process of data observation, classification, analysis, and generalization. This process is cyclical: data are observed, classified, analyzed logically (e.g., mathematically), and the results used to test generalizations. Since tests of generalizations rarely if ever are utterly satisfactory, the process immediately begins again. It need not proceed strictly in the order stated. The investigator always finds some work of all four kinds already done and can go on further with any of the four tasks. Classifications are useful which can sort out data in such a way as to make them most amenable to analysis and most parsimoniously generalizable. This last statement is axiomatic, resting on the nature of scientific investigation as an attempt to explain the largest number and variety of observations with the fewest logically and empirically consistent general principles.

For anthropologists today, the most urgent need is a standard set of categories and terms. On many topics, such as kinship, there is wide agreement about the theoretical importance of a number of categories but wide disagreement about the names to use for them. Consider the variety of inconsistent technical meanings given to the word "clan." We need to standardize usage to follow the most general and most nearly validated system at hand. In kinship, for example, Murdock's *Social Structure* (39), with all its faults and shortcomings, is the closest thing we have to a generally validated system, and consequently Murdock's terminology should be followed as standard. Where theoretical results support the importance of a *new* category, not found in existing literature, then and only then should new terms be introduced. Old terms should not, however, in such cases be given new meanings, for this compounds confusion.

The problem of comparability of categories baffles many anthropologists trained to work in one culture at a time. In describing a single culture, the ethnographer soon learns to use the categories of the culture being studied, rather than those of his own culture, wherever they differ. In cross-cultural comparisons, where dozens or hundreds of cultures are compared, the narrowly trained ethnographer does not see how he can work with dozens or hundreds of different sets of categories—one set for each culture in the sample.

The solution to this problem was worked out satisfactorily in practice by the Yale school a couple of decades ago [see, for example, Ford (17)]. But only recently has the Yale principle been given clear statement in Goodenough's rule. Goodenough (21, p. 37) puts it this way:

> What we do as ethnographers is, and must be kept independent of, what we do as comparative ethnologists. An ethnographer is constructing a theory that will make intelligible what goes on in a particular social universe. A comparativist is trying to find principles common to many

different universes. His data are not the direct observations of an ethnographer, but the laws governing the particular universe as an ethnographer formulates them. It is by noting how these laws vary from one universe to another, and under what conditions, that the comparativist arrives at a statement of laws governing the separate sets of laws which in turn govern the events in their respective social universe.

For the tyro, anthropologically unsophisticated, the danger to avoid is the danger of supposing that the special categories of one's own culture are suitable for cross-cultural use. They may be, or they may not. The English kin term "mother," for example, denoting as it does a unique relationship always present in every society, is perfectly suitable for cross-cultural comparative use even though in many societies no comparable term is found. Whether or not the Hawaiian language provides a single term distinguishing mother from mother's sister or father's sister, the distinction is theoretically a clear and useful one. On the other hand, as every anthropology freshman knows, the English terms "uncle" and "aunt" are quite ambiguous; the English term "cousin" even more so. In order to decide whether a given concept is cross-culturally useful, one must be clearly aware of the range of functional variation in categorization found in known human societies. Only through systematic comparative study itself can such an awareness be gained. Thus only after carefully examining a wide sample of cultures can one confidently proceed to construct categories. The Human Relations Area Files are a sample particularly convenient for study from this point of view.

The comparativist in cross-cultural surveys, however, need not be further anxious about the problem of cultural context, so widely and properly publicized by Ruth Benedict (1, p. 42) in her critique of Frazer's *Golden Bough*. Frazer put together a functionally linked system in which each element in the system might come from a different culture. He offered no evidence that the elements ever occurred together. Field anthropologists familiar with his data often could see immediate and obvious rival hypotheses to explain the functional setting of a given trait. Frazer's method is now, however, no longer in use. Cross-cultural surveys have never used it. By their nature, cross-cultural studies are studies of cultural context, in which one trait from a given culture is compared with another trait of the same culture.

But it is not enough for a category to be theoretically suitable for cross-cultural comparison. It must be operational. That is to say, one must be able to find out enough about a typical society by studying existing library materials so that in practice the classification can be applied. Definitions need to be made extremely precise, so that coders use as little discretion as possible in classifying particular cultures from field reports. One way out of this difficulty may be to treat the ethnographer as a measuring instrument and to study the characteristics of his report as such. For example, I am currently trying to measure suicide frequency simply by counting the number of words devoted to suicide by ethnographers who mention it at all. Validating such a measure is obviously a difficult matter. Common sense protests immediately that many other factors unrelated to suicide frequency would influence the attention an ethnographer gives to the topic. Yet if suicide wordage is consistently correlated—as it seems to be—with traits not so irrelevantly influenced, such as divorce rules and marriage restrictions, this correlation itself provides validation for such a content analysis approach.

In fact, cross-cultural surveys are studies of ethnographies rather than of living people. They observe indirectly, "through a glass, darkly." There may well be a methodological advantage to putting our cards on the table faceup, as we do when we study a trait like suicide wordage. For when we do so, it is unmistakably and unforgettably clear that we are directly studying the behavior of field workers, and only indirectly and by inference are we studying the behavior of the people in whom we are interested and whom we seek to understand. Astronomers have long since learned to study photographic plates of the stars, rather than to observe the stars directly. If we think of our work as a study of ethnographies rather than as a study of the native peoples, we will be constantly anxious. We know that ethnographies are immensely less-faithful reproducing instruments than astronomical photographs. And our anxiety will be all to the good, for it will lead us to take great care to detect and allow for the large measures of error and distortion which are inevitably involved.

Another problem which we need to keep constantly in mind in constructing categories and developing coding plans is the problem of actual versus theoretical behavior. The peasants of Kaunertal in Tyrol insist that they follow the stem family plan of multigenerational household. In fact, however, a village census reveals no single instance of a stem family household, although several families are eligible (55). The comparativist must consider separately for each trait whether he is studying the plan or pattern which the people have in mind or whether he is studying the system they actually follow. Either choice may be called for by the theoretical problem which interests him.

In any case, however, he should take care to avoid creating spurious correlations by confounding the definitions of two traits, so that his definitions themselves produce correlations. For example, in an earlier study (45) it was necessary to eliminate occupational subdivision of labor, as found, say, in a Samoan canoe-building crew, from a craft-specialty count in order to see if occupational division of labor was correlated with team ramification. Otherwise, the study would have learned nothing, since a correlation between subdivision of labor organized into work crews and team ramification is implied by the very concepts themselves.

Finally, the comparativist must consider carefully whether he cannot somehow quantify his variables. For some sorts of problems this may well be utterly impossible. If he is relating residence rules and descent rules, for example—working with the theoretical plans rather than with the actual behavior—he is dealing inescapably with attributes and cannot quantify. Often, however, ingenuity and care can yield a practical method of quantification.

Quantification has four main advantages. These will be clear from the other chapters in this book. First, significance tests of increased sensitivity can be used. Since carefully conducted cross-cultural surveys are quite expensive, and since, further, Galton's problem usually limits the size of the usable sample, quantification could make the difference between a study whose significance tests attain conventional levels of significance and one whose tests do not.

Second, an advantage newly discovered by H. M. Blalock (3, chap. 4) can be applied. He shows that as data on the relationship between percentage of Negroes and delinquency rate in the United States are successively grouped by counties, states, and regions, increased homogeneity leads to a steady increase in coefficient of correlation. But slope of the data remains constant. It might then be useful to compute slopes as well as correlation coefficients—especially if the computation is being performed by a computer. However, slopes can be computed only between two quantitative variables.

A third advantage of quantification to the comparativist is the fact that if variables are in quantitative form, he can see whether their relationship is linear or curvilinear. If curvilinear, he can often use some transformation to attain linearity. Linearity is a key assumption of parametric partial correlations. Parametric partial correlations, in turn, form a key element of multiple-variable causal analysis.

A fourth advantage of quantification to the comparativist lies in the freedom from artifacts of arbitrary and varying dichotomy cuts. True, where attributes are all cut near the 50 percent level, these artifacts constitute no problem. But more often than not, they vary widely from 50 percent. Difference in dichotomy cuts of this sort can produce spurious factors in factor analysis.

Several methods of quantification are discussed at length in other chapters in this book. The variable itself may be directly expressible in quantitative form. A Guttman scale may be possible; if not, then usually a Likert scale can be worked out. If several attributes are in quantified form, perhaps they can be combined into an index.

Another method is also possible in cross-cultural surveys. Where the trait concerned can reasonably be supposed to vary in impact upon the ethnographer in direct relationship to its elaboration or importance among the people being studied, the investigator can, as already suggested, attempt to measure this impact by counting the number of words devoted to that topic as well as the number of words in the ethnographer's entire report; he can thus compute a wordage ratio. Obviously such a ratio would be influenced by the ethnographer's conscious or subconscious interests and attitudes as well as by the culture studied. Where, however, the other factors seem irrelevant to the coding of other variables in the study, the factors would not lead to spurious correlations. For this reason, the wordage ratio method is more useful for *one* only of two variables in a correlation than for both together. In an influence analysis research design, wordage ratio might well be considered for use as the measure of the dependent variable. Obviously, however, where direct quantitative measures of the variable itself are available, they are much to be preferred to the indirect measure of the ethnographer's reactions.

## 7.9 CONCLUSION

Development of the cross-cultural survey method is one of the chief tasks of present-day anthropology. Its problems are many and difficult but all of them can be solved if we keep at the work. Solutions to the six problems just discussed will provide social science with a tool for the rigorous testing of generalizations about all human society and culture. Only through their solution can we validate such generalizations. Studies conducted within a single society, or comparing a small number of societies, can be stimulating and informative, but they can never be conclusive. Therefore, while a healthy social science requires a wide variety of research methods, in scientific controversies about rival theories of society or culture, the cross-cultural survey method will sooner or later have the last word.

## REFERENCES

1 Benedict, Ruth: *Patterns of Culture* (New York: Mentor Books, New American Library, 1946).

2 Blalock, Hubert M., Jr.: "Correlational Analysis and Causal Inferences," *American Anthropologist,* **62** (August, 1960), 624–631.

3 Blalock, Hubert M., Jr.: *Causal Inferences in Nonexperimental Research* (Chapel Hill, N.C.: University of North Carolina Press, 1964).

4 Boas, Franz: "Die Entwickelung der Mythologien der Indianer der Nordpacifischen Küste Americas," *Zeitschrift für Ethnologie,* **27** (1895), 487–523.

5 Boudon, Raymond: "A Method of Linear Causal Analysis," *American Sociological Review,* **30** (1965), 365–374.

6 Campbell, Donald T.: "From Description to Experimentation: Interpreting Trends in Quasi-experiments." Paper read at Social Science Research Council Conference on Problems in Measuring Change, Madison, Wis., 1962.

7 Capell, Arthur: *A Linguistic Survey of the Southwestern Pacific,* rev. ed. (Noumea: South Pacific Commission, 1962).

8 Carneiro, Robert L., and Stephen F. Tobias: "The Application of

Scale Analysis to the Study of Cultural Evolution," *Transactions of the New York Academy of Sciences,* ser. II, **26** (1963), 196–207.

9 Davie, Maurice R.: *The Evolution of War* (New Haven, Conn.: Yale, 1929).

10 Driver, Harold E.: "Statistics in Anthropology," *American Anthropologist,* **55** (1953), 50–51.

11 Driver, Harold E.: *Indians of North America* (Chicago: University of Chicago Press, 1961).

12 Driver, Harold E., and William C. Massey: "Comparative Studies of North American Indians," *Transactions of the American Philosophical Society,* **47** (1957).

13 Driver, Harold E., and Karl F. Schuessler: "Factor Analysis of Ethnographic Data," *American Anthropologist,* **59** (1957), 655–663.

14 Eggan, Fred: "Some Aspects of Culture Change in the Northern Philippines," *American Anthropologist,* **43** (1941), 11–18.

15 Eggan, Fred: *Social Organization of the Western Pueblos* (Chicago: University of Chicago Press, 1950).

16 Ember, Melvin: "The Relationship between Economic and Political Development in Non-industrialized Societies," *Ethnology,* **2** (April, 1963), 228–248.

17 Ford, Clellan S.: "A Sample Comparative Analysis of Material Culture," in George P. Murdock (Ed.), *Studies in the Science of Society* (New Haven, Conn.: Yale, 1937), pp. 225–246.

18 Fortune, Reo F:. "Arapesh Warfare," *American Anthropologist,* **41** (1939), 22–41.

19 Freeman, Linton C.: *An Empirical Test of Folk Urbanism* (Ann Arbor: University Microfilm, N.23502), 1957.

20 Freeman, Linton C., and Robert F. Winch: "Societal Complexity: An Empirical Test of a Typology of Societies," *American Journal of Sociology,* **62** (1957), 461–466.

21 Goodenough, Ward H.: "Residence Rules," *Southwestern Journal of Anthropology,* **12** (1956), 37.

22 Greenway, John: *Bibliography of the Australian Aborigines and the Native People of Torres Strait to 1959* (Sydney: Angus and Robertson, 1963).

23 Hobhouse, L. T., G. C. Wheeler, and M. Ginsberg: *The Material Culture and Social Institutions of the Simpler Peoples* (London: Chapman & Hall, 1930).

24 Hoijer, Harry: "Athapaskan Kinship Systems," *American Anthropologist,* **58** (1930), 309–333.

25 Holmberg, Allan: *Nomads of the Long Bow* (Washington, D.C.: Institute of Social Anthropology, 1953).

26 Hsu, Francis L. K.: *Clan, Caste and Club* (Princeton, N.J.: Van Nostrand, 1963).

27 Hymes, Dell: "Lexicostatistics So Far," *Current Anthropology,* 1 (1960), 3–44.

28 Kenney, John F., and E. S. Keeping: *Mathematics of Statistics,* 2d ed. (Princeton, N.J.: Van Nostrand, 1951), part II.

29 Kluckhohn, Clyde: "On Certain Recent Applications of Association Coefficients to Ethnological Data," *American Anthropologist,* 41 (1939), 345–377.

30 Köbben, Andre J.: "New Ways of Presenting an Old Idea: The Statistical Method in Social Anthropology," *Journal of the Royal Anthropological Institute,* 82 (1952), 129–146.

31 Kroeber, Alfred L.: "Culture Area Distributions: III. Area and Climax," University of California Publications in *American Archeology and Ethnology,* 37 (1936), 111–112.

32 Leach, E. R.: *Political Systems of Highland Burma* (Boston: Beacon Press, 1964).

33 Lewis, Oscar: *Life in a Mexican Village* (Urbana, Ill.: University of Illinois Press, 1951).

34 Lowie, Robert H.: "Evolution in Cultural Anthropology: A Reply to Leslie White," *American Anthropologist,* 48 (1946), 227–230.

35 Man, E. H.: "On the Aboriginal Inhabitants of the Andaman Islands," *Journal of the Anthropological Institute of Great Britain and Ireland,* 2 (1883), 69–175, 327–434.

36 Mead, Margaret: *Sex and Temperament in Three Primitive Societies* (New York: Mentor Books, New American Library, 1935).

37 Miller, L. Keith: "A Methodological Note on Determining the Causal Priority of Two Variables," in Alvin W. Gouldner and Richard A. Peterson (Eds.), *Technology and the Moral Order* (Indianapolis, Bobbs-Merrill, 1962), pp. 67–78.

38 Moore, Frank W. (Ed.): *Readings in Cross-cultural Methodology* (New Haven, Conn: Human Relations Area Files, 1961).

39 Murdock, George P.: *Social Structure* (New York: Macmillan, 1949).

40 Murdock, George P.: "World Ethnographic Sample," *American Anthropologist,* 59 (1957), 664–687.

41 Murdock, George P.: *Outline of World Cultures,* 2d ed. rev. (New Haven, Conn.: Human Relations Area Files, 1958).

42 Murdock, George P.: *Ethnographic Bibliography of North America,* 3d ed. (New Haven, Conn.: Human Relations Area Files, 1960).

43 Murdock, George P., Clellan S. Ford, Alfred E. Hudson, Raymond Kennedy, Leo W. Simmons, John W. M. Whiting: *Outline of Cultural Materials,* 4th rev. ed. (New Haven, Conn.: Human Relations Area Files, 1961).

44 Nadel, S. F.: "Witchcraft in Four African Societies," *American Anthropologist,* 54 (1952), 18–29.

45 Naroll, Raoul: "A Preliminary Index of Social Development," *American Anthropologist,* 58 (1956), 687–715.

46 Naroll, Raoul: "Two Solutions to Galton's Problem," *Philosophy of Science,* 28 (1961), 15–39.

47 Naroll, Raoul: "Two Stratified Random Samples for a Cross-cultural Survey," 1961. (Mimeographed.)

48 Naroll, Raoul: *Data Quality Control* (New York: Free Press, 1962).

49 Naroll, Raoul: "Thwarting Disorientation and Suicide," 1963. (Mimeographed.)

50 Naroll, Raoul: "A Fifth Solution to Galton's Problem," *American Anthropologist,* 66 (1964), 863–867.

51 Naroll, Raoul: "On Ethnic Unit Classification," *Current Anthropology,* 5 (1964), 283–312.

52 Naroll, Raoul: "Galton's Problem: The Logic of Cross Cultural Research," *Social Research,* 32 (Winter, 1965), 428–451.

53 Naroll, Raoul, and Roy G. D'Andrade: "Two Further Solutions to Galton's Problem," *American Anthropologist,* 65 (1963), 1053–1067.

54 Naroll, Raoul, and Ronald Cohen (Eds.): *A Handbook of Method in Cultural Anthropology* (New York: Natural History Press, in preparation).

55 Naroll, Raoul, and Frada Naroll: "Social Development of a Tyrolean Village," *Anthropological Quarterly,* 35 (1962), 103–120.

56 Naroll, Raoul, and Frada Naroll: "On Bias of Exotic Data," *Man,* no. 25 (1963).

57 Needham, R.: "Siriono and Penan: A Test of Some Hypotheses," *Southwestern Journal of Anthropology,* 10 (1954), 228–232.

58 Pilling, Arnold R.: "Statistics, Sorcery and Justice," *American Anthropologist,* 64 (1962), 1057–1059.

59 Polk, Kenneth, Hubert M. Blalock, Jr., and W. S. Robinson: "Asymmetric Causal Models: A Three-way Discussion," *American Sociological Review,* 27 (1962), 539–548.

60 Radcliffe-Brown, A. R.: *The Andaman Islanders* (New York: Cambridge, 1933).

61 Redfield, Robert: *Tepoztlan* (Chicago: University of Chicago Press, 1930).

62 Redfield, Robert: *Folk Culture of Yucatan* (Chicago: University of Chicago Press, 1941).

63 Segall, Marshall H., Donald T. Campbell, and Melville J. Herskovits: "Cultural Differences in the Perception of Geometric Illusions," *Science,* 139 (1963), 769–771.

64 Segall, Marshall H., Donald T. Campbell, and Melville J. Herskovits: *The Influence of Culture on Visual Perception* (Indianapolis: Bobbs-Merrill, 1966).

65 Sapir, Edward: *Time Perspective in Aboriginal American Culture:*

*A Study in Method,* Memoir 90, Anthropological Series no. 13 (Ottawa: Department of Mines, Geological Survey, 1961).

66 Schapera, I.: *Government and Politics in Tribal Societies* (London: Watts, 1956).

67 Simon, H. A.: "Spurious Correlation: A Causal Interpretation," *Journal of the American Statistical Association,* 49 (1954), 467–479.

68 Spicer, Edward H.: *Pascua: A Yaqui Village in Arizona* (Chicago: University of Chicago Press, 1940).

69 Spicer, Edward H.: *Potam: A Yaqui Village in Sonora,* American Anthropological Association, Memoir no. 77 (1954).

70 Spier, Leslie: "The Sun Dance of the Plains Indians," *Anthropological Papers, American Museum of Natural History,* 16 (1921), 451–527.

71 Stewart, Omer C.: "Culture Element Distributions: XVIII. Ute-Southern Paiute," *Anthropological Records,* 6 (Berkeley, 1942).

72 Tukey, John W.: "Causation, Regression and Path Analysis," in Oscar Kempthorne et al. (Eds.), *Statistics and Mathematics in Biology* (Ames, Iowa: Iowa State College Press, 1954), pp. 35–66.

73 Turner, Malcolm E., and Charles D. Stevens: "The Regression Analysis of Causal Paths," *Biometrics,* 15 (1959), 236–258.

74 Tylor, Edward B.: "On a Method of Investigating the Institutions Applied to the Laws of Marriage and Descent," *Journal of the Royal Anthropological Institute,* 18 (1889), 272.

75 Whiting, John W. M., and Irving L. Child: *Child Training and Personality* (New Haven, Conn.: Yale, 1953).

76 Wright, Sewall: "The Method of Path Coefficients," *Annals of Mathematical Statistics,* 5 (1934), 161

77 Zeisel, Hans: *Say It with Figures* (New York: Harper & Row, 1947).

CHAPTER 8

# Sampling Theory and Procedures

BERNARD LAZERWITZ

In the social sciences, sampling considerations and complications are thrust upon the researcher by the very nature of his data-gathering conditions. In the United States, for example, social scientists face the expensive and time-consuming task of investigating a vast and differentiated population spread over a large territory. Despite the obvious need to avoid measuring every member of such a vast population, why the monumental concern over the way a part of this whole is selected? Is not getting a part out of a whole—from which to comment upon the whole—an artistic affair? Unfortunately, leaving the sampling process to such a judgmental approach winds up with various researchers presenting different sampling recipes which usually give poor measurements of beliefs and behavior because of the vagaries operating in judgmental sampling. The junkyard of this subjective approach is filled with the twisted remains of the *Literary Digest* prediction that Landon would win the Presidency in 1936, the pollsters' declaration that Dewey would win the 1948 presidential election, and the market research that gave the Ford Motor Company the go-ahead signal on the Edsel. The failings of subjective approaches can be overcome by the procedures of statistics which eliminate the guesswork in sampling and obtain information of determinable precision about the whole from a part of the whole.

What should be the desired characteristics of a sample? First of all, a proper sample must give a precise picture of the population from which it is drawn. Second, the sample must be obtained by a probability process. This permits the use of statistical procedures to describe and analyze the data of the sample and to relate it to the population from which it came. Finally, the sample should be as small as precision considerations permit, as economical as possible, and gathered as swiftly as its various measurement techniques permit. Bear in mind that the sampling process not only should yield estimations of population means, percentages, and totals, but must also obtain measurements on subclasses of a population. In the social sciences, the emphasis is more often upon the relations among subclasses than upon a description of the entire population. For instance, students of the sociology of religion are more concerned with the church-attendance patterns of United States Protestants, Catholics, and Jews than with the overall frequencies of church attendance for the entire country.

In short, then, a proper sample should be a small piece of the population obtained by a probability process that mirrors, with known precision, the various patterns and subclasses of the population.

## 8.1 SIMPLE RANDOM SAMPLING

The most basic and least complicated probability sampling procedure is simple random sampling, which is the sampling model employed for most of statistical inference.[1] It requires a clear definition of a population to be sampled, a complete listing of all its elements, and the assumption that all such elements are statistically independent of one another. For social scientists, the requirement of statistical independence means that the elements can engage in only a very small amount of interaction. The variables being measured must relate to each other very much like the successive outcomes obtained by flipping a coin.

The two basic requirements of complete listing and little or no interaction seriously restrict the opportunities for the use of simple random sampling. Much of the time, complete listing is prohibitively expensive, and the groups under investigation have large amounts of interaction among all or some of their component parts. Nevertheless, knowledge of simple random sampling is necessary for an understanding of the more complicated types of sample design which use more realistic assumptions.

A simple random sample can be selected by the following steps:

**1** List all the elements in the population and assign them consecutive numbers from 1 to $N$ (where $N$ stands for the total number of elements in the population). These elements are often referred to as the listing elements of a population.

**2** Decide upon the desired sample size—$n$ (where $n$ stands for the number of listing elements sampled). Procedures for approximating sample size are given in Sec. 8.2.

---

[1] It is assumed that the reader has some acquaintance with both descriptive statistics and statistical inference. The more difficult sections of the chapter are indicated by asterisks and may be skipped by the more casual reader.

**3** Then, using a table of random numbers, select $n$ different random numbers that fall between 1 and $N$.

**4** The listing elements in the population that have been assigned these various $n$ random numbers constitute the sample. One can next interview the people or measure the items designated by the sampled elements.

With the interviewing or measuring completed, the several sample means, totals, and proportions estimate their corresponding population values through these formulas:

$$\bar{x} = \sum_{i=1}^{n} \frac{x_i}{n} \tag{8.1}$$

A sample mean is the estimator of its corresponding population mean; $x_i$ is the measurement value on the $i$th sample element; $n$ is the number of elements selected into the sample.

$$p = \sum_{i=1}^{n} \frac{x_i}{n} \tag{8.2}$$

A sample proportion is the estimator of its corresponding population proportion; $x_i = 1$ when the sample element possesses the characteristic under investigation, i.e., is an Episcopalian; or $x_i = 0$ when the sample element *does not* possess the characteristic under investigation, i.e., *is other than* an Episcopalian.

$$T = N\bar{x} \qquad \text{or} \qquad Np \tag{8.3}$$

A total is the estimator of its corresponding population total where $N$ is the number of listing elements in the population.

Since probability samples of an entire population also give probability samples of subclasses of that population, the above formulas can be used to compute estimators of population subclass means, proportions, and totals. In such cases, the summation is across only the subclass members; $x_i$ involves only the subclass members in the sample; $n$ becomes $n_g$, the number of subclass members falling into the sample; and $N$ becomes $N_g$, the subclass population size. For example, if one wants to get an estimate of the proportion of the Episcopalian population that are white-collar Episcopalians, $x_i$ becomes the number of sample Episcopalians who have white-collar occupations and $n_g$ becomes the number of Episcopalians in the sample. Then the estimator of the proportion of the Episcopalian population that has white-collar occupations is obtained by dividing the number of white-collar Episcopalians within the sample by the number of Episcopalians within the sample.

In addition to estimating population means, proportions, and totals, only probability sampling permits calculation of their precision. Such precision calculations are derived from the operations of the mathematical laws called the *law of large numbers* and the *central limit theorem*. In essence, these laws show that sample means, proportions, and totals vary about their population equivalents very much like a normal probability distribution (provided the sample size is not too small). Hence, confidence intervals can be formed about these sample estimators which will encompass their population equivalents (e.g., means or totals) with a specific, known chance of error. This chance of error is the probability that confidence intervals fail to encompass the population values. Confidence limits are expressed as multiples of the standard errors (also abbreviated SE) of these means, proportions, or total estimators. A typical confidence interval statement is that a sample mean of $1,000 plus or minus $600 will include its population value 95 times out of 100 in the long run. This declares that the sample mean value of $1,000 (obtained by this particular sample) plus or minus twice the value of the sample mean's standard error ($300) will encompass its population mean in 95 out of 100 samples of this kind.[2] Only 5 samples out of the 100 will have sample means whose confidence intervals fail to include the population mean. The phrase, in the long run, refers to the process of obtaining and measuring the results of 100 (or more) samples. The standard error formulas for the above sample estimators are given below.

Standard error of a mean is

$$\text{SE}(\bar{x}) = \sqrt{(1-f)\frac{\sum_{i=1}^{n}(x_i - \bar{x})^2}{n(n-1)}} \tag{8.4}$$

In this formula $f = \dfrac{n}{N}$ is the sampling fraction and $1 - f$ is the finite population correction factor.

Standard error of a proportion is

$$\text{SE}(p) = \sqrt{(1-f)\frac{pq}{n-1}} \tag{8.5}$$

where $q = 1 - p$.

Standard error of a total is

$$\text{SE}(T) = N\text{SE}(\bar{x}) \quad \text{or} \quad N\text{SE}(p) \tag{8.6}$$

The finite population correction factor operates as sort of a bonus term in that it reflects the size of the bite a sample takes from its population. The greater the bite, the less the standard error. If the entire population is selected (a 100 percent sample), then $f$ equals 1, the finite population correction factor becomes zero, and the standard error reduces to zero.[3] This zero value makes

[2] Actually a more correct value for the 95 times out of a 100 condition is 1.96 times the standard error of a sample mean. In this chapter, for simplification, 2 will be used instead of 1.96.

[3] Of course, it is possible to sample from a population whose elements are infinite in number. Then $f$ is zero and the finite population correction factor vanishes. Such an infinite population can also be generated by sampling with replacement, in other words, permitting an element to be selected into a sample more than once. Clearly, this is not a feasible

sense when one realizes that a 100 percent sample yields population means, proportions, and totals and not just estimators of these quantities.

Again, the standard error of the means, proportions, and totals of subclasses can be obtained by letting $n$ and $N$ become $n_g$ and $N_g$; by restricting the values of $x_i$ and $p$ to those of a subclass, i.e., $x_{gi}$ and $p_g$; and by summing across a subclass.

## An Illustration

As an example, let us draw a sample of 200 students from a high school student body of 1,000 and interview them about their study habits. As part of the analysis of the data, let us estimate the proportion of the high school that is Protestant, Catholic, and Jewish, and the proportion getting good grades (A's and B's) among Protestant students whose fathers are white-collar workers.

To obtain the sample, we assign the students numbers from 1 to 1,000; then we select 200 different random numbers between 1 and 1,000 from a table of random numbers. The students assigned the selected random numbers constitute the sample and are interviewed. After the interviews are coded and the data processed, assume that the following sample information is obtained:

**1** Proportion of sample that is
Protestant: 0.53
Catholic: 0.30
Jewish: 0.17

**2** Number of Protestant students whose fathers have white-collar occupations: 86

**3** And of these 86, 37 have good grades

Then applying Eq. (8.2), we estimate that in the high school, as a whole, 53 percent of the students are Protestants, 30 percent are Catholics, and 17 percent are Jewish. Furthermore, the standard errors for these estimations are, from Eq. (8.5):

for Protestants $\qquad \sqrt{(1 - 0.2)\dfrac{(0.53)(0.47)}{199}} = 0.03 \qquad\qquad (8.7)$

for Catholics $\qquad \sqrt{(1 - 0.2)\dfrac{(0.3)(0.7)}{199}} = 0.03 \qquad\qquad (8.8)$

for Jews $\qquad \sqrt{(1 - 0.2)\dfrac{(0.17)(0.83)}{199}} = 0.025 \qquad\qquad (8.9)$

---

model for most kinds of social research; thus, only sampling without replacement will be discussed.

On the other hand, certain forms of statistical analysis require generalizing to an infinite population from a sample selected without replacement. In such circumstances, the finite population correction factor must be dropped.

Hence, one can state, at the 95 percent confidence level (two standard errors), that the percentages of the entire high school which embrace the three faiths are: for Protestants, between 47 and 59 percent; for Catholics, between 24 and 36 percent; for Jews, between 12 and 22 percent.

Applying Eq. (8.2) to the Protestant subclass, we obtain $\frac{37}{86} = 0.43$ as the estimate for the high school of the proportion getting good grades among Protestant students having white-collar fathers. This proportion has a standard error of 0.05 which means, for 95 samples out of 100, the actual proportion can be expected to be between 0.33 and 0.53.

## Some Definitions

The word "precision" has been used in this discussion of simple random sampling. Its meaning needs to be enlarged upon. Suppose the 1,000 people composing the adult population of a village were asked if they were registered voters, and their answers indicated that 86 percent were. Now, the researcher goes to the local board of election commissioners and determines who are actually the registered voters among the village's adult population. This research reveals that only 75 percent of the adult population of the village is legally registered. Finally, the researcher selects a simple random sample of 100 adults out of the 1,000 in the village for reinterviewing. In the course of the interviews, he again asks the various respondents whether or not they are registered voters. This time 89 percent state that they are registered. One now has three sets of figures:

**1** Results of interviewing the entire adult population of the village indicate that 86 percent claim to be registered voters.

**2** Results of interviewing a simple random sample of these same adults indicate that 89 percent claim to be registered voters.

**3** Actually, only 75 percent are legally registered voters.

The first figure, 86 percent, is the precise estimate and is the value obtained by measuring the entire population in the same manner as the sample. The second figure, 89 percent, is the sample estimate for the population and differs from 86 percent because of sampling error. Note that both the precise figure and the sample estimate are subject to the error factors arising out of an equivalent measurement process. The third figure, 75 percent, is the true registration percentage; the difference between it and 86 percent results from the various nonsampling errors arising from the measurement technique used to ascertain the proportion registered. Unfortunately, one can seldom determine true figures or answers. Typically, a researcher can compute only his sampling error and use it to set confidence limits around *the precise not the true figure.* Lastly, the degree to which the sample estimate approaches the true figure is referred to as the *accuracy* of a sample and reflects both sampling and measurement errors.

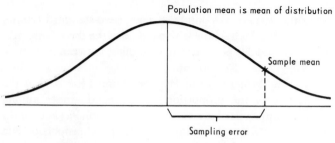

Population mean is mean of distribution

Sample mean

Sampling error

(a) Unbiased distribution

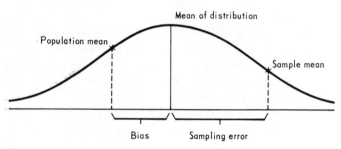

Mean of distribution

Population mean

Sample mean

Bias     Sampling error

(b) Biased distribution

**Fig. 8.1.   An Unbiased and a Biased Distribution of a Sample Mean.**

Still another important sampling concept is *bias*.   Bias refers to whether or not the operation of the law of large numbers produces a curve whose mean is the population value being estimated.   Figure 8.1 pictures a biased and an unbiased distribution.   Figure 8.1*a* shows an unbiased sample mean falling on a normal (or nearly normal) curve.   The mean of this normal curve is the population mean estimated by the sample value.   Here, these two means differ because of sampling error.   If the mean of the normal curve is not the same as the population mean, as shown by the biased distribution of Fig. 8.1*b*, then the difference between the actual mean of the normal curve and the population mean would be called the bias.   When a bias does exist, the estimator of a population value will not average out to that population value throughout many different samples.   Then, to the sampling error difference between a sample estimator and the mean of its distribution would have to be added the bias in order to obtain the value of the population mean.

When can the sample mean be considered to fall on a sufficiently normal distribution?   It is suggested that a minimum sample size of 100 should be obtained before any mean or proportion can be considered to have a sufficiently normal distribution.[4]   The same requirement of 100 should be applied to the

---

[4] Another precaution for proportions is to avoid the normality assumption when $p$ is less than 0.05 or greater than 0.95.   For such extreme values, one needs to use the *binomial expansion formula* to obtain confidence limits or, better still, to base these very small or large proportions on considerably larger samples.

size of subclasses. For both the total sample or any subclass, the requirement of 100 represents a conservative level and a skilled statistician can readily work with smaller samples. But let the semiskilled seek the more cautious level of 100 cases.

## 8.2 SAMPLE SIZE DETERMINATION

Just how does one go about deciding upon the sample size that is best suited to his investigation? While there are several procedures available for the determination of sample size, there is one which is, by far, the easiest to apply. Consider the fact that the numerator in the formula for the variance of a sample proportion reaches its maximum value when the proportion is 0.5. With much of the analysis of sample survey data being concerned with proportions, it is simple to obtain a conservative level for sample size by use of the formula for the standard error of a proportion.

Starting with this modified form of Eq. (8.5):

$$\text{SE}(p) = \sqrt{\frac{pq}{n}} \qquad \text{set } p \text{ and } q \text{ at } 0.5 \qquad (8.10)$$

Next, the researcher has to decide how wide a confidence interval around 0.5, at the 95 percent confidence level (if he chooses this), he wants to work with. Suppose he decides to seek a sample size in which these confidence limits are 0.45 and 0.55 which makes twice $\text{SE}(p)$ equal to 0.05. Now the only unknown in the equation is the sample size, which can be solved by

$$n = \frac{(2)^2 pq}{[2\text{SE}(p)]^2} = \frac{(4)(0.5)(0.5)}{(0.05)^2} = \frac{1}{(0.05)^2} = 400 \qquad (8.11)$$

Hence, a sample size of 400 will yield the specified confidence interval for 0.5. The general sample size formula is

$$n = \frac{1}{k^2} \qquad (8.12)$$

where $k$ is the desired interval about 0.5 at a 95 percent confidence level.

Since the numerator of the standard error formula for a proportion of 0.5 will be larger than that of any other proportion, this procedure has the advantage of providing even smaller confidence intervals for percentages other than 50 percent.

Because of the many possibilities, seldom does an investigator know which statistics to base confidence intervals upon. Hence, the procedure of establishing confidence intervals about 50 percent is a reasonable and conservative rule-of-thumb approach.

A large enough finite population correction factor can appreciably reduce the variance. When this occurs, the procedure just described will give more than the minimum number of sample cases needed to yield the desired confidence.   Unfortunately, the bite taken out of the population has to be pretty sizable, say, about 20 percent, for the $1 - f$ factor to carry any major reducing influence.   Almost all the time, the finite population correction factor is quite small and has a negligible effect.[5]

Another question which must be answered before this approach to total sample size can be accepted is what will a sample subclass size be if Eq. (8.12) is used?   If subclass analysis is important to a survey, then the necessary way to set total sample size is to apply Eq. (8.12) to that subclass, among those to be analyzed, which has the smallest proportion of the population.   For instance, if the smallest population subclass to be analyzed is one-fourth of the population, then Eq. (8.12) would require that this particular subclass have 400 cases in the sample and that the total sample size be 1,600.   Still another way of doing it is to set, arbitrarily, the smallest subclass size at 100 cases.

The trouble with desired subclass sizes is that they quickly require a large total sample.   If the total sample becomes too large, some subclasses will have to be dropped from analysis, or only as much analysis performed on them as the number of subclass sample cases permit after cost, time, and manpower requirements are considered.

When the sample size is finally decided upon, it is possible to translate the number of cases into minimal cost estimates.   Suppose the method of measurement is to be an hour-long interview (a fairly common survey objective).   If the sample size is 400 and travel time per interview is estimated at half an hour, then 600 man-hours of interview time are required.   If 10 interviewers are employed for twenty hours a week, the field work will take at least three weeks and quite likely four to five weeks.   If all interviewing costs run $3 an hour, at least $1,800 (and probably more) will be spent on field work.

Experience has shown that survey costs, including analyst's time and overhead, can easily amount to $50 per interview.   Of course, costs per interview will be less if the analyst's time is not paid for and if overhead is absorbed by a sponsoring agency.   Nevertheless, the minimum amount of time, money, and manpower required for a survey of a given sample size can be approximated by the above rule-of-thumb statements.   With such quick and simple estimates before him, a researcher can decide whether or not he can afford the levels of sample size, length of interview, or amount of field activity thus indicated.   If not, then sample size and length of interview should be reduced.   Survey quality must not be permitted to suffer through such things as permitting a higher rate of interview refusals or poorer interviewer training.

A final point to note about the sample size formula is its omission of any population term.   The formula for sample size is actually composed of an estimate of the population *variance* and a predetermined level for the confidence interval.[6]   This omission is possible because the size of a population has nothing

---

[5] Similarly, a large enough total sample, or subclass, size permits $n$ to replace $n - 1$.

[6] The term "variance" refers to the square of the standard error of an estimator or, for actual interview measurements, to the square of the standard deviation.

to do with the size of a probability sample from that population.  Of vital importance is the heterogeneity of the population.  No matter how large the population, if everybody in it held the same position, behaved the same way, or possessed the same values, a sample of one would give as much information about this fully homogeneous population as would a sample of many thousands. If the members of a population differ widely in their behavior or characteristics, then a fairly large sample is needed to mirror the population precisely.

## 8.3   NONSAMPLING ERRORS

Not all the errors encountered in survey work are a result of the sampling process.  An important class of errors, called nonsampling errors, arises out of such things as poor schedule questions, refusals or incomplete respondent answers, inability to contact the proper respondents, even clerical errors in processing or coding interviews, and mistakes in data processing or analysis. These errors can best be distinguished from the standard errors of sampling by realizing that they are the kinds of errors that would still be there even if the entire population were interviewed.

Nonsampling errors can be classified into two basic divisions.  (1) Random errors consist of those kinds of mistakes which tend to cancel one another out in the long run.  Examples are clerical mistakes in coding or data processing and minor interviewer errors.  (2) Biases consist of those kinds of mistakes which have cumulative effect and do not cancel out.

The standard way to combine sampling and nonsampling errors is by the right-triangle approach of Fig. 8.2.  Total error is equal to the square root of the sum of the square of the sampling standard error and the square of the nonsampling errors.  The drawback to this kind of approach is the difficulty of measuring the nonsampling errors.  Indeed, the sizes of the most important sources of nonsampling errors, such as interviewer effects, the errors due to nonresponse, or incorrect answers by respondents, are ordinarily never known.

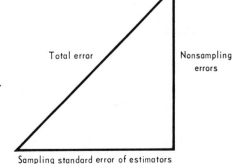

Total error          Nonsampling errors

**Fig. 8.2.   Combining Sampling and Non-sampling Errors to Get Total Error.**

Sampling standard error of estimators

Hence, the best survey strategy is to allocate resources so as to minimize the factors which contribute most to total error. In practice, this means that after the construction of a well-designed sample, a survey staff should work hard to ensure that measurement instruments work properly, that the field force is well trained, and that nonresponse is reduced through sufficient call-backs and few refusals. Even though one has a well-designed sample to analyze, large nonsampling errors can easily add up to large total errors which can cast serious doubts upon the results of a survey.

## 8.4  STRATIFIED SIMPLE RANDOM SAMPLING

### Basic Design

Stratified simple random sampling involves dividing the population into separate, more homogeneous strata and then selecting simple random samples from each of the strata. Therefore, the new design points that need consideration are (1) the criteria for forming strata, (2) the variance reduction possible with stratified sampling, and (3) modified formulas for means, proportions, totals, and their standard errors.

Actually, any method of dividing the population into strata can be used *provided* the resultant strata are relatively homogeneous. Among possible stratifying criteria can be number of years of education, age, life cycle, sex, family income, occupation, religion, race, or any other item relevant to a research problem. To stratify, simply place every member of the population into its proper stratum as determined by the stratifying criterion. Suppose the stratifying criterion is education and consists of the following strata:

> Eight grades of education or less
> Some high school
> High school graduate
> Some college or other post high school formal education
> College graduate
> Graduate or professional education

It becomes necessary to determine the amount of education of each member of the population, and then to place each member into one of these six education strata. After stratification has been performed, six simple random samples are selected from the six population strata and combined into one sample.

The sample design advantage of stratified sampling over simple random sampling is best expressed by the word "homogeneity." Through stratification, the researcher cuts the total variance of the population into two parts—the variance within strata and the variance between strata. If the stratification criterion works well, the increased homogeneity within strata results in an appreciable part of the total variance falling between strata. Since the modified formulas for the standard errors of means, proportions, and totals exclude between-strata variance, their resultant sizes are lessened. Ordinarily, stratification results in moderate standard error reductions.[7]

## *Disproportionate Stratified Simple Random Sampling*

Stratified simple random sampling consists of a general type, disproportionate stratified sampling, and two special types, proportionate stratified sampling and optimum allocation. In disproportionate stratified simple random sampling, the within-strata sampling fractions vary from stratum to stratum. Let the symbol $f_h$ be used for the within-strata sampling fractions where $f_h = n_h/N_h$ or the proportion of the listing elements of the $h$th population stratum selected for the $h$th sample stratum. Perhaps 1 percent of the listing elements of the first population stratum might be selected to compose the sample from the first stratum, 3 percent of the listing elements of the second population stratum could be selected into the second sample stratum, 5 percent of a third stratum, and so forth.

The formulas for means, proportions, and totals for disproportionate stratified simple random sampling are as follows. The mean is

$$\bar{x}_{DS} = \sum_{h=1}^{L} W_h\bar{x}_h \tag{8.13}$$

In this formula for means, $\sum\limits_{h=1}^{L}$ indicates summation over all $L$ strata;

$$\bar{x}_h = \frac{\sum\limits_{i=1}^{n_h} x_{hi}}{n_h}$$

is the mean of the $h$th sample stratum; $\sum\limits_{i=1}^{n_h}$ indicates summation over all the sample values of the $h$th sample stratum; $n_h$ is the sample size of the $h$th sample stratum; $W_h = N_h/N$ is the ratio of the number of listing elements in the $h$th *population* stratum to the number of listing elements in the *entire population;* the subscript $DS$ stands for disproportionate stratified simple random sampling.

---

[7] This reduction in standard error is illustrated by analysis of variance which resolves the overall variance into a between-strata component and a within-strata component.

The proportion is

$$p_{DS} = \sum_{h=1}^{L} W_h p_h \qquad (8.14)$$

Here $p_h$ is the value of a proportion in the $h$th sample stratum. The total is

$$T_{DS} = N\bar{x}_{DS} \text{ or } Np_{DS} \qquad (8.15)$$

The formulas for the standard errors of means, proportions, and totals for this type of sample design are as follows.

The standard error of a mean is

$$\text{SE}(\bar{x}_{DS}) = \sqrt{\sum_{h=1}^{L} \frac{W_h{}^2(1 - f_h)s_h{}^2}{n_h}} \qquad (8.16)$$

Here $s_h{}^2 = \sum_{i=1}^{n_h} (x_{hi} - \bar{x}_h)^2/(n_h - 1)$ is the $h$th sample stratum variance.

The standard error of a proportion is

$$\text{SE}(p_{DS}) = \sqrt{\sum_{h=1}^{L} \frac{W_h{}^2(1 - f_h)p_h q_h}{n_h - 1}} \qquad (8.17)$$

The standard error of a total is

$$\text{SE}(T_{DS}) = \sqrt{\sum_{h=1}^{L} \frac{N_h{}^2(1 - f_h)s_h{}^2}{n_h}} \qquad (8.18)$$

For an example of this type of sample design, suppose that a religious census has been taken in a high school with 1,000 students. The religious census shows that 550 of the high school's students are Protestants, 260 are Catholics, and 190 are Jews. The students are then stratified by religious affiliation, and within affiliation, are listed in alphabetical order by the first letter of their last names. From a machine print-out of this stratified listing of the student body, a simple random sample is then drawn from each of the three religious strata. The Protestant sample consists of 44 students, the Catholic sample contains 26 students, and the Jewish sample has 30 students. These 100 students are interviewed and their political party preferences and their fathers' ages are obtained. From these data the principal of the high school would like to obtain the proportion of the school that prefers the Republican party and the average age of students' fathers. These figures can be obtained as follows.

Having ascertained from the sample survey that 65 percent of the sample's Protestants, 35 percent of the Catholics, and 20 percent of the Jews prefer the Republican party, the proportion of the entire high school student body that prefers the Republican party can be estimated by Eq. (8.14):

$$p_{DS} = \left(\frac{550}{1,000}\right)(0.65) + \left(\frac{260}{1,000}\right)(0.35) + \left(\frac{190}{1,000}\right)(0.20) = 0.49 \quad (8.19)$$

The mean paternal ages and variances as determined from the three sample strata are:

| Sample strata | Average age of father, years | Variance of paternal age |
|---|---|---|
| Protestants | 38 | 10 |
| Catholics | 44 | 7 |
| Jews | 40.5 | 8 |

Then the estimated average paternal age for the entire high school is calculated from Eq. (8.13):

$$\bar{x}_{DS} = \left(\frac{550}{1,000}\right)(38) + \left(\frac{260}{1,000}\right)(44) + \left(\frac{190}{1,000}\right)(40.5) = 40 \text{ years} \quad (8.20)$$

The standard error for the 49 percent of the school that is Republican is obtained from Eq. (8.17):

$$SE(p_{DS}) = \left\{ \left[ (0.55)^2 \left(1 - \frac{44}{550}\right) \frac{(0.65)(0.35)}{43} \right] \right.$$
$$+ \left[ (0.26)^2 \left(1 - \frac{26}{260}\right) \frac{(0.35)(0.65)}{25} \right]$$
$$\left. + \left[ (0.19)^2 \left(1 - \frac{30}{190}\right) \frac{(0.20)(0.80)}{29} \right] \right\}^{\frac{1}{2}} = 0.06 \quad (8.21)$$

Also, the standard error for the estimated average paternal age of 40 years is derived from Eq. (8.16) as:

$$SE(\bar{x}_{DS}) = \left\{ \left[ (0.55)^2 \left(1 - \frac{44}{550}\right) \frac{(10)}{44} \right] + \left[ (0.26)^2 \left(1 - \frac{26}{260}\right) \frac{(7)}{26} \right] \right.$$
$$\left. + \left[ (0.19)^2 \left(1 - \frac{30}{190}\right) \frac{(8)}{30} \right] \right\}^{\frac{1}{2}} = 0.29 \text{ years} \quad (8.22)$$

## Proportionate Stratified Simple Random Sampling

When the same sampling fraction is used throughout all population strata, the sample design is called *proportionate stratified simple random sampling*. Obviously, this kind of sample design is a special case of the more general disproportionate technique.

If the same overall sampling fraction is used, $f_1 = f_2 = f_3 = \cdots f_h = f$. Also, as a result of using the same overall sampling fraction, $n_h/n = N_h/N$ since the sample strata sizes bear the same ratio to the total sample size as do the population strata sizes to the total population size.[8]  With the substitution of sample weights for population weights, Eqs. (8.13) and (8.14) are modified as follows: A mean is

$$\bar{x}_{ps} = \sum_{h=1}^{L} \frac{n_h}{n} \sum_{i=1}^{n_h} \frac{x_{hi}}{n_h} = \sum_{h=1}^{L} \sum_{i=1}^{n_h} \frac{x_{hi}}{n} \tag{8.23}$$

Here the subscript $ps$ stands for proportionate stratified simple random sampling. A proportion is

$$p_{ps} = \frac{1}{n} \sum_{h=1}^{L} n_h p_h = \sum_{h=1}^{L} \sum_{i=1}^{n_h} \frac{x_{hi}}{n} \tag{8.24}$$

Here $x_{hi} = 1$ when the sample element possesses the characteristic under investigation, and $x_{hi} = 0$ where the sample element does not possess the characteristic under investigation.

Both Eqs. (8.23) and (8.24) are the same as the corresponding simple random sampling Eqs. (8.1) and (8.2), except for the summation within strata and across strata, because the stratification weight, $N_h/N$, in the form of $n_h/n$, cancels out.  Hence proportionate stratified sampling is often called *self-weighting sampling.*

The formulas for the standard errors of means, proportions, and totals simplify to the following.

The standard error of a mean is

$$SE(\bar{x}_{ps}) = \sqrt{\sum_{h=1}^{L} \frac{n_h^2}{n^2} \frac{(1-f)s_h^2}{n_h}} = \sqrt{\frac{(1-f)}{n^2} \sum_{h=1}^{L} n_h s_h^2} \tag{8.25}$$

The standard error of a proportion is

$$SE(p_{ps}) = \sqrt{\frac{(1-f)}{n^2} \sum_{h=1}^{L} \frac{n_h^2 p_h q_h}{n_h - 1}} \tag{8.26}$$

The standard error of a total is

$$SE(T_{ps}) = \sqrt{(1-f)\frac{N^2}{n^2} \sum_{h=1}^{L} n_h s_h^2} \tag{8.27}$$

[8] Of course, this equivalence of the sample weights to the population weights ignores a slight sampling variation and assumes the same response rate in all strata.  For example, if a population stratum has 897 listing elements, an overall sampling fraction of one-fifth can yield 179 or 180 cases for the sample stratum size.  Again, if 50 percent of the respondents in stratum 1 refuse to be interviewed, but only 20 percent refuse in stratum 2, the ratios to total sample size of the yields from strata 1 and 2 will not be the same as their population strata ratios.

With a proportionate sample design that uses an overall sampling fraction of one-tenth, the previous example would yield the following results.

| Strata | Sample size | Prefer Republican Party | Average age of father, years | Variance of paternal age |
|---|---|---|---|---|
| Protestants | 55 | 0.65 | 38 | 10 |
| Catholics | 26 | 0.35 | 44 | 7 |
| Jews | 19 | 0.20 | 40.5 | 8 |

$$p_{ps} = \frac{1}{100} [(55)(0.65) + (26)(0.35) + (19)(0.20)] = 0.49 \qquad (8.28)$$

$$SE(p_{ps}) = \left[ \frac{1 - \frac{1}{10}}{(100)^2} \right]^{\frac{1}{2}} \left[ (55)^2 \frac{(0.65)(0.35)}{54} + (26)^2 \frac{(0.35)(0.65)}{25} \right.$$
$$\left. + (19)^2 \frac{(0.20)(0.80)}{18} \right]^{\frac{1}{2}} = 0.045 \quad (8.29)$$

$$\bar{x}_{ps} = \frac{55}{100} (38) + \frac{26}{100} (44) + \frac{19}{100} (40.5) = 40 \text{ years} \qquad (8.30)$$

$$SE(\bar{x}_{ps}) = \left[ \frac{1 - \frac{1}{10}}{(100)^2} \right]^{\frac{1}{2}} [(55)(10) + (26)(7) + (19)(8)]^{\frac{1}{2}} = 0.28 \text{ years} \quad (8.31)$$

If the focus of investigation is some subclass, then the sampling fractions must be sufficiently large to yield an adequate number of subclass cases throughout the entire sample. Often the strata are focal points of investigation. When this occurs, the problem of getting enough strata cases for adequate analysis often demands disproportionate stratified sampling. If the rule of thumb is followed that at least 100 cases should be present in a stratum to permit proper stratum analysis, small population strata will require relatively large sampling fractions. On the other hand, the fairly large population strata can readily yield adequate sample numbers with fairly small sampling fractions. In such a situation, the best compromise is to use disproportionate stratified sampling with larger sampling fractions applied in the small population strata and smaller sampling fractions applied in the large population strata.

As a general rule, it is wise to use proportionate stratification whenever analysis requirements can be met in order to gain the calculation simplifications this sampling design allows. It is clearly awkward to work on the basic card-sorting machines with the various weights demanded by disproportionate stratified sampling. Counter sorters can be used only with great caution and more complicated tabulator wiring must be employed to insert weight factors. The weighting-simplification procedures presented in the subsection entitled "Disproportionate Cluster Sampling" in Sec. 8.6 ease the complications of machine operations.

It is possible to establish a conservative level for the total sample size of a proportionate stratified sample with the procedure of Sec. 8.2 by ignoring the variance reduction through stratification.

A good way to close this section is to introduce the concept of *efficiency*. Efficiency refers to the ratio of the variances of two sample estimates which have the same sample size.  The more efficient of the two sample estimates is the one with the smaller variance.  Another way of stating it is to say that the more efficient of two estimates based on the same sample size is the one with the smaller variance.  For example, suppose a simple random sample of 100 yielded a mean of 9.5 years of education for adults twenty-five years old or older with a variance of 4, while a stratified proportionate sample of 100 yielded a mean of 9.8 years with a variance of 2.  Then the stratified sample would be considered twice as efficient as the simple random sample for estimating mean years of education.

## * Strata Subclasses

Calculation formulas for strata subclasses can readily be obtained by making the following substitutions in stratification Eqs. (8.13) to (8.18).

| *From* | *To* |
|---|---|
| $N$—total population size | $N_g$—subclass population size |
| $n$—total sample size | $n_g$—subclass sample size |
| $N_h$—population size within a stratum | $N_{gh}$—subclass population size within a stratum |
| $n_h$—sample size within a stratum | $n_{gh}$—subclass sample size within a stratum |
| $s_h{}^2$—variance of a sample stratum | $s_{gh}^2$—variance for a subclass of a sample stratum |
| $p_h$—proportion of a sample stratum | $p_{gh}$—proportion for a subclass of a sample stratum |

For the standard error of totals, multiply the standard error of a subclass mean by $N_g$.  However, various statistical considerations prevent use of the simplified proportionate sampling formulas for any subclasses.

## * Optimum Allocation

Another important stratified sampling variation is optimum allocation. With this design, the object is to allocate parts of the total sample size to the various sample strata so that the strata with the larger variances receive the larger number of sample cases. This means that as $s_h^2$ increases in value, so should its divisor $n_h$. Optimum allocation is reached when the term $\sum_{h=1}^{L} s_h^2/n_h$ is as small as it can be as a result of the particular combination of $n_h$'s assigned to the various strata.

Use of optimum allocation requires fairly reliable information on the various strata variance terms. This information is then fed into an optimum allocation equation to determine the optimum strata sample sizes. Such information is difficult to come by in advance of data collection, and its lack greatly handicaps a researcher's ability to use an optimum allocation design. Furthermore, the optimum allocation is for one variable. Since a survey gathers very many variables, it becomes necessary to establish some compromise allocation of strata sample sizes. This further involves the researcher in formula complications and increases demand for knowledge of population characteristics that are hard to obtain if, indeed, such data exist. Finally, analysis needs frequently require minimum strata sizes which handicap the application of optimum allocation techniques. All these problems combine to reduce greatly the opportunities to use this type of sample design in research.

## 8.5 SYSTEMATIC SELECTION

There is a more practical way of selecting sample elements from a population or the strata of a population. This more practical technique is systematic selection. It is obtained by determining the overall sampling fraction or the various strata sampling fractions, as has been shown above, and then doing what the sampling fraction indicates. Suppose a sampling fraction is one-fiftieth. If this fraction is read as 1 in 50 and from every 50 listing elements of the population one element is selected at random, a systematic sample is obtained. Consider a population of 1,039 listing elements to which a 1 in 50 sampling fraction is to be applied. First select a random number, say 15, between 1 and 50.[9] Starting with 15, add 50 to 15 to get 65 and then add 50 to 65 to obtain 115. Keep adding 50 until the resultant sum exceeds 1,039. Then these various numbers—15, 65, 115, 165, and so forth—represent the listing numbers of the elements to be selected into a 1 in 50 probability sample. The number 15 is called the *random start*, and the number 50 is called the *selection interval*. Whatever listing procedure is used to number the population elements from 1 to 1,039, systematic selection has determined that the 21 population elements numbered 15, 65, 115, 165, and so on up to 1,015 compose the probability sample. Now 50 divided into 1,039 gives a quotient of 20.78; therefore 20 sample elements must be obtained by this technique and a twenty-first sample element has 78 chances in 100 of being selected. If the random start falls anywhere from 1 to

[9] Remember to select a random number between 1 and 50 by using two columns (or rows) of a table of random numbers. This requires the eligible random numbers to range from 01 to 50.

39, a twenty-first sample element will be selected. If the random start falls anywhere from 40 to 50, the twenty-first sampling element will not be selected. The probability of selection of a block that contains 50 housing units is obviously 1; the probability of selection of a block that contains 40 housing units is 0.8. The probability of selection of a block that contains 125 housing units is still 1. Such a block will have two of its housing units selected with certainty, and it has a 50-50 chance of having a third housing unit selected into the sample. If systematic selection is not used but, instead, all the sample elements are determined from a table of random numbers, there is no certainty that any of the above blocks will yield any sample housing units. If a table of random numbers is employed, determining the probabilities of varying numbers of housing units being sampled from these blocks involves a complex application of the binomial theorem.[10] Therefore, another value of the systematic selection technique, besides clerical ease, is that it enables one to determine clearly and easily the probabilities of various sample selections from a population.[11]

Systematic selection may also be viewed as a kind of stratified sampling. Group the listing elements of the population into strata equal in number to the systematic selection interval. The random start selects a sample element from the first population group. Then, the random start plus the systematic selection interval determines a sample element from the second population group and so on throughout all the population groups. For instance, if the random start is 10 and the selection interval is 50, a population of 1,039 elements is divided into 20 full strata of 50 elements each and one stratum of 39 elements. The random start of 10 selects the element numbered 10 in the first stratum of 50, and, applying the interval of 50, the elements numbered 60, 110, 160, 210, etc., until 1,010 are systematically selected into the sample. The partial stratum of 39 is the last stratum and has 0.78 chances out of 1 of having a sample element selected from it. With sampling without replacement from the population of 1,039 elements, there are 50 different samples that can be systematically obtained. Clearly, these 50 different samples consist of all the elements numbered 1 within each group, or all the elements numbered 2 within each group, or, finally, all the elements numbered 50 within each group. Since 20 groups contain 50 elements and one group has 39, 39 out of the 50 possible samples will contain 21 sampling elements and 11 samples will contain only 20 sampling elements.

What effect does systematic selection have on the sample designs previously

[10] Actually, a binomial model should be used for infinite universes and a hypergeometric model should be used for finite universes.

[11] It is also possible to work with a fractional interval. Suppose, in the example just given, that the systematic selection interval is 47.3. Then a random start must be selected between 00.1 and 47.3. If the random start is 11.1, it selects population element number 11 into the sample. Applying the systematic selection interval of 47.3 gives additional selection numbers 58.4, 105.7, 153, 200.3, etc., to 1,004.4. These numbers select into the sample the population elements numbered 58, 105, 153, 200, etc., to 1,004. In other words, the selection numbers are rounded down to the last whole number, and the fractional components are ignored. When these fractional components build up to a whole number, there results a one-unit jump for some of the sample selection numbers.

discussed? For all practical purposes, none. Remember, systematic selection, like the use of a table of random numbers, is just a way of selecting elements into a sample *after* the conditions and rules of selection have been determined by a probability sample design. No new equations are required for simple random sampling or the various forms of stratified simple random sampling if sample elements are chosen by systematic selection. Indeed, in order to gain the various advantages of systematic selection, investigators employ it as much as possible.[12]

There are a couple of drawbacks to systematic selection that must be guarded against. One of these is the danger of *periodicity*. The essence of systematic selection is the selection into a sample of the same numbered elements from each of the groups formed by applying an interval such as 50. If there are any unusual properties associated with the similarly numbered elements that form a sample, the characteristics of such a sample can be drastically affected. For example, suppose a particular characteristic has its values varying in a periodic cycle (say, a sine curve) throughout its population. If sample selections fall on equivalent parts of a periodic cycle, one would get a sample view of the characteristic being investigated that differs considerably from another systematically selected sample consisting of an element located on the negative part of the periodic curve, then one on the positive part, then the negative, and so on.

While curves of such full periodicity do not occur too often in the social sciences, less perfect periodic variations do occur with fair frequency. Fortunately, it is fairly simple to avoid the effects of periodicity by changing random starts every now and then. Such shifts of random start will move the within-strata element selections around the curve of periodicity and give a sample that properly pictures the variations in value of a population characteristic.

If an investigator is aware of certain periodic tendencies, he should treat the problem by skillful design of both his sample and selection techniques. For example, on every sample block it would be unwise to select a house located in the same position, say, a corner house. Instead, a separate random start should be used with every sample block to obtain sample houses occupying a variety of locations. This same rule applies to selection of apartments within an apartment building or of buildings within a complex of structures.

Again, in case of a time trend in the characteristics under investigation, one must determine the temporal periodicity and cut across it. It would be clearly unwise to limit data gathering or study to the same day each week or the same week each month or the same month each year. In such cases, it is absolutely necessary to sample several different days, or weeks, or months to guarantee proper picturing of activities.

Another source of danger arises out of *linear trends*. For example, values

---

[12] In employing systematic selection with stratified sampling designs, one must obtain a different random start for each stratum. The selection interval can be different in each stratum, which gives a disproportionate stratified sample design.

can continually increase or decrease with the passage of time or distance.   This is illustrated by the decrease in traffic flow as one moves out of a metropolitan area.   To avoid improper estimations, under such circumstances, the investigator should again employ many random starts as beginning points for systematic selection and should try to employ a stratified sample design which could take advantage of such linear trends.   Finally, it is always possible to use only a table of random numbers to select sample elements when it is feared that either periodicity or linearity cannot be overcome by the mixture of systematic and random number selection procedures suggested here.

## 8.6   CLUSTER SAMPLING

### Basic Design

In the sample designs treated thus far, the listing elements of the population have been selected one at a time.   Only one element is designated to be a sample member for each random number or within each systematic selection stratum.   But it is entirely feasible to group the listing elements of a population into clusters of elements.   Then the clusters are listed, and a probability sample of such clusters is selected by either random numbers or a systematic technique.   When such group selections are made, the sample design is called *cluster sampling*.

Listing elements can be clustered by many criteria.   The clusters can be army squads, school classrooms, or industrial work teams, city blocks, geographic areas, or all employees at a given level of management in a business or governmental structure.   Clusters can be artificially created apart from functional or social criteria.   For instance, the sample elements of a systematic sample can be viewed as a cluster of listing elements having the same numerical position within the groups formed by systematic selection.   When a systematic sample of 1 in 50 is selected, the various groups of 50 can be thought of as placed in layers one above the other with all number 1s directly under each other, all number 2s directly under each other, and so on.   Then obtaining a random start between 1 and 50, say 10, is akin to selecting a cluster of all the tenth elements out of the groups of 50.

After the initial clusters, customarily called *primary sampling units* (abbreviated psu's), are sampled, it is possible to subdivide each selected primary sampling unit into clusters.   Within each psu, new items can be used as the listing units for cluster formation.   Then a sample of clusters can be selected from within primary sampling units.   These clusters within the first clusters are called *secondary sampling units*.   Again, clusters can be formed within the secondary sampling units with still another listing element utilized for cluster formation.   This process of creating and sampling clusters within clusters within clusters can be continued as long as required by whatever sampling design is being created.   Such a process of continuous cluster sampling is called *multistage cluster sampling*.   When the clusters are successive geographic units, the sample design is a special form of multistage sampling called *area sampling*. An example of multistage area sampling is the following design:

**1** Divide the United States into counties and select a sample of counties. This is the first sampling stage, and the counties are the primary sampling units.

**2** Within each selected psu (sampled counties), let three strata be formed. Stratum 1 consists of all large cities, stratum 2 consists of all small cities and villages, and stratum 3 contains the remainder of the county divided into clusters through use of U.S. Bureau of the Census enumeration districts. Within each of the three strata, select samples of the large cities, small cities and villages, and enumeration districts. This obtains the secondary selection units.

**3** Divide each secondary unit into blocks or other small geographic areas. Then select a sample of them to obtain the third stage of sampling.

**4** Within each of the third-stage clusters, select a sample of housing units for the fourth stage of sampling.

**5** Finally, within each sampled housing unit select one adult to be interviewed. This is the fifth and final sampling stage.

Note that it is readily possible to use stratification within clusters for any part of a multistage process. When stratification is used, the sample design is called a *multistage, stratified cluster sample*. Any form of stratification—disproportionate, proportionate, or optimum—can be used with multistage designs. Obviously, multistage sampling can be both a quite complicated and flexible procedure. To actually select clusters from any particular stage, one may employ either random numbers or systematic selection. Because its advantages offer considerable gains, systematic selection is almost always used in multistage sampling.

A good criterion to guide the designation of clusters is heterogeneity within clusters. Ideally, the elements forming clusters should be equally as heterogeneous as a simple random sample of the same number of elements.

There are major cost and time gains from the use of cluster sampling. First of all, the use of different types of listing elements permits clusters to be designated on the basis of readily available information. When one wants to select a probability sample of the adult population of the United States, it clearly is not possible to get a listing of all adults in the country in order to use a simple random sample or a stratified simple random sample design. By using the easily available list of counties in the country, one can, however, design a multistage probability sample of adults. Furthermore, any sample design whose interviews are geographically widely spread requires the expenditure of considerable time and money to support interviewer travel. Cluster sample design permits concentration of interviews within far fewer geographic areas and, thereby, greatly reduces travel time and costs. Again, such clustering allows field work to be completed in a shorter time.

## Statistical Analysis Complications

Naturally, there are disadvantages to clustering. First of all, it is a complicated sample design and its creation and execution demand a skilled practitioner
of the sampling art. Then, as we shall see later on, its various formulas are
complex and require electronic data-processing equipment. Again, its standard
errors are almost inevitably larger than those of simple random sampling.
Indeed, sometimes the variance increases are quite appreciable. Finally, its
design precludes the use of a fixed sample size. In simple random sampling
with systematic selection, one knows that a rate of 1 in 50 will yield 20 sample
cases out of a population of 1,000 listing units. Cluster sampling causes the
actual size of the sample of listing elements to vary randomly; it introduces a
*sampling error component* into the final sample size. Since clusters are randomly
selected into the sample, the final sample size depends upon actual cluster sample sizes which, in turn, vary, depending upon the specific clusters coming into
a sample.

For instance, while 1,000 housing units might be on 50 city blocks, there
would be different numbers on these blocks. Suppose two different sample
selections could give the following yields:

| Sample No. | Block numbers | Number of housing units per block |
|:---:|:---:|:---:|
| 1 | 5 | 15 |
|  | 15 | 30 |
|  | 25 | 10 |
|  | 35 | 51 |
|  | 45 | 20 |
| 2 | 3 | 28 |
|  | 13 | 19 |
|  | 23 | 5 |
|  | 33 | 80 |
|  | 43 | 24 |

If sample 1 is selected, 126 housing units are in the sample; if sample 2 is
selected, 156 housing units are in the sample. Again, if still another block
sample is selected, the number of sample housing units will vary with the specific
sample blocks.

The combined effects of this sampling variation in the actual sample size
and the greater variances and cluster homogeneity of cluster sampling force a
drastic revision in the way analytical statistical procedures can be applied to its
sample data. Practically all statistical analysis theory assumes simple random
sampling; this assumption is no longer feasible with cluster sampling. Some
ways of modifying statistical analysis to cope with the changed conditions of
cluster sampling have been presented in a series of recent publications (4;6,
chap. 14; 10; 11; 13; 14). In general, these new procedures: (1) use more

complicated variance terms in place of simple random sampling variances, and (2) require greater differences between cluster sample means and proportions to reach statistical significance than are needed with simple random sampling designs.

Since clusters are almost always formed by the various operations of social systems, the elements within clusters tend either to be or to become more alike. People holding the same or similar views, values, and beliefs join the same voluntary associations. Members of the same army squad or work team tend to become more alike in their various social characteristics because they do things under the same conditions and have considerable social interaction. These increases in homogeneity within clusters enlarge the variances of cluster sampling.

A sample of 50 can be selected from a population of 1,000 by simple random sampling (which can also be looked upon as a form of cluster sampling where the cluster sizes are all one). Suppose the same sample of 50 is obtained by forming clusters of five and selecting 10 sample clusters. If there is a fair amount of homogeneity within clusters, one obtains a less precise picture of the population from the cluster sample than from the same size simple random sample. This arises out of the homogeneous nature of the clusters. An investigator clearly obtains less information if he interviews the relatively similar five members of a single cluster than if he selects one member from five different clusters. Stated in other words, the effective sample size is greater with the simple random sample than it is with the corresponding cluster sample. However, when costs and time are considered, cluster samples customarily give more information per dollar, more quickly, and with less variance per dollar than do the frequently more expensive simple random or stratified random samples.

This increase in cluster homogeneity as a result of interaction or differential selection can be measured by the intraclass correlation which can be obtained from[13]

$$\frac{\text{var } \bar{x}_c}{\text{var } \bar{x}} = 1 + \text{rho}(\bar{b} - 1) \tag{8.32}$$

where var $\bar{x}_c$ = variance for a mean of a cluster sample of $n$ final-stage units (i.e., the respondents interviewed or objects measured).

var $\bar{x}$ = variance for a mean of a simple random sample of size $n$.

rho = estimated value of the intraclass correlation.

$\bar{b}$ = average number of final-stage units per primary sampling unit. For example, if a sample yields 500 interviews from 50 primary sampling units, $\bar{b} = \frac{500}{50} = 10$.

When rho equals 1, the efficiency of the cluster sample is at its lowest point with the cluster variance equal to the simple random sampling variance mul-

[13] More complicated formulas can be used for three or more stage cluster samples or for the determination of $\bar{b}$ where the number of interviews per primary sampling unit exhibits considerable variation from primary sampling unit to primary sampling unit. Nevertheless, the formula given for the intraclass correlation is a sufficiently close approximation to its more complicated versions for almost all purposes.

tiplied by $\bar{b}$. An intraclass correlation of 1 means that each cluster is fully homogeneous. For example, if the members of every cluster are all Republicans or Democrats and there are no mixtures of adherents of these two political parties, one would obtain as much information on party preference from one interview per cluster as from $\bar{b}$ interviews. As rho approaches zero, the efficiency of the cluster sample improves, and there are more mixtures of party preference within clusters. When rho is zero, the cluster sample is as efficient as a simple random sample of the same size. In such a case, the party mixture within the clusters is equivalent to the mixture that would be obtained by selecting simple random samples of size $\bar{b}$. Finally, in those rare instances where rho becomes negative, a cluster sample is more efficient than a simple random sample.

The effects of these various cluster sampling conditions can best be seen by an examination of the formula for a sample mean. Up to now, the sample mean has been equal to the sum of the measurements of a particular random quantity $\Sigma x_i$ for all respondents divided by the number $n$ of such respondents. Also, the sample size $n$ has been a constant. But for cluster sampling, $n$ also becomes a random variable, which changes the formula for the sample mean into the ratio of two random variables. Even though a sample mean is calculated in the same way, its statistical nature is changed for cluster samples. Furthermore, the numerator and denominator of the mean cannot be considered independent of one another within cluster samples whose components engage in interaction. This gives another condition which has to find its way into cluster sampling formulas. Finally, when the differences between two cluster sample means are investigated, the fact that these means may not be statistically independent must be properly reflected in the involved formulas.[14]

As a result of these various effects of cluster sampling, the ordinary sample mean has to be considered a sample ratio which is an estimator of the corresponding ratio in the population. Consequently, the previous formulas for sample means and proportions now become one formula, called the *sample ratio estimator*, which is

$$r = \frac{\Sigma x_i}{n} \qquad (8.33)$$

In this equation, $\Sigma x_i$ equals the sum of the measurements upon the various final-stage sample elements. These measurements can be either numerical values or the 1 and 0 elements that form proportions. The number of final-stage listing elements selected into the sample is $n$. The formula for a total becomes

$$Nr = \frac{N\Sigma x_i}{n} \qquad (8.34)$$

So far, obviously, all that has been done is to give new names and symbols to the previous formulas for means, proportions, and totals. Clearly, the ratio

---

[14] The Kish-Hess article (11) gives formulas for the variance of the difference between two cluster sample means or percentages.

estimator of a cluster sample estimates the corresponding ratio, $\sum_{i=1}^{N} x_i/N$, of the population. A ratio estimator can be formed from any two sample values and need not involve the number of sample elements as a denominator. For example, a ratio estimator can be formed by dividing the total of respondents' annual earnings by the total number of years of education received by those interviewed. This latter type of ratio estimator can be developed for any of the previously discussed sample designs in addition to cluster sample means, proportions, or totals.

## Proportionately Stratified Cluster Sampling

As an example of a proportionately stratified cluster sample, consider this sample design for a large city. The city's area has been divided into three status groups, high, middle, and low, based upon median rents within census tracts. These three status groups constitute three strata. Within each of the three strata, all census tracts are listed in order of declining median rent, and two tracts are systematically selected from each stratum. Hence, the six census tracts (two to a stratum) become the primary sampling units of the sample design. Within each census tract, a sample of blocks has been drawn and within each block a sample of housing units has been selected. Finally, within each sample housing unit, the head of the resident family has been interviewed. The sample design yields respondents at the overall sampling fraction of $\frac{1}{2,000}$; hence the sample is proportionately stratified. Family income and the religious preference of each family head have been ascertained among a number of other survey measurements. The summation of the number of Protestant family heads and total family incomes for each sample primary sampling unit is as follows.

| *Sample primary sampling unit* | *Number of Protestant family heads* | *Family income* | *Number of interviews* |
|---|---|---|---|
| *High-income stratum* | | | |
| Tract 101 | 33 | $315,000 | 40 |
| Tract 106 | 43 | 295,000 | 45 |
| *Middle-income stratum* | | | |
| Tract 209 | 19 | 150,210 | 35 |
| Tract 225 | 26 | 142,987 | 41 |
| *Low-income stratum* | | | |
| Tract 353 | 10 | 75,800 | 37 |
| Tract 375 | 18 | 62,300 | 40 |
| *Total* | 149 | $1,041,297 | 238 |

The estimated proportion of Protestant family heads within the city is $r = \dfrac{149}{238} = 0.63$. The estimated mean income per family for the city is $r = \dfrac{\$1,041,297}{238} = \$4,375.20$.

For such a proportionately stratified cluster sample, the formula for a ratio estimator is

$$r = \frac{\displaystyle\sum_{h=1}^{L}\sum_{a=1}^{m_h}\sum_{i=1}^{n_{ha}} x_{hai}}{\displaystyle\sum_{h=1}^{L}\sum_{a=1}^{m_h} n_{ha}} \tag{8.35}$$

where $x_{hai}$ = the measurement of the $i$th final-stage sample element within the $a$th sample primary sampling unit within the $h$th sample stratum

$n_{ha}$ = the number of final-stage sampling elements from the $a$th sample primary sampling unit within the $h$th sample stratum

$\displaystyle\sum_{i=1}^{n_{ha}}$ = summation over all the sample measurements within the $a$th sample primary sampling unit

$\displaystyle\sum_{a=1}^{m_h}$ = summation over all the $m_h$ sample primary sampling units within the $h$th sample stratum

$\displaystyle\sum_{h=1}^{L}$ = summation over all the $L$ strata

The variance of such a ratio estimator is

$$\text{var }(r) = \frac{1-f}{\left(\displaystyle\sum_{h=1}^{L}\sum_{a=1}^{m_h} n_{ha}\right)^2}\left[\sum_{h=1}^{L}\frac{m_h}{m_h-1}\sum_{a=1}^{m_h}\left(x_{ha}-\frac{x_h}{m_h}\right)^2\right.$$

$$+\ r^2 \sum_{h=1}^{L}\frac{m_h}{m_h-1}\sum_{a=1}^{m_h}\left(n_{ha}-\frac{n_h}{m_h}\right)^2$$

$$\left.-\ 2r \sum_{h=1}^{L}\frac{m_h}{m_h-1}\sum_{a=1}^{m_h}\left(x_{ha}-\frac{x_h}{m_h}\right)\left(n_{ha}-\frac{n_h}{m_h}\right)\right] \tag{8.36}$$

and $$\text{SE }(r) = \sqrt{\text{var }(r)} \tag{8.37}$$

where $x_{ha} = \displaystyle\sum_{i=1}^{n_{ha}} x_{hai}$ or the sum of the measurements within the $a$th sample primary sampling unit within the $h$th sample stratum

$m_h$ = the number of sample primary sampling units within the $h$th sample stratum

$$x_h = \sum_{a=1}^{m_h} \sum_{i=1}^{n_{ha}} x_{hai} \text{ or the sum of the measurements throughout all the } m_h$$

sample primary sampling units within the $h$th sample stratum

$$n_h = \sum_{a=1}^{m_h} n_{ha} \text{ or the number of final-stage sampling elements from all the}$$

$m_h$ sample primary sampling units within the $h$th sample stratum

Applying Eqs. (8.35) and (8.36) to the data of the above example gives the following for the variance of the estimated proportion of Protestant family heads in the city:

$$\text{var } (r) = \text{var } (0.63) = \left(1 - \frac{1}{2,000}\right) \frac{1}{(238)^2} [213 + (0.63)^2(70)$$
$$- 2(0.63)(116)] = 0.001670 \quad (8.38)$$

where

$$213 = 2\left[\left(33 - \frac{33 + 43}{2}\right)^2 + \left(43 - \frac{33 + 43}{2}\right)^2 + \cdots\right.$$
$$\left. + \left(10 - \frac{10 + 18}{2}\right)^2 + \left(18 - \frac{10 + 18}{2}\right)^2\right] \quad (8.39)$$

$$70 = 2\left[\left(40 - \frac{40 + 45}{2}\right)^2 + \left(45 - \frac{40 + 45}{2}\right)^2 + \cdots\right.$$
$$\left. + \left(37 - \frac{37 + 40}{2}\right)^2 + \left(40 - \frac{37 + 40}{2}\right)^2\right] \quad (8.40)$$

$$116 = 2\left[\left(33 - \frac{33 + 43}{2}\right)\left(40 - \frac{40 + 45}{2}\right) + \cdots\right.$$
$$\left. + \left(18 - \frac{10 + 18}{2}\right)\left(40 - \frac{37 + 40}{2}\right)\right] \quad (8.41)$$

As shown by Eq. (8.34), the estimated total family income for the entire city is $501,610(\$4,375.20) = \$2,194,644,072$, where $501,610$ is the total number of families in the city.[15] The variance of this totality estimate is $N^2[\text{var}(\$4,375.20)] = (501,610)^2(6,453.45)$. This gives a standard error of $\$40,296,037$ for the estimated total family income of the entire city.

Actually, a sample ratio estimator is a slightly biased estimator of its population equivalent. However, with a moderate number of sample primary sampling units, say about 20, this bias is quite small and can readily be ignored. Also, with enough final-stage sample cases, say at least 100, the law of large

[15] Since the overall sampling fraction is 1 in 2,000, it is possible to estimate total family income for the entire city by multiplying $\$1,041,297$ by 2,000 to obtain $\$2,082,594,000$. This new totality estimation has a variance equal to the first term in the brackets of Eq. (8.36) multiplied by $(1 - f)/f^2$ which gives a standard error of $\$50,363,130$. Its advantages are that it readily gives totality estimators without the need to know a population value such as $N$ (which is required to estimate totals with the ratio estimator) and that it is unbiased. Its disadvantage is that it has an appreciably larger variance than the ratio estimator.

numbers operates to make the sample ratio estimators vary about their population equivalents in a normal or nearly normal probability distribution.

## *Disproportionate Cluster Sampling

The best procedure to employ for disproportionate cluster sampling is to weight to proportionality.  To accomplish this:

**1** Form ratios between the largest sampling fraction for a stratum and all the other strata sampling fractions.  For example, if there are three different strata sampling fractions of $\frac{1}{20}$, $\frac{1}{40}$, and $\frac{1}{80}$, form these ratios—$\frac{1}{20}:\frac{1}{80} = 4$ and $\frac{1}{20}:\frac{1}{40} = 2$.

**2** Then use these ratios as weights to be multiplied times their strata measurements.  Here, the measurements from the stratum with the sampling fraction of $\frac{1}{80}$ would be weighted by 4, and the measurements from the stratum with the sampling fraction of $\frac{1}{40}$ would be weighted by 2.  The other stratum used as the reference factor receives a weight of 1.

**3** Applying these weights to the various strata results in weighting them to the same overall sampling fraction of $\frac{1}{20}$.

This weighting procedure establishes frequency factors to be applied to the various strata.  It also makes it appear, as far as calculations are concerned, that all strata have the same sampling fraction, $\frac{1}{20}$.  When these weights are applied as frequency factors to actual measurements on the various sampling elements, a respondent with an income of $10,000 might appear in the calculations as four respondents with incomes of $10,000 each.  There is no change in those parts of the various estimation and variance formulas that require division by the actual number of sample interviews or primary sampling units.

Since disproportionate stratification customarily takes place within primary sampling units, the weights should be directly applied to the actual measurements, i.e., the various $x_{hai}$ and $n_{ha}$ measures are directly multiplied by their strata weights.  The ratio estimator for a disproportionately stratified cluster sample becomes

$$r_w = \frac{\sum_{h=1}^{L} \sum_{a=1}^{m_h} \sum_{h_s=1}^{L_s} w_{hs} \sum_{i=1}^{n_{has}} x_{hasi}}{\sum_{h=1}^{L} \sum_{a=1}^{m_h} \sum_{h_s=1}^{L_s} w_{hs} n_{has}} \qquad (8.42)$$

where $x_{hasi}$ = the measurement upon the $i$th final-stage sampling element from the $s$th internal stratum of the $a$th sample primary sampling unit

$n_{has}$ = the number of final-stage sampling elements from the $s$th internal stratum of the $a$th sample primary sampling unit

$w_{hs}$ = the weight for the $s$th internal stratum of the $a$th sample primary sampling unit as described above

the subscript $w$ stands for weighting

The formula for the variance of the ratio estimator of a disproportionately stratified cluster sample becomes[16]

$$
\text{var}(r_w) = \frac{1}{\left(\sum\limits_{h=1}^{L} \sum\limits_{a=1}^{m_h} \sum\limits_{h_s=1}^{L_s} w_{hs} n_{has}\right)^2} \left[ \sum\limits_{h=1}^{L} \frac{m_h}{m_h - 1} \sum\limits_{a=1}^{m_h} \left( \sum\limits_{h_s=1}^{L_s} w_{hs} x_{has} - \frac{x_h}{m_h} \right)^2 \right.
$$

$$
+ (r_w)^2 \sum\limits_{h=1}^{L} \frac{m_h}{m_h - 1} \sum\limits_{a=1}^{m_h} \left( \sum\limits_{h_s=1}^{L_s} w_{hs} n_{has} - \frac{n_h}{m_h} \right)^2
$$

$$
\left. - 2r_w \sum\limits_{h=1}^{L} \frac{m_h}{m_h - 1} \sum\limits_{a=1}^{m_h} \left( \sum\limits_{h_s=1}^{L_s} w_{hs} x_{has} - \frac{x_h}{m_h} \right)\left( \sum\limits_{h_s=1}^{L_s} w_{hs} n_{has} - \frac{n_h}{m_h} \right) \right] \quad (8.43)
$$

where $\sum\limits_{h_s}^{L_s}$ indicates summation across the $L_s$ internal strata *within* sample primary sampling units

$n_h = \sum\limits_{a=1}^{m_h} \sum\limits_{h_s=1}^{L_s} w_{hs} n_{has}$ or the weighted number of final-stage sampling elements throughout all the $m_h$ sample primary sampling units of the $h$th sample stratum

$x_{has} = \sum\limits_{i=1}^{n_{has}} x_{hasi}$ or the sum of the measurements throughout the $s$th internal stratum of the $a$th sample primary sampling unit

$x_h = \sum\limits_{a=1}^{m_h} \sum\limits_{h_s=1}^{L_s} w_{hs} x_{has}$ or the sum of the weighted sample primary sampling unit measurements throughout all the $m_h$ sample primary sampling units of the $h$th sample stratum

Note that the $1 - f$ factor is absent from Eq. (8.43). The nature of the mathematics of disproportionate sampling makes it inadvisable to use the sampling fraction to which the various strata data are being weighted. Obviously, for most variance calculations the $1 - f$ factor is negligible. For the rare occasions when it cannot be ignored, an averaging procedure is given in Kish's *Survey Sampling* (6, pp. 432–433).

As an example, consider a situation in which each sample psu is internally stratified by religion. Three religious strata, Protestants, Catholics, and Jews, are established within every sample psu. Then a sampling fraction of $\frac{1}{80}$ is applied to Protestants, of $\frac{1}{40}$ to Catholics, and of $\frac{1}{20}$ to Jews. In applying Eqs. (8.42) and (8.43), weights of 4 are applied to all measurements on Protestant respondents, weights of 2 are applied to all measurements on Catholic respondents, and weights of 1 to all measurements on Jewish respondents. This process

[16] Note that in either Eq. (8.36) or (8.43) the term involving $n_{ha}$ or $n_{has}$ would be zero if these quantities were constant for all primary sampling units. Similarly, the term involving the cross products of $x_{ha}$ and $n_{ha}$ or $x_{has}$ and $n_{has}$ would be zero if the quantities forming the numerator and denominator of the ratio estimator were statistically independent.

results in a weighted overall sampling fraction of $\frac{1}{20}$ appearing at the primary sampling unit level.

## *Cluster Sample Subclasses

A note on subclasses is a good way to conclude this difficult section. If a subclass, such as a geographic group, is found only in a portion of the sample psu's, the $m_h$ factors in the preceding formulas are replaced by the number of psu's that contain the subclass. Otherwise the formulas hold as they are. If a subclass, such as blue-collar workers, is spread throughout all of the sample psu's, the adjustment is the standard one of confining the calculations to members of that subclass. Hence, the $x$ terms become $x_g$ terms and the $n$ terms become $n_g$ terms, both of which are inserted in the various cluster sampling formulas.

### 8.7 SAMPLING WITH PROBABILITY PROPORTIONAL TO A MEASURE OF SIZE

Out of the circumstances of cluster sampling arises the ability to assign measures of size to clusters which directly reflect the number of next-stage elements contained within the clusters. Since this design device is accomplished with systematic selection, its main outlines have already been introduced. Consider a sampling situation in which one desires to select a sample of housing units from blocks where these blocks obviously contain varying numbers of housing units. One controls sample size variations from these blocks by giving the blocks with larger numbers of housing units greater chances of selection than are given blocks with relatively few housing units. At the same time, all sample housing units are selected with the same overall sampling fraction. The following example illustrates how this is done.

| Block number | Number of housing units on block | Cumulative total | Selection numbers |
|:---:|:---:|:---:|:---:|
| 1 | 55 | 55 | |
| 2 | 83 | 138 | 72 |
| 3 | 100 | 238 | 172 |
| 4 | 21 | 259 | |
| 5 | 225 | 484 | 272, 372, 472 |

If the selection interval is 100 and its random start is 72, the numbers selected into the sample are 72, 172, 272, 372, and 472. Here, each block is assigned a measure of size equal to the number of housing units it contains. Hence, block 1 has a probability of 0.55 of being selected into the sample; block 2 has 0.83; block 3 is selected with certainty; block 4 has 0.21; and block 5 is selected with certainty. Nevertheless, only blocks 2, 3, and 5 are actually selected into the sample. With an interval of 100, clearly blocks 1 and 2 cannot both be selected unless the random start is from 1 to 38. Similarly, block 4 will be selected only if the random start is from 39 to 59. Since block 5 contains 225 housing units, it forms two full selection strata and 0.25 of a third stratum. Therefore, block 5 will always be selected by an interval of 100; it will enclose two selection numbers and have a probability of 0.25 of enclosing a third selection number.

The number of selection numbers enclosed by a sample block determines the number of housing units that block furnishes to the sample. However, the blocks with the larger number of enclosed selection numbers also have the larger number of housing units. This results in the housing units within such larger blocks having a smaller within-block chance of selection than do housing units within the smaller blocks. This combination of a larger chance of selection for the blocks with the larger number of housing units, together with a smaller within-block selection rate for their housing units, produces a housing unit sample with the same overall selection rate. For instance, the within-block selection rate for the one sample housing unit obtained from block 2 is $\frac{1}{83}$, the within rate for the one sample housing unit of block 3 is $\frac{1}{100}$, and the within rate for the three sample housing units furnished by block 5 is $\frac{3}{225}$. Multiplying the block selection rate by the within-block selection rate for these three sample blocks gives:

Block 2: $\frac{1}{100} = \frac{83}{100} \times \frac{1}{83}$
Block 3: $\frac{1}{100} = \frac{100}{100} \times \frac{1}{100}$
Block 5: $\frac{3}{100} = \frac{225}{100} \times \frac{3}{225}$

Why the $\frac{3}{100}$ rate for the housing units of block 5? Since block 5 contains two full selection strata and one-fourth of a third stratum, each full stratum must furnish one housing unit to the sample, and depending on the random start, the third stratum can be called upon to furnish an additional sample housing unit. Hence, the equation for block 5 really consists of two equations like that for block 3 plus $\frac{1}{100} = \frac{25}{100} \times \frac{1}{25}$. When these three strata equations are added together, there results the above combined equation for block 5.

The within-block selections for blocks 2 and 3 can be done by random numbers. The within-block selections for block 5 are obtained by employing a systematic selection interval of 3 in 225 proceeding from a random start.[17]

---

[17] Strictly speaking, the housing units of block 5 should be divided into two groups of 100 each and one group of 25. Then one sample housing unit should be selected from each of the two 100 housing unit groups and, if the random start results in a third selection number being enclosed by block 5, one sample housing unit from the group of 25. In practice this can also be accomplished without any alteration of probabilities by selecting two, or three (depending on the random start), housing units out of the 225 in block 5.

## 8.8 THE SAMPLING EQUATION

A good way of picturing a multistage cluster sample design is to write down its stage-by-stage probabilities. By way of an example, take this sampling equation.

$$\frac{1}{1,100} = \frac{(80)(1,000)}{100,000} \times \frac{(100,000)(20)}{(1,100)(80)(1,000)(4)} \times \frac{4}{20} \quad (8.44)$$

$$\underset{\text{tracts}}{\phantom{x}} \qquad \underset{\text{blocks within tracts}}{\phantom{x}} \qquad \underset{\substack{\text{housing units} \\ \text{within blocks}}}{\phantom{x}}$$

This shows the stages in selecting (1) four housing units from (2) a block with 20 housing units in (3) a tract with 1,000 housing units in (4) a city that has 100,000 housing units. It also represents the sample design for the selection of a housing unit sample at an overall rate of 1 in 1,100.

Stage 1 of the design calls for the selection of 80 census tracts as sample primary sampling units from among all the census tracts of the area. The entire group of tracts can be listed in any predetermined manner such as a socioeconomic order of low, medium, and high status and within the three status groups by geographic location. This particular tract is sampled with a probability proportionate to its number of housing units: $\frac{(80)(1,000)}{100,000} = \frac{4}{5}$. The interval for the selection of any tract is $\frac{100,000}{80} = 1,250$. Stage 3 calls for the selection of 4 out of 20 of the housing units on this particular block.

Stage 2 is the catchall stage, for its probability must be such as to ensure an overall sampling fraction of $\frac{1}{1,100}$ after the rates for the first and third stages have been determined. Indeed, almost every sampling equation will have such a catchall intermediate sampling stage. In the probability term for the second stage are found all the terms of stages 1 and 3 plus the overall sampling fraction. The specific block selection probability is $\frac{(100,000)(20)}{(1,100)(80)(1,000)(4)} = \frac{1}{176}$. Blocks are to be assigned measures of size equal to their number of housing units so that selection is with probability proportionate to a measure of size.

When the probabilities of the three stages are multiplied together, one obtains the probability of selecting a sample housing unit from within a sample block which has been selected from within a sample census tract; the overall probability for each sample housing unit is $\frac{1}{1,100}$.

The within-housing-unit sampling stage is not included in the above sampling equation. If there is only one eligible respondent per sample housing unit, the within-housing-unit rate is 1. If within each housing unit one adult is selected from among all the adults, the various interview measurements should be weighted by the number of adults within each sample housing unit. For instance, the measurements resulting from interviewing the sole adult within a sample housing unit receive a weight of 1; the results from interviewing one adult selected out of two adults within a sample housing unit must receive a weight of 2 since the interview stands for two adults, and so on for one adult selected from three or more adults within a sample housing unit.[18]

The sampling equation strongly illustrates the basic concept of probability sampling which is to *fix the rates* at which elements are sampled, *never the numbers to be sampled*. Measures of size are used solely to establish sampling rates. Insofar as the measures are inaccurate, sample yields will vary, but such sample yields will all be obtained at a known, fixed probability. Nonprobability samples commit a major error by wrongly reversing this principle to fix yields at the cost of varying probabilities. Then, the resultant jumble of probabilities is ignored in data analysis, which creates bias and prevents the application of statistical inference.

## *8.9  A SIMPLIFIED MODEL FOR THE SAMPLING ERRORS OF CLUSTER SAMPLES

When stratified cluster sampling is employed, it is customary to select only one primary sampling unit per stratum. Since variance components cannot be computed on the basis of a single psu, the sample psu's are paired (or, better still, adjacent strata are collapsed) to obtain the minimum two psu's per stratum required for the computation of variances. This procedure is facilitated when the stratification of the psu's places similar strata adjacent to each other so that the paired sample units will be as alike as possible. In this way, the largest possible amount of the variance will be found between collapsed strata and, hence, eliminated from the sampling error.

This paired, or collapsed, strata model permits simplification of (8.36) into the following for the variance of a ratio estimator with two sample primary sampling units per stratum:[19]

$$\text{var }(r) = \frac{(1-f)}{\left(\sum\limits_{h=1}^{L} n_h\right)^2} \left[ \sum\limits_{h=1}^{L} (x_{h1} - x_{h2})^2 + r^2 \sum\limits_{h=1}^{L} (n_{h1} - n_{h2})^2 \right.$$

$$\left. - 2r \sum\limits_{h=1}^{L} (x_{h1} - x_{h2})(n_{h1} - n_{h2}) \right] \quad (8.45)$$

---

[18] A discussion of a technique for the selection of one respondent from among several within a sample housing unit can be found in Kish (6, pp. 396–401; or 7).

[19] This simplification comes from $m_h = 2$ and $x_h/m_h = (x_{h1} + x_{h2})/2$. With these terms substituted into $\sum\limits_{a=1}^{m_h} \left(x_{ha} - \frac{x_h}{m_h}\right)^2$, one gets $\left(x_{h1} - \frac{x_{h1}+x_{h2}}{2}\right)^2 + \left(x_{h2} - \frac{x_{h1}+x_{h2}}{2}\right)^2$

$= \left(\frac{x_{h1}-x_{h2}}{2}\right)^2 + \left(\frac{x_{h2}-x_{h1}}{2}\right)^2 = \frac{2(x_{h1}^2 - 2x_{h1}x_{h2} + x_{h2}^2)}{4} = \frac{(x_{h1}-x_{h2})^2}{2}.$

If the sample primary sampling units are selected by systematic selection, the following can be used for the variance of a ratio estimator:

$$\text{var } (r) = \frac{(1 - f)L}{2(L - 1)\left(\sum\limits_{h=1}^{L} n_h\right)^2} \left[ \sum_{h=1}^{L-1} (x_h - x_{h+1})^2 + r^2 \sum_{h=1}^{L-1} (n_h - n_{h+1})^2 \right.$$

$$\left. - 2r \sum_{h=1}^{L-1} (x_h - x_{h+1})(n_h - n_{h+1}) \right] \quad (8.46)$$

where $L$ = the number of strata from which the primary sampling units have been systematically selected

$x_h$ = the sum of the measurements for that sample primary sampling unit selected from the $h$th stratum

$x_{h+1}$ = the sum of the measurements for that sample primary sampling unit selected from the $h + 1$ stratum

$n_h$ = the number of final-stage sampling elements from the sample primary sampling unit selected from the $h$th stratum

$n_{h+1}$ = the number of final-stage sampling elements from the sample primary sampling unit selected from the $h + 1$ stratum

As an illustration of Eq. (8.46), let us redo the cluster sampling example given in the subsection entitled "Proportionately Stratified Cluster Sampling" in Sec. 8.6. Note that the term $\sum\limits_{h=1}^{L-1} (x_h - x_{h+1})^2$ refers to successive differences, i.e., $(x_1 - x_2)^2 + (x_2 - x_3)^2 + \cdots + (x_h - x_{h+1})^2 + (x_{h+1} - x_{h+2})^2 + \cdots$. The same thing applies to $\sum\limits_{h=1}^{L-1} (n_h - n_{h+1})^2$ and $\sum\limits_{h=1}^{L-1} (x_h - x_{h+1})(n_h - n_{h+1})$. In this modified example, a systematic selection design would be able to reflect six strata with one sample tract per stratum instead of three strata with two sample tracts per stratum. Or one can consider the original example to have been formed by collapsing six strata into three.

While the ratio estimator of mean income per family does not change, the systematic selection calculations for its variance become:

$$\sum_{h=1}^{L-1} (x_h - x_{h+1})^2 = (\$315,000 - \$295,000)^2$$

$$+ (\$295,000 - \$150,210)^2$$
$$+ \cdots + (\$75,800 - \$62,300)^2$$
$$= \$26,112,658,798 \quad (8.47)$$

$$\sum_{h=1}^{L-1} (n_h - n_{h+1})^2 = (40 - 45)^2 + (45 - 35)^2 + (35 - 41)^2$$

$$+ (41 - 37)^2 + (37 - 40)^2 = 186 \quad (8.48)$$

$$\sum_{h=1}^{L-1} (x_h - x_{h+1})(n_h - n_{h+1}) = (\$315{,}000 - \$295{,}000)(40 - 45) + \cdots$$

$$+ (\$75{,}800 - \$62{,}300)(37 - 40)$$
$$= \$1{,}900{,}486 \qquad (8.49)$$

$$\text{and the SE of } \$4{,}375.20 = \left\{ \left[ \frac{\left(1 - \dfrac{1}{2{,}000}\right) 6}{2(6-1)(238)^2} \right] [13{,}043{,}127{,}854] \right\}^{\frac{1}{2}} \qquad (8.50)$$

$$= \$371.60$$

## 8.10  SPECIFIC SAMPLE DESIGN TECHNIQUES[20]

There are several basic design techniques that can be employed in the selection of an area sample. These can be generalized into a combination of sampling from a list coupled with an area sample that picks up items not included in the list. An advanced version of this combination is the use of a city directory address sample supplemented by a block sample to pick up dwelling units either missed by the city directory or constructed since the directory was compiled. For territory not covered by a city directory, a complete area sample must be devised. Such an area sample might consist of an enumeration district and housing unit cluster design for open country, or a census tract and blocks-within-census-tracts type of design. In this section, various aspects of these types of design techniques will be discussed.

### Population Definition and Boundaries

The first step in any sampling process is a clear definition of the population to be sampled. For area sampling this definition must also include the geographic boundaries enclosing the population. It is wise to use boundaries employed or established by the most recent national census, for this permits the use of the maps, population, and housing unit counts obtained by the U.S. Bureau of the Census. Of course, this census information should be brought up-to-date through data obtained from local community sources and, if necessary, field trips to small areas. For discussion purposes, let it be assumed that the population to be sampled consists of all adults living in the housing units of that part of a standard metropolitan statistical area which has been subdivided into census tracts.

In practice, one large city directory will cover the major city of a metropolitan area and, often, several smaller directories will cover some of the suburban communities. The full extent of city directory coverage is established by comparing outlying addresses and cross streets and determining the locations

---

[20] For an excellent and detailed treatment of the design techniques presented in this section refer to Kish (6, chap. 9).

where such outlying directory address listings cease.   Whatever final boundaries are established should be coincident with some Census Bureau boundary.

With city directory boundaries established, the remaining territory to be sampled can be covered by an enumeration district selection procedure. Typically, the city directory stratum includes much of the built-up area.

## Overall Sampling Fraction

To establish an overall sampling fraction, we shall assume illustratively that 92 percent of the area's housing units (hu's) are occupied, that 98 percent of the selected housing units will be found by interviewers, and that 86 percent of the occupied sample housing units found by interviewers will yield interviews.[21] If the sample design is to provide 700 interviews and the population to be sampled contains 993,300 housing units, the overall sampling fraction will be

$$\frac{700}{\dfrac{(0.92)(0.98)(0.86)}{993,300}} = \frac{1}{1,100} \tag{8.51}$$

## City Directory Sample

With the overall sampling fraction determined, it is possible to establish a sampling rate for the selection of pages and lines from the street address section of the various city directories.   Table 8.1 illustrates how this can be done. Columns 1 and 2 of Table 8.1 give a list of hypothetical city directory places together with the estimated number of housing units in each place;[22] column 3 gives the number of sample housing units expected from each place at the overall sampling fraction of 1 in 1,100; column 4 gives the number of three-line city directory clusters expected from each place.   A three-line directory cluster consists of three contiguous directory lines formed by selecting one line and taking the following two.   The degree of clustering can vary to suit various design criteria such as desired travel costs or expected number of eligible respondents per housing unit.

Experience has indicated that, on the average, 80 percent of the city directory lines are housing units, with the remainder being commercial addresses, street names, telephone numbers, and so forth.   Therefore, an enlargement factor of 0.8 is employed to increase the size of the housing unit sample.[23]   Con-

---

[21] Bear in mind that these assumed occupancy, coverage, and response figures will vary from place to place and should be estimated anew for new survey operations.

[22] Sometimes one city directory covers several communities.   If each such community is listed separately in the directory, it can be entered separately in Table 8.1.   If the street address section does not separate the addresses of the several communities, they should be listed in Table 8.1 as if they composed one community.

[23] This enlargement factor should be varied to fit experience with local city directories.

TABLE 8.1    The Determination of Sampling Rates for City Directory Pages and Lines

| (1) | (2) | (3) | (4) | (5) | (6) | (7) |
|---|---|---|---|---|---|---|
| *Places in city directory* | *Estimated no. hu's in place* | *Estimated no. sample hu's from place* $\dfrac{col.\ (2)}{1,100}$ | *Estimated no. city directory clusters from place* $\dfrac{col.\ (3)}{3\times 0.8}$ | *No. pages in city directory street address section for place* | *Page interval* $\dfrac{col.\ (5)}{col.\ (4)}$ | *Line interval* $\dfrac{3\times 1,100}{col.\ (6)}$ |
| Central City | 581,000 | 528 | 220 | 2,610 | 11.86 | 278.25 |
| Dormitory Downs | 75,000 | 68 | 28 | 375 | 13.39 | 246.45 |
| Lower Suburbia | 51,700 | 47 | 20 | 208 | 10.40 | 317.31 |
| Cheapside, Jones, and Johnstown | 40,500 | 37 | 15 | 200 | 13.33 | 247.56 |
| Aviv Acres | 31,700 | 29 | 12 | 161 | 13.42 | 245.90 |
| Credit Cove | 24,800 | 23 | 10 | 123 | 12.30 | 268.29 |
| Noveau Ridge | 15,600 | 14 | 6 | 82 | 13.67 | 241.40 |
| Hidebound Hills | 13,400 | 12 | 5 | 67 | 13.40 | 246.27 |
| Mishmash Lanes | 7,500 | 7 | 3 | 42 | 14.00 | 235.71 |
| Xepzzphiary Woods | 3,300 | 3 | 1 | 17 | 17.00 | 194.12 |

sequently, column-4 entries are formed by dividing the number of sample housing units expected from a place by 3 and by 0.8 to get the number of clusters of three city directory lines needed for the housing unit sample.

Column-5 entries are the number of pages in the street address section of the various city directories. Dividing column-5 entries by their corresponding column-4 entries gives the intervals for selecting sample pages from the various street address directory sections which are shown in column 6. The intervals of column 7 are the selection rates for the first line of each sample cluster within a sample page. They are calculated by dividing the reciprocal of the overall sampling fraction, 1 in 1,100, by the page interval and multiplying by the clustering factor. With the first line in each sample cluster having a probability of selection of 1 chance in 3,300, the three lines composing a cluster will have a probability of 1 in 1,100 of being selected. This probability of 1 in 1,100 arises out of the fact that each line in a cluster can be selected in three different ways—by being selected as the first line of a sample cluster at a rate of 1 in 3,300 or by being one line or two lines below the first line of a sample cluster with a 1 in 3,300 chance of selection. Hence, the probabilities for the three ways of coming into a sample cluster add to a total of 1 in 1,100. After selecting sample clusters, one need draw only one random number from among numbers 1, 2, or 3 to obtain a subsample of one-third of the sample lines at an overall rate of 1 in

3,300.[24]   The use of clusters of lines, such as three in this example, facilitates subsampling from an original sample.   It also permits the directory sample to be selected in clusters so that there is a more adequate number of housing units awaiting an interviewer, and travel is minimized.

Sample clusters are selected by an address scale which is constructed by placing a sheet of paper alongside a column of directory lines and placing a mark on the paper corresponding to each printed line.   The unit of count is the space covered by one line.   Larger print and blank spaces within columns of addresses must be counted and may yield several counting units.   The counting of units of line print space proceeds cumulatively from column to column and sample page to sample page.   Consequently, the various selection numbers obtained by adding the line-sampling interval to a random start determine the specific line numbers that form the first lines of clusters.

The city directory address scale identifies these selected line numbers on the sample pages.   For example, suppose one is selecting a sample from pages in the street directory section which contain two columns of house addresses so that the first sample page has units of count numbers 1 to 50 in its first address column and 51 to 100 in its second column, and the second sample page has units of count numbers 101 to 150 in its first column and 151 to 200 in its second column.   If the random start is 10 and the selection interval 100, sample line number 10 would be the tenth unit of count in the first column on the first sample page as measured by the scale.   It is also the first line of the first sample cluster.   The next two units of count, the eleventh and twelfth, form the remaining two lines of a three-line cluster.   All printed matter and blank space between the mark for the tenth unit of count on the scale and the mark for the thirteenth unit of count compose a city directory cluster selection.   Next the 110th, 111th, and 112th units of count are identified on the second sample page by the scale, the second cluster selection is determined, and its listings recorded.   This process is continued until all the units of count on all the sample pages are counted and sample clusters determined and recorded.[25]

It may happen that the space between the marks for the first and third units of count include parts of lines of print.   These parts of lines can be allocated by including within a cluster any line of print which has any part below the mark for the beginning of the cluster and by excluding any line of print which is not completely above the mark for the end of the cluster.

Since a city directory sample results in the selection of whatever is contained in the street directory section, one obtains a sample of addresses of occupied

---

[24] If only one line per cluster is subsampled for a survey, the variances of the various ratio estimators will be quite near a simple random sample level.   As more than one line per cluster is subsampled, the variances increase because of increased clustering.

[25] If all the units of count of a cluster are not on the same sample page, just carry over the counting to the next sample page.   In other words, it is possible to have a three-line cluster consisting of the last one or two lines of address print on one sample page and the first one or two lines of address print on the next sample page.

housing units and vacant housing units as well as industrial and commercial addresses. All such addresses must be checked to determine which are housing units. As a result of familiarity with a given metropolitan area, one may know that certain addresses are definitely industrial or commercial and can be eliminated from the sample.

It is possible for city directory addresses to have differing probabilities of selection. This can occur whenever a given address occupies several lines in a directory. Suppose 703 Jefferson Street appears in a city directory like this:

> 703 Jefferson St., Harding Apartments
> Apt. 1
> Apt. 2
> Apt. 3
> Apt. 4

This address, 703 Jefferson, has several times the chance of selection as an address that occupies only one line of print. To adjust for such situations, apply the following procedure:

**1** Ascertain how many lines have been selected from the listings for a multiline address. For instance, if only Apartment 1, 703 Jefferson Street, has been selected into the sample, just one housing unit out of the four listed for that address should come into the sample.

**2** Next, visit 703 Jefferson and list all the housing units actually at that address. Assume that six apartments are found and listed.

**3** Sample the same proportion of the housing units found at a multiline address as the proportion of its lines that have been selected into the sample. Again, one housing unit out of the four listed in the city directory for 703 Jefferson has been selected. Hence, type the address on a field form, instruct the interviewer to list all housing units at this sample address and to interview at the first listed housing unit, the fifth listed housing unit, the ninth listed housing unit, etc. This results in a one-fourth sample of housing units at 703 Jefferson and corrects for the four-times chance the address has of being selected in comparison with one-line addresses. One starts with the first listed housing unit because the first apartment printed in the directory for that address has been sampled. This one-fourth sample yields two housing units instead of the expected one because the directory listing was incomplete. Nevertheless, the six housing units actually at this address all have a four-times chance of selection from the city directory. The two housing units obtained by the one-fourth subselection come into the sample at the desired probability of 1 in 1,100.

It is recommended that hotels, motels, and trailer courts be excluded from the city directory sample and placed in the block supplement sample. The handling of these facilities is discussed in the next section.

## Block Supplement Sample

Of course, all housing units within the area assigned to the city directory
will not appear in it.  Some will have been missed by the field workers who
compiled the information published in the city directory, some will have been
built since the directory was prepared, and some may have been excluded from
the directory by a policy decision of its publishers.  To obtain a sample of
those housing units not in the city directory street address section, one must
employ a block supplement sample.  The combination of a city directory list
sample and an area block supplement sample completes the proper representation of the geographic area assigned to the city directory stratum.  For this
supplement to the city directory to work correctly, housing units must be drawn
into the sample by *either* the city directory sample or the block supplement
sample.

The sample of blocks should be selected at the overall rate of 1 in 1,100.
In this way, the blocks can be sampled singly or in clusters depending upon
travel problems and costs.  For present design purposes, let blocks be individually selected.

Within each community of the city directory stratum, every block is
assigned an identifying number.  Blocks, or areas such as parks, which have
no dwelling units, should be combined with residential blocks and the grouping
assigned one block number.  Sparsely built-up blocks can be assigned several
block unit numbers to allow for future growth or possible subdividing.

Table 8.2 illustrates a method of selecting blocks.  Table column 2 gives
the total block numbers assigned to each community, and column 3 gives the
cumulative total of column 2.  From a block interval of 1 in 1,100 and a random
start of 217 are derived the various selection numbers indicated in column 4.
Column 5 gives the number of selections falling within the cumulative range of
each community, which determines the number of block numbers sampled for
that community.  Since the block unit numbers for each municipality are
known, it is a simple matter to subtract the cumulative total of the previous
community from the selection numbers within the succeeding one and obtain
the actual sampled block numbers, which are indicated in column 6.

After this, each sampled block should be visited, block boundaries verified,
street names checked and corrected, any additional bounding or internal streets
placed on the map, the within-block range of housing numbers for all streets
obtained, and the number of housing units on the block estimated.  Next, one
copies the city directory address listings shown for the various streets bounding
or falling within the sampled blocks.  Field verification of bounding streets and
block house number ranges permits the correct transcription of all addresses
that a city directory shows for a block.  Do not transcribe directory descriptions
for hotels, motels, or trailer courts if these categories have been assigned to the
block supplement.

TABLE 8.2  Selection of Blocks for a City Directory (Supplementary Sample)

| (1) Places in city directory | (2) Assigned no. of blk units | (3) Cum. total | (4) Selection numbers | (5) No. of blk units selected | (6) Within-place sampled blk unit numbers |
|---|---|---|---|---|---|
| Central City | 5,708 | 5,708 | 217; 1,317; 2,417; 3,517; 4,617 | 5 | 217; 1,317; 2,417; 3,517; 4,617 |
| Dormitory Downs | 753 | 6,461 | 5,717 | 1 | 9 |
| Lower Suburbia | 517 | 6,978 | 6,817 | 1 | 356 |
| Cheapside, Jones, and Johnstown | 405 | 7,383 | | 0 | |
| Aviv Acres | 319 | 7,702 | | 0 | |
| Credit Cove | 248 | 7,950 | 7,917 | 1 | 215 |
| Noveau Ridge | 156 | 8,106 | | 0 | |
| Hidebound Hills | 134 | 8,240 | | 0 | |
| Mishmash Lanes | 75 | 8,315 | | 0 | |
| Xepzzphiary Woods | 41 | 8,356 | | 0 | |

The number of reported housing units on each supplementary block can be estimated from the block address listings given by the directory. Then, this reported number of housing units is subtracted from the number obtained on the field count to give the approximate number of housing units per block that appear to have been missed by the city directory. To minimize travel and provide a more adequate work load for interviewers, it would be best to select the suspected missed housing units in clusters. For illustrative purposes, clusters of three are used here. Again, clustering is accomplished by dividing the estimates of missed housing units by 3.

Table 8.3 gives a procedure for sampling block measures and determining within-block sampling intervals for Central City. Any block, or group of physical blocks, that has fewer than an expected three missed housing units is automatically assigned one measure. Two or three sample blocks can be combined and assigned one measure if the blocks are built-up and have little chance of changing, provided the directory lists nearly as many housing units on the blocks as estimated by the field check.

In Table 8.3, column 1 gives the selected block unit numbers for Central City, and column 2 gives the field numbers assigned to the blocks. Column 3 gives the estimated number of housing units on a sample block as determined by the field check, and column 4 gives the number estimated for the block from city directory listings. Column 5 gives the difference between columns 3 and 4 divided by three. Column 6 gives the number of clusters of a suspected three missed housing units assigned to a block. Column 7 indicates which ones of these clusters are subsampled; column 8 gives the within-block sampling intervals to be applied to blocks with two or more clusters in order to obtain the

TABLE 8.3    Establishing and Subsampling Block Supplement Measures
            for Central City

| (1) | (2) | (3) | (4) | (5) | (6) | (7) | (8) |
|---|---|---|---|---|---|---|---|
| *Within-place block unit no.* | *Field block no.* | *Estimated no. hu's on blk* | *No. hu's listed in city directory for blk* | *Col. (3) minus col. (4) ÷ 3* | *No. clusters* | *Sub-select.* | *Sample line numbers* |
| 217 | 1 | 75 | 75 | 0 | | | Take all |
| 1,317 | 2 | 90 | 89 | 0.33 $\Big\}$ 1 | 1 | | Take all |
| 2,417–2,418 | 3 | 68 | 50 | 6 | 3 | 2 | 1,3,5,7, |
| | | | | (double interval—2,417) | | | 9, . . . |
| 3,517 | 4 | 30 | 27 | 1 | 1 | | Take all |
| 4,617 | 5 | 43 | 39 | 1.33 | 1 | | Take all |

subsampled number of clusters, e.g., to get one sample cluster out of an available three sample clusters.

Because of a large number of possibly missed housing units, the physical field block 3 has been assigned two block unit numbers, 2,417 and 2,418, the first of which has been selected into the sample. The table notation, double interval, calls this to our attention. Hence, only three out of the six clusters assigned to this field block are eligible to be selected into this sample. Since the first block number (2,417) was the one sampled, an interval of 2 with a random start of 1 is applied to the missed housing units found on this block. All the missed housing units on blocks not requiring such subsampling fall into the supplementary sample.

Finally, interviewers go to the supplementary blocks, check the list of city directory addresses against the addresses actually found on the blocks, and list and interview at all housing units found at addresses not on the city directory lists. The missed housing units on blocks with subsampled line numbers should be transcribed on field forms. Then an interviewer is to interview at all housing units falling on the form lines corresponding to the block's sample line numbers. All missed housing units obtained by these procedures come into the sample at an overall rate of 1 in 1,100. If any hotels, motels, or trailer courts are found on supplementary blocks, all their housing units or trailer units which are occupied by nontransients are to be listed on field forms as missed housing units since, by previous definition, they cannot come in through city directory listings.

## The Segment Sample

Now that the sample has been designed for the city directory stratum and its block supplement component, the remaining territory can be sampled by an area sample design.   The first step is to divide the remaining territory into primary sampling units composed of communities, tracts, townships, or other minor civil subdivisions.   The boundaries of these areas should be as of the last census, and care should be taken to ensure that no piece of territory is left out of the segment stratum because its boundaries do not fully mesh with the boundaries of the city directory stratum.

After psu's are formed, they should be assigned measures of size based upon their current number of housing units.   Next, for stratification purposes, the data from the last census and local information can be used to rate each psu on a 3-point economic scale as high, medium, and low.   Then (1) make a complete listing of all these psu's starting with the highest economic rating; (2) within economic ratings, list psu's by geographic location (north, east, south, and west); and (3) within geographic location, list the psu's by the number of housing units.   It would be best to reverse the order of listing psu's from one subgroup to the next, i.e., to list psu's from north to west and then west to north in succeeding economic groups; to list psu's by those with large to small numbers of housing units and then by those with small to large numbers of housing units within successive geographic groups.   Table 8.4 shows this suggested listing of psu's.

TABLE 8.4   Selection of Primary Sampling Units within the Segment Stratum

| (1) psu's | (2) Economic rating | (3) Geographic location | (4) Estimated no. of hu's | (5) Strata | (6) Cumulative total within stratum | (7) Sample psu's | (8) Probability of sample psu's |
|---|---|---|---|---|---|---|---|
| Gelt Towers | high | north | 12,000 | | 12,000 | * | 0.35 |
| Tract 81 | high | east | 5,000 | | 17,000 | | |
| Township Ten | high | south | 6,000 | 1 | 23,000 | | |
| Tract 70 | high | south | 4,000 | | 27,000 | | |
| Tract 71 | high | south | 3,000 | | 30,000 | | |
| Tract 52 | high | west | 4,500 | | 34,500 | | |
| Medium Manors | med. | west | 4,500 | | 4,500 | | |
| Tract 75 | med. | west | 3,200 | | 7,700 | | |
| Tract 66 | med. | west | 2,500 | | 10,200 | | |
| Tract 18 | med. | north | 2,700 | 2 | 12,900 | * | 0.09 |
| Tract 19 | med. | north | 2,800 | | 15,700 | | |
| Tract 25 | med. | north | 3,500 | | 19,200 | | |
| Township Two | med. | east | 12,000 | | 31,200 | | |
| Low Lanes | low | east | 17,500 | | 17,500 | | |
| Mortgage Manors | low | south | 5,700 | 3 | 23,200 | | |
| Tract 22 | low | west | 10,000 | | 33,200 | * | 0.30 |

Primary sampling units can then be grouped into strata of approximately 33,000 housing units.   This stratum size gives an expected work load for one or more interviewers of 30 sample housing units per stratum.   Within each stratum, one psu is sampled with probability proportional to its measure of size. These sample psu's are indicated by asterisks in column 7; the probability of selection for each sample psu is shown in column 8.   Primary sampling units having around 33,000 housing units form their own strata, represent just themselves in the sample, and are selected with certainty.   Otherwise, the sample psu's represent other psu's in addition to themselves and have probabilities of selection proportional to their share of the housing units of their strata.

The first step in the subsampling process is to subdivide each sampled psu into still smaller secondary units which will, in turn, be sampled.   These secondary units can be either U.S. Bureau of the Census enumeration districts[26] or election precincts.[27]   If enumeration districts are used, measures of size can be housing unit counts.   With election precincts, measures of size can be number of registered voters as of the last presidential election.[28]

After establishing secondary selection units for each sampled psu, select one secondary selection unit per primary sampling unit with probability proportional to secondary unit measures of size.   The procedure for doing this is the same as that previously described for the selection of sample psu's.

Having obtained a sample of secondary units, one must then subdivide them.   The first phase of subdivision consists in visiting each sampled secondary unit and dividing it into groups of around 28 to 30 housing units.   This activity is frequently referred to as *chunking*.   Division should be along block boundaries, roads, streams, creeks, or any easily recognizable physical boundary.   Where it is not possible to divide an area into chunk units of around 28 to 30 housing units, divide it into multiples of 28 or 30 and assign multiple chunk units numbers.

The rate of selection of sample chunks can well be three times the overall sampling fraction or, in this design, 3 in 1,100.   Then, the within-chunk rate for selection of housing units will be 1 in 3.   Such a subsampling rate tends to

---

[26] U.S. Bureau of the Census enumeration districts are the geographic work areas assigned to various census enumerators.   Their exact boundary descriptions and last census housing unit counts can be obtained from the Bureau of the Census.   The boundaries of the enumeration districts are created at the time of the last census, which is another reason for the emphasis upon the use of previous census boundaries.

[27] The boundaries and voter-registration data of election precincts can be obtained from local boards of election.   Care must be exercised in fitting election precinct boundaries to sample psu boundaries.   Where an exact fit cannot be obtained, parts of precincts must be used and voter estimations changed accordingly.

[28] It is assumed that the various social forces operating to produce voter registration do not vary significantly from precinct to precinct within the same primary sampling unit.   It is also assumed that the number of registered voters in each precinct is directly proportional to the number of dwelling units in each precinct.   Since these assumptions are more likely to be fulfilled in presidential election years, it is recommended that the data for such years be utilized.   It is possible to use other election data if they fulfill the above assumptions.

maximize the use of field materials and listings and helps spread the selection of housing units over more chunks.

The sampling equation for chunks might be expressed as

$$\frac{3}{1,100} = \frac{1}{1.833} \times \frac{1}{7} \times \frac{1}{28.577}$$

where $\frac{3}{1,100}$ is the overall sampling rate for chunks

$\frac{1}{1.833}$ is the probability of selection of a primary sampling unit

$\frac{1}{7}$ is the probability of selection of a secondary unit within the primary sampling unit

and $\frac{1}{28.577}$ is the probability of selection of chunks within the secondary unit

Then, to obtain the final sample at 1 in 1,100, just use a 1 in 3 rate within a sampled chunk.

Tables 8.5 and 8.6 show the procedures for selection of sample chunks within secondary units and for selection within chunks. In columns 1 and 2 of Table 8.5 are indicated the sampled primary and secondary units—Gelt Towers and enumeration district 1 of Gelt Towers. The various chunks composing enumeration district 1 are listed in column 3; column 4 indicates the number of chunk units assigned to the various chunks; column 5 gives the cumulative total of column 4. The sampled chunk units are recorded in column 6; column 7 indicates the proportion of the housing units belonging to a chunk to be accepted into the sample. For example, since chunk 5 has only one chunk unit, all the housing units of chunk 5 are to be accepted. But only one chunk unit has been selected out of the two units composing chunk 3, and only one chunk unit has been selected out of the four composing chunk 6. Consequently, only one-half the housing units within chunk 3 and one-fourth of those within chunk 6 can be accepted into the sample.

After the sample chunks have been selected, they should be visited and the second phase of subdivision performed. This second phase is frequently called *segmenting* and consists in subdividing a chunk into contiguous groups of approximately four housing units. Each such group of four housing units represents one segment measure. If segments of four housing units cannot be established, then segments can be multiples of four housing units and receive multiple measures of size. As with chunks, segment boundaries should be physical boundaries, easily located structures, or, if necessary, even imaginary lines projected between two clearly identified landmarks. Above all else, boundaries must be clearly and easily identified by interviewers in their field activities. Segmenting

TABLE 8.5   Selection of Chunks within Secondary Units

| (1) Primary sampling unit | (2) Secondary selection | (3) Chunk | (4) No. of chunk units | (5) Cumulative total of col. (4) | (6) Samples chunk units | (7) Selected portion |
|---|---|---|---|---|---|---|
| Gelt Towers | E.D. 1 | 1 | 1 | 1 | | |
| | | 2 | 1 | 2 | | |
| | | 3 | 2 | 4 | 3 | One-half |
| | | 4 | 1 | 5 | | |
| | | 5 | 1 | 6 | 6 | Take all |
| | | 6 | 4 | 10 | 9 | One-fourth |
| | | 7 | 1 | 11 | | |

TABLE 8.6   Selection of Segments

| (1) Chunk | (2) Segment | (3) Segment measures | (4) Cumulative total of col. (3) | (5) Sample selections | (6) Sample line numbers |
|---|---|---|---|---|---|
| 5 | A | 1 | 1 | | |
| | B | 2 | 3 | 3 | 2,4,6,8,10, . . . |
| | C | 1 | 4 | | |
| | D | 4 | 8 | 6 | 2,6,10,14,18, . . . |
| | E | 1 | 9 | 9 | Take all |
| 6 | A | 1 | 10 | | |
| | B | 1 | 11 | | |

minimizes interviewer travel and spreads housing unit listing work over several surveys.

Table 8.6 shows how to obtain a segment subsample at a rate of 1 in 1,100. In line with the previous discussion, every third segment measure must be selected. Columns 1 and 2 contain chunk-identifying numbers and segment-identifying letters. Columns 3 and 4 indicate the number of segment measures assigned to each segment and their cumulative totals. Columns 5 and 6 indicate the sample selections from an interval of 3 and a random start of 3 together with resultant sample line numbers. When an interviewer visits each sample segment, he lists all its housing units on a field form. The interviewer refers to the segment sample line numbers which are transcribed on the segment's field form. He then interviews at those housing units listed on the form line numbers corresponding to the sample line numbers.

## *New Construction

One of the great advantages of a city directory—segment sample—design is its excellent ability to pick up new construction. The block supplement approach will reflect all changes from the city directory listings; the area sample approach of the segment design will give a proper sample of all housing unit changes occurring in the segment stratum. In addition, by careful field work in establishing and assigning block supplement measures and chunk and segment measures, one can avoid getting too many highly clustered, newly constructed housing units into the sample.

If no city directories are available, a segment sample design can be used throughout the metropolitan area. In such a situation, the central city of the area comes into the design with certainty. Its census tracts become primary sampling units which can be stratified as desired. Within the sampled census tracts, blocks are selected; within sample blocks, housing units are selected. It is also possible to regard city blocks as chunks and to form block housing units into segment groups.

The various suburban communities which otherwise would be listed in city directories can become primary sampling units within the segment stratum. Then, only some of them will come into the sample in contrast to all of them when city directories are available.

## *Standard Errors

In calculating standard errors, one assumes the psu's are city directory clusters and supplementary blocks and the various primary sampling units of the segment stratum. Equation (8.46), the systematic selection formula, should be applied to the primary sampling unit summations within the major sampling error groups and then these group values should be added. The first major sampling error group consists of city directory sample clusters ordered by community and within communities in city directory page order. In other words, the city directory clusters from Central City would appear first, with the first cluster being that from the initially selected city directory page, then the second cluster would be that from the second selected city directory page, and so on. Next would come the clusters from Dormitory Downs, etc., until all the directory clusters from Xepzzphiary Woods had been listed. With order thus specified Eq. (8.46) is readily applied to these clusters. The second major sampling error group is composed of the data from the various blocks forming the block supplement sample with these blocks listed in order of community size and within community in block-number order. Finally, the third major sampling error group consists of the various primary sampling units of the segment stratum listed in their order of appearance in Table 8.4. After the three major group calculations are obtained, they should be added together to complete variance computations.

If city directories are not used, then the various census tracts which become the sample primary sampling units within Central City would be listed in order of selection and Eq. (8.46) applied with the Central City tracts forming the first major sampling error group. Then, the remaining primary sampling units, listed in order of selection, would compose the second major sampling error group. If any other community was of fairly large size (say, 33,000 or more housing units) and was self-representing in the sample design, it, too, might well have its sample census tracts form a separate major sampling error group for calculation purposes.

## 8.11 CONCLUDING REMARKS

### Design Problems

By this time, having plowed through a varied and detailed array of concepts, formulas, and techniques, one realizes the relatively advanced level of sampling theory and procedures. Employing the concepts and techniques written about in this chapter, one can readily select a representative probability sample of just about any population and generalize to the characteristics of that population from the statistics of this sample.

Nevertheless, there should be no surprise with the statement that much work remains to be done in the field of sampling. Clearly, there is need for more than rules of thumb in such design areas as:

**1** Cluster sizes required for various multistage sample levels. For example, how many secondary selections should there be per primary sampling unit or how many housing units should there be in segments or chunks in order to minimize standard errors and costs?

**2** Subclass sizes required for multiquestion surveys. What subclass sizes need there be for the best efficiency on data derived from the many question items obtained by survey interviews of half an hour, one hour, or more than one hour in length? Sample design can be optimized for one question, but how can it best be done over dozens of questions?

**3** Minimal costs for surveys. As with cluster and subclass sizes, here, too, there is concern over the reduction of the costs of travel time, call-backs to not-at-home respondents, lengths of interviews, refusal rates, and the costs of housing unit listings and other aspects of sample selection.

The very large number of survey variables helps to make the design of samples a matter for considerable experience. Once one goes to the trouble and expense of selecting a respondent and getting him to agree to being interviewed, it is obviously sensible to ask him as much as possible despite the varying nature of the questions. Surveys are meant to obtain lots of data through asking lots of questions.

Often social science surveys are unique events which are undergone to get data on some topic of contemporary importance. If surveys are repeated, they are frequently done at such intervals as to result in almost complete, or complete, turnover in research personnel. Hence, learning experiences must be repeated and mistakes replicated. Typically, survey records are so fragmentary as to be of little use the next time around. Then, too, survey analysis permits, indeed, demands, radical redesign and improvement of previous survey schedules. Hence, it takes several surveys on the same topics by the same organization to develop and stabilize efficient and effective methods of selecting and questioning respondents.

The problems of continuity of research organizations, topics, and survey instruments are being resolved in such excellent research groups as the Survey Research Center of the University of Michigan and the National Opinion Research Center. Progress is being made in cost accounting records for surveys. It is to be hoped that gains in knowledge as a result of regularly repeated surveys by stable research institutes will soon result in more rules to guide the solutions for the above-mentioned sampling design problems.

## Other Survey Problems

The various links in the chain of survey research data gathering and analysis are strong in sample design, of medium strength in data analysis, and weakest in the art of interviewing.

The activities of questioning respondents, building rapport, and reducing refusals remain somewhat of an art which is acquired by experience and a sensitivity for these tasks. Research text after research text cries out for improved interviewing techniques based on generalized survey research information. Yet progress is slow and difficult in this area, with much important work still to be done.

While survey data can be analyzed by presently available statistical methods, there remains a most alarming gap between the perceptive, often brilliant, analysis techniques originated by survey researchers and the concerns of mathematical statisticians. Far too often the available mathematical concepts make overly simple assumptions such as the possibility of repeated interviews of the same person, statistical independence among survey respondents, or simple random sampling. Social science researchers stand in sore need of better thinking and more help from mathematicians.

Indeed, one feels the need for the development of a new mathematics curriculum for social scientists. Such a mathematical curriculum should break away from a traditional physical science orientation and humdrum obsession with teaching mathematical proofs. Instead a sequence of courses ought to be developed which reflect the nature of social dynamics and which teach mathematics as a source of logical models for social scientific thinking. Such a course sequence could also make full use of the manipulative and organizing capabilities of electronic computers.

# REFERENCES

1 Bergsten, Jane: "A Nationwide Sample of Girls from School Lists," *Journal of Experimental Education*, **26** (March, 1958), 197–208.

2 Cochran, William: *Sampling Techniques*, 2d ed. (New York: Wiley, 1963).

3 Deming, W. Edwards: *Some Theory of Sampling* (New York: Wiley, 1950).

4 Deming, W. Edwards: "On Simplification of Sample Design through Replication with Equal Probability and without Stages," *Journal of the American Statistical Association*, **51** (March, 1956), 40–43.

5 Hansen, Morris, William Hurwitz, and William Madow: *Sample Survey Methods and Theory* (New York: Wiley, 1953), vols. I and II.

6 Kish, Leslie: *Survey Sampling* (New York: Wiley, 1965).

7 Kish, Leslie: "A Procedure for Objective Respondent Selection within the Household," *Journal of the American Statistical Association*, **44** (September, 1949), 380–387.

8 Kish, Leslie: "A Two-stage Sample of a City," *American Sociological Review*, **17** (December, 1952), 761–769.

9 Kish, Leslie: "Selection of the Sample," in Leon Festinger and Daniel Katz (Eds.), *Research Methods in the Behavioral Sciences* (New York: Holt, 1953), chap. 5.

10 Kish, Leslie: "Confidence Intervals for Clustered Samples," *American Sociological Review*, **22** (April, 1957), 154–165.

11 Kish, Leslie, and Irene Hess: "On Variances of Ratios and of Their Differences in Multi-stage Samples," *Journal of the American Statistical Association*, **54** (June, 1959), 416–446.

12 Lazerwitz, Bernard: "A Sample of a Scattered Group," *Journal of Marketing Research*, **1** (February, 1964), 68–71.

13 Lazerwitz, Bernard: "A Comparison of Major United States Religious Groups," *Journal of the American Statistical Association*, **56** (September, 1961), 568–579.

14 Lazerwitz, Bernard, and Louis Rowitz: "The Three Generations Hypothesis," *American Journal of Sociology*, **69** (March, 1964), 529–538.

15 Sharp, Harry, and Allan Feldt: "Some Factors in a Probability Sample Survey of a Metropolitan Community," *American Sociological Review*, **24** (October, 1959), 650–661.

16 Stephan, Frederick: "History of the Uses of Modern Sampling Procedures," *Journal of the American Statistical Association*, **43** (March, 1948), 12–39.

17 Sukhatme, Pandurang: *Sampling Theory with Applications* (Ames, Iowa: Iowa State College Press, 1954).

18 Woolsey, Theodore: *Sampling Methods for a Small Household Survey*, Public Health Monograph no. 40 (United States Public Health Service, 1956).

19 Yates, Frank: *Sampling Methods for Censuses and Surveys*, 2d ed. (London: Griffin, 1953).

# PART 3

# EXPERIMENTAL DESIGNS
# AND THE ANALYSIS OF
# CHANGE DATA

Experimental designs and the analysis of change data provide the ideal way of studying causal interrelationships and of isolating the effects of limited numbers of variables for more systematic investigation. Yet change and experimental studies present their own peculiar problems, some of which overlap those discussed in Part 2. The study of *long-run* changes involves many of the same sorts of difficulties encountered in comparative analyses: lack of comparability in measurement, simultaneous changes in large numbers of variables, and the necessity of including exogenous variables as possible disturbing influences. The focus of attention in Part 3 is mainly the relatively simpler problem of investigating *short-run* changes that can be studied through experimental manipulations or panel studies.

One of the major advantages of experimental designs consists in the ability to focus on a small number of variables. The symmetrical properties of these designs make it possible to create experimental effects that are statistically independent of each other. Randomization then enables one to make certain simplifying assumptions regarding disturbing influences which, in turn, permit one to separate the main effects of each variable from certain classes of interaction effects. In Chap. 9, on experimental designs, Ross and Smith show how choice of design affects the number of quantities one may estimate from the data, as well as the number of assumptions one must make in order to estimate the desired quantities. In general, the more complex the design the smaller the number of unknowns that must be assumed a priori, and the authors compare various alternative designs with this in mind.

Short-run change studies are particularly sensitive to errors of measurement, since induced (or real) changes in the independent variables are likely to be small as compared with measurement errors. For this reason, it is essential to study possible sources of measurement error as well as ways of separating the measurement error component analytically, once data have been collected. In Chap. 11, James Coleman suggests an ingenious method of achieving the latter objective. The major portion of Chap. 10, by James Wiggins, is devoted to the problem of controlling variation in order to maximize internal validity. The discussion is focused on methods for the control of extraneous variables in experimental research which affect the degree of validity of the investigator's inferences. Wiggins deals with variation due to such extraneous variables as the investigator's biases, the subjects themselves, faulty communication between subject and investigator, and instrumentation.

Coleman's chapter, which deals with the conceptual and analytical element to be mastered in the study of change, provides an appropriate conclusion to the volume, although readers will find this chapter relatively technical. Coleman's purpose is to indicate how the investigator can extract from his observations the best description and explanation of change through the use of mathematical models constructed to mirror the processes of change. These models involve a comparison of various states of an object or situation measured at different points in time, and employ calculus as a basic tool.

Dynamic formulations, as noted in the introduction to Part 2, provide a general theoretical framework of which static models are a special case. Undoubtedly, sociologists and other social scientists will in the future need to address themselves more systematically to such dynamic theories.

# CHAPTER 9

# Orthodox Experimental Designs

JOHN ROSS

PERRY SMITH

For causal research, the experiment offers primarily two advantages over the survey: first, the investigator can manipulate stimuli as he wishes, determining their intensity and duration; and second, he can decide which subjects shall receive each stimulus. The experimental approach permits the random assignment of subjects to stimuli, averaging out differences among subjects before the stimuli act. But experiments also differ among themselves depending on whether they are conducted in the laboratory or in the field. In the field, the investigator may find it hard to exclude miscellaneous stimuli, which unfortunately can affect his subjects much more than the stimulus under test.

Experimentation in both field and lab is sometimes avoided in the belief that subjects do not behave naturally when they know they are under analysis. Many ways to avoid unnatural behavior are set forth below. A more subtle objection is that experiments are atomistic, separating factors which in reality always occur together. This is occasionally a danger in applying experimental results to the real world (10,11,43), but for strictly causal analysis it nevertheless clarifies how factors interact.

Except for small-group research, sociologists have neglected the experiment. This is a serious mistake, for the experimental method can be a valuable tool in the field. It has already advanced field research in political sociology, demography, medical sociology, small-group conflict, industrial sociology, methodology, and other fields (3,5,6,12,16,26,27,38,44). It made major contributions as early as the 1930s in the Hawthorne studies and 1934 in Dodd's Syrian experiment and it won vastly expanded scope as late as

1963 when it was extended to several groups of rural villages and one entire city. Some notable examples of recent field experiments follow.

The largest, and probably the most successful, field experiment thus far was conducted in 1963 on the island of Taiwan. Faced with high population growth rates officials there permitted a pilot project in Taichung, a city of 300,000. The stimulus was a nine-month action program to encourage family planning, with city-wide measurements taken before and after. About 36,000 married women, or 2,400 neighborhoods, were allocated to a 12-cell design. These cells received various combinations of stimuli: 19,000 home visits, 24,000 letters, 105,000 pamphlets, and 51,000 street posters. A probability sample of 2,500 women was interviewed before and after. Birth-control services were maintained at all health clinics in the city, which over 5,000 women visited. Ten percent of all women in the childbearing ages accepted contraception, most of them choosing the simple insertion of an intrauterine device. The 10 percent figure assumes greater significance when one realizes that these 10 percent are 40 percent of all eligible women: those not sterile, not already practicing contraception, not pregnant, and not wanting more children (5, issues 4 and 6; and 6).

To this historic effort may be added others, which also induced changes in reproductive behavior. In Singur, India, a rural area north of Calcutta, over twenty villages were made the target of a family-planning experiment (5, issue 1). Another fertility experiment was conducted for four years in the Ludhiana District of northwest India, using 16 villages containing about 16,000 people (5, issue 1). In 1962, near Seoul, Korea, 14 villages became the target of two birth-control programs (5, issue 2; and 49).

To the documentation in demographic research may be added innumerable field experiments in education, industry, and advertising. In addition, the testing of new medicines and drugs uses ordinary people in clinical trials, with enough scope to support an entire profession. Research in medical sociology and public health offers such field experiments as the following. In New York City, Jolliffe obtained lifetime commitments from over 650 persons to join an anticoronary club and stick to a special prudent diet. Overweight and blood cholesterol levels fell, dropouts were minimal, and more persons applied for the program than could be accepted (27). Matthew Lee and associates contrasted a new plan of home treatment against conventional treatment for randomly selected stroke victims. Many agencies around Philadelphia gave their endorsement, and specialists from several health disciplines collaborated. Kronick (29) showed that responses to the two plans of treatment followed dissimilar patterns in different social classes. Irvine Page and associates have begun a project to assign randomly some 5,000 middle-aged males either to their customary diet or to a special diet for five years. They plan to watch the consequences for heart disease rates and general mortality

(3). A considerable diversity of experimental applications is found in Campbell's writings (12,14).

## Terminology

Some of the terminology found in survey research will be used in this chapter. The causal stimuli under test are termed *independent variables* or *treatments*. These stimuli affect certain subject characteristics of interest, the *dependent variables*. It must be understood that *subjects* is merely a convenient term for the units upon which observations are made; they are not necessarily human individuals. If the experiment directs special propaganda at randomly selected census tracts in order to increase the percentage voting Democratic, then census tracts are the subjects. Similarly, subjects may be entire villages, schools, or sales organizations, whatever is acted upon by the independent variable.

A distinction is also employed between property variables and forcing variables (7). *Property variables* are characteristics of the subjects (such as attitudes for persons, morale for school classes, or fertility rates for cities) and include the dependent variable(s). The property variables are subject to change by *forcing variables*, which are simply all the outer stimuli. Forcing variables include the independent variable(s), the procedures adopted by the investigator (e.g., the special instructions he gives to his subjects), and all the uncontrolled stimuli present in the environment. Many uncontrolled stimuli will have no effect whatever in any particular experiment, and many properties of the subjects will remain unchanged during any particular experiment. It will be noted later that random assignment of subjects to stimuli helps control only the property variables. It has no effect on the forcing variables.

## Outline

The plan of this chapter is straightforward. If an experiment is to be well planned, the important variables involved should be sorted into their major types (Sec. 9.1). Frequently, special devices will be necessary to avoid unnatural behavior, and some of these devices are described for measurement procedures and for creating treatments that will seem real to the subjects (Sec. 9.2). Then certain pitfalls in interpreting experimental data are presented, which should be carefully watched while the research is being planned (Sec. 9.3). Some limits to the generalization of results are given brief mention (Sec. 9.4). Then, two major sections are devoted to designs, the first giving a systematic set of simple designs (Sec. 9.5), and the second introducing classic experimental designs, which sociological training frequently omits (Sec. 9.6).

## 9.1  TYPES OF VARIABLES

The investigator, his topic in mind, should begin by sorting out the kinds of variables with which he will deal. This is generally a helpful discipline, since it frequently suggests variables that would otherwise be overlooked and shows the investigator where dangerous uncontrolled variables may lie. He may then attempt to move some of the variables into more desirable classifications. The types of variables below[1] are illustrated from O'Rourke's dissertation research (34), a summary of which follows.

> O'Rourke hypothesized that the behavior of small groups in a laboratory is often unlike that in natural surroundings, especially with reference to interpersonal affect. To test this he obtained 24 families who worked on similar tasks, once at home and once in a lab. Though each family contained two or more children, he used only the parents and one child from each family. The families were all volunteers, contacted through two churches of the same denomination in one Eastern city. Twelve families came from each church, six with a son and six with a daughter. All children used were age fifteen to seventeen.
>
> Every group worked first at home, and later in the lab. The investigator was invariably present at each of the two sessions, during which he set the family to discussing two decision problems with specified alternatives. Four different problems were thus required. Their sequence was different for different families, but they were so ordered that for all families taken together, each problem would occur an equal number of times in each session. The dependent variables were frequency and positivity of affect during the session, as exhibited by each person (and within each pair relationship) among the three subjects. The Bales short form of the Interaction Process Analysis was employed.

From this brief summary we can illustrate the main types of variables and draw out some general lessons for experimental practice.

## *Independent and Dependent Variables*

Every experiment manipulates one or more variables to see the effect upon other variable(s). In the experimental literature, independent variables are called *treatments* or *factors,* and the dependent variable is customarily

---

[1] This classification is similar to that presented in Leslie Kish, "Some Statistical Problems in Research Design," *American Sociological Review,* **24** (June, 1959), 328–338.

called the *criterion*. [This is an appropriate name, since the impact of the factor(s) is judged by it.]

For O'Rourke, the independent variable was *setting* (home versus lab). There were two dependent variables, positivity and frequency of affect. The experiment focused on the manner in which these two variables changed as the subjects shifted from one setting to the other.

The values of a variable are divided into groups called *categories*. If the number of values is small, there may be only one value in each category. If the variable is, for example, the length of practice at some task, the categories might be "less than one hour," "one hour to two hours," and so on.

## One-category Controls

These are variables controlled by restricting all subjects to one category of them. If males only are used, then sex is controlled. When more than one category of a variable is considered, there is a rapid increase in the number of cells as other variables are cross-tabulated, and consequently it is often more efficient to use subjects from only one category. If all subjects are college juniors, both age and education are controlled. The price paid for this control by restriction is that, strictly speaking, all the findings can be generalized only to college juniors. Sooner or later, the experiment should be run on subjects in *other* categories of these variables, just as the chemist might run his experiment first at room temperature and later at an extremely hot or cold temperature.

In O'Rourke's experiment, one-category controls were group size (three), age of participating child (fifteen to seventeen), nature of group (intact family), and various background characterisics (a single city, language, religion, etc.).

## Block Variables (Multicategory Controls)

Block variables are controlled as in one-category controls, except that the experiment is run separately within two or more categories of the variable. With sex, for example, the experiment would be run in the same way for both males and females. This permits a broader generalization of results, beyond either sex alone. This tactic is sometimes used on a variable that not only needs to be explicitly controlled but is also of some theoretical interest, since the pattern of results across categories of the variable will shed light on its causal role. If control is the only motive, it is called a *block variable*, where each of its categories is a block.[2]

[2] Using such a variable must reduce error variance enough to justify the sacrifice it causes in degrees of freedom. If it does not, its control function is worthless or harmful.

In the example, both categories of the variable, sex of the participating child, were used. The motive here was more than control. There was theoretical interest in the child's sex, since the father-son relationship might experience a special kind of change in the transfer from home to an outside setting.

Another block variable, and a better illustration of block, is the two churches. A separate sample was taken from each. They amount to two locations for obtaining subjects, each of which should yield an internally homogeneous sample, thereby controlling numerous unspecified variables.

## Randomized Variables

Because subjects are randomly assigned to treatments, a large number of property variables are controlled. But the term "control" has many meanings and does not denote the same thing here as in either one-category controls or multicategory controls above. Randomization is simply a blanket device to give every experimental group the same distribution on each of the innumerable property variables. If it worked perfectly, one could pick out any property variable he pleased, and he would find the same mean, standard deviation, and distribution in every group in the experiment. This being so, any differences among the groups after the experiment could not be due to any property variables, and in that sense they would be controlled. In practice, of course, randomization works imperfectly.

In O'Rourke's experiment, the randomization device was not used because of the nature of the design. Note that it is basically a one-group repeated-measurements design. All subjects receive two treatments: first a problem-solving session at home, and then in the lab. Two groups could have been used, created by random division, one for each setting (treatment). Then randomization would be assumed to have created identical groups. The use of a single group for both treatments is merely another way of offering two identical groups (the same group at two different points in time) to the treatments. Each device has its risks; randomization relies on chance, and using the same group twice assumes that experiencing the first treatment has no effect on response to the second treatment. If this latter assumption is safe, the second procedure is to be preferred, since no closer comparison can be achieved than the same person or family with itself. Both heredity and environment are covered totally, whereas randomization is certain to fail for at least some variables. O'Rourke's single-group design was a wise choice, therefore, assuming that the results would have been unchanged with a reverse sequence of treatments.[3]

[3] A test for this can be incorporated in the design, by subjecting a random half of the sample to each sequence. In a sufficiently large sample, this not only balances the two sequence efforts, if any, but also affords an opportunity to examine them.

## Ignored Variables

The experimenter, at last, must leave a group of unrecognized or untouched variables. The subjects possess an infinite number of properties, and no experimenter can possibly restrict his sample to a tiny range on each of many traits—genetic, mental, familial, economic, political, religious, and social. He would be lucky to find even one subject who would qualify, leaving no one to generalize to. He can only try to balance purity against breadth in the sample, judging shrewdly which are the important variables. He gets, finally, a collection of subjects who are haphazard in some respects. There are, moreover, ignored forcing variables. Innumerable stimuli are constantly at work, and it is fortunate that experiments are impervious to most of them. They range from the day's headlines to noises outside the laboratory to the color of the investigator's shirt. It is a matter of judgment which of these must be controlled and which condition the generalization of results.

In the example, one could speculate at length on the importance of ignored property variables. Interaction between husband and wife might have been affected by their relative ages, or by the occupation of the husband, or by their social classes of origin. (Many such variables were partially controlled through obtaining all subjects from two churches of the same denomination in one city and by using only intact families with a child aged fifteen to seventeen).

Notwithstanding the potential superiority of repeated measurements of one group over the random creation of two groups, both plans are vulnerable to variables left unattended. In the example, it was possible to control explicitly the birth order of the participating child. If the distribution of birth orders for the sample was a peculiar one, and if this variable had strong conditioning powers over the results, then all findings might have quite limited generalizability. The point is that one *cannot be free of the risk* that some unrecognized variable is playing just such a role.

Regarding procedural variables, uniform practices are illustrated by the investigator being present at every session, by using the same sequence of home-then-lab for every family, and by the introduction of standardized stimuli in different phases of the research (Thematic Apperception Test cards, the four problems, etc.). Careful attention was given to the sequence of stimuli within each session and to the time permitted for each.

Uncontrolled events would not, one would assume, play a significant role in this experiment, since the focus is role relationships of a long-standing nature. Unusual disturbances to these relationships, occurring between the home and lab sessions, would be cause for worry. A son might quit school, a husband might lose his job, a wife might discover infidelity by her spouse, etc. The investigator should be on the lookout for such disturbances and eliminate bizarre cases, replacing them by a continuation of the original procedure used to obtain subjects.   It is a matter of judgment when a disturbance is severe enough to justify dropping the subject.

## 9.2   UNOBTRUSIVE MEASUREMENTS AND TREATMENTS

In many experiments there is a danger that subjects will behave artificially.   Volunteers for an experiment know that it is not for real and may unconsciously fall into certain poses (35).   Cast into a let's-pretend role they often respond according to their perception of what is socially normal.[4] Or subjects may balk at being manipulated and try to outthink the experimenter.   They may be hypercooperative or hypercompetitive with their fellow subjects.   The most famous example of a laboratory effect is the Hawthorne study (38), in which selected factory workers were so pleased at the experimental attentions of the management that they produced steadily more with each new change, regardless of whether it was an improvement.   The highest productivity came with the final change, which took away all breaks, hot lunches, and incentive payments.   Needless to say, generalization to all factory workers was rather unsafe.   This form of guinea-pig reaction, where subjects respond much more to the fact of being subjects than to the treatment, has been dubbed the Hawthorne effect.

In the following paragraphs, we shall discuss some measurement procedures that will not signal to the subjects that an experiment is in progress and some ways of administering treatments that do not reveal the presence of an experiment.

## *Unnoticed Measurements*

**Natural measurements.**   This device is best explained by an example. Gosnell (26) equated two groups and then conducted a preelection campaign in one to stimulate a higher percentage of voting.   The election returns constituted posttest scores, a fine natural measurement [see also Campbell (13)]. The researcher obtained the data needed without any expenditure of his own resources, and the subjects saw nothing unusual in the measurement process.

Such opportunities are extensive.   Registration and voting statistics are published in great detail.   Census results down to the county, city, and town levels are published, with block statistics often included or available on special request.   Such information might, for example, assess the results of an intracity experiment using blocks as units.   State and national vital statistics, covering births, deaths, migration, and marriages, may assess various action programs using political entities as units [e.g., Bogue (8) and Bogue and Palmore (9) report on efforts to reduce fertility rates in parts of Chicago].   A great body of information appears every year on business, manufacturing, financial activi-

---

[4] This may be a valuable opportunity of studying just those perceptions.

ties, and labor union membership. Within corporations there is routine reporting of such natural targets for experiments as sales, numbers of new clients, etc. Many professions publish data on themselves, or the government does it for them.[5]

**False auspices.** Measurement is sometimes more accurate when subjects do not connect it with the treatments. Let us say that a Planned Parenthood chapter has mounted an action experiment to increase knowledge about birth control. Pamphlets are mailed to the home and, later, are supplemented by house-to-house contacts. Because all action has been openly connected with Planned Parenthood, its staff members should not be used as interviewers, since housewives might not wish to say that they had discarded the pamphlets, etc. Better auspices would be a local university, which could gain the desired information by a survey on family matters, thus measuring the program effect by indirection. Such cooperation can work both ways. To make a treatment appear real, a university might conduct an experiment exactly like this under the Planned Parenthood name.

**Secret measurement.** Bugged rooms and one-way mirrors are extreme examples of this and have been used frequently for experiments on children. Hidden cameras and tape recorders also permit unperceived measurement. It must be stressed that these techniques and certain others discussed here hold a controversial status among researchers. They raise important questions of propriety and of the continued good reputation of social research.

**Disguised measurement.** Within the school, many kinds of intellectual and psychological tests can be presented as part of the routine testing program. This may afford an unnoticed measure of a set of treatments, such as new teaching techniques. The same is true in the examination programs given by some corporations to job applicants. A special test might be added to evaluate an experimental effort to recruit applicants with high-achievement drives. The key characteristic is not the presence of a routine testing program, but the disguising of the true reason for testing, so as to conceal the existence of an experiment.

## Ostensibly Real Treatments

The presence of an experiment is sometimes concealed by arranging treatments so that they seem real to the subjects. Examples follow.

[5] For example, "American Science Manpower" is published each year by the National Science Foundation. It covers over 200,000 scientists, 11 major professional societies, and through them, about 200 specialized societies.

The famous experiments started by Asch and others depended on deception to create their treatments. Subjects might be put into a dark room and told to focus on a pinhole of light some distance away, noting how far it moved and in which direction. Actually the light never moved, but because accurate perception is impossible under such conditions, subjects had no guide but the investigator's implication. Substantial movement was regularly reported. A thoroughly ambiguous stimulus of this type is good for studies of interpersonal influence, and these were quickly explored. Individual judgments were studied first alone and then under the influence of group discussion or of disagreement by stooges.

**False reporting.** Another way to produce desired treatments is to have subjects undergo an experience difficult for them to assess, and then to provide them with a seemingly authoritative interpretation. In one experiment, Dittes (20) misinformed subjects on their standing among their peers, thus bringing to bear, at will, either a high or low sense of acceptance by others.[6] Self-esteem was apparently affected, leading to differential scoring on subsequent tests. In another experiment (21), Dittes (a university professor) wanted to induce a sense of failure and inadequacy among graduate students. Using a normal classroom situation, he distributed folders of instructions and asked each student to work confidentially. A random portion of the class received paragraphs saying that the test they were about to take was a proven indicator of personal and intellectual promise, thereby involving their egos. All students took the test (a difficult space relations test) and were then given a key for self-scoring. Some keys were contrived to produce numerous wrong answers, while others made most questions right. The easy keys included a generous percentile distribution, putting subjects high relative to graduate students. The severe keys included a discouraging percentile rating, putting subjects low relative to candidates for bachelor degrees. This kind of written false reporting very effectively induced the treatments, a sense of success and a sense of failure. Performance on subsequent tasks in the folder differed markedly between the two groups and by whether or not the student was in the ego-involved group.

**Covert randomization.** This technique permits acquisition of data on a random half of a population without subject awareness, simply by investigating the other half. Given sufficient numbers, chance will ensure that the investigated half is representative of the total group. It is also used in many field experiments, without subject awareness, to compare two treatments. For example, an advertising concern wishing to determine which of two appeals is superior may arrange for an issue of a magazine to be run with each appeal in alternate copies. Each advertisement contains some pretext for

---

[6] See Festinger and Katz (23, p. 161) for an attempt at this which failed.

a coupon return, which serves as a posttest measure of effectiveness. (No pretest is needed, by the logic of design 2b in Sec. 9.5.)

The same device exactly may be used in door-to-door, or patient-to-patient, or customer-to-customer contacts. Different methodological instruments, within a single study, may also be compared by subject-to-subject alternation.

Covert randomization has administrative uses. Frequently, programs in which the public has strong interest cannot be openly tested. The first mention of an evaluation of the program may touch off intense conflict. Consider, for example, the director of a city's urban renewal program who believes that homeowners in transitional neighborhoods will be inspired to fix up their dwellings if the worst houses in the neighborhood are removed. He arranges the removals in a number of areas, and a furor breaks out. This obviously affects any conclusions drawn from the study. Even if the neighbors do spend sizable sums in home repair, critics may argue that these improvements were not inspired by the program, that they would have been carried out anyway. In the future, the director follows an alternative course of quietly selecting a larger number of blocks for his program, and executing it only in a random 50 percent of them. Comparison of the two halves gives more convincing evidence.

Thus covert randomization has potential for action research in the continuing improvement of a program. It is significant that all resources can still be fully used for the altruistic aim at stake. If, let us say, 25 counties can be served, one might quietly select 50 or more counties, using randomization within this larger group to select the 25. This affords a comparison which permits rational program evaluation. Just as important, it represents an administrative decision-making principle that is totally democratic. It cuts any nexus between the administrator's prejudices and the selections made (14).

**Fabricated treatments.** Sometimes the effect of a given stimulus cannot be fairly assessed except in the field and with people who suspect nothing artificial. Then the investigator may need to play a special role, to present fabricated treatments as real, and to use covert randomization. Schwartz and Skolnick (41) used these devices in their Catskill study of convicts' chances for employment. Four folders were prepared setting forth identical characteristics of a job applicant, except that in one he had been sentenced for assault, in one he had been tried but acquitted, in one not only had he been acquitted but the judge had written a complimentary letter, and in one no mention was made of criminal activity. According to the plan, employers were listed randomly and visited for reactions to such an applicant. Procedures were nicely devised to give the visit an authentic cast for the employer. The percentage of offers declined regularly with the applicant's criminal involvement.

## 9.3  PITFALLS

It is often said that, compared with observational studies, the experimental method is very powerful.   Randomization presumably ensures that all groups begin the experiment on an equal basis, so that any posttest differences are due strictly to the treatments.   If true, this would make cause-effect inference quite rigorous.

What can go wrong?   What besides the treatments might be responsible for the posttest differences?   It is granted that other stimuli run concurrently with the treatments and that these uncontrolled events may share responsibility for the posttest differences or lack of them.   It is also granted that one can never be sure *what aspect* of the treatments deserves credit for the treatment effects.[7]   But apart from this, there are certain pitfalls which should come to mind when one asks, Did the treatments produce the posttest differences among groups, or did something else do it?   Following is a checklist of things that can go wrong, which should be thoroughly considered during the planning of an experiment.

### *Unlucky Randomization*

Random allocation of subjects to treatments should make the groups equal on the dependent variable before the experiment begins.[8]   Whether or not it does this depends on chance, which with careful planning will be reliable *in most cases*.   When chance fails, any posttest differences may simply be a carry-over of original inequalities.   The *probability* of this occurring is evaluated by standard significance tests and confidence intervals, and decisions based on them of course err occasionally.   This is an important pitfall, one which is certain to occur sometimes.[9]

To make randomization more reliable on all variables, including those of interest, one may:

**1** Enlarge the number of subjects.   The probability that this will equalize the groups rises with the square root of the number of subjects being allocated to each group.

**2** Match the subjects on an important variable(s) before randomization, so as to place them into a number of categories, containing approximately equal numbers of subjects.   Then randomize separately the subjects in each

[7] Two examples: (1) When *The American Soldier* study of integrated Army units showed them to be highly successful, a white colonel remarked that he had always known Negroes would soldier better under white officers (31, p 25).   (2) There is the apocryphal story of the investigator who carefully followed Mill's canon of similarity. His subjects became intoxicated from scotch and water, whisky and water, and gin and water.   He blamed the water.

[8] "Equal" denotes substantially the same means, variances, and distribution shapes.

[9] In some experiments, a pretest of all subjects can be conducted, permitting a check on how similar the groups are.

category. (See classic design b in Sec. 9.5.) This is often called *precision matching*.

**3** Another technique, which may be called *frequency matching*, works in a looser fashion. Subjects are allocated so as to create groups with similar distributions on *each* of two or more variables but not necessarily on all of them simultaneously. Thus two groups might have the same age distribution and the same sex distribution, but not the same age-by-sex distribution. This kind of similarity is less rigorous, but it can be attained with less loss of subjects.

**4** Sometimes, an efficient way of getting a set of $n$ similar subjects is to use each subject $n$ times. This is the *repeated-measurements* design.

**5** Human twins can often be used to create equivalent groups. When there are two treatments, identical twins are simply allocated randomly, thereby controlling all genetic factors. Either identical or same-sex fraternal twins may be used to control substantially all environmental factors. In particular, it is fortunate that both fraternal and identical twins exist, since by comparison with each other and with siblings they permit the separation of hereditary and environmental influences. The only case of equal heredity is identical twins, but there are two cases of nearly equal environment—identical and same-sex fraternal twins. Siblings are considered to have neither heredity nor environment equal, for they differ in birth order, peer groups, parents' maturity at a given age, etc. Suppose then that intrapair differences on any variable are determined for siblings, same-sex fraternal twins, and identical twins. If these differences average about the same for siblings and fraternal twins but are much smaller for identical twins, heredity will be considered the primary determinant of that variable. But if fraternal and identical twins average about the same, and siblings' differences average considerably more, environment must be determinative. For human behavior, no other research strategy can so elegantly separate the effects of environment and genetics.[10]

## Erroneous Assumed Values

In order to compute the treatments' effects in an experiment, one must often assume values for other quantities. As indicated in some of the simple designs set forth below (Sec. 9.5), this can be an uncertain business.

## Faulty Measurement

All inferences drawn from an experiment are premised on the accurate measurement of variables. Yet no variable is exempt from measurement er-

[10] Summaries of all twin studies supported currently or previously by over eighty Federal and private agencies are available from the Science Information Exchange, Washington, D.C.

ror.  Even a simple variable like sex suffers from imprecision, as census experience shows.  In general, measurement error has a large random component, which attenuates correlations.[11]  Measurement error can exaggerate correlations, however.  (This might occur if teachers were asked to judge two
variables, intelligence and creativity, among their students.  Subjective tendencies toward consonance would be expected to produce more agreement
between these two variables than actually exists.)

Measurement is far too broad a topic to discuss briefly.  Above all, errors
that change the mean of one group more than others are to be feared.  This
undermines inference far more than equal error across all groups.  There
are techniques to handle the latter; i.e., true intergroup differences can still
be detected through a general policy of a large sample size and an efficient
design.

## Biased Mortality

In almost any experiment which runs more than a few days, some subjects
drop out, impairing the representativeness of the sample used (if any).
Worse, there may be *biased* mortality, wherein the dropouts from one group
in the experiment possess different characteristics from other dropouts.  This
upsets the *prior equality*, or comparability, of the groups,[12] leaving the investigator with the defect of observational studies, that the groups differ in unknown ways.

How should one reduce the number of dropouts?  This will vary with
the experiment, but one should consider such options as impressing subjects
with the significance of the research, requesting a firm commitment of faithful-
ness from them, paying them, using invisible research (they do not withdraw
from the project because they do not know they are in it), and deliberate
creation of a Hawthorne effect to stir up enthusiasm for the project.  One
should request that each dropout at least agree to a posttest on important
variables, including the dependent variable.  This permits an estimate of how
atypical the dropouts are and how much differential bias they create between
experimental and control groups.

## Contamination

Field experiments especially may suffer from subjects telling each other
about the treatments they are undergoing.  If, for example, treatment A is
intended for certain census tracts and treatment B for others, news of the

[11] See Chap. 5, especially remarks on how attenuation depends on the relative
magnitude of measurement error and true variation in the independent variable.

[12] In the discussion below of the technical aspects of designs, note that the possibility
of dropouts favors design 2a, not 2b.

experiment may travel widely. Consequently, treatment A may affect both sets of tracts, as may treatment B. The general problem is that the results cannot be clearly interpreted, since each group is subjected in unknown degree to more than one treatment.

Where treatments vary only in degree, not in kind, contamination causes a spillover of influences, thus helping along the weaker treatments. This reduces the apparent differences between treatments and induces conservative decisions in significance testing. If therefore one finds, in spite of contamination, a difference between a control and an experimental group, he may infer an even stronger real effect. If the treatments represent two or more levels on a quantitative variable, the observed effect should increase regularly with each level.

To prevent contamination, one can use subjects or areas widely separated in status or space. The key is to select different treatment groups so that contamination among them is unlikely. Sometimes one can take advantage of an ecological barrier, though this may impair randomization. A fertility-control experiment in Chicago used a long, high embankment supporting the el to separate control and experimental areas (8,9). Similar experiments have used a large river and a mountain range to separate control from experimental villages (5, issues 1 and 2; and 49). Other means of retarding contamination are the avoidance of all publicity about the research, the use of natural measurements and other devices which do not let the subjects suspect that they are part of an experiment.

## *The Regression Fallacy*[13]

For experimental work, the regression phenomenon becomes important if subjects are selected because of their extreme scores on some variable, which is to be remeasured at a later time (12,15).

Suppose that a group of retarded children receive IQ tests, and the lowest scorers are selected for remedial training. After some time they are again tested and their IQ scores show improvement. The fallacy is that the contribution of the training program is unknown, since the scores would be expected to rise anyway. Any set of lowest, or highest, scores is created partly by chance factors in the testing situation, by measurement error, and by other temporary influences, all of which have worked in one direction for those few subjects. Such factors have come together in unusual combinations (for, indeed, only a *few* subjects appeared with such extreme scores). One low score, for example, might result partly because of slight illness, a misunderstanding of instructions, a broken pencil, and the hardest chair in the room. At a later time, such a combination of difficulties would not likely

---

[13] See Chap. 11 for a fuller discussion. Campbell and Clayton (15) should also be consulted.

strike that same child.    In this way, initial extreme scorers tend toward the mean at retest.    The reverse is also true, that extreme scorers on the second test will have been at an original position closer to the mean.

There are two checks to detect the regression phenomenon, if one has test-retest scores on all subjects (not just on the initial extreme scores).    The first is to keep track of what is happening to the total dispersion (variance) of all scores, over time.    The other is to measure the reverse regression—the behavior of cases who show up as extreme at the second testing.    If at the first testing, these cases were only moderately removed from the mean (in the same direction as at the second testing), ordinary regression is probably at work.

## 9.4    GENERALIZABILITY

Faced with the power of experimental logic, one can easily forget that the responses observed in one experiment might never recur in another group of subjects.    Every experiment occurs at its own time and place, within a single culture, and under a myriad of conditions defining the methods, sample, and procedures.    Change any one of these and the results *might* be different. Unique factors abound: subjects drop out, a pretty girl administers the treatments, an assistant forgets to take subjects in random order.    The unchangeable fact is that some undetected peculiarity about the experiment *may* have materially affected the results.    The art of transferring one's findings to other subjects in other circumstances is called *generalization*.    The potential for doing so, as seen by an objective outsider, is the *generalizability* of the results.

Campbell (12) has clarified quite nicely three of the limits we must set on the generalizability of findings: (1) sampling of subjects, (2) sampling of treatments, and (3) sampling of measurement devices.    The following discussion is drawn partly from his comments.

## *Sampling of Subjects*

In the unusual experiments where subjects are drawn as a probability sample from a known population, all results are subject to sampling error.    It is this aspect of generalizability that we are best equipped to handle; the battery of statistical techniques worked out is, in fact, too great for any one person to master completely.    Strictly speaking, generalizing beyond the subjects actually used cannot be done rationally unless probability sampling is employed.    Yet many investigators fail to sample, relying instead on such groups as their academic classes.    This is sometimes a reluctant concession to necessity; at other times it is quite satisfactory.    Why this difference?

First, it should be noted that assigning experimental subjects randomly to the various experimental groups does not compensate for failure to select subjects randomly from the population. The experimental findings may be safely generalized only to a population of which the experimental subjects are representative members. If the subjects are not representative, no amount of randomization within the experiment will make them so.

Second, there are situations where sampling may be unnecessary. If the experiment focuses on fundamental responses rooted very deeply in the biological or psychological character of human subjects, then broad generalization from a few subjects may be safe. Thus almost anyone jumps when burned, and almost everyone tries to avoid an electric shock. Certain learning experiments with young children build on their native curiosity and would seem to give results of very wide applicability (32,45). The investigator must judge how sensitive his findings will be to the kinds of subjects used and decide whether to sample and, if so, from what population.

Finally, the experimenter should not be too easily discouraged in trying to sample. True, randomly picked individuals will sometimes not submit to the demands of an experiment, and sometimes it may not be feasible to bring all subjects to one place. Large time requirements are frequent, causing scheduling problems. But with more vigorous efforts, samples often can be obtained. The inability or unwillingness of subjects to cooperate can be met in numerous ways, such as paying them (with due regard to the effect of money on subject objectivity). An appeal to the furtherance of science may be persuasive in gaining cooperation (19). Some institutions, like military installations, large industrial plants, schools, and prisons, offer a sufficiently large captive population from which to draw a specialized sample.

## Sampling of Treatments

Treatments are not always sampled. If, for example, the independent variable concerns polio vaccines, and only three kinds exist, then three treatment groups exhaust the possibilities (plus a fourth, perhaps, for a placebo). If, however, the independent variable is amount of sleep, it will be too cumbersome to have one treatment group for every possible duration. The investigator may use only the even numbers from two to ten hours, or the odd numbers, or a random sample of three numbers. Then the question is, would the findings have been the same with a different sample of numbers?

Formulas for statistical analysis can set probabilities on the answers to such a question. Winer offers a lucid presentation (48, pp. 140ff.). He points out that for statistical purposes we should identify three kinds of treatment sampling. If there are $P$ possible levels of the variable, and one actually uses only $p$ levels, one may create the $p$ levels by combining adjoining levels or by selection, or both. When $p = P$, the variable is called *fixed*. It is also fixed if $p < P$ and the $p$ levels are selected by a nonrandom procedure. But if $p < P$ and the $p$ levels are selected randomly, then the variable is called *random*. The ratio $p/P$ is called the *sampling fraction* for a variable. In many situations, especially where the variable is a continuous one, $P$ is so large that $p/P$ is nearly zero. Winer expands all these considerations, giving formulas whereby the results for the $p$ levels actually used may be generalized to the population of all $P$ treatments for that variable.

## Sampling of Measurement Devices

Because different procedures can be used to measure the same variables, the investigator must often choose one arbitrarily. This would not matter if all procedures gave the same answers, but unfortunately they do not. Where investigators disagree and use different procedures, their results often cannot be compared. And each investigator is troubled by the thought that his conclusions might have been different if he had followed a different procedure.

There is no easy solution to this problem. If excessive energy is devoted to repeating an experiment several times with different measurement procedures, very little headway will be made on the substantive questions. In practice, measurement devices are rarely sampled in any strict sense; rarely is more than one procedure used. This has the unfortunate result that conclusions may be drawn and widely generalized when they are only an artifact of measurement.

A compromise deserving serious consideration is to replicate one group in the experiment, trying an alternative measurement device on it. This practice would give many investigations double significance and, in time, would considerably improve methodology.

To review, generalizability is technically restricted by each and every aspect of the experiment and the milieu encompassing it. Going no further than this, however, leads to a hopeless particularism in research. Most researchers generalize, but they do so more rationally in some aspects than others.

## Summarizing Illustration

Ingenious field research is nowhere better illustrated than in the boys' camp experiments of Sherif, Sussman, and associates (44). Wanting to study the dynamics of conflict and concord between groups, they arranged an investigation of eleven- and twelve-year-old boys in an isolated summer camp.

To exclude variation in numerous property variables, they accepted only boys in good physical and emotional health, somewhat above average in intelligence, and from middle-class, white, stable, Protestant homes. Obtaining such a purified group required extensive labor in studying school records and watching the boys at play.

To avoid any Hawthorne effects, invisible research was used throughout.

All measurements in the field were concealed or natural: all the investigators assumed roles as camp staff, permitting close daily observation. Certain games were worked into the schedule of activities to reveal pecking orders and shifts in leadership under the pressure of conflict with another group (in much the same way as bowling scores told Whyte about leadership in his street corner gang). At times, unobtrusive cameras and microphones were used. Interviews and sociometric ratings were also employed, but the boys seemed to perceive these as part of the ordinary procedures of such a camp.

All treatments were presented as part of the summer program. Upon arrival in the camp area, the boys were permitted to live together for a while in order that natural friendships and cliques might form. Soon, each boy was asked informally who his best friends were. Then, best friends and cliques were deliberately split up, with each boy assigned to one of two large groups. This was done to keep yet another variable from disturbing the free play of repetitive group dynamics, that of special cliques. For the same reason, only boys who were strangers to one another had been accepted into the camp, and it was on the buses taking them to the camp area that they first met.

The two large groups, immediately after formation, lived in separate cabins and had no contact with each other, so that each could develop its own informal structure. Leaders appeared, followers sifted down to varying levels of influence, and an *esprit de corps* developed.

Then, conflict between the two groups was experimentally produced, following the hypothesis that well-adjusted individuals will become hostile toward one another if they belong to groups with conflicting aims. A tournament of games was arranged, continually pitting each group against the other. Soon the boys were calling each other names, giving each other negative ratings, snubbing former best friends, and conducting raids against each other. Within each group, solidarity and good feeling rose.

The investigators then introduced treatments to replace conflict with concord. At first, the strategy was to build up pleasant social contacts through joint meals and movies. But the boys merely seized on these new opportunities to "berate and attack each other." Next, the hypothesis was investigated that harmony will follow the pursuit of overarching goals which neither group can achieve without the other. A series of urgent, seemingly natural emergencies occurred: the water supply broke; the movie budget ran low; the food-supply truck balked and required pushing. Things were so arranged as to make cooperation easy. The boys pitched in on one endeavor after another, and slowly their hostilities were replaced by good feeling. Finally, they were actively suggesting joint activities.

Why do we find this account scientifically convincing? The design is, after all, characterized by impressive limitations, in that the unit employed was a single pair of groups. For conflict studies this represents a sample size of one, and even this single unit was not selected to represent any specific population of such units. There was no second unit serving as a control, which means that the investigators assumed that chance and all concurrent events were of negligible influence.[14] Without checks and compensating strengths, such a design can be rather promiscuous in fallacious inference.

Sherif and associates used several effective field methods. Notice how they eliminated numerous alternative explanations for the findings:

**1** *Physical insulation* from outside stimuli.

**2** *Invisible research:* hidden or natural measurement coupled with treatments that seemed real.

**3** *Field execution* providing a backdrop that in essentials was consistent with the environment to which results were to be generalized.

**4** *Purification of the sample:* homogeneity on numerous property variables. Changes in behavior during the experiment could not plausibly be attributed to the unfolding interplay of a strange mix of characteristics among the boys.

**5** *Elimination of unique nonreplicatable influences.* The best example here is the avoidance of cliques by splitting up best friends. With a small sample (only one pair of groups) it was critically important to control as many sources of variation as possible. Had a peculiar clique congealed in one of the two groups, it might have dominated activities and badly obscured more general group dynamics.

Certain strengths of the experimental method itself also serve to convince us. The time order of treatments and effects is known, and the investigators had the subjective assurance that all nontreatment influences seemed stable during the experiment.

In addition, good research canons were exemplified by using multiple and diversified measurements and by using a full circle of treatment effects, from harmony to conflict and back to harmony.

### 9.5   SIMPLE DESIGNS

In this section we discuss experiments which aim at determining the effect of a single stimulus on a single property of the experimental subjects. For example, the experimental subjects might be sixth-grade school children, and the experimenter might want to determine how effective a certain speed-reading course is in increasing their average reading speed.[15] The most direct approach is to (1) give the children a *pretest* to determine their average

---

[14] Or at least that their effects could be estimated and subtracted.

[15] The experimental subjects will have been randomly selected from all the sixth-grade children in an area.

reading speed before the course is given, (2) give the course, (3) give the children a *posttest* to determine their new average reading speed, and (4) assume that the difference in average reading speed before and after the course is entirely due to the course. But there are many reasons why this simple experiment may give incorrect results. We shall discuss several of these reasons and present more elaborate experiments which will give better results.

Some possible sources of error in the above experiment are these:

**1** Some of the improvement in reading speed between the beginning and the end of the experiment might have nothing to do with the course, but be the natural result of reading ability improving as the children grow older (maturation of subjects, one kind of uncontrolled event).

**2** Testing the reading speed of the children before giving the course may increase their interest in improving their speed, so that they work harder at the course and profit more from it than they would if they had not been pretested. If the course is given to other children who are not pretested, it may be less effective (*interaction* of pretest with experimental stimulus).

**3** Some of the children's parents may decide to give their children extra reading practice at home, either using the techniques being taught in the course or not. Such extra practice in itself would probably increase reading speed, but it could also tend either to reinforce or to interfere with the children's learning of the techniques taught in the course, thus increasing or decreasing the effectiveness of the course. (The extra reading practice is an *uncontrolled event,* which has an effect all by itself. It can also interact with the experimental stimulus and/or the pretest.)

We can give a more systematic analysis of the factors at work in this experiment. Let $d$ be the difference in average reading speed observed when the experiment is performed. That is, $d$ = average posttest score minus average pretest score. Let $E$, $P$, and $U$ be the changes in average reading speed due to the effects, acting alone, of the experimental stimulus (the course), the pretest, and uncontrolled events, respectively. Let $I_{PE}$ be the change in average reading speed due to the interaction of the pretest with the experimental stimulus, and define $I_{PU}$ and $I_{EU}$ similarly. Also there is $I_{PEU}$, the three-way interaction among the pretest, the experimental stimulus, and uncontrolled events simultaneously. We now have in the above experiment:

$$d = P + E + U + I_{PE} + I_{PU} + I_{EU} + I_{PEU} \qquad (9.1)$$

which is considerably more complicated than the naïve assertion that $d = E$. In Eq. (9.1), $d$ is known and there are seven unknowns, so to solve the equation we must assume values for six of them. Assuming that $P = U = I_{PE} = I_{PU} = I_{EU} = I_{PEU} = 0$, as was done in the above experiment, is obviously dangerous.

Consider the three possible sources of error listed above.

The first, maturation of subjects, is an uncontrolled event.
The second is one of the contributions to the $I_{PE}$ term.
The third involves contributions to the $U$ and $I_{EU}$ terms.

There are other possible experiments which will not require us to make so many assumptions. If we are given a group of subjects, we can choose whether or not to pretest the group and whether or not to apply the experimental stimulus to the group. So a group can be treated in any of four different ways: (1) pretest and stimulus, (2) pretest only, (3) stimulus only, and (4) neither pretest nor stimulus. We always posttest the group.

These four different options give rise to four basic group types, with an equation for each. We have already seen that the equation for group (1) is

$$d = P + E + U + I_{PE} + I_{PU} + I_{EU} + I_{PEU} \qquad (9.1)$$

In group 2 there is no experimental stimulus, so the terms $E$, $I_{EU}$, and $I_{PEU}$ drop out, leaving

$$d = P + U + I_{PU} \qquad (9.2)$$

For group 3 we have

$$d = E + U + I_{EU} \qquad (9.3)$$

We do not know the value of $d$ in this equation, because we do not have a pretest score to subtract from the posttest score, but if we have pretested another group and both groups are large random samples from the same population, then it is safe to use the pretest score from the pretested group to obtain a value of $d$ for the group receiving treatment 3. As described below, probability formulas can tell how safe this is. For group 4 we have simply

$$d = U \qquad (9.4)$$

and the remark made under group 3 again applies.

These four fundamental equations are summarized in Table 9.1. A design may contain from one to four of the groups. Drawing from the four options above, there are four possible designs which contain one group only. There are six possible two-group designs, four possible three-group designs, and one four-group design. Whenever a design contains two or more groups, it is assumed that subjects are assigned to the groups randomly, thus making them equal at the pretest within probability expectations. Of all the possible designs, only the more useful ones are discussed here, though all are shown in Table 9.2. For a full account consult Ross and Smith (40). Table 9.2 is the basis of the following presentation of designs.

TABLE 9.1  Possible Experimental Groups

| Group | Pretest | Experi-mental stimulus | Uncon-trolled events | Posttest | Equations |
|-------|---------|------------------------|----------------------|----------|-----------|
| 1 | $P$ | $E$ | $U$ | $T$ | $d_1 = P + E + U + I_{PE}$ $+ I_{PU} + I_{EU} + I_{PEU}$ |
| 2 | $P$ | ... | $U$ | $T$ | $d_2 = P + U + I_{PU}$ |
| 3 | ... | $E$ | $U$ | $T$ | $d_3 = E + U + I_{EU}$ |
| 4 | ... | ... | $U$ | $T$ | $d_4 = U$ |

## One-group Designs

**1a.**  The name PEUT means that the group is exposed to a pretest, the experimental stimulus, uncontrolled events, and a posttest. This experimental design has already been discussed. We saw that six assumptions must be made to solve Eq. (9.1), which is the equation for this design. There are seven unknowns, and the number 7 in column 3 of Table 9.2 means that there are seven ways to choose which six unknowns to assume values for. (Choosing which six unknowns to assume values for is equivalent to choosing which unknown to solve for.) Normally the experimenter wants the value of $E$ to be computed, not assumed, so we list in column 4 the number of sets of assumed values which leave $E$ to be computed. Here there is only one such set. Column 5 lists the unknowns which do not occur in any of the equations for the design being discussed. All the unknowns occur in Eq. (9.1), so "none" is entered in column 5.

This design leans so heavily on guesswork that it is scarcely better than the zero-group design (in which the experimenter simply guesses the values of all the unknown quantities).

**1b, 1c, 1d.**  These designs are useless for finding $E$, because either there is no pretest, so that $d$ cannot be found, or there is no experimental stimulus, so that $E$ does not even occur in the equation for the design. Design 1b can be used for determining $P$ in exactly the manner indicated for $E$ in design 1a.

## Two-group Designs

**2a. Groups 1 and 2.**  This is the so-called classic two-group design, where the experimental stimulus is withheld from one group and given to the other.

TABLE 9.2    Summary of 15 Designs

| (1) Design | (2)* Assumptions required to solve for all unknowns | (3)* Legitimate sets of assumed values | (4) Legitimate sets which do not assume a value for E | (5) Quantities ignored | (6) Comment |
|---|---|---|---|---|---|
| 1a. PEUT | 6 | 7 | 1 | none | |
| 1b. P..UT | 2 | 3 | (omits E) | $E,I_{PE},I_{EU},$ $I_{PEU}$ | Cannot find E |
| 1c. ..EUT⎱ dis- <br> 1d. ....UT⎰ card | | | | | |
| 2a. PEUT <br>     P..UT | 5 | 12 | 3 | none | The classic 2-group design. 2b is generally superior |
| 2b. ..EUT <br>     ....UT | 1 | 2 | 1 | $P,I_{PE},I_{PU},$ $I_{PEU}$ | Best design for finding a mean value for E |
| 2c. `PEUT <br>     ..EUT | 5 | 12 | 4 | none | |
| 2d. PEUT <br>     ....UT | 5 | 6 | 1 | none | Can never assume a value for U.† Only one set of assumptions permits finding E |
| 2e. P..UT <br>     ..EUT | 3 | 8 | 3 | $I_{PE},I_{PEU}$ | |
| 2f. P..UT <br>     ....UT | 1 | 2 | (omits E) | $E,I_{PE},I_{EU},$ $I_{PEU}$ | Cannot find E |
| 3a. PEUT <br>     P..UT <br>     ..EUT | 4 | 20 | 8 | none | Popular design but generally inferior to 3b |
| 3b. P..UT <br>     ..EUT <br>     ....UT | 2 | 4 | 2 | $I_{PE},I_{PEU}$ | Usually the best 3-group design, if $I_{PE}$ and $I_{PEU}$ can be ignored |
| 3c. PEUT <br>     P..UT <br>     ....UT | 4 | 8 | 2 | none | Can never assume a value for U† |
| 3d. PEUT <br>     ..EUT <br>     ....UT | 4 | 8 | 4 | none | Can never assume a value for U† |

TABLE 9.2    Summary of 15 Designs *(Continued)*

| (1) | (2)* | (3)* | (4) | (5) | (6) |
|-----|------|------|-----|-----|-----|
| Design | *Assumptions required to solve for all unknowns* | *Legitimate sets of assumed values* | *Legitimate sets which do not assume a value for E* | *Quantities ignored* | *Comment* |
| 4a.  PEUT<br>P..UT<br>..EUT<br>....UT | 3 | 8 | 4 | none | Incorporates every other design, though at extra cost. Requires the fewest assumptions (3) to get values for all 7 quantities |

* This table summarizes all the designs under discussion. Columns 2 and 3 require explanation. Each design of two groups or more possesses a system of equations. The number of equations is the same as the number of groups, and this number minus the number of different unknowns involved in all equations gives the number of assumptions necessary to solve the equations (col. 2). Since there are more quantities than assumptions, a number of different sets of assumed quantities are possible. However, one is not entirely free in choosing which quantities shall take assumed values. Some sets of assumptions are mathematically illegitimate, since they either will be inconsistent with the data or will merely replicate the data and thus be redundant. (Col. 3 shows the number of legitimate sets.) For example, in any design containing group four, in which $U = d_4$, it is illegitimate to assume a value for $U$. Doing so will contradict the value of $d_4$ yielded by the data or else will duplicate it. This is redundant and useless, and the equations cannot be solved without adding yet another assumption.

† Designs in which one cannot assume a value for $U$. These designs should be avoided whenever the investigator believes uncontrolled events to have negligible influence, since he cannot assume $U = 0$.

Both groups are pretested and posttested. In our opinion it has been overrated and misunderstood. The group receiving treatment 1 is usually called the *experimental* group, and the other is called the *control* group. The equations are

$$d_1 = P + E + U + I_{PE} + I_{PU} + I_{EU} + I_{PEU} \qquad (9.5)$$
$$d_2 = P + U + I_{PU} \qquad (9.6)$$

We are assuming, as we will always do in designs with more than one group, that uncontrolled events act equally on all the groups. Otherwise we would have a $U_1$ for the first group and a $U_2$ for the second group instead of a single $U$ for both.

From these equations we obtain

$$d_1 - d_2 = E + I_{PE} + I_{EU} + I_{PEU} \qquad (9.7)$$

We have four unknowns in this equation, and any set of assumptions which permits us to solve the equations must assume values for three of these unknowns. In all, there are seven unknowns and two (original) equations, so values must be assumed for five unknowns. A legitimate set of assumptions therefore assumes values for five unknowns, three of which are taken from the list $E$, $I_{PE}$, $I_{PU}$, $I_{PEU}$, and two from the list $P$, $U$, $I_{PU}$. There are twelve legitimate ways to choose the five unknowns for which to assume values, as column 3 states; there are three legitimate ways in which $E$ is not chosen, as column 4 states.

Many discussions of this design have ignored $P$ and all the interactions. This omission has amounted to writing the equations for this design as

$$d_1 = E + U \qquad d_2 = U \qquad (9.8)$$

Then $d_1 - d_2 = E$. As in our reading-speed experiment, there is often reason to suspect that $I_{PE}$, $I_{EU}$, or other omitted quantities are not zero, and neglecting them cannot be justified.

If used with proper attention to all quantities, this design provides the advantage of a known pretest score on each subject. This permits the calculation of individual pretest-to-posttest difference scores, which give statistically significant results with a much smaller sample size than when differences in group means are compared (see design 2b). Another strength of pretesting is that individuals' responses to the experimental stimulus can be correlated with their various personal characteristics, thus clarifying why they react as they do.[16] But these gains come at the cost of adding $P$ and its three interactions to the equations, and the correlations may involve the additional stimuli of more question asking. Unless the values of these extra quantities can be safely estimated, the final calculations will contain considerable guesswork.

**2b. Groups 3 and 4.** The equations are

$$d_3 = E + U + I_{EU} \qquad d_4 = U \qquad (9.9)$$

(We use the symbols $d_3$ and $d_4$ rather than $d_1$ and $d_2$ to agree with Table 9.1.) Subtracting, we have

$$d_3 - d_4 = E + I_{EU} \qquad (9.10)$$

Only three of the seven possible unknowns occur in the equations (column 5 lists the other four) so it is only these three whose values we are concerned

---

[16] In observational studies, where subjects are not randomly assigned to groups, it is valuable, if possible, to know what the values of the dependent variable were before the stimulus acted. These pretest scores can show whether the groups involved were roughly equal before receiving the stimulus and can also give the advantages mentioned in the text for experiments.

with. We have two equations in three unknowns (or, since the equation $d_4 = U$ is trivial, one equation in two unknowns), and only one assumption is required, rather than five as in design 2a. With the present design all the effort and expense of pretesting are also avoided. The one apparent drawback is that $d_3$ and $d_4$ are not known. Let $X_3$ and $X_4$ be the actual average posttest scores for the two groups, and let $Y_3$ and $Y_4$ be the average scores which would have been obtained had the groups been pretested. Then

$$d_3 = X_3 - Y_3$$
$$d_4 = X_4 - Y_4 \qquad (9.11)$$
$$\text{and} \qquad d_3 - d_4 = (X_3 - X_4) - (Y_3 - Y_4)$$

Since both groups are large random samples from the same population, we may assume $Y_3 = Y_4,$[17] so that $d_3 - d_4 = X_3 - X_4$. We now have the equation

$$X_3 - X_4 = E + I_{EU} \qquad (9.12)$$

and $E$ is found with only one assumption.

Uncontrolled events are always present, so whenever $E$ occurs in our equations $U$ and $I_{EU}$ will also occur. By using option 4 above, we can isolate $U$, but we can never separate $E$ from $I_{EU}$ in our equations. If the uncontrolled events in an experiment are a normal part of the environment, then for practical purposes $E + I_{EU}$ may be the quantity whose value is desired, rather than $E$ alone. In this case, design 2b requires no assumptions of values for unknowns at all. Suppose that in our reading-speed experiment maturation of subjects is the only significant uncontrolled event. Probably $I_{EU} \neq 0$, because the maturity of the students may well be important in determining the effectiveness of the course. There is no interest in determining the effectiveness of the course when taught to imaginary sixth-graders whose development remains frozen while the course is being given; it is $E + I_{EU}$ which is important. In evaluating the course, we must still remember the natural increase in reading speed as the students mature (i.e., we must separate $U$ from $E + I_{EU}$), and design 2b permits this separation.

We conclude that design 2b is definitely superior to design 2a for the purpose of calculating $E$ or $E + I_{EU}$. For other purposes design 2a is superior. For example, no pretesting is done in design 2b, so that changes in individual scores cannot be studied. An admirable discussion of design 2b, with references to both experimental and observational studies, is found in Campbell (12, pp. 304–306).

2c–2f. We shall not discuss these designs.

[17] That is, that $Y_3 - Y_4$ is probably small and can safely be ignored. Directions are given below for setting probability limits on the differences.

## Three-group Designs

**3a. Groups 1, 2, and 3.**   The equations are

$$d_1 = P + E + U + I_{PE} + I_{PU} + I_{EU} + I_{PEU} \qquad (9.13)$$
$$d_2 = P + U + I_{PU} \qquad (9.14)$$
$$d_3 = E + U + I_{EU} \qquad (9.15)$$

This design was first discussed by Solomon (46) and is the only three-group design mentioned in the literature prior to the work of Ross and Smith (40). There are seven unknowns and three equations, so four assumptions are required. Values may not be assumed for all three of the unknowns $P$, $U$, and $I_{PU}$, because when values for two of them are assumed the value of the third is determined by Eq. (9.14). When allowance is made for this and similar restrictions on the selection of unknowns for which to assume values, there are found to be 20 legitimate sets of four unknowns for which values may be assumed, and 8 such sets not containing $E$.

**3b. Groups 2, 3, and 4.**   The equations are

$$d_2 = P + U + I_{PU} \qquad (9.16)$$
$$d_3 = E + U + I_{EU} \qquad (9.17)$$
$$d_4 = U \qquad (9.18)$$

Avoiding treatment 1 eliminates interactions of the pretest with the experimental stimulus, so the unknowns $I_{PE}$ and $I_{PEU}$ do not occur in the equations. There are three equations in five unknowns and only two assumptions are required. There are only four legitimate pairs of unknowns for which values may be assumed: $E$ and $I_{PU}$, $E$ and $P$, $I_{EU}$ and $I_{PU}$, $P$ and $I_{EU}$. Only two of these do not assume a value for $E$.

This design is superior to design 3a for the purpose of computing $E$ and $P$, since it requires fewer assumptions (and less pretesting). But for the purpose of computing $E$ alone, design 2b is preferable to any three- or four-group design because it is less costly and requires no more assumptions. The purpose of the three- and four-group designs is to yield empirical values for more of the unknowns, not to yield more accurate values for $E$.

**3c and 3d.**   These designs have no special merits and will not be discussed.

## Four-group Designs

The characteristics of this design are stated in Table 9.2.   It yields values for all seven unknowns with only three assumptions, but requires more time, effort, and subjects than the other designs.

As a convenience for the researcher, solutions are given in Tables 9.3–9.11 for the system of equations under each permissible set of assumptions, for most designs. Values for unassumed quantities (unknowns) are stated in terms of the $d$'s (which are known) and assumed values. (See p. 371.)

Finally, the analysis should not be frozen by any initial set of assumed values. As long as the researcher conscientiously separates his before thinking from his after-the-fact thinking, he should fully exploit his data. Typically, he will execute an initial analysis based on the views he had in selecting his hypotheses and in settling on a particular design. In that process he will almost certainly have painfully considered what assumptions to make. Following those decisions, he may or may not regard the results of this initial analysis as plausible. In either case, he should identify his prior analysis

TABLE 9.3  Assumptions for Design 2a*
$$P\ E\ U\ T\!:\ d_1 = P + E + U + I_{PE} + I_{PU} + I_{EU} + I_{PEU}$$
$$P\,.\,.\ U\ T\!:\ d_2 = P + U + I_{PU}$$
(5 Assumptions)

| Case no. | $U$ | $E$ | $P$ | $I_{EU}$ | $I_{PU}$ | $I_{PE}$ | $I_{PEU}$ |
|---|---|---|---|---|---|---|---|
| 1 | $D_2$ | $D_1 - D_2$ | | | | | |
| 2 | | $D_1 - D_2$ | $D_2$ | | | | |
| 3 | | $D_1 - D_2$ | | | | $D_2$ | |
| 4 | $D_2$ | | | $D_1 - D_2$ | | | |
| 5 | $D_2$ | | | | | $D_1 - D_2$ | |
| 6 | $D_2$ | | | | | | $D_1 - D_2$ |
| 7 | | | $D_2$ | $D_1 - D_2$ | | | |
| 8 | | | $D_2$ | | | $D_1 - D_2$ | |
| 9 | | | $D_2$ | | | | $D_1 - D_2$ |
| 10 | | | | $D_1 - D_2$ | $D_2$ | | |
| 11 | | | | | $D_2$ | $D_1 - D_2$ | |
| 12 | | | | | $D_2$ | | $D_1 - D_2$ |

* In this and all later tables, an empty space signifies an assumed value, to be filled in for each experiment by the investigator. Only legitimate sets of assumptions are included; for each design, additional sets are logically possible but the assumptions comprising them would make the system of equations mathematically unpermissible, by failing to meet the requirements of independence of, and consistency with, the data. For example, in design 2a, it would be illegitimate to assume values for $P$, $U$, and $I_{PU}$, thereby specifying the sum of these quantities, because Eq. (2) says that the sum, $P + U + I_{PU}$, is equal to $d_2$, a figure produced by the data. If the assumed values happened to add to $d_2$ then they would simply be redundant (nonindependent), adding no new information, and if they did not add to $d_2$, they would be inconsistent with the data. In short, additional assumptions are logically possible in each table, but they lead to results that can be confirmed or denied empirically, making it either redundant or erroneous to produce the same result by assumptions. For an explanation of the $D_i$, see p. 371.

TABLE 9.4 Assumptions for Design 2c

$P \; E \; U \; T:\; d_1 = P + E + U + I_{PE} + I_{PU} + I_{EU} + I_{PEU}$

$.. \; E \; U \; T:\; d_2 = E + U + I_{EU}$

(5 Assumptions)

| Case no. | $U$ | $E$ | $P$ | $I_{EU}$ | $I_{PU}$ | $I_{PE}$ | $I_{PEU}$ |
|---|---|---|---|---|---|---|---|
| 1 | | $D_2$ | $D_1 - D_2$ | | | | |
| 2 | | $D_2$ | | | $D_1 - D_2$ | | |
| 3 | | $D_2$ | | | | $D_1 - D_2$ | |
| 4 | | $D_2$ | | | | | $D_1 - D_2$ |
| 5 | $D_2$ | | $D_1 - D_2$ | | | | |
| 6 | $D_2$ | | | | $D_1 - D_2$ | | |
| 7 | $D_2$ | | | | | $D_1 - D_2$ | |
| 8 | $D_2$ | | | | | | $D_1 - D_2$ |
| 9 | | | $D_1 - D_2$ | $D_2$ | | | |
| 10 | | | | $D_2$ | $D_1 - D_2$ | | |
| 11 | | | | $D_2$ | | $D_1 - D_2$ | |
| 12 | | | | $D_2$ | | | $D_1 - D_2$ |

as such and proceed to work toward a best fit of assumed values with the data. It is wise first to try whatever seems the safest set of assumptions and see what values result for the unassumed quantities. If these seem unreasonable, the researcher will modify the most suspect assumption to see what results follow, and continue this iterative process until the values for all quantities, assumed and unassumed, become least offensive. Then it is time for another experiment.

TABLE 9.5 Assumptions for Design 2d

$P \; E \; U \; T:\; d_1 = P + E + U + I_{PE} + I_{PU} + I_{EU} + I_{PEU}$

$.... \; U \; T:\; d_2 = U$

(5 Assumptions)

| Case no. | $U$ | $E$ | $P$ | $I_{EU}$ | $I_{PU}$ | $I_{PE}$ | $I_{PEU}$ |
|---|---|---|---|---|---|---|---|
| 1 | $D_2$ | $D_1 - D_2$ | | | | | |
| 2 | $D_2$ | | $D_1 - D_2$ | | | | |
| 3 | $D_2$ | | | $D_1 - D_2$ | | | |
| 4 | $D_2$ | | | | $D_1 - D_2$ | | |
| 5 | $D_2$ | | | | | $D_1 - D_2$ | |
| 6 | $D_2$ | | | | | | $D_1 - D_2$ |

TABLE 9.6   Assumptions for Design 2e
$$P \ldots U \ T: d_1 = P + U + I_{PU}$$
$$\ldots E \ U \ T: d_2 = E + U + I_{EU}$$
(3 Assumptions)

| Case no. | $U$ | $E$ | $P$ | $I_{EU}$ | $I_{PU}$ |
|---|---|---|---|---|---|
| 1 | $D_1$ | $D_2 - D_1$ | | | |
| 2 | | $D_2$ | $D_1$ | | |
| 3 | | $D_2$ | | | $D_1$ |
| 4 | $D_2$ | | $D_1 - D_2$ | | |
| 5 | $D_1$ | | | $D_2 - D_1$ | |
| 6 | $D_2$ | | | | $D_1 - D_2$ |
| 7 | | | $D_1$ | $D_2$ | |
| 8 | | | | $D_2$ | $D_1$ |

## One-quantity Aims

When research is undertaken to assess only one of the seven quantities described above, the following procedures are suggested. [When two quantities are to be assessed, and one of them is $E$, refer to Ross and Smith (40).]

TABLE 9.7   Assumptions for Design 3a
$$P \ E \ U \ T: d_1 = P + E + U + I_{PE} + I_{PU} + I_{EU} + I_{PEU}$$
$$P \ldots U \ T: d_2 = P + U + I_{PU}$$
$$\ldots E \ U \ T: d_3 = E + U + I_{EU}$$
(4 Assumptions)

| Case no. | $U$ | $E$ | $P$ | $I_{EU}$ | $I_{PU}$ | $I_{PE}$ | $I_{PEU}$ |
|---|---|---|---|---|---|---|---|
| 1 | $D_2 + D_3 - D_1$ | $D_1 - D_2$ | $D_1 - D_3$ | | | | |
| 2 | $D_2 + D_3 - D_1$ | $D_1 - D_2$ | | | $D_1 - D_3$ | | |
| 3 | $D_2$ | $D_3 - D_2$ | | | | $D_1 - D_3$ | |
| 4 | $D_2$ | $D_3 - D_2$ | | | | | $D_1 - D_3$ |
| 5 | | $D_3$ | $D_2$ | | | $D_1 - D_2 - D_3$ | |
| 6 | | $D_3$ | $D_2$ | | | | $D_1 - D_2 - D_3$ |
| 7 | | $D_3$ | | | $D_2$ | $D_1 - D_2 - D_3$ | |
| 8 | | $D_3$ | | | $D_2$ | | $D_1 - D_2 - D_3$ |
| 9 | $D_2 + D_3 - D_1$ | | $D_1 - D_3$ | $D_1 - D_2$ | | | |
| 10 | $D_3$ | | $D_2 - D_3$ | | | $D_1 - D_2$ | |
| 11 | $D_3$ | | $D_2 - D_3$ | | | | $D_1 - D_2$ |
| 12 | $D_2 + D_3 - D_1$ | | | $D_1 - D_2$ | $D_1 - D_3$ | | |
| 13 | $D_2$ | | | $D_3 - D_2$ | | $D_1 - D_3$ | |
| 14 | $D_2$ | | | $D_3 - D_2$ | | | $D_1 - D_3$ |
| 15 | $D_3$ | | | | $D_2 - D_3$ | $D_1 - D_2$ | |
| 16 | $D_3$ | | | | $D_2 - D_3$ | | $D_1 - D_2$ |
| 17 | | | $D_2$ | $D_3$ | | $D_1 - D_2 - D_3$ | |
| 18 | | | $D_2$ | $D_3$ | | | $D_1 - D_2 - D_3$ |
| 19 | | | | $D_3$ | $D_2$ | $D_1 - D_2 - D_3$ | |
| 20 | | | | $D_3$ | $D_2$ | | $D_1 - D_2 - D_3$ |

TABLE 9.8    Assumptions for Design 3b
$$P .. U\ T:\ d_1 = P + U + I_{PU}$$
$$.. E\ U\ T:\ d_2 = E + U + I_{EU}$$
$$.... \ U\ T:\ d_3 = U$$
(2 Assumptions)

| Case no. | U | E | P | $I_{EU}$ | $I_{PU}$ |
|----------|------|-----------|-----------|-----------|-----------|
| 1 | $D_3$ | $D_2 - D_3$ | $D_1 - D_3$ | | |
| 2 | $D_3$ | $D_2 - D_3$ | | | $D_1 - D_3$ |
| 3 | $D_3$ | | $D_1 - D_3$ | $D_2 - D_3$ | |
| 4 | $D_3$ | | | $D_2 - D_3$ | $D_1 - D_3$ |

For finding $E$ design 2b is best. It produces the desired result with the minimum number of groups and assumptions (one), though it may require a sizable sample. When the only aim is to evaluate $I_{EU}$, design 2b is again best. Ordinarily it would *not* be best for the *double* aim of evaluating both $E$ and $I_{EU}$, since finding a value for either one demands an assumed value for the other. But no design whatever can separate the effects of $E$ and $I_{EU}$, i.e., create a group subject to one and not the other. Therefore, design 2b remains the best when one is interested in both quantities. It can only give the *sum*, $E + I_{EU}$, but it does so with no assumed values.

TABLE 9.9    Assumptions for Design 3c
$$P\ E\ U\ T:\ d_1 = P + E + U + I_{PE} + I_{PU} + I_{EU} + I_{PEU}$$
$$P .. U\ T:\ d_2 = P + U + I_{PU}$$
$$.... \ U\ T:\ d_3 = U$$
(4 Assumptions)

| Case no. | U | E | P | $I_{EU}$ | $I_{PU}$ | $I_{PE}$ | $I_{PEU}$ |
|----------|------|-----------|-----------|-----------|-----------|-----------|-----------|
| 1 | $D_3$ | $D_1 - D_2$ | $D_2 - D_3$ | | | | |
| 2 | $D_3$ | $D_1 - D_2$ | | | $D_2 - D_3$ | | |
| 3 | $D_3$ | | $D_2 - D_3$ | $D_1 - D_2$ | | | |
| 4 | $D_3$ | | $D_2 - D_3$ | | | $D_1 - D_2$ | |
| 5 | $D_3$ | | $D_2 - D_3$ | | | | $D_1 - D_2$ |
| 6 | $D_3$ | | | $D_1 - D_2$ | $D_2 - D_3$ | | |
| 7 | $D_3$ | | | | $D_2 - D_3$ | $D_1 - D_2$ | |
| 8 | $D_3$ | | | | $D_2 - D_3$ | | $D_1 - D_2$ |

TABLE 9.10 Assumptions for Design 3d
$P\ E\ U\ T:\ d_1 = P + E + U + I_{PE} + I_{PU} + I_{EU} + I_{PEU}$
$..\ E\ U\ T:\ d_2 = E + U + I_{EU}$
$....\ U\ T:\ d_3 = U$
(4 Assumptions)

| Case no. | U | E | P | $I_{EU}$ | $I_{PU}$ | $I_{PE}$ | $I_{PEU}$ |
|---|---|---|---|---|---|---|---|
| 1 | $D_3$ | $D_2 - D_3$ | $D_1 - D_2$ | | | | |
| 2 | $D_3$ | $D_2 - D_3$ | | | $D_1 - D_2$ | | |
| 3 | $D_3$ | $D_2 - D_3$ | | | | $D_1 - D_2$ | |
| 4 | $D_3$ | $D_2 - D_3$ | | | | | $D_1 - D_2$ |
| 5 | $D_3$ | | $D_1 - D_2$ | $D_2 - D_3$ | | | |
| 6 | $D_3$ | | | $D_2 - D_3$ | $D_1 - D_2$ | | |
| 7 | $D_3$ | | | $D_2 - D_3$ | | $D_1 - D_2$ | |
| 8 | $D_3$ | | | $D_2 - D_3$ | | | $D_1 - D_2$ |

Exactly the same comments apply to $P$ and $I_{PU}$ in design 2f. Note, however, that for $P$ or $I_{PU}$ or their sum, design 1b is a strong second choice. In it, $d_1 = P + U + I_{PU}$. Whenever the value of $U$ can be assumed, e.g., as zero, only two unknowns are left, the same two that design 2f yields. The costs of a second group are avoided, at the price of possible error in $U$.

In the rare cases where the only aim is to assess $U$, either design 2b or 2f is best. Group 1 can be dismissed after the pretest.

To find either $I_{PE}$ or $I_{PEU}$, one must use a design that includes group

TABLE 9.11 Assumptions for Design 4
$P\ E\ U\ T:\ d_1 = P + E + U + I_{PE} + I_{PU} + I_{EU} + I_{PEU}$
$P..\ U\ T:\ d_2 = P + U + I_{PU}$
$..\ E\ U\ T:\ d_3 = E + U + I_{EU}$
$....\ U\ T:\ d_4 = U$
(3 Assumptions)

| Case no. | U | E | P | $I_{EU}$ | $I_{PU}$ | $I_{PE}$ | $I_{PEU}$ |
|---|---|---|---|---|---|---|---|
| 1 | $D_4$ | $D_3 - D_4$ | $D_2 - D_4$ | | | $D_1 - D_2 - D_3 + D_4$ | |
| 2 | $D_4$ | $D_3 - D_4$ | $D_2 - D_4$ | | | | $D_1 - D_2 - D_3 + D_4$ |
| 3 | $D_4$ | $D_3 - D_4$ | | | $D_2 - D_4$ | $D_1 - D_2 - D_3 + D_4$ | |
| 4 | $D_4$ | $D_3 - D_4$ | | | $D_2 - D_4$ | | $D_1 - D_2 - D_3 + D_4$ |
| 5 | $D_4$ | | $D_2 - D_4$ | $D_3 - D_4$ | | $D_1 - D_2 - D_3 + D_4$ | |
| 6 | $D_4$ | | $D_2 - D_4$ | $D_3 - D_4$ | | | $D_1 - D_2 - D_3 + D_4$ |
| 7 | $D_4$ | | | $D_3 - D_4$ | $D_2 - D_4$ | $D_1 - D_2 - D_3 + D_4$ | |
| 8 | $D_4$ | | | $D_3 - D_4$ | $D_2 - D_4$ | | $D_1 - D_2 - D_3 + D_4$ |

1 (PEUT), thus incorporating all seven quantities. To find $I_{PE}$ or $I_{PEU}$, use design 2a:

$$d_1 - d_2 = E + I_{EU} + I_{PE} + I_{PEU} \qquad (9.19)$$

To find either quantity, three assumptions are required. An alternative route is design 2c. But in no design whatever can $I_{PE}$ and $I_{PEU}$ be separated. Obtaining a value for either requires an assumed value for the other. Finally, note that if one is willing to pay the costs of design 4, he can obtain

$$d_1 - d_2 - d_3 + d_4 = I_{PE} + I_{PEU}$$

thereby obtaining the sum with no assumed values. The three three-group designs which contain group 4 offer other possibilities but require one assumption each.

## Statistical Note

Only in designs 1a and 2a is every experimental subject pretested. In the other designs involving more than one group, we have assumed that if all the subjects were pretested the average pretest scores for the various groups would be equal, or at least that their differences would be negligible. In this section we discuss methods of estimating these differences. For definiteness we consider design 2b. The quantities $X_3$, $X_4$, $Y_3$, and $Y_4$ were defined in our discussion of 2b.

The assumption that the two pretest means are identical is rarely true, but they will not differ very much if the groups are large enough and if the variance of the dependent variable is modest. The question is whether the sum $E + I_{EU}$ (i.e., $X_3 - X_4$, the difference between the two posttest means) is so small that it might have been created by a mere chance difference in the pretest means. Frequently one can look at the individual posttest scores and see immediately that the variability within either group is so large that any difference between posttest means could be accidental. But this depends on informal judgment and assumes that the variability at pretest survived the experiment unchanged and shows up accurately in the posttest scores. If the investigator feels insecure about these aspects, he has two ways to formalize the use of posttest scores and one way to use pretest scores. We shall discuss the three approaches in that order.

The aim in all three devices is to estimate the probable difference between the pretest means $(Y_3 - Y_4)$. Hence we want $\hat{\sigma}_{Y_3 - Y_4}$. This depends on $\sigma_{Y_3}$ and $\sigma_{Y_4}$ in the population from which the subjects were drawn; and these two quantities have identical values. Thus the problem reduces to estimating $\sigma_{Y_3} = \sigma_{Y_4}$. The three devices below differ by their manner of obtaining this estimate.

**1** Compute the standard deviation, $s_4$, for the posttest scores in the control and let it estimate $\sigma_{Y_3} = \sigma_{Y_4}$. Then

$$\hat{\sigma}_{Y_3-Y_4} = s_4 \sqrt{\frac{N_3 + N_4}{N_3 N_4}} \qquad (9.20)$$

where $N_3$ and $N_4$ = the numbers of subjects in the two groups

$s_4$ = the standard deviation of the dependent variable in the control group

$\hat{\sigma}_{Y_3-Y_4}$ = the standard deviation of the difference between the two pretest means

Ninety-five percent confidence limits for $E$ are then

$$E = X_3 - X_4 - I_{EU} - 1.96 s_4 \sqrt{\frac{N_3 + N_4}{N_3 N_4}} \qquad (9.21)$$

Ideally our estimate, $s_4$, would come from pretest instead of posttest scores. $s_4$ *may* change considerably during the experiment under the impact of uncontrolled events. If this seems to be the case, one should not use this approach.

**2** Use both sets of posttest scores to estimate $\sigma_{Y_3} = \sigma_{Y_4}$. This assumes that $s_3$ (the standard deviation for the experimental group) and $s_4$ change little during the experiment, i.e., that $E$, $U$, and $I_{EU}$ leave $s_3$ unaffected and that $U$ leaves $s_4$ unaffected (regardless of whether the two means vary from pretest to posttest). In judging this assumption, the experimenter may be guided partly by the fact that, within chance limits, $s_3$ and $s_4$ were equal at the time of pretest, owing to random creation of the groups. If they were indeed unaffected by the experiment, they will be about equal at posttest.[18]

Since this method uses a pooled estimate, each $s$ must be weighted by its own $N$. Usually, $N_3$ and $N_4$ will be equal.

$$\hat{\sigma}_{Y_3-Y_4} = \sqrt{\frac{N_3 s_3{}^2 + N_4 s_4{}^2}{N_3 + N_4 - 2}} \sqrt{\frac{N_3 + N_4}{N_3 N_4}} \qquad (9.22)$$

Using this equality, one again has

$$E = X_3 - X_4 - I_{EU} \pm 1.96 \hat{\sigma}_{Y_3-Y_4} \qquad (9.23)$$

We now leave the second approach. The reader might expect a third approach to use an estimate based on group 3 posttest scores. This, of course, is a possibility, and the formulas would follow procedure 1. But one would

[18] To illustrate a situation where $s_3$, the experimental group's standard deviation, would be a poor estimate of pretest variability, imagine a very dogmatic, antimarriage film shown to newlyweds. If the dependent variable is agreement with the film, responses would probably cluster tightly at one end of the scale, whereas pretest scores, if taken, would show more dispersion.

be assuming that the net impact of $E$, $U$, and $I_{EU}$ upon $s_3$ was negligible. If this were so, then $s_4$ would probably *also* have come through the experiment intact and one should pool the two groups to exploit the larger $N$, which is procedure 2. The third procedure we shall suggest, therefore, is something quite different.

**3** Finally, one can create three instead of two groups in the original random division. The third group is pretested, and its $s$ is taken as an estimate of the standard deviation of the population and hence of the other two groups. The formula is, as in procedure 1, Eq. (9.21); the standard deviation of the third, pretested group, replaces $s_4$. An extra advantage of using a third group is that its mean estimates the pretest means of the other two groups. Then the pretest-posttest change within each group can be figured, again with confidence limits if the investigator desires.

To summarize, the first and second procedures require no additional subjects. To use either requires the assumption that the posttest scores possess about the same standard deviation as pretest scores would have shown if obtained. This is less likely in the experimental than in the control group because two additional influences, $E$ and $I_{EU}$, affect the scores. The third procedure is best if additional subjects come cheaply; though once involved, they might as well be kept on and posttested. This transforms the experiment into a three-group design. Finally, note that none of these procedures is necessary if $E$ (or $E + I_{EU}$) is so large as to be obviously real. The methods of obtaining estimates in the other designs are similar.

## Generalizations

In the preceding discussion, we have thought of $P$ as representing the effect of pretesting, $E$ the effect of the experimental stimulus, and $U$ the effect of uncontrolled events on the value of the dependent variable (e.g., reading speed) in an experiment. The equations apply more generally. $P$, $E$, and $U$ can be thought of as the effects of any three stimuli whatever on the dependent variable, except that $U$ must be a stimulus to which every group is exposed.

**Example 1.** It is suggested that keeping hens in a constantly illuminated environment will increase their egg production. An experiment is arranged to determine the effectiveness of a particular level of illumination in conjunction with the presence or absence of a certain diet supplement and of background music. Uncontrolled events may be neglected. The hens' present performance is known, so no pretesting is required. The experimenter can use design 2b, with $U$ representing the effect of the illumination, $P$ the effect of the diet supplement, and $E$ the effect of the music. Using assumed or previously determined values for $E$ and $P$, he can calculate $U$, $I_{PU}$, and $I_{EU}$ from the equations for design 2b.

**Example 2.** It is found that taking the usual pretest of reading speed (a timed reading) significantly increases students' reading speed. It is thought that another test, which appears to be a test of comprehension, will be more neutral. Design 2e is used, with $P$ standing for the effect of the first pretest and $E$ the effect of the second pretest on reading speed.

As in design 2b, pretests are often unnecessary if only differences between groups are needed, rather than absolute changes in scores for the groups separately. In this case, $P$ can represent the effect of a second experimental stimulus. It will then be necessary to subtract the equations for the experiment from one another so that differences between $d$'s occur rather than the unknown $d$'s themselves. These differences can then be replaced by the known differences in posttest scores.

We have been considering experimental stimuli which must be either present or absent, as opposed to stimuli which may be present at different levels. It is possible to let $P$ and $E$ represent two different levels of the same stimulus. Then no group can be subject to both $P$ and $E$, so only designs which do not use group 1 may be used.

More elaborate experiments than those we have discussed can be created, involving several experimental stimuli. If a group is pretested and exposed to experimental stimuli $E$, $F$, and $G$ then its equation is

$$d = P + U + E + F + G + 26 \text{ interaction terms} \qquad (9.24)$$

By choosing whether or not to expose a group to $P$, to $E$, to $F$, and to $G$, we obtain 16 different groups. With 16 groups, the number of possible four-group designs is 1,820. Adding additional stimuli creates an even more unmanageable situation.[19]

Some simplifications are possible. We have three suggestions: (1) Do no pretests. Then $P$ and all interactions involving $P$ can be deleted from all equations. They can also be deleted even if pretests are done, providing that the pretests and all their interactions are considered innocuous. (2) Try to refine environmental conditions to the point where uncontrolled events and their interactions can be neglected. Then $U$ and its interactions can be deleted. (3) Minimize the number of stimuli acting on each group. This greatly reduces the number of interaction terms in the equations. In more detail:

**1** If the method of dispensing with pretest scores entirely and using differences in posttest scores cannot be used, it may be desirable to create and

---

[19] These additional stimuli may be new kinds of stimuli or new levels of old stimuli. There are no interactions between different levels of the same kind of stimulus because the different levels never occur together.

pretest an extra group of sufficient size to yield a reliable assumed pretest score for all the experimental groups. If in addition the experimenter needs to know $P$, the impact of the pretest on the dependent variable, he should have two groups, of the form

$$P..UT \qquad d_1 = P + U + I_{PU} \qquad (9.25)$$
$$....UT \qquad d_2 = U \qquad (9.26)$$

and should not pretest any others. Then $d_1 - d_2 = P + I_{PU}$, and $P$ is found with one assumption (or $P + I_{PU}$ is found with none), and $P$ and its interactions do not occur in the remaining equations.

**2** Refining the environment to the point of effectively eliminating $U$ is, of course, the great virtue of the lab. Moving toward this goal in the field will challenge the researcher's ingenuity. He should first decide, however, that he *wants* to eliminate uncontrolled events. They may be a normal part of the environment to which he plans to generalize his findings, in which case his efforts will be aimed not at eliminating them but at obtaining them as accurately as possible, so that his value of $E + U + I_{EU}$ will be close to the natural environmental value. For example, he may be studying ways of increasing voter participation in large cities, and the uncontrolled factor of newspaper headlines may be a major factor in determining such participation. If he eliminates this uncontrolled event, his conclusions may be valid only during newspaper strikes.

**3** If the experimenter wants to determine an interaction, say, $I_{FG}$, then he must have a group in which both $F$ and $G$ are present. But if this interaction does not interest him, then if possible he should avoid groups in which both are present. In particular, he may wish to avoid groups which are subjected to an experimental stimulus and also pretested. (If the experimenter is interested in pretest-to-posttest difference scores for individuals, however, he will have to pretest.)

Let us now sum up the general principles followed in the preceding material. Once these are mastered, the investigator can handle more complex situations than those discussed.

**1** It is recognized that uncontrolled events may be present and may interact with other stimuli. $U$ is assumed to be negligible only by an explicit decision.

**2** It is recognized that a pretest may itself change behavior and that it often is better *not* to pretest (unless one wants to determine the effect of pretesting or obtain individual change scores).

**3** Once the direct effects are identified (including the pretest and uncontrolled events), one identifies all the possible groups he can create by varying the presence and absence of these quantities (except uncontrolled events).

The number of such groups will be two to a power equal to the number of manipulatable main effects. For example, in the model presented, $P$ and $E$ could be manipulated, so there were $2^2$, or four, possible groups. One can then, if the number of possibilities does not become too large, identify all possible designs based on these groups by taking them one at a time, two at a time, three at a time, and so forth, just as was done with the model. This pattern follows the binomial distribution, with $n$ equal to the number of groups, and $u$ varying from 1 to $n$. Note that with $n$ equal to 8 ($2^3$, produced by three manipulatable quantities) one can generate 255 designs containing from one to eight groups. Thus the situation rapidly gets out of hand. One cannot look at each design individually as we did in the model with only 15 designs. One must fall back on judgment and insight, but the following considerations will aid greatly:

($a$)  Decide precisely for which direct effects and interactions you want to find values. In general, the fewer values to be found, the smaller the number of experimental groups required.

($b$)  Judge carefully which of the unknowns you feel safe in assuming values for and what those values should be. Toward this end, exploit any related literature and expert opinion. A preliminary experiment may even be indicated. Remember especially that the more assumptions you can make, the fewer the number of groups needed, but that a design wisely chosen can often simply omit uninteresting quantities.

($c$)  List several candidate designs if you can. Analyze each rigorously and thoroughly. Write the formula for each group in each design, showing the quantities responsible for any difference between pretest and posttest. Work with the system of equations created by all groups taken at once in order to discover which assumptions are mathematically impermissible and to solve for each unknown. After this is done for all candidate designs, select the best one to minimize costs and risks involved in the assumptions.

For reference we list in Tables 9.3–9.11 the permissible sets of assumptions for the two-, three-, and four-group designs of Table 9.2 and the solutions of the equations using these assumptions. In each table, the sets of assumptions which leave $E$ to be empirically determined are listed above the line. We omit designs 2b and 2f because the equations are trivial. To simplify the presentation of the solutions, we introduce new variables $D_1$, $D_2$, $D_3$, and $D_4$. Consider case 1 of Table 9.11. The blanks in this line under $I_{EU}$, $I_{PU}$, and $I_{PEU}$ mean that these are the three unknowns whose values are being assumed in this case. Assume values for them. Now the known quantities are $d_1$, $d_2$, $d_3$, $d_4$, $I_{EU}$, $I_{PU}$, and $I_{PEU}$, and the unknowns are $U$, $E$, $P$, and $I_{PE}$. Rewrite the four equations in Table 9.11 so that the known quantities are on the left and the unknowns on the right, and introduce the $D$'s as follows:

$$D_1 = d_1 - I_{EU} - I_{PU} - I_{PEU} = P + E + U + I_{PE} \qquad (9.27)$$
$$D_2 = d_2 - I_{PU} \qquad\qquad\quad = P + U \qquad\qquad (9.28)$$
$$D_3 = d_3 - I_{EU} \qquad\qquad\quad = E + U \qquad\qquad (9.29)$$
$$D_4 = d_4 \qquad\qquad\qquad\quad\ = U \qquad\qquad\qquad (9.30)$$

Now $D_1$, $D_2$, $D_3$, and $D_4$ can be found at once, and in terms of them we find $U = D_4$, $E = D_3 - D_4$, $P = D_2 - D_4$, and $I_{PE} = D_1 - D_2 - D_3 + D_4$. Whenever all assumed values are zero, each $D$ reduces to the corresponding $d$. Note that the meanings of the symbols $D_1$ to $D_4$ change in every line as the quantities for which values are assumed change.

## *Examples*[20]

Two examples follow. In the first, all assumed values are zero, and each $D$ therefore reduces to the corresponding $d$. In the second example, nonzero assumptions are used in order to illustrate computation of the $D$'s.

Suppose the impact of a speed-reading course is to be measured. After appropriate forethought the investigator decides that uncontrolled events ($U$) will have negligible influence and that, furthermore, he can neglect all interactions involving $U$.[21] This provides the four zero assumptions $U = I_{PU} = I_{EU} = I_{PEU} = 0$. The investigator is, of course, interested in measuring $E$, and he would also like to obtain measures for $P$ and $I_{PE}$. He therefore selects design 3a, Table 9.7, line 5.

Subjects are randomly divided into three groups. Pretests of groups 1 and 2 show mean reading speeds of 245 and 255 words per minute, respectively. The grand mean of 250 words per minute becomes the inferred pretest score of group 3. The 95 percent confidence limits for this mean are, say, $250 \pm 20$, or 230 and 270 words. The speed-reading course is then administered. Posttest scores of the three groups are 765, 295, and 650, respectively, giving $d_1 = 520$, $d_2 = 40$, and $d_3 = 400 \pm 20$.

The three unknowns $P$, $E$, and $I_{PE}$ are now found by reference to Table 9.7, line 5. Since only zero assumptions were used, the large $D$'s can simply be replaced with the small $d$'s. Thus $P = d_2 = 40$, $E = d_3 = 400 \pm 20$, and $I_{PE} = d_1 - d_2 - d_3 = 80 \pm 20$.

The investigator thus calculates that his experimental stimulus, the speed-

---

[20] Entire section, and Tables 9.3–9.11, are quoted from Ross and Smith (40). Used by permission.

[21] Note that when a main effect is *present but has no effect on the dependent variable*, it may nevertheless interact with other main effects. If the main effect is *totally absent* (as $P$ is absent when no pretest is done), however, it cannot interact with anything else; then all interactions involving that factor must be zero (e.g., $I_{PE}$, $I_{PU}$, and $I_{PEU}$). The two cases are quite different but easily confused.

reading course, produced an average gain of 400 words per minute. The pretest experience by itself ($P$) produced a separate gain of 40 words per minute, most probably through the aroused interest and sustained vigor that learning one's reading speed can create. Finally, $I_{PE}$ (the interaction between $P$ and $E$) produced a separate gain of 80 words per minute. The investigator reasons that the pretest experience sensitizes subjects to the reading program and causes them to react to it differently than had they not been pretested. This is in addition to the independent effect of the pretest on reading speed.

Now consider an example using nonzero assumptions. Suppose the experiment is again concerned with a speed-reading course. After appropriate advance study the four-group design is selected (Table 9.11, line 4). From other research these assumed values are chosen:

$$P = 15 \text{ words per minute}$$
$$I_{PE} = 20 \text{ words per minute}$$
$$I_{EU} = -25 \text{ words per minute}$$

After the experiment is executed, the $d$'s are calculated in the same manner as before, with the results that

$$
\begin{array}{ll}
d_1 = 615 & d_3 = 510 \pm 25 \\
d_2 = \phantom{0}70 & d_4 = \phantom{0}40 \pm 25
\end{array}
\tag{9.31}
$$

Each of the four $D$'s equals the counterpart $d$, minus all assumed quantities in the formula for that $d$. We obtain

$$
\begin{array}{lll}
D_1 = 615 - 15 - 20 + 25 & = 605 \\
D_2 = \phantom{0}70 - 15 & = \phantom{0}55 \\
D_3 = 510 \pm 25 + 25 & = 535 \pm 25 \\
D_4 = \phantom{0}40 \pm 25 & = \phantom{0}40 \pm 25
\end{array}
\tag{9.32}
$$

Line 4, Table 9.11, gives the values of the unknowns:

$$
\begin{array}{lll}
U = D_4 & = \phantom{0}40 \pm 25 \\
E = D_3 - D_4 & = 495 \pm 50 \\
I_{PU} = D_2 - D_4 & = \phantom{0}15 \pm 25 \\
I_{PEU} = D_1 - D_2 - D_3 + D_4 = & \phantom{0}55 \pm 50
\end{array}
\tag{9.33}
$$

As before, this gives the impact of each quantity in words per minute gained.

## 9.6 CLASSIC DESIGNS

We now take up a somewhat different approach to experimental designs. This is intended to introduce the classic designs developed in agriculture, genetics, and biology and already made a part of standard graduate training in psychology.

Under the proper conditions designs of this kind are very powerful and useful. Because innumerable varieties and adaptations of them exist, they can serve a wide range of research aims. The researcher who is conversant with them has access to some of the best investigatory tools offered by science. We are indebted for their invention mainly to R. A. Fisher and his disciple F. Yates. The relevant materials are definitively presented in several sources (17,18,24,30,48).

These designs, in general, possess the following characteristics, not all of which are favorable.

**1** No pretests are done.[22]

**2** Therefore, the estimate of the standard deviation in each experimental group (cell) must be based fundamentally on posttest scores. This is especially important, because all F tests, t tests, and confidence intervals require an accurate estimate of the within-cell variation *prior* to the experiment. When posttest scores are used without qualification, one assumes that the experiment does not affect the within-cell standard deviation, though it may change the cell mean. Unless the experiment is arranged to permit certain special analyses, the assumption is that a stimulus pushes all subjects in the same direction by roughly the same amount, which leaves their dispersion unchanged. This is by no means a safe assumption in psychological and sociological matters. Often, subjects respond to a stimulus by hyperactivity or hypoactivity or by some other kind of opposite responses. If, for example, a stimulus is an extremist speech on socialism, with listener agreement as the dependent variable, responses may polarize sharply, producing an enormous standard deviation within the group (cell).

**3** $U$ (uncontrolled events) and its interactions are virtually ignored by being subsumed under other quantities. The symbol $E$ now includes what we previously designated as $E + I_{EU}$. Since the classic designs often include several cells, we may think of the stimuli as $E_1$, $E_2$, $E_3$, etc. $U$ itself is sometimes represented by the posttest mean of the group (cell) receiving no stimulus, when such a group is part of the experiment. Otherwise, $U$ may go unmentioned and will actually be one component responsible for the posttest mean of each cell. This is not a serious difficulty, though, because the analysis typically works on differences between cell means, and $U$ cancels out in the subtractions.

There are, of course, pros and cons to the disappearance of separate terms for $U$ and its interactions. On the favorable side, we have already

---

[22] Campbell notes (12, p. 304) that Fisher did not totally ignore pretests. In the first edition (1953) of *The Design of Experiments*, p. 176, Fisher argued that in agriculture their value did not justify their use.

mentioned that it is empirically impossible to separate the effects of $E$ and $I_{EU}$, and in the context which the investigator accepts for any particular experiment, all cells are equally subject to $U$. Why not, then, use a single symbol? For the pair, all we can ever get empirically is the sum anyway. A single symbol permits simplified formulas, which are in common use throughout the immense literature on classic designs. Besides, in the lab, or by careful planning in the field, we may avoid unusual disturbances, so that the summed figure faithfully indicates how the treatments perform against a normal backdrop of conditions and concurrent influences. And this is exactly what we want, at least for practical purposes.

And yet, to be conceptually tidy, we should identify all components of variation. Certainly, one should fully display all symbols if he wishes to make separate estimates for all components. This will often be the case in the field, where the dangerous clutter of uncontrolled events needs constant attention. Two field experiments done on similar subjects and using similar procedures, but differing in their settings, may disagree in results because of $U$ and its interactions. In fact, these components may be necessary to explain any differences between the two $E$ values.

We have simplified the above discussion by letting $E$ refer to a typical cell in a design. It should be recognized of course that one design may contain many cells. The above comments apply to each such cell.

In the brief introduction to classic designs below, general usage is followed by ignoring $U$ and its interactions. This is done partly because it is so easy to transfer back into the more complete set of symbols: merely replace the symbol for the main effect of any cell (e.g., $E$) by $E + I_{EU}$, and replace the symbol for any interactive effect (e.g., $I_{E_1 E_2}$) by that symbol plus the symbol for the next higher-order interaction with $U$ (e.g., $I_{E_1 E_2} + I_{E_1 E_2 U}$). For every cell, $U$ must be added to the list of components responsible for posttest scores.

## An Overview of Some Common Designs

It is more important to set forth the outstanding features separating the major types of designs than to give each design in detail. For a first acquaintance with the literature on classic designs it is best to consult only a few sources; otherwise one's effort is dissipated in learning different symbols and organization of material. The discussion below, therefore, is based almost entirely on the standard text by Cochran and Cox (17) for designs and on Winer's definitive work (48) for statistical aspects. A simpler introduction to the field is Lindquist (30), which has the virtue of illustrations taken from human behavior, not agriculture and biology. The reader searching for additional detail will find it easiest to consult these authorities.

One change in terminology is necessary for the classic designs. An independent variable is called a *factor*. A factor may have several categories, or treatments. Sometimes "treatments" refers to all the categories of several factors.

## The Single-factor Design

The simplest and sometimes the best design pools all subjects and then by a random procedure assigns them to the various treatments. If extra reliability on the effect of selected treatments is needed, the number of subjects in those cells may, of course, be easily enlarged without compromising randomness. Inequalities among cell sizes affect the statistical analysis, however (48, pp. 96ff.), and it is helpful to keep them equal. This design maximizes the number of degrees of freedom ($df = t - 1$, where $t$ is the number of treatments), since it puts the fewest constraints possible on the assignment of subjects to treatments. This, of course, is a highly desirable feature; but it does not permit the division of subjects into homogeneous subgroupings. In the statistical analysis, a straightforward analysis of variance is applied, using a t test for two cells or an F test for three or more cells. In the latter case, if the overall comparison turns out to be significant, one may wish to decide whether a particular two of the several treatments differ significantly in their effects. This is by no means a simple task, for usually the data are testing a hypothesis suggested by the selfsame data (47, p. 105). One is often tempted to fix on whatever pair of treatment means happens to differ most. This capitalizes on chance, and it would be fallacious to use an ordinary t test. The question no longer concerns the probability that two samples drawn from the same population will differ by a preset amount, but rather the probability that of all the pairs drawn,[23] the members of at least one pair will differ by that amount. This is a considerably higher probability and will occur by chance more frequently. [Procedures for conducting these a posteriori tests are thoroughly discussed by Winer (48, pp. 65ff. and 85ff.).] All findings are tentative, however, and ideally will be tested deliberately in a new experiment planned specifically for that purpose (47, p. 105).

## The Single-factor Design with Blocks

A block is simply a homogeneous group of subjects. Instead of pooling all subjects before randomizing, divide them into a number of homogeneous groups. The entire experiment is then repeated in each of these groups. Sometimes the results are similar in all the groups. This is neat, and makes it easier to state conclusions. But sometimes the results contradict one another, and if all subjects had been pooled into a single experiment, the trends might have canceled out, leading to the appearance of no trend at all. It

---

[23] There will be $[n(n-1)]/2$ pairs, where $n$ is the number of treatments.

may be wise to put males into one block and females into another, or the married into one and the unmarried into another. The point is to break the overall group of subjects into smaller, homogeneous groups, and then to repeat the entire experiment within each group. Within each block, variation is less in confounding property variables, permitting a clear view of treatment effects. This is excellent experimental strategy, providing the blocks do indeed meaningfully purify the material. If they are irrelevant to the

TABLE 9.12

*a. Single-factor design*

Factor 1
Treatments 1–$n$

1  2  3  4 . . . $n$

| | | | | |
|---|---|---|---|---|

*b. Single-factor design with blocks*

Factor 1
Treatments 1–$n$

| Blocks | 1 | 2 | 3 | 4 . . . $n$ |
|---|---|---|---|---|
| $a$ | | | | |
| $b$ | | | | |
| $c$ | | | | |
| $d$ | | | | |
| . | | | | |
| . | | | | |
| . | | | | |

*c. Full factorial*

Factor 3

| Treat-ments I–IV | Factors 1 and 2 Treatments 1–2; A–C | | | | | |
|---|---|---|---|---|---|---|
| | 1 | | | 2 | | |
| | A | B | C | A | B | C |
| I | | | | | | |
| II | | | | | | |
| III | | | | | | |
| IV | | | | | | |

*d. Multiple-factor design with blocks*

Factors 1 and 2
Treatments 1–3; A–B

| Blocks | 1 | | 2 | | 3 | |
|---|---|---|---|---|---|---|
| | A | B | A | B | A | B |
| $a$ | | | | | | |
| $b$ | | | | | | |
| $c$ | | | | | | |
| $d$ | | | | | | |
| . | | | | | | |
| . | | | | | | |
| . | | | | | | |

*e. Latin Square*

| Row effects | Column effects | | | |
|---|---|---|---|---|
| | 1 | 2 | 3 | 4 |
| I | A | B | C | D |
| II | B | C | D | A |
| III | C | D | A | B |
| IV | D | A | B | C |

criterion, then the loss of degrees of freedom[24] in this design makes it inferior to the single-factor design.

Perhaps the easiest way to apply the block concept in sociology is to think of city blocks. Usually the people living within a single block are more homogeneous than are people across the entire city. This is generally true for many socioeconomic indicators, race, nationality, etc. Imagine a field experiment which deals with housewives as units. Replicating the entire experiment within one block, then another, etc., reduces confounding differences among subjects. It is also a geographically convenient plan.

Experimental blocks may be general in nature, presenting homogeneity on many variables (families, census tracts, neighborhoods), or they may be deliberately created to achieve homogeneity on a special variable. The latter is often called *matching,* as when subjects are classed together by IQ. Such a block variable may be an interesting *factor,* too. Suppose, e.g., that an experiment is to be done on school children, and each school is a block. (In Table 9.12, panel *b,* each row would be one school). In the city, the schools would vary in the economic level of their neighborhood, and for some investigations this would be of interest in its own right. What distinguishes a block variable from a factor is that the block variable is not itself of interest—it is only a way to purify the experimental material.

When does it pay to use blocks instead of simple random assignment (design *a,* the single-factor design)? Using blocks *always* sacrifices degrees of freedom (undesirable), and *sometimes* reduces error variance (desirable). In general, how can we tell whether or not any design with fewer degrees of freedom justifies itself by sufficient reduction in error variance? Cochran and Cox review this question (17, p. 32), showing that there is no exact answer. But Table 9.13 is a general guide:

TABLE 9.13   Estimated Variances Which Provide Equal Amounts of Information

| Number of error degrees of freedom (n) | | | | | | | |
|---|---|---|---|---|---|---|---|
| 1 | 2 | 3 | 4 | 5 | 6 | 7 | 8 |
| 0.500 | 0.600 | 0.667 | 0.714 | 0.750 | 0.778 | 0.800 | 0.818 |

| Number of error degrees of freedom (n) | | | | | | | |
|---|---|---|---|---|---|---|---|
| 9 | 10 | 11 | 12 | 15 | 20 | 30 | ∞ |
| 0.833 | 0.846 | 0.857 | 0.867 | 0.889 | 0.913 | 0.939 | 1.000 |

Source: Fisher (24).

[24] $df = rt - 1$, where $t$ is the number of treatments and $r$ is the number of replications or blocks. Cochran and Cox (17, p. 107ff.) illustrate the statistical analysis.

The standard of comparison is at the extreme right, which assumes an infinite number of degrees of freedom and variance of 1. Each of the two or more designs under consideration may be compared with this standard. Suppose one of them has an error *df* equal to 5 and the other has a *df* equal to 10. Then, to be as good as the standard, the first design must have a variance only 0.750 as great as the imaginary standard design; the second one must have a variance 0.846 as great as the same standard. Thus the first design is superior to the second only if its error variance is less than 0.750/0.846 times the error variance of the second. We already knew that the first design, with fewer degrees of freedom, would have to have less error variance to be as good as the second. This procedure gauges how much less. For precise work, it requires knowledge of the two error variances, something the researcher may not know in advance. In such a case he must rely on the literature and on experience. Lacking either, he may still use the above table to see whether the design with fewer *df* must produce a large or small reduction in variance to be worthwhile.

**Incomplete blocks.** A special-purpose tool of considerable importance is the incomplete block design, meaning that only some of the treatments are used in each block. Thus one does not need as many subjects per block, which is especially handy when the blocks most conveniently available contain fewer subjects than there are treatments. A good example is the situation where human twins are used (to control numerous hereditary and environmental differences) in an experiment with three treatments. Or one may wish to apply five treatments to siblings. Since five-child families may not be plentiful, one could use three-child groups in the incomplete block design. See Cochran and Cox (17, p. 181 and chap. 9) for an authoritative treatment; also see Winer (48, p. 379).

## Full Factorial

Here, unlike the block designs, all dimensions are factors. Superficially, in Table 9.12 the full factorial design looks like the single-factor design with blocks, and indeed, the formats are similar. To grasp the difference, remember that everything turns on the experimenter's aims. The block variable is merely a tactic of purification, the better to observe the really important effects. Though it produces an arrangement on paper like that of a factorial, the questions being asked are different. In the full factorial design, every dimension is a variable of substantive interest. The statistical analysis also proceeds differently, since block effects are not of interest.

The factorial design contains several single-factor designs, one in every row and in every column. In addition, the marginal (total) row is a single-factor design containing all the subjects. So is the marginal (total) column.

But tying the row design and column design together by crossing them yields great dividends.   There are, of course, administrative efficiencies: every subject does double duty, serving in a row design as well as in a column design, and many single-factor designs are executed all at once.   But more valuable, one can observe the row factor effects over and over again *at varying levels of the column factor* (and vice versa).   This yields great versatility for generalizing, since one knows each factor's behavior over a greater range of conditions.   Fortunately, this still lets each main effect be estimated as precisely as though the entire experiment were devoted to it alone.   Finally, interaction effects among all factors will be exposed in a factorial design, but never in separate single-factor designs.   This wholly distinct aspect is indispensable to understanding many phenomena.

The factorial design has unusual strengths.   Yet it easily becomes a major undertaking, since the number of cells mounts so rapidly with the addition of more factors and levels of factors.   For what purposes is the factorial design best fitted?   Cochran and Cox (17, p. 152) offer a summary: [25]

1. In exploratory work where the object is to determine quickly the effects of each of a number of factors over a specified range.

2. In investigations of the interactions among the effects of several factors.   From their nature, interactions cannot be studied without testing *some* of the combinations formed from the different factors.   Frequently, information is best obtained by testing all combinations.

3. In experiments designed to lead to recommendations that must apply over a wide range of conditions.   Subsidiary factors may be brought into an experiment so as to test the principal factors under a variety of conditions similar to those that will be encountered in the population to which recommendations are to apply.

On the other hand, if considerable information has accumulated, or if the object of the investigation is specialized, it may be more profitable to conduct intensive work on a single factor or on a few combinations of factors.   For instance, some investigations are directed towards finding the combination of the levels of the factors that will produce a maximum response. . . .   A well-planned series of single-factor experiments will often reach the maximum more quickly than a single large factorial experiment.   An alternative strategy for this problem . . . does use experiments in which all the factors appear, but for studying the nature of the response in the neighborhood of the maximum [there are] special designs. . . .

Statistical analysis is introduced particularly well in Winer (48, pp. 141–143) and in Cochran and Cox (17, pp. 148ff.).

**Factorial designs with confounding.**   The full factorial design just discussed incorporates every possible combination of treatments.   Each level of

---

[25] Quoted by courtesy of John Wiley & Sons, Inc.

each factor is combined with every level of every other factor. While this is admirably thorough, it can also be quite wasteful. One may have no interest in certain combinations of treatments and, in addition, may not need them for the statistical analysis. Omitting such cells reduces costs.

A great variety of specialized factorial designs are available in which some cells are empty. Such designs are based on the principle of *confounding*, a term which nicely reflects the inevitable drawback accompanying the reduced costs. Because some cells are not used, a complete statistical analysis is impossible. Certain effects will always be confounded with each other. One can, however, choose which effects these will be. Usually, it does no harm to confound two or more uninteresting effects, since there is no reason to separate them anyway. Also, if the investigator is sure that one effect is zero, he may confound it with a second effect, measuring the second effect by the sum. Full discussions are found in Cochran and Cox (17) and in Winer (48).

## Multiple-factor Design with Blocks

This design is exactly like the single-factor design with blocks, except that two or more factors are investigated. As Table 9.12 shows, the option of a block variable is retained. This points up the way designs may be pyramided. Note that a full factorial design (two factors) is contained within every block in design *d* of Table 9.12. In turn, each factorial design is built up from crossed single-factor designs. Thus we have single-factor designs within factorial designs within blocks. This is only the beginning of possible elaborations, for each cell can always contain another design, producing an infinite regression. Empty cells, if any, can be chosen by either random or systematic procedures, and can be planned to highlight efficiently almost any aspect of the analysis one prefers. According to the evolving aims of the investigator as he proceeds through the analysis, a block variable may become a factor, and vice versa. Specialized significance tests may be used at appropriate points in the analysis to decide whether to omit or include lengthy subanalyses on higher-order interactions. There are many other kinds of designs, such as lattice designs, which may be further classified as balanced, partially balanced, and cubic. This perhaps indicates the versatility and ramifications of the small number of simple designs under discussion.

One should note in Table 9.12 that design *d* is identical in format to design *c*. The only difference is in the view taken toward the rows: if they are nothing more than a device for homogenizing the subjects, they constitute a block variable. If, however, they are of causal interest, they constitute a factor and should be recognized in the statistical analysis. They are discussed and illustrated in Cochran and Cox (17, pp. 175ff.).

## Latin and Greco-Latin Squares

Despite their fancy names, these designs are not difficult. They are simply devices for controlling two or three confounding factors in an experiment. They do this by ensuring that each of the confounding factors acts with equal strength on every treatment. Their limitation is that they fail to prevent the confounding factors from acting in *unlike combinations* on the various treatments. When this happens, their net impacts differ, undermining the attempt at control.

A Latin Square may be regarded as a double grouping and a Greco-Latin Square as a triple grouping. This is best understood after we explain a single grouping (Table 9.14). Consider an experiment where a single factor has three treatments, which are applied to nine subjects. The factor might be three propaganda films directed at army privates. To avoid large differences among subjects, the investigator divides the subjects into three homogeneous groups (rows) by education, and runs the experiment separately within each. That is, within each row, each of the three treatments, *A, B,* and *C,* is applied to one subject. The separation by rows protects against one confounding variable.

The double grouping, or Latin Square, is a specialized way of protecting against a second confounding variable. It simply adds another grouping, which adds more cells to the design, but the number of subjects is not increased. This means that some cells must now be empty. Table 9.15 shows a $3 \times 3$ Latin Square in two different formats, with the empty cells exposed in the lower version. *A, B,* and *C* denote the treatments, the three propaganda films, as before. There are two confounding factors, with three categories each, I, II, III and 1, 2, 3, which are education as before and, let's say, years of service in the army. The upper format is the standard arrangement and is more concise. The lower one conforms to the conventional way of cross-classifying for three variables and shows frequencies in the cells. (We

TABLE 9.14

| Row | | | |
|-----|---|---|---|
| I   | A | B | C |
| II  | A | B | C |
| III | A | B | C |

Note: Each treatment is applied to one subject in each row. The three subjects in a row are homogeneous; the rows are heterogeneous when compared with one another.

assume that only one subject falls into each of the nine cells used in the design, though it is quite acceptable to have *n* subjects per cell.) The lower format reveals the Latin Square's main features:

**1** Each treatment appears exactly once in every row and in every column.

**2** Each row (or each column), taken by itself, repeats the entire series of treatments, but confounds each treatment with a different column (or row).

**3** The number of rows, number of columns, and number of treatments are all identical. In many cases, the number of subjects will be the same. Finding variables that meet this restriction is often difficult.

**4** Every time a treatment occurs, it does so under a different row-column combination (cell), and no row-column combination is brought to bear on more than a single treatment. (Treatment *B*, for example, uniquely occurs in row II-column 1, row I-column 2, row III-column 3.)

These features produce both the strength and weakness of a Latin Square. In one sense, any row influence on the three treatments cancels out, since each row affects the action of each treatment exactly once. Or if one thinks only of the column influences, they, too, cancel out in the sense that each column affects each treatment exactly once. But the three actions of each treatment occur under a unique set of three row-column combinations (cells). Treatment *A* occurs in three different cells from either treatment *B* or treatment *C*. Consequently, there is no way to disentangle the impact of treatment *A* from the unique impact, if any, of its three cells.

The three cells may possess no unique impact, in the sense that one can interchange the letters *A, B,* and *C* in the design and get identical results. If this is so, we say the row-column effects are merely *additive,* that they do not *interact.*[26] If additive, the Latin Square controls effects of the row and column factors very efficiently; note that the investigator needs no subjects whatever in 18 of the 27 cells shown in Table 9.15, bottom panel. But if interactions are present, the Latin Square may lead one astray. The question is particularly important because the Latin Square offers little if any way to detect interactions if they are indeed present. By and large it assumes their absence. Complex refinements permit the partial study of interactions, but they are treacherous unless one has expert guidance [e.g., see Winer (48, pp. 521 and 527ff.)].

All the above comments on strengths and weaknesses of the Latin Square apply directly to the Greco-Latin Square, or triple grouping. It is a way

---

[26] When effects are additive, the impact of a row is the same regardless of which column it is combined with, and vice versa. Latin Squares assume this to be the case. But when effects interact, a row's impact will change, depending on which column it is combined with, and vice versa. A Latin Square may lead to the wrong conclusions when this occurs.

TABLE 9.15

| Row influence | Column influence 1 | 2 | 3 | |
|---|---|---|---|---|
| I | A | B | C | (Cell letters denote treatments) |
| II | B | C | A | |
| III | C | A | B | |

|  | Column influence | | | | | | | | |
|---|---|---|---|---|---|---|---|---|---|
|  | 1 Treatment | | | 2 Treatment | | | 3 Treatment | | |
| Row influence | A | B. | C | A | B | C | A | B | C |
| I | X | | | | X | | | | X |
| II | | X | | | | X | X | | |
| III | | | X | X | | | | X | |

Note: The two formats give identical information. The upper one is the customary Latin Square format, but the lower one may be clearer. It is the conventional format for three variables where frequencies appear in the cells. It exposes more clearly the unused cells and shows how the Latin Square is a partial factorial design. If all cells were filled, it would be a full factorial design. The upper format assumes one subject per cell unless otherwise specified.

of protecting against a third confounding variable. Adding to the two control groupings of the Latin Square, it places the same number of subjects into a simultaneous third grouping, or block variable, which might be type of duty assignment for the soldiers. One may think of this as simply arranging for each treatment to appear once in a row variable, once in a column variable, and once in a layer variable. The level of the layer variable is shown by the subscript in Table 9.16. The arrangement given is only one of many that would satisfy the requirements of the Greco-Latin Square.

It is easy to generate more squares from any given square (48, pp. 516–519). One way is to rotate the symbols in each row to the right, moving the rightmost symbol to the left end. The same may be done, quite independently, for columns. Or one may simply interchange rows or columns. Winer presents a concise and interesting summary of devices for obtaining many varieties in these squares. He points out that in 6 × 6 Latin Squares there are 812,851,200 possible varieties. With so many arrangements to choose

TABLE 9.16

| $A_3$ | $B_1$ | $C_2$ |
|-------|-------|-------|
| $B_2$ | $C_3$ | $A_1$ |
| $C_1$ | $A_2$ | $B_3$ |

Note: An alternative format can be written, which corresponds to the lower panel of Table 9.15, but with one added dimension.

from, one must avoid any kind of bias in the choice. A random selection may readily be made by reference to Fisher and Yates (25) or Cochran and Cox (17).

We shall not discuss any complexities beyond the Greco-Latin Square. One could, of course, go to quadruple groupings and beyond, but in practice even triple groupings are rare. The reason for this is the main practical shortcoming of these squares—that the number of treatments and the number of levels in each block variable must all be identical. This is very hard to arrange in most actual research. It is easier if all control variables are forcing rather than property variables, since the investigator can manipulate forcing variables more easily, and if they are continuous, which lets the experimenter select any number of values he pleases. For example, with three treatments, if time strongly affects the treatments' action, one could create a $3 \times 3 \times 3 \times 3$ Greco-Latin Square where the three control variables were time of day (e.g., 10 A.M., 3 P.M., 8 P.M.), day of the week (Monday, Wednesday, Friday), and time of the month (first third, middle third, last third). There would be nine subjects, and each treatment would be applied to three of these subjects.

Every time one adds a control variable, whether through a single, double, or triple grouping, one loses degrees of freedom. The reduction in the error term must be sufficient to justify this, or else the additional grouping is a net loss.

## 9.7 CONCLUSION

Some of the major advantages and disadvantages of alternative experimental designs have been discussed in this chapter. It should not be overlooked, however, that certain important practical considerations will also influence the researcher's choice of design. This is particularly true where the experimenter has less than complete control over the assignment of subjects to treatments or over the number and types of treatment groups. It is not possible to design a strategy that will always be appropriate. The investigator is by necessity required to combine a knowledge of principles with practical experience and sound judgment.

Sources of error introduced in the course of an experiment have been dealt with abstractly in this chapter and are summarized in the $U$ term in the equations. Since some of the interactions involving these uncontrolled events will inevitably be confounded with the effects of the experimental variable, it becomes essential that the effects of uncontrolled events be reduced to a minimum. The next chapter, by James Wiggins, is devoted primarily to a discussion of possible sources of experimental error and how such error may be reduced.

## REFERENCES

1 American Psychological Association: "Ethical Standards in Research," in *Ethical Standards of Psychologists* (Washington, D.C., 1953), pp. 113–124.

2 Anderson, R. L., and T. A. Bancroft: *Statistical Theory in Research* (New York: McGraw-Hill, 1952).

3 Baker, Benjamin M., et al.: "The National Diet-Heart Study," *The Journal of The American Medical Association,* 185 (July 13, 1963), 105–106.

4 Bavelas, A.: "Communication Patterns in Task-oriented Groups," in D. Cartwright and A. Zander (Eds.), *Group Dynamics: Research and Theory* (New York: Harper & Row, 1953).

5 Berelson, Bernard (Ed.): *Studies in Family Planning* (New York: Population Council, Inc., 1964).

6 Berelson, Bernard, and Ronald Freedman: "A Study in Fertility Control," *Scientific American,* 210 (May, 1964), 3–11.

7 Blalock, Hubert M.: *Causal Inferences in Nonexperimental Research* (Chapel Hill, N.C.: University of North Carolina Press, 1961).

8 Bogue, Donald J.: "Experiments in the Use of Mass Communication and Motivation to Speed Adoption of Birth Control in High Fertility Populations." Paper discussed at the Annual Meeting of the Sociological Research Association, Washington, D.C., 1962.

9 Bogue, Donald J., and James A. Palmore, Jr.: "The Chicago Fertility Control Experiments: Some Preliminary Findings." Paper prepared for the Epidemiology and Population Dynamics section, Annual Meeting of the American Public Health Association, 1964.

10 Brunswik, E.: *Perception and the Representative Design of Psychological Experiments* (Berkeley, Calif: University of California Press, 1956).

11 Brunswik, E.: "Representative Design and Probabilistic Theory in a Functional Psychology," *Psychological Review,* 62 (1955), 193–217.

12 Campbell, Donald T.: "Factors Relevant to the Validity of Experiments in Social Settings," *Psychological Bulletin*, 54 (1957), 297–312.

13 Campbell, Donald T.: "On the Possibility of Experimenting with the 'Bandwagon' Effect," *International Journal of Opinion Attitude Research*, 5 (1951), 251–260.

14 Campbell, Donald T.: "Quasi-experimental Designs," in David L. Sills (Ed.), *International Encyclopedia of the Social Sciences* (New York: Macmillan, Free Press, and Crowell-Collier, in press).

15 Campbell, Donald T., and Keith N. Clayton: "Avoiding Regression Effects in Panel Studies of Communication Impact," *Studies in Public Communication*, no. 3 (1961), 99–118.

16 Cannell, Charles F., and Morris Axelrod: "A Study of Special Purpose Medical-history Techniques," *Health Statistics from the U.S. National Health Survey*, ser. D, no. 1, Public Health Service Publication no. 584-D1, 1960.

17 Cochran, William G., and Gertrude M. Cox: *Experimental Designs*, 2d ed. (New York: Wiley, 1957).

18 Cox, D. R.: *Planning of Experiments* (New York: Wiley, 1958).

19 Deasy, Leila C.: "Socio-economic Status and Participation in the Poliomyelitis Vaccine Trial," *American Sociological Review*, 21 (1956), 185–191.

20 Dittes, J. E.: "Effect of Changes in Self-esteem upon Impulsiveness and Deliberation in Making Judgments," *Journal of Abnormal and Social Psychology*, 58 (1959), 348–356.

21 Dittes, J. E.: "Impulsive Closure as Reaction to Failure-induced Threat," *Journal of Abnormal and Social Psychology*, 63 (1961), 562–569.

22 Dodd, Stuart C.: *A Controlled Experiment on Rural Hygiene in Syria* (Beirut, Lebanon: American Press, 1934).

23 Festinger, Leon, and Daniel Katz (Eds.): *Research Methods in the Behavioral Sciences* (New York: Holt, 1953).

24 Fisher, R. A.: *The Design of Experiments*, 7th ed. (New York: Hafner, 1960).

25 Fisher, R. A., and F. Yates: *Statistical Tables for Biological, Agricultural, and Medical Research*, 4th ed. (London: Oliver & Boyd, 1953).

26 Gosnell, H. F.: *Getting Out the Vote: An Experiment in the Stimulation of Voting* (Chicago: University of Chicago Press, 1927).

27 Jolliffe, Norman, S. H. Rinzler, and Morton Archer: "Anti-coronary Club: Including a Discussion of the Effects of a Prudent Diet on the Serum Cholesterol Level of Middle-aged Men," *American Journal of Clinical Nutrition*, 7 (1959), 451–462.

28 Kelman, Herbert: "The Human Use of Human Subjects." Paper read at the American Psychological Association meetings, September, 1965.

29 Kronick, Jane C.: "Social Class Variation in Family Response to

a Stroke and Patient Recovery." Paper read at the Eastern Sociological Society meetings, Philadelphia, April, 1962.

30 Lindquist, E. F.: *Design and Analysis of Experiments in Psychology and Education* (Boston: Houghton Mifflin, 1953).

31 Miller, Delbert C.: *Handbook of Research Design and Social Measurement* (New York: McKay, 1964).

32 Moore, Omar K.: *Autotelic Responsive Environments and Exceptional Children* (Hamden, Conn.: Responsive Environment Foundation, 1963).

33 Morse, N., and E. Reimer: "The Experimental Change of a Major Organizational Variable," *Journal of Abnormal and Social Psychology,* **52** (1956), 120–129.

34 O'Rourke, John F.: "Field and Laboratory: The Decision-making Behavior of Family Groups in Two Experimental Conditions," *Sociometry,* **26** (1963), 422–435.

35 Orne, Martin: "On the Social Psychology of the Psychological Experiment: With Particular Reference to Demand Characteristics and Applications," *American Psychologist,* **17** (1962), 776–783.

36 Postman, Leo, and Edward C. Tolman: "Brunswik's Probabilistic Functionalism," in S. Koch (Ed.), *Psychology: The Study of a Science* (New York: McGraw-Hill, 1958), vol. I.

37 Riley, Matilda White: *Sociological Research: I. A Case Approach* (New York: Harcourt, Brace & World, 1963).

38 Roethlisberger, F. J., and W. J. Dickson: *Management and the Worker* (Cambridge, Mass.: Harvard, 1939).

39 Rosenthal, R.: "The Effect of the Experimenter on the Results in Psychological Research," in B. Mahr (Ed.), *Progress in Experimental Personality Research* (New York, Academic, 1964), Vol. I.

40 Ross, John A., and Perry Smith: "Experimental Designs of the Single-stimulus, All-or-nothing Type," *American Sociological Review,* **30** (1965), 68–80.

41 Schwartz, R. D., and J. H. Skolnick: "Two Studies of Legal Stigma," *Social Problems,* **10** (1962), 133–142.

42 Seashore, Stanley E.: "Field Experiments with Formal Organizations," *Human Organization,* **23** (1964), 164–170.

43 Selltiz, Claire, M. Jahoda, M. Deutsch, and S. W. Cook: *Research Methods in Social Relations* (New York: Holt, 1959).

44 Sherif, Muzafer: "Experiments in Group Conflict," *Scientific American,* **195** (1956), 54–58.

45 Skinner, B. F.: "A Case History in Scientific Method," *American Psychologist,* **11** (1956), 221–233.

46 Solomon, R. L.: "Extension of Control Group Design," *Psychological Bulletin,* **46** (1949), 137–150.

47 Tate, Merle, W., and Richard C. Clelland: *Nonparametric and Short-*

*cut Statistics in the Social, Biological, and Medical Sciences* (Danville, Ill.: Interstate Printers and Publishers, 1957).

48 Winer, B. J.: *Statistical Principles in Experimental Design* (New York: McGraw-Hill, 1962).

49 Yang, J. M., S. Bang, M. H. Kim, and M. G. Lee: "Fertility and Family Planning in Rural Korea," *Population Studies,* 28 (March, 1965), 237–250.

50 Zelditch, Morris, Jr., and T. K. Hopkins: "Laboratory Experiments with Organizations," in Amitai Etzioni (Ed.), *Complex Organizations: A Sociological Reader* (New York: Holt, 1961).

# CHAPTER 10

# Hypothesis Validity and Experimental Laboratory Methods

JAMES A. WIGGINS

Let us begin with an assumption: *the probability that one dependent variable* (or variation thereof) *has multiple causes* (independent variables) *is greater than the probability that it is caused by a single independent variable.* For example, conformity is influenced by reward exchange, low self-esteem, democratic leadership, and affiliation motivation, as opposed to just one of these variables. The majority of empirical studies do not contradict this. Following this assumption, if a hypothesis were disproved through the prescribed scientific procedure, it could be discarded in favor of other possible alternative (rival) hypotheses predicting the dependent variable. If a second hypothesis were not disproved by the same procedures, it would not be discarded; however, neither could it be considered proved. It would remain, with slightly higher status, among the multiple undisproved hypotheses. From this point of view, the task of science is not accepting or proving hypotheses. Rather it is rejecting or disproving hypotheses. A second assumption is: *hypotheses can only be discarded.* Therefore, empirical investigations should test as many alternative hypotheses as possible.

The *internal validity* of a hypothesis is the number of its alternative hypotheses disproved. Hypotheses are disproved by observing the lack of association (contiguity or concomitance in time) between variations of the independent and dependent variables. If there is variation in one without variation in the other, there is no relationship. If there is variation in both independent and dependent variables but they are not systematically related (fit to a mathematical equation), there is no relationship. However, two important conditions must be met: (1) there must be a wide range of variation in the independent variable so as to allow for the possibility of high and low threshold effects (e.g., frustration may produce interpersonal aggression only at very high values of frustration); (2) there must be sufficient time to allow for the possibility of delayed effects (e.g., untrustworthy communicators may have a sleeper effect on attitude change).

The critical problem for the researcher is to have some way of controlling the variation in the variables. How this is done in laboratory experiments will be discussed shortly. If the researcher could control all the variation in the independent and dependent variables, hypothetically he could associate all the variation in the dependent variable with the variation in one or more independent variables. *Controlled variation* is the proportion of the variation in the dependent variable which shows some systematic relationship with the variation in the independent variable(s). *Uncontrolled variation* (Ross's and Smith's $U$) is the proportion of the variation in the dependent variable which does not show such a relationship.

The *external validity* of a hypothesis is the degree of similarity between the variation in the independent variables (and interactions thereof) and the variation in the population variables. Under conditions of low external validity, the researcher has difficulty in generalizing his findings to situations in which the variation is dissimilar to that in the research situation. For example, if it is found that under a high degree of leader competence, group morale increases group productivity, would this hypothesis generalize to a low degree of leader competence? Similarly, if it is found that with a Negro researcher, frustration increases the hostility of Negroes, would this hypothesis generalize to white researchers?

Two points of clarification are probably necessary. First, external validity is being used in reference to variables, not people per se. Although people are the source of data, social science is interested in the variables which people represent. Second, external validity is being used in reference to the variations (scaled values) of a variable, or more specifically, to the variations of an operation or measure of that variable. It could have been used more broadly in referring to all operations or measures relevant to a particular conceptual variable. Then the question of generalization would apply to the similarity between the operations in an experiment and all the operations which are theoretically relevant to the conceptual variable under investigation. This is usually called *concept validity*.

*Sometimes* internal and external validity conflict. If a researcher wants to control the effects of a variable on a dependent variable by minimizing the variation in the former (internal validity), he may not be able to generalize to situations in which there is greater variation or a different mean value (external validity). For example, the use of college sophomores as subjects may decrease the variation in several variables, but hypotheses tested using these subjects may not generalize to individuals of greater variation. Conversely, if a researcher wants to test alternative hypotheses by producing a large variation in several independent variables (internal validity), he is not able to generalize directly to situations in which there is less variation (external validity). Although the randomization assumption is violated, the researcher can generalize solely from the data where the variation in the independent variable is similar to that in the population.

Any investigation risks external validity to some degree because it is conducted in a relatively low-variation environment, sampled from a relatively low-variation population, and measured with relatively low-variation instruments.[1] Of course, the risk increases as the variation in the population increases. Because of this inevitable risk, a third assumption is required: *the probability that the variations in the independent variables are independent of one another is greater than the probability that they are caused by the interactions among the independent variables* (main effects or additive effects are more probable than nonadditive effects).[2] Although internal validity sometimes involves interactions, external validity always involves interactions between the experimental manipulation and other conditions of the experiment. Because of this and the fact that the pursuit of external validity frequently disallows the testing of alternative hypotheses, external validity becomes of secondary importance to internal validity. Thus, a fourth, very important assumption can be made: *hypotheses can be generalized.*

Therefore, research from which validity about hypotheses can be drawn maximizes, first, internal validity, and second, external validity.

## Definition of Experimental Method

The *experimental method* involves the experimenter's manipulation of the variation in one or more independent variables and the randomization of other independent variables, followed by the measurement of the variation in one or more dependent variables.[3] For example, an experimenter, using randomization, assigns half of his subjects to a cooperative task and half to a competitive task, and then measures the interpersonal aggression. Or the experimenter has several stooges agree with one another when half of his subjects are present and disagree when the other half are present (subjects

---

[1] Whereas measurement is usually considered a problem of internal validity, it may be somewhat difficult to perceive its relationship to external validity. Measurement may be a population variable. For example, in many situations people are accustomed to being observed or questioned or to taking paper-and-pencil tests. The degree to which the measurements in the research situation resemble measurements in the population, the greater the external validity.

[2] One must be aware that some interactions are only pseudo interactions because they result from independent variables that are related to one another.

[3] Sometimes the variation in the independent variable(s) is not produced by the experimenter's manipulation but instead results from more natural factors (e.g., classrooms being taught by different procedures).

again being assigned by randomization), and then measures the subjects' agreement with the stooges. The experimental method is designed primarily for the study of change. At time 1, the variations in the independent and dependent variables are measured or assumed. The assumption (the fifth) is: *through randomization the means and/or variations in these variables are equally distributed among the manipulated variations in the independent variable* (experimental variations). At time 2, the variation in the independent variable is manipulated, while the variation in the dependent variable is (re)measured. (Although the manipulation is continued throughout time 2, the measurement may actually occur at the end of time 2 or, in the case of a postexperimental questionnaire or interview, after time 2.)

It has been assumed that the strength of the laboratory experiment, relative to other research methods, has been its internal validity and that its weakness has been its external validity. The external validity cry has been raised because of the particular homogeneity of the laboratory settings and the sampled population (e.g., the college sophomore). The stimulus environments of the laboratory do not involve variations in relevant variables. They are artificial, unlike the real world. The experimentalist has responded that he was more concerned with internal validity or concept validity.

These positions have undergone great change in recent years. The experimentalist has become more interested in external validity with research done in laboratory simulations and field experiments. However, at the same time, experimenters themselves have increasingly questioned the internal validity of experimentation. Whereas an experimental design can control most extraneous variables which are present prior to the experiment (what is of primary concern to Ross and Smith), there are many extraneous variables occurring *during* an experiment which until recently have been unperceived and/or uncontrolled.[4] For purposes of discussion, these extraneous variables will be categorized as (1) the experimenter, (2) the subjects, (3) the manipulations, and (4) the measurements.

## Methods of Controlling Variation Due to Extraneous Variables

In order to increase controlled variation, the experimenter must, with some certainty, control the variations in the possible extraneous variables in his investigation. The following are three general procedures by which experimenters control the variations in these extraneous variables: nonvariation, similar variation, and variation differences.

[4] Extraneous variables (Ross's and Smith's $U$ factor) are independent variables which, because the experimenter does not intentionally manipulate or measure them, decrease controlled variation. They are the source of important alternative hypotheses. Experimenters who first called attention to extraneous variables are Rosenzweig (50), Riecken (40), and Campbell and Stanley (13).

**Nonvariation.**   This general method involves minimizing the variation in the extraneous variables.   By minimizing this variation, the experimenter reduces the variation in the dependent variable which is caused by these particular extraneous variables.   If there is shown to be variation in the dependent variable, then it is not associated with variation in the extraneous variables (because the latter is absent), and the hypotheses involving these particular extraneous variables are disproved.   Thus, the internal validity of the hypothesis involving the independent variable is increased.   However, there remains the possibility that the variation in the dependent variable is caused by the *interaction* between the independent variable (actually the experimental manipulation) and the extraneous variables (being held constant), as opposed to the independent variable alone.

Additional problems may result from the mean value of the extraneous variable used.

**1** *Population value.*   If the population variation in the extraneous variable is small, an experimenter may be able to produce the same variation in the experimental situation.   For example, if one-way mirrors are never found in the population, he may simply not use them in an experiment.   If paper-and-pencil testing on an intermittent basis is always found in the population, the experimenter may gather some of his data using such testing.

**2** *Nonpopulation value.*   If an experimenter cannot replicate the particular population variation in the laboratory, he may produce a small variation which is different from that found in the population.   He hopes that the effects of the extraneous variable(s) in each experimental variation will be constant; thus the variation in the dependent variable cannot be attributed to the extraneous variable(s).   For example, an experiment may be conducted in the same laboratory by the same experimenter when there are no laboratories or experimenters in the population.   Then, of course, external validity may be decreased if the independent and extraneous variables interact (produce nonadditive effects).

**Similar variation.**   This general method involves creating similar mean values of extraneous variables among all experimental variations.   It is accomplished by three procedures: first, the matching of extraneous variables (actually the matching of subjects, observers, etc., in terms of the extraneous variables) and then randomizing them among the experimental variations; second, simply randomizing the extraneous variables among the experimental variations; third, using the same variation in the extraneous variables in all experimental variations (e.g., using the same subjects and same observers).   The first two procedures require the assumption that randomization of subjects, observers, and so forth similarly randomizes the extraneous variables.   For example, if age is expected to affect a subject's response, the first procedure would require that the number of subjects of the same age be the same as the number of experimental variations. The subjects of the same age would be assigned to an experimental variation through randomization. The second procedure would just randomize subjects and assume that age was similarly randomized (approximately equal age means). Again, this method does not allow for the test of alternative hypotheses involving interactions between independent and extraneous variables. This is true because the experimenter regards the mean value of the extraneous variable as the only true value represented in the experimental variations. Therefore, as the means are approximately equal among the experimental variations, this method resembles the nonvariation method. However, *since variation exists within the experimental variations, uncontrolled variation will be greater than in the nonvariation method.*

As was true of the nonvariation method, this method involves the use of sample means and/or variations which may either take (1) *population values* or (2) *nonpopulation values.* In other words, the sample means and variations are either representative or unrepresentative of the population means and variations. In the latter case, the possible resulting interactions would decrease external validity. In practice most experimenters do not use this control method with any intention of increasing external validity. Therefore, the population value and nonpopulation value distinction will not be emphasized in the following discussion.

**Variation differences.** This method involves treating the extraneous variable(s) as independent variables in a factorial design. For example, if the experimenter anticipates that the sex of a stooge will affect the subjects' aggressive responses to the stooge's interference responses, he could use a four-cell design with two interference variations (high and low interference) for each of two sex variations (male and female). This method maximizes internal validity because it provides the opportunity to disprove alternative hypotheses involving interactions between independent and extraneous variables; thus the experimenter does not have to rely on the interaction assumption (the probability of main effects is greater than that of nonadditive effects) *as far as these particular extraneous variables are concerned.* Controlled variation is increased because of the small variation in the *particular* extraneous variables *within* each experimental variation. Neither does the experimenter have to rely *so strongly* on the randomization assumption, as these *particular* extraneous variables are distributed through experimental manipulation. This becomes more crucial as the sample size decreases. A less effective, but more practical, procedure is simply to measure the extraneous variables (or the subjects' perceptions of the extraneous variables) and control them statistically.

The specific application of these general methods to the control of specific extraneous variables will now be discussed. In this discussion, the methods will be ranked according to the number of their attributes which contribute to hypothesis validity.[5]

**1. Variation differences.** This method tests some interaction hypotheses involving extraneous variables thereby increasing internal validity and decreasing the dependence on the interaction (nonadditive) assumption. It decreases the extraneous variation within the experimental variations thereby not increasing the uncontrolled variation. This method increases external validity. Finally, it decreases the dependence on the randomization assumption.

**2. Nonvariation: population value.** This method decreases the extraneous variation within the experimental variations thereby not increasing the uncontrolled variation. It increases external validity and decreases the dependence on the randomization assumption. However it has one great disadvantage. This method does not test interaction hypotheses involving extraneous variables thereby decreasing internal validity and increasing the dependence on the interaction assumption.

**3. Nonvariation: nonpopulation value.** This method has one added disadvantage over the previous method. It decreases external validity.

**4. Similar variation.** Compared with the other methods, this method has all the disadvantages. It does not test interaction hypotheses involving extraneous variables thereby decreasing internal validity and increasing the dependence on the interaction assumption. It does not decrease the extraneous variation within the experimental variations and thereby increases the uncontrolled variation. It does not increase external validity. Finally, this method increases the dependence on the randomization assumption.

## 10.1 EXPERIMENTER VARIATION

### *Experimenter's Conceptualizations*

As social psychologists have found that a person's perceptual categories affect his behavior and as a consequence the behavior of those interacting

---

[5] The attributes themselves may be ranked according to their importance to hypothesis validity. I would rank them in order of importance as: (1) the method tests some interaction hypotheses involving would-be extraneous variables thereby increasing internal validity and decreasing dependence on the interaction (nonadditive) assumption; (2) the method decreases the extraneous variation within the experimental variations thereby not increasing the uncontrolled variation; (3) the method increases external validity; (4) the method decreases dependence on the randomization assumption (randomizing subjects, etc., randomizes the extraneous variables).

with him as well as his interpretation of others' behavior, it should not be particularly surprising that an experimenter's conceptualizations affect the behavior of his subjects as well as his interpretations of this behavior. If different experimenters have different conceptualizations, it is quite possible that they will obtain different experimental results. Back (2) demonstrated that when cohesiveness was used as an independent variable the experimental results were a function of which of three different conceptualizations were employed. In a review of research literature, Burgess (12) found that when group productivity was used as a dependent variable the acceptance or rejection of hypotheses concerning the effects of different communication networks on productivity was a function of the particular experimenter's conceptualization of group productivity.

Possible explanations for the experimenter's conceptualizations are many. His *methodological attitudes* are one. This chapter began with several assumptions. One stated that hypotheses can only be *dis*proved. Most experimenters conduct research as though they did not accept this assumption. They do not provide simultaneous tests of alternative hypotheses, and more importantly, they frequently interpret their data as proving a hypothesis. (A more conservative interpretation is that the data provide support for the hypothesis.) This would not be the interpretation of an experimenter whose orientation included the disproof assumption. Also, if the experimenter thinks that external validity is a more crucial question than internal validity in hypothesis testing, his interpretation of laboratory data might always be more conservative than that of an experimenter who is more concerned with internal validity. A closely related issue is the differential evaluation of the crucial experiment and replication. An experimenter who places high value on replication (an attitude probably correlated with a concern with external validity) will make more conservative interpretations of a single experiment than will an experimenter who evaluates experiments on the basis of their pioneering a new theoretical approach or providing the missing link which would integrate several approaches.

A second factor is the *theoretical attitudes* of the experimenter. Some scientists argue that science is a matter of curiosity and explanation; others argue that science concerns prediction and control. Criswell (18) suggests that the latter attitude results in the experimenter's using a machine model of behavior and being unconcerned with how his subjects perceive the experiment. In other words, such an experimenter's interpretations would not be a function of some of the uncontrolled extraneous variables. Bakan (4) proposes that the same attitude produces a scientific norm that research consists in the testing of *pre*conceived hypotheses and that findings which were not thought of beforehand are rejected or accepted as tentative.

An experimenter's discipline may also affect his conceptualizations and consequently his interpretations. Take, for example, the concept of *norm*.

Psychologists frequently conceive of norms as uniformities of behavior in a group. Social psychologists generally conceive of norms as attitudes or frames of reference shared by individuals. Sociologists conceive of them as ideal behavior or functional standards for accomplishing group goals. Each of these could produce different interpretations of the same data. A very common difference of interpretation in laboratory experimentation concerns so-called small-group experiments. There are differences in conceptualizing *group*. A psychologist may use only two criteria in defining group—two or more individuals interacting. However, a sociologist may have numerous criteria—interaction, norms, differentiation, goal, member replacement, persistence, organizational levels, and so forth. Such conceptualizations affect not only the experimenter's interpretation but also his choice of experimental settings. For example, a sociologist may feel it unfeasible to establish a real group in the laboratory.

An experimenter's conceptualizations may be a function of his occupation. For example, Levy and Orr (30) compared the work of academic and non-academic experimenters on the validity of the Rorschach. They concluded that the former conceived of concept validity in terms of construct validity (what property of the instrument controls the variation of the instrument responses), whereas the latter perceived it as criterion or pragmatic validity (how well the instrument predictably controls the variation of another instrument). As a result they devised their experiments differently and interpreted the outcomes quite differently.

Finally, a well-established principle in social psychology is that the credibility of a source increases the probability of his influence over others, particularly if the stimuli involved are ambiguous. This principle suggests that an experimenter may have adopted the conceptualizations of one who has prestige in his discipline and/or is respected by the experimenter, for example, an instructor in the department of which the experimenter is a graduate (most likely his major professor). It is doubtful that students of Kurt Lewin and Robert Bales see eye to eye. Sad to say, the ambiguity of the conceptualization may maximize the credibility effect.

## Experimenter Characteristics and Behavior

Several studies have suggested that the sex of the experimenter influences the subjects' behavior. Sarason and Harmatz (52) produced data showing that a subject's learning speed was faster if the experimenter was male. Binder, McConnell, and Sjoholm (6) studied variations of the verbal conditioning of hostile verbs produced by using two experimenters, one a small and very feminine girl and the other a large and masculine boy. The results showed a much faster rate of conditioning for the female experimenter when the reinforcer (the word "good") was given each time the subject uttered a hostile word. The interpretation was that she provided a less threatening environment. (If the results had been reversed, the explanation might have been that the male subjects chose to act more gentlemanly in her presence.)

The experimenter's race may affect the behavior of the subjects. Katz, Roberts, and Robinson (26) found that when using Negro subjects (1) the race of the experimenter and (2) the interaction between the experimenter's race and the instructional set (motor coordination or intelligence) affected the subject's performance.

The experimenter's personality (or the subjects' perception of his personality) also may affect the subjects' behavior. Sapolsky (51) demonstrated that the effect of reinforcement on verbal conditioning was increased by the compatibility of the personalities of the experimenter and the subjects. This might suggest that the greater the compatibility or similarity between experimenter and subject, the more the experimenter's behavior affects the subject's behavior in the direction of confirming the experimenter's hypothesis.

Several aspects of the experimenter's behavior may affect that of the subjects. The experimenter's verbalizations (words or inflections) may tip off the subject as to how he is supposed to behave in the experiment. A similar effect may be produced by the experimenter's gestures and facial expressions. For example, if the experimenter either demonstrates or verbalizes to the subjects examples of how the experiment works, he can be sure that the subjects will become particularly sensitive to how the experimenter did it or would do it. Sarason and Minard (53) showed that the hostile behavior of the experimenter influenced the verbal conditioning of his subjects. However, Bryan and Lichtenstein (10) found that the negative attitudes of the subjects did not have this effect. Winkel and Sarason (62) found that the experimenter's anxiety increased the performance of his subjects.

This suggests the possibility of an *experimenter-modeling effect*. As was suggested concerning the effect of source credibility on experimenter's conceptualizations, it may be that the probability of the subjects' imitating the experimenter's behavior increases with (1) the ambiguity of the experimental situation and (2) the prestige of the experimenter. Age and professor-graduate status may be important stimuli in the latter respect. If, in an experimental investigation of aggression, the experimenter projects a friendly or passive image to the subjects, he may decrease the amount of aggression expressed by the subjects. If he becomes irritated at what he regards as the stupid questions asked by a few of the subjects in the preliminary session, he may increase the amount of their aggression.

How can the behavioral differences in experimenters be explained? Social psychologists have found that a person's expectation of others' behavior affects his own behavior in such a way as to increase the probability of his expectation being confirmed. In an experimental situation, this effect may occur in two ways: (1) the behavior of the experimenter produces the behavior of the subjects consistent with the former's expectation or hypothesis; (2) the experimenter's hypothesis causes him to perceive the behavior of his subjects as consistent with the experimenter's hypothesis.

Rosenthal (44) has provided a discussion of several different theoretical notions which suggest the effects of the experimenter's hypothesis on the subjects' behavior. He and Fode (46) performed three experiments on what they call experimenter bias. The first experiment involved pictures of people which had been previously rated as neutral (0) and which were presented to subjects by different experimenters. The experimenters were in five matched pairs and were told that the ratings of the subjects would probably be close either to $+5$ or to $-5$. All $+5$ biased experimenters obtained from their subjects significantly higher mean ratings than did the $-5$ biased experimenters. In the second experiment using the same picture procedure, they found that the biased experimenters who read the instructions to the subjects and showed the pictures to them obtained ratings more similar to their own bias than did the biased experimenters who read the instructions to the subjects but then retired behind a screen while the subjects looked at the pictures. The third experiment found that the experimenter's motivation (the experimenter having been paid different amounts of money for his services) did not produce differences in the effect of experimenter bias. However, Insko and Schopler (25) have not been able to replicate these findings. Interestingly, Rosenthal and Lawson (48) found that experimenter bias was as important in experiments using animals (rats) as subjects as in experiments using humans.

It is quite possible also that the experimenter's analysis of the data between the beginning and end of data collection can produce a change in the strength of his hypothesis. As a consequence, this could cause a change in his behavior during the experiment.

Finally, there is the effect of experimenter maturation. As the experimenter becomes more socialized into his role as experimenter through his participation in an increasing number of experimental sessions, his behavior may change. At the same time that he is becoming socialized, he may also be feeling fatigued or bored with the experiment. Bernard (5) has shown that subjects' performance on a projective test was influenced by the number of experimental sessions in which the experimenter had participated.

## Methods of Controlling Experimenter Variation

**Variation differences.** The use of this method of control is straightforward. For each experimental variation of the independent variable, there may be experimental variations of the extraneous variables.[6] The extraneous variables may be either variations of the experimenter's conceptualizations, sex,

---

[6] Ross and Smith have discussed both complete and incomplete factorial designs.

personality, or behavior *or*, except for a few variables such as sex, variations in assumed determinants of these variables. As was discussed previously, this method of control has several advantages over the other methods: (1) tests for possible interactions between experimenter variables and the independent variable(s) thereby increasing internal validity and decreasing the dependence on the interaction assumption relative to the particular experimenter variables; (2) decreases the variation of the experimenter variable(s) within the variations of the independent variable(s) thereby not increasing the uncontrolled variation in the dependent variable; (3) increases external validity; (4) decreases dependence on the randomization assumption relative to the particular experimenter variables.

**Nonvariation: population value.** The elimination of the experimenter's conceptualizations is close to impossible. The best procedure is to minimize the involvement of the experimenter. His involvement may be limited to the presession and postanalysis parts of the experiment. The experimenter should make the analysis and interpretation decisions in the beginning stages of the experiment so that the analysis speaks for itself as much as possible. Starting with alternative hypotheses facilitates this procedure. (It is also possible, though not probable, that the experimenter can start with no preconceived hypothesis.) McGuigan (33) suggests that the experimenter's sex, personality, and behavior are best controlled by eliminating the experimenter from experimental sessions. He suggests the use of taped instructions as an alternative. This procedure would be useful except where the experimenter's verbalizations have an effect or where the subjects can infer other experimenter characteristics from his (*or her*) voice. If the experimenter cannot be eliminated entirely, Rosenthal (45) suggests that face-to-face interaction be eliminated. One could argue that this procedure could still have the problems of the taped instructions. However, in an experiment previously discussed, Rosenthal and Fode (46) do demonstrate the effect of eliminating the experimenter-subject interaction as soon as possible.

Of course, by eliminating the experimenter, one also eliminates the effects of his hypotheses on the subjects' behavior. These effects may also be eliminated by two additional procedures: (1) the experimenter's lack of awareness of the hypothesis being tested (use of a naïve substitute experimenter); (2) the experimenter's lack of awareness of the particular experimental variation. If the experimenter is a social scientist, it is quite probable that he will have made some fairly accurate guesses about the hypothesis being tested, and this may have an effect on his behavior and, in turn, the subjects' behavior. Therefore, it is advisable that he not be a social scientist or even particularly familiar with the social sciences. The effects of premature examination of the data can be eliminated only by the experimenter's not doing it. Finally, the only procedure for eliminating experimenter maturation is to eliminate the experimenter's participation in experimental sessions or to limit each experimenter's participation to a single session.

**Nonvariation: nonpopulation value.**  There are two procedures which minimize the variation of experimenter variables at values not representative of those of the population: first, use of the same experimenter in all experimental sessions and, second, sampling from a population of homogeneous experimenters. However, the first procedure will not minimize the variation of the experimenter's behavior due to his reactions to the behavior of individual subjects, premature examination of data, or experimenter maturation.  The second procedure will control experimenter maturation only as long as each experimenter participates in no more than one experimental session.

Additional advantages and disadvantages of the nonvariation method of control have been discussed previously.  The advantages are (1) the decrease in the variation of the experimenter variable(s) within the experimental variations of the independent variable(s) and (2) the decrease in the dependence on the randomization assumption relative to the particular experimenter variables.  The disadvantage is the impossibility of testing possible interactions between experimenter variables and the independent variable(s) and the increase in the dependence on the interaction assumption.  Whether the method has the advantage of greater external validity is a function of whether the value of the experimenter variables is similar to that found in the population.

**Similar variations.**  McGuigan (33) suggests that a second procedure for controlling the effects of the experimenter is to sample randomly from a population of experimenters and randomize them among the experimental variations.  This procedure would in most cases require several assumptions: (1) that the population represents all variations of the experimenter variables; (2) that the sample represents the population in the same respect (population value as opposed to nonpopulation value) thereby increasing external validity; (3) that the randomization procedures are successful in distributing the experimenter variables among the experimental variations (including the behaviors of the experimenters once in the experimental sessions) thereby increasing internal validity.  Experimenter maturation could be controlled by randomizing the order of the experimental sessions.  If the experimenter's behavior is, in part, a function of his subjects' behavior or characteristics, randomization of the subjects provides some control.  Again, the general disadvantages of the similar-variations method of control have already been mentioned.  They are (1) the impossibility of testing possible interactions between experimental variables and independent variable(s) and the increase in the dependence on the interaction assumption; (2) the increase in the variation of the experimenter variables within the experimental variations; and (3) the increase in the dependence on the randomization assumption. Whether the method has the advantage of greater external validity is a function of the similarity between the means, variations, and distributions of the experimenter variables in the experimental situation and in the population.

**10.2  SUBJECT VARIATION**

## Selection and Mortality

The major question here is, What are the extraneous variables which can be attributed to the particular individuals who are the subjects in an experiment? *Selection* refers to the extraneous variables introduced by the choice of individuals to participate as subjects. *Mortality* concerns the extraneous variables introduced by the elimination of chosen subjects once the experiment has begun. Mortality may be the choice of the experimenter. The experimenter may choose to eliminate subjects on the basis of their failing to cooperate, their awareness of experimental deceptions or experimental hypotheses, and so forth.

## Subject's Motivation: Basis of Volunteering and Cooperating

One of the major criticisms of laboratory experimentation concerns the involvement of the subject. Are the subjects really involved in what they are doing? The criticism should be based on the assumption that one always wants to generalize to an involved population. However, as involvement is a variable and itself worthy of investigation as an independent variable, the real question should be, With what is the subject involved? and only then, How much? These questions suggest at least four *involvement variables* varying in their importance for valid inference.

**1** *The amount of involvement with extraneous variables.* The most crucial involvement variable is the amount of attention the subjects give to those experimental stimuli which are not manipulated as the independent variables. The more the subject attends to these extraneous variables, the greater the probability his behavior is a result of these extraneous variables.

**2** *The amount of involvement with the independent variable(s).* Even if the subject's attention is not focused on extraneous variables, the degree to which it is focused on the desired independent variables may vary. The less the subject's involvement with the independent variables, the greater the probability his behavior will be the result of the cognitive attributes (beliefs, attitudes) with which the subject enters the experiment.

**3** *The generality of the involvement.* A subject's motivations may increase his attention to a wide range of stimuli or pinpoint it to just a few. It is important that the experimental stimuli fall within the range of attended stimuli. Considering the many different stimuli that experimenters employ in their research, the use of subjects with general motivations may provide greater assurances of attention. Therefore, the greater the generality of the subject's motivation, the greater the probability he will attend to the independent variables. (Of course, this same generality may increase the subject's attention to extraneous variables.)

**4** *The permanency of the involvement.* It is important that the subject's attention be maintained throughout an experimental session. This is particularly true if the measurements of the dependent variable occur at the end of time 2. Even if one argues that a subject need not be involved with postexperimental questions (a topic to be discussed later), it is quite possible that a subject's answers may be a function of his most recent experiences which occur at the end of the session and where involvement is most questionable. Of course, the longer an experimental session, the less the probability of continued involvement. This proposition is conditional in two respects: (*a*) the subject's involvement may be equally low at the very beginning of a session; (*b*) his involvement may be highest at the point where he is most rewarded, assuming that he does not become saturated with rewards.

A subject may enter an experiment with a number of motivations or he may actually acquire motivations during an experimental session. For example, Back, Hood, and Brehm (3) found that the motives for volunteering for experiments vary with the subject's sex. Some motivations may affect the subject's involvement with the experimental stimuli. They will be discussed in terms of the amount of involvement with the independent variable they produce.

**High positive involvement.** There is only one motivation which may produce high involvement with the independent variables—scientific welfare. A subject who values the scientific approach and believes that the experiment serves the purposes of science may (1) not attend to extraneous variables (assuming that he knows what these are); (2) attend to independent variables (particularly if pointed out by the experimenter-scientist); (3) attend to any number of possible experimental operations of an independent variable; (4) attend to the independent variable throughout the experimental session. In the only empirical investigation of this proposition, Fillenbaum (22) found that neither scientific value nor perceived importance of the experiment affected the subjects' performance. This may suggest that while it is quite possible that an individual can report a positive or negative attitude toward the scientific approach, his ability to translate his attitude into appropriate behavior in the laboratory is less probable. However, it would seem possible to educate individuals in this respect.

**Potentially positive involvement.** There are two motivations—achievement and affiliation—whose involvement effects are a function of the particular independent variable being manipulated. If the motivation and the independent variable are related, attention may be high. If they are not related, the involvement may be in the direction of the related extraneous variables. If a subject has high achievement motivation and the independent variable involves the performance of a task, the subject will probably be very much involved. This is not meant to imply that a high achiever can be enticed by just any task. Some individuals are specific-task oriented, i.e., mechanical, mathematical, physical, etc. Some are specific success-probability oriented. For example, high achievers generally like tasks which have about a 50 percent probability of being solved. Similarly, if the subject has high affiliation motivation and the independent variable involves the subject's interaction with other subjects, he will probably be highly involved. Capra and Dittes (14) found that firstborn (assumed high affiliation motivation) volunteered more frequently where the appeal of the experimenter was one of guaranteed participation and affiliation in a group performing a common task cooperatively. However, if it is the experimental arrangements and not the independent variable which involve task performance or intersubject interactions, the subject will be highly involved with the extraneous variables.

**Low involvement.** The motivations of peers' approval and escape from other tasks provide low involvement. If a subject is motivated to cooperate in an experiment because of the approval he will receive from his peers, his involvement with an experimental variable will probably be very general, but low and temporary. Rosenbaum and Blake (42) and Rosenbaum (41) found that the volunteering of a stooge significantly increased the volunteering of others. No one has investigated how such procedures may affect the subject's behavior in the experimental session. Blake, Berkowitz, Bellamy, and Mouton (7) found that volunteering could be increased by such avoidance suggestions as holding class and quizzes for those not volunteering. However, once in the experimental session, the subject has successfully escaped from these tasks and his involvement will probably diminish.

**Potentially negative involvement.** A subject may be motivated by a grade or money which is contingent on his cooperation. The involevement produced by such motivations is a function of whether the experimenter is the grade or money giver. If the experimenter is the giver, the subjects will probably be more attentive to the experimenter than to the independent variable. Some subjects are more attentive toward the experimenter because of any possible approval or disapproval he might show of the subject's behavior. If the experimenter is the giver, but the grade or money is contingent on only the subject's participation and not his performance (the usual situation), the subject will probably remain uninvolved with any of the experimental stimuli. If the experimenter is not the giver, the subjects will not be likely to be involved with any variable, independent or extraneous.

**High negative involvement.** At least three motivations produce high involvement with extraneous variables. The first concerns authoritative approval. Some subjects may be motivated to achieve the approval of an authority such as the experimenter might represent. As a result, these subjects will be particularly attentive to the behavior of the experimenter. For example, Rosenberg (43) proposed that it was quite conceivable that in certain cognitive dissonance experiments the use of surprisingly large monetary rewards for eliciting counterattitudinal arguments may suggest that the experimental situation is one in which the subject's autonomy, his honesty, his resoluteness in resisting a special kind of bribe were being tested. The subject will resist giving evidence of attitude change for large rewards because it might convey something negative about himself to the experimenter. Block and Block (8) found that middle-class subjects almost invariably structure the experimental situation as one calling for a submissive role in relation to an authority figure.

Second, some subjects may be motivated to outwit the experimenter. This motivation may be particularly common among subjects who perceive that the experimenter is attempting some form of deception himself. Such subjects will attend to all variables but particularly those to which they think the experimenter does not want them to attend. Of course, these will be extraneous variables. Third, there is the subject motivated by simple curiosity. Although this motivation is only temporary, it does increase involvement with extraneous variables. With time this involvement decreases with a *possible* resulting increase in the subject's involvement with the independent variable.

## Subject's Beliefs

It is quite probable that a subject's beliefs concerning laboratory experimentation, specifically, and interpersonal situations, generally, affect his behavior in the laboratory. There are two principal belief areas concerning laboratory experimentation: (1) experimental laboratory procedures and (2) the experimental hypothesis.

The subject may have several beliefs concerning laboratory procedures. The first concerns the subject's belief as to the role of an experimental subject. Some individuals may conceive of the experimental subject as a guinea pig, whose role it is to subordinate himself to the experimenter. If he has a positive attitude toward such a role, a subject will probably behave very passively, attend primarily to the experimenter, and wait for him to present some dramatic stimulus such as an electric shock. Other individuals may believe the subject role to be a matter of role playing or acting as though one were in another (real) situation. Here there is a possible problem of a difference between the subject's and experimenter's interpretation of the experimental stimuli. Then again some individuals may believe the role involves behaving naturally in order to provide greater understanding of human behavior. Such a belief should minimize the effects of extraneous variables.

Another belief has been mentioned briefly. Does the subject believe the experimenter is deceiving him? If so, what are the subject's attitudes toward deception? Do populations differ in their attitudes toward deception? For example, Burchard (11) found that sociologists were more favorable toward the use of concealed listening devices in jury deliberations than political scientists, who were more favorable than lawyers, who in turn were more favorable than editors and commentators. Rosenthal, Kohn, Greenfield, and Carota (47) suggest that subjects with a greater need for approval may not report their awareness of the deceptive reinforcement contingencies in verbal conditioning experiments because such reports would be inappropriate to the perceived situational demands. It is quite probable that whether a subject has a positive or negative attitude toward deception, his belief that it exists will direct his attention to many extraneous variables. If he has a negative attitude, he may try to outwit the experimenter as a means of harming the experiment or maintaining his own self-esteem.

On the other hand, does the subject trust the experimenter not to harm him with the experimenter's deception? Criticizing a previous experiment in which it was found that hypnotized subjects were willing to carry out such *apparently* dangerous action as grasping a dangerous reptile, plunging their hand into concentrated acid, and throwing the acid at an assistant, Orne and Evans (38) found that unhypnotized subjects complied with the same requests. The subjects invariably reported they were convinced the activities were safe because they were participating in research conducted by competent, responsible scientists. Thus it appears that the belief most favorable to valid inference is one which neither overly trusts nor distrusts the experimenter.

If a subject has a belief about the hypothesis being tested, his belief may affect his behavior. This proposition is similar to the experimenter-hypothesis effect. However, it is also different in that the experimenter-hypothesis proposition predicts that the experimenter will behave in ways that will increase the probability of his belief being confirmed. The subject's belief may produce just the opposite effect, depending on his other beliefs and motivations. In other words, the subject's belief will interact with the other variables and magnify their effects. Orne (36) and Spielberger (56) found that certain experimental effects were present only when the subjects were aware of the experimental hypothesis. In a sensory deprivation experiment, Orne and Scheibe (39) found different effects between subjects who were exposed to preexperimental conditions designed to imply that sensory deprivation effects were expected to emerge and subjects who were exposed to the same physical conditions in such a way as to lead them to expect nothing to happen. However, Orne (37) optimistically suggests that if the subject is *acutely* aware of the experimenter's hypothesis, he may lean over backward to be honest. Fillenbaum (22) found that the subject's previous knowledge of the tested hypothesis did not affect his behavior. Therefore, these apparently contradictory results may be explained in terms of the interaction between a subject's awareness of the hypothesis and his other beliefs and motivations.

These and other beliefs of the subject may result from experimental experiences. The beliefs may be a function of the subject's own experiences in previous experiments. Fillenbaum (22), however, found that a subject's previous experience in a deception experiment did not affect his behavior. Brock and Becker (9) found that a deception experience did affect the subject's behavior if the original deception situation was *similar* to the present experimental situation. Our previous discussion of deception suggested that the effect is also a result of the subject's attitude toward deception. A subject may not have had any experience in an experiment but still have well-developed beliefs about typical experimental procedures and hypotheses as a result of exposure in social science classrooms. The college sophomore subject is frequently recruited from introductory courses in psychology or sociology where experiments are a matter of discussion. Owing to the educational attractiveness of deception experiments, the instructor usually uses them as examples and the students remember them more frequently. Similarly an individual may be educated by his peers. If there is a cute, exciting, or challenging experiment on campus, most students soon learn something about it.

Finally, the beliefs a subject brings to an experiment may not have resulted from his exposure to experimental situations. I have suggested that subjects' consistent behavior in the early phases of a longitudinal experiment is probably the result of the beliefs which were developed outside the experimental situation (61). For example, an attempt to produce two types of reward distribution in small groups—egalitarian and differentiated—found that when each session began all groups (college students) used an egalitarian distribution system. I suggested that such behavior may be the result of two extraneous variables: (1) the general egalitarian beliefs found in most university communities; (2) the egalitarian beliefs found in most of the groups (usually informal groups) with which young people had previously had experience. Other beliefs such as those concerning cooperation or competition may affect experimental results if they are closely related to independent or dependent variables.

## Methods of Controlling Subject Variation

**Variation differences.** Again, this method of control involves experimental variations of the extraneous variable(s) for each experimental variation of the independent variable. A less complicated and, as a result, riskier method involves experimental variations of one extraneous variable which presumably summarizes the subject-related extraneous variables—the simulated subject or the placebo. Here the subject is simply asked to pretend he is confronted with a variation of the independent variable (e.g., an intense shock, a competitor, an attractive female experimenter). Because the subject is not confronted with the real independent variable but is confronted with the extraneous variables, the between-group variation is a function of the real independent variable.

Another less desirable method is to measure the extraneous variables and employ statistical controls. For example, if the extraneous variable is the subject's hypothesis developed during the session, some attempt may be made to measure it. Spielberger (56) found that this sometimes requires very intensive interviewing. It is possible that too much pressure may cause the subject to exaggerate his insights into the experimental situation.

If variation in the dependent variable is expected prior to the manipulation of the independent variable, a premanipulation (or pretest) measurement may be taken. The difference between the premanipulation and postmanipulation measurements can be used as an indicator of the effect of the independent variable, or the premanipulation scores may be used as the covariate in an analysis of covariance. However, this method may create a more important extraneous variable than the one it is intended to eliminate. This pretest effect was discussed in Chap. 9 and will be briefly reviewed in the discussion of measurement variation. These methods will allow for the control of error due to subject mortality (as far as those extraneous variables which are manipulated are concerned) by simply eliminating all the data on these subjects.

**Nonvariation: population value.** There are two ways of reducing subject-related extraneous variables to a value near that found in the population. One involves eliminating the undesirable motivations and beliefs; the other, eliminating the experimental stimuli which elicit these motivations and beliefs. There are several ways to accomplish the former. The most utopian procedure would be to educate individuals to be good subjects. It may be possible to socialize them to accept the value of the scientific approach and the belief in behaving naturally (as opposed to socializing them to cognitions associated with extraneous variables, e.g., the previously mentioned classroom emphasis on deception experiments). This would provide experimenters with a large pool of subjects from which to draw.

A more realistic procedure is the screening process. This involves selecting subjects on the basis of the most desirable motivations and beliefs (desirable in the sense of internal and external validity). One could use any number of selection devices such as paper-and-pencil tests, projective techniques, and simulated-experiment techniques. Of course, the best device is one from which the subject cannot draw any inference about what the experimenter is measuring. If he can guess, the same problem arises as with the premanipulation measurement. If this does arise, or if the experimenter cannot get such measurements, he may select subjects on the basis of the assumed determinants of the motivations and beliefs. This would involve selecting those individuals who have not been exposed to experimentation involving deception (actual experience, classroom or peer exposure). Some exposure is probably desirable in order to minimize the effects of curiosity, but it should involve neither deception nor identical experimental stimuli. The probability of the undesirable effects of information acquired through peers' experience may be decreased by requesting that each subject not discuss the experiment with anyone because "it could be very detrimental to the success of the experiment and a waste of *your* time as well as ours."

The second method of reducing subject-related extraneous variables to a value near that of the general population involves the elimination of the experimental stimuli which elicit the undesirable cognitions. The two principal stimuli of concern are stimuli which imply deception and the experimenter himself. It was suggested earlier that neither a subject's belief in (and negative attitude toward) deception nor his having too much trust in the experimenter was desirable. If the experimenter suspects the former, he should use no deception (e.g., pointing out one-way mirrors and the observers they hide) or use it only when he can successfully divert the subject's attention from it. If either the risk or the consequences of deception are too great, the experimenter should refrain from its use. On the other hand, if the experimenter suspects the subject is too trusting, he should demonstrate the absence of artificiality with respect to the particular procedure (e.g., a practice shock).

If the experimenter is the problematic stimulus, he can be eliminated in two ways. As was suggested as a control of experimenter variation, taped instructions may be similarly used as a means of eliminating authoritative approval. The second way would be to use two experimenters. The effects of course grades or money may be minimized by disassociating them from the experimenter participating in the experimental sessions. This can be accomplished by using another experimenter to do the recruiting and to provide the grade or money. Further control may be provided by stressing that the grade or money is not contingent on the subject's performance. Two experimenters could be used to control authoritative approval—one for the manipulation of the independent variable and the other for the measurement of the dependent variable. Rosenberg (43) has shown that this procedure is particularly effective if these two events can be made to appear as two independent situations, i.e., two different and unrelated experiments.

Finally, it may be possible to reduce uncontrolled variation due to these extraneous variables by using a high-value variation of the independent variable and giving it enough time to achieve its full effect. Longitudinal experimentation provides an opportunity to utilize such a procedure, but, at the same time, it creates the possibility of such problems as the temporary nature of the subject's involvement and the maturation of the experimenter, subjects, and instruments. However, a counterbalance design could be used at least to explore such a possibility (61). For example, if one is interested in the differential variations in group productivity produced under cooperative and competitive interaction, the subjects in one variation may interact cooperatively, then competitively, and then again cooperatively. The subjects in a second variation would experience the reverse order—competition, cooperation, and then competition.

Of course, using the nonvariation method of control theoretically eliminates the possible effects of mortality. Because each subject represents the same value of the extraneous variables, the loss of a subject will not change the value of the extraneous variables presented by the remaining subjects.

**Nonvariation: nonpopulation value.** Procedures similar to those for controlling experimenter variation may be used to control subject variation. These involve (1) the use of the same subjects in all experimental variations and (2) sampling from a supposedly homogeneous population. In addition to the previously mentioned difficulties with this method, the former procedure creates a new extraneous variable, subject maturation. This variable is analogous to experimenter maturation. Some check on this and other possible extraneous variables is provided by repeated dependent-variable measurements both before and after the experimental manipulation. The procedure of sampling from a homogeneous population may also create another extraneous variable, statistical regression. It will be discussed in the section on measurement variation. Again, mortality is not an extraneous variable.

**Similar variations.** This method of control again relies on the faith in randomization. The three assumptions mentioned in the section on experimenter variation must be employed in the use of this method. Of particular concern is the assumption that the randomization procedures are successful in randomly distributing a priori the extraneous variables which become manifest once the subject is in the experiment session. Of course this assumption has to be made. But one is in extremely deep water if the standard deviation of the extraneous variable is large. Assuming that the extraneous variable does have an effect on the dependent variable, the smaller the within-group variation of the latter the greater the assurance in assuming the success of the randomization procedure. However, as this evaluation procedure is an *ad hoc* method, one should rely as much as possible on minimizing the possibility of the problems of a large standard deviation through the use of a sample size as large as practicably possible. If the experimenter is aware of a *small* number of subject-related extraneous variables, it would be particularly effective if he chose to match subjects on this basis and then randomized the pairs. A combination of too many extraneous variables and too small population size will make this procedure impractical.

Finally, mortality could wreak havoc with the method of similar variation. The typical procedure is to eliminate all the data of those subjects who failed to complete the experiment. But one should, at least, compare the available data of the dropouts with the same data of those who completed the experiment before drawing any conclusions about the effects of mortality.

## 10.3   MANIPULATION VARIATION

### Situation Equivalence or Realism

Again, the artificiality of the experimental situation may be a problem. Although many, such as Criswell (18) and Cicourel (15), have raised the question, a few, such as Weick (59) and Drabek and Haas (20), have attempted to specify the variables which would make the laboratory situation equivalent to nonlaboratory (or real) situations. On the other hand, Festinger (21) argues that a laboratory experiment need not, and should not, be an attempt to duplicate a real situation, but rather an attempt to create a situation in which the operation of experimentally manipulated variables can be viewed without the extraneous variables of the group's past history or other current events.

Probably no one, particularly the macrosociologist, will agree that the following discussion exhausts the variables which, if present in a laboratory experiment, would make the experimental situation equivalent to the real world. The fact remains that experimenters and nonexperimenters alike should be explicit about these variables, and the experimenters should be making greater attempts to operationalize some of them in the laboratory.

**Subject's reaction to other subjects.**   If the subject perceives that all the other subjects have volunteered for the experiment, the experiment is not equivalent to a real situation. This assumption is suggested by Milgram (34) in his explanation that subjects who administered what they thought to be severe electric shocks to other subjects did so, in part, because they perceived that the victim had voluntarily submitted to being shocked. Such perceptions of volitional participation may liberalize a subject's interpersonal behavior in ways which are called antisocial in a real situation.

**Subject's reaction to participating in an experiment.**   If the subject perceives that he is participating in an experiment, the experimental situation is not equivalent to a real situation. Such awareness may introduce numerous extraneous variables ranging from a feeling of importance as a result of being selected for an experiment (Hawthorne effect) to the previously mentioned motivation to outwit the experimenter.

**Subject's reaction to the experimental task.** If the subject does not perceive the experimental task as related to some activity with which he has some familiarity, the experimental situation is not equivalent to a real situation. This is based on the assumptions that if the subject does not perceive the task as meaningful, the chances are that (1) he will not become involved with the task or (2) his behavior will be a function of the particular activity and, being dissimilar to any of his activities in the real world, his responses, as reflected in the experimental findings, cannot be generalized.

**Subject's reaction to the experimental consequences.** If the subject's behavior is not met with consequences similar to those he experiences in real life, the experimental situation is not equivalent to a real situation. If the experimental consequences are not like those consequences which normally have an effect on the individual's behavior, the subject will probably exhibit behavior of two extremes. Either he will be completely uninvolved with the experimental situation or he will behave uninhibitedly (or at least differently than he would were he not in the experimental situation).

**Subject's reaction to ecological arrangements.** If the ecological arrangements (i.e., seating arrangements, communication networks, isolation) are not similar to real ecological arrangements, the experimental situation is not equivalent to a real situation. Similarly, if the variables concomitant with the ecological variables in the experimental situation are not similar to those associated with ecological arrangements in the real world, the experimental situation is not equivalent. For example, high status is usually associated with some degree of isolation but with being central to seating arrangements and the communication network. Also Sommer (54) found that the group task affected spatial arrangements.

**Subject's reaction to social arrangements.** If the social arrangements of the experimental group are not similar to those in a real group, the experimental situation is not equivalent to a real situation. However, as was discussed in the section on experimenter variation, there is a problem in defining the variables of a real group. Must a collectivity have interaction, norms, interdependent differentiation, goals, member replacement, persistence, and organization levels in order to be a group? Of course, the wrong question has been asked. The question should be, Assuming that collectivities vary to a great degree in terms of these variables, are the variables of the experimental group equivalent to the social arrangement variables of the groups *to which* *the experimenter wishes to generalize?* This recognizes that the identification of a group is itself a complicated composite of variables and even real groups vary in terms of it.

## Subject's Information

In order to effect predicted subject behavior, the experimenter attempts to provide the subject with some information through the experimental manipulation and, at the same time, attempts to withhold other information by various controls. Sometimes either or both attempts fail and the subject's behavior becomes an effect, in part, of incomplete information or unintended information.

There are several possible determinants of incomplete information. First, as the number of independent variables manipulated simultaneously increases, the probability of a subject attending to and understanding them decreases. Thus, the variation-differences method of controlling extraneous variables may itself produce additional extraneous variables. Second, the amount of tension created by an experimental situation may affect the subject's behavior by decreasing the amount of intended information. Tension may cause the subject to focus intensely on some aspect of the manipulation but not all of it. Spence (55) and Winkel and Sarason (62) found that anxiety affected subjects' performance in a conditioning experiment. However, Fillenbaum, Singleton, and Hull (23) found no such effect in another conditioning experiment. Third, if it is assumed that many manipulations require the transmission of information from one individual to another, the subject must be looking at the informer (i.e., experimenter or stooge) in order to make the manipulation effective. In a review of the research literature on eye contact, Argyle and Dean (1) point out that eye contact is less when the potential perceiver (1) is speaking as opposed to listening, (2) is female, (3) is of the same sex as the other, (4) dislikes the other, (5) is deceived by the other, (6) is tense, (7) is competing with the other as opposed to cooperating, or (8) when the topic of discussion is personal. Sommer (54) proposed that, because of these variables, spatial arrangements are an attempt to facilitate or hinder eye contact. The fourth determinant may involve either incomplete or unintended information. A subject and the experimenter may simply not interpret the experimental manipulation the same way (60).

There are two sources of unintended information—one inside the experimental session (instructional set) and the other outside the experiment (history). The instructional set usually results from statements made by the experimenter. These may include statements about the importance of or reasons for the experiment as well as the examples the experimenter may use to illustrate what the subject is expected to do. Sarason and Harmatz (52) found that an experimenter's statement that the experiment was concerned with performance as it reflects intelligence increased the subject's learning speed. They also found that evaluative statements made during the experiment affected the subject's behavior. DiVesta and Blake (19) and Norris and Grant (35) found that instructional set affected subjects' performance in conditioning experiments. History refers to the extraneous variables originating outside the experimental session between time 1 and time 2. These could include loud noises, laughter, classroom examinations, or a fight with a girl friend. Any of these events, in addition to the experimental manipulation, could affect a subject's behavior.

## The Stooge

Very little work has been done on the extraneous effects of a stooge on subjects' behavior; however, any proposition concerning interpersonal behavior can be applied to this relationship. Leik (29) investigated the effects of variations in a stooge's dress and behavior on the subject's reactions to the stooge. He found that both neat (as opposed to sloppy) dress and confident (as opposed to hesitant) behavior increased the subject's (1) perception of good task performance by the stooge, (2) perception of the value of the stooge's ideas, and (3) liking of the stooge.

## Methods of Controlling Manipulation Variation[7]

**Variation differences.** The only distinction between the use of the variation-difference method for the control of manipulation variation and experimenter or subject variation is that the method itself becomes a possible extraneous variable because incomplete information increases as the number of independent variables increases. Therefore, as it is impossible to investigate this variable through the factorial design procedures, an attempt may be made to control this variable statistically through measurement. This procedure is also particularly crucial in examining the effects of possible differences in the experimenter's and subjects' perceptions of the experimental manipulations as well as the subjects' perception of a stooge.

**Nonvariation: population value.** This method of control when applied to possible problems of situational inequivalence involves two procedures: (1) structuring an experimental situation so that the values of its variables are

---

[7] The effect of the variables just discussed concerning manipulation variation may be expressed in a reverse way by a single assumption: there is the possibility that a subject has certain behavior alternatives which are actually ruled out by the nature of an experimental situation. Criswell (18) expresses it, "In some experiments the interpretation of the subject's responses is similar to the expression of wonder over an ape who might obtain a banana with a stick instead of a shepherd's crook or a ski pole, when no shepherd's crook or ski pole had been supplied him."

equivalent to those in the population structures; (2) selecting subjects who have experience with these population structures (as experience may be one of the structural variables it may not always be a desirable selection criterion). This would include establishing a situation on the basis of the following criteria. (1) Use a task with which the subjects are familiar and have measurable degrees of experience. (2) Conduct the task in an environment similar to that in which it is usually conducted (i.e., classroom, counseling office, family living room) under the pretenses in which it is normally conducted (i.e., examination, choosing a career, family decision making) and with the same apparent consequences (passing or failing, taking precollege courses, making application for a job or university, buying a set of encyclopedias). Of course, if the subject is not familiar with the laboratory as a laboratory, in many cases it may be possible to simulate the environment in the laboratory. (3) Structure the situation to be ecologically and socially similar to the population situations. This would include the concomitance of the ecological and social variables. However, this method would not control for structures which might emerge during an experimental session. Randomization of subjects may provide some control if the emergent structures are a function of the subject's behavior external to the experiment (in the real world). There would be less risk of increasing uncontrolled variation due to these structures if one were to be interested in the development of unstructured groups or were to use preexisting groups than if one were to structure a group experimentally.

The procedures for controlling subjects' incomplete information are straightforward. The number of independent variables should be small and compatible with the abilities of the subjects. Procedures should increase eye contact (unless, of course, eye contact is used as an independent variable). If the experimental situation is one with which *both* the experimenter and the subjects have had common experiences (e.g., the university classroom), the possibility of different perceptions of the manipulations may be minimized.

Instructional set is controlled by careful wording of instructions and information given to the subjects both before (including the recruiting information) and during the session. This would, in particular, include anything that would (1) indicate to the subject what the experimenter thinks the subject will or should do during the session, (2) cause the subject to develop any hypotheses regarding his own behavior (e.g., that there might be a relationship between intelligence and task performance), or (3) reinforce his performance (e.g., praise). History is controlled by isolating the experimental laboratory from the outside world or conducting all the sessions simultaneously or in as short a period as possible. The former procedure is very difficult if a longitudinal design is used where the subject is in the laboratory for only one hour each day for a period of several days.

Three procedures may be used to control for the effects of a stooge. The first is to make sure the stooge looks and behaves like an individual whom the subjects might find in the situation. This does not mean he should be a stereotype, but he should not be unlike anyone the subjects might expect to find in such a situation. In order that variations in a stooge's behavior may be controlled, the stooge should not be aware of the experimental hypothesis. Neither should he be aware of the particular experimental variation until the manipulation is made. A prearranged signal should be flashed to the stooge at the time the independent variable is to be manipulated.

**Nonvariation: nonpopulation value.** The two procedures of this method of control that have been discussed are (1) sampling from a homogeneous population and (2) using the same sample in all experimental variations. However, neither procedure is satisfactory for the control of situation inequivalence because the criticism is one of external validity. These procedures are not useful in controlling history, as one cannot be sure that each subject is experiencing the same history, unless each is locked up in a room for the duration of the experiment. Standardized instructions provide some control of instructional set unless its effects are due to an interaction with the independent variable. Using the same experimental procedures and the same subjects in all experimental variations would provide some control over the subjects' incomplete information. However, as was discussed in the section on subject variation, the use of the same subjects produces an additional extraneous variable, subject maturation. Finally, the stooge's behavior should be standardized and checked observationally for reliability since he, too, may mature.

**Similar variations.** There is very little the similar-variation method can do to control variation resulting from extraneous variables. Ideally, an experimental hypothesis should be tested in a series of experiments, each single experiment being assigned to particular settings through randomization. The few examples of experimentally testing the same hypothesis in different countries is a step in this direction. Randomizing subjects may randomize their different perceptions of the experimental manipulations.[8] Randomizing the experimental sessions will provide some control on errors due to history. Finally, if two or more stooges are used, they should be assigned to an experimental session through randomization procedures.

## 10.4   MEASUREMENT VARIATION

### *Instrumenter's Conceptualization, Characteristics, Behavior, and Maturation*

The three most commonly used measuring instruments are observation, the questionnaire, and the interview. The instrumenter, i.e., the observer, questionnaire constructor, or interviewer, may suffer from the same perils

---

[8] Again, if the experimenter is going to rely on such an assumption, the $N$ should be as large as possible.

as the experimenter.   In some cases he is the experimenter.   The instrumenter's conceptualizations, hypotheses, personal characteristics, and behavior may affect his observations, his wording of questions, his interpretation of the subject's behavior (including the subject's answers to questions) as well as the subject's behavior (5,28,57).   Although the questionnaire constructor is naturally immune, both the observer and the interviewer may be subject to instrumenter maturation, sometimes referred to as instrument decay or unreliability.   Learning and fatigue may produce differences in the measuring instruments between time 1 and time 2 as well as between experimental sessions.

## Reactive Measurement

The process of measuring may itself change that which is hypothetically being measured.   It becomes another stimulus in the total experimental situation affecting the subject's behavior.   There are several ways that measurements can affect the subject's behavior.

*Interpolated measurement* is an extraneous variable which could have been discussed in the section on situational equivalence.   It concerns the effects of using a particular measurement in a situation in which there are usually no such measurements.   The measurement may be disguised as a natural part of the experimental situation or inserted during a momentary interruption during the session or, more typically, administered at the end of the session.   It is also possible to use a measurement in making an experimental manipulation.   The artificiality of these measurements may affect the subject's behavior and the external validity of the experimental findings.

The premanipulation or pretest effect has already been discussed extensively in Chap. 9.   In order to control the effects of the dependent variable which exist prior to the experimental manipulation (the motivations, beliefs, and real-world behavior patterns a subject brings into the laboratory), the investigator may administer a premanipulation measurement of these variables.   However, the taking of the premanipulation measurement may affect the subject's performance on the postmanipulation measurement, particularly if the former gives him a clue to the purpose of the experiment.   The experimental manipulation itself may help the subject interpret the actual purpose of the measurement.

Both the questionnaire and the interview methods require the subject to act as an instrumenter.   Of course, this maximizes the probability of error because both the subject variation and the instrumenter variation are centered in one individual, thereby creating an almost certain probability of uncontrolled variation due to the interaction between the two variables.   For example, a student-subject faced with a professor-instrumenter will probably want to present himself as knowledgeable.   Therefore, when asked whether he saw a particular stimulus in the experimental session, e.g., a deception procedure, he will probably indicate that he did perceive it. In such a situation, the effects of Rosenberg's (43) evaluation apprehension or Couch's and Keniston's (17) social desirability would be optimal. Even if there were no independent sources of error, Lyons (32) argues that a subject cannot successfully play the role both of the subject, the truth-representing role, and of the instrumenter, the information-giving role, because the two roles are incompatible.

The questionnaire and interview methods not only increase the possibility of a social-desirability effect but they also make it possible for the subject's style of answering questions to have an effect on the measurement. Of course, not everyone has such a style, or response set as it is usually called, but some individuals will give positive answers to almost any question, the aye sayers, while others will give negative answers, the nay sayers. Some individuals offer extreme answers; others offer answers of moderation.

## Statistical Regression

*Statistical regression* is an extraneous variable which may result from the use of premanipulation measurements as a basis for sample assignment using the similar-variation method of controlling subject variation. It is based on the assumption that there will always be a degree of uncontrolled measurement variation. Each subject's performance on a test will vary with each administration. Some subjects' performances will increase, and others will decrease. Now, if the subjects are selected on the basis of their extreme scores, the uncontrolled variation could only go in the direction of the mean of all the subjects' scores. Therefore, there would be fewer extreme scores on the second measurement, not because of the experimental manipulation but because of the between-measurement variation and the method of sample selection.

## Time of Measurement

The time at which a measurement is made is of great importance because the effect produced by an experimental manipulation *may* (1) occur only immediately after the manipulation and then extinguish or (2) not occur immediately after the manipulation but be delayed until sometime later. The observational method usually involves continuous measurement of the dependent variable throughout time 2 so that manipulation effects can be of minimal consequence as long as time 2 is extensive enough to cover possible delayed effects. However, if all the measurements are then totaled across time 2, the real strength of the manipulation effects may be hidden by these summarizing procedures. Questionnaires and interviews are usually administered at the end of time 2 and, in many cases, the subject is asked to reflect on his behavior during time 2. Such procedures are both an asset and a liability. The asset is that if the subject reports the behavior, the time it occurred is ignored. This avoids the problem of summarizing procedures. The liability is that the subject may not have attended to his behavior or cannot remember it. If the effect occurred immediately after the manipulation and extinguished rapidly, the probability of this liability is increased.

## Methods of Controlling Measurement Variation

**Variation differences.** The variation-difference method again involves treating the extraneous variables as independent variables in a factorial design. More has been written on the control of the premanipulation or pretest effect than any other measurement error. The variation-difference method of controlling for this effect is the Solomon Four-group design. If practical concerns negate the possibility of this procedure, statistical controls may be applied to measurements of the extraneous variables, e.g., the subjects' interpretations of the measurements. However, one may be adding insult to injury by using measurements to control for measurement variation.

**Nonvariation: population value.** This method of controlling instrumenter variation is the same as that for controlling experimenter variation. The interaction between instrumenter and subject may be minimized by the use of questionnaires or mechanical measuring devices similar to those developed by psychophysicists or operant conditioners. No matter how much the interaction between the instrumenter and the subject, the former should not be aware of (1) the experimental hypotheses or (2) the particular experimental manipulation.

The only procedure for controlling interpolated-measurement variation is to use as a criterion of situational equivalence an experimental situation in which measurements are similar to those occuring in a real situation, for example, examinations in a classroom, ability or intelligence tests in a university testing bureau, teacher or parent observers in a classroom or family. The effects of premanipulation or pretest may be eliminated by simply not using it and, instead, relying on randomization procedures and a larger sample size.

The possible solutions to problems of social desirability and response set are many and are well reviewed by Cook and Selltiz (16). They suggest three general approaches to the control of social desirability. First, the purpose of the questionnaire or interview can be made less apparent by the following procedures: (1) the inclusion of items not relevant to the dependent variable, and (2) the inclusion in each item of a number of aspects in addition to the dependent variable (for example, What did you think of that person's looks, ideas, and behavior?). Second, it is possible to make it easier for the subject to give undesirable answers by the following procedures: (1) assurances of anonymity; (2) stating that there is no right or wrong answer; (3) stating that subjects differ in their views of these things; (4) emphasizing the importance of honest answers in order to contribute to scientific knowledge; (5) increasing rapport in order to create the impression that the instrumenter will not disapprove of any answer; (6) including items to which an unfavorable reply is likely to be considered acceptable (for example, Would you be willing to invite such an antisocial person to join your fraternity?); (7) wording items in such a way that they assume that the subject holds certain attitudes (such as, When did you first become angry with the person?). Third, it could be made harder to falsify a desirable answer by using forced-choice items matched in social desirability.

Cook's and Selltiz's suggestions for controlling response set include the following: (1) varying the wording of items in such a way that for half of them agreement represents a favorable attitude and for half an unfavorable attitude; (2) using pairs of statements representing roughly opposed points of view on a given issue, both statements being worded positively or negatively, and asking the subject to indicate which is nearer his own position or to indicate his position on a scale running between the two statements; (3) using free response items (e.g., open-ended, sentence stubs); (4) using matched pairs of items, one referring to the experimental stimulus, and the other referring to some control stimulus, and scoring in terms of the discrepancy between the two responses. The latter technique is particularly important as it can be used to control for both types of response set (aye sayers–nay sayers and extreme-moderate) as well as social desirability. The authors also suggest that observational techniques are less susceptible to these types of errors.

It is impossible to control for statistical regression by nonvariation methods, as the assumption behind the problem is that there are always changes between administrations of the same measurement. Problems due to the time of measurement may be controlled by repeated measurement over a period long enough to catch delayed effects. However, each repeated measurement increases the probability of reactive measurement error.

**Nonvariation: nonpopulation value.** This method controls for instrumenter variation by using the same instrumenter for all sessions (but thereby increases instrumenter-maturation variation) or by sampling several instruments from a population of homogeneous instrumenters and limiting each to just one experimental session. Reactive measurement is controlled by (1) periodic reliability checks of standardized measuring instruments, (2) pretesting all subjects, and/or (3) using the same subjects in all experimental variations. The latter may provide minimal control of time of measurement by achieving the same attention and recall characteristics. Of course, this method provides no control for statistical regression.

**Similar variations.** Instrumenter variation may be controlled by randomizing different instrumenters among the experimental variations. Nothing can be done to control interpolated measurement error other than to assume that one is randomizing perceptions of the measurements by randomizing the subjects. The same thing applies to the other reactive measurement errors. Statistical regression is controlled by not selecting subjects on the basis of their extreme scores but using all subjects or a random sample of subjects. One should also examine the total dispersion of scores over time. Finally, the problems of time of measurement may be controlled by randomizing the measurement time, thereby decreasing the problems created by repeated measurement, and by randomizing the subjects, assuming, in turn, that the subjects' attention and recall are being randomized (an extremely tenuous assumption).

## 10.5  CONCLUDING REMARKS

Assuming the possible effects of all the extraneous variables just discussed, the traditional advice has been to maximize the differences in the variations of the independent variable. Thus, even with all the uncontrolled variation of the dependent variable, there was a chance, or hope, that some difference could be discriminated as a result of the independent variable. At the same time, it has been recognized that it is either impractical or unethical to produce extreme variations of some variables, either independent or dependent. Therefore, the development and use of methods for the control of extraneous variables is the only apparent answer to this problem.

Some researchers are not so optimistic. The method of throwing in the towel has not gone unsuggested. Lyons (32) has argued that it is not possible to do experiments on experiments because the method doing the testing is just like the method being tested. He states that "they [experimenters] are in the unhappy position of having no cure but the hair of the dog that bit them." Criswell (18) is just slightly less pessimistic when she suggests that the subject can learn as fast as the experimenter in that each new method of control devised by an experimenter is quickly followed by a new extraneous reaction by the subject. Cicourel (15) may be suggesting that experimentation can be used by some disciplines but not by sociology when he asks whether sociological variables are so obscure that we are unable to specify how they can be manipulated in an experiment.

There may be some validity in these criticisms, but not necessarily in the way the authors intended. The last criticism simply has not been disproved, at least not yet. Continuous experimentation on experimental laboratory methods can keep the experimenter that one step ahead of the subject. And the first criticism only draws our attention to the fact that experiments, and experiments on experiments, are social situations whose principles are the same as those principles of social behavior in real social situations. They are both real situations. It is possible to examine social behavior experimentally only by using the principles of social behavior. However, there is no reason why this should in any way discourage experimental laboratory research.

There is much to be done. The first step is simply to become more attentive to extraneous variables. This step has already been taken. The next step is to test the hypotheses involving these extraneous variables and to develop new, more imaginative methods of controlling the variables. Most of the hypotheses suggested in this discussion have not been subjected to empirical test. For example, one can only speculate about the determinants and effects of (1) researcher and instrumenter conceptualizations, (2) subject motivations and beliefs, (3) situational inequivalence, (4) incomplete or unintended information, and (5) stooge characteristics. Most researchers with negative attitudes toward laboratory research speculate in favor of the worst; that is, they believe that extraneous variables produce uncontrolled variation. A few laboratory researchers simply don't speculate because they ignore the possibility of such problems.

A few hypotheses have been met with conflicting evidence. For example, the effects of (1) researcher, or instrumenter, hypotheses and (2) subject hypotheses are still in question. Some research indicates no such effect. I think it safe to assume that much research involving the disproof of hypotheses has never been reported.

Finally, a few hypotheses are well supported. For example, the effects of the experimenter or instrumenter characteristics, e.g., sex, race, personality, anxiety, are well documented in laboratory as well as field research. Research has demonstrated the effects of reactive arrangements, particularly premanipulation or pretest and response-set effects. Suggestions for nonreactive research have been made by Webb, Campbell, Schwartz, and Sechrest (58).

All are researchable topics. Some of the reluctance to investigate them may be a function of their being regarded as problems in methods as opposed to theory. At least two factors are beginning to change this situation. First, social scientists are receiving as much status for being methodologists as for being theorists. Second, and more recently, the distinction between methodology and theory is decreasing. As mentioned previously, both methodology and theory involve social behavior, and therefore they are subject to the same laws. Probably the major distinction lies in the researcher's conceptualizations.

There is one final point which is very important. Whether or not a particular hypothesis has already been researched, there are methods of controlling the extraneous variables involved. One must make the disproof assumption mentioned at the beginning of this discussion and use procedures whereby alternative hypotheses may be eliminated. In laboratory experiments, this requires more time and energy than money. These are a small price to pay for greater validity.

## REFERENCES

1 Argyle, M., and J. Dean: "Eye Contact, Distance and Affiliation," *Sociometry,* **28** (September, 1965), 289–304.

2 Back, Kurt W.: "Influence through Social Communication," *Journal of Abnormal and Social Psychology,* **46** (January, 1951), 9–23.

3 Back, Kurt W., Thomas C. Hood, and Mary L. Brehm: "The Subject Role in Small Group Experiment," *Social Forces,* **43** (December, 1964), 181–187.

4 Bakan, D.: "The Mystery-mastery Complex in Contemporary Psychology," *American Psychologist,* **20** (February, 1965), 186–191.

5 Bernard, P.: "Interaction Effects among Certain Experimenter and Subject Characteristics on a Projective Test," unpublished doctoral dissertation, University of Washington, Seattle, Wash., 1963.

6 Binder, A., D. McConnell, and N. Sjoholm: "Verbal Conditioning as a Function of Experimenter Characteristics," *Journal of Abnormal and Social Psychology,* **55** (November, 1957), 309–314.

7 Blake, R., H. Berkowitz, R. Bellamy, and J. Mouton: "Volunteering as an Avoidance Act," *Journal of Abnormal and Social Psychology,* **53** (September, 1965), 154–156.

8 Block, J., and J. Block: "An Interpersonal Experiment on Reactions to Authority," *Human Relations,* **5** (February, 1952), 91–98.

9 Brock, Timothy, and Lee Alan Becker: "Debriefing and Susceptibility to Subsequent Experimental Manipulations," *Journal of Experimental Social Psychology,* **2** (July, 1966), 314–323.

10 Bryan, James H., and E. Lichtenstein: "Effects of Subject and Experimenter Attitudes in Verbal Conditioning," *Journal of Personality and Social Psychology,* **3** (February, 1966), 182–189.

11 Burchard, W.: "A Study of Attitudes towards the Use of Concealed Devices in Social Science Research," *Social Forces,* **36** (December, 1957), 111–115.

12 Burgess, Robert L.: "Communication Structures and Contingencies," unpublished manuscript, University of Washington, Seattle, Wash., 1965.

13 Campbell, Donald T., and J. Stanley: "Experimental Designs and Quasi-experimental Designs for Research on Teaching," in Nataniel Gage (Ed.), *Handbook of Research on Teaching* (Chicago: Rand McNally, 1963).

14 Capra, P., and J. Dittes: "Birth Order as a Selective Factor among Volunteer Subjects," *Journal of Abnormal and Social Psychology,* **64** (April, 1962), 302.

15 Cicourel, A.: "Method and Measurement in Sociology," in *Experimental Designs in Sociology* (New York: Free Press, 1964), chap. 7.

16 Cook, Stuart W., and Claire Selltiz: "A Multiple-indicator Approach

to Attitude Measurement," *Psychological Bulletin,* **62** (July, 1964), 36–55.

17 Couch, A., and K. Keniston: "Agreeing Response Set and Social Desirability," *Journal of Abnormal and Social Psychology,* **62** (January, 1961), 175–179.

18 Criswell, J.: "The Psychologist as Perceiver," in R. Tagiuri and L. Petrullo (Eds.), *Person Perception and Interpersonal Behavior* (Stanford, Calif.: Stanford, 1958).

19 DiVesta, F., and K. Blake: "The Effects of Instructional 'Sets' on Learning and Transfer," *American Journal of Psychology,* **72** (March, 1959), 57–67.

20 Drabek, T., and J. Haas: "Realism in Laboratory Simulation: Myth or Method?" Paper presented at the annual meeting of the American Sociological Association in Chicago, 1965.

21 Festinger, L.: "Laboratory Experiments," in L. Festinger and D. Katz (Eds.), *Research Methods in the Behavioral Sciences* (New York: Holt, 1953).

22 Fillenbaum, S.: "Prior Deception and Subsequent Experimental Performance: The 'Faithful' Subject," *Journal of Personality and Social Psychology,* 4 (November, 1966), 532–537.

23 Fillenbaum, S., R. Singleton, and J. Hull: "Situational Manipulations in Eyelid Conditioning," unpublished manuscript, University of North Carolina, Chapel Hill, N.C., 1965.

24 French, J.: "Experiments in Field Settings," in L. Festinger and D. Katz (Eds.), *Research Methods in the Behavioral Sciences* (New York: Holt, 1953).

25 Insko, Chester, and John Schopler: Unpublished research notes, University of North Carolina, Chapel Hill, N.C., 1966.

26 Katz, Irwin, S. Oliver Roberts, and James Robinson: "Effects of Task Difficulty, Race of Administrator, and Instructions on Digit-symbol Performance of Negroes," *Journal of Personality and Social Psychology,* 2 (July 1965), 53–59.

27 Kintz, B., D. Delprae, D. Mettee, C. Persons, and R. Schapp: "The Experimenter Effect," *Psychological Bulletin,* 63 (April, 1965), 223–323.

28 Krasner, Leonard: "Studies of the Conditioning of Verbal Behavior," *Psychological Bulletin,* 55 (May, 1958), 148–170.

29 Leik, R.: " 'Irrelevant' Aspects of Stooge Behavior: Implications for Leadership Studies and Experimental Methodology," *Sociometry,* 28 (September, 1965), 259–271.

30 Levy, L., and T. Orr: "The Social Psychology of Rorschach Validity Research," *Journal of Abnormal and Social Psychology,* 58 (January, 1959), 79–83.

31 Lord, E.: "Experimentally Induced Variations in Rorschach Performance," *Psychology Monograph,* 64 (1950), no. 316.

32 Lyons, J.: "On the Psychology of the Psychological Experiment," in C. Scheerer, *Cognition: Theory, Research, Promise* (New York, Harper & Row, 1964).

33 McGuigan, F.: "The Experimenter: A Neglected Stimulus Object," *Psychological Bulletin,* 60 (July, 1963), 421–428.

34 Milgram, S.: "Behavioral Study of Obedience," *Journal of Abnormal and Social Psychology,* 67 (October, 1963), 371–378.

35 Norris, E., and D. Grant: "Eyelid Conditioning as Affected by Verbally Induced Inhibitory Set and Counter-reinforcement," in C. Eriksen, *Behavior and Awareness* (Durham, N.C.: Duke, 1962).

36 Orne, M.: "The Nature of Hypnosis: Artifact and Essence," *Journal of Abnormal and Social Psychology,* 58 (March, 1959), 277–299.

37 Orne, M.: "On the Social Psychology of the Psychological Experiment: With Particular Reference to Demand Characteristics and Their Implications," *American Psychologist,* 17 (November, 1962), 776–783.

38 Orne, M., and F. Evans: "Social Control in the Psychological Experiment: Antisocial Behavior and Hypnosis," *Journal of Personality and Social Psychology,* 1 (March, 1965), 189–200.

39 Orne, M., and Scheibe, K.: "The Contribution of Nondeprivation Factors in the Production of Sensory Deprivation Effects," *Journal of Abnormal and Social Psychology,* 68 (January, 1964), 3–12.

40 Riecken, H.: "A Program for Research on Experiments in Social Psychology," in N. Washburne, *Decision, Values and Groups* (New York: Pergamon Press, 1962), vol. II.

41 Rosenbaum, M.: "The Effect of Stimulus and Background Factors on the Volunteering Response," *Journal of Abnormal and Social Psychology,* 53 (July, 1956), 118–121.

42 Rosenbaum, M., and R. Blake: "Volunteering as a Function of Field Structure," *Journal of Abnormal and Social Psychology,* 50 (March, 1955), 193–196.

43 Rosenberg, M.: "When Dissonance Fails: On Eliminating Evaluation Apprehension from Attitude Measurement," *Journal of Personality and Social Psychology,* 1 (January, 1965), 28–42.

44 Rosenthal, R.: "Experimenter Outcome-orientation and the Results of the Psychological Experiment," *Psychological Bulletin,* 61 (December, 1964), 405–412.

45 Rosenthal, R.: "The Effect of the Experimenter on the Results of Psychological Research," in B. A. Maher (Ed.), *Progress in Experimental Personality Research* (New York: Academic, 1964).

46 Rosenthal R., and K. Fode: "Psychology of the Scientist: V. Three Experiments in Experimenter Bias," *Psychological Reports,* 12 (April, 1963), 491–511.

47 Rosenthal, Robert, Paul Kohn, Patricia M. Greenfield, and Noel

Carota: "Data Desirability, Experimenter Expectancy, and the Results of Psychological Research," *Journal of Personality and Social Psychology,* **3** (January, 1966), 20–27.

48 Rosenthal, Robert, and R. Lawson: "A Longitudinal Study of the Effects of Experimenter Bias on the Operant Learning of Laboratory Rats," *Journal of Psychiatric Research,* **2** (1963), 61–72.

49 Rosenthal, Robert, G. W. Persinger, Linda L. Vikan-Kline, and K. L. Fode: "The Effect of Experiment Outcome-bias and Subject Set on Awareness in Verbal Conditioning Experiments," *Journal of Verbal Learning and Verbal Behavior,* **2** (1963), 275–283.

50 Rosenzweig, S.: "The Experimental Situation as a Psychological Problem," *Psychological Review,* **40** (July, 1933), 337–354.

51 Sapolsky A.: "Effect of Interpersonal Relationships upon Verbal Conditioning," *Journal of Abnormal and Social Psychology,* **60** (February, 1960), 241–246.

52 Sarason, I., and M. Harmatz: "Test Anxiety and Experimental Conditions," *Journal of Personality and Social Psychology,* **1** (May, 1965), 499–505.

53 Sarason, I., and J. Minard: "Interrelationships among Subjects, Experimenter, and Situational Variables," *Journal of Abnormal and Social Psychology,* **67** (July, 1963), 87–91.

54 Sommer, Robert: "Further Studies of Small Group Ecology," *Sociometry,* **28** (December, 1965), 337–348.

55 Spence, K.: "Anxiety (Drive) Level and Performance in Eyelid Conditioning," *Psychological Bulletin,* **61** (February, 1964), 129–139.

56 Spielberger, C.: "The Role of Awareness in Verbal Conditioning," in C. Eriksen, *Behavior and Awareness* (Durham, N.C.: Duke, 1962).

57 Symons, R.: "Specific Experimenter-subject Personality Variables Pertinent to the Influencing Process in a Verbal Conditioning Situation," unpublished doctoral dissertation, University of Washington, Seattle, Wash., 1964.

58 Webb, Eugene W., D. T. Campbell, R. D. Schwartz, and L. Sechrest: *Unobtrusive Measures: Nonreactive Research in the Social Sciences* (Chicago: Rand McNally, 1966).

59 Weick, K.: "Laboratory Experimentation with Organizations," in J. March (Ed.), *Handbook of Organizations* (Chicago: Rand McNally, 1965).

60 Wiggins, James A.: "Interaction Structure, Frustration, and the Extensiveness and Intensity of Aggression," *Sociometry,* **28** (March, 1965), 89–98.

61 Wiggins, James A.: "Status Differentiation, External Consequences, and Alternative Reward Distributions," *Sociometry,* **29** (June, 1966), 89–103.

62 Winkel, G., and I. Sarason: "Subject, Experimenter, and Situational Variables in Research on Anxiety," *Journal of Abnormal and Social Psychology,* **68** (June, 1964), 601–608.

# CHAPTER 11

# The Mathematical Study of Change

JAMES S. COLEMAN

A number of elements are necessary to develop a methodology for the study of change. Ordinarily, the study of change is the study of factors which produce change. One of the classical research techniques to discover these factors is experimentation. Another is continued or periodic observation of an ongoing situation. There are many variations upon these techniques, and combinations of them.

One of the elements that must be mastered in the study of change is the research design: how one can carry out experiment or observation so that valid inferences can be drawn about the factors that produce change. Much work has been devoted to this element. See Chap. 9 and also Campbell and Stanley (6), which discusses various designs and the dangers in inference that attend each.

A second element that must be mastered is more nearly conceptual and analytical: how one can extract from his observations the best description and explanation of change. The present chapter is concerned with this element, proceeding through the construction of models that attempt to mirror the processes of change. The varieties of change make inference difficult without such models.

## The Concept of Change

The concept of change in science is a rather special one, for it does not immediately follow from our sense impressions. The concept of number, of course, is a direct abstraction from sets of objects; and geometric concepts derive directly from spatial configurations. But the concept of change is a second-order abstraction. It is based on a comparison, or difference, between two sense impressions, and, simultaneously, a comparison of the times at which the sense impressions occurred. Thus the concept of change requires an extra intellectual leap beyond the mere formation of concepts that reflect a state of the world. Historically, it had also to wait upon a systematic concept of time, for observations of differences in time have always to run alongside the observations of differences in the state for which change is of interest.

Perhaps because of this, a systematic concept of change came late in the development of Western society and is quite absent in the cultural development of certain primitive tribes. As a mathematical concept, it came about through man's attempt to study the motion of physical objects. The study of motion requires at its very base an idea of change. Such an idea existed in ancient times, but the precise statement of uniform change of position was first made evident in the works of Galileo. Galileo (13) defined uniform motion in this way: "By steady or uniform motion, I mean one in which the distances traversed by the moving particle during any equal intervals of time, are themselves equal." But one of the reasons Galileo was unable to develop the laws of motion beyond such verbal statements is that the formal conceptual tools he had were limited to geometry and were totally static. In particular, there existed no formal conceptual tools—that is, no mathematics—for representing change.

It remained for Isaac Newton to lay the precise conceptual framework for representing change and thus motion. Newtonian mechanics of motion required a mathematical structure for representing change. Thus just as the concepts of line and point and the postulates of geometry developed through attempts to study physical space and the concept of number grew out of attempts to comprehend other aspects of the physical world, the concept of change arose in the study of motion of physical objects. This concept was the differential calculus.

The double abstraction involved in the concept of change has made it a difficult one to comprehend. A paradox occurs: the concept depends intrinsically on a *difference* between states and is thus directly derivative from the concept which measures the states. Yet the concept of change must, as any concept, itself reflect a state of an object at a point in time. An example will show the paradox. Consider a bird in motion. To characterize this bird as having a certain velocity, or quantity of motion, we must observe its position at two points in time and note the difference in position as well as the difference in time. But then can we say the bird had this velocity at the first time or at the second time? Neither, of course, for the quantity depended on measurements at both points in time. Thus what can we say about the bird's velocity at any given point in time?

Consider a more systematic example. Suppose we think of the motion of an object along a line. We measure the position of the object and note the time at which the measurement is taken. Let us call the position, measured from some reference point, $s$ and the time $t$. Thus we can represent the position at time $t$ symbolically by $s_t$. Then at a later time, $\tau$, we note the position again, which we can label $s_\tau$, measured from the same reference point. A primitive idea of change, then, exists when we compare these two positions, say, by subtraction, $s_\tau - s_t$. This gives somehow the idea of change, or motion, yet the concept is far from representing a state of the object in the way that other concepts do. It is necessary, somehow, to pinpoint this concept so that it can be associated with a particular point in time. We have two differences, $s_\tau - s_t$ and $\tau - t$, the difference in position and the difference in time. But only if we pinpoint this concept in time, so that it can be said to represent the state of an object, can we empirically associate it with the factors that produce it.

Newton's solution of this problem took a very ingenious direction. Since what was necessary was a concept at a point in time, he proposed the intellectual experiment of letting the time difference, $\tau - t$, become smaller and smaller, with the result that the space difference, $s_\tau - s_t$, would also become smaller and smaller. As this intellectual experiment proceeds, $\tau - t$ becomes vanishingly small, as does $s_\tau - s_t$. Thus as $\tau$ approaches $t$, the concept of change or motion seems to evaporate, with nothing left. But then Newton proposed, since both these entities would become vanishingly small, that we could arrive at a concept for the quantity of motion by their *ratio*, by $(s_\tau - s_t)/(\tau - t)$ as $\tau - t$ became vanishingly small. One could represent the resulting ratio in any of a variety of ways, such as $ds/dt$, or $\dot{s}$, to use two common representations. But however represented, it could stand as a representation of the quantity of change or motion which characterized the object at a given point in time. Since this quantity is an abstraction not directly measurable, however, it is necessary to relate it to quantities that are directly measurable, that is, to states of the object at particular points in time. This Newton accomplished through the integral calculus, which derives the state quantity $s$, at a particular time $\tau$, from knowledge of the state at an earlier time, say, $s$ at time $t$, and the expression for the derivative, $ds/dt$. For example, if $ds/dt$ is a constant $c$, then the integral calculus gives $s_\tau = s_t + c(\tau - t)$.[1]

Newton's construction can be seen as two steps: first, development of the differential calculus to create a theoretical concept representing the quantity of motion, or velocity, contained by an object; and second, development of the integral calculus to provide a bridge between this theoretical quantity and the observables that can be measured at a given point in time. Thus by this neat trick, Newton attempted to overcome the paradox which attended any conception

---

[1] In this chapter, it will regularly be necessary to shift between the differential equation, which gives the theoretical expression or the model governing change, and the integrated equation, which expresses this model in terms that are directly observable, that is, measurement of states of the object at given points in time. This shift is fundamental to the present chapter: the model for change is expressed theoretically by the differential equation; but to test the model requires a shift to the integrated form, which gives observable quantities. However, the reader need not understand the operation of integration, since the results of that operation will always be given.

of change associated with a particular point in time and to make possible incorporation of such a conception in testable theories. Such an idea found violent objections from mathematicians and natural philosophers, but it had in fact resolved the paradox, and in time was accepted.

In social science as in natural science, the study of change must proceed from such fundamental considerations. It becomes necessary, just as in natural science, to use this concept, which is the only concept we have for systematically studying change. It is, of course, possible to talk or write about change without using this basic mathematical tool. In fact, methods of statistics based on static models of association have been applied to the study of change. But because they are based on static models, the approach is both *ad hoc* and more complicated than necessary. For quantitative research techniques, a failure to base the study of change upon the mathematical tools appropriate to it can lead only to confusion and unnecessary complications. This will become evident later in the chapter when we examine approaches that start from statistical ideas rather than from this mathematical concept.

At the outset, it is necessary to recognize that, although the tool of calculus was first developed for use in the study of motion, it still constitutes the basic tool in the study of change and is the only conceptual tool we have for representing change in any quantity (except for the special case of discontinuous jumps, or instantaneous changes of state, which will be examined subsequently).

## Variations in the Quantitative Study of Change

There are at least two fundamental cases in the application of calculus to the study of change, and these require different mathematical treatment. The classical case, and the simplest to study mathematically, is the study of changes in a quantity. A quantity is measured by a number, and change in the quantity can be measured by change in the number. An example is the case of motion, since distance (from a reference point) is a quantity representable by a number. (We will consider here only scalar quantities, although the treatment is easily generalized to vector quantities.)

Some concepts which sociologists use are quantities, represented by a number. The most common one of these is numerical size, such as the size of a group or the size of a city.[2] Others are the number of acts of a certain kind,

---

[2] Size is a concept which can be considered either a quantity, representable by a number, or a state, representable by a probability of being in the state. Treatment as a number involves discontinuities, since number changes only in integral values. Treatment as a state, however, requires a whole set of probabilities, one to represent each of the possible size states that the group can be in. It is the more exact treatment, and its use is indicated whenever the numerical treatment introduces too much approximation. See James Coleman (7, chaps. 10, 11) for mathematical treatment of the state probability approach in sociology. For similar treatment in related fields, showing both approaches (the deterministic and the stochastic), see N. T. J. Bailey (1).

the amount of time spent in a given activity, and so on.    Much behavior which sociologists study in research, however, is not a quantity at all, but a state: responding yes or no to an attitude question, acting or failing to act, voting for candidate A, B, or C, migrating or remaining, entering job x, y, or z, etc. Change in such behavior must be studied as change from one state to another and requires a different mathematical treatment.    This is necessary because such change of state is not regular, but discontinuous: it proceeds in jumps, and thus the strategy of calculus, which lets the difference $s_\tau - s_t$ diminish to the vanishing point, is no longer possible, as it is when change is regular.    Discontinuous change, however, may be studied by the same tool of calculus, but applied to the *probability* of being in a given state.    In such treatment, the quantity of change is the rate of change of the probability with respect to time, $dp/dt$, or $\dot{p}$.

These two cases must be treated separately in the examination below. The classical case, change in a quantity, will be treated first, and then the case of change in state.    But before proceeding, we shall classify somewhat more precisely the study of change.    For the formal treatment, three dimensions are important.    These will allow locating the treatment to be undertaken in this chapter.    The dimensions are:

> $a$: continuous variable $(+)$ or qualitative state $(-)$
> $b$: continuous time $(+)$ or discrete time $(-)$
> $c$: stochastic $(+)$ or deterministic $(-)$

There are eight configurations of change generated by these dimensions, and they require different mathematical treatment.    These are indicated below.

*Dimension*

| Type | a | b | c | Treatment |
|------|---|---|---|-----------|
| 1 | + | + | + | diffusion processes in stochastic theory |
| 2 | + | + | − | differential equations |
| 3 | + | − | + | random-walk processes in stochastic theory |
| 4 | − | + | + | continuous-time discrete-space stochastic theory |
| 5 | + | − | − | difference equations |
| 6 | − | + | − | step functions |
| 7 | − | − | + | discrete-time discrete-space stochastic theory |
| 8 | − | − | − | permutation matrices and other Boolean matrices |

The exposition in this chapter concentrates upon types 2 and 4 of change, although type 7 is treated at some points together with 4.    The major organization of the chapter is along dimension $a$, continuous variables versus qualitative states.    The organization corresponds also, however, to a difference in deterministic and stochastic treatment.    The deterministic treatment is taken for continuous variables and the stochastic treatment for qualitative states, because these approaches allow the fullest treatment for the respective types of variables.

## 11.1 CHANGE IN QUANTITATIVE VARIABLES[3]

### *Change Solely as a Function of Time*

The simplest instance of change is that which Galileo described, in the case of motion, as uniform change of position. Much of the study of change in elementary statistics texts is confined to such description of change, though the actual data show variability around such uniform change. The assumption of uniform change may be stated very simply as

$$\frac{dx_1}{dt} = b \tag{11.1}$$

where $b$ is a constant.

As indicated earlier, to test this assumption empirically requires expression of Eq. (11.1) in terms of values of $x_1$ that can be measured. This is carried out through integrating Eq. (11.1) to give

$$x_{1t} = x_{10} + bt \tag{11.2}$$

where $x_{10}$ expresses the value of $x_1$ at the time taken as $t = 0$. The value of $b$ may be found by regression analysis, given values of $x_1$ at a variety of times. (If desired, a best-fitting value of $x_{10}$ can be estimated at the same time.)

Moving a step beyond this analysis would allow the rate of change to be described as a more general function of time. For example, Eq. (11.3) postulates that the rate of change $dx_1/dt$ is a nonlinear function of time:

$$\frac{dx_1}{dt} = b_1 + b_2 t + b_3 t^2 + b_4 t^3 \tag{11.3}$$

In this case, integration gives as the equation for $x_1$ as a function of time:

$$x_{1t} = x_{10} + b_1 t + \frac{b_2}{2} t^2 + \frac{b_3}{3} t^3 + \frac{b_4}{4} t^4 \tag{11.4}$$

By using multiple regression techniques, we may obtain the estimates of $b_1$, $b_2$, $b_3$, and $b_4$ (and $x_{10}$ if desired). Often data do not fit the hypothesis of uniform change, and an equation like Eq. (11.3) is necessary to adequately describe the change.

Having carried out such an examination, we can study the coefficients of the powers of $t$ to examine whether a particular series, such as an exponential, is approximated by the data. Alternatively, it is possible to *assume* some particular nonuniform rate of change, and proceed by estimating the coefficients for that case, and test the fit of the data. For example, we might assume that the

[3] Not until page 453 will the possibility of measurement error be introduced. Thus for any data likely to contain measurement error, the methods discussed in the subsection "Measurement Error or Unreliability" (beginning on page 453) should be used.

rate of increase of the number of actions of a given kind in a group would be proportional to the number of actions already taken:

$$\frac{dx}{dt} = bx \tag{11.5}$$

After integration, the number of actions may be expressed as a function of time:

$$x_{1t} = x_{10}e^{bt} \tag{11.6}$$

or

$$\ln x_{1t} = \ln x_{10} + bt$$

By using this approach, one can estimate $b$ (and if desired, a best-fitting value for $x_{10}$) by regression procedures. It becomes possible also to get a preliminary estimate by plotting $\ln x_{1t}$ versus $t$. If the assumption is an appropriate one, this plot will approximate a straight line.

This general approach, which merely uses time [or a particular growth function such as Eq. (11.5)] for explaining change, is not a very satisfactory one. It describes the change without giving any good ideas about the factors that may have brought it about. Thus it is necessary to introduce some of these factors to get insight into which ones contributed to the change. First, however, it is useful to examine more generally the possibility introduced above, that change in a quantity depends upon its own size.

**Fig. 11.1**    $x_{1t} = x_{10}e^{bt}$

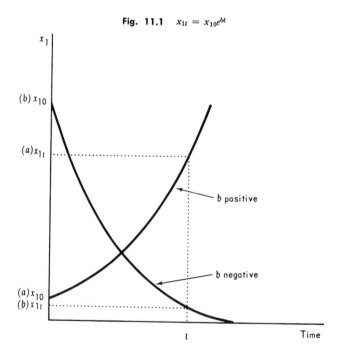

## Immanent Change

The next step in explaining change beyond the assumption of uniform change or change dependent on time alone is the assumption that change depends on the value of the variable itself undergoing change.

Perhaps the most primitive approach in explaining $dx_1/dt$, where $dx_1/dt$ is not merely uniform, is explanation in terms of the existing value of $x_1$. If $dx_1/dt$, the rate of change, depends on the value of $x_1$ in a linear fashion, then the equation for such dependence is

$$\frac{dx_1}{dt} = a + bx_1 \qquad (11.7)$$

This expression relates the amount of change, $dx_1/dt$, to the existing value of $x_1$. But we wish to explain $dx_1/dt$, that is, to estimate $b$, the coefficient showing the dependence of the amount of change upon $x_1$, and $a$, the coefficient showing the amount of change if the value of $x_1$ were zero. This necessitates expressing $a$ and $b$ in terms of values of $x_1$ at various times. That is, we do not observe directly the quantity of change, $dx_1/dt$, but rather we observe the values of $x_1$ at particular points in time. Thus as before we cannot simply estimate $a$ and $b$ by use of Eq. (11.7) but must transform Eq. (11.7) in such a way that $a$ and $b$ are expressed as functions of $x_1$ at different times.

Suppose time is labeled so that 0 and $t$ are the values of time at two successive observations. Then the solution of Eq. (11.7) gives $x_{1t}$ as a function of $x_{10}$ and the two coefficients $a$ and $b$, letting $\Delta t = t - 0$:

$$x_{1t} = \frac{a}{b}\left(e^{b\Delta t} - 1\right) + x_{10}e^{b\Delta t} \qquad (11.8)$$

If the observations are equally spaced so that $t - 0$ is the same for all adjacent observations, this equation is in the form

$$x_{1t} = a^* + b^* x_{10} \qquad (11.9)$$

Thus when one can estimate $a^*$ and $b^*$ by use of Eq. (11.9), then it becomes possible to use these to estimate the coefficients of change, $a$ and $b$. This will be the general strategy throughout this chapter. The integrated form of the differential equation can be fitted to data to estimate parameters such as $a^*$ and $b^*$. But the differential equation itself expresses the model, in terms of fundamental parameters of change, such as $a$ and $b$. Thus the general procedure is to set up the model as the differential equation, then to use the data to estimate $a^*$ and $b^*$, test the goodness of fit of the model by the amount of variance in $x_{1t}$ explained, and then use $a^*$ and $b^*$ to estimate the basic parameters of change, $a$ and $b$. The minimum data necessary for estimating $a^*$ and $b^*$ are three observations. With three values of $x_1$ taken at equal intervals of time, it is possible to write two equations of the form of Eq. (11.9), and thereby solve for $a^*$ and $b^*$. Ordinarily, however, one has many values of $x_1$, taken at equal

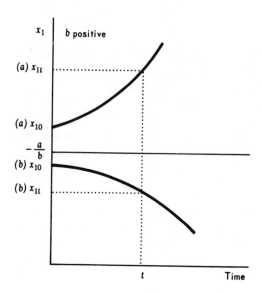

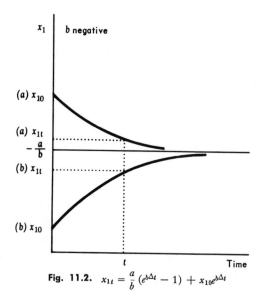

**Fig. 11.2.**    $x_{1t} = \dfrac{a}{b}\left(e^{b\Delta t} - 1\right) + x_{10}e^{b\Delta t}$

intervals in time, and the methods of regression analysis can be used to obtain $a^*$ and $b^*$. The data may be two waves of a panel with two observations on many individuals or many observations on the same individual.

After the values of $a^*$ and $b^*$ have been estimated, they may be used to calculate the value of the coefficients of change, $a$ and $b$. These equations [found by using Eqs. (11.8) and (11.9) to solve for $a$ and $b$] are

$$a = \frac{a^* \ln b^*}{\Delta t \, (b^* - 1)} \tag{11.10}$$

$$b = \frac{\ln b^*}{\Delta t} \tag{11.11}$$

These values, $a$ and $b$, constitute the fundamental parameters of change. The dimensions on $a$ are units of change in $x_1$ per unit time, and the dimensions on $b$ are units of change per unit time per unit of $x_1$ existing.

If the assumptions of this model are met, the values of $a$ and $b$ will not be dependent on the length of time taken in the regression analysis based on Eq. (11.9). The values of $a^*$ and $b^*$ will be dependent on the length of time, however. If, for example, the period of time $\tau - 0$ is twice that of $t - 0$, then by using observations at times 0 and $\tau$ we can estimate another set of parameters:

$$x_\tau = a^0 + b^0 x_{10} \tag{11.12}$$

It can be shown through Eq. (11.8) that the relation between $a^0$, $b^0$, and $a^*$, $b^*$, is as follows:

$$b^0 = b^{*2} \tag{11.13}$$

$$a^0 = a^*(1 + b^*) \tag{11.14}$$

Thus if we double the interobservation period, we should expect to find the relationships shown in Eqs. (11.13) and (11.14) between the regression coefficients found for these periods. If this relation does not hold, it may be a sign of measurement error (see below, page 453).

It is important to note some of the assumptions implicit in this technique. When the technique utilizes data from a number of persons (for example, each observed at time 0 and $t$) to estimate a single pair of coefficients, the implicit assumption is made that the process is identical for all persons. That is, a two-wave panel would give a pair of observations $x_{1t}$ and $x_{10}$ for each individual. These data could be used in conjunction with Eq. (11.9) to estimate $a^*$ and $b^*$, and thereby $a$ and $b$. But in so doing, we assume that $a$ is identical for all individuals and that $b$ is identical for all individuals. If they are not equal, our estimates of $a$ and $b$ are some kind of average over the set of individuals in the sample.

Similarly, if a set of values of $x_1$ for one individual over many points in time is used to estimate $a$ and $b$ for that individual, then this implies an assumption of constancy of $a$ and $b$ over time.

Third, a strong assumption implied by Eq. (11.7) is the linearity of $dx_1/dt$'s dependence on $x_1$. This is always the simplest kind of dependence, but one which may not be true in a given case.

A fourth assumption is that the dependence of $dx_1/dt$ is upon the present value of $x_1$. If there is a lag, then $dx_1/dt$ depends upon earlier values of $x_1$, perhaps upon the value of $x_1$ at a particular time interval, perhaps upon values of

$x_1$ over a period of time extending from the present backward.   The existence of such a lag often means that one or more other variables intervene in the process and that the process itself is more complex than has been assumed.

All these assumptions are difficult to eliminate by making the model more general.   The first may be partly tested by comparing estimates of $a$ and $b$ made over subsamples of the values of $x_1$.   However, the development of the more general models, with nonlinearity and with heterogeneity of the coefficients $a$ and $b$, goes beyond the scope of this chapter.   The overall test of this explanation of change is effected in a standard way, by obtaining predicted values of $x_{1t}$ to compare with the actual ones and using this comparison to show how much of the variance in $x_{1t}$ is explained by $x_{10}$ through Eq. (11.9).

**Regression effects and the sign of the coefficient $b$.**   One of the most prominent and pervasive phenomena in the study of change is generally labeled *regression effect*.   It is the tendency for a second measurement on an individual who was initially above the mean to be lower than the first, and a second measurement on an individual who was initially below the mean to be higher.   This is sometimes explained in terms of measurement error, since measurements that are higher than average will often be so partly because they contain positive measurement error, but on a second measurement the distribution of measurement error will lead them less often to contain positive measurement errors, and thus tend away from the extreme toward the mean.   To cite an example, if a man's IQ is measured as very high, the best guess about its value on a subsequent measurement is that it will be lower.

In many cases of regression effect, however, something more than measurement error, some actual change, is involved.   For example, the same regression phenomenon holds for a man's weight, even though his weight can be measured without appreciable error.   In this case, the explanation requires something more than a consideration of measurement error.

It is here that an examination of Eq. (11.7) becomes relevant.   If the sign of $b$ is positive, this means that the larger is $x_1$, the greater the positive change will be, as in the growth process examined on page 434.   If $x_1$ is large in a negative direction, the change will be great in the negative direction.   In short, a positive value of $b$ leads to an unstable situation: the magnitude of the variable increases without limit, in a positive or negative direction, depending on whether it begins above its mean or below.

Such a quantity is rare in any scientific discipline.   It does occur, and there are examples of such unstable growth processes, some of which will be considered in a later section.   However, most quantities are part of equilibrating processes, so that once far from the mean, they will tend to return.   When this is so, the sign of $b$ is negative.   This may be thought of as negative feedback, for this is precisely what is meant by negative feedback.   This is also the condition that produces regression toward the mean.   If the value of $b$ is large and negative, this will produce a regression effect which is large.   The result is that

$x_1$ will always be kept close to its mean. Figure 11.1 shows the time path of $x_1$ under the two conditions of positive and negative feedback.

The analysis of a regression effect in this way allows for the clarification of certain issues that surround this effect. In particular, there is always one puzzling aspect of regression effects: Why should the value of $x_1$ regress toward the mean of a particular population, when the effects are all at the level of the individual? For example, if an individual is in a population with mean $\bar{x}_1$, the principle of regression toward the mean would dictate that his value $x_1$ should regress toward $\bar{x}_1$. But if he is in a population with mean $\bar{x}_1'$, the principle would dictate that the $x_1$ should regress toward $\bar{x}_1'$. Yet clearly this is a process stated at the level of the individual, in which the population mean should have no effect.

The answer to this puzzle lies in two assumptions besides negative feedback that are implicit in the regression principle: (1) that the variable is in aggregate equilibrium, and (2) that each individual is characterized by the same values of the parameters which govern the process.

If these two assumptions are true, then the mean value of $x_1$ is $-a/b$, and this is the equilibrium value for *each* individual, toward which $x_1$ will regress. However, often assumption 2 is not met in practice, and individuals are in fact characterized by different values of $a$ and $b$, dependent upon the other variables that characterize them. As a consequence, each will be tending toward his own mean, although with data of the sort usually gathered, we have no way of knowing what that mean is. That is, our data ordinarily allow only an estimate of an overall $a$ and $b$ for the total sample, unless we introduce additional variables, as discussed in a subsequent section. Thus we expect regression toward the mean of this particular sample, but only because we implicitly assume that all persons in the sample are characterized by the same coefficients governing movement.

**Negative feedback and functional analysis.**[4] The case of Eq. (11.7) where $b$ has a negative value provides a useful explication of functional analysis. The general character of functional explanations is something like this:

Condition $x$ exists in order to carry out function $y$.

For example, a popular functional explanation of the differential status accorded different occupations goes as follows:

A differential reward system exists in order to motivate persons into those occupations most necessary to the society's functioning.

In terms of such an explanation, an element exists not through its causes, but through its consequences. If its consequences are important to the functioning of society (or whatever other social unit is under consideration), then in

---

[4] I am grateful to H. M. Blalock, Jr., for pointing out to me the relationship discussed in this section.

functional explanations, this is sufficient to explain its existence.[5]   In its most radical form, a functional explanation states:

Condition $x$ exists because it has functions necessary to the survival of society.

Most persons would argue that this is no explanation at all, for it implies a reification of society into an actor with goals of survival which it can implement. Nevertheless, this does describe certain relationships, and as such is closely related to the description given by Eq. (11.7) when $b$ has a negative value.

Consider Eq. (11.7), which states that $dx_1/dt = a + bx_1$.   If $b$ has a negative value, then this means two things: when $x_1$ is above its equilibrium value of $-a/b$, then it will decrease to this equilibrium value, because the rate of change, $dx_1/dt$, will be negative.   And when $x_1$ is below its equilibrium value, it will increase to the equilibrium.   There is no statement whatever of the causal process through which this might occur.   When such negative feedback exists, then there is a chain of effects, somewhat as follows: $x_1 \rightarrow x_2 \rightarrow x_3 \rightarrow x_1$, where there is an odd number of negative effects.[6]   That is, $x_1$ may affect $x_2$ positively, which affects $x_3$ positively, which affects $x_1$ negatively.   This would produce a system that would come to stable equilibrium.[7]   The statement of Eq. (11.7) constitutes a kind of shortcut to this system, leaving out variables $x_2$ and $x_3$ altogether.   Thus in such a system which comes to stable equilibrium, an equation expressing change in each variable as a function only of its own value can be stated for each of the variables in the system—so long as it is closed and not subject to exogenous shocks.

In this case, the variable acts as a surrogate for all the variables involved in cycles leading back to itself—in the example, $x_2$ and $x_3$.   In the same way, functional analysis takes a shortcut, letting the variable itself stand for the chain of variables which it affects that in turn affect it.   If the system were closed and if it had a stable equilibrium point, then there would be no danger in this shortcut.   Unless these two conditions are true, however, this approach does incur dangers, for if one of the hidden intervening variables changes, the self-equilibrating relation might not hold.   Even without such danger, of course, this approach does not aid much in the development of theory, because it obscures the relationships of which the system is composed.   Thus it allows no possibility of seeing how an exogenous change in one of the variables may bring about changes in other variables in the system.   This has always been a major defect

---

[5] There are some watered-down versions of functional analysis that make it scarcely distinguishable from ordinary explanation.   See Kingsley Davis (11).

[6] A chain of effects exists also in growth processes, where there is positive feedback, and the sign of $b$ is positive.   Even in population growth, where the variable $x_1$ is number of persons, there are implicit mechanisms, so that the rate of growth of population is not *directly* dependent on population size.   It is dependent on the number of conception-producing interactions, which is dependent on the number of males and the number of females in a certain age segment of the population.

[7] A system with a stable equilibrium point could also be produced by configurations of coefficients other than that stated, if each variable had a negative effect upon its own change. But at this point, we want to explicitly exclude such self-effects.

of functional analysis and accounts for its unsuitability for the study of change.

In nearly all systems of linear differential equations, there is a term in each equation for the negative feedback of the variable on itself. This can be seen as a surrogate for all the chains of feedback in the empirical system that remain implicit in the formal system. As the formal system becomes more complete, this coefficient should approach zero. Thus the size of the coefficient allows a way of evaluating the completeness of any representation of the empirical system by a system of differential equations.

## *Exogenous Change: Explaining Change in One Variable by Values of Other Variables*

The type of change described above is very special, for it is change explained only in terms of previous values of the quantity undergoing change. The coefficient $a$ includes some of the change due to other factors that were constant over the sample of time or the sample of individuals studied. The coefficient $b$ includes some of the change due to factors which are affected by $x_1$ and in turn affect it in such a way as to give negative (or possibly positive) feedback. The unexplained variance in $x_{1t}$ includes the change due to those factors which varied over the sample of time or individuals. Ordinarily in the study of change, it is these other factors whose effect is of interest.

The simplest introduction of such factors is in a form analogous to Eq. (11.7), a simple linear equation. For the case of a single independent variable, $x_2$, which we will assume first to be constant, the equation is

$$\frac{dx_1}{dt} = a + b_1 x_1 + b_2 x_2 \qquad (11.15)$$

In the same way as with Eq. (11.7), this equation may be solved to give $x_{1t}$ as a function of $x_{10}$, $x_2$, and the parameters $a$, $b_1$, $b_2$. The solution is

$$x_{1t} = \frac{a}{b_1} (e^{b_1 \Delta t} - 1) + e^{b_1 \Delta t} x_{10} + \frac{b_2}{b_1} (e^{b_1 \Delta t} - 1) x_2 \qquad (11.16)$$

This equation is again in linear form, so that regression analysis may be used:

$$x_{1t} = a^* + b_1^* x_{10} + b_2^* x_2 \qquad (11.17)$$

After estimating the values of $a^*$, $b_1^*$, and $b_2^*$ by regression methods, then if for convenience we set $C^* = b_1 \Delta t / (e^{b_1 \Delta t} - 1) = \ln b_1^* / (b_1^* - 1)$, the coefficients of change are

$$a = \frac{a^* C^*}{\Delta t} \qquad (11.18)$$

$$b_1 = \frac{\ln b_1^*}{\Delta t} \qquad (11.19)$$

$$b_2 = \frac{b_2^* C^*}{\Delta t} \qquad (11.20)$$

The meaning of $a$, $b_1$, and $b_2$ should be made explicit, because these are the fundamental coefficients that express the dependence of $x_1$ on various factors. They are defined as follows:

$a$ = the number of units change per unit time in $x_1$ when it is zero and $x_2$ is also zero.

$b_1$ = the number of units change per unit time in $x_1$ for each unit of $x_1$. Most often, the sign of $b_1$ will be negative, which expresses the tendency for $x_1$ to reach an equilibrium, that is, for change to be negative when the value of $x_1$ is positive, or for change to be positive when the value of $x_1$ is negative.

$b_2$ = the number of units change per unit time in $x_1$ for each unit of $x_2$. This is a direct measure of the dependence of $x_1$ on $x_2$. The ratio $b_2/b_1$ shows the relative dependence of $x_1$ on itself and on $x_2$.

Figure 11.3 shows the relation between $x_1$ and $t$ for two different values of $x_2$, when $b_1$ is negative. This approach can obviously be directly generalized to a dependence of $x_1$ on a set of other variables. The relative sizes of the regression coefficients $b_i{}^*$ for all independent variables other than the dependent variable reflect the relative sizes of the true coefficients of change, $b_i$, since each, multiplied by $\ln b_1{}^*/(b_1{}^* - 1)\Delta t$, is equal to the corresponding $b_i$.

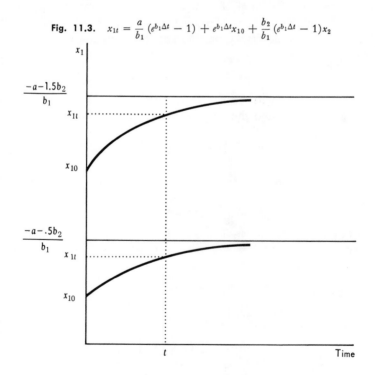

**Fig. 11.3.**  $\displaystyle x_{1t} = \frac{a}{b_1}(e^{b_1\Delta t} - 1) + e^{b_1\Delta t}x_{10} + \frac{b_2}{b_1}(e^{b_1\Delta t} - 1)x_2$

**Exogenous change when the independent variables are not constant.**[8]
The preceding section assumed that independent variables $x_2$, $x_3$, . . . were
constant through time. Often, however, they are not constant, even though we
can assume they are unaffected by the dependent variable under study, $x_1$. In
this case, a somewhat more complex formulation is necessary. If $x_2$ is a function
of time, then integration of Eq. (11.15) gives

$$x_{1t} = \frac{a}{b_1} (e^{b_1 \Delta t} - 1) + e^{b_1 \Delta t} x_{10} + b_2 e^{b_1 \Delta t} \int_0^t x_{2\tau} e^{-b_1 \tau} d\tau \qquad (11.21)$$

Without explicit knowledge of the functional dependence of $x_2$ upon time,
we assume some arbitrary function. Probably the most reasonable assumption
in most cases is that $x_2$ varies linearly with time between the two values of $x_{20}$ and
$x_{2t}$. With such an assumption, Eq. (11.21) can be integrated to give

$$x_{1t} = \frac{a}{b_1} (e^{b_1 \Delta t} - 1) + e^{b_1 \Delta t} x_{10} + \frac{b_2}{b_1} (e^{b_1 \Delta t} - 1)x_{20} + \frac{b_2}{b_1} \left[ \frac{e^{b_1 \Delta t} - 1}{b_1 \Delta t} - 1 \right] \Delta x_{2t}$$
$$(11.22)$$

In this equation, compared with Eq. (11.16), there is an additional variable
$\Delta x_{2t}$, which is simply the change in $x_2$ between time 0 and $t$. In using empirical
data with regression analysis, one would estimate $a^*$, $b_1^*$, $b_2^*$, and $b_{2\Delta}^*$ in Eq.
(11.23):

$$x_{1t} = a^* + b_1^* x_{10} + b_2^* x_{20} + b_{2\Delta}^* \Delta x_{2t} \qquad (11.23)$$

Comparison of Eq. (11.22) with Eq. (11.16) shows that $a^*$, $b_1^*$, and $b_2^*$ are
related in the same way to the coefficients of change $a$, $b_1$, and $b_2$. This gives
an extra degree of freedom, $b_{2\Delta}^*$, to test the fit of the model. The relation of
$b_{2\Delta}^*$ to the other parameters should be

$$b_{2\Delta}^* = \frac{b_2^*(1 - C^*)}{(b_1^* - 1)C^*} \qquad (11.24)$$

After solving for the regression coefficients, we should find that $b_{2\Delta}^*$ is
related to the others as indicated by Eq. (11.24). If this is not so, then there is
good evidence that the model does not fit the data.

The overall result of including the possibility of exogenous change in $x_2$
leaves the original relationships between observations and coefficients of the
model undisturbed, but adds a new relation that makes possible a further test
of the model. Alternatively, $b_{2\Delta}^*$ can be used with $b_2^*$ in estimating $b_2$, with
$b_2 = [C^*/2\Delta t][b_2^* + b_{2\Delta}^* C^*(b_1^* - 1)/(1 - C^*)]$, from Eqs. (11.22) and
(11.23).

---

[8] I am thankful to Mr. T. Robert Harris for pointing out to me that the preceding section
is valid only for the case when the independent variables are constant, and for suggesting the
method on which this section is based.

*The Relation of Coefficients of Change to Regression Coefficients in Cross-sectional Analysis*

Most often, statistical analysis must be based on cross-sectional data. When the analysis is carried out with the aim of establishing causal inferences, it ordinarily results in regression coefficients from cross-sectional data, as in Blalock (3). With $x_1$ as the dependent variable and with all observations made at time 0, the regression equation would be (using Greek symbols for representing the regression coefficients in this case):

$$x_{10} = \alpha + \beta_2 x_{20} + \beta_3 x_{30} + \cdots \qquad (11.25)$$

The relation between these coefficients and those obtained from the change analysis is simple and direct. The cross-section analysis assumes, either implicitly or explicitly, that the causal processes have resulted in an equilibrium state. That is, the implicit assumption in regression analysis is that this is a stable relationship, which would give the same values for the regression coefficients in a later cross section unless an exogenous factor disturbed the situation. This assumption implies that $dx_1/dt = 0$, and thus that Eq. (11.15) becomes

$$0 = a + b_1 x_1 + b_2 x_2 \qquad (11.26)$$

Transposing to let $x_1$ be the dependent variable gives

$$x_1 = -\frac{a}{b_1} - \frac{b_2}{b_1} x_2 \qquad (11.27)$$

Similarly, in multivariate explanation, $-b_3/b_1$ would be the coefficient for $x_3$, and in general, $-b_i/b_1$ for $x_i$.

Thus the relationship between the change coefficients $a$, $b_1$, and $b_i$, and the regression coefficients $\alpha$ and $\beta_i$, is

$$\alpha = -\frac{a}{b_1} \qquad (11.28)$$

$$\beta_i = -\frac{b_i}{b_1} \qquad (11.29)$$

It is useful to see intuitively the meaning of $\beta_i$ or $-b_i/b_1$ under this assumption of equilibrium. As indicated earlier, equilibrium implies that $b_1$ is negative. Therefore $b_i$ is positive. Then $\beta_i$ represents simply the relative size of $b_i$, the coefficient of effect of $x_i$ on $x_1$, compared with $b_1$.

The coefficients of change are not fully identifiable from the regression coefficients. It should be noted that the relation of either to the lagged regression coefficients $a^*$ and $b_i^*$ is quite different, because the lagged coefficients are a (nonlinear) function of the time between observations. The relation of Eqs. (11.28) and (11.29) holds, of course, only under the assumption of aggregate equilibrium, and more important, assumes prior knowledge of the direction of causality, which the coefficients $b_i$ in the change model do not.

## Change as a Function of Contextual Variables

In the examination above, change in a quantity that describes behavior was assumed a function of other variables describing the individual or the social unit under consideration. But a special case often arises in which an individual's behavior is affected by the behavior of those around him.[9]

Such a variation can be easily handled by this approach. Consider a group of individuals, each characterized by $x_1, x_2, \ldots$ on variables 1, 2, .... Then the group itself is characterized by the means of these variables: $\bar{x}_1, \bar{x}_2,$ .... Now the behavior of each individual in the group may be affected not only by the quantities that describe him, but also by the others' behavior. That is, a change in $x_1$ may depend on $x_1, x_2, \ldots$, but also upon $\bar{x}_1 - x_1/n, \bar{x}_2 - x_2/n, \ldots,$ where $\bar{x}_i - x_i/n = \tilde{x}_i$ is the average of *others* in the group on variable $i$. In cross-sectional analysis, the methods for such treatment have been labeled *structural effects* analysis, or *compositional effects* analysis (4,10). Yet the possibility of various statistical artifacts, such as those introduced by measurement error, makes valid inferences about effects difficult to draw from cross-sectional analysis alone. With panel data, and the methods presented here, one can relate the change itself to contextual variables, and thus have a much stronger basis for inference.

The general equation describing such change in $x_1$ as a function of individual and contextual variables is

$$\frac{dx_1}{dt} = a + b_1 x_1 + b_2 x_2 + b'_1 \tilde{x}_1 + b'_2 \tilde{x}_2 + \cdots \qquad (11.30)$$

The solution of this equation is exactly as in the preceding case, indicated by Eq. (11.16). The relevant regression equation is

$$x_{1t} = a^* + b_1^* x_{10} + b_2^* x_{20} + b_1'^* \tilde{x}_{10} + b_2'^* \tilde{x}_{20} + \ldots \qquad (11.31)$$

In this regression equation, the relation of $a^*$, $b_i^*$, and $b_i'^*$ to $a$, $b_i$, and $b_i'$ is given by Eqs. (11.18) for $a$, (11.19) for $b$, and (11.20) for other $b_i$ and $b_i'$.

This dynamic formulation of contextual effects allows the possibility that a quantity may be affected in one direction by the individual variable and in another by the contextual variable. The most common example of this is the case of a variable's effect on itself. That is, a quantity representing some behavior will be negatively affected by its own size, but positively affected by the average level of the group. A child's boisterousness (for example, as measured by the noise he creates) will show the usual regression effect: it is negatively affected by its own level to produce some equilibrium value. But in a group context, the child's boisterousness is positively affected by the average level of boisterousness in the group.

---

[9] I am grateful to Herbert Costner for raising in a seminar the problem of contextual effects via regression analysis, which suggested to me its study through regression analysis of changes, as outlined in this section.

A similar phenomenon holds in many areas. An attitude is usually subject to the regression effect: the more extreme it is, the more likely it is to move toward the center. But in the context of others, the more extreme they are, the more extreme it will tend to be. Thus under certain conditions an explosive effect could occur, where attitudes or behavior go quite out of control.

The process can be characterized quite easily. If $b_{1i}$ is the coefficient of effect of one's own behavior in damping itself, and $b_{1j}$ is the positive effect of each other person $j$'s behavior, then we have, for individual $i$ in a group of size $n$,

$$\frac{dx_{1i}}{dt} = a_i + b_{11}x_{11} + \cdots + b_{1i}x_{1i} + \cdots + b_{1n}x_{1n} \qquad (11.32)$$

This equation can be viewed simply as a case of $n - 1$ independent variables and one dependent variable, as above, page 441. In the situation described here, $b_{1i}$ is negative, and all other $b_{1j}$'s positive. However, a difficulty arises. Unless one controls the behavior of the other individuals in the group, the other quantities, $x_{1j}$, are subject to change as well, by a process like that of Eq. (11.32). Such a process becomes difficult to analyze, and in part because of this, some experimenters studying influence processes in small groups have carried out such control. They have fixed the behavior of some group members by making them accomplices, and then studied only the behavior of the one dependent group member. Sherif's experiments (25) with social influence in the autokinetic effect provide a good example of this. None of these experimenters, however, have analyzed the data with mathematical models of this sort, and as a consequence there is a whole field of exploration to be carried out. For example, the estimates of $b_{1i}$ and $b_{1j}$ for various persons in a group would show the leadership and follower patterns. A leader has a very high value of $b_{1i}$ and a low value of $b_{1j}$ for all other persons $j$; a follower has a low value of $b_{1i}$.

To analyze such processes in detail when other group members are not held constant would require treating the equations as a system of simultaneous differential equations and estimating the coefficients by the techniques discussed on pages 448–452. However, in some cases, one will have less extensive data than this and will be interested only in the *group* behavior when such processes are operative. A few simplifications will allow such treatment. First, assume that for individual $i$, each other individual $j$ has the same effect: $b_{1j} = b_{1k}$. Let us call this coefficient of effect $b_{2i}$, that is, the effect of each other person on individual $i$. Then Eq. (11.32) becomes

$$\frac{dx_{1i}}{dt} = a_i + b_{1i}x_{1i} + b_{2i}(x_{11} + x_{12} + \cdots + x_{1i-1} + x_{1i+1} + \cdots x_{1n}) \qquad (11.33)$$

This equation can be reduced to

$$\frac{dx_{1i}}{dt} = a_i + (b_{1i} - b_{2i})x_{1i} + nb_{2i}\bar{x}_1 \qquad (11.34)$$

where $\bar{x}_1$ is the group average.

Summing these equations over all individuals $i$ and dividing by $n$ gives the rate of change of the group:

$$\frac{d\bar{x}_1}{dt} = \bar{a} + \frac{1}{n} \sum_{i=1}^{n} (b_{1i} - b_{2i})x_{1i} + n\bar{b}_2\bar{x}_1 \qquad (11.35)$$

where $\bar{a}$ is the average of $a_i$, and $\bar{b}_2$ is the average of $b_{2i}$. If there are data on each individual through time and if one wishes to solve for the individual values of $a_i$, $b_{1i}$, and $b_{2i}$, then the system of equations consisting of the $n$ equations of the form of Eq. (11.34) plus Eq. (11.35) can be used, together with the technique described on page 448 to obtain these. However, this requires difficult computations; results approximating these may be obtained much more simply by treating Eqs. (11.34) and (11.35) as if the independent variables in them were truly independent of the system. The relatively simple methods discussed on page 441 can be used for approximating the coefficients. This strategy, of course, can be used as a first approximation in Eq. (11.32) as well, and for any equations that are part of a system. What is not known is just how much error is incurred by such treatment.

To deal only with movements in the group mean, Eq. (11.35) can be simplified by the assumption that $b_{1i} = b_{1j}$ and $b_{2i} = b_{2j}$ for all $i$ and $j$. This gives, in place of Eq. (11.35),

$$\frac{d\bar{x}_1}{dt} = \bar{a} + b_1\bar{x}_1 + (n-1)\bar{b}_2\bar{x}_1$$

or simplifying,
$$\frac{d\bar{x}_1}{dt} = \bar{a} + [b_1 + (n-1)\bar{b}_2]\bar{x}_1 \qquad (11.36)$$

where $b_1$ equals $b_{1i}$ for all individuals $i$. This equation is simply an equation of immanent change, with $\bar{x}_{1t}$ dependent on previous values of $\bar{x}_1$, and subject to the methods described on page 435. These methods would allow solution for the coefficients $\bar{a}$ and $b_1 + (n-1)\bar{b}_2$, but would not allow separate estimation of the values of $b_1$ and $\bar{b}_2$. However, it is useful to examine the conditions of stable equilibrium and the conditions of explosive group behavior. For the usual situation as described earlier, $b_1$, the feedback from each person's own behavior is negative, while $b_2$ is positive. Thus stability is ensured if the absolute value of $b_1$ is greater than $(n-1)\bar{b}_2$, that is, if the negative feedback from each person's own behavior is greater than the sum of the positive feedback from others.[10] By setting $d\bar{x}/dt = 0$, we find the equilibrium point to be

$$\bar{x} = -\bar{a}/[b_1 + (n-1)\bar{b}_2]$$

The conditions under which stability does not occur are rather special ones in social behavior, labeled fad, rage, riot, panic, and the like. These situations

[10] In certain situations, where there is imperfect communication in the group, we might expect $b_2$ to decrease with group size. If this decrease is large enough to make $(n-1)\bar{b}_2$ decline as $n$ increases, then the larger the group, the less likely such explosive behavior would be.

have in common a temporarily heightened value of $\bar{b}_2$, that is, of positive effect from others' behavior.   Such a temporary increase in $\bar{b}_2$, brought on from whatever cause, will allow the group's behavior to jump wildly out of control.

More generally, different persons' coefficients of dependence on own and others' behavior will differ, creating a variety of situations of leadership and followership in a group.   Equations such as these could be used, but only in conjunction with intensive observation of group members over time, to study such behavior.   For present purposes, it is enough to note that the explanation of change can profit from the use of contextual variables; and in a complementary fashion, the study of contextual effects can profit from the introduction of explicit models of change.

## Changes in Several Variables

In the above examination, the necessity arose for treating more than one variable as dependent, requiring techniques more complex than those developed earlier.   This is but one example of a system of interdependent variables.   The simplest case is the two-variable case, which has been extensively studied.   Such a case is described by Eqs. (11.37) and (11.38):

$$\frac{dx_1}{dt} = a_1 + b_{11}x_1 + b_{21}x_2 \tag{11.37}$$

$$\frac{dx_2}{dt} = a_2 + b_{12}x_1 + b_{22}x_2 \tag{11.38}$$

When sociologists study such problems of interdependence, they often ask whether $x_1$ affects $x_2$, or $x_2$ affects $x_1$ [see, for example, Pelz and Andrews (20)]. However, it is evident that this is not really the right question, for these two effects are not mutually exclusive.   The effect of $x_2$ on $x_1$ is given by the size of $b_{21}$ (either absolutely or relative to $b_{11}$), and the effect of $x_1$ on $x_2$ is given by the size of $b_{12}$, either absolutely or relative to $b_{22}$.   Thus the effects of $x_2$ on $x_1$ and $x_1$ on $x_2$ are two separate questions.   In addition, there are several other kinds of questions that can be asked about such a system of equations.   For example, the questions of equilibrium points, stability of equilibrium, and kinds of approach to equilibrium may be important in a given investigation.   To consider only the most common case, take the situation where $b_{11}$ and $b_{22}$ are negative, and $b_{12}$ and $b_{21}$ are positive.   This is the case where both $x_1$ and $x_2$ have positive effects on each other, but there is a negative feedback of each variable's value upon itself ($b_{11}$ and $b_{22}$).   For this configuration of parameters, each of the variables by itself would behave as in Eq. (11.15) and Fig. 11.4.   But when the two sets of effects are put together to form a system, the system might behave as shown in either Fig. 11.5$a$ or 11.5$b$.   In these figures, the arrows represent

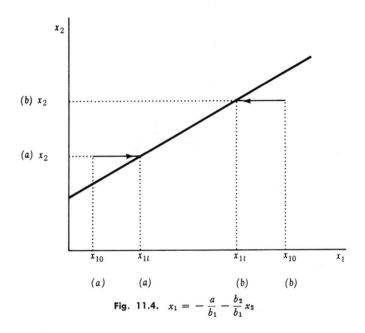

**Fig. 11.4.** $x_1 = -\dfrac{a}{b_1} - \dfrac{b_2}{b_1} x_2$

the movement of this system of two variables. The essential question which determines the behavior of the system is whether the product $b_{12}b_{21}$ is greater or less than the product $b_{11}b_{22}$. Intuitively, we see that this is the same as asking whether the positive effects of each variable on the other are greater than the negative damping effects of each variable on itself. If $b_{12}b_{21}$ is greater than $b_{11}b_{22}$, the explosive condition of Fig. 11.5$b$ holds; if $b_{12}b_{21}$ is less than $b_{11}b_{22}$, the stable condition of Fig. 11.5$a$ exists.

There are various texts on nonlinear differential equations which may be used to go beyond these elementary points. For our purpose here, it is of interest only to ask how we estimate the parameters of the system, $a_i$ and $b_{ij}$, as we did in the simpler case of a single dependent variable.

The pair of equations, (11.37) and (11.38), is only a special case of a system of $n$ linear differential equations. Since the estimation of parameters is conceptually as difficult in the two-variable case as in the general case, we will consider the general case.[11] In the general case, we will call the vector with elements $dx_i/dt$, $\dot{X}$; the vector with elements $a_i$, $A$; the vector with elements $x_{jt}$, $X_t$; and the matrix with elements $b_{ij}$, $B$. In matrix notation, the system of equations is represented by

$$\dot{X} = A + X_t B \qquad (11.39)$$

[11] I am indebted to Mr. T. Robert Harris for suggesting the procedure outlined here for estimating the parameters $a_i$ and $b_{ij}$ from the values of $a_i{}^*$ and $b_{ij}{}^*$ calculated from observation.

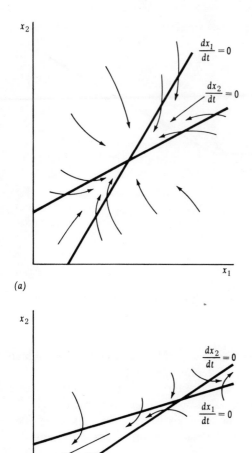

(a)

(b)

**Fig. 11.5**

and the solution to such a set of equations is

$$X_t = X_0 e^{Bt} - AB^{-1} \qquad (11.40)$$

where the exponent of the matrix, $e^{Bt}$, is defined as the series expansion of $Bt$, as follows:

$$e^{Bt} = I + Bt + \frac{B^2 t^2}{2!} + \frac{B^3 t^3}{3!} + \cdots \qquad (11.41)$$

Equation (11.40) gives $X_t$ as a linear function of $X_0$, which can be written as

$$X_t = A^* + X_0 B^* \tag{11.42}$$

where $A^*$ is a vector with elements $a_i{}^*$, and $B^*$ is a matrix with elements $b_{ij}{}^*$. This equation is in the form of a linear regression of $x_{it}$ upon $x_{10}, x_{20}, \ldots, x_{n0}$, with coefficients $a_i{}^*$ and $b_{ji}{}^*$. Thus with data on all variables at times 0 and $t$, it is possible to estimate the regression coefficients.

The data may consist either of observations of $x_1, x_2, \ldots, x_n$ on a number of individuals at times 0 and $t$ (under the assumption that the behavior of all individuals is governed by the same parameters, $b_{ij}$ and $a_i$), or of observations on one individual at many points in time, equally spaced (under the assumption that the parameters governing the individual's behavior do not change over this time). The minimal data required for estimation consist of observations at two time periods for a number of individuals equal to the number of variables plus one $(n + 1)$, or $n + 1$ pairs of observations on one individual separated by time period $\Delta t$. The latter can consist of $n + 2$ observations equally spaced in time, so that observations 0 and 1 constitute the first pair, 1 and 2 the second, etc. In general, however, because of correlation between the observations, additional data will provide better estimates.

Once the estimates of $a_i{}^*$ and $b_{ij}{}^*$ are obtained, these can be used, as in the preceding cases, to estimate the fundamental parameters of the process, $a_i$ and $b_{ij}$. This may be done as follows. First, find the eigenvalues of $B^*$, that is, the set of $n$ values of $\lambda^*$ which satisfy the equation

$$|B^* - \lambda^* I| = 0 \tag{11.43}$$

Then, if these eigenvalues are all distinct, a set of $n$ linearly independent eigenvectors may be found, each satisfying the equation

$$B^* H_j = \lambda_j{}^* H_j \tag{11.44}$$

where $H_j$ is the $j$th eigenvector (corresponding to the $j$th eigenvalue, $\lambda_j{}^*$). From this, it is possible to calculate the values of $b_{ij}$ directly, by first calculating

$$\lambda_j = \frac{\ln \lambda_j{}^*}{\Delta t} \tag{11.45}$$

and then creating a diagonal matrix $\Lambda$, in which the diagonal entries are $\lambda_j$. Then, if $H$ is the matrix whose $j$th column is $H_j$,

$$B = H \Lambda H^{-1} \tag{11.46}$$

Having found $B$, we then calculate $A$ directly by use of Eqs. (11.40) and (11.42):

$$-AB^{-1} = A^*$$

or postmultiplying by $-B$, $\qquad A = -A^* B \tag{11.47}$

Standard computer programs exist for calculating eigenvalues and eigenvectors and for inverting matrices, and simple computer programs may be constructed to carry out the remaining operations.[12]

It is useful at this point to compare the formulation developed in this section with that of a paper in the sociological literature directed to the study of causal relationships by use of data involving two or more observations on the same individuals. This is a paper by Pelz and Andrews (20) devoted to examining the relative effects of two variables upon each other. Pelz and Andrews used an empirical approach: they used data in which they felt confident about which direction the effects were in, and they examined which measures gave results that most closely fitted their preconceptions. The measures they used were various kinds of correlation coefficients, and their examination depended on a comparison of the relative sizes of these coefficients.

After a number of attempts, they arrived at the use of partial correlation coefficients: the partial correlation of $x_{1t}$ with $x_{20}$, holding constant $x_{10}$, and the partial correlation of $x_{2t}$ with $x_{10}$, holding constant $x_{20}$. These can be labeled $r_{x_{1t}x_{20}, x_{10}}$ and $r_{x_{2t}x_{10}, x_{20}}$. They reasoned that if the former were greater than the latter, $x_2$ affected $x_1$, while if the reverse were true, $x_1$ affected $x_2$. Leaving aside the point that these effects are not mutually exclusive and should not be considered as such, we can examine the relation of these partial correlation coefficients to the results above.

The coefficient $b_{21}^{*}$ for $x_2$'s effect on the change of $x_1$ is closely related to $r_{x_{1t}x_{20}, x_{10}}$, for this is the partial regression coefficient corresponding to that correlation coefficient. The relation is

$$r_{x_{1t}x_{20}, x_{10}} = b_{21}^{*} \frac{\sqrt{1 - r_{x_{20}x_{10}}^{2}}}{\sqrt{1 - r_{x_{1t}x_{10}}^{2}}} \tag{11.48}$$

where $r_{ij}$ is the zero-order coefficient of correlation between $i$ and $j$. The coefficient $b_{21}^{*}$ in turn is directly related through Eqs. (11.43) to (11.46) to $b_{21}$, the fundamental coefficient for the effect of $x_2$ on $x_1$. Thus the partial correlation coefficients used by Pelz and Andrews in an empirical search are directly related to the correct measures. It is evident, of course, that even though the relationship is close, the transformations between the two may make the correlation coefficient a misleading measure of change in any given case.

---

[12] Alternate ways of calculating $B$ from $B^{*}$ may be used. One is by a method analogous to that described on pages 471–472, Eqs. (11.122) to (11.126). Another is an iterative technique which is based on Eq. (11.41). Writing that equation for only an element of the $B^{*}$ matrix gives: $b_{ij}^{*} = \delta_{ij} + b_{ij}\Delta t + \sum_{k}(b_{ik}b_{kj})(\Delta t)^{2}/(2!) \ldots$ By defining time so that $\Delta t = 1$, and transposing, this equation becomes $b_{ij} = b_{ij}^{*} - \delta_{ij} - \sum_{k}(b_{ik}b_{kj})/(2!) \ldots$

With the equation in this form, the values of $b_{ij}$, together with values of $b_{ij}$ calculated on the previous iteration, can be used in the right-hand side of the equation to calculate the next iteration for $b_{ij}$. In carrying out such an iteration, we should extend the equation until the next term in the series is less than some predetermined small value. A computer program for such an iterative technique may be found in Coleman (7, chap. 5).

## Measurement Error or Unreliability

Measurement error causes great difficulties in the study of change.[13]  Suppose a situation exists in which there is a large amount of measurement error in a variable, but no change at all.   Then two measurements, separated in time, will result in two different values for most individuals.   Although the overall distribution will not have changed (except for sampling error),[14] individuals will appear to have changed, some having moved up and others having moved down.   Application of regression analysis by use of Eq. (11.9) and solving for $a$ and $b$ by use of Eqs. (11.10) and (11.11) would show a negative feedback, that is, a negative value for $b$.   This would show that the movement of the variable is a negative function of its own position and would incorrectly suggest a process of change.   In fact, all that would have happened is measurement error, without any change whatsoever taking place.

The potential for being misled is even greater in an analysis of change using one or more independent variables to explain the change.   Again suppose there is nothing but measurement error.   If there are initial correlations between the dependent variable and the independent ones, then on the second observation, these correlations will remain approximately the same, though individuals will appear to have changed.   If, then, an analysis of the supposed change is carried out in order to discover the effects of the independent variables on the dependent variable, apparent effects will be found.   Yet there is no effect whatsoever; instead, measurement error is masquerading as change.   Even more harmful, in this case, it is masquerading as effects of other variables upon change.

The principal way of separating random measurement error from change for models of change such as those discussed in preceding sections requires the use of three or more observations on the same individuals.[15]   We will first examine intuitively how the third observation helps, and then treat the matter more systematically.   Intuitively, we see the matter as follows: if the apparent change is merely measurement error, and if measurement error remains constant, then the relation between the first and third observations should be the same as that between the first and second or the second and third.   But if the apparent change is real, the relation between the first and third observations

---

[13] Blalock has pointed out, in a comment on this section, that such measurement error can cause special difficulties, since in many practical situations absolute amounts of change that can be observed or induced in short time periods are apt to be quite small relative to measurement error.

[14] The concept of sampling from a universe is as follows in this case.   Consider each true value and the distribution around it of values that would be observed over a very large number of observations on the same individual.   The sample consists of a single observation from each one of the error distributions that surround each true value.

[15] If the errors themselves are serially correlated, the results given below for measures of change would appear to be unaffected.   The estimates of the amount of error would be reduced, however, since only the nonserially correlated portion of the error would appear in the regression coefficients.   If, however, the serial correlations of errors decline as $\Delta t$ increases, the serially correlated portion of the error is indistinguishable from true change in the variable.

should be less than the relation between the first and second or second and third, for there has been a greater opportunity for change to occur.

Consider the following equation for the explanation of change:

$$\frac{dx_1}{dt} = a + b_1 x_1 + b_2 x_2 \qquad (11.49)$$

Now let us assume two situations:

**1** $a$ is nonzero, $b_1$ is negative, $b_2$ is positive, and no measurement error exists.

**2** $a$, $b_1$, and $b_2$ are all zero. There is no change at all, but, first, $x_1$ is correlated with $x_2$; and, second, there is measurement error in $x_1$.

Now given data at two observations, $x_{10}$, $x_{20}$, and $x_{1t}$, we can estimate the values of $a^*$, $b_1^*$, and $b_2^*$ in the following equation:

$$x_{1t} = a^* + b_1^* x_{10} + b_2^* x_{20} \qquad (11.50)$$

If we estimate values for $a^*$, $b_1^*$, and $b_2^*$, how can we tell whether they are related to $a$, $b_1$, and $b_2$ in Eqs. (11.15) through (11.19) and (11.20), meaning that condition 1 above holds, or are generated purely by measurement error, under condition 2 above?

Suppose we take the third observation and estimate the values of $a^0$, $b_1^0$, and $b_2^0$ in the following equation:

$$x_{1\tau} = a^0 + b_1^0 x_{10} + b_2^0 x_{20} \qquad (11.51)$$

where $\tau$ is the time of the third observation. Although the general case is easily treated, let us assume for simplicity of exposition that the time intervals are the same: $\tau - 0 = (\tau - t) = 2(t - 0)$.

What will the relation be between $a^0$, $b_1^0$, $b_2^0$, on the one hand, and $a^*$, $b_1^*$, and $b_2^*$, on the other, under conditions 1 and 2?

If condition 2 holds, with only measurement error, then we should find that $a^0 = a^*$, $b_1^0 = b_1^*$, and $b_2^0 = b_2^*$. That is, there is only measurement error; consequently, the time separating the two measurements is totally irrelevant. Thus subject only to sampling error, the regression coefficients should be alike in the two cases.

If condition 1 holds, however, this should no longer be true. If the period $\tau - 0$ is twice that of $t - 0$, then Eq. (11.16) becomes

$$x_{1\tau} = \frac{a}{b_1}(e^{b_1 2\Delta t} - 1) + e^{b_1 2\Delta t} x_{10} + \frac{b_2}{b_1}(e^{b_1 2\Delta t} - 1)x_{20} \qquad (11.52)$$

This becomes, after algebraic manipulations, and substituting $a^*$, $b_1^*$, and $b_2^*$,

$$x_{1\tau} = a^* + b_2^* x_{20} + b_1^*(a^* + b_1^* x_{10} + b_2^* x_{20}) \qquad (11.53)$$

Thus if condition 1 holds, with no measurement error, we should obtain the following relationships:

$$a^0 = a^*(b_1{}^* + 1) \tag{11.54}$$

$$b_1{}^0 = b_1{}^{*2} \tag{11.55}$$

$$b_2{}^0 = b_2{}^*(b_1{}^* + 1) \tag{11.56}$$

Therefore, if the use of the third observation results in identical regression coefficients for $x_{1t}$ on $x_{10}$ and for $x_{1t}$ on $x_{10}$, we know that the apparent change is wholly measurement error. If on the other hand, the regression coefficients are related as in Eqs. (11.54), (11.55), and (11.56), this shows that there is no measurement error.

It is probably most frequent, however, that neither of these extremes is met: that the data exhibit both measurement error and change. The problem then is to estimate the component of the change parameters $a$, $b_1$, and $b_i$ due to change and the component due to measurement error. These components can be estimated as follows. Assume that we describe the parameters of change as estimated over time period $\Delta t$, in terms of two components, one due to measurement error and the other due to change:

$$a_{\Delta t} = a_{e\Delta t} + a_c \tag{11.57}$$

$$b_{1\Delta t} = b_{1e\Delta t} + b_{1c} \tag{11.58}$$

$$b_{2\Delta t} = b_{2e\Delta t} + b_{2c} \tag{11.59}$$

Now if there were no error component, our estimates of $a_1$, $b_1$, and $b_2$ from the data would be independent of the length of period, since $a_c$, $b_{1c}$, and $b_{2c}$ are independent of $\Delta t$. But if the apparent change were totally due to error component, then we would find $a_1 \Delta t$, $b_1 \Delta t$, and $b_2 \Delta t$ to be constant, where $\Delta t$ is the time period over which the lagged regression is calculated. This follows from Eqs. (11.18), (11.19), (11.20) and the fact that $a^*$, $b_1{}^*$, and $b_2{}^*$ would be independent of the time period $\Delta t$. Thus our estimates of $a$, $b_1$, and $b_2$ would be inversely proportional to the time period $\Delta t$. Thus, if we define $a_e$, $b_{1e}$, and $b_{2e}$ to be constant over time, we will find that

$$a_{\Delta t} = \frac{a_e}{\Delta t} + a_c \tag{11.60}$$

$$b_{1\Delta t} = \frac{b_{1e}}{\Delta t} + b_{1c} \tag{11.61}$$

$$b_{2\Delta t} = \frac{b_{2e}}{\Delta t} + b_{2c} \tag{11.62}$$

If we let the time period $t - 0 = \Delta t$, and the time period $\tau - 0$ is twice this, we will have

$$a_{\Delta \tau} = \frac{a_e}{2\Delta t} + a_c \tag{11.63}$$

$$b_{1\Delta \tau} = \frac{b_{1e}}{2\Delta t} + b_{1c} \tag{11.64}$$

$$b_{2\Delta \tau} = \frac{b_{2e}}{2\Delta t} + b_{2c} \tag{11.65}$$

These equations can be used in conjunction with Eqs. (11.18), (11.19), (11.20) and the regression estimates $a^*$, $b_1^*$, $b_2^*$ and $a^0$, $b_1^0$, $b_2^0$ to estimate the measurement error component and the change component:

$$b_{1e} = 2 \ln \frac{b_1^*}{b_1^0} \tag{11.66}$$

$$b_{1c} = \frac{1}{\Delta t} \ln \frac{b_1^0}{b_1^*} \tag{11.67}$$

$$a_e = 2a^*C^* - a^0C^0 \tag{11.68}$$

$$a_c = \frac{1}{\Delta t} (a^0C^0 - a^*C^*) \tag{11.69}$$

$$b_{2e} = 2b_2^*C^* - b_2^0C^0 \tag{11.70}$$

$$b_{2c} = \frac{1}{\Delta t} (b_2^0C^0 - b_2^*C^*) \tag{11.71}$$

where, as before, $C^* = \ln b_1^*/(b_1^* - 1)$.

Thus by comparison of the change over time $\Delta t$ and $2\Delta t$, we can separate the measurement error from the change, through Eqs. (11.66)–(11.71). If the time period $\tau - 0$ is not $2\Delta t$, but is some other interval $s\Delta t$ (where $s$ need not be an integer), the equations above are modified slightly. In Eqs. (11.66), (11.68), and (11.70), $s$ replaces 2, and the right-hand side of all equations is multiplied by $1/(s - 1)$.

It should be noted that this approach, as well as the very concept of measurement error, may oversimplify reality. Where we have partitioned the change into two components, one instantaneous and the other uniform through time (in the sense that $a_c$, $b_{1c}$, and $b_{2c}$ are independent of time), it may be true in some instances that the rate of change is very rapid immediately after a measurement, but declines as time passes. Where the measurement is a response, as on a test or questionnaire, there is some evidence to suggest that this is so. To identify this declining rate of change would require, however, measurement at a number of time points.

## Various Nonlinear Models in the Study of Change

The examination in earlier sections is one which follows the same general purpose as linear regression analysis, but with a more powerful model: to describe the change and analyze the effects on change which are implicit in a set of data. To do so, it makes the simplest assumption about the form such effects take, that is, an assumption of linearity.

This strategy is useful for data analysis. However, there are other times at which one has definite assumptions about the nature of change. Population growth is one such case; diffusion of information is another. In such cases, it is appropriate to make other assumptions about the form that effects will take, and develop a more specific model embodying these assumptions.[16]

A few such cases will be presented here, to show the way one proceeds with such a strategy. There is, however, a rather extensive literature on such models, and any serious examination of these models should begin with that literature, which will be cited at appropriate points.

A very simple model of population growth is one that assumes if the population size is $x$, the rate of births is proportional to it, $ax$, as is the rate of deaths, $bx$. The rate of change of the population thus is

$$\frac{dx}{dt} = ax - bx \tag{11.72}$$

and depending on whether $a$ is greater or less than $b$, the population will grow exponentially or die out. The population size at time $t$ is

$$x_t = x_0 e^{(a-b)t} \tag{11.73}$$

Such a model, however, does not correspond to known shapes of population growth among human beings or other species, for most population curves have a tendency to grow more slowly after a certain point. An assumption made by Verhulst in the nineteenth century was that the rate of growth of the population would be inhibited proportionally to the square of its size. This gives rise to the following equation for the rate of change of the population:

$$\frac{dx}{dt} = ax - bx^2 \tag{11.74}$$

where $a$ is now the difference between birth and death rates, and $b$ is the coefficient of inhibition. This assumption leads to the logistic equation of population growth:

$$x = \frac{a/b}{1 + ke^{-at}} \tag{11.75}$$

where $k$ is a constant related to the population size at time 0 $[k = (a/b - x_0)/x_0]$. This model has been shown to fit quite well population growth of insects in limited environments, as well as human populations in various countries over limited time periods (17,21).

Work in the size of human population has developed in the direction of the use of much richer data, involving fertility rates, age cohorts, and other variables. Developments in this direction may be found in Ryder (22–24), Lopez (16), and Boulding (5).

[16] The variables under consideration here and in most of the models of this section are not truly continuous variables, but numbers of persons, and thus discontinuous. The model of continuous change is therefore an approximation. The processes can also be studied by models which treat each size as a state and examine the probability of shifting from one state to another. For small populations, such a treatment is necessary. See Coleman (7, chaps. 10, 11, 17) for such models.

Models involving the interaction of populations have been developed, beginning with Lotka (17) and Volterra (26). Volterra considered the situation of a predator-prey relationship between two populations 1 and 2, of size $x_1$ and $x_2$. Population 1, the prey, is assumed to subsist in an unlimited environment, and thus have a growth rate, except for the predator, of $ax_1$. But the population diminishes proportionally to the number of contacts between the predator and the prey, assumed to be $kx_1x_2$. Thus the overall growth rate for $x_1$ is

$$\frac{dx_1}{dt} = ax_1 - kx_1x_2 \tag{11.76}$$

The predator population grows proportionally to these contacts (since this constitutes its food) thus at the rate $bkx_1x_2$, where $b$ is a constant between zero and 1 (since there must be more than one of the prey to sustain one predator). The death rate is assumed proportional to the population size, $cx_2$. The overall rate is then

$$\frac{dx_2}{dt} = bkx_1x_2 - cx_2 \tag{11.77}$$

The solution of this pair of equations to find the population sizes at any time $t$ provides interesting results. Under certain conditions, cyclical patterns exist, with growth in the prey population leading to growth in the predator population, which depletes the prey population and thereby itself. Then the prey population is free to rise again, leading to another cycle [see Davis (9, Fig. 6, p. 109)]. Some pairs of animal populations have been studied from this point of view by Gause (14). H. T. Davis (9) has developed this theory in several directions. However, further work in the interaction of populations quickly reaches mathematical difficulties.

Another area of work with nonlinear models of change is diffusion or contagion of some behavior or knowledge. A simple model of diffusion assumes that the rate of diffusion is proportional to the number of interactions between those who have and those who have not, and that this in turn is proportional to the product of these two numbers of persons. Equation (11.78) expresses such a model:

$$\frac{dx}{dt} = kx(N - x) \tag{11.78}$$

where $N$ is the total population size and $x$ is the number of haves. This model has been used and developed in various directions by a number of authors. The principal contributions to this field, however, have been made by statisticians working in a related area, the theory of epidemics. Much of this work (including the stochastic theory, which treats each size of the epidemic as a discrete state) is summarized by Bailey (1). A weakening of the assumption of a homogeneously interacting population has been carried out by Coleman (7, chap. 17).

A third area of change for which specific mathematical models of change have been developed is in intergenerational occupational mobility. This work, however, does not treat continuous change, but rather change at discrete points in time, that is, each generation. Rather than introduce this different mathematical treatment here, we refer the reader to other publications which treat such models (2,15,18,19).

## 11.2 CHANGE IN QUALITATIVE STATES

In Sec. 11.1, attention has been focused upon quantitative variables. However, individuals are often characterized by qualitative states, and it is necessary to examine the means for treating change in these states. As indicated on page 432, the mathematics necessary for this treatment encompasses a wide range. Of the four cases outlined on page 432, the three most important are:

**1** Change which is *determinate*. An example is prescriptive marriage patterns and descent patterns in certain primitive tribes, as treated by White (27). A man is classified as a member of one of several classes, and a woman is classified as a member of one of these same classes. Where marriage of a man in class $i$ is allowed only with a woman of class $j$, the marriage rules of the tribe can be described by a matrix of 1s and 0s with an entry of 1 in column $i$ to represent the allowable marriage. When coupled with a similar matrix showing the class $j$ of a son of a man in class $i$, the matrices can be employed to show the various types of kinship relationships that can occur between members of each pair of classes.

The scope of this determinate change is quite limited. For example, in modern society, there are few such prescriptions or proscriptions, so that the same processes as those described above would be characterized by probabilities of marriage between categories of persons instead of 0s or 1s. Some work in occupational mobility from father to son has used such interclass stochastic marriage matrices (2).

**2** Change which is *probabilistic, but fixed in time at discrete points*. This type of change occurs in psychological experiments that employ trials at which a subject is presented with a stimulus. Any situation in which there is periodic presentation of a stimulus or other event is of this type. Similarly, periodic behavior that occurs only at weekly, yearly, or other intervals, requires the study of probabilistic change at discrete points in time. Often it is true, however, as in intergenerational mobility, that the time intervals are not uniform. In such cases, a continuous-time model is probably more appropriate than a discrete-time model. The mathematics for treating periodic change of the type described above is the theory of discrete-time stochastic processes. This will be discussed briefly in subsequent sections.

**3** Change which is *probabilistic, and may occur at any point in time*. A wide variety of change lies in this area. Most behavior in natural settings, except that which occurs at fixed intervals, is of this type. The change at fixed times, described in 2 above, can be considered a special case of this change; and the mathematics for treating change of this type can be derived as a special case of change that is continuous in time. Most of the exposition below will assume change that is both probabilistic and continuous in time.

Each section below will parallel the comparable section for continuous variables, because in the study of change in state there is a direct analog for each of the problems treated for continuous variables.

In all the treatment below, individuals (or other units) will be characterized according to the *probability* of being in a given state. Thus the change that is of concern is a change in this probability (or set of probabilities, for if the individual may be in any of $m$ states, he is described by $m - 1$ independent probabilities). In most of the exposition below, only qualitative attributes with two states will be considered. Treatment for attributes with more than two states becomes more complex and is beyond the scope of this chapter. The same limitation will be made for independent attributes which may affect change in the dependent attribute. Treatment for attributes with more than two states may be found in Coleman (7,8). The values of the attributes will be labeled $x_1, x_2, \ldots$, as above, with the possible values of $x$ limited to 1 and 0, for the two states. The probability of an attribute having the value $x_i = 1$ will be labeled $p$, and the probability that $x_i = 0$ is $1 - p$. Since we will consider only a single dependent attribute until we reach the subsection entitled "Changes in a System of Interdependent Attributes," no subscript for attribute 1 will be used until then, always implicitly taking attribute 1 as the dependent variable.

In the discrete-time case, the change in the probability is described by a discrete difference $p_n - p_{n-1}$, where $p_n$ is the probability that attribute 1 is in state 1 on trial $n$. In the continuous-time case, the rate of change in the probability is continuous, and is described by a derivative with respect to time, $dp/dt$.

## Change as a Function of Time

The process of stochastic change in state most directly analogous to uniform change in a continuous variable is that in which the probability of change per unit time is constant, given that the individual is in the relevant state. If the individual is in state 0 on attribute 1 and there is a constant rate of change into state 1 (but no change from 1 to 0), the process is described as follows:

For continuous change:

$$\frac{dp}{dt} = a(1 - p) \tag{11.79}$$

For discrete change:

$$p_n - p_{n-1} = a(1 - p_{n-1}) \tag{11.80}$$

The coefficient $a$ for the transition from state 0 to 1 is ordinarily called a transition rate or transition intensity; it is called a transition probability in the case of discrete change.

Comparison of these two equations with the corresponding Eq. (11.1) for continuous variables shows that here the rate of change becomes dependent upon the state of the individual, because there are only fixed states, and change can occur only if the individual is in state 0.

The probability of being in state 1 at time $t$ (or on trial $n$) as a function of the probability of being in state 1 at time 0 (on trial $n - 1$) is obtained by integrating Eq. (11.79) or solving Eq. (11.80) for $p_n$:

$$p_t = (1 - e^{-a\Delta t}) + e^{-a\Delta t}p_0 \tag{11.81}$$

$$p_n = a + (1 - a)p_{n-1} \tag{11.82}$$

These equations are both of the form

$$p_t = a^* + b^*p_0 \tag{11.83}$$

which allows linear regression methods to be applied in estimating the rate of change $a$. Given sufficient values of $p_t$ and $p_0$, it is possible to obtain two estimates of $a$ from the regression coefficients, by use of Eq. (11.83) with (11.81) or (11.82).

For continuous change

$$a = -\frac{1}{\Delta t} \ln b^* \tag{11.84}$$

$$a = -\frac{1}{\Delta t} \ln (1 - a^*) \tag{11.85}$$

For discrete change:

$$a = 1 - b^* \tag{11.86}$$

$$a = a^* \tag{11.87}$$

It often **happens**, however, that only one value of $p_0$ and one value of $p_t$ are obtained from the data. For example, if the probabilities are estimated by proportions over a sample at two interview waves, then only one estimate of $p_t$ and one estimate of $p_0$ are obtained for the sample as a whole. In such a case, the fact that $a^* = 1 - b^*$ [from Eq. (11.81) or (11.82)] allows these estimates to be used in obtaining an estimate of $a$.

Another strategy in estimating transition rates or transition probabilities will prove to be valuable in later sections. This strategy is to separate the sample into two segments, individuals who began in state 1 and those who began in state 0. By treating these as separate samples and obtaining $p_t$ separately for each, we can write a general equation:

$$p_t = a^* + b^*x_1 \tag{11.88}$$

where $x_1$ has the value 0 for one sample, and 1 for the other.   For the sample in which $x_1 = 1$, there can be no change, and $p_t$ is 1; for the sample in which $x_1 = 0$, $p_t = a^*$, and thus $a$ can be directly estimated from $p_t$, by use of Eq. (11.81) or (11.85).   For the case of discrete change this estimate of $a^*$ gives directly the estimate of the transition probability.   Obviously, with a larger amount of data (such as several samples, or samples with more than two waves of data), the assumption of a constant rate of change can be tested.

As in the case of continuous variables, it is possible to consider change as a more general function of time.   The function of most empirical interest is one in which the rate of change is decreasing proportionally to its own size:

$$\frac{da}{dt} = -ka \tag{11.89}$$

or integrating,

$$a = e^{-k\Delta t} \tag{11.90}$$

where $\Delta t$ is the time since the start of the process of change.   Such an exponentially declining rate of change appears to occur when the change follows an event.   The impact of the event declines over time, and there is some indication that Eq. (11.89) describes the decline in the rate of change in many empirical cases.

## Change as a Function of Present State

In the simple case above, the transition rate or transition probability was constant, so long as the individual was in state 0.   However, in many cases, there is change in either direction, depending on one's state.   When such change is constant over time, then the rate of change in the continuous case is[17]

$$\frac{dp}{dt} = -bp + a(1 - p) \tag{11.91}$$

where $b$ is the transition rate from state 1 to state 0, and $a$ is, as before, the transition rate from state 0 to state 1.   Just as in the case of immanent change in continuous variables with negative feedback, this leads to an equilibrium state different from $p = 0$ or 1.

The probability of being in state 1 at time $t$ as a function of the probability of being in state 1 at time 0 is given by integrating Eq. (11.91), which gives

$$p_t = \frac{a}{a + b} (1 - e^{-(a+b)\Delta t}) + e^{-(a+b)\Delta t} p_0 \tag{11.92}$$

This equation is again in the form of a linear regression equation:

$$p_t = a^* + b^* p_0 \tag{11.93}$$

---

[17] We shall not continue to treat the case of discrete change because of its lesser range of applicability.   It can always be treated as a special case of continuous change where $\Delta t$ is always constant, and thus $e^{-a\Delta t}$ can be treated as a single constant.

Estimating $a^*$ and $b^*$ from the data will allow estimating of $a$ and $b$ by

$$a = \frac{a^*}{\Delta t} \frac{\ln b^*}{(b^* - 1)}$$
$$= \frac{a^* C^*}{\Delta t} \tag{11.94}$$

$$b = \frac{(1 - a^* - b^*)}{\Delta t} \frac{\ln b^*}{b^* - 1}$$
$$= \frac{(1 - a^* - b^*)C^*}{\Delta t} \tag{11.95}$$

where as before $C^* = \ln b_1^* / (b_1^* - 1)$.

Comparison of these equations with the case of continuous variables [Eqs. (11.10) and (11.11)] shows that the estimate for $a$ is exactly the same function of $\Delta t$, $a^*$, and $b^*$, while the estimate for $b$ is somewhat different in this case.

Given appropriate data, these two equations will give estimates for the transition rates, which are the fundamental parameters of change. However, the strategy suggested in the preceding section, of dividing the sample according to initial state, allows estimates in many cases where the data are not otherwise sufficient for estimation. For example, if a system is in aggregate equilibrium, $p_t$ will differ from $p_0$ only by sampling error, and Eq. (11.93) cannot be used for estimation. However, by dividing the sample according to the initial state, estimation can be carried out. Using this strategy, and considering separately two samples, in which $x_1 = 0$ and $x_1 = 1$, gives

$$p_t = a^* + b^* x_1 \tag{11.96}$$

If the values of $p_t$ from the two samples are labeled $p_{0t}$ and $p_{1t}$, then Eqs. (11.94) and (11.95) can be used directly with the data to estimate $a$ and $b$:

$$a = -\frac{p_{0t}}{\Delta t} \frac{\ln (p_{1t} - p_{0t})}{(1 - p_{1t} + p_{0t})} \tag{11.97}$$

$$b = -\frac{(1 - p_{1t})}{\Delta t} \frac{\ln (p_{1t} - p_{0t})}{(1 - p_{1t} + p_{0t})} \tag{11.98}$$

It should be noted that the assumptions in making such estimates as these are similar to those in the case of continuous variables. The transition rates $a$ and $b$ are assumed alike over all the individuals (if the proportions $p_t$ are taken over individuals) or over the range of time (if the proportions $p_t$ are taken for one individual over a number of time points). The process is assumed to take the simple form of Eq. (11.91), comparable to the linearity assumption in the continuous-variable case.

If these assumptions are met, then a number of conditions will hold. Probably the most important is the constancy of $a$ and $b$ when different periods of time are taken for estimation. As $\Delta t$ becomes larger, the values of $a^*$ and $b^*$ should change in such a way that $a$ and $b$ remain constant. Examination of

Eq. (11.92) shows that if the time interval $\tau - 0$ is twice that of $t - 0$, and the values $a^0$ and $b^0$ are obtained in place of $a^*$ and $b^*$ in Eq. (11.96), using $p_\tau$, the relation between these coefficients is as in the continuous-variable case:

$$b^0 = b^{*2} \tag{11.99}$$

$$a^0 = a^*(b^* + 1) \tag{11.100}$$

If this is not the case, but instead $a^0$ and $b^0$ are closer to the values of $a^*$ and $b^*$, this is evidence suggesting response unreliability (i.e., measurement error). This problem will be discussed on page 472.

## Exogenous Change: Changes in State as a Function of Other Attributes

The more important aspects of the examination of change require the introduction of other attributes. The effect of these other attributes is to add to the transition rates, either adding to the rate $a$ toward state 1 or adding to the rate $b$ toward state 0. Let us label $x_2$ in such a way that the effect of state 1 of $x_2$ is toward state 1 of $x_1$, and the effect of state 0 of $x_2$ is toward state 0 of $x_1$.[18] Then the transition rates can be conceived as due to the sum of two components: random shocks ($a$ toward state 1, $b_1$ toward state 0), and effects of $x_2$ ($b_2$ toward state 1 when $x_2$ is in state 1, and $b_2$ toward state 0 when $x_2$ is in state 0).

When $x_2$ is 1:

toward state 1: $a$ (random shocks) $+ b_2$ (effect of $x_2 = 1$)
toward state 0: $b_1$ (random shocks)

When $x_2$ is 0:

toward state 1: $a$ (random shocks)
toward state 0: $b_1$ (random shocks) $+ b_2$ (effect of $x_2 = 0$)

These assumptions parallel those of linear effects for continuous variables. The coefficient $b_2$ is an added component of the transition rate due to $x_2$, its direction depending upon the state of $x_2$.

A single equation expressing these effects on the rate of change is

$$\frac{dp}{dt} = -[b_1 + b_2(1 - x_2)]p + (a + b_2 x_2)(1 - p) \tag{11.101}$$

This may be put into the form

$$\frac{dp}{dt} = -b_1 p + b_2(x_2 - p) + a(1 - p) \tag{11.102}$$

---

[18] An alternative model may be introduced, which assumes that the effect of $x_2$ occurs only when $x_2 = 1$, so that there is no effect of $x_2$ in the direction of state 0 of $x_1$. Such a model will give rise to somewhat different estimates of $b_2$. It should be used whenever the effect of $x_2$ seems, on theoretical grounds, to act only toward state 1 of $x_1$.

which roughly parallels the analogous equation for continuous variables [see Eq. (11.15)]. When integrated, this equation takes the form of Eq. (11.83) and conforms to the general form

$$p_t = a^* + b_1^* p_0 + b_2^* x_2 \qquad (11.103)$$

where $a$, $b_1$, and $b_2$ may be found by equations analogous to Eqs. (11.94) and (11.95):

$$a = \frac{a^* C^*}{\Delta t} \qquad (11.104)$$

$$b_1 = \frac{(1 - a^* - b_1^* - b_2^*) C^*}{\Delta t} \qquad (11.105)$$

$$b_2 = \frac{b_2^* C^*}{\Delta t} \qquad (11.106)$$

Again by dividing the total sample into samples based on the initial state of $x_1$ (as well as the initial state of $x_2$), we can obtain estimates of $a$, $b_1$, and $b_2$ from data in a two-wave panel:

$$p_t = a^* + b_1^* x_1 + b_2^* x_2 \qquad (11.107)$$

Since there are four such equations (for the four combinations of status of $x_1$ and $x_2$), and three parameters to estimate, there are excess data. By least-squares techniques [see Coleman (7, p. 199) for such a procedure], we can obtain estimates of $a^*$, $b_1^*$, and $b_2^*$ from the four values of $p_t$. If we label $p_{ijt}$ the value of $p_t$ calculated over the segment of the sample which began in state $i$ on $x_1$ and $j$ on $x_2$, then the estimates are

$$b_1^* = \tfrac{1}{2}(p_{10t} - p_{00t} + p_{11t} - p_{01t}) \qquad (11.108)$$
$$b_2^* = \tfrac{1}{2}(p_{01t} - p_{00t} + p_{11t} - p_{10t}) \qquad (11.109)$$
$$a^* = \tfrac{1}{4}(3p_{00t} + p_{01t} + p_{10t} - p_{11t}) \qquad (11.110)$$

The use of Eqs. (11.104), (11.105), and (11.106) will give estimates of $a$, $b_1$, and $b_2$. The value of $b_2$ shows the effect of $x_2$ on $x_1$.

This procedure generalizes directly to higher numbers of independent attributes. The equations for $b_3$, $b_4$, etc., are identical to Eq. (11.106) for $b_2$. Thus by this procedure, the explanation of changes in state by other dichotomous attributes can be accomplished. It differs only slightly from the procedure for explanation of change in continuous variables.

## The Relation of Coefficients of Change to Measures of Association for Dichotomous Attributes

It is quite valuable to establish techniques of analysis that use the same mathematical model though the form of the data is different. In particular, it is valuable to use measures for analysis of cross-sectional data that derive from the same models used in analysis of data at two or more points in time. By so doing, we are able to compare directly measures obtained from cross-sectional data with measures obtained from over-time data. The comparison, when the measures derive from the same model, can quickly show whether the effects shown in the sample are at aggregate equilibrium, and if not, whether the relationships are increasing or decreasing.[19]

The correspondence between a dynamic model and cross-sectional relationships is similar for data on qualitative states to that for data on quantitative variables. That is, the cross-sectional measures should be based on the assumption of aggregate equilibrium, implying that $dp/dt$ is zero. This gives as a special case of Eq. (11.102):

$$0 = -b_1 p + b_2(x_2 - p) + a(1 - p) \tag{11.111}$$

To examine the use of this equation, consider a usual cross tabulation with a dependent attribute $x_1$, and an independent attribute $x_2$, with the sample divided into two on the value of $x_2$, and proportions calculated for each subsample separately. The proportion for which $x_1 = 1$, for the subsample with $x_2 = 1$, will be labeled $p_1$, and the corresponding proportion for $x_2 = 0$ will be labeled $p_0$. The tabulation of data would look like this:

|         |   | $x_2$ |   |   |
|---------|---|-------|---|---|
|         |   | 0 | 1 |   |
| $x_1$ | 1 | $n_{10}$ | $n_{11}$ | $n_{1.}$ |
|         | 0 | $n_{00}$ | $n_{01}$ | $n_{0.}$ |
|         |   | $n_{.0}$ | $n_{.1}$ | $n$ |

and the proportions formed by dividing through by $n_{.0}$ and $n_{.1}$ would give

|         |   | $x_2$ |   |
|---------|---|-------|---|
|         |   | 0 | 1 |
| $x_1$ | 1 | $p_0$ | $p_1$ |
|         | 0 | $1 - p_0$ | $1 - p_1$ |

For these two subsamples, Eq. (11.111) would take on two different forms:

$$0 = -b_1 p_0 + b_2(0 - p_0) + a(1 - p_0) \tag{11.112}$$
$$0 = -b_1 p_1 + b_2(1 - p_1) + a(1 - p_1) \tag{11.113}$$

These two equations may be used to find, not the absolute sizes of $b_1$, $b_2$, and $a$, but their relative sizes, i.e., each relative to the sum $a + b_1 + b_2$. Such calculation gives

$$\frac{b_2}{a + b_1 + b_2} = p_1 - p_0 \tag{11.114}$$

[19] This correspondence, together with examples, is shown in Coleman (7, chap. 5). The model is the same as that described here, though the treatment there is somewhat more general.

$$\frac{b_1}{a + b_1 + b_2} = 1 - p_1 \qquad (11.115)$$

$$\frac{a}{a + b_1 + b_2} = p_0 \qquad (11.116)$$

Thus the measure of effect of attribute 2, $b_2/(a + b_1 + b_2)$, is merely the percentage difference that is commonly used to measure the effect of one attribute upon another.[20] The generalization of this to more than one independent attribute is given, for independent attribute $i$, merely by the *average* percentage difference, taken over all those pairs of subsamples that differ only in the state of attribute $i$. [See Coleman (7, chap. 6) for a detailed discussion.]

## Change in State as a Function of Other Individuals' States

In the situation in which the individual's change is a function only of the states of his own attributes, and these attributes are themselves independent of the one under study, the approach discussed on page 464 is relevant. When the attribute is a function of the state of others' attributes, then under certain conditions the same treatment is possible. The mere fact that the attributes characterize an individual in his environment rather than himself does not change their logical status.

However, for such treatment, these attributes must themselves be independent of his own; otherwise, their treatment as independent attributes is unwarranted and may lead to incorrect conclusions. When the attributes are, like his own, dependent on the state of others in the group, then an interdependent system exists, one that becomes mathematically difficult.

Consider the case in which there are $n$ individuals in the group, that is, $n - 1$ others. Of these, $n_1$ are in state 1 and $n_0$ are in state 0 at time $t$ (so that $n_1 + n_0 = n - 1$). Then if there is an effect of each of these others on his own state, the equation for change is similar to Eq. (11.101) for change as a function of other attributes:

$$\frac{dp}{dt} = -(b_1 + n_0 b_2)p_1 + (a + n_1 b_2)(1 - p_1) \qquad (11.117)$$

This equation assumes change in both directions and assumes that in either direction, the increment to the transition rate due to each other individual's being in that state is $b_2$.

If $n_1$ and $n_0$ were fixed, this equation would give rise to a solution similar to that of Eq. (11.101). However, if each individual is characterized by a similar equation of change, then this no longer can be done. If each individual is characterized by the same transition rates $a$, $b_1$, and $b_2$, then the system can be

[20] Using the alternative model described in footnote 18 in which there is an effect toward $x_1 = 1$ only when $x_2 = 1$, and no effect when $x_2 = 0$, the derived measure would be another commonly used measure, the percentage difference corrected for a ceiling effect $(p_1 - p_0)/(1 - p_0)$.

treated as a unit, with $n + 1$ states. The states of the group would not distinguish *which* individuals were in state 1, but only *how many*. That is, the states would be 0, 1, . . . , $n$. Solution of such a system is beyond the scope of the present treatment. Solutions of certain portions of the problem, such as the expected equilibrium state and the case where movement is entirely from state 0 to state 1, may be found in Coleman (7, chaps. 10, 11). A few comments may be made concerning the system, however. When movement is in both directions, as in Eq. (11.117), then the expected equilibrium state for the group is unchanged from what it would be if $b_2$ were 0 and no contagion existed.[21] However, there are two major differences: individual changes in a given period of time will be more numerous, owing to the increased transition rates in both directions; and the average deviation of groups from the expected equilibrium will be greater; that is, the group is less stable. In fact, if $b_2$ is twice the size of $a + b$, then even in groups as small as 5, most groups will spend most of their time in state 0 or state 5. As the group size increases, the value of $b_2$ necessary for such extremes reduces proportionately.

If the change is only in the direction of state 1, so that the first term on the right of Eq. (11.117) vanishes, then the path of the group is approximated by the logistic curve.[22] This differs from the negative exponential curve describing the state of the group if all individuals were independent in that it shows an accelerating rate of change up to the point that half the group is in state 1, and consequently the group moves to state $n$ more quickly.

The primitive state of work in these most sociological processes indicates the amount of further work to be done. For example, it ought to be possible to specify the observations on members of groups necessary to estimate $a$, $b_1$, and $b_2$, and to provide the equations for estimation; however, that work remains to be done.

## Changes in a System of Interdependent Attributes

As in the case of continuous variables, change in a system of attributes is more difficult to analyze than change in a single attribute. The difficulties reside in the fact that it is difficult to separate the direct effects and the indirect ones. When the same attributes are both dependent and independent variables, both acted upon and acting on others, then indirect effects may proliferate. Nevertheless, such a situation of interdependence is frequent (for example, interdependence of two attitudes), and often one is interested in disentangling such interdependence. The most frequent problem is that of the relative effect

---

[21] This can be seen by setting $dp/dt = 0$ for equilibrium, and noting that the contagion term drops out, since $(n_0 + n_1)p_1 = n_1$.

[22] The approximate solution, giving the logistic curve, may be found by substituting $np_1$ for $n_1$, since the expected number of persons in state 1 at any time is $np_1$, where $p_1$ is the probability that any individual is in state 1. Obviously, this approximation will be better as the expected approaches the actual, i.e., with increase in $n$.

of attribute 1 on 2 versus the effect of 2 on 1.   The transitions in a system of two interdependent attributes are as illustrated by the diagram below.

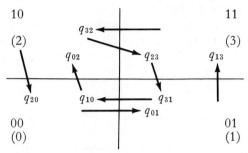

State 1 of attribute 1 is to the right, and state 0 to the left.   State 1 of attribute 2 is above, and state 0 below.   The question of interdependence between these attributes is one of comparison between the transition rates. There is evidence of an effect of attribute 2 on attribute 1, for example, if $q_{32}$ is different from $q_{10}$, and $q_{23}$ is different from $q_{01}$.   These differences express the fact that movement on $x_1$ differs depending on the state of $x_2$.

To analyze this system as a linear system, we can partition the transition rates for each of the two attributes into components as on page 464.   For changes in attribute 1, these components are:

to state 0:
$$b_{11} + (1 - x_2)b_{21} \qquad (q_{32} \text{ or } q_{10})$$
to state 1:
$$a_1 + x_2 b_{21} \qquad (q_{23} \text{ or } q_{01})$$

For changes in attribute 2:

to state 0:
$$b_{22} + (1 - x_1)b_{12} \qquad (q_{31} \text{ or } q_{20})$$
to state 1:
$$a_2 + x_1 b_{12} \qquad (q_{13} \text{ or } q_{02})$$

With this notation, $p_1$ is the positive state on attribute 1 (incorporating both states 11 and 01); $p_2$ is similarly defined.   The coefficients $b_{ij}$ represent the effects of attribute $i$ on attribute $j$, and the coefficient $a_i$ represents uniform change toward state 1 of attribute $i$.

The first approximation to estimation of these parameters is treatment of each attribute as a dependent variable by the method presented on page 464. This uses equations analogous to Eq. (11.101):

$$\frac{dp_1}{dt} = -[b_{11} + b_{21}(1 - p_2)]p_1 + (a_1 + b_{21}p_2)(1 - p_1) \qquad (11.118)$$

$$\frac{dp_2}{dt} = -[b_{22} + b_{12}(1 - p_1)]p_2 + (a_2 + b_{12}p_1)(1 - p_2) \qquad (11.119)$$

Thus when these attributes constitute an interdependent system, the system may be characterized by Eqs. (11.118) and (11.119) which specify the changes for each attribute in the probability of being in state 1.

These equations can be put in the same form as the analogous equations for a system of interdependent variables, treated deterministically, that is, Eqs. (11.37) and (11.38). Rearranging coefficients, these equations become

$$\frac{dp_1}{dt} = a_1 - (a_1 + b_{11} + b_{21})p_1 + b_{21}p_2 \qquad (11.120)$$

$$\frac{dp_2}{dt} = a_2 + b_{12}p_1 - (a_2 + b_{22} + b_{12})p_2 \qquad (11.121)$$

However, these equations are somewhat more specific than those treated on page 448, because of constraints upon the coefficients. First, all transition rates $a_i$ and $b_{ij}$ are positive. Second, the coefficient of $p_1$ in the first equation is larger than the coefficient of $p_2$, while the reverse is true in the second equation. Also, we have assumed that the effects of each variable on the other are positive.[23] Under these assumptions, only one of the possible types of systems discussed on pages 448–450 can occur. This is a stable system, with movement toward stability as shown in Fig. 11.6. The mutual effects of these attributes can be seen by first focusing on the line at which $dp_1/dt = 0$. If attribute 1 were

---

[23] If the effects of both are toward the opposite states of the other, then redefining one of the attributes by reversing states 1 and 0 will produce Eqs. (11.120) and (11.121). On the other hand, if the first attribute affects the second positively, and the second affects the first negatively, then a truly different system exists. In this case, the equation for $dp_1/dt$ becomes: $dp_1/dt = a_1 + b_{21} - (a_1 + b_{11} + b_{21})p_1 - b_{12}p_2$. The characteristic roots of the system of equations are conjugate complex numbers with the real part negative, and the trajectories of the system will be spirals toward the equilibrium point, as indicated in Fig. 11.7.

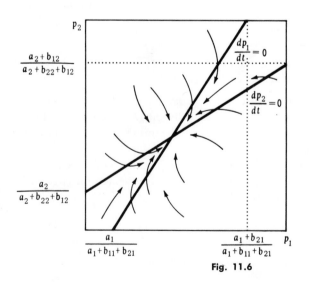

Fig. 11.6

the only dependent variable, then the probability of being in state 1 would (at equilibrium) lie along that line, the point determined by the probability that attribute 2 was in state 1, that is, by $p_2$. But when there is also an effect of attribute 1 on attribute 2, then $p_2$ is itself subject to change, either up or down until the single equilibrium point is reached.

The task of estimating the coefficients $a_i$ and $b_{ij}$ requires a considerable amount of computation, so that in some cases, the approximation using the method discussed on page 464 will be preferable.

For such estimation, let us return to the $p$'s that treat states on both attributes simultaneously: $p_{11}, p_{10}, p_{01}, p_{00}$. Now consider a more general system with any number of such states (for $m$ attributes, $2^m$ states). Then it can be shown (using matrix algebra) that

$$P_t = P_0 e^{Qt} \tag{11.122}$$

where $P$ is the row vector of $p$'s, $Q$ is the matrix of transition rates $q_{ij}$, and $e^{Qt}$ is interpreted as the matrix analog of an exponential series. Two methods for using Eq. (11.122) to estimate the $q_{ij}$'s are given in Coleman (7, chap. 5). One of those is given below.

We may also write in place of Eq. (11.122):

$$P_t = P_0 R_t \tag{11.123}$$

where $R_t$ is a transition matrix over the time $t$ for a Markov process. The elements in this transition matrix can be estimated directly by use of two-wave

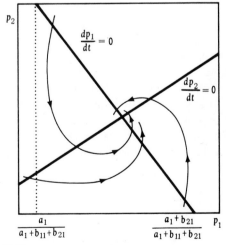

**Fig. 11.7**

panel data.   Then, using Eqs. (11.122) and (11.123),

$$R_t = e^{Qt} \tag{11.124}$$

or         $$\ln R_t = Qt \tag{11.125}$$

where      $$\ln R_t = (R_t - I) - \tfrac{1}{2}(R_t - I)^2 + \tfrac{1}{3}(R_t - I)^3 - \cdots \tag{11.126}$$

Equation (11.126) can be used, when it converges, for estimating $Qt$.[24]   The elements of the matrix formed by summing the terms in Eq. (11.126) are the elements $q_{ij}$, multiplied by $t$.

   After estimating the separate $q_{ij}$'s, we may then use them for estimating the $a_i$'s and $b_{ij}$'s.   For a two-attribute system, the estimating equations are as follows, using the notation from the diagram on page 469.

$$a_1 = \tfrac{1}{2}(q_{01} + q_{23} + q_{32} - q_{10}) \tag{11.127}$$
$$b_{11} = \tfrac{1}{2}(q_{32} + q_{10} + q_{01} - q_{23}) \tag{11.128}$$
$$b_{21} = \tfrac{1}{2}(q_{23} - q_{01} + q_{10} - q_{32}) \tag{11.129}$$
$$a_2 = \tfrac{1}{2}(q_{02} + q_{13} + q_{31} - q_{20}) \tag{11.130}$$
$$b_{22} = \tfrac{1}{2}(q_{20} + q_{31} + q_{02} - q_{13}) \tag{11.131}$$
$$b_{12} = \tfrac{1}{2}(q_{13} - q_{02} + q_{20} - q_{31}) \tag{11.132}$$

   This estimation, once the $q_{ij}$'s have been found, provides the necessary estimates of the coefficients of change, $a_i$ and $b_{ij}$.   Comparison of the sizes of these coefficients shows the amounts of effect of each of the attributes on the other.

### Unreliability for Qualitative Attributes

   Response unreliability is an even more common problem for qualitative attributes than for continuous variables.   For qualitative attributes, there is often a high degree of unreliability.   For example, in an item on psychological tests, an individual may give a correct response one time and an incorrect response a second time, owing to chance factors present at the two times.   Or on an attitude question, the influences of the moment may lead a respondent to reply differently at different moments, though he had not changed his attitude in any way that could be detected by subsequent responses (that is, subsequent responses would show stable probabilities of a given response).   For example, consider three successive responses to the same question by a sample of individuals.   Suppose they showed the following distributions:

|          |     | *Time* |    |    |
|----------|-----|--------|----|----|
|          |     | 0      | 1  | 2  |
| *Response* | 1 | 60     | 60 | 60 |
|          | 0   | 40     | 40 | 40 |

[24] When it does not converge, this means either that the data are not compatible with the assumptions of a continuous-time Markov process, or that the waves of the panel are too widely spaced.

The distributions at these times are the same, which suggests that there has not been any change. But to detect this, we must examine the individual's succession of responses. For example, in this case, we might find either of the results shown below in a cross tabulation of times 0 and 1.

|  |  | *a* Response at time 1 | | | *b* Response at time 1 | | |
|---|---|---|---|---|---|---|---|
|  |  | 1 | 0 | | 1 | 0 | |
| Response at time 0 | 1 | 60 | 0 | 60 | 48 | 12 | 60 |
|  | 0 | 0 | 40 | 40 | 12 | 28 | 40 |
|  |  | 60 | 40 | 100 | 60 | 40 | 100 |

In the tables above, *a* shows no change at all, while *b* suggests that change of attitude did occur. Clearly in the second case there is change of response; but *b* might be regarded in either of two ways. It might be conjectured either that there had indeed been change of attitude or that the attitude had remained the same, with nothing more than response unreliability. To assess what has in fact happened, we must examine the third response, to see whether the attitudes have remained the same or have changed. If they have remained the same, then the third response should show this, especially at one critical point: those who responded 1 and then 0 should be just as likely to respond 1 as are those who responded 0 and then 1 between the first two times, and thus be more likely to respond 1 than the group which changed to 0. The two opposite expectations can be represented by the tables below, which cross-tabulate all three responses.[25]

|  |  | *a* Unreliability Response at time 2 | | |  | *b* Change (Markovian) Response at time 2 | | |
|---|---|---|---|---|---|---|---|---|
|  |  | 1 | 0 | | | 1 | 0 | |
|  | 11 | 42 | 6 | 48 | 11 | 38.4 | 9.6 | 48 |
|  | 10 | 6 | 6 | 12 | 10 | 3.6 | 8.4 | 12 |
| Response at times 0 *and* 1 | 01 | 6 | 6 | 12 | 01 | 9.6 | 2.4 | 12 |
|  | 00 | 6 | 22 | 28 | 00 | 8.4 | 19.6 | 28 |
|  |  | 60 | 40 | 100 |  | 60 | 40 | 100 |

As indicated on pages 463–464, and as in the continuous-variable case, the regression coefficients $a^0$ and $b^0$ calculated over two units of time (e.g., from time 0 to 2) should be related to $a^*$ and $b^*$ calculated over a single time period

---

[25] Part *a* is only one of the possible tables showing pure unreliability, while *b* is the only possible table showing regular change which is Markovian. The condition that must be met by the table showing pure unreliability is that collapsing for any one of the three times gives the same table, identical to that for times 0 and 1 shown in *b* earlier. This implies that the response patterns 101, 011, and 110 have the same frequency, and 001, 010, and 100 have the same frequency.

as follows, if there is only change without unreliability: $a^0 = a^*(b^* + 1)$, and $b^0 = b^{*2}$ [and if there is an independent variable, $b_2{}^0 = b_2{}^*(b_1{}^* + 1)$]. When this is not true, we can estimate the components of change and unreliability, as in the continuous-variable case, by separating the transition rates into two components, as shown below for the case of a single independent attribute:

$$a = a_e + a_c \tag{11.133}$$

$$b_1 = b_{1e} + b_{1c} \tag{11.134}$$

$$b_2 = b_{2e} + b_{2c} \tag{11.135}$$

If there were no response unreliability, our estimates of $a$, $b_1$, and $b_2$ would be independent of $\Delta t$. But if there were only unreliability, then $a\Delta t$, $b_1\Delta t$, and $b_2\Delta t$ should be constant, since $a^*$, $b_1{}^*$, and $b_2{}^*$ would be independent of $\Delta t$. Thus the estimates of $a$, $b_1$, and $b_2$ would be inversely proportional to $\Delta t$. Consequently, defining $a_e$, $b_{1e}$, and $b_{2e}$ to be constant over time gives the following equations for $a$, $b_1$, and $b_2$ calculated over time $\Delta t$:

$$a_{\Delta t} = \frac{a_e}{\Delta t} + a_c \tag{11.136}$$

$$b_{1\Delta t} = \frac{b_{1e}}{\Delta t} + b_{1c} \tag{11.137}$$

$$b_{2\Delta t} = \frac{b_{2e}}{\Delta t} + b_{2c} \tag{11.138}$$

This means that if we have two time intervals (say between time 0 and $t$, and 0 and $\tau$), then we can solve for the two sets of estimates $a_{\Delta t}$, $b_{1\Delta t}$, $b_{2\Delta t}$ and $a_{\Delta \tau}$, $b_{1\Delta \tau}$, and $b_{2\Delta \tau}$, thereby giving enough information to solve for the error components and the change components of the transition rates. By calculations similar to those for continuous variables, we arrive at the following equations, which express the error and change components as a function of the regression coefficients estimated over the two time intervals.

If $a^*$, $b_1{}^*$, and $b_2{}^*$ are calculated over the time interval $\Delta t$, which is taken as the time unit, and $a^0$, $b_1{}^0$, and $b_2{}^0$ are calculated over the time period $\Delta \tau$, which is $s$ times $\Delta t$, and if we again simplify notation by setting

$$C^* = \ln b_1{}^*/(b_1{}^* - 1)$$

then the equations are

$$a_e = \frac{1}{s-1}(sa^*C^* - a^0C^0) \tag{11.139}$$

$$a_c = \frac{1}{(s-1)\,\Delta t}(a^0C^0 - a^*C^*) \tag{11.140}$$

$$b_{2e} = \frac{1}{s-1}(sb_2{}^*C^* - b_2{}^0C^0) \tag{11.141}$$

$$b_{2c} = \frac{1}{(s-1)\,\Delta t}(b_2{}^0C^0 - b_2{}^*C^*) \tag{11.142}$$

$$b_{1e} = \frac{1}{s-1} [s(1 - a^* - b_1{}^* - b_2{}^*)C^* - (1 - a^0 - b_1{}^0 - b_2{}^0)C^0] \quad (11.143)$$

$$b_{1c} = \frac{1}{(s-1)\,\Delta t} [(1 - a^0 - b_1{}^0 - b_2{}^0)C^0 - (1 - a^* - b_1{}^* - b_2{}^*)C^*] \quad (11.144)$$

If one has data in which the individuals can be classified according to their position on attributes 1 and 2 at time 0, then the estimation of $a^*$, $b_1{}^*$, and $b_2{}^*$ is carried out simply by use of Eqs. (11.108), (11.109), and (11.110), and the estimation of $a^0$, $b_1{}^0$, $b_2{}^0$ is carried out in the same way, by use of $p_{ijr}$ instead of $p_{ijt}$.

The investigation of response unreliability is an almost totally undeveloped field, because of the lack of mathematical models to encompass both unreliability and change. For example, there is evidence that the so-called unreliability is not in fact instantaneous. Rather than a transition rate split into an instantaneous and constant component, as in this chapter, there may be transition rates that are some declining function of the passage of time after a response.[26]

## 11.3   CONCLUSION

The investigation of causal relations is a difficult task. Even more difficult is the task of uncovering the causal relations in a system of variables. One approach to these tasks is by the use of cross-sectional data; the investigator may infer causal relations from statistical associations when the causal ordering is known or can be safely assumed. This approach has been developed at some length and has resulted in sophisticated techniques, as the chapters by Blalock and Boudon in this volume indicate.

Another approach to the problem of inferring causal relations or mapping out a system of causal relations is the use of data gathered at two or more points in time. When variables are observed at two or more points in time, additional information exists beyond that obtained in cross-sectional data. This is information which, if used properly, can indicate what factors bring about change in a variable. These changes will, of course, create or maintain the relationships that may be found in cross-sectional data, and thus provide information about the dynamics of a system beyond that provided by cross-sectional data.

In an ideal world, with no constraints on data collection, the observation of sets of variables over time would provide all the information necessary for laying out the system of causal relations which tied these variables together. In the usual situation, however, data consist of two or more observations on a set of individuals (where individuals may be persons, groups, or other entities). It is for such observations that the methods of this chapter are relevant. By use of the calculus for continuous variables, and continuous-time stochastic

---

[26] One model for unreliability mixed with change is given in Coleman (8). This is derived from a different conceptual basis, but is isomorphic to the model presented here.

processes for qualitative attributes, these methods provide a means for measuring the *quantity of change* in a given variable that characterizes a set of individuals, and then a means for *explaining* the change by other variables. These methods combine the use of calculus and multiple regression techniques. Multiple regression is used to regress the state of a variable at the later time on the states of variables at an earlier time; then the methods of calculus are used to relate the state equation (for which regression coefficients will have been obtained) to the dynamic equation which expresses change in the variable as a function of states of the other variables. By this two-part technique, one can estimate (from the regression coefficients) the parameters in the dynamic equation.

However, there are many pitfalls in the use of such over-time data. One of the most serious is that of measurement error, which can sometimes be larger than the change itself. Measurement error is particularly destructive, because if the dependent variable is correlated with the independent variable, an apparent effect of the independent variable on the dependent variable will arise solely through measurement error on the latter.

A technique, for both continuous variables and qualitative attributes, is given to separate change from measurement error when there are three or more observations on the same individuals. Yet this only begins to solve the problem, because no account is taken of correlations between the measurement error at different times (error is assumed serially independent), and no account is taken of measurement error in the independent variables.

In other ways as well, the methods of this chapter mark only a start in the inference of cause from over-time data on a set of individuals. The causal equations presented are simple ones, usually assuming linear and additive effects, and assuming that effects on the rate of change are instantaneous. (This does not, of course, imply instantaneous adjustment of the state of the dependent variable to its equilibrium position; the time period to reach such adjustment depends on the rate of change.) In some causal systems, the change in one variable may depend, not on the present state of another, but upon a previous state.

In these ways and others, the methods presented in this chapter provide only starting points for the study of causal relations with observations at two or more times on a set of individuals. Yet both the data appropriate to these methods and further development of the methods are necessary if research is to provide the basis for assessment of causal relations.


## REFERENCES

1 Bailey, N. T. J.: *The Mathematical Theory of Epidemics* (London: Griffin, 1957).

2 Beshers, James M., and S. Reiter: "Social Status and Social Change," *Behavioral Science*, **8** (January, 1963), 1–14.

3 Blalock, Hubert M.: *Causal Inferences in Nonexperimental Research* (Chapel Hill, N.C.: University of North Carolina Press, 1964).

4 Blau, Peter M.: "Structural Effects," *American Sociological Review*, **25** (April, 1960), 178–193.

5 Boulding, Kenneth E.: "Toward a General Theory of Growth," in J. J. Spengler and O. D. Duncan (Eds.), *Population Theory and Policy* (New York: Free Press, 1956), pp. 109–124.

6 Campbell, Donald T., and Julien S. Stanley: "Experimental and Quasi-experimental Designs for Research on Teaching," in N. L. Gage (Ed.), *Handbook of Research on Teaching* (Chicago: Rand McNally, 1963), pp. 171–246.

7 Coleman, James S.: *Introduction to Mathematical Sociology* (New York: Free Press, 1964).

8 Coleman, James S.: *Models of Change and Response Uncertainty* (Englewood Cliffs, N.J.: Prentice-Hall, 1964).

9 Davis, Harold T.: *Introduction to Nonlinear Differential and Integral Equations* (Washington, D.C.: Atomic Energy Commission, 1960).

10 Davis, James A., J. L. Spaeth, and Carolyn Huson: "A Technique for Analyzing the Effects of Group Composition," *American Sociological Review*, **26** (April, 1961), 215–225.

11 Davis, Kingsley: "The Myth of Functional Analysis as a Special Method in Sociology and Anthropology," *American Sociological Review*, **24** (December, 1959), 757–772.

12 Durkheim, Emile: *Suicide* (New York: Free Press, 1951).

13 Galileo, Galilei: *Two New Sciences* (New York: Dover, n.d.). First published in Italian, 1638.

14 Gause, George F.: *The Struggle for Existence* (Baltimore: Williams & Wilkins, 1934).

15 Kemeny, John G., and J. Laurie Snell: *Mathematical Models in the Social Sciences* (Boston: Ginn, 1962).

16 Lopez, Alvaro: *Problems in Stable Population Theory* (Princeton, N.J.: Office of Population Research, 1961).

17 Lotka, A. J.: *Elements of Physical Biology* (Baltimore: Williams & Wilkins, 1925). Republished as *Elements of Mathematical Biology* (New York: Dover, n.d.).

18 Matras, Judah: "Comparison of Intergenerational Occupational Mobility Patterns: An Application of the Formal Theory of Social Mobility," *Population Studies*, **14** (November, 1960), 163–169.

19 Matras, Judah: "Differential Fertility, Intergenerational Occupational Mobility, and Change in the Occupational Distribution: Some Elementary Relationships," *Population Studies*, **15** (November, 1961), 187–197.

20 Pelz, Donald C., and Frank M. Andrews: "Causal Priorities in Panel Study Data," *American Sociological Review*, **29** (December, 1964), 836–848.

21 Pearl, Raymond: *The Biology of Population Growth* (New York: Knopf, 1925).

22 Ryder, N. B.: "The Structure and Tempo of Current Fertility," in *Demographic and Economic Change in Developed Countries*, National Bureau of Economic Research (Princeton, N.J.: Princeton, 1960), pp. 117–136.

23 Ryder, N. B.: "The Translation Model of Demographic Change," in *Emerging Techniques in Population Research* (New York: Millbank Memorial Fund, 1963).

24 Ryder, N. B.: "The Process of Demographic Translation," *Demography Annual* (1964).

25 Sherif, Muzafer: *The Psychology of Social Norms* (New York: Harper & Row, 1936).

26 Volterra, Vito: *Leçons sur la théorie mathématique de la lutte pour la vie* (Paris: Gauthier-Villars, 1931).

27 White, Harrison: *An Anatomy of Kinship* (Englewood Cliffs, N.J.: Prentice-Hall, 1963).

**INDEXES**

# Name Index

Where authors have been designated only by a reference number in the text, the reference number is given in parentheses following the appropriate text page number.

# Subject Index

Abstraction models, 121
Accuracy of estimators, 283
Additive effects of variables, 392, 395
Affective attitude scales, 71–72, 89, 93–97
    (*See also* Guttman scalogram model;
        Likert scale; Thurstone scale)
Ambiguity criterion, 91–93
Ambivalence, 72
American Psychological Association, 386
Anthropological studies (*see* Cross-cultural
        studies; Cross-cultural survey)
Area sampling, 299
    (*See also* Cluster sampling)
Assessment, 64–67, 74
Association, coefficient of, 142
Attenuation, correction for, 46–49, 52
Attitude measurement, 60–69
Attitude measurement models (*see* Atti-
        tude scales)
Attitude scales, 69–80
    cognitive, behavioral, affective, 69–73,
        75, 91
    direct, indirect, 74–80
    nominal, ordinal, interval, ratio, 74–78
Attitude variables, 60, 69–73, 94, 98, 107
Attributes, and change analysis, 459–475
    and dependence coefficients, 212,
        216–220, 226–233
Autocorrelation, 172
Autonomous behaving units, 165–166
Auxiliary theory, 7, 23–26, 172

Background variables, 173, 175–176

Behavioral attitude scales, 70–71, 75
Bias, 284, 287
    of estimators, 284, 287
    reporting, 264, 265
    sampling, 93, 253–258, 265
Block supplement samples, 318, 319, 320
Blocks, 337, 338, 376–379, 381
Boundaries of populations, 313, 314

Calculus, 429–431
Categorical judgment law, 78, 86, 90–93
Categorization of traits, 267–273
Category boundaries, 84–89, 105, 106
Category scale, 76, 77, 85, 86, 91
Causal chains, simple, 158, 170, 187
Causal laws, 187–189
    versus generalizations to populations,
        192–196
Causal models, construction of, 161–174
    in cross-cultural studies, 242, 244–248,
        262, 266, 272, 273
    (*See also* Dependence coefficients; Path
        coefficients)
Ceiling effects, 35–36, 50
Change, concept of, 428–431
    and dependence analysis, 227–233
    exogenous, 441–443, 464, 465
    as function of time, 433, 434, 460–462
    immanent, 435–441, 447, 462–464
    in laboratory experiments, 393–397
    and nonlinear models, 456–459
    parameters of, 435–437, 442, 463
    in qualitative states, 459–475